WILLIAM JAMES McKNIGHT

1780   A   1850

PIONEER OUTLINE HISTORY

OF

Northwestern Pennsylvania

EMBRACING

THE COUNTIES OF TIOGA, POTTER, McKEAN, WARREN,
CRAWFORD, VENANGO, FOREST, CLARION, ELK, JEFFERSON,
CAMERON, BUTLER, LAWRENCE, AND MERCER

ALSO

A PIONEER SKETCH OF THE CITIES OF ALLEGHENY, BEAVER, DU BOIS,
AND TOWANDA

My First Recollections of Brookville, Pennsylvania, 1840-1843,
when my feet were bare and my cheeks were brown

BY

W. J. McKNIGHT, M.D.

BROOKVILLE, PA.

AUTHOR OF "MY FIRST RECOLLECTIONS OF BROOKVILLE, PENNSYLVANIA," "RECOLLECTIONS OF
RIDGWAY, PENNSYLVANIA," ALSO OF THE "PIONEER HISTORY OF
JEFFERSON COUNTY, PENNSYLVANIA"

Philadelphia
PRINTED BY J. B. LIPPINCOTT COMPANY
1905

F
157
.A18M15

THESE PAGES

ARE

AFFECTIONATELY DEDICATED

TO

MRS. MARY (McKNIGHT) TEMPLETON

Née THOMPSON

PREFACE

To write a pioneer history years and years after all the fathers and mothers have gone to that "country from whose bourn no traveller returns" is a task to appall the most courageous. To say it mildly, it is a task requiring a vast amount of labor and research, untiring perseverance, great patience, and discrimination. In undertaking this task I realized its magnitude, and all through the work I have determined that, if labor, patience, and perseverance would overcome error and false traditions and establish the truth, the object of this book would be fully attained. This book is not written for gain, nor to laud or puff either the dead or the living. It is designed to be a plain, truthful narrative of pioneer men and events in the northwest.

I have compiled, wherever I could, from the writings of others. This book it is hoped will enable you to

> "Lift the twilight curtains of the past
> And, turning from familiar sight and sound,
> Sadly and full of reverence, cast
> A glance upon tradition's shadowy ground."

To accomplish this I have taken no account of travel, time, or expense, expecting all that to be a financial loss, but only working and desiring to make a true, reliable history.

I am indebted to the following historical works,—viz., " Jefferson County Atlas," " Jefferson County History," Day's " Historical Recollections," Egle's " History of Pennsylvania," McKnight's pioneer history, and histories of Butler, Crawford, Clarion, Cameron, Elk, Forest, Lawrence, Mercer, McKean, Venango, Tioga, Potter, and Warren.

I am also indebted to J. Sutton Wall for map tracings, and to the State Report of Public Instruction of 1877.

PREFACE

A few errors in the "Pioneer History of Jefferson County" have since been discovered, and are corrected in this work.

In every instance, as far as possible, credit has been given to the writings of those who have preceded me. But, dear reader,

> "Whoever thinks a faultless work to see,
> Thinks what ne'er was, nor is, nor e'er shall be.
> In every work regard the writer's end,
> Since none can compass more than they intend,
> And if the means be just, the conduct true,
> Applause, in spite of trivial faults, is due."

W. J. McKNIGHT.

BROOKVILLE, PENNSYLVANIA, 1905.

CONTENTS

CONTENTS

8

CONTENTS

9

CONTENTS

CONTENTS

LIST OF ILLUSTRATIONS

LIST OF ILLUSTRATIONS

LIST OF ILLUSTRATIONS

LIST OF MAPS

LIST OF ILLUSTRATIONS

A PIONEER OUTLINE HISTORY OF NORTHWESTERN PENNSYLVANIA

CHAPTER I

"The deeds of our fathers in times that are gone,
Their virtues, their prowess, the toils they endured."

At this time all the pioneers have passed away, and the facts here given are collected from records and recollections. Every true citizen now and in the future of the northwest must ever possess a feeling of deep veneration for the brave men and courageous women who penetrated this wilderness and inaugurated civilization where savages and wild beasts reigned supreme. These heroic men and women migrated to this forest and endured all the hardships incidental to that day and life, and through these labors and tribulations they have transmitted to us all the comforts and conveniences of a high civilization. The graves have closed over all these pioneer men and women, and I have been deprived of the great assistance they could have been to me in writing this history.

In 1780 railroads were unknown. To-day there are in the United States one hundred and seventy thousand miles of railroad. Over these roads there were carried, in 1897, five hundred million people and six hundred million tons of freight. Employed upon them are one million men, thirty thousand locomotives, twenty-one thousand passenger cars, seven thousand baggage cars, and one million freight cars. The total capital invested is eight billion dollars. The disbursements for labor and repairs are yearly six hundred and fifty million dollars. And now, in 1905, as a Pennsylvanian, I am proud to say our own Pennsylvania road is the greatest, the best, and most perfect in management and construction of any road in the world. We have smoking-cars, with bath-room, barber-shop, writing-desks, and library; we have dining-cars in which are served refreshments that a Delmonico cannot surpass; we have parlor cars with bay-windows and luxurious furniture; and we have cars with beds for sleeping soft as the "eider down."

In the year 1780 men were imprisoned for debt and kept in prison until the last farthing was paid. The jails of that day were but little better than dungeons. There was no woman's Christian temperance union, no woman's relief corps, no society for the prevention of cruelty to animals or children.

In 1780 domestic comforts were few. No stove had been invented. Large, deep fireplaces, with cranes, andirons, and bake-ovens, were the only

Northwestern Pennsylvania in 1780

"A savage place—as lonely and enchanted
As e'er beneath a waning moon was haunted."

modes of heating and cooking. Friction-matches were unknown. If the fire of the house went out, you had to rekindle with a flint or borrow of your neighbor. I have borrowed fire. House furniture was then meagre and rough. There were no window-blinds or carpets. Rich people whitewashed their ceilings and rooms, and covered their parlor-floors with white sand. Hence the old couplet:

"'Oh, dear mother, my toes are sore
A dancing over your sanded floor.'"

18

HISTORY OF NORTHWESTERN PENNSYLVANIA

Pine-knots, tallow-dipped candles burned in iron or brass candlesticks, and whale oil burned in iron lamps were the means for light in stores, dwellings, etc. Food was scarce, coarse, and of the most common kind, with no canned goods or evaporated fruits. In addition to cooking in the open fireplace, women had to spin, knit, dye, and weave all domestic cloths, there being no mills run by machinery to make woollen or cotton goods. Mrs. Winslow's soothing syrup and baby-carriages were unknown. The bride of 1790 took her wedding-trip on foot or on horseback behind the bridegroom on a " pillion."

Men wore no beards, whiskers, or moustaches, their faces being as clean shaven and as smooth as a girl's. A beard was looked upon as an abomination, and fitted only for Hessians, heathen, or Turks. In 1780 not a single cigar had ever been smoked in the United States. I wish I could say that of to-day. There were no aniline dyes, no electric lights, no anæsthetics and painless surgery, no gun-cotton, no nitroglycerine, no dynamite, giant powder, audiphones, pneumatic tubes, or type-writers, no cotton-gin, no planting-machine, no mower or reaper, no hay-rake, no hay-fork, no corn-sheller, no rotary printing-press, no sewing-machine, no knitting-machine, no envelopes for letters, no india-rubber goods, coats, shoes, or cloaks, no grain-elevator except man, no artificial ice, no steel pens, no telegraph or telephone, no street-cars, no steam-mills, no daguerreotypes or photographs, no steam-ploughs, no steam-thresher (only the old hand-flail), no wind-mill, and no millionaire in the whole country. General Washington was the richest man, and he was only worth eight hundred thousand dollars.

Previous to 1800, or the settlement of Northwestern Pennsylvania, there were about nine inventions in the world,—to wit, the screw, lever, wheel, windlass, compass, gunpowder, movable type, microscopes, and telescopes. About everything else has been invented since. To-day France averages about nine thousand and the United States twelve thousand a year.

In 1800 the United States contained a population of 5,305,925.

In 1800 Philadelphia and New York were but overgrown villages, and Chicago was unknown. Books were few and costly, ignorance the rule, and authors famed the world over now were then unborn; now we spend annually one hundred and forty million dollars for schools. Then there was no telegraph, telephone, or submarine cable; now the earth is girdled with telegraph wires, and we can speak face to face through the telephone a thousand miles apart, and millions of messages are sent every year under the waters of the globe. To-day in the United States an average of one to twelve telegraphic messages are sent every minute, day and night, the year through.

In 1800 emigrants to America came in sailing-vessels. Each emigrant had to provide his own food, as the vessel supplied only air and water. The trip required a period of from thirty days to three months. Now this trip can be made by the use of Jefferson County coal in less than six days. Now ocean travel is a delight. Then canals for the passage of great ships and transatlantic steamers were unknown.

In 1800 electricity was in its infancy, and travel was by sail, foot, horse-back, and by coach. Now we have steamers, street-cars, railroads, bicycles, and horseless carriages. Gas was unheard of for stoves, streets, or lights. Pitch-pine, fat, and tallow candles gave the only light then.

In 1800 human slavery was universal, and irreligion was the order of the day. Nine out of every ten workingmen neither possessed nor ever opened a Bible. Hymn-books were unknown, and musical science had no system. Medicine was an illiterate theory, surgery a crude art, and dentistry unknown. No snap shots were thought of. Photography was not heard of. Now this science has revealed " stars invisible" and microscopic life beyond computation.

In 1800 there were but few daily papers in the world, no illustrated ones, no humorous ones, and no correspondents. Modern tunnels were unknown, and there was no steam-heating. Flint and tinder did duty for matches. Plate-glass was a luxury undreamed of. Envelopes had not been invented, and postage-stamps had not been introduced. Vulcanized rubber and celluloid had not begun to appear in a hundred dainty forms. Stationary washtubs, and even washboards, were unknown. Carpets, furniture, and household accessories were expensive. Sewing-machines had not yet supplanted the needle. Aniline colors and coal-tar products were things of the future. Stem-winding watches had not appeared; there were no cheap watches of any kind. So it was with hundreds of the necessities of our present life.

In the social customs of our day, many minds entertain doubts whether we have made improvements upon those of our ancestors. In those days friends and neighbors could meet together and enjoy themselves, and enter into the spirit of social amusement with a hearty good-will, a geniality of manners, a corresponding depth of soul, both among the old and young, to which modern society is unaccustomed. Our ancestors did not make a special invitation the only pass to their dwellings, and they entertained those who visited them with a hospitality that is not generally practised at the present time. Guests did not assemble then to criticise the decorations, furniture, dress, manners, and surroundings of those by whom they were invited. They were sensible people, with clear heads and warm hearts; they visited each other to promote mutual enjoyment, and believed in genuine earnestness in all things. We may ignore obligations to the pioneer race, and congratulate ourselves that our lot has been cast in a more advanced era of mental and moral culture; we may pride ourselves upon the developments which have been made in science and art; but, while viewing our standard of elevation as immeasurably in advance of that of our forefathers, it would be well to emulate their great characteristics for hospitality, honor, and integrity.

The type of Christianity of that period will not suffer by comparison with that of the present day. If the people of olden times had less for costly apparel and ostentatious display, they had also more for offices of charity and benevolence; if they did not have the splendor and luxuries of wealth, they at least had no infirmaries or paupers, very few lawyers, and but little use for jails. The vain and thoughtless may jeer at their unpretending manners and customs, but in all the elements of true manhood and true womanhood it may be safely averred that they were more than the peers of the generation that now occupy their places. That race has left its impress upon our times,— whatever patriotism the present generation boasts of has descended from them. Rude and illiterate, comparatively, they may have been, but they possessed strong minds in strong bodies, made so by their compulsory self-denials, their privations and toil. It was the mission of many of them to aid and participate in the formation of this great commonwealth, and wisely and well was the mission performed. Had their descendants been more faithful to their noble teachings, harmony would now reign supreme where violence and discord now hold their sway in the land.

The pioneer times are the greenest spot in the memories of those who lived in them; the privations and hardships they then endured are consecrated things in the recollection of the survivors.

Our fathers established the first Christian, non-sectarian government in the world, and declared as the chief corner-stone of that government Christ's teaching, that all men are " born free and equal;" love your neighbor as your- self. Since this thought has been carried into effect by our non-sectarian government, it has done more to elevate and civilize mankind in the last one hundred years than had ever been accomplished in all time before. Under the humane and inspiring influence of this grand idea put into practice, the wheels of progress, science, religion, and civilization have made gigantic strides, and our nation especially, from ocean to ocean, from arctic ice to tropic sun, is filled with smiling, happy homes, rich fields, blooming gardens, and bright firesides, made such by Christian charity carried into national and State con- stitutional enactment.

CHAPTER II

OUR ABORIGINES—THE IROQUOIS, OR SIX NATIONS—INDIAN TOWNS, VILLAGES, GRAVEYARDS, CUSTOMS, DRESS, HUTS, MEDICINES, DOCTORS, BARK-PEELERS, BURIALS, ETC.

AQUANUSCHIONI, or "united people," is what they called themselves. The French called them the Iroquois; the English, the Six Nations. They formed a confederate nation, and as such were the most celebrated and power-ful of all the Indian nations in North America. The confederacy consisted of the Mohawks, the fire-striking people; the Oneidas, the pipe-makers; the Onondagas, the hill-top people; the Cayugas, the people from the lake; the Tuscaroras, unwilling to be with other people; and the Senecas, the mountaineers.

The aborigines were called Indians because Columbus thought he had discovered India, and they were called Red Men because they daubed their faces and bodies with red paint.

The Iroquois, or Six Nations, were divided into what might be called eight families,—viz., the Wolf, Bear, Beaver, Turtle, Deer, Snipe, Heron, and Hawk. Each of the Six Nations had one of each of these families in their tribe, and all the members of that family, no matter how wide apart or of what other tribe, were considered as brothers and sisters, and were forbidden to marry in their own family. Then a Wolf was a brother to all other Wolves in each of the nations. This family bond was taught from infancy and enforced by public opinion.

"If at any time there appeared a tendency toward conflict between the different tribes, it was instantly checked by the thought that, if persisted in, the hand of the Turtle must be lifted against his brother Turtle, the toma-hawk of the Beaver might be buried in the brain of his kinsman Beaver. And so potent was the feeling that, for at least two hundred years, and until the power of the league was broken by the overwhelming outside force of the whites, there was no serious dissension between the tribes of the Iroquois.

"In peace, all power was confined to 'sachems;' in war, to 'chiefs.' The sachems of each tribe acted as its rulers in the few matters which required the exercise of civil authority. The same rulers also met in council to direct the affairs of the confederacy. There were fifty in all, of whom the Mohawks

NOTE.—For much in this chapter I am indebted to Rupp's History.

22

had nine, the Oneidas nine, the Onondagas fourteen, the Cayugas ten, and the Senecas eight. These numbers, however, did not give proportionate power in the councils of the league, for all the nations were equal there. There was in each tribe, too, the same number of war-chiefs as sachems, and these had absolute authority in time of war. When a council assembled, each sachem had a war-chief near him to execute his orders. But in the war-party the war-chief commanded and the sachem took his place in the ranks. This was the system in its simplicity.

" The right of heirship, as among many other of the North America tribes of Indians, was in the female line. A man's heirs were his brother,— that is to say, his mother's son and his sister's son,—never his own son, nor his brother's son. The few articles which constituted an Indian's personal property—even his bow and tomahawk—never descended to the son of him who had wielded them. Titles, so far as they were hereditary at all, followed the same law of descent. The child also followed the clan and tribe of the mother. The object was evidently to secure greater certainty that the heir would be of the blood of his deceased kinsman. The result of the application of this rule to the Iroquois system of clans was that if a particular sachemship or chieftaincy was once established in a certain clan of a certain tribe, in that clan and tribe it was expected to remain forever. Exactly how it was filled when it became vacant is a matter of some doubt; but, as near as can be learned, the new official was elected by the warriors of the clan, and was then inaugurated by the council of the sachems.

" If, for instance, a sachemship belonging to the Wolf clan of the Seneca tribe became vacant, it could only be filled by some one of the Wolf clan of the Seneca tribe. A clan council was called, and, as a general rule, the heir of the deceased was chosen to his place,—to wit, one of his brothers, reckoning only on the mother's side, or one of his sister's sons, or even some more distant male relative in the female line. But there was no positive law, and the warriors might discard all these and elect some one entirely unconnected with the deceased, though, as before stated, he must be one of the same clan and tribe. While there was no unchangeable custom compelling the clan council to select one of the heirs of the deceased as his successor, yet the tendency was so strong in that direction that an infant was frequently chosen, a guardian being appointed to perform the functions of the office till the youth should reach the proper age to do so. All offices were held for life, unless the incumbent was solemnly deposed by a council, an event which very seldom occurred. Notwithstanding the modified system of hereditary power in vogue, the constitution of every tribe was essentially republican. Warriors, old men, and women attended the various councils and made their influence felt. Neither in the government of the confederacy nor of the tribes was there any such thing as tyranny over the people, though there was a great deal of tyranny by the league over conquered nations. In fact, there was very little government of any kind, and very little need of any. There was substantially no property interests to guard, all land being in common, and each man's personal property being limited to a bow, a tomahawk, and a few deer-skins. Liquor had not yet lent its disturbing influence, and few quarrels were to be traced to the influence of women, for the American Indian is singularly free from the warmer passions.

" His principal vice is an easily aroused and unlimited hatred; but the tribes were so small and enemies so convenient that there was no difficulty in gratifying this feeling (and attaining to the rank of a warrior) outside of his own nation. The consequence was that although the war-parties of the Iroquois were continually shedding the blood of their foes, there was very little quarrelling at home.

" Their religious creed was limited to a somewhat vague belief in the existence of a Great Spirit and several inferior but very potent evil spirits. They had a few simple ceremonies, consisting largely of dances, one called the ' green-corn dance,' performed at the time indicated by its name, and others at other seasons of the year. From a very early date their most important religious ceremony has been the ' burning of the white dog,' when an unfortunate canine of the requisite color is sacrificed by one of the chiefs. To this day the pagans among them still perform this rite.

" In common with their fellow-savages on this continent, the Iroquois have been termed ' fast friends and bitter enemies.' Events have proved, however, that they were a great deal stronger enemies than friends. Revenge was the ruling passion of their nature, and cruelty was their abiding characteristic. Revenge and cruelty are the worst attributes of human nature, and it is idle to talk of the goodness of men who roasted their captives at the stake. All Indians were faithful to their own tribes, and the Iroquois were faithful to their confederacy; but outside of these limits their friendship could not be counted on, and treachery was always to be apprehended in dealing with them.

" In their family relations they were not harsh to their children and not wantonly so to their wives; but the men were invariably indolent, and all labor was contemptuously abandoned to their weaker sex.

" Polygamy, too, was practised, though in what might be called moderation. Chiefs and eminent warriors usually had two or three wives, rarely more. They could be discarded at will by their husbands, but the latter seldom availed themselves of their privilege.

" Our nation—the Senecas—was the most numerous and comprised the greatest warriors of the Iroquois confederacy. Their great chiefs, Cornplanter and Guyasutha, are prominently connected with the traditions of the head-waters of the Allegheny, Western New York, and Northwestern Pennsylvania. In person the Senecas were slender, middle-sized, handsome, and straight. The squaws were short, not handsome, and clumsy. The skin was reddish brown, hair straight and jet-black.

"After the death of a Seneca, the corpse was dressed in a new blanket or petticoat, with the face and clothes painted red. The body was then laid on a skin in the middle of the hut. The war and hunting implements of the deceased were then piled up around the body. In the evening after sunset, and in the morning before daylight, the squaws and relations assembled around the corpse to mourn. This was daily repeated until interment. The graves were dug by old squaws, as the young squaws abhorred this kind of labor. Before they had hatchets and other tools, they used to line the inside of the grave with the bark of trees, and when the corpse was let down they placed some pieces of wood across, which were again covered with bark, and then the earth thrown in, to fill up the grave. But afterwards they usually placed three boards, not nailed together, over the grave, in such a manner that the corpse lay between them. A fourth board was placed as a cover, and then the grave was filled up with earth. Now and then a proper coffin was procured.

"At an early period they used to put a tobacco-pouch, knife, tinder-box, tobacco and pipe, bow and arrows, gun, powder and shot, skins and cloth for clothes, paint, a small bag of Indian corn or dried bilberries, sometimes the kettle, hatchet, and other furniture of the deceased, into the grave, supposing that the departed spirits would have the same wants and occupation in the land of souls. But this custom was nearly wholly abolished among the Delawares and Iroquois about the middle of the last century. At the burial not a man shed a tear; they deemed it a shame for a man to weep. But, on the other hand, the women set up a dreadful howl." They carried their dead a long way sometimes for burial.

THE ORIGINAL BARK-PEELERS

An Indian hut was built in this manner. Trees were peeled abounding in sap, usually the linn. When the trees were cut down the bark was peeled with the tomahawk and its handle. They peeled from the top of the tree to the butt. The bark for hut-building was cut into pieces of six or eight feet; these pieces were then dried and flattened by laying heavy stones upon them. The frame of a bark hut was made by driving poles into the ground, and the poles were strengthened by cross-beams. This frame was then covered inside and outside with this prepared linn-wood bark, fastened with leather-wood bark or hickory withes. The roof ran upon a ridge, and was covered in the same manner as the frame; and an opening was left in it for the smoke to escape, and one on the side of the frame for a door.

HOW THE INDIAN BUILT LOG HUTS IN HIS TOWN OR VILLAGE

They cut logs fifteen feet long and laid these logs upon each other, at each end they drove posts in the ground and tied these posts together at the top with hickory withes or moose bark. In this way they erected a wall of logs fifteen feet long to the height of four feet. In this same way they raised a wall opposite to this one about twelve feet away. In the centre of each end of this log frame they drove forks into the ground, a strong pole was then laid upon these forks, extending from end to end, and from these log walls they set up poles for rafters to the centre pole; on these rafters they tied poles for sheeting, and the hut was then covered or shingled with linn-wood bark. This bark was peeled from the tree, commencing at the top,

Captain George Smoke and his cousin John Smoke, who stood for this picture as a special favor for the author. They are Seneca Indians dressed and equipped as the Senecas of Northwestern Pennsylvania four hundred years ago

with a tomahawk. The bark-strips in this way were sometimes thirty feet long and usually six inches wide. These strips were cut as desired for roofing.

At each end of the hut they set up split lumber, leaving an open space at each end for a door-way, at which a bear-skin hung. A stick leaning against the outside of this skin meant that the door was locked. At the top of the hut, in place of a chimney, they left an open place. The fires were made in the inside of the hut, and the smoke escaped through this open space. For bedding they had linn-wood bark covered with bear-skins. Open places between logs the squaws stopped with moss gathered from old logs.

There was no door, no windows, and no chimney. Several families occupied a hut, hence they built them long. Other Indian nations erected smaller huts, and the families lived separate. The men wore a blanket and went bare-headed. The women wore a petticoat, fastened about the hips, extending a little below the knees.

Our nation, the Senecas, produced the greatest orators, and more of them than any other. Cornplanter, Red Jacket, and Farmer's Brother were all Senecas. Red Jacket once, in enumerating the woes of the Senecas, exclaimed,—

" We stand on a small island in the bosom of the great waters. We are encircled, we are encompassed. The evil spirit rides on the blast, and the waters are disturbed. They rise, they press upon us, and the waters once settled over us, we disappear forever. Who then lives to mourn us? None. What marks our extinction? Nothing. We are mingled with the common elements."

The following is an extract from an address delivered by Cornplanter to General Washington in Philadelphia, Pennsylvania, in 1790:

" FATHER,—When you kindled your thirteen fires separately the wise men assembled at them told us that you were all brothers, the children of one Great Father, who regarded the red people as his children. They called us brothers, and invited us to his protection. They told us he resided beyond the great waters where the sun first rises, and he was a king whose power no people could resist, and that his goodness was as bright as the sun. What they said went to our hearts. We accepted the invitations and promised to obey him. What the Seneca nation promises they faithfully perform. When you refused obedience to that king he commanded us to assist his beloved men in making you sober. In obeying him we did no more than yourselves had bid us promise. We were deceived; but your people, teaching us to confide in that king, had helped to deceive us, and we now appeal to your breast. Is all the blame ours?

" You told us you could crush us to nothing, and you demanded from us a great country as the price of that peace which you had offered us, as if our want of strength had destroyed our rights."

" Drunkenness, after the whites were dealing with them, was a common vice. It was not confined, as it is at this day among the whites, principally to the ' strong-minded,' the male sex; but the Indian female, as well as the male, was infatuated alike with the love of strong drink; for neither of them knew bounds to their desire: they drank while they had whiskey or could swallow it down. Drunkenness was a vice, though attended with many serious conse-quences, nay, murder and death, that was not punishable among them. It was a fashionable vice. Fornication, adultery, stealing, lying, and cheating, principally the offspring of drunkenness, were considered as heinous and scandalous offences, and were punished in various ways.

27

"The Delawares and Iroquois married early in life; the men usually at eighteen and the women at fourteen; but they never married near relations. If an Indian man wished to marry he sent a present, consisting of blankets, cloth, linen, and occasionally a few belts of wampum, to the nearest relations of the person he had fixed upon. If he that made the present, and the present pleased, the matter was formally proposed to the girl, and if the answer was affirmatively given, the bride was conducted to the bridegroom's dwelling without any further ceremony; but if the other party chose to decline the proposal, they returned the present by way of a friendly negative.

"After the marriage, the present made by the suitor was divided among the friends of the young wife. These returned the civility by a present of Indian corn, beans, kettles, baskets, hatchets, etc., brought in solemn procession into the hut of the new married couple. The latter commonly lodged in a friend's house till they could erect a dwelling of their own.

"As soon as a child was born, it was laid upon a board or straight piece of bark covered with moss and wrapped up in a skin or piece of cloth, and

Indians moving

when the mother was engaged in her housework this rude cradle or bed was hung to a peg or branch of a tree. Their children they educated to fit them to get through the world as did their fathers. They instructed them in religion, etc. They believed that Manitou, their God, 'the good spirit,' could be propitiated by sacrifices; hence they observed a great many superstitious and idolatrous ceremonies. At their general and solemn sacrifices the oldest men performed the offices of priests, but in private parties each man brought a sacrifice, and offered it himself as priest. Instead of a temple they fitted up a large dwelling-house for the purpose.

"When they travelled or went on a journey they manifested much carelessness about the weather; yet, in their prayers, they usually begged ' for a clear and pleasant sky.' They generally provided themselves with Indian meal, which they either ate dry, mixed with sugar and water, or boiled into a kind of mush; for they never took bread made of Indian corn for a long journey, because in summer it would spoil in three or four days and be unfit for use. As to meat, that they took as they went.

"If in their travels they had occasion to pass a deep river, on arriving at it they set about it immediately and built a canoe by taking a long piece of bark of proportionate breadth, to which they gave the proper form by fastening it to ribs of light wood, bent so as to suit the occasion. If a large canoe was required, several pieces of bark were carefully sewed together. If the voyage was expected to be long, many Indians carried everything they wanted for their night's lodging with them,—namely, some slender poles and rush-mats, or birch-bark."

When at home they had their amusements. Their favorite one was dancing. "The common dance was held either in a large house or in an open field around a fire. In dancing they formed a circle, and always had a leader, to whom the whole company attended. The men went before, and the women closed the circle. The latter danced with great decency and as if they were engaged in the most serious business; while thus engaged they never spoke a word to the men, much less joked with them, which would have injured their character.

"Another kind of dance was only attended by men. Each rose in his turn, and danced with great agility and boldness, extolling their own or their forefathers' great deeds in a song, to which all beat time, by a monotonous, rough note, which was given out with great vehemence at the commencement of each bar.

"The war-dance, which was always held either before or after a campaign, was dreadful to behold. None took part in it but the warriors themselves. They appeared armed, as if going to battle. One carried his gun or hatchet, another a long knife, the third a tomahawk, the fourth a large club, or they all appeared armed with tomahawks. These they brandished in the air, to show how they intended to treat their enemies. They affected such an air of anger and fury on this occasion that it made a spectator shudder to behold them. A chief led the dance, and sang the warlike deeds of himself or his ancestors. At the end of every celebrated feat of valor he wielded his tomahawk with all his might against a post fixed in the ground. He was then followed by the rest; each finished his round by a blow against the post. Then they danced all together; and this was the most frightful scene. They affected the most horrible and dreadful gestures; threatened to beat, cut, and stab each other. They were, however, amazingly dexterous in avoiding the threatened danger. To complete the horror of the scene, they howled as dreadfully as if in actual fight, so that they appeared as raving madmen. During the dance they sometimes sounded a kind of fife, made of reed, which had a shrill and disagreeable note. The Iroquois used the war-dance even in times of peace, with a view to celebrate the deeds of their heroic chiefs in a solemn manner.

" The Indians, as well as ' all human flesh,' were heirs of disease. The most common were pleurisy, weakness and pains in the stomach and breast, consumption, diarrhœa, rheumatism, bloody flux, inflammatory fevers, and occasionally the small-pox made dreadful ravages among them. Their general remedy for all disorders, small or great, was a sweat. For this purpose they had in every town an oven, situated at some distance from the dwellings, built of stakes and boards, covered with sods, or dug in the side of a hill, and heated with some red-hot stones. Into this the patient crept naked, and in a short time was thrown into profuse perspiration. As soon as the patient felt himself too hot he crept out, and immediately plunged himself into a river or some cold water, where he continued about thirty seconds, and then went again into the oven. After having performed this operation three times successively, he smoked his pipe with composure, and in many cases a cure was completely effected.

" In some places they had ovens constructed large enough to receive several persons. Some chose to pour water now and then upon the heated stones, to increase the steam and promote more profuse perspiration. Many Indians in perfect health made it a practice of going into the oven once or twice a week to renew their strength and spirits. Some pretended by this operation to prepare themselves for a business which requires mature deliberation and artifice. If the sweating did not remove the disorder, other means were applied. Many of the Indians believed that medicines had no efficacy unless administered by a professed physician ; enough of professed doctors could be found ; many of both sexes professed to be doctors.

"Indian doctors never applied medicines without accompanying them with mysterious ceremonies, to make their effect appear supernatural. The ceremonies were various. Many breathed upon the sick ; they averred their breath was wholesome. In addition to this, they spurted a certain liquor made of herbs out of their mouth over the patient's whole body, distorting their features and roaring dreadfully. In some instances physicians crept into the oven, where they sweat, howled, roared, and now and then grinned horribly at their patients, who had been laid before the opening, and frequently felt the pulse of the patient. Then pronounced sentence, and foretold either recovery or death. On one occasion a Moravian missionary was present, who says, 'An Indian physician had put on a large bear-skin, so that his arms were covered with the forelegs, his feet with the hind legs, and his head was entirely concealed in the bear's head, with the addition of glass eyes. He came in this attire with a calabash in his hand, accompanied by a great crowd of people, into the patient's hut, singing and dancing, when he grasped a handful of hot ashes, and scattering them into the air, with a horrid noise, approached

30

the patient, and began to play several legerdemain tricks with small bits of wood, by which he pretended to be able to restore him to health.'

" The common people believed that by rattling the calabash the physician had power to make the spirits discover the cause of the disease, and even evade the malice of the evil spirit who occasioned it.

" Their materia medica, or the remedies used in curing diseases, were such as rattlesnake-root, the skins of rattlesnakes dried and pulverized, thorny ash, toothache-tree, tulip-tree, dogwood, wild laurel, sassafras, Canada shrubby elder, poison-ash, wintergreen, liverwort, Virginia poke, jalap, sarsaparilla, Canadian sanicle, scabians or devil's-bit, bloodwort, cuckoo pint, ginseng, and a few others.

" Wars among the Indians were always carried on with the greatest fury, and lasted much longer than they do now among them. The offensive weapons were, before the whites came among them, bows, arrows, and clubs. The latter were made of the hardest kind of wood, from two to three feet long and very heavy, with a large round knob at one end. Their weapon of defence was a shield, made of the tough hide of a buffalo, on the convex side of which they received the arrows and darts of the enemy. But about the middle of the last century this was all laid aside by the Delawares and Iroquois, though they used to a later period bows, arrows, and clubs of war. The clubs they used were pointed with nails and pieces of iron, when used at all. Guns were measurably substituted for all these. The hatchet and long-knife was used, as well as the guns. The army of these nations consisted of all their young men, including boys of fifteen years old. They had their captains and subordinate officers. Their captains would be called among them commanders or generals. The requisite qualifications for this station were prudence, cunning, resolution, bravery, undauntedness, and previous good fortune in some fight or battle.

" ' To lift the hatchet,' or to begin a war, was always, as they declared, not till just and important causes prompted them to it. Then they assigned as motives that it was necessary to revenge the injuries done to the nation. Perhaps the honor of being distinguished as great warriors may have been an ' ingredient in the cup.'

" But before they entered upon so hazardous an undertaking they carefully weighed all the proposals made, compared the probable advantages or disadvantages that might accrue. A chief could not begin a war without the consent of his captains, nor could he accept of a war-belt only on the condition of its being considered by the captains.

" The chief was bound to preserve peace to the utmost of his power. But if several captains were unanimous in declaring war, the chief was then obliged to deliver the care of his people, for a time, into the hands of the captains, and to lay down his office. Yet his influence tended greatly either to prevent or encourage the commencement of war, for the Indians believed

31

that a war could not be successful without the consent of the chief, and the captains, on that account, strove to be in harmony with him. After war was agreed on, and they wished to secure the assistance of a nation in league with them, they notified that nation by sending a piece of tobacco, or by an embassy. By the first, they intended that the captains were to smoke pipes and consider seriously whether they would take part in the war or not. The embassy was intrusted to a captain, who carried a belt of wampum, upon which the object of the embassy was described by certain figures, and a hatchet with a red handle. After the chief had been informed of his commission, it was laid before a council. The hatchet having been laid on the ground, he delivered a long speech, while holding the war-belt in his hand, always closing the address with the request to take up the hatchet, and then delivering the war-belt. If this was complied with, no more was said, and this act was considered as a solemn promise to lend every assistance; but if neither the hatchet was taken up nor the belt accepted, the ambassador drew the just conclusion that the nation preferred to remain neutral, and without any further ceremony returned home.

" The Delawares and Iroquois were very informal in declaring war. They often sent out small parties, seized the first man they met belonging to the nation they had intended to engage, killed and scalped him, then cleaved his head with a hatchet, which they left sticking in it, or laid a war-club, painted red, upon the body of the victim. This was a formal challenge. In consequence of which, a captain of an insulted party would take up the weapons of the murderers and hasten into their country, to be revenged upon them. If he returned with a scalp, he thought he had avenged the rights of his own nation.

"Among the Delawares and Iroquois it required but little time to make preparations for war. One of the most necessary preparations was to paint themselves red and black, for they held it that the most horrid appearance of war was the greatest ornament. Some captains fasted and attended to their dreams, with the view to gain intelligence of the issue of the war. The night previous to the march of the army was spent in feasting, at which the chiefs were present, when either a hog or some dogs were killed. Dog's flesh, said they, inspired them with the genuine martial spirit. Even women, in some instances, partook of this feast, and ate dog's flesh greedily. Now and then, when a warrior was induced to make a solemn declaration of his war inclination, he held up a piece of dog's flesh in sight of all present and devoured it, and pronounced these words, ' Thus will I devour my enemies!' After the feast the captain and all his people began the war-dance, and continued till daybreak, till they had become quite hoarse and weary. They generally danced all together, and each in his turn took the head of a hog in his hand. As both their friends and the women generally accompanied them to the first night's encampment, they halted about two or three miles from the town, danced the war-dance once more, and the day following began their march.

Before they made an attack they reconnoitred every part of the country. To this end they dug holes in the ground; if practicable, in a hillock, covered with wood, in which they kept a small charcoal fire, from which they discovered the motions of the enemy undiscovered. When they sought a prisoner or a scalp, they ventured, in many instances, even in daytime, to execute their designs. Effectually to accomplish this, they skulked behind a bulky tree, and crept slyly around the trunk, so as not to be observed by the person or persons for whom they lay in ambush. In this way they slew many. But if they had a family or town in view, they always preferred the night, when their enemies were wrapped in profound sleep, and in this way killed, scalped, and made prisoners of many of the enemies, set fire to the houses, and retired with all possible haste to the woods or some place of safe retreat. To avoid pursuit, they disguised their footmarks as much as possible. They depended much on stratagem for their success. Even in war they thought it more honorable to distress their enemy more by stratagem than combat. The English, not aware of the artifice of the Indians, lost an army when Braddock was defeated.

" The Indian's cruelty, when victorious, was without bounds; their thirst for blood was almost unquenchable. They never made peace till compelled by necessity. No sooner were terms of peace proposed than the captains laid down their office and delivered the government of the state into the hands of the chiefs. A captain had no more right to conclude a peace than a chief to begin war. When peace had been offered to a captain he could give no other answer than to mention the proposal to the chief, for as a warrior he could not make peace. If the chief inclined to peace, he used all his influence to effect that end, and all hostility ceased, and, in conclusion, the calumet, or peace-pipe, was smoked and belts of wampum exchanged, and a concluding speech made, with the assurance 'that their friendship should last as long as the sun and moon give light, rise and set; as long as the stars shine in the firmament, and the rivers flow with water.' "

The weapons employed by our Indians two hundred years ago were axes, arrows, and knives of stone. Shells were sometimes used to make knives.

The Indian bow was made as follows: the hickory limb was cut with a stone axe, the wood was then heated on both sides near a fire until it was soft enough to scrape down to the proper size and shape.

A good bow measured forty-six inches in length, three-fourths of an inch thick in the centre, and one and a quarter inches in width, narrowing down to the points to five-eighths of an inch. The ends were thinner than the middle. Bow-making was tedious work.

" The bow-string was made of the ligaments obtained from the vertebra of the elk. The ligament was split, scraped, and twisted into a cord by rolling the fibres between the palm of the hand and the thigh. One end of the string was knotted to the bow, but the other end was looped, in order that the bow could be quickly strung."

Quivers to carry the arrows were made of dressed buckskin, with or without the fur. The squaws did all the tanning.

The arrow-heads were made of flint or other hard stone or bone; they were fastened to the ash or hickory arrows with the sinews of the deer. The arrow was about two feet and a half in length, and a feather was fastened to the butt end to give it a rotary motion in its flight.

Poisoned arrows were made by dipping them into decomposed liver, to which had been added the poison of the rattlesnake. The venom or decomposed animal matter no doubt caused blood-poisoning and death.*

Bows and arrows were long used by the red men after the introduction of fire-arms, because the Indian could be more sure of his game without revealing his presence. For a long time after the introduction of fire-arms the Indians were more expert with the bow and arrow than with the rifle.

Their tobacco-pipes were made of stone bowls and ash stems. Canoes were made of birch or linn-wood bark, and many wigwam utensils of that bark. This bark was peeled in early spring. The bark canoe was the American Indian's invention.

When runners were sent with messages to other tribes the courier took an easy running gait, which he kept up for hours at a time. It was a "dog-trot," an easy, jogging gait. Of course he had no clothes on except a breech-clout and moccasins. He always carried both arms up beside the chest with the fists clinched and held in front of the breast. He ate but little the day before his departure. A courier could make a hundred miles from sunrise to sunset.

When a young squaw was ready to marry she wore something on her head as a notice.

Then kettles were made of clay, or what was called "pot stone."

The stone hatchets were in the shape of a wedge; they were of no use in felling trees. They did this with a fire around the roots of the tree. Their stone pestles were about twelve inches long and five inches thick. They used bird-claws for "fish-hooks." They made their ropes, bridles, nets, etc., out of a wild weed called Indian hemp.

The twine or cords were manufactured by the squaws, who gathered stalks of this hemp, separating them into filaments, and then taking a number of filaments in one hand, rolled them rapidly upon their bare thighs until twisted, locking, from time to time, the ends with fresh fibres. The cord thus made was finished by dressing with a mixture of grease and wax, and drawn over a smooth groove in a stone.

---

* It was originally the practice of our Indians, as of all other savage people, to cut off in war the heads of their enemies for trophies, but for convenience in retreat this was changed to scalping.

Their hominy-mills can be seen yet about a mile north of Samuel Temple's barn, in Warsaw Township, Jefferson County. Corn, potatoes, and tobacco were unknown until the discovery of America.

All the stone implements of our Indians except arrows were ground and polished. How this was done the reader must imagine. Indians had their mechanics and their workshops or " spots" where implements were made. You must remember that the Indian had no iron or steel tools, only bone, stone, and wood to work with. The flint arrows were made from a stone of uniform density. Large chips were flaked or broken from the rock. These chips were again deftly chipped with bone chisels into arrows, and made straight by pressure. A lever was used on the rock to separate chips,—a bone tied to a heavy stick.

From Jones's " Antiquities of the Southern Indians" the writer has gleaned most of the following facts : They had a limited variety of copper implements, which were of rare occurrence, and which were too soft to be of use in working so hard a material as flint or quartzite. Hence it is believed that they fashioned their spear- and arrow-heads with other implements than those of iron or steel. They must have acquired, by their observation and numerous experiments, a thorough and practical knowledge of cleavage,— that is, " the tendency to split in certain directions, which is characteristic of most of the crystallizable minerals." Captain John Smith, speaking of the Virginia Indians in his sixth voyage, says, " His arrow-head he quickly maketh with a little bone, which he weareth at his bracelet, of a splint of a stone or glasse, in the form of a heart, and these they glue to the ends of the arrows. With the sinews of the deer and the tops of deers' horns boiled to a jelly they make a glue which will not dissolve in cold water." Schoolcraft says, " The skill displayed in this art, as it is exhibited by the tribes of the entire continent, has excited admiration. The material employed is generally some form of horn stone, sometimes passing into flint. No specimens have, however, been observed where the substance is gun-flint. The horn-stone is less hard than common quartz, and can be readily broken by contact with the latter." Catlin, in his " Last Ramble among the Indians," says, " Every tribe has its factory in which these arrow-heads are made, and in these only certain adepts are able or allowed to make them for the use of the tribe. Erratic bowlders of flint are collected and sometimes brought an immense distance, and broken with a sort of sledge-hammer made of a rounded pebble of horn-stone set in a twisted withe, holding the stone and forming a handle. The flint, at the indiscriminate blows of the sledge, is broken into a hundred pieces, and such flakes selected as from the angles of their fracture and thickness will answer as the basis of an arrow-head. The master-workman, seated on the ground, lays one of these flakes on the palm of his hand, holding it firmly down with two or more fingers of the same hand, and with his right hand, between the thumb and two forefingers, places his chisel or punch on the point that is to be broken off, and a co-operator—a striker—in front of him, with a mallet of very hard wood, strikes the chisel or punch on the upper end, flaking the flint off on the under side below each projecting point that is struck. The flint is then turned and chipped in the same manner from the opposite side, and that is chipped until required shape and dimensions are obtained, all the fractures being made on the palm of the hand. In selecting the flake for the arrow-head a nice judgment must be used or the attempt will fail. A flake with two opposite parallel, or nearly parallel, planes of cleavage is found, and of the thickness required for the centre of the arrow-point. The first chipping reaches nearly to the centre of these planes, but without quite breaking it away, and each clipping is shorter and shorter, until the shape and edge of the arrow-head is formed. The yielding elasticity of the palm of the hand enables the chip to come off without breaking the body of the flint, which would be the case if they were broken on a hard substance. These people have no metallic instruments to work with, and the punch which they use, I was told, was a piece of bone, but on examining it, I found it to be of substance much harder, made of the tooth—incisor—of the sperm whale, which cetaceans are often stranded on the coast of the Pacific."

" A considerable number of Indians must have returned and settled along the Red Bank as late as 1815–16. James White, of ' Mexico,' informed the writer that three hundred of them, about that time, settled along this stream below Brookville, partly in Armstrong-County. Respecting their return to this section, Dr. M. A. Ward wrote to Eben Smith Kelly, at Kittanning, from Pittsburg, January 18, 1817,—

" ' I am not at all surprised that the sober, industrious, religious inhabitants of Red Bank should be highly incensed at their late accession of emigrants, not only because by them they will probably be deprived of many fat bucks and delicious turkeys, to which, according to the strict interpretation of all our game laws, they have as good a right, if they have the fortune to find and the address to shoot them, as any " dirty, nasty" Indians whatever, but because the presence and examples of such neighbors must have a very depraving influence upon the morals. Their insinuating influence will be apt to divert the minds of the farmers from the sober pursuits of agriculture and inspire a propensity for the barbarous pleasures of the chase. . . . But what is worse than all, I have heard that they love whiskey to such an inordinate degree as to get sometimes beastly drunk, and even beat their wives and behave unseemly before their families, which certainly must have a most demoralizing tendency on the minds of the rising generation.' "—*History of Armstrong County.*

The Delaware Indians styled themselves " Lenni Lenape," the original or unchanged people. The eastern division of their people was divided into three tribes,—the Unamies, or Turtles of the sea-shore; the Unochlactgos, or Turkeys of the woods; and the Minsi-monceys, or Wolves of the mountains.

A few of the Muncy villages of this latter division were scattered as far west as the valley of the Allegheny.

From Penn's arrival in 1682 the Delawares were subject to the Iroquois, or the confederacy of the Six Nations, who were the most warlike savages in America. The Iroquois were usually known among the English people as the *Five* Nations. The nations were divided and known as the Mohawks, the fire-striking people, having been the first to procure fire-arms. The Senecas, mountaineers, occupied Western New York and Northwestern Pennsylvania. They were found in great numbers along the Allegheny and its tributaries. Their great chiefs were Cornplanter and Guyasutha. This tribe was the most numerous, powerful, and warlike of the Iroquois nation, and comprised the Indians of Northwestern Pennsylvania.

" But these were Indians pure and uncorrupted. Before many a log fire, at night, old settlers have often recited how clear, distinct, and immutable were their laws and customs; that when fully understood a white man could transact the most important business with as much safety as he can to-day in any commercial centre.

" In this day and age of progress we pride ourselves upon our railroads and telegraph as means of rapid communication, and yet, while it was well known to the early settlers that news and light freight would travel with incomprehensible speed from tribe to tribe, people of the present day fail to understand the complete system by which it was done.

" In many places through the western counties you will find traces of pits, which the early settlers will tell you were dug by white men looking for silver, which, as well as copper, was common among the Indians, and was supposed by first comers to be found in the vicinity; but experience soon proved the copper came, perhaps, from Lake Superior, by this Indian express, as we might term it, and the silver, just as possible, from the far West. Our railroads wind along the valleys, almost regardless of length or circuit, if a gradual rise can only be obtained. To travellers on wheels straight distances between points are much less formidable than is generally supposed. We find traces of the example of the Indian in the first white men. The first settlers of 1799 and 1805 took their bags of grain on their backs, walked fifty miles to a mill, and brought home their flour the same way."

" The following is taken from the 'Early Days of Punxsutawney and Western Pennsylvania,' contributed a few years ago to the *Punxsutawney Plaindealer* by the late John K. Coxson, Esq., who had made considerable research into Indian history, and was an enthusiast on the subject. According to Mr. Coxson, ' More than eighteen hundred years ago the Iroquois held a lodge in Punxsutawney (this town still bears its Indian name, which was their sobriquet for "gnat town"), to which point they could ascend with their canoes, and go still higher up the Mahoning to within a few hours' travel of the summit of the Allegheny Mountains. There were various Indian trails

37

traversing the forests, one of which entered Punxsutawney near where Judge Mitchell now (1898) resides.

" ' These trails were the thoroughfares or roadways of the Indians, over which they journeyed when on the chase or the " war-path," just as the people of the present age travel over their graded roads. " An erroneous impression obtains among many at the present day that the Indian, in travelling the interminable forests which once covered our towns and fields, roamed at random, like a modern afternoon hunter, by no fixed paths, or that he was guided in his long journeyings solely by the sun and stars, or by the course of the streams and mountains; and true it is that these untutored sons of the woods were considerable astronomers and geographers, and relied much upon these unerring guide-marks of nature. Even in the most starless nights they could determine their course by feeling the bark of the oak-trees, which is always smoothest on the south side and roughest on the north. But still they had their trails, or paths, as distinctly marked as are our county and State roads, and often better located. The white traders adopted them, and often stole their names, to be in turn surrendered to the leader of some Anglo-Saxon army, and, finally, obliterated by some costly highway of travel and commerce. They are now almost wholly effaced or forgotten. Hundreds travel along, or plough over them, unconscious that they are in the footsteps of the red men." * It has not taken long to obliterate all these Indian landmarks from our land; little more than a century ago the Indians roamed over all this western country, and now scarce a vestige of their presence remains. Much has been written and said about their deeds of butchery and cruelty. True, they were cruel, and in many instances fiendish, in their inhuman practices, but they did not meet the first settlers in this spirit. Honest, hospitable, religious in their belief, reverencing their Manitou, or Great Spirit, and willing to do anything to please their white brother,—this is how they met their first white visitors; but when they had seen nearly all their vast domain appropriated by the invaders, when wicked white men had introduced into their midst the " wicked fire-water," which is to-day the cause of many an act of fiendishness perpetrated by those who are not untutored savages, then the Indian rebelled, all the savage in his breast was aroused, and he became pitiless and cruel in the extreme.

" ' It is true that our broad domains were purchased and secured by treaty, but the odds were always on the side of the whites. The " Colonial Records" give an account of the treaty of 1686, by which a deed for " walking purchase was executed, by which the Indians sold as far as a man could walk in a day. But when the walk was to be made the most active white man was obtained, who ran from daylight until dark, as fast as he was able, without stopping to eat or drink. This much dissatisfied the Indians, who expected to walk leis-

* This paragraph was taken from Judge Veech.

urely, resting at noon to eat and shoot game, and one old chief expressed his dissatisfaction as follows: 'Lun, lun, lun; no lay down to drink; no stop to shoot squirrel, but lun, lun, lun all day; me no keep up; lun, lun for land.' That deed, it is said, does not now exist, but was confirmed in 1737."

" 'When the white man came the Indians were a temperate people, and their chiefs tried hard to prohibit the sale of intoxicating drinks among their tribes; and when one Sylvester Garland, in 1701, introduced rum among them and induced them to drink, at a council held in Philadelphia, Shemeken-whol, chief of the Shawnese, complained to Governor William Penn, and at a council held on the 13th of October, 1701, this man was held in the sum of one hundred pounds never to deal rum to the Indians again; and the bond and sentence was approved by Judge Shippen, of Philadelphia. At the chief's suggestion the council enacted a law prohibiting the trade in rum with the Indians. Still later the ruling chiefs of the Six Nations opposed the use of rum, and Red Jacket, in a speech at Buffalo, wished that whiskey would never be less than "a dollar a quart." He answered the missionary's remarks on drunkenness thus: "Go to the white man with that." A council, held on the Allegheny River, deplored the murder of the Wigden family in Butler County by a Seneca Indian while under the influence of whiskey, approved the sentence of our law, and again passed their prohibitory resolutions, and implored the white man not to give rum to the Indian.'

" Mr. Coxson claims that the council of the Delawares, Muncys, Shawnese, Nanticokes, Tuscorawas, and Mingos, to protest against the sale of their domain by the Six Nations, at Albany, in 1754, was held at Punxsutawney, and cites Joncaire's 'Notes on Indian Warfare,' 'Life of Bezant,' etc. 'It is said they ascended the tributary of La Belle Riviere to the mountain village on the way to Chinklacamoose (Clearfield) to attend the council.' * At that council, though Sheklemas, the Christian king of the Delawares, and other Christian chiefs, tried hard to prevent the war, they were overruled, and the tribes decided to go to war with their French allies against the colony. 'Travellers, as early as 1731, reported to the council of the colony of a town sixty miles from the Susquehanna.' †

" 'After the failure of the expedition against Fort Duquesne, the white captives were taken to Kittanning, Logtown, and Pukeesheno (Punxsutawney). The sachem, Pukeesheno (for whom the town was called), was the father of Tecumseh and his twin brother, the Prophet, and was a Shawnese. We make this digression to add another proof that Punxsutawney was named after a Shawnese chief as early as 1750.' ‡

" 'I went with Captain Brady on an Indian hunt up the Allegheny River. We found a good many signs of the savages, and I believe we were so much like the savages (when Brady went on a scouting expedition he always dressed

---

* Joncaire.   † Bezant.   ‡ History of Western Pennsylvania, p. 302.

39

in Indian costume) that they could hardly have known us from a band of Shawnese. But they had an introduction to us near the mouth of Red Bank. General Brodhead was on the route behind Captain Brady, who discovered the Indians on the march. He lay concealed among the rocks until the painted chiefs and their braves had got fairly into the narrow pass, when Brady and his men opened a destructive fire. The sylvan warriors returned the volley with terrific yells that shook the caverns and mountains from base to crest. The fight was short but sanguine. The Indians left the pass and retired, and soon were lost sight of in the deepness of the forest. We returned with three children recaptured, whose parents had been killed at Greensburg. We immediately set out on a path that led us to the mountains, to a lodge the savages had near the head-waters of Mahoning and Red Bank.

" ' We crossed the Mahoning about forty miles from Kittanning, and entered a town, which we found deserted. It seemed to be a hamlet, built by the Shawnese. From there we went over high and rugged hills, through laurel thickets, darkened by tall pine and hemlock groves, for one whole day, and lay quietly down on the bank of a considerable stream (Sandy Lick). About midnight Brady was aroused by the sound of a rifle not far down the creek. We arose and stole quietly along about half a mile, when we heard the voices of Indians but a short distance below us; there another creek unites its waters with the one upon whose banks we had rested. We ascertained that two Indians had killed a deer at a lick. They were trying to strike a light to dress their game. When the flame of pine-knots blazed brightly and revealed the visages of the savages, Brady appeared to be greatly excited, and perhaps the caution that he always took when on a war-path was at that time disregarded. Revenge swallowed and absorbed every faculty of his soul. He recognized the Indian who was foremost, when they chased him, a few months before, so closely that he was forced to leap across a chasm of stone on the slippery rock twenty-three feet; between the jaws of granite there roared a deep torrent twenty feet deep. When Brady saw Conemah he sprang forward and planted his tomahawk in his head. The other Indian, who had his knife in his hand, sprang at Brady. The long, bright steel glistened in his uplifted hand, when the flash of Farley's rifle was the death-light of the brave, who sank to the sands. . . . Brady scalped the Indians in a moment, and drew the deer into the thicket to finish dressing it, but had not completed his undertaking when he heard a noise in the branches of the neighboring trees. He sprang forward, quenched the flame, and in breathless silence listened for the least sound, but nothing was heard save the rustling of the leaves, stirred by the wind. One of the scouts softly crept along the banks of the creek to catch the faintest sound that echoes on the water, when he found a canoe down upon the beach. The scout communicated this to Brady, who resolved to embark on this craft, if it was large enough to carry the company. It was found to be of sufficient size. We all embarked and took the deer along. We had not gone forty rods down the stream when the savages gave a war-whoop, and about a mile off they were answered with a hundred voices. We heard them in pursuit as we went dashing down the frightful and unknown stream. We gained on them. We heard their voices far behind us, until the faint echoes of the hundreds of warriors were lost; but, unexpectedly, we found ourselves passing full fifty canoes drawn up on the beach. Brady landed a short distance below. There was no time to lose. If the pursuers arrived they might overtake the scouts. It was yet night. He took four of his men along, and with great caution unmoored the canoes and sent them adrift. The scouts below secured them, and succeeded in arriving at Brodhead's quarters with the scalps of two Indians and their whole fleet, which disabled them much from carrying on their bloody expeditions.'

" In the legend of Noshaken, the white captive of the Delawares, in 1753, who was kept at a village supposed to have been Punxsutawney, occurs the following: ' The scouts were on the track of the Indians, the time of burning of the captives was extended, and the whole band prepared to depart for Fort Venango with the prisoners. . . . They continued on for twenty miles, and encamped by a beautiful spring, where the sand boiled up from the bottom near where two creeks unite. Here they passed the night, and the next morning again headed for Fort Venango.

" ' This spring is believed to have been the " sand spring" at Brookville.' "

The Indian wampum, or money, was of two kinds, white and purple; the white is worked out of the inside of the great shells into the form of a bead, and perforated, to string on leather; the purple is taken out of the inside of the mussel shell; they are woven as broad as one's hand and about two feet long; these they call belts, which they give and receive at their treaties as the seals of friendship; for lesser matters a single string is given. Every bead is of known value, and a belt of a less number is made to equal one of a greater by fastening so many as is wanting to the belt by a string.

PUNXSUTAWNEY

Punxsutawney was an Indian town for centuries and, like all other towns of the Indian before the white man reached this continent with fire-arms, was stockaded.

The word " punxsu" means gnat. The land was a swamp, and alive with gnats, mosquitoes, turtles, and reptiles. For protection against the gnats the Indians anointed themselves with oil and ointments made of fat and poisons. Centuries ago the Indians of Punxsutawney dressed themselves in winter with a cloak made of buffalo, bear, or beaver skins, with a leather girdle, and stockings or moccasins of buckskin. It might be well to state here that the beavers were of all colors, white, yellow, spotted, gray, but mostly black. The Indian subsisted mostly on game, but when pressed for food ate acorns, nuts, and the inside bark of the birch-tree. As agriculturists each was apportioned a piece of land outside of the stockade, which was planted by the squaws in corn, squashes, and tobacco. A hole was made in the ground with a stick and a grain of corn put in each hole. Population among Indians did not increase rapidly. Mothers often nursed their papooses until they were five, six, and seven years old.

Not knowing how to dig wells, they located their ga-no-sote and villages on the banks of runs and creeks, or in the vicinity of springs. About the period of the formation of the league, when they were exposed to the inroads of hostile nations, and the warfare of migratory bands, their villages were compact and stockaded. Having run a trench several feet deep around five or ten acres of land, and thrown up the ground on the inside, they set a continuous row of stakes, burned at the ends, in this bank of earth, fixing them at such an angle that they inclined over the trench. Sometimes a village was surrounded by a double or even triple row of stakes. Within this enclosure they constructed their bark houses and secured their stores. Around it was the village field, consisting oftentimes of several hundred acres of cultivated land, which was subdivided into planting lots; those belonging to different families being bounded by uncultivated ridges.

The entrances to the stockade were anciently contrived so that they could be defended from assault by a very few men.

The Iroquois were accustomed to live largely in villages, and the stockades built about these villages protected them from sudden assaults and rendered it possible for the houses within to be built according to a method of construction such that they might last for a long time.

At the two ends of the houses were doors, either of bark hung on hinges of wood, or of deer- or bear-skins suspended before the opening, and however long the house, or whatever number of fires, these were the only entrances. Over one of these doors was cut the tribal device of the head of the family. Within, upon the two sides, were arranged wide seats, also of bark boards, about two feet from the ground, well supported underneath, and reaching the entire length of the house. Upon these they spread their mats of skins, and also their blankets, using them as seats by day and couches at night. Similar berths were constructed on each side, about five feet above these, and secured to the frame of the house, thus furnishing accommodations for the family. Upon cross-poles near the roof were hung in bunches, braided together by the husks, their winter supply of corn. Charred and dried corn and beans were generally stored in bark barrels and laid away in corners. Their implements for the chase, domestic utensils, weapons, articles of apparel, and miscellaneous notions were stored away, and hung up wherever an unoccupied place was discovered. A house of this description would accommodate a family of eight, with the limited wants of the Indian, and afford shelter for their necessary stores, making a not uncomfortable residence. After they had

42

The above cut shows an Indian stockade (bark houses) cut in two, showing the long house and ga-no-sote within. This is the mode of building the Indian villages of Northwestern Pennsylvania four hundred years ago. Painted for and presented to the author by Mr. Beaver, or the man who runs around, a Seneca Indian

learned the use of the axe, they began to substitute houses of logs, but they constructed them after the ancient model.

Our Indians were the Senecas, and they had six yearly festivals. These festivals consisted of dancing, singing, and thanksgiving to the Great Spirit for his gifts. The New Year was an acknowledgment for the whole year, and the white dog was sent to the Great Spirit to take to him their messages. The dog was the only animal they could trust to carry their messages.

1. The Maple Festival, for yielding its sweet water.
2. The Planting Festival.
3. The Strawberry Festival.
4. Green Corn Festival.
5. The Harvesting Festival.
6. New Year or White Dog Sacrifice.

The Indians had no Sunday. Our Indians called themselves Nun-ga-wah-gah, "The Great Hill People," and their legend was that they sprung from the ground. The civil chiefs wore horns as an emblem of power.

The moccasin was an Indian invention, and one of great antiquity. The needle was made from a bone taken from the ankle-joint of the deer, and the thread was from the sinews. The deer-skin was tanned by the use of the brains of the deer. The brains were dried in cakes for future use. Bear-skins were not tanned, but were used for cloaks and beds.

Indian corn was red and white flint. They ground it in mortars and sifted it in a basket, and then baked it in loaves an inch thick and about six inches in diameter. They had a way of charring corn so it would keep for years. They would pick ears while green, roast it, dry it in the sun, mix with it about a third of maple sugar, and pound it into flour. This they carried with them on long trips.

For ropes and straps, raw hide and barks were used; the bark made the best ropes. The inside bark of the elm or bass-wood was boiled in ashes, separated into filaments, and then braided into rope.

Their knives were made of flint and horn-stone. Tomahawks were made of stone. They buried food with their dead.

Their cooking-vessels could not be exposed to fire, hence they used large upright vessels made of birch-bark, in which to boil food. Repeatedly putting stones red-hot into the water in these vessels, forcing them to boil.

The Indian was a great ball-player and fond of games, swift in races; in truth, the Indian was built for fleetness and not for strength; his life of pursuit educated him that way. Their feathers and war-paint was nothing else than crude heraldry. The squaws did the work, they were more apt than the braves. Paint spread upon the face and body indicated the tribe, prowess, honor, etc., of the individual and family, and the arbitrary methods employed by the squaws made their heraldry hard to understand. The facial heraldry was unique both in representation and subject. Every picture had its significance. If a squaw was in love she daubed a ring around one of her eyes. This meant I am ready for a proposal. This symbol worn by a buck indicated he was in the market, too. When love matters were running smoothly with a squaw she painted her cheeks a cherry-red, and a straight mark on her forehead, which meant a happy road. A zigzag mark on the forehead meant lightning. In case of a death in the family the squaw painted her cheeks black. Before a battle each warrior had smeared on the upper part of his body a wolf, herron, snipe, etc., to indicate his tribe, so that if he was killed his tribe could recognize his body and come for it.

In 1762 the great Moravian missionary, Rev. John Heckewelder, may have, and probably did, spend a day or two in Punxsutawney. In or about the year 1765 a Moravian missionary—viz., Rev. David Zeisberger—established a mission near the present town of Wyalusing, Bradford County, Pennsylvania. He erected forty frame buildings, with shingle roofs and chimneys, in connection with other improvements, and Christianized a large number of the savages. The Muncy Indians were then living in what is now called Forest County, on the Allegheny River. This brave, pious missionary determined to reach these savages also, and, with two Christian Indian guides, he traversed the solitude of the forests and reached his destination on the 16th of October, 1767. He remained with these savages but seven days; they were good listeners to his sermons, but every day he was in danger of being murdered. Of these Indians he wrote,—

"I have never found such heathenism in any other parts of the Indian country. Here Satan has his stronghold. Here he sits on his throne. Here he is worshipped by true savages, and carries on his work in the hearts of the children of darkness." These, readers, were the Indians that roamed over our hills, then either Lancaster or Berks County. In 1768 this brave minister returned and put up a log cabin, twenty-six by sixteen feet, and in 1769 was driven back to what is now called Wyalusing by repeated attempts on his life. He says in his journal, "For ten months I have lived between these two towns of godless and malicious savages, and my preservation is wonderful."

In 1768 the six Indian nations having by treaty sold the land from "under the feet" of the Wyalusing converts, the Rev. Zeisberger was compelled to take measures for the removal of these Christian Indians, with their horses and cattle, to some other field. After many councils and much consideration, he determined to remove the entire body to a mission he had established on the Big Beaver, now Lawrence County, Pennsylvania. Accordingly, "on the 11th of June, 1772, everything being in readiness, the congregation assembled for the last time in their church and took up their march toward the setting sun." They were "divided into two companies, and each of these were subdivided. One of these companies went overland by the Wyalusing path, up the Sugar Run, and down the Loyal Sock, *via* Dushore. This company was in charge of Ettwein, who had the care of the horses and cattle.

The other company was in charge of Rothe, and went by canoe down the Susquehannah and up the west branch." The place for the divisions to unite was the Great Island, now Lock Haven, and from there, under the lead of Rev. John Ettwein, to proceed up the west branch of the Susquehanna, and then cross the mountains over the Chinklacamoose path, through what is now Clearfield and Punxsutawney, and from there to proceed, *via* Kittanning, to the Big Beaver, now in Lawrence County, Pennsylvania. Reader, just think of two hundred and fifty people of all ages, with seventy head of oxen and a greater number of horses, traversing these deep forests, over a small path sometimes scarcely discernible, under drenching rains, and through dismal swamps, and all this exposure continued for days and weeks, wild beasts to the right and to the left of them, and the path alive with rattlesnakes in front of them, wading streams and overtaken by sickness, and then, dear reader, you will conclude with me that nothing but " praying all night in the wilderness" ever carried them successfully to their destination. This story of Rev. Ettwein is full of interest. I reprint a paragraph or two that applies to what is now Jefferson County,—viz.:

" *1772, Tuesday, July 14.*—Reached Clearfield Creek, where the Buffaloes formerly cleared large tracts of undergrowth, so as to give them the appearance of cleared fields. Hence the Indians called the creek ' Clearfield.' Here we shot nine deer. On the route we shot one hundred and fifty deer and three bears.

" *Friday, July 17.*—Advanced only four miles to a creek that comes down from the Northwest." This was and is Anderson Creek, near Curwensville, Pennsylvania.

" *July 18.*—Moved on . . .

" *Sunday, July 19.*—As yesterday, but two families kept up with me, because of the rain, we had a quiet Sunday, but enough to do drying our effects. In the evening all joined me, but we could hold no service as the Ponkies were so excessively annoying that the cattle pressed toward and into our camp to escape their persecutors in the smoke of the fire. This vermin is a plague to man and beast by day and night, but in the swamp through which we are now passing, their name is legion. Hence the Indians call it the Ponsetunik, *i.e.*, the town of the Ponkies." This swamp was in what we now call Punxsutawney. These people on their route lived on fish, venison, etc.

CHAPTER III

CORNPLANTER—OUR CHIEF—CHIEF OF THE SENECAS, ONE OF THE SIX NATIONS
—BRIEF HISTORY—SOME SPEECHES—LIFE AND DEATH

In the year 1784 the treaty to which Cornplanter, or Beautiful Lake, was a party was made at Fort Stanwix, ceding the whole of Northwestern Pennsylvania to the Commonwealth, with the exception of a small individual reserve to Cornplanter. The frontier, however, was not at peace for some years after that, nor, indeed, until Wayne's treaty in 1795.

Notwithstanding his bitter hostility, while the war continued, he became the fast friend of the United States when once the hatchet was buried. His sagacious intellect comprehended at a glance the growing power of the United States, and the abandonment with which Great Britain had requited the fidelity of the Senecas. He therefore threw all his influence at the treaty of Fort Stanwix, now Rome, New York, and Fort Harmar in favor of peace. And notwithstanding the large concessions which he saw his people were necessitated to make, still, by his energy and prudence in the negotiation, he retained for them an ample and beautiful reservation. For the course which he took on those occasions the State of Pennsylvania granted him the fine reservation upon which he resided on the Allegheny. The Senecas, however, were never satisfied with his course in relation to these treaties, and Red Jacket, more artful and eloquent than his elder rival, but less frank and honest, seized upon this circumstance to promote his own popularity at the expense of Cornplanter.

Having buried the hatchet, Cornplanter sought to make his talents useful to his people by conciliating the good will of the whites and securing from further encroachment the little remnant of his national domain. On more than one occasion, when some reckless and bloodthirsty whites on the frontier had massacred unoffending Indians in cold blood, did Cornplanter interfere to restrain the vengeance of his people. During all the Indian wars from 1791 to 1794, which terminated with Wayne's treaty, Cornplanter pledged himself that the Senecas should remain friendly to the United States. He often gave notice to the garrison at Fort Franklin of intended attacks from hostile parties, and even hazarded his life on a mediatorial mission to the Western tribes.

The following is an extract from a speech of Cornplanter to representatives of the United States government appointed to meet him at Fort Franklin, 8th of March, 1796:

" I thank the Almighty for giving us luck to meet together at this time, and in this place as brethren, and hope my brothers will assist me in writing to Congress what I have now to say.

" I thank the Almighty that I am speaking this good day. I have been through all Nations in America, and am sorry to see the folly of many of the

people. What makes me sorry is they all tell lies, and I never found truth amongst them. All the western Nations of Indians, as well as white people, have told me lies. Even in Council I have been deceived, and been told things which I have told to my chiefs and young men, which I have found not to be so, which makes me tell lies by not being able to make good my word, but I

4   49

hope they will all see their folly and repent. The Almighty has not made us to lie, but to tell the truth one to another, for when two people meet together, if they lie one to the other, them people cannot be at peace, and so it is with nations, and that is the cause of so much war.

"General Washington, the father of us all, hear what I have now to say, and take pity on us poor people. The Almighty has blest you, and not us. He has given you education, which enables you to do many things that we cannot do. You can travel by sea as well as by land, and know what is doing in any other country, which we poor people know nothing about. Therefore you ought to pity us. When the Almighty first put us on this land he gave it to us to live on. And when the white people first came to it they were very poor, and we helped them all in our power; did not kill them, but received them as brothers. And now it appears to me as though they were agoing to leave us in distress."—*Pennsylvania Archives.*

"After peace was permanently established between the Indians and the United States, Cornplanter retired from public life and devoted his labors to his own people. He deplored the evils of intemperance, and exerted himself to suppress it. The benevolent efforts of missionaries among his tribe always received his encouragement, and at one time his own heart seemed to be softened by the words of truth, yet he preserved in his later years many of the peculiar notions of the Indian faith.

"In 1821-22 the commissioners of Warren County assumed the right to tax the private property of Cornplanter, and proceeded to enforce its collection. The old chief resisted it, conceiving it not only unlawful, but a personal indignity. The sheriff again appeared with a small posse of armed men. Cornplanter took the deputation to a room around which were ranged about a hundred rifles, and, with the sententious brevity of an Indian, intimated that for each rifle a warrior would appear at his call. The sheriff and his men speedily withdrew, determined, however, to call out the militia. Several prudent citizens, fearing a sanguinary collision, sent for the old chief in a friendly way to come to Warren and compromise the matter. He came, and after some persuasion, gave his note for the tax, amounting to forty-three dollars and seventy-nine cents. He addressed, however, a remonstrance to the governor of Pennsylvania, soliciting a return of his money and an exemption from such demands against lands which the State itself had presented to him. The Legislature annulled the tax, and sent two commissioners to explain the affair to him. He met them at the court-house in Warren, on which occasion he delivered the following speech, eminently characteristic of himself and his race:

"'Brothers, yesterday was appointed for us all to meet here. The talk which the governor sent us pleased us very much. I think that the Great Spirit is very much pleased that the white people have been induced so to assist the Indians as they have done, and that he is pleased also to see the great men of this State and of the United States so friendly to us. We are much pleased with what has been done.

" ' The Great Spirit first made the world, and next the flying animals, and found all things good and prosperous. He is immortal and everlasting. After finishing the flying animals, he came down on earth and there stood. Then he made different kinds of trees and weeds of all sort, and people of every kind. He made the spring and other seasons and the weather suitable for planting. These he did make. But stills to make whiskey to be given to the Indians he did not make. The Great Spirit bids me tell the white people not to give Indians this kind of liquor. When the Great Spirit had made the earth and its animals, he went into the great lakes, where he breathed as easily as anywhere else, and then made all the different kinds of fish. The Great Spirit looked back on all that he had made. The different kinds he had made to be separate and not to mix with or disturb each other. But the white people have broken his command by mixing their color with the Indians. The Indians have done better by not doing so. The Great Spirit wishes that all wars and fightings should cease.

" ' He next told us that there were three things for our people to attend to. First, we ought to take care of our wives and children. Secondly, the white people ought to attend to their farms and cattle. Thirdly, the Great Spirit has given the bears and deers to the Indians. He is the cause of all things that exist, and it is very wicked to go against his will. The Great Spirit wishes me to inform the people that they should quit drinking intoxicating drink, as being the cause of disease and death. He told us not to sell any more of our lands, for he never sold lands to any one. Some of us now keep the seventh day, but I wish to quit it, for the Great Spirit made it for others, but not for the Indians, who ought every day to attend to their business. He has ordered me to quit drinking intoxicating drink, and not to lust after any woman but my own, and informs me that by doing so I should live the longer. He made known to me that it is very wicked to tell lies. Let no one suppose that I have said now is not true.

" ' I have now to thank the governor for what he has done. I have informed him what the Great Spirit has ordered me to cease from, and I wish the governor to inform others what I have communicated. This is all I have at present to say.' "—Day's Collections.

The old chief appears after this again to have fallen into entire seclusion, taking no part even in the politics of his people. He died at his residence on the 7th of March, 1836, at the age of one hundred and four years. " Whether at the time of his death he expected to go to the fair hunting-grounds of his own people or to the heaven of the Christian is not known."

" Notwithstanding his profession of Christianity, Cornplanter was very superstitious. ' Not long since,' says Mr. Foote, of Chautauqua County, ' he said the Good Spirit had told him not to have anything to do with the white people, or even to preserve any mementos or relics that had been given to him from time to time by the pale-faces, whereupon, among other things, he burnt up his belt and broke his elegant sword.' "

In reference to the personal appearance of Cornplanter at the close of his life, a writer in the *Democratic Arch* (Venango County) says,—

" I once saw the aged and venerable chief, and had an interesting interview with him about a year and a half before his death. I thought of many things when seated near him, beneath the wide-spreading shade of an old sycamore, on the banks of the Allegheny,—many things to ask him, the scenes of the Revolution, the generals that fought its battles and conquered, the Indians, his tribe, the Six Nations, and himself. He was constitutionally sedate, was never observed to smile, much less to indulge in the luxury of a laugh. When I saw him he estimated his age to be over one hundred; I think one hundred and three was about his reckoning of it. This would make him near one hundred and five years old at the time of his decease. His person was stooped, and his stature was far short of what it once had been, not being over five feet six inches at the time I speak of. Mr. John Struthers, of Ohio, told me, some years since, that he had seen him near fifty years ago, and at that period he was at his height,—viz., six feet one inch. Time and hardship had made dreadful impressions upon that ancient form. The chest was sunken and his shoulders were drawn forward, making the upper part of his body resemble a trough. His limbs had lost size and become crooked. His feet (for he had taken off his moccasins) were deformed and haggard by injury. I would say that most of the fingers on one hand were useless; the sinews had been severed by the blow of a tomahawk or scalping-knife. How I longed to ask him what scene of blood and strife had thus stamped the enduring evidence of its existence upon his person! But to have done so would, in all probability, have put an end to all further conversation on any subject. The information desired would certainly not have been received, and I had to forego my curiosity. He had but one eye, and even the socket of the lost organ was hid by the overhanging brow resting upon the high cheek-bone. His remaining eye was of the brightest and blackest hue. Never have I seen one, in young or old, that equalled it in brilliancy. Perhaps it had borrowed lustre from the eternal darkness that rested on its neighboring orbit. His ears had been dressed in the Indian mode, all but the outside ring had been cut away. On the one ear this ring had been torn asunder near the top, and hung down his neck like a useless rag. He had a full head of hair, white as the driven snow, which covered a head of ample dimensions and admirable shape. His face was not swarthy, but this may be accounted for from the fact, also, that he was but half Indian. He told me he had been at Franklin more than eighty years before the period of our conversation, on his passage down the Ohio and Mississippi with the warriors of his tribe, in some expedition against the Creeks or Osages. He had long been a man of peace, and

I believe his great characteristics were humanity and truth. It is said that Brandt and Cornplanter were never friends after the massacre of Cherry Valley. Some have alleged, because the Wyoming massacre was perpetrated by Senecas, that Cornplanter was there. Of the justice of this suspicion there are many reasons for doubt. It is certain that he was not the chief of the Senecas at that time. The name of the chief in that expedition was Ge-en-quah-toh, or He-goes-in-the-smoke. As he stood before me—the ancient chief in ruins—how forcibly was I struck with the truth of that beautiful figure of the old aboriginal chieftain, who, in describing himself, said he was ' like an aged hemlock, dead at the top, and whose branches alone were green'! After more than one hundred years of most varied life,—of strife, of danger, of peace,—he at last slumbers in deep repose on the banks of his own beloved Allegheny.

"Cornplanter was born at Conewongus, on the Genesee River, in 1732, being a half-breed, the son of a white man named John O'Bail, a trader from the Mohawk Valley. In a letter written in later years to the governor of Pennsylvania he thus speaks of his early youth: 'When I was a child I played with the butterfly, the grasshopper, and the frogs; and as I grew up I began to pay some attention and play with the Indian boys in the neighborhood, and they took notice of my skin being of a different color from theirs, and spoke about it. I inquired from my mother the cause, and she told me my father was a resident of Albany. I still ate my victuals out of a bark dish. I grew up to be a young man and married a wife, and I had no kettle or gun. I then knew where my father lived, and went to see him, and found he was a white man and spoke the English language. He gave me victuals while I was at his house, but when I started to return home he gave me no provisions to eat on the way. He gave me neither kettle nor gun.'

"Little further is known of his early life beyond the fact that he was allied with the French in the engagement against General Braddock in July, 1755. He was probably at that time at least twenty years old. During the Revolution he was a war chief of high rank, in the full vigor of manhood, active, sagacious, brave, and he most probably participated in the principal Indian engagements against the United States during the war. He is supposed to have been present at the cruelties of Wyoming and Cherry Valley, in which the Senecas took a prominent part. He was on the war-path with Brandt during General Sullivan's campaign in 1779, and in the following year, under Brandt and Sir John Johnson, he led the Senecas in sweeping through the Schoharie and Mohawk Valleys. On this occasion he took his father a prisoner, but with such caution as to avoid an immediate recognition. After marching the old man some ten or twelve miles, he stepped before him, faced about, and addressed him in the following terms:

"'My name is John O'Bail, commonly called Cornplanter. I am your son. You are my father. You are now my prisoner, and subject to the custom of Indian warfare; but you shall not be harmed. You need not fear. I am a warrior. Many are the scalps which I have taken. Many prisoners have I tortured to death. I am your son. I was anxious to see you and greet you in friendship. I went to your cabin and took you by force; but your life shall be spared. Indians love their friends and their kindred, and treat them with kindness. If you now choose to follow the fortunes of your yellow son and to live with our people, I will cherish your old age with plenty of venison, and you shall live easy. But if it is your choice to return to your fields and live with your white children, I will send a party of trusty young men to conduct you back in safety. I respect you, my father. You have been friendly to Indians, and they are your friends.' The elder O'Bail preferred his white children and green fields to his yellow offspring and the wild woods, and chose to return.

"Cornplanter was the greatest warrior the Senecas, the untamable people of the hills, ever had, and it was his wish that when he died his grave would remain unmarked, but the Legislature of Pennsylvania willed otherwise, and erected a monument to him with this beautiful inscription:

"'GY-ANT-WA-CHIA, THE CORNPLANTER,
JOHN O'BAIL, ALIAS CORNPLANTER,
DIED
AT CORNPLANTER TOWN, FEB. 18, A.D. 1836,
AGED ABOUT 100 YEARS.'

"Upon the west side is the following inscription:

"'Chief of the Seneca tribe, and a principal chief of the Six Nations from the period of the Revolutionary War to the time of his death. Distinguished for talent, courage, eloquence, sobriety, and love for tribe and race, to whose welfare he devoted his time, his energy, and his means during a long and eventful life.'"

CHAPTER IV

I REPRODUCE from McKnight's "Pioneer History of Jefferson County" the following:

"At the close of the war of the Revolution, in the year 1783, the ownership of a large area of the territory within the charter boundaries of Pennsylvania was still claimed by the Indians of the several tribes that were commonly known as the Six Nations. The last purchase of lands from the Six Nations by the proprietary government of the province was made at Fort Stanwix in November, 1768, and the limit of this purchase may be described as extending to lines beginning where the northeast branch of the Susquehanna River crosses the northern line of the State, in the present county of Bradford; thence down the river to the mouth of Towanda Creek, and up the same to its head-waters; thence by a range of hills to the head-waters of Pine Creek, and down the same to the west branch of the Susquehanna; thence up the same to Cherry Tree; thence by a straight line, across the present counties of Indiana and Armstrong, to Kittanning,* on the Allegheny River, and thence down the Allegheny and Ohio Rivers to the western boundary line of the province. The Indian claim, therefore, embraced all that part of the State lying to the northwest of the purchase lines of 1768, as they are here described. With the close of the Revolutionary struggle, the authorities of the new Commonwealth, anxiously looking to its future stability and prosperity, soon found themselves confronted with duties and responsibilities different in many respects from those that had engaged their serious attention and earnest effort during the previous seven years of war. They were to enact just and equitable laws for the government of a new State, and to devise

---

* "Canoe Place," so-called in the old maps of the State to designate the head of navigation on the west branch of the Susquehanna River, is the point at which the purchase line of 1768 from that river to Kittanning, on the Allegheny River, begins. A survey of that line was made by Robert Galbraith in the year 1786, and a cherry-tree standing on the west bank of the river was marked by him as the beginning of his survey. The same cherry-tree was marked by William P. Brady as the southeast corner of a tract surveyed by him "at Canoe Place," in 1794, on warrant No. 3744, in the name of John Nicolson, Esq. The town of Cherry Tree now covers part of this ground. The old tree disappeared years ago. Its site, however, was regarded as of some historic importance, and under an appropriation of fifteen hundred dollars, granted by the Legislature in 1893, a substantial granite monument has been erected to mark the spot where it stood.

55

such measures as would stimulate its growth in wealth and population and promote the development, settlement, and improvement of its great domain.

"As early as the 12th of March, 1783, the General Assembly had passed an act setting apart certain lands lying north and west of the Ohio and Allegheny Rivers and Conewango Creek to be sold for the purpose of redeeming the depreciation certificates given to the officers and soldiers of the Pennsylvania Line who had served in the war of the Revolution, and also for the purpose of making donations of land to the same officers and soldiers in compliance with a promise made to them by a resolution passed in 1780. It will be observed that when this act was passed the Indian claim of title to the lands mentioned was still in force; but the State authorities, though seemingly slow and deliberate in their actions, were no doubt fully alive to the necessity of securing as speedily as possible the right to all the lands within the State—about five-sixteenths of its area—that remained unpurchased after the treaty at Fort Stanwix in 1768. With that purpose in view, the first movement made by the General Assembly to be found on record was on the 25th day of September, 1783. This action is in the form of a resolution passed on that day by the recommendation of the report of a committee that had been previously appointed 'to digest such plans as they might conceive necessary to facilitate and expedite the laying off and surveying of the lands' set apart by the act of the previous March. The resolution reads,—

"'Resolved, unanimously, That the supreme executive council be, and they are hereby authorized and empowered to appoint commissioners to hold a meeting with the Indians claiming the unpurchased territory within the acknowledged limits of the State, for the purpose of purchasing the same, agreeable to ancient usage, and that all the expenses accruing from the said meeting and purchase be defrayed out of the Treasury of the State.'—*Pennsylvania Archives*, vol. x. p. 111.

"It next appears by a minute of the Supreme Executive Council, of February 23, 1784, that Samuel John Atlee, William Maclay, and Francis Johnston were on that day chosen commissioners to treat with the Indians as proposed in the resolution of the General Assembly. The gentlemen named— all of them prominent citizens—were informed on the 29th of the same month of their appointment, but they did not acknowledge the receipt of President Dickinson's letter until the 17th of May following. On that day Messrs. Atlee and Johnston reply in a letter of thanks for the honor conferred upon them, and explain the delay as having been caused by circumstances that required Mr. Maclay and Colonel Atlee to visit their families, the first named still remaining absent. The letter also contains a statement of their views upon various matters pertaining to the mission upon which they are about to enter. They suggest Samuel Weiser, a son of Conrad Weiser, the noted Indian missionary, as a proper person to notify the Indians of the desire to treat with them, and, from his familiarity with their language and customs, to act as interpreter. The time and place for holding the treaty are mentioned, but nothing definite suggested, owing to the fact that the Continental Congress had likewise appointed commissioners to meet the Six Nations for the purpose of treating with them in relation to the lands of the Northwest, beyond the limits of Pennsylvania, and it was deemed proper to permit the representatives of Congress to arrange for the meeting.* Fort Stanwix, in the State of New York, was finally agreed upon as the place where the meeting should be held, and thither the commissioners on the part of Pennsylvania were directed to proceed. On the 25th of August, 1784, a committee of the General Assembly, having Indian affairs under consideration, made the following report:

" ' That weighty reasons have occurred in favor of the design for holding a conference with the Indians on the part of this State, and if under the present situation of Continental affairs that measure can be conducted on sure ground and without too unlimited an expense, it ought to take place and be rendered as effective as this House can make it, under whose auspices a foundation would thus be laid of essential and durable advantage to the public, by extending population, satisfying our officers and soldiers in regard to their donation lands and depreciation certificates, restoring that ancient, friendly, and profitable intercourse with the Indians, and guarding against all occasions of war with them.'—*Pennsylvania Archives*, vol. x. p. 316.

" To aid the commissioners in their efforts to attain objects so worthy and laudable, the above report was accompanied by a resolution that authorized the Supreme Executive Council to expend nine thousand dollars in the purchase of ' such goods, merchandise, and trinkets' as would be acceptable to the Indians, to be given them as part of the consideration in the event of a purchase being made. In pursuance of this resolution the council promptly ordered a warrant to be issued by the treasurer in favor of the commissioners for the sum of £3375 (equivalent in Pennsylvania currency to nine thousand one hundred dollars), to be expended by them in purchasing the necessary articles.†

" After a tedious and fatiguing journey, in which they met with a number of unexpected delays, the commissioners reached Fort Stanwix early in the month of October, where they found some of the tribes already assembled, and with them the commissioners of the Continental Congress. In a letter to President Dickinson, dated October 4, 1784, they announce their arrival, and state that the negotiations had already commenced, and while they would not venture an opinion as to the final issue, they say the disposition of the Indians appeared to be favorable. The negotiations continued until the 23d of

---

* Pennsylvania Archives, vol. x. p. 265.
† For a list of the articles designated in the order see Colonial Records, vol. xiv. p. 186. After the negotiations at Fort Stanwix had been concluded the commissioners gave an obligation for an additional thousand dollars in goods, to be delivered at Tioga. For this list see Pennsylvania Archives, vol. x. p. 496.

the same month, and on that day ended in an agreement by which the Indian title to all the lands within the boundaries of the State that remained after the treaty of 1768 was extinguished. The Indians represented at the conference were the Mohawks, the Oneidas, the Onondagas, the Senecas, the Cayugas, and the Tuscaroras. The consideration fixed for the surrender of their rights was five thousand dollars. The deed is dated October 23, 1784, is signed by all the chiefs of the Six Nations and by the Continental commissioners as witnesses. The boundaries of the territory ceded are thus described: ' Beginning on the south side of the river Ohio, where the western boundary of the State of Pennsylvania crosses the said river, near Shingo's old town, at the mouth of Beaver Creek, and thence by a due north line to the end of the forty-second and the beginning of the forty-third degrees of north latitude, thence by a due east line separating the forty-second and the forty-third degree of north latitude, to the east side of the east branch of the Susquehanna River, thence by the bounds of the late purchase made at Fort Stanwix, the fifth day of November, Anno Domini one thousand seven hundred and sixty-eight, as follows: Down the said east branch of Susquehanna, on the east side thereof, till it comes opposite to the mouth of a creek called by the Indians Awandac, and across the river, and up the said creek on the south side thereof, all along the range of hills called Burnet's Hills by the English and by the Indians ——, on the north side of them, to the head of a creek which runs into the west branch of Susquehanna, which creek is by the Indians called Tyadaghton, but by the Pennsylvanians Pine Creek, and down the said creek on the south side thereof to the said west branch of Susquehanna, thence crossing the said river, and running up the south side thereof, the several courses thereof to the forks of the same river, which lies nearest to a place on the river Ohio called Kittanning, and from the fork by a straight line to Kittanning aforesaid, and thence down the said river Ohio by the several courses thereof to where said State of Pennsylvania crosses the same river at the place of beginning.' After the commissioners had accomplished in so satisfactory a manner the object for which they had journeyed to Fort Stanwix, it became necessary to appease the Western Indians, the Wyandots and the Delawares, who also claimed rights in the same lands. The same commissioners were therefore sent to Fort McIntosh, on the Ohio River, at the site of the present town of Beaver, where, in January, 1785, they were successful in reaching an agreement with those Indians for the same lands. This deed, signed by the chiefs of both tribes, is dated January 21, 1785, and is in the same words (except as to the consideration money, which is two thousand dollars) and recites the same boundaries as the deed signed at Fort Stanwix in the previous month of October.*

* The conference of the commissioners at Fort Stanwix and Fort McIntosh with the deeds signed at those places are published in the Appendix to the General Assembly for the session of February to April, 1785.

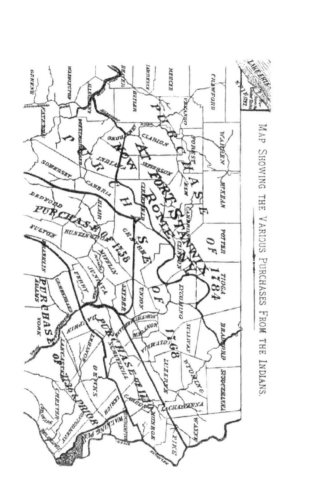

MAP SHOWING THE VARIOUS PURCHASES FROM THE INDIANS.

" After the purchase of 1768 a disagreement arose between the proprietary government and the Indians as to whether the creek flowing into the west branch of the river Susquehanna, and called in the deed ' Tyadaghton,' was intended for Lycoming Creek or Pine Creek. The Indians said it was the former, and that the purchase only extended that far ; the proprietaries claimed the latter stream to be the extent of the purchase, but, in order to avoid any trouble that might arise from the dispute, it was wisely determined that no rights should be granted for lands west of Lycoming Creek. This determination, however, did not deter or prevent adventurous pioneers from entering upon and making settlements within the disputed territory, and from their persistency in so doing arose an interesting, not to say serious, condition of affairs, to which reference will again be made. The commissioners at Fort Stanwix were instructed to ascertain definitely from the Indians which of the two streams they meant by ' Tyadaghton.' They then admitted that it was Pine Creek, being the largest emptying into the west branch of the Susquehanna.

" The Indian claim of right to the soil of Pennsylvania, within its charter limits, had thus, in a period of a little more than one hundred years, ceased to exist. A glance at a map of the State will show that within the magnificent domain that comprises the purchase of 1784 are to be found at the present day the counties of Tioga, Potter, McKean, Warren, Crawford, Venango, Forest, Clarion, Elk, Jefferson, Cameron, Butler, Lawrence, and Mercer, and parts of the counties of Bradford, Clinton, Clearfield, Indiana, Armstrong, Allegheny, Beaver, and Erie.* This large and important division of our great Commonwealth, now teeming with population and wealth, the abiding-place of a noble civilization, and containing within its boundaries thousands upon thousands of homes of comfort and many of elegance and luxury, fertile valleys to reward the labor of the husbandman, thriving villages, busy towns, and growing, bustling cities, was, in 1784, largely an uninhabited and untraversed wilderness.

" LANDS EAST OF THE ALLEGHENY RIVER AND CONEWANGO CREEK

" The General Assembly of the State did not delay in enacting laws which would open to settlers and purchasers that part of the late acquisition that had not been otherwise appropriated. As a matter of fact, in anticipation of the purchase, an act was passed on the 1st day of April, 1784, in which it was provided that as soon as the Indians were ' satisfied for the unpurchased lands,' the supreme executive council should give official information thereof to the surveyor-general, who was then to appoint district surveyors to survey all such lands within the purchase as should ' be found fit for cultivation.' The tracts were to contain not more than five hundred nor less than two

---

* See accompanying map, which shows the extent of the purchase.

hundred acres each, and were to be numbered on a general draft of each district. When a certain number of lots were surveyed, they were to be sold at public auction, the purchaser having the privilege of paying one moiety at the time of purchase and receiving a credit of two years for the other moiety. The mode of disposing of the lands thus indicated was soon changed by subsequent legislation. By an act passed December 21, 1784, to amend the act of April 1, the provisions of the law for sales by public auction and the giving of credit were repealed. Section 6 of the act provided that the land-office should be open on the 1st day of May, 1785, to receive applications for lands at the rate of £30 * for every hundred acres of the same, and that the survey of an application should not contain more than one thousand acres, with the usual allowance of six per centum for highways. This act was intended to apply to all lands within the purchase, except the lands north and west of the Ohio and Allegheny Rivers and Conewango Creek (which, as already mentioned, had been appropriated for the redemption of depreciation certificates and for the donations of land to the soldiers of the Pennsylvania Line) and the disputed territory between Lycoming and Pine Creeks. By Section 7, a warrant issued in pursuance of the act was not descriptive, and was not confined to any particular place, but could be located on any vacant land, not within the excepted districts, that the applicant might select. Sections 8, 9, and 10 of the act provide for the persons who occupied lands between Lycoming and Pine Creek, in violation of the proprietary mandate. The situation of these settlers was peculiar. When the disagreement in regard to the purchase lines of the purchase of 1768 occurred, the proprietaries, always extremely anxious to avoid giving offence to the Indians, decided to withhold the territory between the two streams from sale and settlement until the differences could be properly adjusted by mutual agreement. Though many applications for land west of Lycoming Creek were on file, surveys would not be accepted, and at the same time stringent orders were issued protesting against persons making settlement beyond that stream, and warning those already there to depart. In defiance of warnings, protests, and proclamations, however, many sturdy, self-reliant men persisted in occupying the forbidden ground, where they found themselves beyond the bounds of lawful authority, and could not expect to receive encouragement or protection from the proprietary government. But with the energy and courage common to pioneer settlers they at once began the work of subduing the wilderness and building homes for their families, and from accounts that have come down to us, the little community, if it did not live in luxury, was at least able to earn a subsistence that was not meagre in quantity, whatever may have been its quality. Being without law or government, the members of the community were compelled by the necessities of their situation and surroundings to adopt a system

---

* In Pennsylvania currency this was at the rate of eighty cents an acre.

of government of their own, the details of which are not fully known. All, however, were under solemn obligations to support and defend their agreement for mutual support and protection. They called themselves Fair-Play Men, and it is known that annually they elected three of their number to constitute a court, which held stated meetings to dispense justice. To this tribunal all disputes and controversies were referred for settlement, and from its decisions there was no appeal. A stranger coming among them was obliged to appear before the court and promise under oath to submit to the laws of the community. If he did this, he could remain, take possession of unoccupied land, and receive assistance in building his cabin. If he would not take the obligation, he was quickly notified to absent himself without delay, which he usually did, without awaiting the call of a committee, whose methods of expulsion might be none too gentle. Many of these brave frontiersmen served in the army during the Revolutionary War, and Section 8 of the act recited that by reason of their services as soldiers, they merited the 'pre-emption of their respective plantations.' Sections 9 and 10 of the same act allowed a pre-emption to all settlers and their legal representatives who had settled on the lands between the two streams prior to the year 1780, limiting each claim to three hundred acres, providing that the application should be made and the consideration paid on or before November 1, 1785. It will be remembered that the time fixed by the act of December 21, 1784, for the land-office to be opened to receive applications was May 1, 1785. Before that day arrived, however, the Legislature passed another act, which, in many respects, changed the policy previously pursued in disposing of unappropriated lands. This act became a law on the 8th day of April, 1785, and with it came the practice, as provided in the act, of numbering all warrants for land in the last purchase to the east of the Allegheny River and Conewango Creek, a change in practice that has always been regarded as a valuable improvement on the old system. The act is entitled 'An act to provide further regulations, whereby to secure fair and equal proceedings in the land-office, and the surveying of lands.' It was believed that when the office was opened on the day fixed by the law, numerous applications would be made at the same time, and that preference would necessarily be given to some persons to the disadvantage of others, and thereby cause dissatisfaction. In order to prevent any one from profiting by such preference, it was enacted in Section 2 of the act that the priority of all warrants to be granted on applications received during the first ten days after the opening of the office should be determined by a lottery to be drawn under the supervision of the Secretary of the Land-Office. Not more than one thousand acres were to be included in one application, and the warrants were to be numbered 'according to the decision of the lottery.' For conducting the lottery the section contains minute directions. All applications made after the expiration of ten days were to have priority according to the order in which they came into the hands of the Secretary, and were to be numbered accordingly. The other sections of the act relate mainly to the duties of the surveyor-general and the deputy-surveyors to be by him appointed, and the way in which surveys were to be made and returned. It also prescribes the fees to be received by the officers of the land-office and the deputy-surveyors, and attaches the territory east of the Allegheny River and Conewango Creek to Northumberland County, a part of which county it remained until Lycoming County was formed in 1795, when it became part of that county. The remaining portion of the purchase was attached to Westmoreland County, and so continued until Allegheny was formed in 1788, when it was included in the boundary of that county. The applications received during the first ten days from the opening of the office were listed and numbered, placed in the lottery-wheel, and drawn therefrom in the manner provided by the second section of the act. They numbered five hundred and sixty-four, and warrants for that number of tracts were issued, and received a number that corresponded with the number drawn from the wheel. These warrants were called ' Northumberland County Lottery Warrants,' and under that designation are yet carried on the warrant registers of the office. They could be, and were, located in such localities within the purchase east of the Allegheny River as the owners might select, except on a reservation of one thousand acres at the forks of Sinnemahoning Creek, for which General James Potter held a pre-emption.

" The surveyor-general had authority to appoint deputy-surveyors, and to fix the number, extent, and boundaries of the districts to which they were to be assigned. The territory was divided into eighteen districts, and a deputy-surveyor appointed for each. These districts were numbered consecutively, beginning with No. 1 on the Allegheny River, and running eastward to No. 18, which extended to the north branch of the Susquehanna in the northeast corner of the purchase. This arrangement of the districts continued until after the year 1790, when a change was made by the surveyor-general. The number of districts was then reduced to six, and were numbered westward from district No. 1, beginning at the mouth of Lycoming Creek. In the new arrangement John Adlum was appointed deputy-surveyor for district No. 1, John Broadhead for No. 2, John Canan for No. 3, James Hunter for No. 4, William P. Brady for No. 5, and Enion Williams for No. 6, on the Allegheny River. In 1793 John Adlum, whose surveys were principally along the northern line of the State, was succeeded by William Ellis, and Enion Williams by John Broadhead. After the drawing of the lottery warrants the business of the land-office does not appear to have been very pressing. It would seem that at the price fixed by the act of December, 1784—£30 per hundred, or eighty cents an acre—purchasers were not numerous. The records show that from the time of the drawing and issuing of the lottery warrants in May, 1785, down to the year 1792, not more than four hundred warrants were granted for these lands, and among these warrants were many to religious and educational institutions issued under various acts of endowment. There were thirty-two to Dickinson College,—twenty-eight of three hundred acres each, and four of four hundred acres each, making in all seven thousand acres; the Episcopal Academy had thirty-three warrants,—thirty-two of three hundred acres each, and one of four hundred acres, making ten thousand acres; the Lutheran congregation, of Philadelphia, ten warrants of five hundred acres each, making five thousand acres; the Pittsburg Academy, ten warrants of five hundred acres each, making five thousand acres; the Washington Academy, ten warrants of five hundred acres each, making five thousand acres; the Reading Academy, seven warrants,—three of one thousand acres each and four of five hundred acres each, making five thousand acres; and Franklin College thirty-three warrants of three hundred acres each, and one of one hundred acres, making ten thousand acres,—making in the aggregate one hundred and twelve warrants for fifty-two thousand acres of land.

"It had now become apparent to the authorities that the price of land was too high to induce investments of money in them, and that the General Assembly must fix a lower rate to promote sales. Benjamin Franklin, the president of the Supreme Executive Council, under date of February 23, 1787, addressed a letter to that body in which he says, ' We are convinced that it will be of advantage to the State to lower the price of land within the late Indian purchase; only eight warrants have been taken out for lands these six months passed.' * The Legislature accordingly passed an act, October 3, 1788, to reduce the price from the rate of £30 per hundred acres to £20. This rate was to be charged after March 1, 1789, and was a reduction from the old rate of eighty cents an acre to fifty-three and one-third cents an acre. This rate continued until April 3, 1792; but, contrary to expectations, did not have the effect of increasing sales, and, therefore, brought little or no change in the business of the office. By another act, passed April 3, 1792, the price was again reduced. The rate fixed by this act was £5, or $13.33⅓, for each hundred acres, and at this rate sales almost astonishing in extent were made, and the years 1792–93–94 proved to be noted and important years for disposing of unappropriated lands. The low price at which lands could now be bought, and the alluring prospect of a large increase in their value, undoubtedly induced many large purchasers to enter their applications. The applications received at the land-office were for a large number of tracts, and in the course of the years named more than five thousand warrants of nine hundred and one thousand acres each, covering almost five million acres, were granted for lands north and west of the purchase line of 1768, and east of the Allegheny River. These were all numbered in consecutive order, as required by the act of April, 1785, and were sent to the deputy-surveyors of the six districts to be executed. They were issued in the names of a comparatively small number

* Colonial Records, vol. xv. p. 167.

of persons, but the holdings, as a rule, were very large. While it would be tedious to give the names of all the holders of these warrants, generally called ' late purchase warrants,' it may not prove uninteresting to mention a few of those whose purchases were more than usually large, if only to show that a spirit of speculation may have existed in those days, even as it does at the present time. The first to be mentioned will be the warrants issued in the names of Wilhelm Willink, Nicholas Van Staphorst, Christian Van Eeghan, Pieter Stadnitski, Hendrick Vollenhoven, and Ruter Jan Schimmelpenninck. These gentlemen were merchants of the city of Amsterdam, Holland. In the land history of Pennsylvania they are known as the ' Holland Land Company,' and through agents they invested a large amount of money in land in the purchase of 1784. The warrant registers show that in the three years, 1792–93–94, they paid for and received eleven hundred and five warrants of nine hundred acres each, aggregating nine hundred and ninety-five thousand four hundred acres of land lying east of the Allegheny River. These warrants were divided among the deputy-surveyors of the six districts. James Wilson was another large owner of warrants, the number held by him being five hundred and ten, of nine hundred acres each, making four hundred and fifty-one thousand acres. Herman Le Roy and Jan Lincklean, A. Z., also of Amsterdam, three hundred and three warrants of nine hundred acres each, making two hundred and seventy-two thousand seven hundred acres. John Nicholson, three hundred warrants of one thousand acres each, making three hundred thousand acres. Thomas M. Willing, three hundred and eleven warrants of one thousand acres each, making three hundred and eleven thousand acres. George Meade, three hundred and six warrants of one thousand acres each, making three hundred and six thousand acres. Robert Gilmore, two hundred warrants of one thousand acres each, making two hundred thousand acres. Samuel Wallis, one hundred warrants of one thousand acres each, making one hundred thousand acres. William Bingham, one hundred and twenty-five warrants of one thousand acres each, making one hundred and twenty-five thousand acres. Robert Morris, one hundred and eighty-five warrants, one hundred and forty-one of one thousand acres each, and forty-four of five hundred acres each, making one hundred and sixty-three thousand acres. The magnitude of the purchases made by a few individuals is here clearly indicated. There were, however, other large purchasers, such as Robert Blackwell, John Olden, Charles Willing, Philip Nicklin and Robert Griffith, James Strawbridge, Jeremiah Parker, and others whose names we are obliged to omit. The surveys generally were carefully and correctly made, and, considering the extent of territory covered by them, and the large interests involved, no great amount of litigation from conflicting locations afterwards grew out of defective or careless work by the surveyor, as was too often the case with surveys made in other sections of the State. In 1817 the price of the lands was again changed to twenty-six and two-thirds cents an acre, to correspond

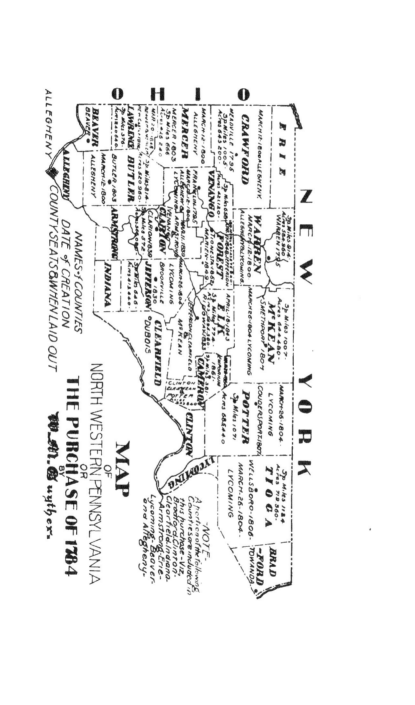

MAP
OF
NORTH WESTERN PENNSYLVANIA
OR
THE PURCHASE OF 1784
BY W. M. Guyther.

NAMES of COUNTIES
DATE of CREATION
COUNTY SEATS & WHEN LAID OUT

-NOTE-
A portion of the following
Counties are included in
this purchase. viz.
Bradford, Clinton,
Clearfield, Indiana,
Armstrong, Erie,
Lycoming, Beaver,
and Allegheny.

OHIO
NEW YORK

with the price in the older purchases. At the same time warrants were made descriptive, and have since been carried in the warrant registers by counties. The surveys made on the numbered warrants did not appropriate all the land within the limits to which they were restricted, and since then many warrants have been granted in all the counties erected from the territory that in 1785 was made to form a part of the county of Northumberland.

"LANDS NORTH AND EAST OF THE OHIO AND ALLEGHENY RIVERS AND CONE-WANGO CREEK

"After the surveys of the tracts to be sold for the redemption of depreciation certificates and the donation lots to be given to the soldiers of the Pennsylvania Line had been made, there remained in this part of the purchase a large surplus of lands to be otherwise appropriated. The Legislature, on the 3d of April, 1792, passed an act for the sale of these lands, entitled ' An act for the sale of vacant lands within this Commonwealth.' This act differs from all previous laws for disposing of the public lands, by providing that they should only be offered for sale to such persons as would ' cultivate, improve, and settle the same, or cause the same to be cultivated, improved, and settled.' The price fixed was £7 10s. in Pennsylvania currency, for every hundred acres, or in other words, twenty cents an acre, and the warrants were limited to four hundred acres each. The surveyor-general was authorized to divide the territory offered for sale into proper and convenient districts and appoint deputy-surveyors, who were to give the customary bond for the faithful performance of their duties. They were to execute warrants according to their priority, but ' not to survey any tract actually settled and improved prior to the date of the entry of such warrant with the deputy, except to the owner of such settlement and improvement.' The territory was divided into eleven districts, and a deputy-surveyor appointed for each; Thomas Reese for district No. 1, William Powers for No. 2, Benjamin Stokely for No. 3, Thomas Stokely for No. 4, John Moore for No. 5, Samuel Nicholson for No. 6, John McCool for No. 7, Stephen Gapen for No. 8, Jonathan and Daniel Leet for Nos. 9 and 10, John Hoge for No. 11.

"By Section 8 of the act, on application being made to the deputy-surveyor of the proper district by any person who had made an actual settlement and improvement, that officer, on being paid the legal fees, was required to survey the lines of the tract, not exceeding four hundred acres, to which such person may have become entitled by virtue of his settlement. Many such surveys were returned to the land-office and constituted pre-emptions to persons for whom they were made. Some of the tracts thus returned still remain unpaid, as a glance at the land lien docket of the land-office will show. By Section 9, no warrant or survey made in pursuance of the act was to vest title to the lands unless the grantee had, ' prior to the date of such warrant made, or caused to be made, or should within the space of two years next after the date of the same, make, or cause to be made, an actual settlement thereon, by clearing, fencing, and cultivating at least two acres for every hundred acres contained in one survey, erecting thereon a messuage for the habitation of man, and residing or causing a family to reside thereon, for the space of five years next following his first settling of the same, if he or she shall so long live.' In default of such actual settlement and residence the right was forfeited, and new warrants, reciting the original warrants and the lack of compliance with the requirements of the act, could be granted to other actual settlers. It was provided, however, ' that if any actual settler or any grantee in any such original or succeeding warrant, shall by force of arms of the enemies of the United States, be prevented from making such actual settlement, or be driven therefrom and shall persist in his endeavors to make such actual settlement as aforesaid, then, in either case, he and his heirs shall be entitled to have and to hold the said lands in the same manner as if the actual settlement had been made and continued.' Under the provisions of this act many surveys, as already stated, were returned for actual settlers, and many warrants were taken out immediately after its passage. The warrants were for four hundred acres each, and immense numbers of them in fictitious names, in which great families of Inks, Pims, etc., appear, were taken out by a few individuals. For instance, the Holland Land Company, previously mentioned, again appears in the territory west of the Allegheny. That company alone took out eleven hundred and sixty-two warrants representing four hundred and sixty-four thousand eight hundred acres of land, and making the entire purchases of the company from the State amount to more than one million five hundred thousand acres. John Nicholson was another purchaser who held a large number of these warrants. To the ' Pennsylvania Population Company' he assigned one hundred thousand acres lying principally in the present County of Erie, and proposed to assign two hundred and fifty thousand acres lying along Beaver Creek and the western line of the State to another of his land schemes called the ' North American Land Company.' The warrants all contained the actual settlement clause, but not any of the large owners of warrants made the slightest pretence of complying with it. Owing to the disturbed condition of the western border at the time it was impossible to do so. A state of war existed with the western Indians. The United States forces had met with serious reverses in the defeat of Harmer and St. Clair in 1791, and it was not until after Wayne's treaty, in December, 1795, gave peace and safety to the borders that settlers with their families could enter upon those lands free from the fear and danger of Indian incursions.

" But with the settling of the Indian disorders and the return of peace, there soon came other troubles, with expensive and vexatious litigation, to annoy and harass settlers and warrantees by the uncertainty that was cast upon their titles. This uncertainty grew out of differences of opinion in relation to the construction the two years' clause of the law requiring actual settlement, after the termination of the Indian hostilities that had prevented such settlement from being made, should receive. The opposite views held by those interested in titles are clearly stated in Sergeant's ' Land Laws,' page 98: ' On one side it was contended that the conditions of actual settlement and residence, required by the act, was dispensed with, on account of the prevention for two years after the date of the warrant * by Indian hostilities; and that the warrant-holder was not bound to do anything further, but was entitled to a patent. On the other side it was insisted that the right under the warrant was forfeited, at the expiration of two years, without a settlement, and that actual settlers might then enter on such tracts and hold them by making a settlement. On this and other constructions, numbers of persons entered on the lands of warrantees and claimed to hold under the act, as settlers, after a forfeiture.' The authorities of the State at the time—1796 to 1800—held to the first opinion, and by the advice of Attorney-General Ingersoll, the Board of Property devised what was called a ' prevention certificate,' which set forth the fact of the inability of the warrantee or settler to make the required settlement. This certificate was to be signed by two justices, and on its presentation, properly signed, the land officers freely granted a patent for the land described. Under prevention certificates of this kind many patents were granted. The Holland Land Company received more than one thousand, and John Field, William Crammond, and James Gibson, in trust for the use of the Pennsylvania Population Company, more than eight hundred. These patents all contained a recital of the prevention certificate. as follows: 'And also in consideration of it having been made to appear to the Board of Property that the said (name of warrantee) was by force of arms of the enemies of the United States prevented from making settlement as is required by the ninth section (act of April 3, 1792), and the assignees of the said (warrantee) had persisted in their endeavors to make such settlement,' etc. With a change of administration in October, 1799, there followed a change of policy. The new authorities did not regard the policy and proceedings of the former Board of Property binding, and the further issuing of patents on prevention certificates was refused. In the mean time, the contentions between the owners of warrants and settlers were carried into the courts, where a like difference of opinion in regard to the rights of the contending parties under the act of 1792 soon manifested itself, the judges disagreeing as widely in their construction of the ninth section as the parties in interest. It was only after years of exciting and troublesome litigation, and the enactment of a number of laws by the Legislature of the State to facilitate an adjustment of the contentions, that titles became settled and owners felt secure in their possessions. It may be said that while the judges of the courts often differed in their opinions on the points at issue, the litiga-

* Nearly all of these warrants were granted in 1792-93.

tion ended generally in favor of the holders of the warrants. The Holland Land Company, being composed of foreigners, could appeal to the courts of the United States. In one case carried to the Supreme Court, the company was actually absolved from making the settlement prescribed by the ninth section, Chief Justice Marshall holding that a warrant for a tract of land under the Act of 1792 'to a person who, by force of arms of the enemies of the United States, was prevented from settling and improving the said land, and from residing thereon from the date of the warrant until the 1st of January, 1796, but who, during the said period, persisted in his endeavors to make such settlement and residence, vests in such grantee a fee-simple in said land.' * That the uncertainty in regard to land titles during these years did much to retard the growth and prosperity of this northwestern section of the State cannot be doubted; but, under the influence of better conditions, brought about by the adjustment of land rights and the allaying of local strife, it afterwards made marvellous strides forward in the march of progress and improvement.

"The dispositions made of the unsold depreciation and the undrawn donation lots in this part of the purchase were fully treated of in former papers, and, therefore, need no further notice. It may not, however, be amiss to say a word in relation to the purchase of the Erie triangle, an acquisition that was of vast importance to Pennsylvania by reason of the outlet of Lake Erie. The triangle was claimed by the States of New York and Massachusetts, but was ceded by both States, in the years 1781 and 1785, to the United States. The Pennsylvania authorities, anticipating its possession, had, through a treaty made at Fort McIntosh by General St. Clair, Colonel Harmer, and others, secured a deed from the Indians by which their claim of title was extinguished. This deed, signed by the chiefs of the Six Nations, is dated January 9, 1789, and the consideration paid was two thousand dollars. It was then, by a deed dated March 3, 1792, ceded by the United States to Pennsylvania. This deed is signed by George Washington, President, and Thomas Jefferson, Secretary of State. In 1790, Andrew Ellicott made a survey of the triangle and found it to contain two hundred and two thousand two hundred and eighty-seven acres, and the purchase-money paid to the United States, at the rate of seventy-five cents an acre, amounted to $151,640.25. This purchase having been completed before the passage of the act of April 3, 1792, the lands within it, except the reservations, were sold under the provisions of that act. Before the completion of the purchase, John Nicholson had made application for the entire tract, and probably held a larger number of warrants for lands within its boundaries than any other individual.

* Smith's Laws, vol. ii. p. 228.

" In the act of March 12, 1783, setting apart the depreciation lands, two reservations for the use of the State were made,—one of ' three thousand acres, in an oblong of not less than one mile in depth from the Allegheny and Ohio Rivers, and extending up and down the said rivers, from opposite Fort Pitt, so far as may be necessary to include the same;' and the other ' three thousand acres on the Ohio, and on both sides of Beaver Creek, including Fort McIntosh.' There was also reserved on Lake Erie for the use of the State the peninsula of Presque Isle, a tract extending eight miles along the shores of the lake and three miles in breadth, and another tract of two thousand acres on the lake at the mouth of Harbor Creek; and also tracts at the mouth of French Creek,.at Fort Le Bœuf, and at the mouth of Conewango Creek. For the purpose of raising an additional sum by the sale of town lots to be used in paying the debts of the State, the President of the Supreme Executive Council was authorized by an act passed the 11th day of September, 1787, to cause a town to be laid out on the reservation opposite Fort Pitt. The tract, except three hundred and twelve acres within its boundaries, was accordingly surveyed into town and out lots and sold at public auction. The regular lots of the town, as laid down in the survey, were in dimensions sixty by two hundred and forty feet, while the out lots contained from five to ten acres. The part containing three hundred and twelve acres, not included in the plan of the town, was patented to James O'Hara on the 5th day of May, 1789. This town has grown into the large and flourishing city of Allegheny. By another act, passed September 28, 1791, the governor was given power to authorize the surveyor-general to cause a part of the reservation at the mouth of Beaver Creek to be laid out in town lots, ' on or near the ground where the old French town stood,' in such manner as commissioners, to be appointed by the governor, should direct. By this act two hundred acres were to be surveyed into town lots, and one thousand acres, adjoining on the upper side, into out lots to contain not less than five acres, nor more than ten acres. Daniel Leet, a deputy-surveyor, who had previously surveyed district No. 2, of the depreciation lands and one of the donation districts, was employed to lay out these town and out lots, and his survey of the town and out lots was confirmed by an act passed in March, 1793. The same act directed the governor to proceed to make sale of the lots and grant conveyances for them, in the manner prescribed by the act authorizing the laying out of the town. The town was called Beavertown, and when the county of Beaver was erected in 1800 was made the county seat. The act erecting the county appropriated five hundred acres of the reservation for the use of such school or academy as might thereafter be established in the town. The town then called Beaver was incorporated into a borough in 1802, and the boroughs of Rochester and Bridgewater, on opposite sides of the creek, also occupy parts of this reservation.

"The towns of Erie, Franklin, Waterford, and Warren were established by an act passed on the 18th day of April, 1795. Of the large reservation on Lake Erie, at Presque Isle, the governor was authorized to appoint two commissioners to survey sixteen hundred acres for town lots and three thousand four hundred, adjoining thereto, for out lots, with such streets, alleys, lanes, and reservations for public uses as the commissioners should direct. The town lots were to contain not more than one-third of an acre,* the out lots not more than five acres, the reservations for public uses not to exceed twenty acres, and the town was to be called Erie. After the survey of the town, made by General William Irvine and Andrew Ellicott, was filed in the office of the secretary of the Commonwealth, the governor was directed to sell at public auction one-third of the town lots and one-third of the out lots to the highest bidders, and grant patents to the purchasers upon the condition that within two years they respectively should 'build a house, at least sixteen feet square, and containing at least one brick or stone chimney,' on each lot purchased, the patent not to be issued until after the expiration of two years, and then only on proof that the condition of the sale had been complied with. In addition to the surveys of the town and out lots, the act provided that three lots—one of sixty acres on the southern side of the harbor, another of thirty on the peninsula, and a third of one hundred acres, also on the peninsula,—should be surveyed for the 'use of the United States in erecting and maintaining forts, magazines, and dock-yards thereon.' Of the tract at the mouth of French Creek, three hundred acres for town lots and seven hundred acres for out lots were to be surveyed for the town of Franklin; and of the tract at the mouth of Conewango Creek, three hundred acres for town lots and seven hundred acres for out lots were to be surveyed for the town of Warren. At the time the act providing for the laying out of these towns became a law a settlement had been made at Fort Le Bœuf. Andrew Ellicott had surveyed and laid out a town, and his draft of the town was accepted and confirmed by the Legislature. It was provided, however, that in addition to the town lots of Ellicott's survey, five hundred acres should be surveyed for out lots, and that the town should be called Waterford. The size of the town and out lots for Franklin and Warren, the out lots for Waterford, and the provisions for streets, lanes, alleys, and reservations for public use,—the reservations reduced to ten acres,—were the same as for the town of Erie, as were also the regulations for the sale of the lots. At Waterford a number of settlers who had built houses were given a right of pre-emption to the lots on which they settled. A subsequent act passed April 11, 1799, provided that surveys should be made of the reserved tracts adjoining Erie, Franklin, Warren, and Waterford, not laid out in town or out lots, into lots not to exceed one hundred and

* The regular town lots of Erie as laid down in the map of the town are eighty-two feet six inches front and one hundred and sixty-five feet in depth.

fifty acres in each, to be sold by commissioners, one of whom was to reside in each town. The tracts were to be graded in quality, and no sale was to be made at less than four dollars an acre for land of the first quality, three dollars for the second quality, and two dollars for the third quality; and purchasers, before title could vest in them, were required within three years from the date of their purchases to make an actual settlement on the land ' by clearing, fencing, and cultivating at least two acres for every fifty contained in one survey, and erect on each lot or tract a messuage for the habitation of man and reside thereon for the space of five years following their first settlement of the same.' The same act required five hundred acres in each of the reserved tracts to be surveyed for the use of schools or academies, and provision was made for the appraisement of the residue of the town and out lots, and for their sale by the commissioner residing in the town. It was also provided in this act that the reserved lot in the town of Erie, at the mouth of Cascade Creek, was to be sold at public sale, on consideration of settlement and improvement, provided it brought fifty dollars an acre. By an act passed February 19, 1800, the clause of the act that required settlement and improvement of lots was repealed. The other reservation of two thousand acres in the Erie triangle, at the mouth of Harbor Creek, was donated by an act of the Legislature to General William Irvine to indemnify him for the loss of Montour's Island (now called Neville Island), in the Ohio River below the city of Pittsburg. General Irvine held the island under a Pennsylvania patent, but was divested of his title by a judgment of the Supreme Court of the United States in an ejectment suit brought against him by a party who claimed ownership under a Virginia right, which, under the agreement between Pennsylvania and Virginia for settling the southwestern boundary dispute, was held by the court to be good."

INDIAN TREATIES AT FORTS STANWIX (ROME, N. Y.) AND M'INTOSH

For a full history of the proceedings of the treaties held at Forts Stanwix and McIntosh, between the commissioners of the Commonwealth of Pennsylvania and the deputies of the *Six Nations* and the *Wyandott* and *Delaware Indians*, claiming the unpurchased territory within the acknowledged limits of the northwest of Pennsylvania, see McKnight's " Pioneer History of Jefferson County, Pennsylvania."

CHAPTER V

TITLES AND SURVEYS—PIONEER SURVEYS AND SURVEYORS—DISTRICT LINES—
LAWS, REFERENCES, AND REPORTS—STREAMS AND HIGHWAYS—DONATION
LANDS

"In 1670 Admiral Sir William Penn, an officer in the English navy, died. The government owed this officer sixteen hundred pounds, and William Penn, Jr., fell heir to this claim. King Charles II. liquidated this debt by granting to William Penn, Jr., 'a tract of land in America, lying north of Maryland and west of the Delaware River, extending as far west as plantable.' King Charles signed this deed March 4, 1671. William Penn, Jr., was then proprietor, with power to form a government. Penn named the grant Pennsylvania, in honor of his father. In 1682 Penn published his form of government and laws. After making several treaties and visiting the Indians in the interior as far as Conestoga, Penn sailed for England, June 12, 1684, and remained away till December 1, 1699. On his return he labored to introduce reforms in the provincial government, but failed. He negotiated a new treaty of peace with the Susquehanna Indians and also with the Five Nations. In the spring of 1701 he made a second journey into the interior, going as far as the Susquehanna and Swatara. Business complications having arisen, Penn sailed for England in the fall, and arrived there the middle of December, 1701. Owing to straitened financial circumstances, he entered into an agreement with Queen Anne, in 1712, to cede to her the province of Pennsylvania and the Lower Counties for the sum of twelve thousand pounds sterling; but before the legal papers were completed he was stricken with paralysis, and died July 30, 1718, aged seventy-four. While Penn accomplished much, he also suffered much. He was persecuted for his religion, imprisoned for debt, and tried for treason. After his death it was found that, owing to the complication of his affairs and the peculiar construction of his will, a suit in chancery to establish his legal heirship was necessary. Several years elapsed before the question was decided, when the Proprietaryship of the province descended to John, Richard, and Thomas Penn. John died in 1746 and Richard in 1771, when John, Richard's son, and Thomas became sole Proprietaries. But the Revolution and the Declaration of Independence soon caused a radical change in the provincial government."—*Meginnis*.

During the Revolution the Penn family were Tories, adherents of England, and on the 27th of November, 1779, the Legislature of Pennsylvania confiscated all their property except certain manors, etc., of which surveys and returns had been made prior to the 4th of July, 1776. The Penns were granted as a compensation for these confiscations one hundred and thirty thousand pounds sterling. This ended the rule of the Penns in America. The treaty of peace between England and what is now the United States was ratified by Congress in January, 1784. All foreign domination or rule in the colonies then ceased, but internal troubles with the savages still continued in this State in the north and northwest.

"The Indians were jealous of their rights, and restive under any real or fancied encroachments that might be made upon them, and it required the exercise of great care, caution, and prudence on the part of the authorities to avert trouble on the northern and western boundaries of the State; and this they did not always succeed in doing, as many adventurous spirits, pushing far out into the unsettled wilderness, discovered to their sorrow. Fortunately, however, by the treaty of October, 1784, with the Six Nations at Fort Stanwix, and that of January, 1785, with the Wyandots and Delawares at Fort McIntosh, the Indian title was extinguished to all the remaining territory within the then acknowledged limits of the State which had been previously purchased. The boundaries of that great northwestern section of the State covered by this purchase may be briefly described as follows: Beginning on the east branch of the Susquehanna River where it crosses the northern boundary of the State in Bradford County; thence down the east branch to the mouth of Towanda Creek; thence up Towanda Creek to its head-waters; thence by a straight line west to the head-waters of Pine Creek; thence down Pine Creek to the west branch of the Susquehanna; thence up the west branch to Cherry Tree in Clearfield County; thence by a straight line to Kittanning, on the Allegheny River, in Armstrong County; thence down the Allegheny River to the Ohio River; thence down the Ohio River to where it crosses the western boundary to Lake Erie; and thence east along the northern boundary of the State to the beginning. And within this territory at the present day we find the counties of Tioga, Potter, McKean, Warren, Crawford, Venango, Forest, Clarion, Elk, Jefferson, Cameron, Butler, Lawrence, and Mercer, and parts of the counties of Bradford, Clinton, Clearfield, Indiana, Armstrong, Allegheny, Beaver, and Erie."—*Annual Report of Internal Affairs.*

The Indians received for this territory ten thousand dollars in cash. Our wilderness was then in Northumberland County. "All land within the late (1784) purchase from the Indians, not heretofore assigned to any other particular county, shall be taken and deemed to be within the limits of Northumberland County and Westmoreland County. And that from Kittanning up the Allegheny to the mouth of Conewango Creek, and from thence up said creek to the northern line of this State, shall be the line between Northumberland County."—*Smith's Laws*, vol. ii. p. 325.

"Under the Proprietary government which ended November 27, 1779, land was disposed to whom, on what terms, in such quantities, and such locations as the proprietor or his agents saw proper. The unoccupied lands were never put in the market, nor their sale regulated by law. Every effort made by the Assembly to secure uniformity in the sale and price of land was resisted by the proprietor as an infringement upon his manorial rights. After the Commonwealth became vested with the proprietary interests, a law was passed April 9, 1781, for establishing the land-office, for the purpose of enabling those persons to whom grants had been made to perfect their titles. July 1, 1784, an act was passed opening the land-office for the sale of vacant lands in the purchase of 1768. The price was fixed at £10 per one hundred acres, or thirty-three and one-third cents per acre, in addition to the warrant survey and patent fees, and the quantity in each warrant limited to four hundred acres and the six per cent. allowance. The purchase of 1784 having been completed and confirmed by the treaty at Fort McIntosh, January, 1785, the land-office was opened for the sale of lands in the new purchase December 21, 1785, at which the price was fixed at £30 per one hundred acres, and warrants were allowed to contain one thousand acres, with ten per cent. overplus, besides the usual allowance." This is the reason why so many old warrants contained eleven hundred acres, with six per cent., or sixty acres more. " Nevertheless, the price of the land was placed so high that but few speculators ventured to invest in the hilly and heavily timbered lands of Northern Pennsylvania. Under the pressure of certain land-jobbers, who were holding important offices (?) in the Commonwealth, like John Nicholson, Robert Morris, and William Bingham, an act was passed April 3, 1792, in which the price of vacant lands was reduced to fifty shillings per one hundred acres, or six and two-thirds cents per acre. Speculation ran wild. Applications for warrants poured into the office by tens of thousands. The law, while it appeared to favor persons of small means, and prevent the wealthy from acquiring large portions of the public domain, was so drawn that by means of fictitious applications and poll deeds—that is, mere assignments of the application without the formalities of acknowledgment—any party could possess himself of an unlimited quantity of the unappropriated lands. Within a year or two nearly all the lands in the county (then Northumberland) had been applied for, Nicholson, Morris, Bingham, James D. Le Roy, Henry Drinker, John Vaughan, Pickering, and Hodgdon being the principal holders."—*Craft's History of Bradford County*, pp. 40, 41.

" When, in the pursuance of this policy which had been adopted by William Penn, by treaties with and by purchases of the Indians, they finally became divested of their original title to all the lands in Pennsylvania; then, under what was called ' The Late Purchase,' which covered all of this section of country and included it in Northumberland County, in the year 1785 certain warrants, called ' Lottery Warrants,' were issued by governmental authority to persons who would pay twenty pounds per hundred acres, authorizing them to enter upon the lands and make selections where they pleased. This was done to some extent, and on those warrants surveys were made; but, as there was no road by which emigrants could come into the country, no settlements could be made except where the sturdy pioneer could push his canoe, ignoring, or overcoming all the privations and difficulties incident to a pioneer life in such a wilderness."

PIONEER SURVEYS

With a desire to give a complete history of the pioneer surveys of the northwest, I addressed a letter to Hon. I. B. Brown, Deputy Secretary of Internal Affairs, asking for all the information possessed by the State. I herewith submit his reply,—viz.:

"DEPARTMENT OF INTERNAL AFFAIRS,
"HARRISBURG, PA., March 7, 1895.

" MR. W. J. McKNIGHT, Brookville, Pa.

" DEAR SIR,—In answer to your letter of the 5th instant, we beg to say that prior to the opening of the land-office in May, 1785, for the sale of lands within the purchase of 1784, that part of the purchase lying east of the Allegheny River and Conewango Creek was divided into eighteen districts, and a deputy-surveyor appointed for each. These districts were numbered consecutively, beginning with No. 1, on the Allegheny River, and running eastward. The southern line of district No. 1 began on the old purchase line of 1768 at Kittanning, and following that line in successive order were districts Nos. 2, 3, 4, 5, and 6, the latter terminating at the marked cherry-tree on the bank of the west branch of the Susquehanna River at Canoe Place. From that point the district line between the sixth and seventh districts, as then constituted, is supposed to be the line that divides the present counties of Indiana and Jefferson from the county of Clearfield as far north as Sandy Lick Creek.

" An old draft and report, found among the records of this department, show that Robert Galbraith, one of the early surveyors of Bedford County, ran the purchase line of 1768 from the cherry-tree to Kittanning for the purpose of marking it and ascertaining also the extent of the several survey districts north of the line and between the two points. This draft and accompanying report are without date, but the survey was presumably made during the summer of 1786. A reference to the appointment of Mr. Galbraith by the surveyor-general to perform this work, and the confirmation of the appointment by the Supreme Executive Council on the 8th of April, 1786, appear in the ' Colonial Records,' vol. xv. pp. 3 and 4. In the same volume, p. 85, is found the record of an order in favor of Galbraith for forty-five pounds, twelve shillings, to be in full for his services in running and marking the line and ' laying off' the districts of the deputy-surveyors. He says in his report, ' I began at the marked cherry-tree and measured along the purchase line seven miles and forty perches for James Potter's district, thence fifty-four perches to the line run by James Johnston for the east line of his district; from the post marked for James Potter's district seven miles and forty perches to a post marked for James Johnston's district, thence fifty-two perches to the line run by James Hamilton for the east line of his district; from Johnston's post seven miles and forty perches to the post marked for James Hamilton's district, thence fifty-two perches to the line run by George Wood, Jr., for the east line of his district; from the post marked for Hamilton's district six miles and one hundred and fifty-two perches to the line run by Thomas B. McClean for the east line of his district, thence two hundred and eight perches to the post marked for George Wood, Jr.'s, district, thence six miles and one hundred and fifty perches to the line run by John Buchanan for the east line of his district, thence two hundred and ten perches to the post marked for Thomas Brown McClean's district, thence two miles and one hundred and twenty perches to the Allegheny River for John Buchanan's district.'

" With the exception of the first, these districts each extended seven miles and forty perches along the purchase line, with the division lines between them running north to the line of New York. Undoubtedly the fourth, fifth, and sixth districts, of which James Hamilton, James Johnston, and General James Potter were respectively the deputy-surveyors, must have embraced, if not all, at least much the larger part of the territory that subsequently became the county of Jefferson, while the earliest surveys were made within that territory during the summer of 1785 by the surveyors named. It is possible, however, that part of the third district, of which George Wood, Jr., was the deputy-surveyor, may have been within these limits, and if so, surveys were no doubt also made by him. These first surveys were principally made and returned on the first warrants granted within the purchase, commonly known as the lottery warrants, and many of them in the name of Timothy Pickering and Company were located on lands that are now within Jefferson County.

" General James Potter died in the year 1789, and was succeeded by his son, James Potter, who was appointed in 1790. One of the reasons given for the appointment of James Potter, second, was that he had filled the position of an assistant to his father, and had done so much of the actual work in the field, and was therefore so thoroughly conversant with the lines of surveys already run, that he would avoid the interferences another person might fall into, thus preventing future trouble arising from conflicting locations. It does not appear, however, that the second James Potter ever did any work in the district, as the deputies' lists of surveys on file in the land-office show no returns from him.

" Soon after the year 1790 a change was made by the surveyor-general in the arrangement of the districts within the purchase of 1784, by which the number was reduced to six, counting west from the mouth of Lycoming Creek to the Allegheny River. In this arrangement the two western districts, Nos. 5 and 6, were assigned respectively to William P. Brady and Enion Williams. Williams was succeeded in 1794 by John Broadhead. Brady's district is described as ' beginning at a cherry-tree of late General Potter's district, and from thence extending by district No. 4 due north to the northern boundary of Pennsylvania, thence by the same west fourteen miles, thence south to the line of purchase of 1768, late the southern boundary of James Johnston's and General Potter's districts, and by the same to the place of beginning.'

" The sixth district comprised all the territory west of Brady's district to the Allegheny River and Conewango Creek. All of the present county of Jefferson must have been within these districts. The surveys made and returned by Brady, Williams, and Broadhead, for the Holland Company, John Nicholson, Robert Morris, and other large purchasers of lands, are so numerous as to practically cover all the lands left unsurveyed by their predecessors within that particular section of the State. A small part of the county, in the vicinity of Brockwayville, was in Richard Shearer's district, No. 7, east of General Potter's line, and a number of lottery warrants was surveyed by Shearer in that locality in 1785. That part of the county subsequently fell within district No. 4, of which James Hunter was the surveyor, who also returned a few surveys.

" In what manner these pioneer surveyors in the wilderness were equipped, and what the outfit for their arduous and difficult labors may have been, we do not know and have no means of ascertaining. Doubtless they had many severe trials and endured many hardships in preparing the way for future settlements and advancing civilization, for which they receive little credit or remembrance at this day. Possibly their only equipment was the ordinary surveyor's compass and the old link chain of those days, but they nevertheless accomplished much work that remains valuable down to the present time. For their labor they were paid by fees fixed by law. The law of that day also provided a per diem wage of three shillings for chain-carriers, to be paid by the purchaser of the land.

" Very truly yours,

" ISAAC B. BROWN,
" Secretary."

You will see from the above that in 1785, Richard Shearer, with his chain-carriers and his axe-men, traversed what is now Brockwayville and the forest east of it; that James Potter, with his chain-carriers and axe-men, traversed the forests near Temples, now Warsaw; that James Johnston, with his chain-carriers and axe-men, traversed the forest where Brookville now is, and that James Hamilton, with his chain-carriers and axe-men, traversed the forest near or where Corsica now is. Each of these lines ran directly north to the New York line. Where these lines ran was then all in Northumberland County. In 1794, James Hunter, with his chain-carriers and axe-men, was in what is now Brockwayville region, William P. Brady, with his chain-carriers and axe-men, was in what is now the Temple region, and Enion

Williams and John Broadhead, with chain-carriers and axe-men, were between where Brookville now is and the Clarion region.

" By an act of the Legislature, passed April 1, 1794, the sale of these lands was authorized. The second section of this law provides that all lands west of the Allegheny Mountains shall not be more than three pounds ten shillings for every hundred acres.

" Section four provides that the quantity of land granted to one person shall not exceed four hundred acres. Section six provides for the survey and laying out of these lands by the surveyor-general or his deputies into tracts of not more than five hundred acres and not less than two hundred acres, to be sold at public auction at such times as the ' Supreme Executive Council may direct.'

" When all claims had been paid, ' in specie or money of the State,' for patenting, surveying, etc., a title was granted to the purchaser. In case he was not ready or able to make full payment at the time of purchase, by paying all the fees appertaining thereto, he was allowed two years to complete the payment by paying lawful interest, and when the last payment was made a completed title was given.

" By the act of April 8, 1785, the lands were sold by lottery, in portions not to exceed one thousand acres to each applicant. Tickets, commencing with number one, were put in a wheel, and the warrants, which were called ' Lottery Warrants,' issued on the said applications, were severally numbered according to the decision of the said lottery, and bore date from the day on which the drawing was finished.

" Section seven of this act allowed persons holding these warrants to locate them upon any piece or portion of unappropriated lands. The land upon each warrant to be embraced in one tract, if possible.

" On the 3d of April, 1792, the Legislature passed an act for the sale of these lands, which, in some respects, differed from the laws of 1784 and 1785. It offers land only to such persons as shall settle on them, and designates the kind and duration of settlement.

" By section two of this act all lands lying north and west of the Ohio and Allegheny Rivers and Conewango Creek, except such portions as had been or should be appropriated to public or charitable uses, were offered to such as would ' cultivate, improve, and settle upon them, or cause it to be done, for the price of seven pounds ten shillings for every hundred acres, with an allowance of six per centum for roads and highways, to be located, surveyed, and secured to such purchasers, in the manner hereinafter mentioned.'

" Section three provided for the surveying and granting of warrants by the surveyor-general for any quantity of land within the said limits, to not exceed four hundred acres, to any person who settled upon and improved said land.

"The act provided for the surveying and division of these lands. The warrants were, if possible, to contain all in one entire tract, and the form of the tract was to be as near, as circumstances would admit, to an oblong, whose length should not be greater than twice the breadth thereof. No warrants were to be issued in pursuance of this act until the purchase-money should have been paid to the receiver-general of the land-office.

"The surveyor-general was obliged to make clear and fair entries of all warrants in a book to be provided for the purpose, and any applicant should be furnished with a certified copy of any warrant upon the payment of one-quarter of a dollar.

"In this law the rights of the citizen were so well fenced about and so equitably defined that risk and hazard came only at his own. But controversies having arisen concerning this law between the judges of the State courts and those of the United States, which the Legislature, for a long time, tried in vain to settle, impeded for a time the settlement of the district. These controversies were not settled until 1805, by a decision of Chief Justice Marshall, of the Supreme Court of the United States.

"At the close of the Revolutionary War several wealthy Hollanders,—Wilhelm Willink, Jan Linklaen, and others,—to whom the United States was indebted for money loaned in carrying on the war, preferring to invest the money in this country, purchased of Robert Morris, the great financier of the country at that time, an immense tract of land in the State of New York, and at the same time took up by warrant (under the law above cited) large tracts in the State of Pennsylvania, east of the Allegheny River. Judge Yeates, on one occasion, said, ' The Holland Land Company has paid to the State the consideration money of eleven hundred and sixty-two warrants and the surveying fees on one thousand and forty-eight tracts of land (generally four hundred acres each), besides making very considerable expenditures by their exertions, honorable to themselves and useful to the community, in order to effect settlements. Computing the sums advanced, the lost tracts, by prior improvements and interferences, and the quantity of one hundred acres granted to each individual for making an actual settlement on their lands, it is said that, averaging the whole, between two hundred and thirty and two hundred and forty dollars have been expended by the company on each tract.'

"An act was passed by the Legislature, March 31, 1823, authorizing Wilhelm Willink, and others of Holland to ' sell and convey any lands belonging to them in the Commonwealth.' "

THE DONATION LANDS OF NORTHWESTERN PENNSYLVANIA

The soldiers of the Pennsylvania Line who served in the War of the Revolution were by act of legislation entitled to the wild lands of the State, and a large part of the northwestern portion of the State north of the depreciation lands and west of the Allegheny River was set apart and surveyed to the officers and soldiers who had served in the Continental army, in the Pennsylvania Line. A description of these lands, reference to the legislation authorizing their survey, and the explorations made in reference to their value, will be of interest to all those who are making a study of the origin of titles in Pennsylvania.

As early as the 7th day of March, 1780, while the war of the American Revolution was still in active progress, and being vigorously waged by the hostile armies in the field, the General Assembly of Pennsylvania by resolution made a promise of " certain donations and quantities of land" to the soldiers of the State, known as the " Pennsylvania Line," then serving in the Federal army. It was provided that these lands should be " surveyed and divided off" at the end of the war, and allotted to those entitled to receive them according to their several ranks. In order to comply with the letter and intention of the resolution of March, 1780, by the same act passed by the General Assembly March 12, 1783, in which it was provided that certain lands should be set apart and sold for the purpose of redeeming the certificates of depreciation given to the soldiers of the Pennsylvania Line, under the act of December 18, 1780, it was also provided that " a certain tract of country, beginning at the mouth of Mogulbughtiton Creek; * thence up the Allegheny River to the mouth of Cagnawaga Creek; † thence due north to the northern boundary of the State; thence west by said boundary, to the northwest corner of the State; thence south, by the western boundary of the State, to the northwest corner of lands appropriated by this act for discharging the certificates ‡ herein mentioned; and thence by the same lands east to the place of beginning; which said tract of country shall be reserved and set apart for the only and sole use of fulfilling and carrying into execution the said resolve."

Under Section VI., of the same act, all rights, titles, or claims to land within the described bounds, whether obtained from the Indians, the late Proprietaries, or any other person or persons, were declared to be null and void, thus reserving the entire tract from sale or settlement until after the allotments of the soldiers were duly made and their claims fully satisfied. By Section VII., officers and privates were to be allowed two years after the declaration of peace in which to make their applications, and in case of death occurring to any one before his application was made, an additional year was allowed to the heirs, executors, or administrators of such person, and thereafter unlocated tracts were to be disposed of upon such terms as the Legislature might direct. It may be said in passing, however, that the period for making applications was a number of times extended by subsequent legislation. By the last section of the act, Section VIII., non-commissioned officers

---

* Now known as Mahoning Creek, in Armstrong County.
† Conewago Creek, in Warren County.
‡ The depreciation certificates.

84

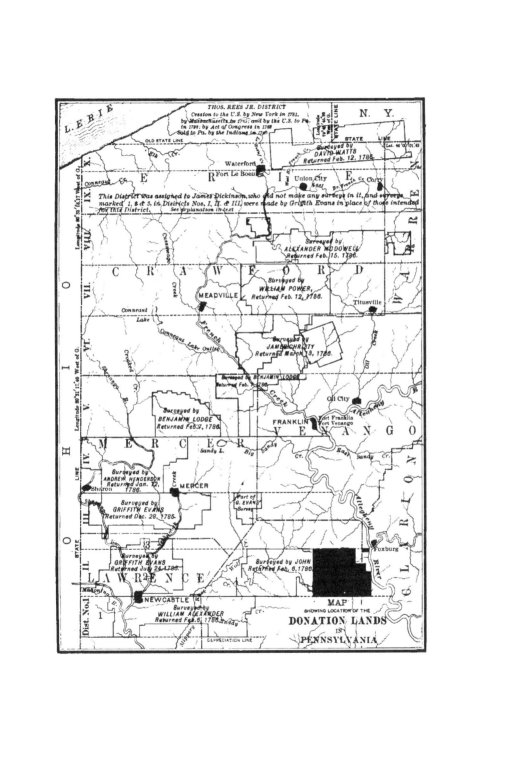

THOS. REES JR. DISTRICT
Cession to the U.S. by New York in 1781,
by Massachusetts in 1785; and by the U.S. to Pa.
in 1792; by Act of Congress in 1788
Sold to Pa. by the Indians in 1789

N. Y.

L. ERIE

OLD STATE LINE

Surveyed by
DAVID WATTS
Returned Feb. 12, 1786.

Waterford
Fort Le Boeuf

Union City

This District was assigned to James Dickinson, who did not make any surveys in it, and surveys
marked 1, 2 & 3, in Districts Nos. I, II, & III, were made by Griffith Evans in place of those intended
for this District. See explanation in text.

C R A W F O R D

Surveyed by
ALEXANDER M'DOWELL
Returned Feb. 15, 1786.

Surveyed by
WILLIAM POWER,
Returned Feb. 12, 1786.

MEADVILLE

Titusville

Conneaut
Lake

Surveyed by
JAMES CHRISTY
Returned March 18, 1786.

Surveyed by BENJAMIN LODGE
Returned Feb. 1786.

Surveyed by
BENJAMIN LODGE
Returned Feb. 3, 1786.

Oil City

V E N A N G O

FRANKLIN Fort Franklin
Fort Venango

M E R C E R

Surveyed by
ANDREW HENDERSON
Returned Jan. 12, 1786.

Sharon

MERCER

Surveyed by
GRIFFITH EVANS
Returned Dec. 28, 1785.

Part of
G. Evans
Survey

Surveyed by
GRIFFITH EVANS
Returned July 24, 1786.

Foxburg

L A W R E N C E

Surveyed by JOHN
Returned Feb. 6, 1786.

NEWCASTLE

Surveyed by
WILLIAM ALEXANDER
Returned Feb. 6, 1786.

Dist. No. I

DEPRECIATION LINE

MAP
SHOWING LOCATION OF THE
DONATION LANDS
IN
PENNSYLVANIA

and privates were prohibited from selling their shares of the land appropriated to their use until after the same had been " actually surveyed and laid off," the act declaring such sales or conveyances absolutely null and void. In this last section of the act a distinction was made between the commissioned officers and the non-commissioned officers and privates, probably under an impression that the former were able to take better care of their interests than the latter. It will be observed that the territory thus set apart under the act of December 12, 1783, for donation purposes, comprises parts of the present counties of Lawrence, Butler, Armstrong, Venango, Forest, and Warren, all of the counties of Mercer and Crawford, and that portion of Erie which lies south of the triangle. The territory was then a wild and unbroken wilderness, and we can at this day, after a century of progress and civilization, truly regard this section of our great Commonwealth, now filled as it is with a prosperous and industrious population that has wrought wonders of advancement and improvement, as a splendid, a princely domain, devoted in our early history to a noble purpose.

As a further reward for the services of the soldiers of the Pennsylvania Line, the next act of the General Assembly was one that exempted from taxation during lifetime the land which fell to the lot of each, unless the same was transferred or assigned to another person, and then follows soon after the purchase of 1784, the acts of March 24, 1785, which directed the mode by which the allowances of lands were to be distributed to the troops, and providing that legal titles, vesting in them the right of ownership, be granted to them. The details of the plan of distribution provided in this act are particular and comprehensive. The surveyor-general was directed forthwith to appoint deputy-surveyors for the purpose of surveying the lots, who were to give bonds in the sum of eight hundred dollars each for the faithful performance of their duties, and to follow such instructions as they might from time to time receive from the surveyor-general and the Supreme Executive Council of the State.

Another section describes the persons who should be entitled to land; and Section V., in order to comply with a previous resolution of the General Assembly, included the names of Baron Steuben, who was to receive a grant equal to that of a major-general of the Pennsylvania Line, and Lieutenant-Colonel Tilghman, a grant equal to that of a lieutenant-colonel of the same line; while by Section VI. other troops, raised under resolutions of February and December, 1780, were also declared to be entitled to lands according to their rank and pay respectively. Section X. enacted that the lots should be of four descriptions: the first to contain five hundred acres each, the second three hundred acres each, the third two hundred and fifty acres each, and the fourth two hundred acres each, with the allowance of six per cent.; and before proceeding to perform their duties under the act the deputies were required to subscribe an oath or affirmation that in making their surveys they would not choose out the best lands for the purpose of favoring any one of the four classes to the prejudice or injury of the others, or of the State. This section also provides for the proper marking of the lines, the numbering of the lots, and the transmission of field notes, drafts, and returns to the surveyor-general's office. Complete lists of all persons entitled to land under the act, with their rank and the quantity of land to be allotted to each, were to be furnished by the comptroller-general to the Supreme Executive Council in order that proper instructions, through the surveyor-general, might be given to surveyors in the field as to the number of lots to be surveyed and the quantities in which they were to be laid off; and when a sufficient number of lots were surveyed and returned, a draft of the whole was to be made and deposited in the rolls-office as a public record to serve in lieu of recording the patents. The wisdom of the last provision may be considered extremely doubtful, as has since been demonstrated in the fact that there are many patents for donation lands in existence of which the patent books of the land-office do not contain a line, and no little trouble in tracing title to certain of these tracts has been experienced in consequence of that defect in the act. The patent books should have contained the enrolment of all. Section VIII. provides minute directions for the distribution of the lots to claimants by lottery. Tickets representing the four classes, carefully numbered and tied " with silken thread," were to be placed in four wheels " like unto lottery wheels," from which the applicants were required to draw for their respective allotments. When not in use for drawing, the wheels were to be sealed and kept in the custody of a committee of the members of the Supreme Executive Council, the same committee having the right to judge and determine the right of every applicant to receive a grant, allowing in cases of doubt or difficulty an appeal to the council, whose decision was to be final. By this section of the act it was further provided that a major-general should draw four tickets from the wheel containing the numbers on the five hundred acre lots; a brigadier-general, three tickets from the same wheel; a colonel, two tickets from the same wheel; a lieutenant-colonel, one ticket from the same wheel and one from the wheel containing the numbers on the three hundred acre lots; a surgeon, chaplain, or major, two tickets from the wheel containing the numbers on the three hundred acre lots; a captain, one ticket from the wheel containing the numbers on the five hundred acre lots; a lieutenant, two tickets from the wheel containing the numbers on the two hundred acre lots; an ensign or regimental surgeon's mate, one ticket from the wheel containing the numbers on the three hundred acre lots; a sergeant, sergeant-major, or quartermaster-sergeant, one ticket from the wheel containing the numbers on the two hundred and fifty acre lots, and a drum-major, fife-major, drummer, fifer, corporal, or private, one ticket from the wheel containing the numbers on the two hundred acre lots. It will be seen that the allotment according to rank was therefore as follows: To a major-general, two thousand acres; a brigadier-general, fifteen hundred acres; a colonel, one thousand acres; a lieutenant-colonel, eight hundred acres; a surgeon, chaplain, or major, six hundred acres; a captain, five hundred acres; a lieutenant, four hundred acres; an ensign or regimental surgeon's mate, three hundred acres; a sergeant, sergeant-major, or quartermaster-sergeant, two hundred and fifty acres; and a drum-major, fife-major, drummer or fifer, or private, two hundred acres. Another section provides for the issuing of patents, to be signed, sealed, and delivered by the president or vice-president of the Supreme Executive Council and prescribing a form for the same, the consideration being " services rendered by ——, in the late army of the United States." The only expense to which applicants were to be subjected was the fee for " surveying, drafting, and returning," including the cost of chain-bearers, markers, etc. The sum fixed was three pounds for a lot of five hundred acres, two pounds for a lot of three hundred acres, and one pound ten shillings for lots of two hundred and fifty and two hundred acres, to be paid by each applicant before he could be permitted to draw for his lot. There were other provisions of the act for the purpose of fully carrying into effect the intentions of the General Assembly in making the grant, especially in Sections XX. and XXI., which provided for the employment of an agent for the purpose of exploration to ascertain and note the quality of the land and the topographic features of the country. This agent was particularly to note such parts of land as he might deem unfit for cultivation.

Three days before the act of March 25, 1785, became a law a committee chosen by the officers of the Pennsylvania Line, who were no doubt acquainted with the provisions of the proposed law, and concerned for their own interests, united in a letter to the Supreme Executive Council, recommending the appointment of General William Irvine, the commanding officer at Fort Pitt, as agent to explore the lands. After calling attention to the provisions in the proposed law for the employment of such agent, they say, " We therefore pray that Council will be pleased to appoint William Irvine, Esq., to that office, if the bill passes in its present state, as he is a gentleman well acquainted with the land appropriated for that purpose, and who is, we humbly conceive, worthy your confidence, as well as that of your most humble servants." (*Pennsylvania Archives*, vol. x. p. 425.) The Supreme Executive Council acted so promptly upon the recommendation of the committee of officers, that two days after the bill became a law, General Irvine was appointed agent, and having on the same day, March 26, 1785, subscribed his oath of office, an order for ninety pounds was issued in his favor as part of his pay. On the same day he received his instructions, which appear in Volume X., page 427, *Pennsylvania Archives*. They read as follows:

In Council, March 26, 1785.

" Sir: By virtue of the authority vested in us by the act of assembly for directing the Mode of distributing the Donation Lands, promised to the troops of this Commonwealth. We have appointed you Agent to perform the duties of this office, it will be necessary that with all possible Dispatch & accuracy, you explore the country to be laid off agreeably to Directions of that Act, noting the quality of the land in the several parts thereof, the hills, mountains, waters, creeks, marshes, uplands, bottom lands, &c., and such other occurrences as may deserve notice with their situation, & distance, but particularly the parts of the land which you may deem unfit for cultivation, &c.; and from time to time transmitting us your remarks, notes, and description of the Country."

This letter is signed by John Dickinson, and addressed to " The Honorable General William Irvine." General Irvine appears to have entered upon his duties of exploration, under the instructions given him, with little delay, and to have exercised good judgment, assiduity, and perseverance in pursuing them. A report of his notes and observations was transmitted to President Dickinson, in a letter dated at Carlisle, August 17, 1785. These papers are replete with interest and are here reproduced as they appear in Volume XI., pages 513 to 520, *Pennsylvania Archives.*

"CARLISLE, August 17, 1785.

" To His Excellency, John Dickinson, Esq.

" Sir: You have herewith transmitted my description of the donation tract of country, together with a sketch. These will, I hope, prove satisfactory to your Excellency and the honorable the council, and answer the public purposes for which they are designed.

" I observed in a former letter that few of the deputy-surveyors attended on my first going into the country, these agreed to postpone the business till September. On my return to Fort Pitt, after my tour, so late as July I found three of the gentlemen preparing to set out to survey. I did not consider it my duty to attend so small a number of them, as it would be spending the public money and my own time to little purpose, besides the law gives me no other control over them than to report to the Surveyor-General should they neglect or delay performing their duty. And I find sundry of them conceive they have not only a right, but are in some measure obliged to survey the land, good or bad, as each of them are instructed to survey a certain number of lots, for instance, two hundred and sixty of different descriptions and sizes, without any regard to water, bottom, upland, or any of the usual modes observed in laying of land. ' Several of the districts has not twenty lots of good land in them, yet the deputies are each instructed to survey upwards of two hundred and sixty, when others contain perhaps double the quantity directed.'

" Unless the Surveyor-General alters his instruction materially, or council, or the Assembly, take order in the premises, the whole end designed will be defeated as no man of common understanding will accept of pay for surveying such land.

" I am of opinion there is more than sufficient of good land on the tract appropriated to answer the purpose, provided the western boundary line of the State strikes the west branch of Beaver Creek as high as is generally supposed. Mr. McLane is of opinion it will cross at least sixteen miles higher than where his line does. In this case I propose this alteration for the consideration of council, that the deputies be instructed to begin at the west line of the State and survey all the land on the several branches of Beaver within the tract, before any other is laid off, if this should not prove sufficient, then proceed to the forks and upper branches of Tunck and Oil Creeks for the remainder. This mode will, I conceive, be better for the troops as their settlement, or vicinity to others will be more compact, consequently the land more valuable and it will certainly be more advantageous to the State, as whatever lands of value may be along the river and upper end of the tract will be reserved unculled, to dispose of as may be judged most expedient; and notwithstanding the spots of good land are detached, yet some of them are of such excellent quality, and so well situated on account of water carriage, easy communication with Lake Erie, and so well calculated for stock-farms, that the State may be much benefited by reserving them for future disposal.

" This mode will occasion an alteration, perhaps, with respect to the number of deputies, as fewer than the present number appointed would execute this mode best, and four or five would doubtless perform the business, provided they are allowed to employ assistants; these four or five might have constant communication with each other, and act as it were superintendents over the assistants, by which they could determine when the number of lots of each class required is done. I know it may be urged, in opposition to this, that sundry of these gentlemen have already gone to considerable expense in equipping themselves for the business and that it will be hard to dismiss them under these circumstances. To this I answer that the private advantage of two or three men ought not to be put in competition with that of as many thousands, particularly where the interest of the State at large is concerned also. I farther answer that these men may be employed by the principals, and will venture to assert that some of them are scarce fit even for this subordinate station, as perhaps the first chain or compass they ever saw was purchased for this occasion. The number, however, that I have proposed may be found among the gentlemen who understand both theory and practice extremely well, and are men of approved integrity, and I believe the State will find their account in this or some such mode, if they even pay the trifling expense the gentlemen have been at.

" I have the honor to be,
" With the greatest respect,
" Sir, Your Excellency's most
" Obedient humble servant,
" WM. IRVINE."

" Notes taken and observations made (by) the Agents appointed to explore the tract of country presented by the State to the late troops of the Pennsylvania Line, of the American Army.

" In exploring the donation land, I began on the Line run by Mr. McLane, between that and the tracts appropriated for redeeming depreciation certificates which he ascertained by a due North Line to be near thirty miles from Fort Pitt, and by the Common computation along the path leading from Fort Pitt to Venango on the mouth of French Creek, which some affirm was actually measured by the French when they possessed that country. I found it forty miles; East of this path along Mr. McLane's Line for five or six miles, the land is pretty level, well watered with small springs, and of tolerable quality, but from thence to the Allegheny River which is about Twenty-five miles due East, there is no land worth mentioning fit for cultivation; as far as French Creek all between the Venango Path and the Allegheny there is very little land fit for cultivation, as it is a continued chain of high barren mountains except small breaches for Creeks and Rivulets to desembogue themselves into the River. These have very small bottoms.

" As I proceeded along the path leading to French Creek about five miles to a Branch of Beaver or rather in this place called Canaghqunese I found the land of a mixed quality, some very strong and broken with large quantities of fallen Chestnut, interspersed with strips covered with Hickory, lofty oak, and for under wood or Brush, Dogwood, Hazel, &c.; along the Creek very fine rich and extensive bottoms in general fit for meadows; from hence to another branch of said Creek called Flat Rock Creek, about ten miles distant, the land is generally thin, stony and broken, loaded, however, with Chestnut Timber, the greatest part of which lies flat on the earth, which renders it difficult travelling—at the usual crossing place on the last named Creek, there is a beautiful fall over a Rock ten or twelve feet high at the fording immediately above the fall, the bottom is one entire Rock, except some small perforations which is capacious enough to receive a horse's foot and leg—it is here about forty yards wide and runs extremely rapid. From Flat Rock to Sandy Creek by Hutchins & Scull called, Lycomie, is about Twenty-four miles; on the first twelve there are a considerable quantity of tolerable level land tho much broken with large stony flats, on which grows heavy burthens of Oak, Beech, and Maple, particularly seven or eight miles from the Creek there is a plain or savannah three or four miles long, and at least two wide, without any thing to obstruct the prospect, except here and there a small grove of lofty Oaks, or Sugar Tree, on the skirts the ground rises gradually to a moderate heighth from which many fine springs descend, which water this fine Tract abundantly—along these Rivulets small but fine spots of meadow may be made, from hence the remaining twelve miles to Sandy Creek is a ridge or mountain, which divides the waters of the Allegheny, the Beaver, and Ohio, and is from East to West at least three times as long as it is broad

—on the whole of this there is little fit for cultivation, yet some of it is well calculated for raising stock. But a person must be possessed of very large Tracts to enable him to do even this to purpose.

" From Sandy to French Creek is about seven or eight miles from the mouth, but it soon Forks into many small runs, and is but a few miles from the mouth to the source—there are two or three small bottoms only on this Creek—to French Creek is one entire hill, no part of which is by any means fit for cultivation.

" On the lower side, at the mouth of French Creek, where the Fort called Venango formerly stood, there is three or four hundred acres of what is commonly called upland or dry bottom, very good land. On the North East side, about one mile from the mouth, another good bottom begins of four or five hundred acres, and on the summits of the hills on the same side tho high, there is a few hundred acres of land fit for cultivation—this is all in this neighborhood nearer than the first fork of the Creek; which is about eight miles distant. On the Road leading from French to Oil Creek, within about three miles and a half of Venango, there is a bottom of fine land on the Bank of the Allegheny, containing four or five hundred acres, there is little beside to Oil Creek fit for cultivation.

" French Creek is one hundred and fifty yards wide.

" From French to Oil Creek is about eight miles—this is not laid down in any map, notwithstanding it is a large stream not less than eighty, or perhaps a hundred yards wide at the mouth, a considerable depth, both of which it retains to the first fork, which is at least twenty miles up, and I am certain is as capable of rafting timber or navigating large boats on as French Creek in the same seasons this high. On the North East or upper side of this creek, at the mouth, is four or five hundred acres of good bottom, and about a mile up there is another small bottom on the South West side, which is all the good land to the first fork.

" Oil Creek has taken its name from an oil or bituminous matter being found floating on the surface. Many cures are attributed to this oil by the natives, and lately by some whites, particularly Rheumatic pains and old ulcers; it has hitherto been taken for granted that the water of the Creek was impregnated with it, as it was found in so many places, but I have found this to be an error, as I examined it carefully and found it issuing out of two places only—these two are about four hundred yards distant from (each) other, and on opposite sides of the Creek. It rises in the bed of the Creek at very low water, in a dry season I am told it is found without any mixture of water, and is pure oil; it rises, when the creek is high, from the bottom in small globules, when these reach the surface they break and expand to a surprizing extent, and the flake varies in color as it expands; at first it appears yellow and purple only, but as the rays of the sun reach it in more directions, the colors appear to multiply into a greater number than can at once be comprehended.

HISTORY OF NORTHWESTERN PENNSYLVANIA

" From Oil Creek to Cuskakushing, an old Indian Town, is about seventeen miles—the whole of this way is barren, high mountains, not fit for cultivation ; the mountain presses so close on the River that it is almost impassable, and by no means practicable when the River is high, then travellers either on foot or horseback are obliged to ascend the mountain and proceed along the summit.

" At Cuskushing there is a narrow bottom about two miles long, good land and a very fine Island fifty or sixty acres, where the Indians formerly planted corn. From Cuskushing to another old Indian Town, also on the Bank of the River, is about six miles ; this place is called Canenacai or Hickory Bottom ; here is a few hundred acres of good land and some small Islands, from hence to a place named by the natives the Burying Ground, from a tradition they have that some extraordinary man was burried there many hundred years ago, is about thirteen miles ; most of this way is also a barren and very high mountain, and you have to travel greatest part of the way in the Bed of the River. To Brokenstraw Creek, or Bockaloons, from the last named place is about fourteen miles, here the hills are not so high or barren, and there are sundry good bottoms along the River. About half way there is a hill called by the Indians Paint Hill, where they find very good red oker. Brokenstraw is thirty yards wide, there is a fine situation and good bottom near the mouth on both sides, but a little way up the creek large hills covered with pine make their appearance. From Brokenstraw to Canewago is eight or nine miles—here is a narrow bottom, interspersed with good dry land, and meadow ground all the way, and there is a remarkable fine tract at the mouth of Conewago, of a thousand or perhaps more acres, from the whole of which you command a view up and down the main branch of Allegheny, and also up Conewago a considerable distance. Conewago is one hundred and fifty yards wide, and is navigable for large boats up to the head of Jadaque Lake, which is upwards of fifty mile from its junction with the east branch of the River. The head of Jadaque Lake is said to be only twelve miles from Lake Erie, where it is also said the French formerly had a Fort, and a good Waggon Road from it to the Lake. Conewago forks about thirty miles from the mouth of the East Branch, is lost in a morass where the Indians frequently carried their canoes across into a large creek called the Cateraque, which empties into the Lake forty or fifty miles above Niagara.

" This account of the branches of Conewago I hade from my guide, an Indian Chief of the Senecas, a native of the place, and an intelligent white man, who traversed all this country repeatedly. I have every reason to believe the facts are so—tho I do not know them actually to be so as I went only a small distance up this creek, being informed there is no land fit for cultivation to the first fork or to the lower end of Jadaque Lake, which begins seven miles up the West Branch, except what has already been mentioned at the mouth of the creek, the appearance of the country, in a view taken from the

92

summit of one of the high hills, fully justified this report, as nothing can be seen but one large chain of mountains towering above another—here, perhaps, it may not be amiss to insert the supposed distances in a collected view—and

first from Fort Pitt to McLane's 40
To fourth branch of Canaghqunese 5
Rocky, or Flat Rock Creek 10
Sandy Creek 24
French Creek 8
Oil Creek, ... 6
Cuskacushing 17
Cananacai 6
The Burying Ground 13
Brokenstraw 14
Conewagoo 9
                                                    ———
                                                    152
Deduct from Fort Pitt to Mc'Lenes line between the depre-
    ciation and donation tracts 40
                                                    ———
Leaves the donation land to be....................... 112 Miles long.

" For the same reason that I did not proceed far up Conawago, I returned the most direct Road to the burying ground—here three old Indian paths take off, one to Cayahaga, on Lake Erie, one to Cuskusky, on the West branch of Beaver Creek, and the third to a Salt Spring, higher up the same branch of Beaver—from hence I crossed the chain of mountains, which runs along the River, and in traveling what I computed to be about twenty five miles, reached the first fork on Oil Creek, on the most easterly Branches there are vast quantities of White Pine, fit for masts, Boards, &c. In this fork is a large Body of tolerable good land, tho high, and along the West Branch very rich and extensive Bottoms fit for meadow, of the first quality—this continues about fifteen miles along the creek, which is a beautiful stream, from thirty to forty yards wide, and pretty deep. From the West Branch of Oil Creek I proceeded on a Westerly course, about ten miles along a ridge which is difficult to ascend, being high and steep, but when you get up it is flat on the summit, four or five miles broad, very level, and fine springs issue from the declivity on both sides, the land heavily loaded with Hickory, large Oak, Maple, and very large Chestnut. From the West end of this ridge several large springs rise, which form the most easterly branch of French Creek—there are five branches of this creek, which is called Sugar Creek, by Mr. Hutchins, all of which have fine Bottoms, excellent for meadow and pasturage, but the upland or ridges between are stony, cold, moist and broken, chiefly covered with Beech, Pine and scrubby Chestnut.

" At the fork or junction of Sugar Creek with the main or West Branch of French Creek (which is only eight miles up from Venango), there is some fine plains or savannahs, and a large quantity of meadow ground—there are but few bottoms, and little or no upland besides what is above mentioned, for twenty miles up this branch, where there is a considerable quantity of excellent meadow ground, beside which there is not much good land until you reach Le Berroff (Boeuf's).

" From Venango, I returned along the path leading to Pittsburg to within about seven miles of Flat Rock Creek, here I took a West course along a large dividing ridge already noticed, about ten miles, where I struck a branch of Canaghquenese or Beaver, about thirty yards wide, and which joins Flat Rock before it empties into the main branch of Canaghquenese—on this creek is very fine and larger bottoms, and in some places some good upland, tho' much broken with high, barren hills and some deep morasses. This creek is not laid down in any map that I have seen. After having explored this creek and lands adjacent, I proceeded on a South course till I struck Mr. McLene's line within eight miles of the great Beaver Creek, which I followed to the Creek; all this distance is very hilly, there are some small bottoms, but the major part of those eight miles is not fit for cultivation.

" From where Mr. McLane's line strikes the great or West Branch of the Beaver, I continued exploring the country up the several western branches of the Beaver, Viz, the most Westerly, and two branches denominated the She-nango. The distance from the above named line to an old Moravian Town is three or four miles, from thence to Shenango, two and a half or three miles; thence to a fork or second branch, two miles; from the mouth of Shenango to Cuskuskey, on the West branch, is six or seven miles, but it was formerly all called Cuszuskey by the natives along this branch as high as the Salt spring, which is twenty-five miles from the mouth of Shenango. There is such a similarity in almost all the lands on all the branches of Beaver Creek, that a particular description of each would be mere (repetition). I shall therefore only briefly observe that the bottoms generally are the most excellent that can be well imagined, and are very extensive—the upland is hilly, and some bad, but most of the hills are fertile and very rich soil—from the falls of the Great Beaver up to the head of the West Branch, and twenty miles up the Shenango branch, is to a considerable distance on either side those creeks there is little land but may be cultivated, and I believe no country is better watered.

" I herewith transmit a sketch of that part of the country only which my duty as agent obliged me to explore. This, together with the remarks herein contained will, I flatter myself give a juster idea of the tract than any map yet published. Tho' I do not pretend to say it is correct, as the distances are all supposed, and there are probably several omissions in this sketch, yet more creeks, hills, &c., are noticed than have been before and their real courses and near connections & division by Hills & Ridges ascertained.

" No Creek is laid down or branch which is not upwards of Twenty yards wide—smaller runs are not noticed—on the whole I have endeavored as well in the remarks as in the sketch,* so far as I have gone, to answer the end for which I was appointed Agent, as well as in my power.

" WM. IRVINE,
" Agent.

" N. B. The dotted lines show the several courses taken in exploring the country on the sketch—besides the several offsets were made to gain summits of hills for the benefit of prospects. All the Branches of Canaghquenese, which are six or seven in number, join and form one large Creek before it enters the Beaver, the junction is about eleven miles above the mouth of Beaver from above the falls and four below McLene's line. I have been unavoidably obliged to leave the North and West lines open in the sketch, as I could not do otherwise till these boundary lines are run; this also prevented my compleating the business, not being able to determine perhaps within several miles, where the line may run. I am persuaded the State of Pennsylvania might reap great advantages by paying early attention to the very easy several communications with Lake Erie from the western parts of their country, particularly Conewago; French Creek and the West Branch of Beaver, from a place called Mahoning to where it is navigable for small craft is but thirty miles to Cayahuga River, which empties into the lake. A good waggon road may be made from Fort Pitt to the mouth of French Creek, & all the way from the mouth of Beaver to Cayuhuga, which is not more than 80 miles. The breadth of the tract cannot be ascertained till the Western Boundary is run. Mr. McLene suspends for this reason extending his line further West than the Great Beaver, which he has found to be 47 miles from the mouth, Mogwolbughtitum, from this part of Beaver Creek it is conjected the West line of the State will run 10 or 12 miles."

In the mean time the authorities of the State were busy in perfecting the machinery necessary for carrying into effect the scheme for the allotment and distribution of the lands to those persons entitled to receive them. On the 3d of May, 1785, John Lukens, the surveyor-general, is informed that by the report of the comptroller-general the number of lots to be surveyed and the quantity of land that each should contain would be " one hundred and seventy-seven lots of the first description, each containing five hundred acres; eighty-eight of the second description, each containing three hundred acres; one hundred and eighty-six of the third description, each containing two hundred and fifty acres, and two thousand one hundred and nineteen of the fourth description, each containing two hundred acres," making two thousand five hundred and seventy lots of the various descriptions, and containing in the

---

* This sketch has not been found.

aggregate five hundred and eighty-five thousand two hundred acres of land. On the second of the same month the surveyor-general informed Council that he had nominated the following persons to Council " for their approbation, to be appointed deputy-surveyors of the donation lands west of the Allegheny River,—viz.: Major William Alexander, Benjamin Lodge, Captain James Christie, Ephraim Douglass, Griffith Evans, James Dickinson, John Henderson, William Power, Junior, Peter Light, Andrew Henderson, James Dickinson, James Hoge, David Watt, of Sherman's Valley, Alexander McDowell." The territory in which the donation surveys were to be made was divided into ten districts by the surveyor-general, after consultation with General Irvine, soon after the latter gentleman had received the appointment of agent. The districts were numbered in regular order to the north from the north line of the depreciation lands,—District No. 1, adjoining that line, and District No. 10, covering parts of the present counties of Erie and Warren. From a letter of the surveyor-general to Secretary Armstrong, dated May 14, 1785, in relation to the districts, there seems to have been some slight friction between the authorities in naming the deputy-surveyors. According to Mr. Lukens, the surveyors were named by him and General Irvine, " four of whom were officers of the Pennsylvania Line, and were recommended by their superior officers and were Practical Surveyors in the back counties, to which we added six more as per List sent to Council ye 5th inst." He then says, " At which Mr. Watts coming in, desired me to enter his son's name, which I did, and have also sent in the names of James Hoge & Peter Light, since for fear some of the first ten should disappoint us; four of the first ten are Commissioned & the others sent for—now why the eleventh should be pushed before we hear some thing from the others, I should be glad to be informed, unless Council have some objection to some of the first." The trouble, whatever it may have been, soon disappeared, and the ten surveyors appointed were William Alexander, for the first district; John Henderson, for the second district; Griffith Evans, for the third district; Andrew Henderson, for the fourth district; Benjamin Lodge, for the fifth district; James Christy, for the sixth district; William Power, for the seventh district; Alexander McDowell, for the eighth district; James Dickinson, for the ninth district; and David Watts, for the tenth district. With a single exception the persons named must have entered upon the performance of their duties very promptly and pursued them with commendable energy. Considering the character of the country in which their work was to be done, its wild and unsettled condition, and the difficulties to be encountered and overcome, the task before them was by no means an easy one. Except a few white traders along the Allegheny River, they would meet only Indians, and with their presence in those days there would always be an apprehension of lurking danger. The surveys of nine districts were, however, made with little or no difficulty so far as the records show, and were returned to the land-office early in the year 1786, one district really on the 28th of December, 1785. There was an equal allotment of the number of tracts of each description to be surveyed to the ten districts,—twenty tracts of five hundred acres each, ten of three hundred each, twenty-one of two hundred and fifty acres each, and two hundred and seventeen of two hundred acres each to each district. The first district, William Alexander, surveyor, was returned in February, 1786; the second, John Henderson, surveyor, February 6, 1786; the third, Griffth Evans, surveyor, December 28, 1785; the fourth, Andrew Henderson, surveyor, January 12, 1786; the fifth, Benjamin Lodge, surveyor, February 7, 1786; the sixth, James Christy, surveyor, March 18, 1786; the seventh, William Power, surveyor, March 13, 1786; the eighth, Alexander McDowell, surveyor, February 15, 1786, and the tenth, David Watts, surveyor, February 12, 1786. The ninth district is omitted from the above statement. The surveyor of that district, James Dickinson, does not appear to have reached the locality assigned to him until after the others had completed their work. He started some time in the fall of 1785 to make his surveys, and reached Venango, at which point it seems he was deterred from proceeding any further by fear of trouble with the Indians. After a consultation with several Indian chiefs, he determined to return home without making any surveys in the district. His explanation of this default on his part is found in a letter to the surveyor-general, dated " Pits Burg, 24th January, 1786," (?) in which he gives a statement of his interview with the Indians, his address to them, and the answer of the Chief Whole Face. The letter of explanation and interview appear in Volume X., pages 740 and 741, *Pennsylvania Archives*, and reads as follows:

" JAMES DICKINSON, TO JOHN LUKENS:
    " DEAR SIR,—Agreeably to Commission and Instructions for Surveying Donation Lands No. 9, District I proceeded on my Errand as far as Venango; but not without hearing on my way a very great uneasiness among the Indians at the procedure of the State in the Purchase of those lands, whereupon I thought it necessary to stop there a few Days & consult some Indians Chief on the subject before I proceeded further where after with the advice of the Pittsburg Traders There, I sent for by a Runner Whole Face, The Corn Planter, & Long Hair, three Senica Chiefs who were then out a hunting, two Days March from Venango. Whole Face & Long Hair came in & the Corn Planter refused,—At their coming in by an interpreter Elijah Matthews I informed them my Errand, they returned for answer, they could not then give me an answer to my Proposal but would in a few Days; I waited on them 4 & then they gave me a Hearing, which was as follows Verbatim.—At Mr. Thomas Wilkey's store at Venango, Present Mr. Thomas Wilkey, Captain Jacob Springer & Elijah Matthews.—Indians, The Chiefs Whole Face & Long Hair, with seven others.—

" My Friend Mr. Whole Face,

" I was sent here by the great Council of the State of Pennsylvania held at Philadelphia, to Measure some Lands a little to the Northward of this Place, which Land I am told the great Council had bought of our Brothers the Indians, whose sole Property they understood it to be—But on my way Here I was told the Indians were not well Pleased we should measure those Lands. I thought it therefore best to stop with you a few Days in Order to know what your uneasiness was if in my Power to remove any obsticle in the Way; being fully assured the Great Council of the State would do every Thing on their side to keep alive Friendship, To maintain Peace, To Increase Friendship, To support a Union & to make Trade Flourish between their Brothers the Indians and themselves, as long as Time shall measure the rolling year, & uttermostly endeavorer the Happiness of both Nations—Now my Brother and Brothers if there is any thing in the way of all these Things I have mentioned, I do wish & intreat you, to inform me frankly and if it can be in my power to serve to removing any such Thing as may obstruct our mutual Happiness, I shall always think myself happy of having it in my power so to do; or if you think some other Person more suitable to represent this Matter should be glad it was soon done & your objections to my Errand sent to the great Council at Philada."

To which Mr. Whole Face after consulting with the others gave the following answer:

" Brother of the Big Knife,

" Several Surveyors have been up here to Measure Lands the Last Summer and have gone Home. We knew not what was their meaning, as none of them told us, but went on without so much as informing their Intent. When they came to our hunting Fires, we used them well without any Question & when they wanted any of our assistance we gave it freely. Many of our young Warriors are dissatisfied with (their) Conduct, who are in the English Interest and also with the Reward we received for the Lands Thinking it inadequate for so large a Body; it not being one pair of Mokosons a piece; they therefore would advise me not to proceed on my Business and to inform the thirteen Fires it was their opinion I was not safe to proceed, though they present would pledge their Faith for my safety against all Indians at Venango & the Hunters to the Southward of that place; yet would not answer for it to the Northward, not even one Mile. That in the Spring as early as possible the six Nations would hold a great Council at Fort Pitt where & when they & all their Brethren hoped to make an endless Peace with their Brothers of the thirteen Fires & hoped till then I would put by every Thought of proceeding on my Errand as being very Dangerous; & then they hoped every obstruction would be removed & we should walk the Woods together as Brothers aught to do, in Love & Pleasure. And now my Brother tell your great Council of the thirteen Fires tis our Fault you do not go on and not yours.

His
" Segonkquas X
mark
His

" Tests,   " Conhonew X

    " Thos. Wilkins.   mark

    " Jacob Springer.

        " Traders.

                " Elijah X. Matthews, Interpreter.

                             " A true copy from the Original.

" This Dear Sir, with much more was pronounced in words and gestures of much warmth & earnest which made me conclude to proceed no further & return—My feet being much bit with Frost detains my not coming at present, but will come down as soon as they are recovered a Little. In the mean time remain yours to serve with the utmost affection?

                                          " JAMES DICKINSON.

    " P. S. I have not wrote you the private conversation Directed.

" To John Lukens, Esqr., Surveyor-General, Philadelphia."

The explanation of Mr. Dickinson was not satisfactory, as will be seen by a reference to the proceedings of the Supreme Executive Council at meetings held in Philadelphia, March 9 and 10, 1786, to be found in Volume XIV., pages 653 and 654, Colonial Records. Among the proceedings of the 9th the following appears: " On consideration of the delinquency of James Dickinson, a deputy-surveyor of donation lands, stated in a letter from Mr. Lukens, it was ordered, That he be removed from office, and that the surveyor-general proceed to nominate a successor thereto;" and on the following day we find that " Griffith Evans, Esquire, was appointed a deputy-surveyor of donation lands, in the room of James Dickinson, removed by an order of yesterday." This accounts for the omission of surveys from the ninth district in the first returns made to the land-office, nor were any surveys for donation purposes subsequently made in the district. The reason for this may be found in a minute of the Supreme Executive Council, May 5, 1786, Volume XV., page 16, Colonial Records. The following appears among the proceedings of that day: " A memorial from sundry officers of the late Pennsylvania Line, stating that large bodies of excellent land remain yet unsurveyed on the waters of Beaver River, in the donation land, very far superior in value, quality, and situation, to the lands in district number nine, and praying that the number of lots designed for the ninth district may be surveyed on the aforesaid waters, by the surveyor appointed to said district, was read and referred to the surveyor-general, who is directed to comply with the prayer of the said petition." Accordingly Griffith Evans, the successor of James Dickinson, immediately proceeded to locate the lots assigned to the ninth district in the unsurveyed parts of districts numbers one, two, and three, and on the 24th of July, 1786, made his returns to the land-office. The return of the surveys made by Mr. Evans, in districts one, two, and three, in place of those originally intended for the ninth district, completed the survey of all the districts and the connected drafts of each district, in a good state of preservation, are now remaining in the Department of Internal Affairs. The number of lots returned was slightly in excess of the number the surveyor-general was directed to have surveyed. There were two hundred lots of five hundred acres, one hundred of three hundred acres, two hundred of two hundred and fifty acres, and two thousand one hundred and seventy of two hundred acres, making two thousand six hundred and eighty lots comprising six hundred and sixteen thousand five hundred acres of land. Preparations were now begun for the distribution of the lots. The surveyor-general made his return to Council, and on the 31st day of August, 1786, the following order was placed upon the minutes: "Ordered, That the drawing of the lottery for, and the patenting of the said (donation) lots, shall commence on the first day of October next, to be continued one year from the 29th instant." The committee of members of the Supreme Executive Council selected to superintend the drawing of the lottery consisted of John Boyd, Jonathan Hoge, Stephen Ballitt, and William Brown, to which was shortly afterwards added Peter Muhlenberg and Samuel Dean. The records do not show definitely how many applicants availed themselves of the privilege of drawing during the period first fixed for the lottery to remain open; but evidently Lieutenant Joseph Collier was early on hand. He drew two lots of two hundred acres each, No. 97 in the first district and No. 1462 in the seventh district. A patent was issued to him on the 2d day of October, one day after the drawing began, and it was probably the first one granted. That a large number of claimants made their drawings during the first period is evident, however, from the number of patents that were granted after the opening in October, 1786, and during the year 1787, though it was found necessary as the closing day approached to grant an extension of time to enable other claimants to appear who had failed to do so. A minute of Council, of August 29, 1787, Volume XV., page 263, Colonial Records, reads as follows: "WHEREAS, It is represented to this Board that there are many of the line of the State intitled to land that have not yet appeared by themselves or sent orders to draw for their lots; and by resolve of the board of the 31st of August, 1786, they will be precluded unless the time be prolonged so as to include one year from the commencement of drawing; therefore, *Resolved*, That the lottery continue open for applicants until the first day of October next, and this resolution be published, so that all concerned may have notice thereof."

The time was again extended for a period of one year by an act passed on the 13th of September, 1788, and by subsequent legislative enactments there were numerous extensions, some of the acts making them also providing for the proper authentication of claims, and for other purposes affecting the rights of claimants. The extensions of time in which to present applications really continued under the various laws until April 1, 1810, which was the last limit of time fixed, and from that day the offices were closed against any further applications.

Owing to the uncertainty which existed in regard to the northern boundary of the State when the tenth district was surveyed, a serious mistake occurred in the location of a large number of lots in that district. It was discovered after the boundary line between Pennsylvania and New York had been located in 1787, that many of the lots fell within the State of New York. This mistake involved * one hundred and twenty lots that were wholly or in part within that State, thirty-one of them lying within the Erie triangle, which did not become a part of Erie County, Pennsylvania, until 1792. Nearly the entire number of these lots had been drawn from the lottery wheels by persons whose claims had been established, and patents had been granted to them before the error in the surveys became known. In order that such persons should not suffer by an unfortunate and mistaken location of the land they had drawn, and thus be deprived of the reward promised to them, the General Assembly on the 30th day of September, 1791, passed a law for their relief. The first section of the act provided that the surveyor-general should ascertain and report to the governor the number of patents that had fallen within the State of New York, together with the number of acres contained in each patent and the names of the persons to whom such patents were issued, which report was to be printed in three newspapers in Philadelphia, with notice to all persons concerned to apply before the first day of December following to the surveyor-general, who was authorized to ascertain by lot the order of priority by which such persons should choose other lots. The second section provided that applicants should in their order of priority choose other lots out of any of the surveyed tracts not otherwise disposed of within any of the donation districts. The third section, that after such persons had made their choice, patents should be granted to them without fees, on the surrender for cancellation of the patents previously granted to them. They were also

* The estimate of the authorities at the time was that one hundred and forty lots fell wholly within the State of New York and twenty-three partly so, making one hundred and sixty-three in all. This was an overestimate. An actual count of the lots as laid down in the map of the district, if the line drawn thereon is correct, shows the number affected by the mistake to have been as above stated. It was also afterwards discovered that a number of lots that had been drawn and released as lying in New York were found to be wholly in Pennsylvania, a fact shown in the preamble of an act passed April 2, 1802.

required to give quit claims to the Commonwealth for compensation on account of any losses they may have suffered. This act was followed by another on the 10th of April, 1792, extending the limit of time fixed for receiving applications from December 1, 1791, to July 1, 1792, and directing the report of the surveyor-general to be printed in newspapers of Philadelphia, Lancaster, York, Chambersburg, Harrisburg, Carlisle, and Pittsburg, with notice that application must be made within the time designated. Other legislation for the purpose of fully indemnifying the persons who held patents to these lots, and to secure to them all the benefits to which they were entitled under the acts of March 12, 1783, and March 24, 1785, followed the acts above mentioned. The acts of April 5, 1793, and February 23, 1801, were of that character. In the last act the comptroller-general was directed to furnish to the secretary of the land-office a list of the names of such persons whose lots fell outside of the State as had received no equivalent. It also provided that applications under the act should be made within three years by the applicant personally, his widow or children, or by his, her, or their attorney. When made by an attorney he was "to declare under oath or affirmation that he had no interest in the claim otherwise than to serve the applicant." The Board of Property was given power to act in all cases of dispute between applicants, and when lots were drawn the secretary of the land-office was directed to grant patents under the inspection of the Board of Property in the same manner as was formerly done by the Supreme Executive Council. There was no further legislation with special reference to the lots that were surveyed within the State of New York. Under the provisions of the laws recited the claims of all applicants who drew such lots were received when made within the limit of time prescribed, and properly adjusted.

Another difficulty arose in relation to a large number of the lots surveyed in the second district because of the alleged inferior quality of the land laid off by the surveyor, John Henderson. In his notes and observations General Irvine says, in reference to the character of the country which became part of that district, that "East of this path * along Mr. McLane's line for five or six miles, the land is pretty level, well watered with small springs, and of tolerable quality, but from thence to the Allegheny River which is about twenty-five miles due east, there is no land worth mentioning fit for cultivation." As it was the expressed intention of the General Assembly when the donation was made that only the best lands within the territory set apart by law should be surveyed for the purpose of the donation, it was thought wrong that so laudable a design on the part of the law-makers should be defeated by giving lands that could not be cultivated. The attention of the surveyor-general had early been called to the poor quality of the land in this district by General Irvine. In a letter to General Armstrong, dated at Carlisle, July

* The path leading from Fort Pitt to Venango.

18, 1786, he recommended that all the surveys made by John Henderson be rejected by Council, and that Major Alexander be appointed to lay off an equal number of lots in other parts of the reserved tracts without being confined to any particular district. He further says in the same letter, " If the surveyor-general has not found my letter in which I complained of John Henderson's surveys as improper to be accepted—he has had sufficient verbal testimony as well from me as sundry other persons to justify his informing Council that the land is not such as the Assembly intended the troops should get, or they could possibly think of receiving, particularly as he surveyed all bad and left a large quantity of good land within his district." The views of General Irvine were not fully adopted, though his representations did to a certain extent influence the action of Council. In the preparations for the drawing of the lottery, one hundred and thirty-four tracts of two hundred acres each, lying in the eastern part of the district, nearest to the Allegheny River, and now part of Butler County, were stricken from the scheme, and the numbers representing the tracts not placed in the wheels. By this action of Council the district became known as the " Struck District" and was ever after so called. The struck numbers remained out of the wheel until after the act of April 2, 1802, the title of which was " An Act to complete the benevolent intention of the Legislature of this Commonwealth, by distributing the donation lands to all who are entitled thereto," became a law. The preamble to this act set forth that some of the officers and soldiers of the Pennsylvania Line had not received their donation land, and that it was represented that among the lots in the tenth district, for which the owners had received patents and which they had released as being in the State of New York, and received other lots in lieu thereof, many were still in Pennsylvania, and also that there were a number of other lots within the bounds of the donated surveys not numbered, returned, or otherwise appropriated. Under this act it was made the duty of the land officers to ascertain the number of such lots of each description that remained undrawn and not otherwise appropriated, or which, having been drawn, had not been applied for within the time prescribed by law, and to cause numbers corresponding to each lot to be made and placed in the wheels from which they were to draw on application being made to them by persons entitled to the donation. Acting under this law the Board of Property, which by this section of the same act was given the same powers relative to donation lands that it exercised over other lands within the Commonwealth, decided to include the lots of the " Struck District," and put corresponding numbers in the wheels. These numbers remained in the wheels until the act of March 25, 1805, directing them to be withdrawn and not again put in. During the years 1803-4-5, many of the lots had been drawn, and patents for them granted, in some instances causing trouble and litigation. Presuming the lands in the eastern part of the district to be vacant and open to settlement and improvement under the act of April 3, 1792, many settlers had gone into the locality and made valuable improvements that interfered with the surveys of the donation lots, thus, of course, involving patentees of donation land and actual settlers in disputes and expensive law-suits. To prevent such undesirable and unfortunate results the act of 1805 was passed. The tickets were taken out of the wheels as directed by the law, and the undrawn lots of the " Struck District" thereafter remained a part of the unappropriated lands north and west of the Ohio and Allegheny Rivers and Conewango Creek open to sale and settlement.

In order to enable the land officers and the Board of Property to execute the duties enjoined upon them by the act of 1802, the Secretary of the Commonwealth was directed to transfer all records relating to the donation lands to the surveyor-general's office, and by the same act the Board of Property was authorized to direct patents to be issued to the widow, heir, or heirs of any deceased officer or soldier on satisfactory proof of their right being made.

The act of March 24, 1785, seemed to require the beneficiaries under its provisions to participate in the drawing in person. To do so was no doubt a serious inconvenience to many, while others, who could not afford the expense of a journey to Philadelphia, would be entirely deprived of the benefits of the act. Be this as it may, it was soon discovered that many persons had not received their land, and in consequence of this condition of the distribution, the Legislature, by an act passed April 6, 1792, directed the land officers, on the 2d day of July following, to draw lots for every person entitled to donation land who had not received the same, agreeably to the list submitted by the comptroller to the Supreme Executive Council, the same as if the person thus entitled to land was present; and the patents were to be granted to such persons or their legal representatives as in other cases. It was also ascertained that there were other persons who had served in the Pennsylvania Line entitled to the donation, but whose names, from some unexplained cause, did not appear in the list prepared by the comptroller-general in 1786. To remedy this defect and enable these persons to receive their quota of land, the Legislature passed an important act relating to them on the 17th of April, 1795. This act directed the comptroller-general to prepare a complete list of such persons entitled to lands whose names were not included in the first list, together with their rank and the quantity of land each should receive. This list was to be transmitted to the surveyor-general, the receiver-general, and the secretary of the land-office, and it was made their duty then to employ a suitable person to prepare tickets and place them in wheels in the same manner as had been done for the first drawing. No greater number of tickets were to be placed in the wheel than would give to each his quantity of land. After these preparations were complete the claimants could attend the drawing in person to draw their lots, or authorize an agent to draw for them, and for such persons as did not attend in person, or by agent, the surveyor-general, receiver-general, and secretary of the land-office were authorized to draw.

When the drawing was finished a report was to be made to the governor, who was directed to prepare and deliver the patents at the expense of the State. The legal representatives of deceased persons entitled to the benefits of the act were permitted to draw lots, or have lots drawn for them, the same as such deceased persons might have done if living. The time allowed for making application under the act was one year from its passage, with a proviso that persons " beyond sea, or out of the United States," shall have two years, and persons serving in the army of the United States at the time of its passage should have three years, of which the surveyor-general was to give notice for six weeks in one of the newspapers of Philadelphia, and in one in each county of the State in which newspapers were published. This was followed by an act passed April 11, 1799, providing among other things for the authentication of claims by the comptroller-general, register-general, and State treasurer, who were to inquire into their lawfulness, ascertain whether they remained unsatisfied, and in each case to transmit to the secretary of the land-office a certificate stating whether the claim should be allowed or rejected, the certificate to be conclusive. After 1805, aside from a number of acts granting donations of land to certain individuals for special reasons, there was no further legislation in reference to these lands of any importance. A question of succession had arisen in the case of an officer who had been killed in the service. He was unmarried, and the land that fell to his share was claimed by a brother as heir-at-law. The Supreme Court decided the claim to be good. The Legislature then, on the 11th of March, 1809, passed an act that no patent was thereafter to issue for donation lands except to the widow or children of any deceased officer or soldier who died or was killed in service.

There had been extensions of the time for filing applications, year by year, until the final limitation as fixed in the previous year, expired on the 1st day of April, 1810. No further applications were received after that date, though patents for lots that had previously been drawn continued to be freely granted for some years longer. After the drawing had been closed, there still remained in the wheels a number of undrawn tickets, and by the act of March 26, 1813, the Legislature made provision for the sale and settlement of such of them as should remain undrawn on the 1st day of October following. It was provided that a person who had made an improvement and settlement, resided with his family on the lot three years previous to the passing of the act, and cleared, fenced, and cultivated at least ten acres of ground; or a person who should after the 1st day of October make an improvement and actual settlement by erecting a dwelling-house, reside with a family on the lot three years from the date of that settlement, and clear, fence, and cultivate at least ten acres of ground, could receive a patent for such donation lot, by paying into the State treasury at the rate of one dollar and fifty cents an acre with interest from three years after the settlement was made, and the usual office fees. The settlement first made and continued, or thereafter made and continued, gave an inception of title to the person making it. These terms are somewhat similar in character to those provided in act of April 3, 1792, for the sale of the unappropriated parts of the lands lying within the donation districts, except that the price fixed for such lands was only twenty cents an acre. This difference in price must be accounted for in the supposition that the lands surveyed for the soldiers were far superior in quality to the other unappropriated parts of the territory originally set apart for donation purposes. The price for the undrawn lots continued to be one dollar and fifty cents an acre until February 25, 1819, when it was reduced to fifty cents an acre. The rate of fifty cents was continued until March 31, 1845, at which time the terms were made in all respects the same as for other vacant lands in the same districts.

This concludes the sketch of the Donation Lands of Pennsylvania and the mode in which they were allotted and conveyed to the persons who came within the provisions of the grant; and we trust it may prove of some interest to the readers of this report. The benefaction was a most worthy and patriotic one to a line of gallant soldiers who served their country well, and endured much in aiding to achieve liberty for the American colonies, from which has since grown our mighty and beneficent American republic. The Pennsylvania Line was an important factor in producing grand results, and rewards to such soldiers were well bestowed.

" Legally, there never was any such thing as the Holland Land Company, or the Holland Company, as they were usually called.

" The company consisted of Wilhelm Willink and eleven associates, merchants and capitalists of the city of Amsterdam, who placed funds in the hands of friends who were citizens of America to purchase a million acres of land in Pennsylvania, which, being aliens, the Hollanders could not hold in their names at that time; and in pursuance of the trust created, there were purchased, both in New York and Pennsylvania, immense tracts of land, all managed by the same general agent at Philadelphia.

" The names of the several persons interested in these purchases, and who composed the Holland Land Company, so called, were as follows: Wilhelm Willink, Nicholas Van Staphorst, Pieter Van Eeghen, Hendrick Vollenhoven, and Ruter Jan Schimmelpenninck. Two years later the five proprietors transferred a tract of about one million acres, so that the title vested in the original five, and also in Wilhelm Willink, Jr., Jan Willink, Jr., Jan Gabriel Van Staphorst, Roelif Van Staphorst, Jr., Cornelius Vollenhoven, and Hendrick Seye."

CHAPTER VI

PIONEER ANIMALS—BEAVERS, BUFFALOES, ELKS, PANTHERS, WOLVES, WILD-
CATS, BEARS, AND OTHER ANIMALS—HABITS, ETC.—PENS AND TRAPS—
BIRDS—WILD BEES

"Nature is a story-book
That God hath written for you."

THE mountainous character of this northwest and the dense forests that covered almost its whole area made the region a favorite haunt of wild beasts. Many of them have disappeared, and it is difficult to believe that animals now extinct on the continent at large were once numerous within the boundaries of this territory.

The beaver, the buffalo, the elk, and the deer were probably the most numerous of the animals. "Beaver will not live near man, and at an early period after the settlement of this State these animals withdrew into the secluded regions and ultimately entirely disappeared." The last of them known in this State made their homes in the great "Flag Swamp," or Beaver Meadow, of Clearfield County, now about and above Du Bois City.

LITTLE CHANGE AMONG BEAVERS

Those who have made them a study assert that, with the exception of man, no other animal now upon the earth has undergone so little change in size and structure as the beaver. Fossil deposits show that in its present form it is at least contemporaneous with and probably antedates the mammoth and the other monsters that once roamed the great forests of the earth. The skeletons of beavers found in this country are the same as those of the same species found in the fossil beds of Europe. Man is the only other mammal of which this is true. How the beaver came to traverse the ocean has never been explained.

"Coarse-fibred, cautious in its habits, warmly protected by nature against climatic influences, simple and hearty in its diet, wise beyond all other forms of lower animal life, prolific and heedful of its young, the beaver has seen changes in the whole function of the world and the total disappearance of countless species of animal and vegetable life.

"The beaver mates but once, and then for a lifetime. There are no divorces, and, so far as has been observed, no matings of beavers who have lost their mates by death. Young beavers are given a place in the family lodge until they are two years old, and are then turned out to find mates and homes for themselves. The age of the beaver is from twelve to sixteen years.

" No other animal has excited so much interest by his home-making and home-guarding as this. 'Wisest of Wild Folk' is the English equivalent for his name in the tongue of the Ojibways.

" Originally a mere burrower in the earth, like his cousins the hedge-hog and the porcupine, he has so improved upon natural conditions that only man is able to reach him in his abiding-places. Indeed, he approaches man in the artificial surroundings that he has adopted for self-preservation.

" The principal engineering and structural works of the beaver are the dam, the canal, the meadow, the lodge, the burrow, and the slide. These are not always found together and some of them are rare."

THEY FORM AN INTERESTING STORY

" Beaver-dams have been found which have been kept in repair by beavers for centuries. It is not unusual to find them more than fifty feet long and so

Beaver

solid that they will support horses and wagons. Fallen trees that have been cut down by the sharp teeth of the beavers are sometimes the foundation. More often branches and a great heap of small stones make the beginning.

" The side toward the water is of mud and pebbles smoothly set by the use of the broad, paddle-like tail of the animal. Interlaced branches and poles make a substantial backing for the earth. A growth of underbrush caps the whole.

" The dam is built for two reasons—to afford a retreat where the home-loving beaver may rest safe from his enemies of the forest, particularly the wolverines, and to give a depth of water that will not freeze to the bottom. A total freeze would effectually lock him in his home and be the cause of death by starvation.

" The dam, in a temperate climate, is usually about four feet deep. It curves up-stream when of great length. Upon the highest part of the submerged area the beaver builds his lodge. This is practically an island capped by a wigwam made of sticks and earth. The outer roof of hardened mud is repaired at the beginning of every winter, and the ceiling of scaling wood and dry earth is removed and taken out of the lodge every spring. Indeed, the beaver is the neatest of housekeepers, only the household nests of dry leaves and sap-bearing wood enough for each meal being allowed within his home.

" Two passages lead from the floor of the lodge into the water. One of these is wide and straight. Through it the members of the family bring the twigs and roots for their meals. The second passage is narrow and winding, and through it the beavers disappear at the first sign of danger.

" The burrows are made in the banks of the artificial lake created by the dam. The entrances to them are beneath the surface of the water. They slope upward with the bank, and, like the lodge, end in snug, dry homes above the water level. The celibate beavers live entirely in burrows; the families in both lodges and burrows.

" To guard against the flooding of their homes the beavers provide outlets for the surplus water. Sometimes the upper part of the dam is purposely left thin and the water trickles through in a steady stream. Where the bank is thick and impervious an overflow gully is cut in its summit, and through this the surplus passes.

" Beaver meadows are made by the rotting and cutting away of timbers within the area of partial flooding. With the passing of the larger vegetation comes a smaller growth of water grasses, upon which the beavers thrive.

" The wonderful beaver canals are streams several feet in width leading from the artificial lake made by the dam into the forest. Upon these the wise little animals float heavy saplings and branches that they would otherwise be unable to transport to the face of the dam.

" The slides are skidways made by beavers down the sides of high, steep banks. Trees and stones are rolled down these for use in home-making.

" In carrying earth, stones, and sticks on land the beaver uses his forefeet as we do our hands, holding what he carries tightly against his throat. In swimming the use of the front feet is unnecessary. He is enabled to hold a heavy branch in front of his breast and to swim swiftly with his tail and his powerful hind feet.

" Most affectionate and intelligent as a pet is the beaver when taken young. When annoyed it gives a querulous cry, like that of an infant. Its beautiful thick coat of reddish brown fur makes it the prey of the trapper.

" Beavers, when caught in traps by the forelegs, almost invariably wrench themselves free, leaving the member in the trap. Many of the pelts brought into the market have one leg and occasionally two legs missing.

"Although their sense of sight is deficient, those of scent and hearing are abnormally developed. The work of construction and repair upon the dams is always done at night, the workers occasionally stopping to listen for suspicious sounds. The one who hears anything to excite his alarm dives instantly, and as he disappears gives warning to his comrades by striking his broad, flat tail upon the surface of the water. The sound rivals a pistol-shot in its alarming loudness."—*Philadelphia North American.*

"The beaver is really a sort of portable pulp-mill, grinding up most any kind of wood that comes in his way. I once measured a white birch-tree, twenty-two inches through, cut down by a beaver. A single beaver generally, if not always, fells the tree, and when it comes down the whole family fall to and have a regular frolic with the bark and branches. A big beaver will bring down a fair-sized sapling, say three inches through, in about two minutes, and a large tree in about an hour.

"One of the queerest facts about the beaver is the rapidity with which his long, chisel-like teeth will recover from an injury."

William Dixon killed a beaver in 1840, near what is now called Sabula, or Summit Tunnel, Clearfield County. This was perhaps the last one killed in the State.

A beaver was reported killed in 1884 on Pine Creek, in Clinton County. It was said to have been chased there from Potter County.

Beavers have four young at a litter, and they are born with eyes open.

THE AMERICAN BISON, OR BUFFALO

Centuries ago herds of wild buffaloes fed in our valleys and on our hills. Yes, more, the "buffalo, or American bison, roamed in great droves over the meadows and uplands from the Susquehanna to Lake Erie," but none north of Lake Erie.

The peculiar distinction of our buffalo was a hump over his shoulders. His eye was black, his horns black and thick near the head, tapering rapidly to a point. His face looked ferocious, yet he was not so dangerous as an elk or deer. The sexual season of the bison was from July to September; after this month the cows ranged in herds by themselves, calved in April, and the calves followed the mother from one to three years. The males fought terrible battles among themselves. The Atlantic seaboards were exceptionally free from them. The flesh of the cow was delicious food, and the hump especially was considered a great delicacy. At what time they were driven from northern Pennsylvania is not known, but two or three hundred years ago the northwest was alive with them.

"Twenty-five or thirty years ago these animals, whose flesh was an important and much prized article of food, the tail especially, and whose pelts were in great demand for robes, buffalo overshoes, and garments to protect both the civilized and uncivilized races from the piercing winter's blasts, were found on our western prairies in countless thousands. To-day, owing to the cruel, wasteful, and greedy skin and meat hunters, there are not, it is asserted, any buffaloes in a wild state in the United States. According to a recent published report, between the years 1860 and 1882 more than fifteen million buffaloes were killed within the limits of the United States." Buffaloes and elks used the same trails and feeding-grounds.

The American elk was widely distributed in this section in 1794. The habitat of this noble game was the forest extending across the northern part of the State. These animals were quite numerous in the thirties.

"When I started, in 1826, to amuse and profit myself by following the chase in Northern Pennsylvania," said Colonel Parker, of Gardeau, McKean County, Pennsylvania, "elks were running in those woods in herds. I have

Buffalo

killed elks a plenty in the Rocky Mountain country and other regions since, but I never ran across any that were as big as those old-time Pennsylvania elks. I have killed elks on the Sinnemahoning and Pine Creek waters, and down on the Clarion River and West Branch, that were as big as horses. A one-thousand-pound elk was nothing uncommon in that country, and I killed one once that weighed twelve hundred pounds. These were bucks. The does would weigh anywhere from six hundred to eight hundred pounds.

"These elks had very short and thick necks, with a short and upright mane. Their ears were of enormous size, so large, in fact, that once Sterling Devins, a good hunter, too, saw a doe elk in the woods on Pine Hill, near Ole

Bull's castle, in the times when elks had begun to grow scarce, and passed without shooting at it, thinking it was a mule. When the elk bounded away, though, and disappeared among the thick timber, Sterling knew what it was, and felt like kicking himself harder than the elk could have kicked him, even if it had been a mule.

"The Pennsylvania elk's eyes were small, but sparkled like jewels. I have often seen a score or more pairs of these bright eyes shining in the dark recesses of the pine-forest, when the shadows might have otherwise obscured the presence there of the owners of those telltale orbs. An infuriated buck elk's eye was about as fearful a thing to look at as anything well imaginable, but so quickly changeable was the nature of these huge beasts that two hours after having captured with ropes one that had, from the vantage ground of his rock, gored and trampled the life out of a half-dozen of dogs, and well-nigh overcome the attacking hunters, it submitted to being harnessed to an improvised sled and unresistingly hauled a load of venison upon it six miles through the woods to my cabin, and took its place among the cattle with as docile an air as if it had been born and brought up among them.

"This same elk that Sterling Devins had mistaken for a mule, he and Ezra Prichard followed all the next day, but lost its trail. Some Pine Creek hunters got on its trail, drove it to its rock, and roped it. When Devins and Prichard got back at night they found the Pine Creek hunters there and the elk in the barn eating hay and entirely at home. That elk had quite an interesting subsequent history. Ezra Prichard had, previous to the capture of this one, secured a pair of elks, broke them, and for a long time drove them in farm work like a yoke of oxen. Sterling Devins was eager for a yoke of elk, and he offered the Pine Creek hunters one hundred dollars for the one they had captured. They refused the offer, but afterwards got into a dispute about its ownership, and it was sold to Bill Stowell and John Sloanmaker, of Jersey Shore. These men took the elk about the country, exhibiting it, and made quite a sum of money. Next fall, although the elk was a doe, it became very ugly and attacked its keeper, nearly killing him before he could get away. No one could go near her, and her owners ordered her shot. The carcass was bought by a man who had a fine pair of elk horns. He was a skilful taxidermist, and he managed to fasten the horns to the head of the doe elk in such a manner that no one was ever able to tell that they hadn't grown there. This made of the head an apparently magnificent head of a buck elk, and it was purchased for one hundred dollars, under that belief, by a future governor of Pennsylvania."

LAST ELK IN THE PINE CREEK REGION

"That doe elk was one of the last family of elks in the Pine Creek country. She and the buck and a fawn had been discovered some time before Sterling Devins ran across the doe, by Leroy Lyman, on Tomer's run, near the Ole Bull settlement. Lyman got a shot at the buck, but the whole three escaped.

The same party of hunters that captured the doe killed the buck afterwards in the woods on Kettle Creek. The fawn the dogs ran into Stowell's mill-pond, and there it was killed.

"Another peculiarity of the elks that used to frequent the Pennsylvania woods was the great size of their nostrils, and the keenness of their scent was something beyond belief. A set of elk antlers of five feet spread, and weighing from forty to fifty pounds, was not an infrequent trophy. George Rae, who was one of the great hunters of Northern Pennsylvania in his day,—and he is one of the greatest in the Rocky Mountains even to this day, in spite of his eighty-five years,—lived along the Allegheny at Portville. He had in his house, and in his barn, the walls almost covered with the antlers of elks he had killed, on the peak of his roof, at one end, being one that measured nearly six feet between the extremities. When George moved West forty years ago he left the horns on the buildings, and only a few years ago many of them were still there, as reminders of what game once roamed our woods.

"It required more skill to hunt the elk than it did to trail the deer, as they were much more cautious and alert. For all that, an elk, when startled from his bed, did not instantly dash away, like the deer, but invariably looked to see what had aroused him. Then, if he thought the cause boded him no good, away he went, not leaping over the brush, like the deer, but, with his head thrown back, and his great horns almost covering his body, plunging through the thickets, his big hoofs clattering together like castanets as he went. The elk did not go at a galloping gait, but travelled at a swinging trot that carried him along at amazing speed. He never stopped until he had crossed water, when his instinct seemed to tell him that the scent of his trail was broken before the pursuing dogs.

"At the rutting season the elk, both male and female, was fearless and fierce, and it behooved the hunter to be watchful. An elk surprised at this season did not wait for any overt act on the part of an enemy, but was instantly aggressive. One blow from an elk's foot would kill a wolf or a dog, and I have more than once been forced to elude an elk by running around trees, jumping from one to another before the bulky beast, unable to make the turns quick enough, could recover himself and follow me too closely to prevent it, thus making my way by degrees to a safe refuge. I was once treed by a buck elk not half a mile from home, and kept there from noon until night began to fall. I haven't the least doubt that he would have kept me there all night if another buck hadn't bugled a challenge from a neighboring hill, and my buck hurried away in answer to it. I didn't wait to see it, but there was a great fight between those two bucks that night.

"I visited the spot the next day. The ground was torn up and the saplings broken down for rods around, and one old buck lay in the brush dead, his body covered with bloody rips and tears. I didn't know whether this was the elk that treed me or not, but I have always been fond of believing it was.

" The whistle of the buck elk, as the hunters used to call it, wasn't a whistle, although there were changes in it that gave it something of a flute-like sound. The sound was more like the notes of a bugle. In making it the buck threw back his head, swelled his throat and neck to an enormous size, and with

Elk

that as a bellows he blew from his open mouth the sound that made at once his challenge or call for a mate. The sound was far-reaching, and, heard at a distance, was weird and uncanny, yet not unmusical. Near by it was rasping and harsh, with the whistling notes prominent.

" The Pennsylvania elks were never much scattered. When I first came to the Sinnemahoning country, nearly seventy years ago, the salt marsh that lay in the wilderness where my residence now is was trampled over by herds of elks and deer that came there to lick the salt from the ground as if a drove of cattle had been there. I have seen seventy-five elks huddled at that marsh. That was ' the great elk lick' of legend, which the reservation Indians have often talked to me about when I lived in Allegheny County, New York, as a boy, and it was to find that lick that my father and I, following the rather indefinite directions of one Johnnyhocks, an old Shongo Indian, entered the Pennsylvania wilderness in 1826."

A TOUGH OLD BUCK

" To follow an elk forty miles before running it down was considered nothing remarkable. I have done it many a time. Leroy Lyman, Jack Lyman, and A. H. Goodsell once started on an elk-hunt from Roulette, Potter County, struck the trail at the head of West Creek, in McKean County, thirty miles from Roulette, followed it through Elk, Clarion, and Clearfield Counties, and finally drove it to its rock eighty or ninety miles from where the trail was first struck. They had followed the elk many days, and finally the quarry was found,—an enormous buck,—with a spread of horns like a young maple-tree. The hunters ran out of rations the second day, and were nearly starved when they ran the elk to its rock. All three of them put a bullet in the defiant elk and ended his career. Visions of elk-meat for supper had haunted the famished hunters, and when the buck fell they shouted for joy. Without delay they started in to carve expected juicy morsels from the carcass to cook for supper, but there was not a knife or a hunting-axe in that party that could make an impression on the old fellow's flesh. He was a patriarch of the woods, and long past use as food. All the starving hunters could manage to make edible of the elk was his tongue, which, roasted, was a grateful offering to hungry men, but would have been impossible of mastication otherwise. The horns were the only trophy that the hunters got from the long and tedious chase, and that trophy was well worth it. It was the largest and next to the finest pair of antlers ever carried by an elk in the Pennsylvania forest, so far as there is any record."

THE ELK VS. WOLVES

" There are scattered through the woods, generally high on the hills, from the Allegheny River down to the West Branch and Clarion River, huge rocks, some detached boulders, and other projections of ledges. These are known as elk rocks, and every one of them has been, in its day, the last resort of some elks brought to bay after a long and hard chase. It was the habit of the hunted elk, when it had in vain sought to throw the hunter and hound from the trail, to make its stand at one of these rocks. Mounting it, and facing its foes, it fiercely fought off the assaults of the dogs by blows of his forefeet or tremendous kicks from its hind feet, until the hunter came up and ended the fight with his rifle. It would be strange if one or more of the dogs were not stretched dead at the foot of the rock by the time the hunter arrived on the scene. I have more than once found dead wolves lying about one of these elk rocks, telling mutely, but eloquently, the tragic story of the pursuit of the elk by the wolves, his coming to bay on the rock, the battle, and the elk's victory. The elk was not always victor, though, in such battles with wolves, and I have frequently found the stripped skeleton of one lying among the skeletons of wolves he had killed before being himself vanquished by their savage and hungry fellows.

" In the winter time the elks would gather in large herds and their range would be exceedingly limited. Sometimes they would migrate to other regions, and would not be seen for months in their haunts, but suddenly they would return and be as plentiful as ever. They had their regular paths or runways through the woods, and these invariably led to salt licks, of which there were many natural ones in Northern Pennsylvania. One of the most frequented of these elk paths started in a dense forest, where the town of Ridgway, the county seat of Elk County, now stands, led to the great lick on the Sinnemahoning portage, and thence through the forest to another big lick, which to-day is covered by Washington Park, in the city of Bradford. I have followed that elk path its whole length, when the only sign of civilization was now and then a hunter's cabin, from the head-waters of the Clarion River to the Allegheny, in McKean County. Hundreds of elks were killed annually at the licks or while travelling to and from them, along their well-marked runways."

HUNTING ELKS AT NIGHT

" Hunting elks by night was an exciting sport. You have heard of persons being scared by their own shadows. If you had ever hunted a Pennsylvania elk at night you would have had an opportunity of seeing something scared by its own shadow, and scared badly. A blazing pine-knot fire would be lighted in the bow of a flat-bottomed boat, and while one man sat near that end with his rifle, another paddled it through the water. Elks were always sure to be standing in the water early in the evening, after darkness had fully set in. When the light of the fire fell on an elk you would not only see his eyes shining like coals, but the whole big spectral spread of his antlers would stand out against the darkness—not only the horns of one, but of perhaps half a dozen. When the hunter fired at one elk all the others would make a break for shore, but the instant they landed, their great black shadows would fall before them from the light of the blazing fires, and back they would rush in terror to the water. Then a hunter might kill every elk in the herd, or several of them, before their fright at the gun overcame the terror of the shadow and the survivors fled to the impenetrable darkness of the woods.

HISTORY OF NORTHWESTERN PENNSYLVANIA

" The biggest set of elk antlers ever captured in the Pennsylvania woods was secured in the Kettle Creek country by Major Isaac Lyman, Philip Tome, George Ayres, L. D. Spoffard, and William Wattles. Philip Tome was a great hunter, and the famous interpreter for Cornplanter and Blacksnake, the great Indian chiefs. He came over from Warren County to help Major Lyman capture an elk alive, and the party started in on the first snow, with plenty of ropes and things. They camped, but the elks were in such big herds that they couldn't get a chance at a single buck for more than a week. Then they got the biggest one they ever saw and gave chase to him. They started him from his bed on Yocum hill. The dogs took him down Little Kettle Creek to Big Kettle, and up that two or three miles. There the elk came to bay on a rock. He kept the dogs at a distance until the hunters came up, when he left the rock and started away again. Tome, knowing the nature of elk, said that all they had to do was to wait and the elk would return to the rock. They dropped poles and fitted up nooses. They waited nearly half a day, and then they heard the buck coming crashing through the woods, down the mountain-sides, the dogs in full cry. He mounted his rock again. The hunters he did not seem to mind, but the dogs he fought fiercely. While he was doing that the hunters got the nooses over his immense horns and anchored him to surrounding trees. They got the elk alive to the Allegheny River, and floated him on a raft to Olean Point. From there they travelled with him through New York State to Albany, exhibiting him with much profit, and at Albany he was sold for five hundred dollars. That elk stood sixteen hands high and had antlers six feet long, and eleven points on each side, the usual number of points being nine on a side."

The last elk killed in this State was in 1864, by Jim Jacobs, an Indian. This elk had been pursued for several days, and in despair sought his " rock" near the Clarion River, and was there shot. He was too old and tough to be used for food. The buffalo, elk, panther, wolf, and beaver are now extinct. The last buffalo killed in the State of which there is a record was about 1799. There were originally in this State over fifty species of wild, four-footed animals. We had three hundred and twenty-five species and sub-species of birds, and our waters, including Lake Erie, had one hundred and fifty species of fish. It may not be amiss to state here that all our wild animals were possessed of intelligence, courage, fear, hate, and affection. They reasoned, had memory, and a desire for revenge. A wolf could be tamed and trained to hunt like a dog. It is recorded in history that a pet snake has been known to travel one hundred miles home. It is undeniable that they could compute time, courses, and distances. Elks, bears, and deer had their own paths. Bears blazed theirs by biting a hemlock tree occasionally.

Elks are polygamous. The chief is a tyrant, and rules the herd like a czar. The does all fear him. Does breed at the age of two years, having but one fawn, but when older often two or three at a time, and these young follow

117

their mother all summer, or from the date of birth in May or June to fall. The elk's whistle varies much and has different meanings; they seem to have a language like all other animals, big or little. A full-grown elk never forgets an injury. They can soon be taught to work like oxen, but it takes from six months to two years to be able to stand in front of an elk and command him.

In 1834, Mike, William, and John Long and Andrew Vastbinder captured a full-grown live elk. Their dogs chased the animal on his high rock, and while there the hunters lassoed him. The elk only lived three weeks in captivity. The last elk in the State was killed in our forests. A noted hunter thus describes a battle between wolves and a drove of elks: " I heard a rush of

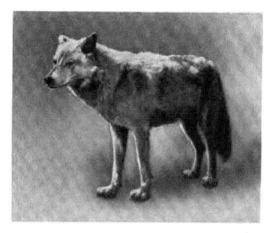

Gray or timber wolf of Pennsylvania

feet from the opposite direction, and the next moment a band of elks swept into sight. Magnificent fellows they were, eight bucks and three does, with a couple of fawns. They had evidently been stampeded by something, and swept past me without seeing me, but stopped short on catching sight of the wolves. The does turned back and started to gallop away in the direction from which they came, but one of the bucks gave a cry, and they stopped short and huddled together with the fawns between them, while the bucks surrounded them. Each buck lowered his horns and awaited the attack. The wolves, seeing the cordon of bristling bone, paused, disconcerted for a moment; then the foremost, a gaunt old wolf, gave a howl and threw himself upon the lowered antlers. He was flung fully ten feet with a broken back, but his fate did not deter the others. They threw themselves upon the elks only to be

118

pierced by the prongs. It was not until fully twenty had in this way been maimed and killed that they seemed to realize the hopelessness of the thing."

The largest carnivorous beast was the panther. After the advent of white men into this wilderness panthers were not common. In the early days, however, there were enough of them in the forests to keep the settler or the hunter ever on his guard. They haunted the wildest glens and made their presence known by occasional raids on the flocks and herds. It is probable that here in our northwestern counties there are still a few of these savage beasts.

The puma, popularly called by our pioneers panther, was and is a large animal with a cat head. The average length of a panther from nose to tip of tail is about six to twelve feet, the tail being over two feet long, and the tip of which is black. The color of the puma is tawny, dun, or reddish along the back and side, and sometimes grayish-white underneath or over the abdomen and chest, with a little black patch behind each ear. The panther is a powerful animal, as well as dangerous, but when captured as a cub can be easily domesticated and will be good until he is about two years old. The pioneers shot them and captured many in panther- and bear-traps. The pelts sold for from one to twelve dollars. The catamount, or bey lynx, was a species of the cat, had tufts on the ears, a cat head, long-bodied, three or four feet long, short-legged, big-footed, and mottled in color. The fur was valuable. The lynx is sometimes mistaken for the panther.

The Longs, Vastbinders, and other noted hunters in Jefferson County killed many a panther. A law was enacted in 1806 giving a bounty of eight dollars for the " head" of each grown wolf or panther killed, and the " pelts," bringing a good price for fur, stimulated these hunters greatly to do their best in trapping, hunting, and watching the dens of these dangerous animals. The bounty on the head of a wolf pup was three dollars. The bounty on the head of a panther whelp was four dollars. The county commissioners would cut the ears off these heads and give an order on the county treasurer for the bounty money. A panther's pelt sold for about four dollars. On one occasion a son of Bill Long, Jackson by name, boldly entered a panther's den and shot the animal by the light of his glowing eyes. In 1833, Jacob and Peter Vastbinder found a panther's den on Boone's Mountain, now Elk County. They killed one, the dogs killed two, and these hunters caught a cub, which they kept a year and then sold it to a showman. In 1819 the Legislature enacted a law giving twelve dollars for a full-grown panther's head and five dollars for the head of a cub.

" Nothing among the wild beasts strikes such terror to the heart of the settler as the cry of the wolf at a lonely spot at night. The pioneers knew very well that on a lonely forest trail at any hour of the day or night the other animals could be frightened by a slight bluff. No other animals go in packs. The wolf would not attack were he alone. It is when reinforced that he is a terror, and then the howl of the wolf is the most blood-curdling of all the noises of the night in the woods. Where he is bent upon attacking a traveller he announces it by a howl from one quarter. The signal is answered from another direction. Another piercing howl comes from somewhere else. The cry of the wolf echoes and rolls from hill to hill in marvellous multiplication of sounds. A small pack of half a dozen wolves will make the mountain seem alive for miles. The cry is anything but reassuring to the timid soul who is shut in safely by the fire of his forest cabin. It is enough to chill the marrow of the man who for the first time hears it when he is in the unprotected open. The wolf is vicious and savage. Hunger gives him any courage that he possesses, and that sort of courage drives him to desperation. That is why the wolf is such a ferocious enemy when once he is aroused to attack man. Death by starvation is no more alluring to him than death by the hand of his possible prey."

The pioneer hunter would sometimes raise a wolf pup. This pup would be a dog in every sense of the word until about three years old, and then he would be a *wolf* in all his acts.

" One hundred years ago wolves were common in Northern and Western Pennsylvania. In the middle of the last century large packs of them roamed over a great portion of the State. To the farmer they were an unmitigated nuisance, preying on his sheep, and even waylaying belated travellers in the forest. After the State was pretty well settled these beasts disappeared very suddenly. Many people have wondered as to the cause of their quick extinction. Rev. Joseph Doddridge in his ' Notes' ascribes it to hydrophobia, and he relates several instances where settlers who were bitten by wolves perished miserably from that terrible disease."

I have listened in my bed to the dismal howl of the wolf, and for the benefit of those who never heard a wolf's musical *soirée* I will state here that one wolf leads off in a long tenor, and then the whole pack joins in the chorus.

Wolves were so numerous that, in the memory of persons still living in Brookville (1898), it was unsafe or dangerous to permit a girl of ten or twelve years to go a mile in the country unaccompanied. In those days the Longs have shot as many as five and six without moving in their tracks, and with a single-barrelled, muzzle-loading rifle, too. The sure aim and steady and courageous hearts of noted hunters made it barely possible for the early settlers to live in these woods, and even then they had to exercise " eternal vigilance." In 1835, Bill Long, John and Jack Kahle captured eight wolves in a " den" near the present town of Sigel. Wolf-pelts sold for three dollars. Wild-cats were numerous; occasionally a cat is killed in the county yet, even within the borough limits.

One of the modes of Mike Long and other pioneer hunters on the Clarion River was to ride a horse with a cow-bell on through the woods over the deer-paths. The deer were used to cow-bells and would allow the horse to come in full view. When the deer were looking at the horse, the hunter usually shot one or two.

Every pioneer had one or more cow-bells; they were made of copper and

Pennsylvania bear

iron. They were not cast, but were cut, hammered, and riveted into shape, and were of different sizes.

The black bear was always common in Pennsylvania, and especially was this so in our wild portion of the State. He was a great road-maker and king of the beasts. The early settlers in the northwest killed every year in the aggregate hundreds of these bears. Bear-skins were worth from three to five dollars apiece. Reuben Hickox, of Perry Township, Jefferson County, as late as 1822, killed over fifty bears in three months. Captain Hunt, a Muncy Indian, living in what is now Brookville, killed sixty-eight in one winter. In 1831, Mrs. McGhee, living in what is now Washington Township, heard her pigs squealing, and exclaimed, " The bears are at the hogs!" A hired man, Philip McCafferty, and herself each picked up an axe and drove the bears away. One pig had been killed. Every fall and winter bears are still killed in our forests.

Peter Vastbinder when a boy shot a big bear through the window of his father's house, and this, too, by moonlight. This bear had a scap of bees in his arms, and was walking away with them. The flesh of the bear was prized by the pioneer. He was fond of bear meat. Bears weighing four or five hundred pounds rendered a large amount of oil, which the pioneer housewife used in cooking.

Trapping and pens were resorted to by the pioneer hunters to catch the panther, the bear, the wolf, and other game.

The bear-pen was built in a triangular shape of heavy logs. It was in shape and build to work just like a wooden box rabbit-trap. The bear steel-trap weighed about twenty-five pounds. It had double springs and spikes sharpened in the jaws. A chain was also attached. This was used as a panther-trap, too. " The bear was always hard to trap. The cautious brute would never put his paw into visible danger, even when allured by the most tempting bait. If the animal was caught, it had to be accomplished by means of the most cunning stratagem. One successful method of catching this cautious beast was to conceal a strong trap in the ground covered with leaves or earth, and suspend a quarter of a sheep or deer from a tree above the hidden steel. The bait being just beyond the reach of the bear, would cause the animal to stand on his hind feet and try to get the meat. While thus rampant, the unsuspecting brute would sometimes step into the trap and throw the spring. The trap was not fastened to a stake or tree, but attached to a long chain, furnished with two or three grab-hooks, which would catch to brush and logs, and thus prevent the game from getting away."

An old settler informs me that in the fall of the year bears became very fat from the daily feasts they had on beechnuts and chestnuts, and the occasional raids they made on the old straw beehives and ripe cornfields. In pioneer times the bear committed considerable destruction to the corn. He would seat himself on his haunches in a corner of the field next to the woods, and then, collecting a sheaf of the cornstalks at a time, would there and then enjoy a sumptuous repast.

Wolves usually hunt in the night, so they, too, were trapped and penned. The wolf-pen was built of small round logs about eight or ten feet high and narrowed at the top. Into this pen the hunter threw his bait, and the wolf could easily jump in, but he was unable to jump out. The wolf-trap was on the principle of the rat-trap, only larger, the jaws being a foot or two long. Wolves would welcome a domestic dog in their pack, but a dog that clung to man, their enemy, they would tear to pieces.

Glutton or sloth wolverines were very rare in the northwest. They were to be found in the most northern tier. The only county reported to have these animals in the northwest was Potter County. Joseph Nelson is reported to have caught one in a trap in 1858, and one is reported to have been killed by J. P. Nelson in 1863. Wolverines were found in Mercer County in 1846.

Trappers rated the fox the hardest animal to trap, the wolf next, and the otter third. To catch a fox they often made a bed of chaff and got him to lie in it or fool around it, the trap being set under the chaff. Or a trap was set at a place where several foxes seemed to stop for a certain purpose. Or a fox could be caught sometimes by putting a bait a little way out in the water, and then putting a pad of moss between the bait and the shore, with the trap hid under the moss. The fox, not liking to wet his feet, would step on the moss and be caught.

THE AMERICAN ELK—DEER AND DEER COMBATS—HUNTERS, PROFESSIONAL AND
    NON-PROFESSIONAL—STALKING AND BELLING DEER—OTHER ANIMALS,
    ETC.

The American elk is the largest of all the deer kind. Bill Long and other noted hunters killed elks in these woods seven feet high. The early hunters found their range to be from Elk Licks on Spring Creek, that empties into the Clarion River at what is now called " Hallton," up to and around Beech Bottom. In winter these heavy-footed animals always " yarded" themselves on the " Beech Bottom" for protection from their enemies,—the light-footed wolves. The elk's trot was heavy, clumsy, and swinging, and would break through an ordinary crust on the snow; but in the summer-time he would throw his great antlers back on his shoulders and trot through the thickets at a Nancy Hanks gait, even over fallen timber five feet high. One of his reasons for locating on the Clarion River was that he was personally a great bather and enjoyed spending his summers on the banks and the sultry days in bathing in that river. Bill Long presented a pair of enormous elk-horns, in 1838, to John Smith, of Brookville, who used them as a sign for the Jefferson Inn.

In looking over old copies of the *Elk County Advocate* I find advertisements something like this:

" HUNTERS.—Several young fawns are wanted, for which a liberal price will be given. Enquire at this office."

In some of the old papers Caleb Dill, of Ridgway, advertised for elks: " For a living male elk one year old I will give $50; two years old, $75;

three years old, $100; and for a fawn three months old, $25." Elks were easily tamed.

"The common Virginia white-tailed deer, once exceedingly numerous in the northwest is still to be found in limited numbers. This deer when loping or running elevates its tail, showing the long white hair of the lower surface. If the animal is struck by a bullet the tail is almost invariably tucked close to the ham, concealing the white.

All deer kind who have branch horns, with one exception, shed their antlers annually every February or March, and have them completely restored by August of the same year.

"The American deer, common deer, or just deer, is peculiar to Pennsylvania. It differs from the three well-known European species,—the red deer, the fallow deer, and the pretty little roe. Of these three, the red deer is the only one which can stand comparison with the American.

"The bucks have antlers peculiar in many cases, double sharp, erect spikes or tines. The doe lacks these antlers. The antlers on the bucks are shed and renewed annually. Soon after the old antlers fall, swellings, like tumors covered with plush, appear; these increase in size and assume the shape of the antlers with astonishing rapidity, until the new antlers have attained their full size, when they present the appearance of an ordinary pair of antlers covered with fine velvet. The covering, or ' velvet,' is filled with blood-vessels, which supply material for the new growth. The furrows in the complete antler show the course of the circulation during its formation, and no sooner is the building process completed than the ' velvet' begins to wither and dry up. Now the buck realizes that he is fully armed and equipped for the fierce joustings which must decide the possession of the does of his favorite range, and he busies himself in testing his new weapons and in putting a proper polish upon every inch of them. He bangs and rattles his horn daggers against convenient trees and thrusts and swings them into dense, strong shrubs, and if observed during this honing-up process he frequently seems a disreputable-looking beast, with long streamers of blood-stained ' velvet' hanging to what will shortly be finely polished antlers with points as sharp as knives. When the last rub has been given and every beam and tine is furbished thoroughly, our bravo goes a-wooing with the best of them. He trails the coy does through lone covers and along favorite runways unceasingly; he is fiery and impetuous and full of fight, and asks no fairer chance than to meet a rival as big and short-tempered as himself. He meets one before long, for every grown buck is on the warpath, and when the pair fall foul of each other there is frequently a long and desperate combat, in which one gladiator must be thoroughly whipped or killed. All deer fight savagely, and occasionally two battling rivals find a miserable doom by managing to get their antlers securely interlocked, when both must perish. Two dead bucks thus locked head to head have been found lying as they fell in an open glade, where the scarred surface of the ground and the crushed and riven shrubs about told an eloquent tale of a wild tourney long sustained, and of miserable failing efforts of the wearied conqueror to free himself of his dead foe."—*Outing.* The Vastbinders, Longs, and all the early hunters found just such skulls in these woods.

Artificial deer-licks were numerous, and made in this way: A hunter would take a coffee-sack and put in it about half a bushel of common salt, and then suspend the sack high on the branch of a tree. When the rain descended the salt water would drip from the sack to the ground, making the earth saline and damp, and to this spot the deer would come, paw and lick the earth. The hunter usually made his blind in this way: A piece of board had two auger-holes bored in each end, and with ropes through these holes was fastened to a limb on a tree. On this board the hunter seated himself to await his game. Deer usually visit licks from about 2 A.M. until daylight. As a rule, deer feed in the morning and evening and ramble around all night seeking a thicket for rest and seclusion in the daytime.

" For ways that were dark and for tricks that were vain" the old pioneer was always in it. When real hungry for a venison steak he would often use a tame deer as a decoy, in this way: Fawns were captured when small, tamed, reared, and permitted to run at large with the cattle. A life insurance was " written" on this tame deer by means of a bell or a piece of red flannel fastened around the neck. Tame deer could be trained to follow masters, and when taken to the woods usually fed around and attracted to their society wild deer, which could then be shot by the secreted hunter. At the discharge of a gun the tame deer invariably ran up to her master. Some of these does were kept for five or six years. Deer generally have two fawns at a time, in May, and sometimes three.

Love of home is highly developed in the deer. You cannot chase him away from it. He will circle round and round, and every evening come to where he was born. He lives in about eight or ten miles square of his birthplace. In the wilds of swamps and mountains and laurel-brakes he has his " roads," beaten paths, and " crossings," like the civilized and cross roads of man. When hounded by dogs he invariably strikes for a creek or river, and it is his practice to take one of these " travelled paths," which he never leaves nor forgets, no matter how circuitous the path may be. Certain crossings on these paths where the deer will pass are called in sporting parlance " stands." These " stands" never change, unless through the clearing of timber or by settlement the old landmarks are destroyed.

" The deer loves for a habitation to wander over hills, through thick swamps or open woods, and all around is silence save what noise is made by the chirping birds and wild creatures like himself. He loves to feed a little on the lowlands and then browse on the high ground. It takes him a long time to make a meal, and no matter how much of good food there may be in any particular place, he will not remain there to thoroughly satisfy his appetite. He must roam about and eat over a great deal of territory. When he has browsed and fed till he is content, he loves to pose behind a clump of bushes and watch and listen. At such times he stands with head up as stanch as a setter on point, and if one watches him closely not a movement of his muscles will be detected. He sweeps the country before him with his keen eyes, and his sharp ears will be disturbed by the breaking of a twig anywhere within gunshot.

Deer and fawn in Mahoning Creek

" Sparkling and bright, in its liquid light, was the water."

" When the day is still the deer is confident he can outwit the enemy who tries to creep up on him with shot-gun or rifle. But when the wind blows, he fears to trust himself in those places where he may easily be approached by man, so he hides in the thickets and remains very quiet until night. To kill a deer on a still day, when he is not difficult to find, the hunter must match the deer in cunning and must possess a marked degree of patience. The deer, conscious of his own craftiness, wanders slowly through the woods; but he does not go far before he stops, and like a statue he stands, and can only be made out by the hunter with a knowledge of his ways and a trained eye.

126

" The deer listens for a footfall. Should the hunter be anywhere within the range of his ear and step on a twig, the deer is off with a bound. He does not stop until he has reached what he regards as a safe locality in which to look and listen again. A man moving cautiously behind a clump of bushes anywhere within the sweep of his vision will start him off on the run, for he is seldom willing to take even a small chance against man. Should the coast be clear, the deer will break his pose, browse and wander about again, and finally make his bed under the top of a fallen tree or in some little thicket.

" To capture the deer by the still-hunting method, the hunter must know his ways and outwit him at his own game. First of all, the still-hunter wears soft shoes, and when he puts his foot on the ground he is careful not to set it on a twig which will snap and frighten any deer that may be in the vicinity. The still-hunter proceeds at once to put into practice the very system which the deer has taught him. He strikes a pose. He listens and looks. A deer standing like a statue two hundred yards away is not likely to be detected by an inexperienced hunter, but the expert is not deceived. He has learned to look closely into the detail of the picture before him, and he will note the difference between a set of antlers and a bush.

" The brown sides of a deer are very indistinct when they have for a background a clump of brown bushes. But the expert still-hunter sits quietly on a log and peers into the distance steadily, examining all details before him. Occasionally his fancy will help him to make a deer's haunch out of a hump on a tree, or he will fancy he sees an antler mixed with the small branches of a bush, but his trained eye finally removes all doubt. But he is in no hurry. He is like the deer, patient, keen of sight, and quick of hearing. He knows that if there are any deer on their feet in his vicinity he will get his eyes on them if he takes the time, or if he waits long enough he is likely to see them on the move. At all events, he must see the deer first. Then he must get near enough to him to bring him down with his rifle."—*Outing*.

Deer will not run in a straight line. They keep their road, and it is this habit they have of crossing hills, paths, woods, and streams, almost invariably within a few yards of the same spot, that causes their destruction by the hounding and belling methods of farmers, lumbermen, and other non-professionals. Deer-licks were numerous all over this county. A " deer-lick" is a place where salt exists near the surface of the earth. The deer find these spots and work them during the night, generally in the early morning. One of the methods of our early settlers was to sit all night on or near a tree, " within easy range of a spring or a ' salt-lick,' and potting the unsuspecting deer which may happen to come to the lick in search of salt or water. This requires no more skill than an ability to tell from which quarter the breeze is blowing and to post one's self accordingly, and the power to hit a deer when the gun is fired from a dead rest."

" Belling deer" was somewhat common. I have tried my hand at it.

The mode was this: Three men were located at proper distances apart along a trail or runway near a crossing. The poorest marksman was placed so as to have the first shot, and the two good ones held in reserve for any accidental attack of "buck fever" to the persons on the first and second stands. An experienced woodsman was then sent into a laurel thicket, carrying with him a cow-bell; and when this woodsman found and started a deer, he followed it, ringing the bell. The sound of this bell was notice to those on the "stand" of the approach of a deer. When the animal came on the jump within shooting distance of the first stand, the hunter there posted would bleat like a sheep; the deer would then come to a stand-still, when the hunter could take good aim at it; the others had to shoot at the animal running. The buck or doe rarely escaped this gauntlet.

"The deer was always a coveted prize among hunters. No finer dish than venison ever graced the table of king or peasant. No more beautiful trophy has ever adorned the halls of the royal sportsman or the humble cabin of the lowly hunter on the wild frontier than the antlers of the fallen buck. The sight of this noble animal in his native state thrills with admiration alike the heart of the proudest aristocrat and the rudest backwoodsman. In the days when guns were rare and ammunition very costly, hunters set stakes for deer, where the animal had been in the habit of jumping into or out of fields. A piece of hard timber, two or three inches thick and about four feet long, was sharpened into a spear shape, and then driven firmly into the ground at the place where the deer were accustomed to leap over the log fence. The stake was slanted toward the fence, so as to strike the animal in the breast as it leaped into or out of the fields. Several of these deadly wooden spears were often set at the same crossing, so as to increase the peril of the game. If the deer were seen in the field, a scare would cause them to jump over the fence with less caution, and thus often a buck would impale himself on one of the fatal stakes, when but for the sight of the hunter the animal might have escaped unhurt. Thousands of deer were killed or crippled in this way generations ago."—*Outing.*

A deer-skin sold in those days for seventy-five to ninety cents. Of the original wild animals still remaining in Northwestern Pennsylvania, there are the fox, raccoon, porcupine, musk-rat, martin, otter. mink, skunk, opossum, woodchuck, rabbit, squirrel, mole, and mouse. Fifty years ago the woods were full of porcupines. On the defensive is the only way he ever fights. When the enemy approaches he rolls up into a little wad, sharp quills out, and he is not worried about how many are in the besieging party. One prick of his quills will satisfy any assailant. When he sings his blood-curdling song, it is interpreted as a sign of rain.

"In fact, when a porcupine curls himself up into the shape of a ball he is safe from the attack of almost any animal, for his quills are long enough to prevent his enemy from getting near enough to bite him.

" Their food is almost entirely vegetable, consisting of the inner bark of trees, tender roots, and twigs. They are fond, however, of the insects and worms found in the bark of pines and hemlocks.

" Provided with powerful jaws and long, sharp teeth, the porcupine gnaws with great speed, stripping the bark from an old tree as though he were provided with weapons of steel. Often he seems to tear in a spirit of sheer destructiveness, without pausing to eat the bark or to search for insects. This is more especially true with the old males.

" The porcupine is not a wily beast. He establishes paths or runways through the forest, and from these he never deviates if he can help it. What is more, he is exceedingly greedy, and stops to investigate every morsel in his way.

" A trap set in the middle of a runway and baited with a turnip rarely fails to catch him." The hunters liked them cooked.

Porcupine

The wholesale prices of furs in 1804 were: Otter, one dollar and a half to four dollars; bear, one to three dollars and a half; beaver, one to two dollars and a half; martin, fifty cents to one dollar and a half; red fox, one dollar to one dollar and ten cents; mink, twenty to forty cents; muskrat, twenty-five to thirty cents; raccoon, twenty to fifty cents; deer-pelts, seventy-five cents to one dollar.

The pioneer hunter carried his furs and pelts to the Pittsburg market in canoes, where he sold them to what were called Indian traders from the East. In later years traders visited the cabins of our hunters in the northwest, and bartered for and bought the furs and pelts from the hunters or from our merchants.

Old William Vastbinder, a noted hunter and trapper in this wilderness, and pioneer in Jefferson County, was quite successful in trapping wolves one season on Hunt's Run, about the year 1819 or 1820; but for some un-known reason his success suddenly stopped, and he could not catch a single wolf. He then suspected the Indians of robbing his traps. So one morning bright and early he visited his traps and found no wolf, but did find an Indian track. He followed the Indian trail and lost it. On looking around he heard a voice from above, and looking up he saw an Indian sitting in the fork of a tree, and the Indian said, " Now, you old rascal, you go home, Ol.l Bill, or Indian shoot." With the Indian's flint-lock pointed at him, Vastbinder immediately became quite hungry and started home for an early breakfast.

Bill Long often sold to pedlers fifty deer-pelts at a single sale. He had hunting shanties in all sections and quarters of this wilderness.

In 1850 the late John Du Bois, founder of Du Bois City, desired to locate some lands near Boone's Mountain. So he took Bill Long with him, and the two took up a residence in a shanty of Long's near the head-waters of Rattle-snake Run, in what is now Snyder Township. After four or five days' rusticating, the provisions gave out, and Du Bois got hungry. Long told him there was nothing to eat here and for him to leave for Bundy's. On his way from the shanty to Bundy's Mr. Du Bois killed five deer.

George Smith, a Washington Township early hunter, who is still (1898) living in the wilds of Elk County, has killed in this wilderness fourteen panthers, five hundred bears, thirty elks, three thousand deer, five hundred catamounts, five hundred wolves, and six hundred wild-cats. He has killed seven deer in a day and as many as five bears in a day. Mr. Smith has followed hunting as a profession for sixty years.

CATAMOUNT—BEY LYNX

The catamount is larger than the wild-cat. They have been killed in this forest six and seven feet long from tip of nose to end of tail. They have tufts on their ear-tips, and are often mistaken for panthers.

MINK

" The mink is an expert at swimming and diving, and able to remain long under water, where it pursues and catches fish, which it frequently destroys in large numbers.

" The mink does much damage to poultry, especially chickens and ducks. Various kinds of wild birds, particularly ground-nesting species, crayfish, frogs, and reptiles are included in the dietary of the mink; and it is also learned from the testimony of different writers and observers that the eggs of domestic fowls are often taken by these nocturnal plunderers.

" The average weight of an adult mink is about two pounds, and for an animal so small it is astonishing to observe its great strength."

WILD-CAT—BOB-CAT

" The wild-cat inhabits forests, rocky ledges, and briery thickets, but its favorite place is in old slashings and bark peelings, where in the impenetrable and tangled recesses it is comparatively safe from pursuit, and is also able to prey upon many varieties of animals which have a permanent or temporary residence in such unfrequented wilds.

" The wild-cat subsists entirely on a flesh diet, and the damage this species does in destroying poultry, lambs, and young pigs of farmers who reside in the sparsely settled mountainous regions is not in any degree compensated by the destruction of other small wild animals which molest the farmer's crops or his poultry."

Wild-cats hunt both by day and by night. A whole family of them will hunt and run down a deer, especially on crusted snow.

" The wild-cat usually makes its domicile or nest in a hollow tree or log. The nest is well lined with leaves, moss, and lichens, called commonly ' hair

Wild-cat

moss.' The nest is also sometimes found in rocky ledges and caves. From two to four constitute a litter. It is stated that the young are brought forth in the middle of May. Wild-cats may be caught in traps baited with rabbits, chicken, grouse, or fresh meat."

THE RIVER OTTER

Our otter was about four feet long, as I recollect him, very heavy and strong; usually weighed about twenty-three pounds, was web-footed, a fisher by occupation, and could whip or kill any dog. On land he had his beaten paths. Big fish eat little fish, little fish eat shrimps, and shrimps eat mud.

Otters ate all kinds of fish, but preferred the speckled trout. Like other animals, otters had their plays and playgrounds. They were fond of strength contests, two or more pulling at the end of a stick something like our " square pull." They made slides, and frolicked greatly in winter time, sliding down hill. They made their slides in this wise: By plunging into the water, then running up a hill and letting the water drip from them to freeze on the slide.

River otter

They lived in excavations on the creek or river bank close to the water. They were hunted and trapped by men for their pelts. John Long, a noted hunter, told me that the most terrific contest he ever had with a wild animal was with an otter near Brookville.

THE FOX

In pioneer times we had in this wilderness the gray, the cross, and the red fox. The gray is now extinct in the northwest, as he can only live in solitude or in a forest. The red fox still lingers in our civilization. Six varieties of foxes are said to be found in the United States, and it is claimed they are all cousins of the wolf. But notwithstanding this relationship, the wolf used to hunt and eat all the foxes he could catch. The wolf's persistence in hunting, and endurance in the race, enabled him at times to overcome the fleetness of the fox. The gray and red fox were about three and one-half feet long. The red fox is the most daring, cunning, and intellectual of all the varieties. You cannot tame him. The term " foxy" originated in connection with him. The red fox has from four to eight puppies in April, and these, like little dogs, are born blind. The red fox has the astounding faculty of creating deep-laid schemes to deceive and thwart his enemies. He is the only animal that will match his intelligence against man, and the only way man can best him is by poison. It was not unusual for the red fox to back-track in such a way while racing for his life as to follow the hunter, and turn the tables from being hunted to being the hunter. He would even feign death— allow himself to be kicked or handled, only waiting and watching for an opportunity to escape. His tricks to outwit man were many and would fill a

Red fox

volume. The fox was very fond of ground-hog eating. Like the bear he would dig them out. His presence in a ground-hog neighborhood created great consternation. All animals have a cry of alarm,—danger,—and if observed by any ground-hog he always gave this cry for his neighbors.

WEASEL

Both sexes have the power to emit a fluid nearly as offensive as that of the polecat. "A glance at the physiognomy of the weasels would suffice to betray their character; the teeth are almost of the highest known raptorial character; the jaws are worked by enormous masses of muscles covering all the sides of the skull; the forehead is low and the nose is sharp; the eyes are small, penetrating, cunning, and glitter with an angry green light. There is something peculiar, moreover, in the way that this fierce face surmounts a body extraordinarily wiry, lithe, and muscular. It ends a remarkably long and slender neck in such a way that it may be held at right angle with the axis of the latter. When the animal is glancing around with the neck stretched up and the flat triangular head bent forward and swaying from one side to the other, we catch the likeness in a moment—it is the image of a serpent.

"His coat changes with the seasons, and while in winter we find it white tinted with sulphur yellow, in summer it is on upper parts of a dark brown not unlike the coloring of a mink; on its under parts it is 'white almost invariably tinged with sulphury yellow' (Coues). The tail partakes of the color of the upper parts, except the bushy end, which, in summer and winter alike, is black. Its legs are short, with slender feet, and are covered all over with fur in winter, but in summer the pads are generally visible.

"Their homes are frequently to be found in a decayed tree-stump and under rocks." He can climb trees with ease.

"The poultry-yard is frequently visited and his apparently insatiable desire for rapine is most clearly shown while on these visits. One chicken will satisfy his appetite, but after that is gratified he does not leave; he kills and slays without mercy all the remainder of the poor frightened chickens, until there are none left and not until then does he leave the scene of carnage.

"He sucks the eggs also, leaving in some instances the unlucky farmer who has unwillingly and unwittingly been his host completely routed as regards his efforts in the poultry line." He also feeds on rats and mice.

THE OPOSSUM

The opossum is an American animal, about the size of a very large cat, eight or ten pounds in weight, twenty inches long, with a prehensile tail, in addition, of fifteen inches. There are said to be three varieties,—viz., the Mexican, Florida, and the Virginia. The last variety is the one found in Northwestern Pennsylvania. They are very prolific, having three litters a year,—viz., in March, May, and July, of twelve to sixteen at a time. At birth they are naked, blind, and about a half inch long, the mother depositing each one with her hands in a pouch or pocket in her abdomen, and there the little creature sucks the mother and sleeps for about eight weeks. When full-grown they are good tree climbers, making great use of their tail in swinging from tree to tree and for other purposes. He is a dull creature, easily domesticated, and the only intelligence he exhibits is when, like the spider and potato-bug, he feigns death. At this he is truly an adept, suffering great abuse waiting for a chance to bite or run. All carnivorous animals eat smaller ones, so the opossum's enemies are numerous, and he in turn is omnivorous and carnivorous, eating everything he can catch that is smaller than himself.

SQUIRRELS

The intelligence of some animals is amazing. Many of them seem to study us as we study them. The squirrel knew that man was his most dangerous enemy, and that man killed him and his race for food. In pioneer times we had several varieties: the principal ones were the black, twenty-

OPOSSUM

two inches long; the gray, eighteen inches long; and the little red, or Hudson Bay, about eight inches long. The red was a bold little beast, liked to be close to man, full of vice and few virtues. He was industrious in season and out. The black and gray were lazy. Whenever a squirrel wanted to cross a creek or river, and didn't want to swim, he sailed over on a piece of bark or wood, using his brushy tail as a sail and to steer by. The skunk did likewise. A single pair of squirrels would inhabit the same tree for years. They had three or four young at a litter. The red or Hudson Bay squirrel was the king of all the squirrels in this forest; although not more than eight inches long, he was the complete master of all the squirrels. The black and gray were as afraid of him as death. With an intellect surprising, he would

Squirrel

chase and capture the black and gray and castrate them, then, in exultation, scold or chickaree to his heart's content.

In pioneer times, every seven or eight years, at irregular intervals in summer, a great army of black and gray squirrels invaded this wilderness from the northwest; a host that no man could number. They were travelling east in search of food. Hundreds of them were killed daily by other animals and by man.

In these pioneer times crows and squirrels were such a menace to the crops of the farmer in Western Pennsylvania that an act was passed by the Legislature to encourage the killing of squirrels in certain parts of this Commonwealth. The pioneer act was passed March 4, 1807, giving a bounty of three cents for each crow scalp and one cent and a half for each squirrel scalp; these scalps to be received in lieu of money for taxes, if delivered to the county treasurer before the 1st day of November of each year.

The first act covered Bedford, Washington, Westmoreland, Armstrong, Indiana, Fayette, and Green Counties. This law was extended in 1811, on the 13th of February, to Butler, Franklin, Mercer, Venango, Somerset, Lycoming, Crawford, and Erie Counties.

One of the cutest things that the red squirrel did was to tap sugar-trees for the sap. He would chisel with his teeth a trough on the top of a limb, and as fast as the trough would fill with the water he would return and drink it.

In the fall of the year a squirrel would hide acorns and nuts outside of his nest, where others of his kind could not easily find the fruit, then in mid-winter, when he became hungry, he would leave his cosey nest and go a long distance through the snow to the identical spot where he had buried his fruit, dig it up, and enjoy his meal.

NATURAL LIFE OF SOME OF OUR WILD AND DOMESTIC ANIMALS

	Years.		Years.
Elk	50	Hog	20
Beaver	50	Wolf	15
Panther	25	Cat	15
Catamount	25	Fox	15
Buffalo	20	Dog	10
Cow	20	Sheep	10
Horse	20	Squirrel	7
Bear	20	Rabbit	7
Deer	20		

BIRDS

" If a bird's nest chance to be before thee in the way in any tree, or on the ground, whether they be young ones, or eggs, and the dam sitting upon the young, or upon the eggs, thou shalt not take the dam with the young: but thou shalt in anywise let the dam go, and take the young to thee; that it may be well with thee, and that thou mayest prolong thy days."—*Deut.* xxii. 6, 7.

With the exception of the wild turkey and raven, which are now about extinct, we have almost the same variety of birds here that lived and sang in this wilderness when the Barnetts settled on Mill Creek. Some of these original birds are quite scarce. We have one new bird,—viz., the English sparrow.

Before enumerating our birds it might be proper to give a few sketches of some of the principal ones.

136

THE RAVEN

A very handsome bird, numerous here in pioneer times, now extinct in Jefferson County, but still to be found in about twenty northern counties of the State. He built his nest on the tallest pine-trees. He belonged to the crow family. He had a wonderful intellect. He could learn to talk correctly, and was a very apt scholar; he was easily tamed, and would follow like a dog. He lived to an extreme old age, probably one hundred years. He was blue-black, like the common crow. He made his home in the solitude of the forest, preferring the wildest and most hilly sections. In such regions, owing to his intellect and strength, his supremacy was never questioned, unless by the eagle. He understood fire-arms and could count five. In the

Raven

fall of the year he would feast on the saddles of venison the hunters would hang on a tree, and the Longs adopted this method to save their meat: Take a small piece of muslin, wet it, and rub it all over with gunpowder; sharpen a stick and pin this cloth to the venison. The raven and crow would smell this powder and keep away from the venison. He was a mischievous bird of rare intelligence. He looked inquiringly at you, as if he understood you. When full grown he measured twenty-two or twenty-six inches from tip of nose to end of tail. In Greenland white ones have been seen. The eggs were from two to seven, colored, and about two inches long.

THE "BALD" EAGLE, OUR NATIONAL EMBLEM

The name "Bald" which is given to this species is not applied because the head is bare, but because the feathers of the neck and head of adults are pure white. In Northwestern Pennsylvania, as well as throughout the United States, we had but two species of eagles, the bald and the golden. The "Black," "Gray," and "Washington" eagles are but the young of the bald eagle. Three years, it is stated, are required before this species assumes the adult plumage. The bald eagle is still found in Pennsylvania at all seasons

Bald eagle

of the year. I have seen some that measured eight feet from tip to tip of wing.

"The nest, a bulky affair, built usually on a large tree, mostly near the water, is about four or five feet in diameter. It is made up chiefly of large sticks, lined inside with grass, leaves, etc. The eggs, commonly two, rarely three, are white, and they measure about three by two and a half inches. A favorite article of food with this bird is fish, which he obtains mainly by strategy and rapine. Occasionally, however, according to different observers, the bald eagle will do his own fishing. Geese and brant form their favorite food, and the address displayed in their capture is very remarkable. The poor victim has apparently not the slightest chance for escape. The eagle's

138

flight, ordinarily slow and somewhat heavy, becomes, in the excitement of pursuit, exceedingly swift and graceful, and the fugitive is quickly overtaken. When close upon its quarry the eagle suddenly sweeps beneath it, and turning back downward, thrusts its powerful talons up into its breast. A brant or duck is carried off bodily to the nearest marsh or sand-bar. But a Canada goose is too heavy to be thus easily disposed of; the two great birds fall together to the water beneath, while the eagle literally tows his prize along the surface until the shore is reached. In this way one has been known to drag a large goose for nearly half a mile.

"The bald eagle occasionally devours young pigs, lambs, and fawns. Domestic fowls, wild turkeys, hares, etc., are also destroyed by this species.

Wild turkey

I have knowledge of at least two of these birds which have killed poultry (tame ducks and turkeys) along the Susquehanna River. Sometimes, like the golden eagle, this species will attack raccoons and skunks. I once found two or three spines of a porcupine in the body of an immature bald eagle. The golden eagle occurs in this State as a winter visitor. The only species with which it is sometimes compared is the bald eagle in immature dress. The two birds, however, can be distinguished at a glance, if you remember that the golden eagle has the tarsus (shin) densely feathered to the toes, while, on the other hand, the bald eagle has a bare shin. The golden eagle breeds in high mountainous regions and the Arctic countries.

139

" Golden eagles are rather rare in this region, hence their depredations to poultry, game, and live-stock occasion comparatively little loss. Domestic fowls, ducks, and turkeys especially, are often devoured; different species of water-birds, grouse, and wild turkeys suffer chiefly among the game birds. Fawns are sometimes attacked and killed; occasionally it destroys young pigs, and frequently many lambs are carried off by this powerful bird. Rabbits are preyed upon to a considerable extent."

Of our birds, the eagle is the largest, swiftest in flight, and keenest-eyed, the humming-bird the smallest, the coot the slowest, and the owl the dullest.

The spring birds, such as the bluebird, the robin, the sparrow, and the martin, were early to come and late to leave.

" Migrating birds fly over distances so great that they must needs have great strength as well as great speed in flight. Bobolinks often rear their young on the shores of Lake Winnipeg, and, like true aristocrats, go to Cuba and Porto Rico to spend the winter. To do this their flight must twice cover a distance of more than two thousand eight hundred miles, or more than a fifth of the circumference of the earth, each year.

" The little redstart travels three thousand miles twice a year, and the tiny humming-bird two thousand. What wonderful mechanism it is that in a stomach no larger than a pea will manufacture its own fuel from two or three slim caterpillars, a fly, a moth, or a spider, and use it with such economy as to be able to propel itself through the air during the whole night at a rate of about fifty miles per hour, and at the same time keep its own temperature at about one hundred and four degrees."

I reproduce from Olive Thorne Miller's Lectures the following,—viz.:

" There are matrimonial quarrels also among birds. As a rule, the female is queen of the nest, but once I saw a male sparrow assert his power. He was awfully angry, and tried to oust his spouse from a hole in a maple-tree in which they had made their home. He did drive her out at last, and absolutely divorced her, for he was back before long with a bride whom, with some trouble and a good many antics, he coaxed to accept the nest.

" The female bird is the queen of the home, and usually selects the place for the nest, the male bird sometimes lending a beak in building it, but most of the time singing his sweet song to encourage his mate.

" That the female is queen is shown by a little story related of a sparrow. She was hatching her eggs, and was relieved now and then by her mate while she went off for exercise and food. One day the male bird was late and the female called loudly for him. He came at last, and she gave him an unmerciful drubbing, which he took without a murmur. Thoroughly ashamed of himself, he sat down meekly on the eggs.

" The robin is the most familiar of our birds. Running over the lawns, with head down, it suddenly grabs a worm, which it shakes as a cat does a mouse. Having swallowed it, the robin looks up with infinite pride. They

BLUE JAY

are great insect-destroyers, though they insist on having the earliest spring peas and the first mulberries, raspberries, and grapes. The robin is the great enemy of the bird observer, giving warning of his approach to every bird in the neighboring thickets. They are brave, and will help any bird in distress. A sparrow-hawk had seized an English sparrow, one of the robin's worst enemies, but the robin attacked the hawk so viciously that it released the sparrow. In another instance a cat had captured a young robin, but was so fearlessly attacked by an older bird that she parted with her tender meal and sought shelter under the barn.

"The robins make charming but most mischievous pets. I heard of a case where a child helped bring up a brood of these birds. When they were fledged they would follow her about the yard like a flock of chickens. The woodpecker, robin, and many other birds have very acute hearing. Did you ever see one of these birds cock his head and listen for the sounds of a worm?

"The wood-thrush or wood-robin is of a shy and retiring nature, frequenting thick woods and tangled undergrowth, and at daybreak and sundown this bird carols forth its thankfulness for a day begun and a day ended. The nest is made in some low tree, with little or no mud in its composition, and contains from four to six eggs. The veery, or tawny thrush, is a wonderful songster, but a most retiring bird.

"The American cuckoo, unlike her English cousin, builds her own nest, and is a most devoted parent. These birds, with white breast, are numerous here in the summer, and the male bird's courting is most grotesque. After each note he makes a profound bow to the mate, and then opens his mouth as wide as possible, as if about to emit a loud cry, but only the feeblest of 'coos' can be heard.

"The blue-jay, though one of our best-known birds, is greatly misunderstood. It is said he is always quarrelling and fighting, whereas really he is only full of frolic and mischief and is a most affectionate bird, and instead of tyrannizing over other birds is most kind to them. These birds have shared a room with a dozen others much smaller than themselves and were never known to molest them. They will defend their young against all comers, and James Russell Lowell tells a story of discovering three young birds who were held to their nest by a string, in which they had got entangled. He determined to cut them loose. The old birds flew at him at first, but on learning what his object was, sat quietly within reach of him, watching the operation, and when the birds were released noisily thanked him.

"A story is told of the frolicsomeness of this bird. One was seated on a fence-rail, and two kittens, having espied him, essayed to stalk him. They got up near him; then he began playing leap-frog over those two kittens until they returned full of offended dignity to the house. The bird tried to coax them out to a game several times afterwards, but the kittens had had enough of it.

"The kingbird is said to fight and drive away every bird that comes near it, but this is a libel. He attends to his own business almost wholly, and though not particularly social, is no more belligerent in the bird world than most birds are when they have nests to protect. He is a character, and interesting to watch.

"The shrike, or butcher-bird, has imputed to him the worst character of any of our birds. He is not only accused of killing birds, but of impaling them afterwards on thorns. That he does kill birds is undoubted, but only when other food is scarce, for he much prefers field-mice, grasshoppers, and other noxious insects. That he impales his prey is certain, and the reason for this is, I think, that he has such small, delicate feet that they are not strong enough to hold down a mouse or insect while he tears it to pieces.

"Blackbirds are gregarious, forming blackbird cities in the tops of trees. He and the fishhawk have a strange friendship for one another, often three or four pairs building their nests in the straggling outskirts of the hawk's large nest, and they unite in protecting one another.

"The red-winged blackbirds are the most independent of birds, as far as the two sexes are concerned. The dull brown-streaked females come up in flocks some time after the males have arrived, and as soon as the breeding season is over they separate again, the males keeping to the marshes, while the females seek shelter in the uplands, but always near water. They nest in marshy places, and insist on plenty of water.

"The cowbird is undoubtedly the most unpopular of this class of birds, simply from the fact that no nest is built, the egg always being placed in the nest of some vireo, warbler, or sparrow, and the rearing of one of these birds means the loss of at least two song-birds, for they always smother the rightful owners. The popular idea that the foster-parents are unaware of this strange egg is doubtful. I believe it to be another instance of the great good nature of the birds to the young of any sort. The cowbirds nearly kill with overwork whatever birds they have been foisted on.

"The bobolink, who later in the year becomes the reed- or rice-bird, is a handsome bird in his plumage of black and white and buff. The female is a quieter-colored bird. While breeding they are voracious insect-eaters, but when they get down to the rice marshes it is almost impossible to drive them away. A hawk seems to be the only thing they are afraid of.

"The Baltimore oriole is one of the most beautiful and best-known birds. Its long, pendant, woven nest is known to every one, and it is wonderful how the bird, with only its beak, can build such a splendid structure. They have been known to use wire in the structure of their nests.

"The meadow-lark, one of the largest of this family, is a wonderful singer, sitting on a fence-rail, carolling forth its quivering silvery song. All these birds, except the oriole, walk while hunting for food, and do not hop as most other birds do.

" The crow does not belong to the blackbird family, but owing to his uniform I will speak about him. Much has been said against him, but the truth is that he is a most useful bird in killing mice, snakes, lizards, and frogs, and is a splendid scavenger. He has been persecuted for so many generations that perhaps he is the most knowing and wary of birds. He will always flee from a man with a gun, though paying little attention to the ordinary pedestrian. These birds are gregarious in their habits, and make their large, untidy nests at the tops of trees.

" They have regular roosting-places, and, curious to say, it is not first come first served. As each flock reaches the sleeping-grove they sit around on the ground, and it is only when the last wanderer returns that they all rise simultaneously and scramble for nests. Crows as pets are intensely funny."

Crow

A crow can be taught to talk. It is said by bird students that crows have a language distinctly their own, and, further, that some of their language can be translated into ours. I have often noticed that while a flock of crows are feeding on the ground, two sentinels are posted to give an alarm of any danger. It is said that if these sentinels fail to perform their duty, the flock will execute one or both of them. A friend of mine living about three miles from Brookville is very fond of raising crows as pets. I visited him several years ago when he had an interesting fellow. This crow used to carry tidbits to the woods to the other crows. When the crows were getting ready to migrate in the fall they called this pet one down to the edge of the woods. After a talk they flew on the pet and tore him to pieces. I asked Mr. McAdoo why they did that. Mr. McAdoo said he thought it was because the " pet" refused to migrate with them. Crows mate for life. A crow knows when Sunday comes.

" In July, when nesting is over, there are no more frolicsome birds than the highholes, or woodpeckers. They are like boys out of school, and actually seem to play games with each other, one that looks very much like ' tag' being a favorite.

" The young of these birds never cease in their clamor for food, and even when they have left their hole-nest they are fed by the parent birds.

" The feeding process is a strange one. The old one half loses its long bill down the throat of the youngster, and from its crop gives up a sufficient supply of half-digested food for a full meal.

" The courtship of these birds is exquisitely quaint, and a correspondent has given an account of a game, or dance, in which they began with a waltz

Woodpeckers

of an odd sort and went through various evolutions, ending with crossing their beaks, and standing so for a moment before they drew back and did the whole thing over.

" The downy woodpecker is particularly fond of apple-trees, and though popularly supposed to be an enemy of the orchard, is in reality one of its greatest friends. They tunnel for the worms, and it has been conclusively proved that trees drilled with their holes have long outlived in usefulness the trees unvisited by these birds.

" The clown of the family is the red-headed woodpecker, which, as well as the others shown, is a Pennsylvanian, and a most original and quaint character. He has been studied for many years in Ohio and many of his tricks described by Mr. Keyser, of that State. He lays up food for the winter, and in places where he has been accustomed to depend on the sweet beechnut for provisions he refuses to stay when the nut crop fails, but at once betakes himself to a more inviting region.

" The sapsucker, or yellow-breasted woodpecker, was shown with his mate and a young one, and his characteristics defended against the charge of sap sucking, which has been made against him. Sufficient evidence from several scientific ornithologists was produced to show that the bird is insectivorous in a great degree, and the small amount of sap he may drink is well paid for by the insects he consumes.

" The junco, or snowbird, is often found in flocks, except in the nesting season. Their favorite resting-place is in the roots of trees that have been blown over. That birds are considerate of one another is certain. I know of a case where a family had fed a flock of juncos during a long spell of cold weather. They got so tame that they would come up to the stoop to be fed; but it was noticed that one bird always remained on the fence and the other ones fed it. On examination, it was found that the bird had an injured wing, and in case of sudden danger would not have been able to leave with the flock in the rush, so it was left in a place of safety and fed.

" The snow-bunting is to be seen in our part of the world only in blizzard times, or when there are snow-scurries around."—*Miller.*

OF HAWKS

The red-shouldered hawk, called by farmers and hunters the hen-hawk, nests in trees in April or May. The eggs are two to four, white and blotched, with shades of brown. The nest is built of sticks, bark, etc.

The goshawk was a regular breeder in our woods and mountains. He is a fierce and powerful bird. The hawk feeds upon wild turkeys, pheasants, ducks, chickens, robins, rabbits, and squirrels. The cooper-hawk, known as the long-tailed chicken-hawk, is an audacious poultry thief, capturing full-grown chickens. This hawk also feeds upon pigeons, pheasants, turkeys, and squirrels. This bird nests about May in thick woods, the nest containing four or five eggs. In about twelve weeks the young are able to care for themselves. The sharp-shinned hawk bears a close resemblance to the cooper, but feeds by choice upon young chickens and pullets, young turkeys, young rabbits, and squirrels. If a pair of these birds should nest near a cabin where chickens were being raised, in a very few days they would steal every one.

When I was a boy large nestings of wild (passenger) pigeons in what was then Jenks, Tionesta, and Ridgway Townships occurred every spring. These big roosts were occupied annually early in April each year. Millions of pigeons occupied these roosts, and they were usually four or five miles long and from one to three miles wide. No other bird was ever known to migrate in such numbers. They fed on beechnuts, etc. In this territory every tree would be occupied, some with fifty nests. These pigeons swept over Brookville on their migration to these roosts, and would be three or four days in passing, making the day dark at times. The croakings of the pigeons in these roosts could be heard for miles.

Red-shouldered hawk

The coopers and the bloody goshawk, the great-horned and barred owls, like other night wanderers, such as the wild bear, panther, wolf, wild-cat, lynx, fox, the mink, and agile weasel, all haunted these roosts and feasted upon these pigeons. The weasel would climb the tree for the pigeons' eggs and the young, or to capture the old birds when at rest. The fox, lynx, mink, etc., depended on catching the squabs that fell from the nests.

Like the buffaloes of this region, the wild pigeon is doomed. These once common birds are only to be seen occasionally. Isolated and scattered pairs still find a breeding-place in our wilds, but the immense breeding colonies that once visited Northwestern Pennsylvania will never be seen again. The extermination of the passenger pigeon has gone on so rapidly that in another decade the birds may become a rarity. The only thing that will save the birds from this fate is the fact that they no longer resort to the more thickly populated States as breeding-places, but fly far into the woods along our northern border. Thirty years ago wild pigeons were found in New York State, and in Elk, Warren, McKean, Pike, and Cameron Counties, Pennsyl-

American goshawk

vania, but now they only figure as migrants, with a few pairs breeding in the beech-woods.

To give an idea of the immensity of these pigeon-roosts, I quote from the *Elk Advocate* as late as May, 1851:

"The American Express Company carried in one day, over the New York and Erie Railroad, over seven tons of pigeons to the New York market, and all of these were from the west of Corning. This company alone have carried over this road from the counties of Chemung, Steuben, and Allegheny fifty-six tons of pigeons."

As late as March, 1854, they came in such clouds for days that I was tired of looking at them and of the noise of the shooters.

The wild pigeon lays usually one or two eggs, and both birds do their

147

share of the incubating. The females occupy the nest from two P.M. until the next morning, and the males from nine or ten A.M. until two P.M. The males usually feed twice each day, while the females feed only during the forenoon. The old pigeons never feed near the nesting-places, always allowing the beechmast, buds, etc., there for use in feeding their young when they come forth. The birds go many miles to feed,—often a hundred or more.

Sharp-shinned hawk

Pigeons do not drink like any other bird. They drink like the ox or cow, and they nourish the young pigeon for the first week of his life from "pigeon milk," a curd-like substance secreted in the crop of both parents profusely during the incubating season. We had but two varieties,—the " wild," and turtle-doves.

Our birds migrate every fall to Tennessee, the Carolinas, and as far south as Florida. Want of winter food is and was the cause of that migration, for those that remained surely picked up a poor living. Migrating birds return year after year to the same locality. In migrating northward in the spring, the males usually precede the females several days, but on leaving their summer scenes of love and joy for the south, the sexes act in unison.

Of the other pioneer birds, there was the orchard-oriole, pine-grosbeak, rose-breasted grosbeak, swallow, barn-swallow, ruff-winged swallow, bank swallow, black and white warbler, chestnut-sided warbler, barn-owl, American long-eared owl, short-eared owl, screech-owl, great-horned owl, yellow-billed cuckoo, black-billed cuckoo, kingbird, crested flycatcher, phœbe-bird, wood-pewee, least flycatcher, ruffed grouse (pheasant, or partridge), quail, also

Wild pigeon

known as the bob-white, marsh-hawk, sparrow-hawk, pigeon-hawk, fish-hawk, red-tailed hawk, American ruff-legged hawk, horned grebe, loon, hooded merganser, wood-duck, buff-headed duck, red-headed duck, American bittern, least bittern, blue heron, green heron, black-crowned night-heron, Virginia

Grouse or Pheasant

rail, Carolina rail, American coot, American woodcock, Wilson's snipe, least sandpiper, killdeer plover, belted kingfisher, turtle-dove, turkey-buzzard, whip-poorwill, nighthawk, ruby-throated humming-bird, blue-jay, bobolink, or reed- or rice-bird, purple grackle, cowbird (cow-bunting), red-winged blackbird, American grosbeak, red-poll, American goldfinch, or yellow-bird, towhee-

149

bunting, cardinal- or redbird, indigo bunting, scarlet tanager, cedar- or cherry-bird, butcher-bird, or great northern scarlet tanager, red-eyed vireo, American

Belted kingfisher

redstart, cootbird, brown thrush, bluebird, house-wren, wood-wren, white-breasted nuthatch, chickadee, golden-crowned knight.

Humming-birds

NATURAL LIFE OF SOME OF OUR BIRDS

	Years.		Years.
Raven	100	Pheasant	15
Eagle	100	Partridge	15
Crow	100	Blackbird	10
Goose	50	Common fowl	10
Sparrowhawk	40	Robin	10
Crane	24	Thrush	10
Peacock	24	Wren	5
Lark	16		

HISTORY OF NORTHWESTERN PENNSYLVANIA

"How doth the little busy bee
Improve each shining hour,
And gather honey all the day
From every opening flower."

In pioneer times these woods were alive with bee-trees, and even yet that condition prevails in the forest part of this region, as the following article on bees, from the pen of E. C. Niver, clearly describes:

"Although the natural range of bee-pasturage in this section is practically unlimited, singular to relate, apiculture is not pursued to any great extent. With all the apparently favorable conditions, the occupation is too uncertain and precarious to hazard much capital or time on it. At the best, apiculture is an arduous occupation, and in the most thickly populated farming communities it requires constant vigilance to keep track of runaway swarms. But in this rugged mountain country, with its thousands of acres of hemlock

Straw bee-scap

slashings and hard-wood ridges, it is virtually impossible to keep an extensive apiary within bounds. The rich pasturage of the forests and mountain barrens affords too great a temptation, and although the honey-bee has been the purveyor of sweets for the ancients as far back as history reaches, she has never yet become thoroughly domesticated. At swarming time the nomadic instinct asserts itself. Nature lures and beckons, and the first opportunity is embraced to regain her fastness and subsist upon her bounty. Never a season goes by but what some swarms escape to the woods. These take up their habitation in hollow trees or some other favorable retreat, and in time throw off other swarms. Thus it is that our mountains and forests contain an untold wealth of sweetness, but little of which is ever utilized by man.

"Here is the opportunity of the bee-hunter. In the backwoods counties of Western Pennsylvania bee-hunting is as popular a sport with some as deer-hunting or trout-fishing. It does not have nearly so many devotees, perhaps, as these latter sports, for the reason that a greater degree of woodcraft, skill, and patience is required to become a proficient bee-hunter. Any backwoodsman can search out and stand guard at a deer runway, watch a lick, or follow a trail; and his skill with a rifle, in the use of which he is familiar from his early boyhood, insures him an equal chance in the pursuit of game. It does not require any nice display of woodcraft to tramp over the mountains to the head of the trout stream, with a tin spice-box full of worms, cut an ash sapling, equip it with the hook and line, and fish the stream down to its mouth. But to search out a small insect as it sips the nectar from the blossoms, trace it to its home, and successfully despoil it of its hoarded stores, requires a degree of skill and patience that comparatively few care to attain. Yet in every community of this section are some old fellows who do not consider life complete without a crockful of strained honey in the cellar when winter sets in. Then, as they sit with their legs under the kitchen-table while their wives bake smoking-hot buckwheat cakes, the pungent flavor of decayed wood which the honey imparts to their palates brings back the glory of the chase. Whenever a man takes to bee-hunting he is an enthusiastic devotee, and with him all other sport is relegated to the background.

"There are many methods employed in hunting the wild honey-bee. The first essential is a knowledge of bees and their habits. This can only be acquired by experience and intelligent observation. The man who can successfully 'line' bees can also successfully 'keep' them in a domestic state, but a successful apiarist is not necessarily a good bee-hunter.

"September and October are the best months for securing wild honey, as the bees have then in the main completed their stores. At that season they can also be most readily lined, for the scarcity of sweets makes them more susceptible to artificial bait. But the professional bee-hunter does not, as a rule, wait until fall to do all his lining. He wants to know what is in prospect, and by the time the honey-bee suspends operations for the winter the hunter has perhaps a dozen bee-trees located which he has been watching all summer in order to judge as near as possible as to the amount of stored honey they contain. If the hunter wants to save the bees he cuts the tree in June and hives the inmates in the same manner as when they swarm in a domestic state. Many swarms are thus obtained, and the hunter scorns to expend any money for a swarm of bees which he can get for the taking. As a matter of course, when the honey is taken in the fall the bees, being despoiled of their subsistence, inevitably perish.

> "'I'll gather the honey-comb bright as gold,
> And chase the elk to his secret fold.'

"The first warm days of April, when the snows have melted from the south side of the hills, and the spring runs are clear of ice, find the bee-hunter on the alert. There is nothing yet for the bees to feed upon, but a few of the advance-guard are emerging from their long winter's hibernations in search of pollen and water, and they instinctively seek the water's edge where the warm rays of the sun beat down. Where the stream has receded from the bank, leaving a miniature muddy beach, there the bees congregate, dabbling in the mud, sipping water and carrying it away. The first material sought for by the bees is pollen, and the earliest pasturage for securing this is the pussy-willow and skunk-cabbage, which grow in the swamps. After these comes the soft maple, which also affords a large supply of pollen. Sugar-maple is among the first wild growth which furnishes any honey. Then come the wild cherry, the locust, and the red raspberries and blackberries. Of course, the first blossoms and the cultivated plants play an important part, but the profusion of wild flowers which are honey-bearing would probably supply as much honey to the acre as the cultivated sections.

" The wild honeysuckle, which covers thousands of acres of the mountain ranges with a scarlet flame in May, is a particular favorite with bees, as is also the tulip-tree, which is quite abundant in this section. Basswood honey has a national reputation, and before the paper-wood cutters despoiled the ridges and forests the basswood-tree furnished an almost unlimited feeding-ground. This tree blooms for a period of two or three weeks, and a single swarm has been known to collect ten pounds of honey in a day when this flower was in blossom. Devil's-club furnishes another strong feed for bees, as well as the despised sumach. Last, but not least, is the golden-rod, which in this latitude lasts from August until killed by the autumn frosts. While these are the chief wild-honey producing trees and plants, they are but a fractional part of the honey resources of the country.

" Having discovered the feeding-ground and haunts of the wild honey-bee, the hunter proceeds to capture a bee and trace it to its habitation. This is done by ' lining,'—that is, following the bee's flight to its home. The bee always flies in a direct line to its place of abode, and this wonderful instinct gives rise to the expression, ' a bee-line.'

" To assist in the chase the hunter provides himself with a ' bee-box,' which is any small box possessing a lid, with some honey inside for bait. Arrived at any favorable feeding-ground, the hunter eagerly scans the blossoms until he finds a bee at work. This he scoops into his box and closes the lid. If he can capture two or more bees at once, so much the better. After buzzing angrily for a few moments in the darkened box the bee scents the honey inside and immediately quiets down and begins to work. Then the box is set down and the lid opened. When the bee gets all the honey she can carry she mounts upward with a rapid spiral motion until she gets her bearings, and then she is off like a shot in a direct line to her habitation. Presently she is back again, and this time when she departs her bearings are located and she goes direct. After several trips more bees appear, and when they get to working the bait and the line of their flight is noted, the box is closed when the bees are inside and moved forward along the direction in which they have been coming and going. The hunter carefully marks his trail and opens the box again. The bees are apparently unconscious that they have been moved, and work as before. This manœuvre is repeated until the spot where the swarm is located is near at hand, and then comes the most trying part of the quest to discover the exact location of the hive. Sometimes it is in the hollow of a dead tree away to the top; sometimes it is near the bottom. Again, it may be in a hollow branch of a living tree of gigantic proportions, closely hidden in the foliage, or it may be in an old stump or log. To search it out requires the exercise of much patience, as well as a quick eye and an acute ear.

" To determine the distance of the improvised hive after a line has been established from the bee-box the hunter resorts to ' cross-lining.' This is done by moving the box when the bees are at work in it some distance to one side. The bees as usual fly direct to their home, the second line of flight converging with the first, forming the apex of a triangle, the distance between the first and second locations of the box being the base and the two lines of flight the sides. Where the lines meet the habitation is to be found.

" Different kinds of bait are frequently used in order to induce the bees to work the box. In the flowering season a little anise or other pungent oil is rubbed on the box to attract the bees and keep them from being turned aside by the wealth of blossoms along their flight. It is a mistake to mix the oil with the bait, as it spoils the honey the bees make and poisons the whole swarm. Sometimes in the early spring corn-cobs soaked in stagnant brine proves an attractive bait, while late in the fall beeswax burned on a heated stone will bring the belated straggler to the bee-box.

" Cutting a bee-tree is the adventuresome part of the sport. An angry swarm is a formidable enemy. Then, too, the treasure for which the hunter is in search is about to be revealed, and the possibilities bring a thrill of anticipation and excitement. So far as the danger goes the experienced hunter is prepared for that, and protects his head and face by a bag of mosquito-netting drawn over a broad-brimmed hat. With gloves on his hands he is tolerably protected, but sometimes a heavy swarm breaks through the netting, and instances are on record where bee-hunters have been so severely stung in despoiling wild swarms as to endanger their lives. In felling a tree great care must be exercised in order that the tree may not break up and destroy the honey. Sometimes trees are felled after night, as bees do not swarm about in the darkness, and the danger of getting stung is not so great.

" The amount of honey secured depends upon the age of the swarm. Frequently much time and labor have been expended in lining and cutting a tree which yielded nothing, while again the returns have been large. There are instances in this community where a single tree yielded over two hundred pounds of good honey. Not long since a hunter cut a tree in which a hollow space about eighteen inches in diameter was filled with fine honey for a length of fifteen feet. Often a tree is cut which has been worked so long that part of the honey is spoiled with age. Often the comb is broken and the honey mingled with the decayed wood of the tree. The bee-hunter, however, carefully gathers up the honey, wood and all, in a tin pail, and strains it, and the pungent flavor of the wood does not in the least detract from the quality in his estimation.

"Bee-hunting as a sport could still be pursued in nearly every section of Western Pennsylvania, particularly in the lumbering and tannery districts. In these sections thousands of acres are annually stripped of timber, extending many miles back from the settled districts. Fire runs through these old slashings every year or so, and a dense growth of blackberry and raspberry briers spring up. These, with the innumerable varieties of wild flowers, afford a rich and vast pasturage for the honey-bee which has thrown off the restraints of civilization. Swarm upon swarm is propagated, the surplus product of which is never utilized. With a little encouragement bee-hunting might become as popular a form of sport with the dweller of the town as with the skilled woodsman."

The bee was imported, and is a native of Asia.

CHAPTER VII

I PAUSE here to tell the story of Bill Long, the "king hunter." William Long, a son of Louis (Ludwig) Long, was born near Reading, Berks County, Pennsylvania, in 1794. His father and mother were Germans. In the summer of 1803, Louis Long, with his family, moved into this wilderness and settled near Port Barnett (now the McConnell farm). Ludwig Long's family consisted of himself, wife, and eleven children,—nine sons and two daughters, —William, the subject of this sketch, being the second child. The Barnetts were the only neighbors of the Longs. Louis Long brought with him a small "still" and six flint-lock guns, the only kind in use at that time. It was not until about the year 1830 that the percussion-cap rifles were first used, and they were not in general use here for some years after that. Guns were invented by a German named Swartz, about 1378. As soon as Mr. Long raised some grain he commenced to operate his "still" and manufacture whiskey, this being the first manufactured west of the mountains and east of the Allegheny River.

This part of Pennsylvania was then the hunting-grounds of the Seneca Indians,—Cornplanter tribe. The still-house of Long soon became the resort for these Indians. Pittsburg was the nearest market for pelts, furs, etc., and the only place to secure flour and other necessaries. From the mouth of Red Bank Creek these goods had to be poled up to Barnett's in canoes. By scooping the channel, wading, and polling, a round trip to the mouth could be made in from one to two weeks. Although the woods swarmed with Seneca Indians, as a rule, they never committed any depredations.

In the summer of 1804, when William was ten years old, he killed his first deer. One morning his father sent him into the woods for the cows. Nature was resplendent with verdure. William carried with him a flint-lock gun, and when a short distance from the house he found the cows and a deer feeding with them. This was William's opportunity. He shot and killed this deer, and, as a reward for merit, his father gave him a flint-lock gun as a present. This circumstance determined his course in life, for from that day until his death it was his delight to roam in the forest and pursue wild animals, and hunting was his only business. He was a " professional hunter," a " still hunter," or a man who hunted alone.

In the summer of 1804 William went with his mother to Ligonier, in Westmoreland County, to get some provisions. The only road was an Indian path, the distance sixty miles. They rode through the brush on a horse, and made the trip in about five days.

Bill Long, the king hunter of Northwestern Pennsylvania

The Indians soon became civilized, as far as drinking whiskey and getting drunk was an evidence. They visited this still-house for debauchery and drunken carnivals. As a safeguard to himself and family, Louis Long had a strong box made to keep the guns and knives of these Indians in while these orgies were occurring. The Indians desired him to do this. Mr. Long never charged the Indians for this whiskey, although they always offered

157

pelts and furs when they sobered up. In consideration of this generosity, the Indians, in broken English, always called Louis Long, " Good man; give Indian whiskey. Indian fight pale-face; Indian come one hundred miles to give ' good man' warning."

Ludwig Long kept his boys busy in the summer months clearing land, farming, etc. The boys had their own time in winter. Then William, with his gun and traps, traversed the forest, away from the ocean's tide, with no inlet or outlet but winding paths used by the deer when he wished to slake his thirst in the clear, sparkling water of the North Fork.

The boy hunter, to keep from being lost while on the trail, followed up one side of this creek and always came down on the opposite. When he grew older he ventured farther and farther into the wilderness, but always keeping the waters of the North Fork, Mill Creek, and Sandy Lick within range until he became thoroughly educated with the country and woods.

In his boyhood he frequently met and hunted in company with Indians. The Indians were friendly to him on account of his father's relations to them, and it was these Indians that gave William his first lessons in the art of hunting. Young William learned the trick of calling wolves in this way. One day his father and he went out for a deer. William soon shot a large one, and while skinning this deer they heard a pack of wolves howl. William told his father to lie down and be ready to shoot, and he would try the Indian method of " howling" or calling wolves up to you. His father consented, and William howled and the wolves answered. William kept up the howls and the wolves answered, coming closer and closer, until his father became scared; but William wouldn't stop until the wolves got so close that he and his father had to fire on the pack, killing two, when the others took fright and ran away. The bounty for killing wolves then was eight dollars apiece. A short time after this William and his father went up Sandy to watch an elk-lick, and at this point they killed an elk and started for home. On the way home they found where a pack of about twenty wolves had crossed their path, near where the town of Reynoldsville now is. Looking up the hill on the right side of Sandy they espied the whole pack, and, both father and son firing into the pack, they killed two of them. William then commenced to " howl," and one old wolf through curiosity came to the top of the hill, looking down at the hunters. For this bravery William shot him through the head. On their return home that day Joseph Barnett treated them both to whiskey and " tansy," for, said he, " the wolves this day have killed one of my cows." When Long was still a young man, one day he went up the North Fork to hunt. About sundown he shot a deer, and when he had it dressed there came up a heavy rain. Being forced to stay all night, he took the pelt and covered himself with it, and lay down under the bank to sleep. After midnight he awoke, and found himself covered with sticks and leaves. In a minute he knew this was the work of a panther hunting food for her cubs, and that she would soon return. He therefore prepared a pitch-pine fagot, lit it, and hid the burning fagot under the bank and awaited the coming of the panther. In a short time after this preparation was completed the animal returned with her cubs, and when she was within about thirty feet of him, Long thrust his torch up and out, and when it blazed up brightly the panther gave out a yell and ran away.

The wild carnivorous animals are found in all parts of the world, except Australia, the Dingo dog being imported there.

John Long and William started out one morning on Sandy Lick to have a bear-hunt, taking with them nine dogs. William had been sent out the day before with two dogs, and had a skirmish with a bear on Sandy Lick, near where Fuller's Station now stands. The two brothers went to this point and found the track, and chased the bear across the creek at Rocky Bend, the bear making for a windfall; but the dogs stopped him before he reached the windfall and commenced the fight. They soon heard some of the dogs giving death-yells. They both hurried to the scene of conflict, and the sight they beheld was three favorite dogs stretched out dead and the balance fighting. William ran in and placed the muzzle of his gun against bruin's breast and fired. The bear then backed up to the root of a large hemlock, sitting upright and grabbing for dogs. John and William then fired, and both balls entered bruin's head, not more than an inch apart. In this *mêlée* three dogs were killed and the other six badly wounded. When William was still a boy he went up the North Fork and killed five deer in one day. On his way home about dark he noticed a pole sticking in the hollow of a tree, and carelessly gave this pole a jerk, when he heard a noise in the hole. The moon being up, he saw a bear emerge from this tree some distance up. Young Long shot and killed it before it reached the earth. In that same fall, William killed in one day, on Mill Creek, nine deer, the largest number he ever killed in that space of time. At that time he kept nothing but the pelts, and carried them home on his back. Panthers often came around Louis Long's home at night, screaming and yelling. So one morning, after three had been prowling around the house all night, William induced his brother John to join him in a hunt for them. There was snow on the ground, and they took three dogs with them. The dogs soon found the " tracks." Keeping the dogs back, they soon found three deer killed by the brutes, and then they let the dogs go. The dogs soon caught these three panthers feasting on a fourth deer and treed two of the panthers. John shot one and Billy the other. The third escaped. The hunters then camped for the night, dining on deer- and panther-meat roasted, and each concluded the panther-meat was the sweetest and the best.

In the morning they pursued the third panther, treed it, and killed it. These were the first panthers the Long boys ever killed. This stimulated young William, so he took one of the Vastbinder boys and started out again, taking two dogs. They soon found a panther, the dogs attacking it. Young

Vastbinder fired, but missed. The panther sprang for Long, but the dogs caught him by the hams and that saved young Long. The panther broke loose from the dogs and ran up on a high root. Long fired and broke the brute's back. The dogs then rushed in, but the panther whipped them off. Then Long, to save the dogs, ran in and tomahawked the creature. Long was now about eighteen years of age. At another time a panther sprang from a high tree for Long. Long fired and killed the panther before it reached him,

Long fires at a panther

but the animal striking Long on the shoulder the weight felled him to the earth.

In 1815 six brothers of Cornplanter's tribe of Indians erected wigwams in the Beaver Meadows, where Du Bois now stands.

In 1826 Ludwig Long moved to Ohio, and young Bill went with the family. He remained there about twenty months; but finding little game, concluded to return to the mountain-hills of Jefferson County, then the paradise of hunters. In 1828, William Long married Mrs. Nancy Bartlett, formerly Miss Nancy Mason, and commenced married life in a log cabin on the North Fork, three miles from where Brookville now is, and on what is now the Albert Horn farm, formerly the Gaup place. About this time, game being plenty, and the scalps, skins, and saddles being hard to carry in, Bill Long induced a colored man named Charles Southerland to build a cabin near him on what is now known as the Jacob Hoffman farm. Long was to provide for Charlie's family. The cabin was built, and Southerland served Long for about five years. Charles never carried a gun. I remember both these characters well in my childhood, and doctored Long and his wife in my early practice and as late as 1862. In 1830, taking Charlie, Long started up the North Fork for bears; it was on Sunday. After Long killed the first bear, he called Charlie to come and bring the dogs. When Charlie reached him he yelled out, " Good God, massa, hab you seed one?" They continued the hunt that day, and before dark had killed seven bears. Charlie had never seen any bears killed before, but after this day was crazy to be on a hunt, for, he said, " if dem little niggers of mine hab plenty of bear-grease and venison, they will fatten well enough." This fall Long killed sixty deer and twenty-five bears, all on the North Fork, and the bears were all killed near and around where Richardsville now is. This locality was a natural home for wild animals,—

> " With its woodland dale and dell,
> Rippling brooks and hill-side springs."

> " A life in the forest deep,
> Where the winds their revels keep;
> Like an eagle in groves of pine,
> Long hunted with his mate."

The day after Long killed the seven bears, he took Charlie Southerland, and travelled over the same ground that he had been over the day before. He heard nothing, however, during the day but the sigh of the breeze or the speech of the brook until near evening, when, within about a mile of home, he saw a large buck coming down the hill. He fired and wounded the buck, and then motioned Charlie to come up to him while he was loading. Charlie came with a large pine-log on his back. Long asked him what he was doing with that log. Southerland replied he wanted it for dry wood. Long told him to throw the wood away, and made him carry the buck home for food. Long then yoked his two dogs up and told Charlie to lead them, but soon discovering bear signs, told Charlie to let the dogs go. The dogs took the trail, and found two bears heading for the laurel on the head of the North Fork. Long knew the route they would take, and beat them to the laurel path. Soon Long heard them coming, the dogs fighting the bears every time the bears would cross a log, catching them from behind. The bears would then turn around and fight the dogs until they could get over the log. When the bears came within about thirty yards of Long, he shot one through the head and killed him. At this time Long only took the pelts, which he always carried home, the meat being of no account. This same year Long took Charlie with him to get some venison by watching a lick, and he took Charlie up a tree with him. In a short time a very large bear came into the lick. Long shot it while he and Charlie were up the tree. Much to Long's amusement, Charlie was so scared that he fell from the tree to the ground, landing on his back with his face up. He was, however, unhurt, and able to carry home to his cabin the pelt and bear oil. The next morning they saw a bear, and Long fired, hitting him in the lungs. This same fall, on the head of the North Fork, Long saw something black in the brush, which, on closer inspection, proved to be a large she bear. On looking up, he saw three good-sized cubs. Long climbed up, and brought the whole three of them down, one at a time. He then handed them to Charlie, who tied their legs. Long put them in his knapsack and carried them home.

Knapsacks were made out of bed-ticking or canvas, with shoulder-strap. One of these young bears Long sold to Adam George, a butcher in Brookville. Even at this late day Long only took the skins and what meat he wanted for his own use. This fall Long was not feeling well, and had to keep out of the wet. He therefore made Charlie carry him across the streams. He also made Charlie carry a wolf-skin for him to sit on at night, when he was watching a lick. At another time Charlie and Long went out on a hunt near the head of the North Fork. In lonely solitude the dog started a bear, and Long could not shoot it for fear of hitting the dog, so he ran up and made a stroke at the bear's head with a tomahawk, wounding it but slightly. The bear jumped for Long, and the dog came to the rescue of his master by catching "the tip of the bear's tail end," and, with the valor and fidelity of a true knight, held it firmly, until Long, who had left his gun a short distance, ran for it. Charlie thought Long was running from the bear, and took to his heels as if the "Old Harry" was after him. Long tried to stop him, but Charlie only looked back, and at this moment his foot caught under a root, throwing him about thirty feet down a hill. Charlie landed on a rock hard enough to have burst a shingle-bolt. Long, seeing this, ran to the bear with his gun and shot him. He then hurried down the hill to see what had become of Charlie, calling to him. Charlie came out from under a bunch of laurel, saying, "God Almighty, Massa Long, I am falled from heben to hell! Are you still living? I tot that ar bar had done gon for you when I seed him come for you with his mouth open. Bless de good Lord you still live, or this nigger would never git out of dese woods!" That night Charlie and Long lay out in the woods. The wolves came up quite close and commenced to howl. Long saw there was a chance for a little fun, so he commenced to howl like a wolf. Charlie became nervous. "When lo! he hears on all sides, from innumerable tongues, a universal howl, and in his fright" said there must be five thousand wolves. Long said he thought there was, and told Charlie that, if the wolves came after them, he must climb a tree. In a few minutes Long made a jump into the woods, yelling, "The wolves are coming," and Charlie bounded like a deer into the woods, too. The night was dark and dreary; but deep in the forest Charlie made out to find and climb a majestic oak. Long, therefore, had to look Charlie up, and when he got near to our colored brother, he heard him soliloquizing thus: " Charles, you have to stick tight, for if this holt breaks you are a gone nigger." Long then stepped up to the tree and told Charlie the danger was over; but coming down the tree was harder than going up, for Charlie fell to the earth like a thunder-bolt and doubled up like a jack-knife.

BILL LONG AND HIS ATTENDANT, " BLACK CHARLIE"

In 1833, on his way home one day, Long saw a bear at the foot of a large tree. He came up close and tried to get a shot at its head, but the bear kept moving about so that he dared not fire. After trying for some time, he knew

Common brown bear

from the action of the bear that there were young ones near, so he bawled like a cub, when the old bear came on the run for him, with her mouth open. Long waited until she came up close, when he rammed the muzzle of the gun in her open mouth and pulled the trigger of the gun with the thumb of his left hand, the load knocking her teeth out and breaking her jaw. She then went back to the tree and commenced walking around in a circle. As soon as Long reloaded the gun he bawled again, and the bear this time came within sixteen feet of him and sat up straight, wiping her mouth with her paws. He then took aim at the stalking place and killed her. Going to the tree she had been walking around and looking up, he saw two cubs. At the sight of Long these cubs commenced to crawl down; one dropped to the ground and ran off. Long fired at the other, breaking its back. This cub then fell to the ground, and Long tomahawked it. Knowing the other cub would not go far away, he reloaded the gun, and espied the cub under a log close by. Taking aim at its head he fired, and the cub fell dead. A bear weighing four hundred pounds would render fifteen gallons of oil.

This same year, on the head of the North Fork, " where rippling waters still flow," Long espied a cub bear on a tree-top. He told his attendant, " Black Charlie," that there was an old bear near, or soon would be, and if

Bear and cubs

the old one did not soon come back he wanted Charlie to make the cub bawl. After waiting for some time for the old bear to come, Long impatiently climbed the tree, caught the cub and gave it to Charlie, telling him to take it by the hind legs and hold it up and shake it, which would make it bawl. After some time the cub was made to bawl. The bear, hearing this, came running with her mouth open. Charlie threw the cub to its mother, but the bear ran by the cub and stopped, looking first at Long and then at the cub. Long fired at her, hitting her in the breast. She then turned and ran toward the cub. After loading again he shot her through the lungs, when she started and ran some distance, and then came back to the cub, which sat still. After firing the second shot Long heard Charlie yell, " What tidings?" Long answered him, " Good." Charlie started for the rear, saying, Long " didn't get dat nigger back dar again till dat brute am killed." As she came up Long shot her in the head, killing her. He then got the cub and took it home alive.

At one time Long took thirteen wolf scalps and five panther scalps to Indiana for the bounty.

Once in this same year, when Long was up on the North Fork, he shot a deer, and it fell apparently dead; but when he went to cut its throat it jumped to its feet and made for him, and threw him on the ground, with a horn on each side of his breast. The stone and gravel stopped the horns from going into the ground to any great depth. Long then called for Charlie and the dogs, but they were slow in coming to his aid. Before Charlie got to him Long had let go of a horn with one hand and had secured his knife, and made a stroke at the neck of the deer, plunging the knife in the throat, and again dexterously clinched the loose horn. The blood came down on him until he was covered and perfectly wet. When the deer commenced to rise Long still held on to both horns until the deer raised him to his feet. The deer then gave a spring, and fell dead. By this time Charlie and the dogs came up, and the negro was crying. Long was angry, and said to Charlie, " You black son of a b——, where have you been?" " Oh, massa, am you killed?" " No, damn you; where have you been?" " Oh, just came as soon as I could. Will I let the dogs go?" Long said, " No, the deer is dead."

Charlie's domestic life was not all peace, as the following newspaper advertisement will explain:

" CAUTION

" Whereas my wife Susey did on the 26th day of March last leave my bed and board, and took with her two of my sons and some property, having no other provocation than ' that I would not consent to my son marrying a white girl, and bring her home to live with us.' Therefore I hereby caution all persons against harboring or trusting her on my account, as I will pay no debts of her contracting.

" If she will come home I promise to do all in my power to make her comfortable, and give her an equal share of all my property.

" CHARLES SOUTHERLAND.

" April 7, 1847."

In a copy of the *Jeffersonian* printed in 1852, I find the following:

" In this day's paper we record the death of Charles Sutherland (colored), who was one of the oldest inhabitants of this county. Sutherland had arrived at the advanced age of nearly one hundred years. He came to what is now Jefferson County upward of forty years ago, when the ground upon which Brookville now stands was but a howling wilderness. Many there are in this borough who will miss the familiar and friendly visits of ' old Charley,' who, with hat in hand, and his venerable head uncovered, asked alms at their hands. No more will they hear from him a description of the ' Father of his Country,' when he, Charley, held his horse at the laying of the corner-stone of the Capitol at Washington City. His breath is hushed, his lips are sealed, and his body is wrapped in the cold habiliments of the grave. *Requiescat in pace.*"

When this wilderness commenced to settle up, Long visited Broken Straw Creek, in Warren County, on the head of the Allegheny River, to see a noted hunter by the name of Cotton, and to learn from him his method of hunting young wolves. He learned much from this man Cotton, and afterwards secured many young wolves by the instruction given him by Cotton. In the winter of' 1835 Mike and Bill Long went to Boone's Mountain to hunt. This mountain was a barren region in those days, that always looked in winter-time like

> " Rivers of ice and a sea of snow,
> A wilderness frigid and white."

During the season Bill killed one hundred and five deer and Mike one hundred and four, and together they killed four bears. At this time there was some local demand in Brookville and other towns for venison, and in this year the Longs sent loads of venison to Harrisburg, making a trip to the capital in seven or eight days. In 1839, Long moved into Clearfield County, and his history in Jefferson County was closed.

Number of animals killed by Long in his life-time: bears, 400; deer (in 1835 one white one), 3500; panthers, 50; wolves, 2000; elks, 125; foxes, 400; wild-cats, 200; catamounts, 500; otters, 75.

In 1824 Bill Long had a thrilling adventure with a huge panther in what is now Warsaw Township. He, in a hand-to-hand encounter, killed the animal near where Bootjack, Jefferson County, now stands.

Long used to catch fawns, mark their ears, turn them loose, and kill them when full-grown deer. Elks were easily domesticated, and sold as follows,— viz.: for a living male elk one year old, $50; two years old, $75; three years old, $100; and for a fawn three months old, $25. In 1835 Long had five wolf-dens that he visited annually for pups, about the 1st of May.

In 1834 Bill Long, his brother Mike, and Ami Sibley started on a hunt for elk near where Portland now is. At the mouth of Bear Creek these three hunters came across a drove of about forty elks. Bill Long fired into the herd and broke the leg of one. This wounded elk began to squeal, and then the herd commenced to run in a circle around the injured one. Sibley's gun had the wiping-stick fastened in it, and he could not use it. Bill and Mike then loaded and fired into the drove as rapidly as they could, the elks continuing to make the circle, until each had fired about twenty-five shots, when the drove became frightened and ran away. On examination, the hunters found eight large elks killed. They then made a raft, ran the load down to where Raught's mill is now, and hauled the meat, pelts, and horns to Brookville. Portland and Bear Creek are now in Elk County.

In 1836 Bill Long took Henry Dull and started on a hunt for a young elk. On the third day Long saw a doe elk and fawn. He shot the mother, and his dog caught the fawn and held it without hurting it. Long removed the udder from the mother, carrying it with the " teats" uppermost, and giving the fawn milk from it until they reached Ridgway, where a jug of milk was secured, and by means of an artificial " teat" the fawn was nourished until Long reached his North Fork home. Dull led the little creature by a rope around its neck. Mrs. Long raised this elk with her cows, feeding it every milking-time, and when the fawn grew to be some size he would drive the cows home every evening for his supper of milk. When this elk was full grown, Long and Dull led him to Buffalo, New York, via the pike westward to the Allegheny River, and up through Warren, and sold the animal for two hundred dollars,—one hundred dollars in cash and a note for the other hundred, that was never paid.

In the fall of 1836 Long took Henry Dull with him to hunt wolves. The second evening Long found an old wolf with six half-grown pups. He shot two and the rest ran away. Long and Dull then climbed a hemlock, and Long began his wolf *howl*. On hearing the howl, two pups and the old wolf came back. Long then shot the mother, and afterwards got all the pups. Dull became so frightened that he fell head first, gun and all, through the brush, striking the ground with his head, producing unconsciousness and breaking his shoulder. "Thanks to the human heart, by which we live," for Long nursed Dull at his home on the North Fork for three months. Scalps then brought twelve dollars apiece. In that same year Fred. Hetrick and Bill killed an elk at the mouth of Little Toby which weighed six hundred pounds.

In the winter of 1834 William Dixon, Mike and Bill Long, with dogs, went out to "rope" or catch a live elk. They soon started a drove on the North Fork, and the dogs chased the drove over to the Little Toby, a short distance up from the mouth. The dogs separated one buck from the drove, and this elk, to protect himself from the dogs, took refuge on a ledge of rocks. Bill Long, while Mike and Dixon and the dogs attracted the attention of the elk from below, scrambled in some way to the top of the rocks and threw a rope over the elk's horns, and then cabled the elk to a small tree. This infuriated the elk, so that he jumped out over the rocks and fell on his side. Mike and Dixon now had the first rope. Bill Long then rushed on the fallen elk and threw another rope in a slip-noose around the elk's neck, and fastened this rope as a guy to a tree. Each rope was then fastened in an opposite direction to a tree, and after the buck was choked into submission, his feet were tied, and the elk was dragged by these three men on the creek ice to where Brockwayville now is. Here they secured a yoke of oxen and sled from Ami Sibley, a mighty hunter. A small tree was then cut, the main stem being left about five feet long and the two forks about three feet in length. Each prong of the tree was fastened to a horn of the buck, and the main stem permitted to hang down in front over the buck's nose, to which it was fastened with a rope. A rope was then tied around the neck and antlers, and the loose end tied around the hind bench of the sled; this drove the elk close up to the hind part of the sled. The ropes around the feet of the elk were then cut, and the buck lit on his feet. After the animal had made many desperate efforts and plunges, he quieted down, and no trouble was experienced until within a few miles of Brookville, when, meeting an acquaintance, Dixon became so much excited over the success in capturing a live elk, that he ran up and hit the elk on the back, exclaiming, " See, we have done it !" and this so scared the elk that he made a desperate jump, upsetting the sled into a ditch over a log. The oxen then took fright, and in the general *mêlée* the elk had a shoulder knocked out of place and the capture was a failure.

There grew in abundance in those days a tree called moose or leatherwood. The pioneers used the bark for ropes, which were very strong.

ELK AND VENISON JERK

This was " venison flesh cut off in a sheet or web about half an inch thick and spread on the tops of pegs driven into the ground, whilst underneath a fire was kindled, fed with chips of sassafras and other odorous woods, that gradually dried it." The web would be removed and replaced until the jerk was thoroughly dried. The old hunter used to carry a little jerk always with him to eat with his bread. This jerk was a delicious morsel. Bill Long gave me many a " cut." I think I can taste it now. Mike and Bill Long would bring it to Brookville and retail it to the people at five cents a cut.

AN INCIDENT ON THE PIKE

In the spring of 1820, when the pike was being constructed, there was an early settler by the name of George Eckler living near Port Barnett. This man Eckler liked a spree, and the Irish that worked on the pike were not averse to "a wee drop at ony time." A jug or two of Long's " Mountain Dew" whiskey, fresh from the still, was secured, and a jolly " Donnybrook Fair" time was had one night in the woods. Eckler came in for the worst of it, for his eyes were blackened and he was battered up generally. On sober reflection he concluded to swear out a warrant before Thomas Lucas, Esq., for the " Paddies of the pike." The warrant was placed in the hands of the constable, John Dixon, Sr. There were about twenty-five in this gang of Paddies, and Constable Dixon summoned a posse of eight to assist in the arrest. This posse consisted of the young Dixons, Longs, and McCulloughs, and when this solid column of foresters reached the Irish on the pike, one of the Paddies told the constable to " go home and attend to his own business."

He then commanded the pike battalion to remove the handles from their picks and charge on the posse. This they did, to the complete rout of the natives, chasing them all in confusion like a herd of deer through and across Mill Creek. Young Bill Long was with this posse, and he ran home, too, but only to arm himself, not with a shillelah, but with his flint-lock, tomahawk, and knife. Thus armed and single-handed he renewed the conflict, keeping in the woods and above the Irish, and sending balls so close to their heads that the whiz could be heard, until he drove the whole pack, with their carts, etc., from above Port Barnett to where Brookville now stands.

In the forties, when Long lived above Falls Creek, he went through wastes of snow and icicled trees to find a buck that he had wounded, and took his son Jack, who was but a boy, along with him. On their way the dog scented some animal that was no deer, and Long told him to go. The dog soon treed a panther, and when the two hunters came to him they found two more panthers on the ground. The dog seized one of the animals, and Jack stopped to shoot the one on the tree, which, after he had shot twice, fell dead. At the same time Long threw his gun down in the snow, as he could not shoot for fear of killing the dog which had seized the panther. Long then ran to the dog's assistance and tomahawked the panther. Jack then came up to his father and said, pointing, " There is the other one looking at us." The dogs were urged on and both took hold of this panther; Jack ran in and caught the panther by the hind legs, the dogs having him in front. Jack was anxious to take this animal home alive and wanted him roped. Long got a rope from his knap-sack and tied it around the hind legs. Making a noose, he put it over the panther's head and tied the rope to a sapling, and Jack pulled back on the other rope, thus stretching the panther full length. The front feet were tied without any danger and the panther was soon secured, but when they had him tied and ready to move home, they discovered he was bleeding at the throat. On looking closely, they discovered the dogs had cut the jugular vein, and before they had the other two animals skinned, the third one was dead.

On Bill Long's first trip over to Chess Creek, he took Colonel Smiley with him. Nearly everybody in those militia days was either a colonel, a major, or a captain. Under this system Pennsylvania had one year forty-eight generals. Colonel Smiley then lived between the town of Du Bois and where Luthersburg now is. They went on this outing for young wolves. On arriving near the head of Chess Creek, they found a very rocky ridge, when it was nearly dark. Long told Smiley they had better lay by for the night, as he thought there must be wolves near there. Smiley wanted to know where they would sleep. " There, upon that," said Long, pointing to a flat rock. Smiley then picked up a pheasant feather, remarking that he was going to have a downy pillow any way. Long, as usual, made a bed of hemlock boughs, and the two slept upon this bed on the rock. Smiley took his feather and there in this deep forest, with nought but the sky above their heads and the shadowy clouds that passed, wrapped in the arms of Morpheus, they slept until about the hour of one, when in the deep stillness of night they were awakened by what proved to be the bark of a dog wolf. Long told Smiley to listen to see if there would be an answer to this bark. Soon they heard an answer in a howl. Long then told the colonel to arise and set the compass for the direction of this howl, for this was a slut, and by this means they could see if the howl was repeated in the morning at the same place. About daylight the dog wolf commenced to bark again, and was answered by the slut with a howl. Long said, "'Set the compass now." This the colonel did, with the remark, "She is at the same place." "Now," said Long, "let us follow the direction," and the colonel, keeping the compass before him, they came, after about three-quarters of an hour, to where a big tree had been blown out of root. There was that she-wolf near to it. On coming up they found nine pups, and while they were getting the pups the old wolf came at them with her mouth wide open. Smiley drew his gun to shoot, but Long told him not to shoot, for that wolf was more to him than a horse, as he wanted to get her pups next year. Long then killed seven of the pups and took two of them to Oldtown, now Clearfield, where he sold the two live ones and got the bounty for the seven he had killed. Long got the pups of this wolf for three years afterwards, always near the same place. Shortly after this Long took his little boy Jack and started up Spring Creek on the Clarion River to the big elk lick there. He stayed at the big lick, and put Jack at a deer lick a short distance further up the creek. Long soon heard elk coming into his lick, when he fired and killed one. Jack, hearing his father's shot, came down to him the next morning. Long left the boy to skin this elk and started for Ridgway to get a drink and some provisions. On his way up to the town he killed five deer. When he returned Jack had finished skinning the elk, which Long then "jerked," took to Brookville, and sold in cuts.

Our elk was what scientists called wapiti. Other common names were red deer, stag, gray moose, or gray elk. They usually lived in families. Their horns were round, with twelve or more regular prongs. A perfectly developed set would weigh twenty or thirty pounds. They calved regularly in May.

Mike and Bill, with their dogs, started for the waters of North Fork, taking a bottle of whiskey with them. When near the head of this stream, the dogs took the scent of wolves and followed them under a large rock. Bill crawled under this rock and took from it eight young wolves. These scalps brought sixty-four dollars. Long went another time and took his son Jack, who was quite small, with him, also his dog, which he called Trim. I remember this dog well. He was most thoroughly trained, and I have seen Long on a drunken jamboree in John Smith's bar-room, in Brookville, command this dog Trim to smell for wolves, when the dog would actively and carefully scent every part of the room. In man the most developed sense is touch, in birds sight, and in dogs smell. While on this trip Long crossed over to the waters of Little Toby, and at a certain point he knew from the actions of Trim that there was game somewhere near. Looking in the same direction as the dog, he saw a big bear on a tree and two large wolves at the foot watching the bear. Long told Jack to hold Trim and he would crawl up and shoot the bear. As he got within shooting distance of the bear, Trim broke loose from Jack and the bear seeing the dog, came down the tree and ran off. The dog then took after the wolves. The slut wolf ran under a rock and the dog wolf ran in a different direction. Long and Trim pursued the dog wolf, and in a short time Trim came back yelping with the wolf at his heels. Trim had about one inch of white at the end of his tail which the wolf had bitten off. The wolf paid no attention to Long, but went straight on. At shooting distance Long shot him through the head. The two, father and son, then went to the rocks, and Bill crawled under, finding there seven young wolves,—six he caught, but the seventh he could not find though he could hear it bark. Long came out and gave his gun to Jack and told him that he would howl like a wolf and the pup would come out, and then for Jack to shoot it. The pup hearing Long howl, and thinking that he was its mother, came out, and Jack shot it. The seven pups and the old male made eight wolves at this time. Bill Long took the pups of that slut every spring for five years, finding them some place between the mouth of Little Toby and Brandycamp. When out on the ridge near where Bootjack, Elk County, now is, Long saw signs of a panther. He had two dogs with him, and soon came on the panther. The dogs were barking at the animal as it sat up on a rock. Long fired at the panther and wounded it. The dogs then rushed upon the panther, but soon let go, though not before one of them was badly crippled. Long at that time had a double-barrelled rifle. He then ran upon the panther, and, putting the muzzle of the gun to its head, killed it on the spot. In this adventure he had not only the skin of the panther to carry home, but the crippled dog also, which was too badly wounded to walk.

About the year 1845 Bill Long and two of Kahle's boys, John and Jacob, caught eight young wolves in a den. This den was on Mill Creek, that empties into the Clarion about three or four miles from where Siegel now is. John Kahle, on going in the ninth time, as he had done eight times before, armed with a torch, a stick four or five feet long with a hook on it to fasten into the wolves, and a rope tied to his foot, to pull him out by, caught the old one. Long and the Kahles thought she was not in. When young Kahle saw the wolf he pulled the rope and Long pulled Kahle out, but Kahle was not able to bring the wolf with him. When he told his story, Long tried to hire him for ten dollars to go in again, but Kahle would not. Long then tried to hire his brother, and he would not go in. Then Long whetted his knife, fixed his gun, and started in, but the way being too narrow for him, he came back before getting out of sight. After the fourth trial by Long, he came out and said he had seen the wolf, but could not shoot her.

As I remember Long, he was about five feet and four inches high, chubby, strongly built, active, athletic, and a great dancer,—danced what he called the "chippers" and the "crack,"—was cheerful, lively, and good-natured. He carried a heavy single-barrelled, muzzle-loading rifle. His belief was that he could shoot better with a heavy rifle than with a light one. Although there were dozens of professional hunters in this wilderness, this man was the king. He had an enduring frame, a catlike step, a steady nerve, keen eyesight, and a ripe knowledge of all the laws governing "still hunts for deer and bears." To reach the great skill he attained in mature life required natural talents, perseverance, sagacity, and habits of thought, as well as complete self-poise, self-control, and quickness of execution.

In these woods Long had great opportunities for perfecting himself in all that pertained to proficiency in a great hunter. Of the other hunters that approached him, I only recall his brothers, the Knapps, the three Vastbinders, the Lucases, the Bells, the Nolfs, Sibley, Fred. Hetrick, Indian Russell, and George Smith.

The professional hunter was created by the law of 1705 under the dynasty of William Penn. The law reads as follows:

"AN ACT FOR THE KILLING OF WOLVES—FOR PREVENTING THE DESTRUCTION OF SHEEP AND CATTLE BY WOLVES

"SECTION 1. *Be it enacted by John Evans, Esquire, by the Queen's royal approbation Lieutenant-Governor under William Penn, Esquire, absolute Proprietary and Governor-in-Chief of the Province of Pennsylvania and Territories, by and with the advice and consent of the freemen of the said Province in General Assembly met, and by the authority of the same,* That if any person within this province shall kill a dog-wolf, he shall have ten shillings, and if a bitch-wolf, fifteen shillings, to be paid out of the county stock. *Provided* such person brings the wolf's head to one of the justices of the peace of that county, who is to cause the ears and tongue of the said wolf to be cut off. And that the Indians, as well as others, shall be paid for killing wolves accordingly.

"SECTION 2. *And be it further enacted by the authority aforesaid,* That all and every person or persons who are willing to make it their business to kill wolves, and shall enter into recognizance before two or more justices of the peace of the respective counties where he or they dwell, with sufficient security in the sum of five pounds, that he or they shall and will make it his or their sole business, at least three days in every week, to catch wolves, shall have twenty-five shillings for every wolf, dog or bitch, that he or they shall so catch and kill within the time mentioned in the said recognizance, to be paid out of the county levies where the wolves are taken as aforesaid."

This act was repealed by the acts of 1782 and 1819.

Long's early dress was a coon-skin cap, moccasin shoes, a hunting-shirt, and generally buckskin breeches. The hunting-shirt was worn by all these early hunters, and sometimes in militia drill. It was a kind of frock, reached down to the thighs, had large sleeves, was open before, and lapped over a foot or so when belted. This shirt was made of linsey, coarse linen, or of dressed buckskin. The deer-skin shirt was cold and uncomfortable in wet and cold rains. The bosom of the shirt served as a receptacle for rye bread, wheat cakes, tow for cleaning the rifle, jerk, punk, flint and knocker to strike fire with, etc. Matches were first made in 1829, but were not used here for many years after that. The belt was tied behind; it usually held the mittens, bullet-bag, tomahawk, and scalping-knife in its long buckskin sheath. The moccasin in cold weather was sometimes stuffed with feathers, wool, and dry leaves. The heavy early rifles carried about forty-five bullets to a pound of lead.

The hand-to-hand conflicts of this noted hunter with panthers, bears, cata-mounts, wolves, elks, and bucks, both on the land and in the streams, if written out in full, would make a large volume. Elk and deer frequently took to the creeks, and a battle royal with knife and horns would have to be fought in the water. Long was several times mistaken while in a thicket for a wild animal, and careless hunters shot at him. Once his cheek was rubbed with a ball. Dozens of Indians and pale-faced men hunted in this wilderness as well as he, and the table giving an exhibit of the aggregate number of animals killed by Long during his life as a hunter only goes to show what a great zoological garden of wild animals this wilderness must have been.

William Long died in Hickory Kingdom, Clearfield County, Pennsylvania, in May, 1880, and was buried in the Conway Cemetery, leaving two sons, —Jack, a mighty hunter, and a younger son, William.

Peace to his ashes. In the haunts of this wilderness, scorched by the summer sun, pinched by the winds of winter wailing their voices like woe, separated for weeks at a time in his lonely cabins from the society of men and women, and then, too, awakened in the dark and dreary nights by the howl of the wolf, the panther's scream, and the owl's to-hoo! to-hoo! Long steadily, year in and year out, for sixty years pursued this wild, romantic life.

THE HABITS OF SOME OF THE GAME LONG HUNTED

Our bears cubbed in February, had two cubs at a birth, and these cubs were about the size of a brown rat, without hair, and blind for nine days. They were suckled by the mother for about three months, when they reached the size of a cat; then the mother took them out and taught them to eat nuts, berries, bugs, little animals, green corn, vegetables, hogs, sheep, and sometimes cattle. A full-grown bear would weigh four hundred pounds. He was exceedingly strong. He could carry a heavy burden and walk on his hind legs for a long distance. He was a good tree-climber and was not quarrelsome, but if other animals trespassed on his rights he became furious and vindictive.

He frequently gnawed himself out of hunters' pens, was a bold, intelligent beast, and his meat was considered a delicacy by the hunters.

Bears lived in "homes," holes, or dens, and sometimes in a rocky place there would be a "community." They, like deer, follow their own paths. He entered his den about Christmas time to hibernate, and remained there

A female panther (Pennsylvania) two years old, not full grown

until about the 1st of May, when he would come out, eat weeds and grass to purge himself, after which he would eat anything.

Our panther was fully as strong as the bear, but was rather cowardly, and especially fearful of dogs. A single blow from one forefoot or a bite from a panther would kill a dog. As a precaution, the panther hunter always had a trained dog with him, for a single bark from a dog would often scare a panther up a tree. The panther, as a rule, sought and sprang upon his

A male panther (Pennsylvania) three years old, full grown

victim in the dark. He could throw a buck, hog, or cow without a struggle. A panther attained sometimes a length of ten feet from nose to end of tail. They lived in dens and had two cubs at a time.

Rowe, of Clearfield, says of the hunter Dan Turner, " Once, when going out to a ' bear wallow,' his attention was attracted by a panther acting in a strange manner. He soon saw a large bear approaching it. With hair erect and eyes glaring, the panther gnashed his teeth, and, waiting until bruin came up, sprang upon him. A mortal struggle ensued. Turner watched with much interest the fight, which lasted some ten minutes or more. At last the growls of the firece combatants became faint, and the struggle ceased. The panther slowly disengaged himself from his dead enemy and took position upon the carcass. It was now Turner's time, and, raising his rifle, he shot the panther in the head. After examining it, he was of the opinion that it could have lived but a very few minutes longer. Nearly every bone in its body was broken, and its flesh was almost reduced to a pulp by the blows and hugs of the bear."

Our wolves always had their dens in the wildest, most hidden part of the wilderness. They always managed to get under the rocks or ground to shelter themselves and young from all storms. The male fed the female when the " pups" were small. He would travel a great distance in search of food, and if what he found was too heavy to carry home, he would gorge himself with it and go home and vomit it up for the family. The wolf and fox were very chary and hard to trap. But Long and other hunters knew their habits so well that they could always outwit them.

A wolf could carry a sheep for miles in this way: seize it by the throat and throw it over or on his back. Wolves hunted the deer in packs; they all hunted together until a deer was started. The pack would keep up the chase until they were tired; then one wolf would keep up the chase at full speed, while the balance of the pack watched, and when the deer turned a circle, fresh and rested wolves struck in and pursued; thus the deer was pursued alternately by fresh wolves and soon tired out, and would then fly to some stream; the wolves would follow, and while the deer would remain in the stream the wolves would separate, a part of the pack forming in line on each side of the stream, when the deer would become an easy prey to these ravenous creatures.

The most dangerous animal or reptile was the rattlesnake. We had two colors,—the black and yellow spotted. Millions of them inhabited these woods, and some were four and five feet long. Snakes, as well as other wild animals, travel and seek their food in the night. To escape this danger, each pioneer kept a large herd of hogs, who would kill and eat snakes with impunity. Dogs, too, were faithful in this direction. But how did the woodsman and hunter escape? Well, he wore woollen stockings, moccasins with anklets, and buckskin breeches. A snake could not bite through these, and at night he usually laid his head on the body of his dog to protect his upper extremities.

It was seldom that the elk or deer had twins. The bear, panther, and wolf always had a litter. Wolves reared in the same pack lived friendly, but strange males always fought.

The deer, when frightened, circled round and round, but never left his haunt. The elk would start on a trot, and never stop under ten or fifteen miles.

The bear was and is a wanderer,—here to-day and away to-morrow. The wolf and panther were fierce and shy. Deer killed the rattler in this way: humping themselves together, and jumping sideways on the snake with all four feet, the hoofs of the deer would cut the snake in pieces. Elk travel in families or herds; the does lead and the bucks bring up the rear. They browse in winter and paw the snow for moss or wild grass.

" When it is remembered that the American elk ofttimes attains a weight of one thousand pounds, a height of sixteen hands, and has spiked antlers of five feet in length and four feet spread. some idea of the offensive capacities of one of these rearing, prancing, snorting creatures may be conceived.

" It must also be remembered that an elk fights with his sharply pointed front hoofs, as well as with his antlers, rearing on his hind legs and delivering swift, terrific lunges right out from the shoulder.

" The bucks become dangerous each fall, at mating time, and in the spring, before their horns drop off; for all male deer shed their horns each spring. By September the prongs are replaced. Each year the male elk grows an extra prong upon his antlers. The expert may ascertain the age of the creature by counting the prongs. However, if the antler should be broken off during a fight, or through any accident, the broken side grows out next season as a straight horn, without the usual prongs.

" During their seasons of anger the bucks will attack any living thing."

LAST PANTHERS AND WOLVES IN NORTHWESTERN PENNSYLVANIA

The last bounty paid for wolves and panthers in Elk County as shown by the books and vouchers on file in the office of the county commissioners,

Wolves.—J. R. Green, November 8, 1871, one; James Bennett, Jr., October 28, 1873, one; A. J. Rummer, December 13, 1874, one; J. R. Green, October, 1874, one; John Myers, December 14, 1874, one; George Smith, April 8, 1874, two; Charles A. Brown, December 28, 1874, one; O. B. Fitch, December, 1877, one; and this was the last wolf killed in Elk County. The last wolf reported killed in Forest County was by Emanuel Dobson, Jenks Township, in 1884. The last wolf killed in McKean County was by J. W. Starks, June 24, 1868. A wolf is reported killed in 1886. The records show that a wolf was killed in Potter County in 1890. A wolf is reported killed in Tioga County by Levi Kissinger in 1885.

Panthers.—Alexander Wykoff, February 18, 1850, one; Thomas Dent, May 20, 1850, one; Peter Smith, January 5, 1852, one; E. G. Deering, February 18, 1852, one; Peter Smith, March 7, 1853, six; Nelson Gardner, June 29, 1857, one. These were all killed in Elk County. Nelson Gardner, who lived above Ridgway, killed the last panther in Elk County.

During the thirties, when Jefferson County still embraced what is now Forest and Elk Counties, the bounties paid for panther, wolf, fox, and wildcat scalps fell a little short of four hundred dollars a year. The last bounties paid for panthers and wolves killed in Jefferson County was in 1856. The record is as follows: March 18, 1856, Jacob Stahlman, one wolf; March 24, 1856, Mike Long, five wolves; May 17, 1856, Andrew Bowers, Gaskill Township, one wolf; November 19, 1856, Adam Hetrick, one panther, killed on Maxwell Run, in Polk Township. George Smith had chased this panther across the line of Elk into Jefferson County. The panther was an old and very large one. Fred. Hetrick, a great hunter, lived then at or near Greenbriar, and this panther commenced to kill and feast on his sheep. The panther made the mistake of his life. Fred. knew at once what was killing his sheep, so he organized a hunting expedition against Mr. Panther, of himself, his son Adam, and four dogs. The dogs soon treed the panther. Fred. shot him while on a limb, in the neck. The panther then sprang from the tree at the dogs, killing one and badly injuring the second. He would soon have killed all four, but Adam gave him a second shot from the rifle, and this shot killed the last panther in Jefferson County.

It is reported that two panthers were killed on the Driftwood in what is now Cameron County by Isaac Rammage in 1851. The last panther in what is now Forest County was killed at Panther Rocks in 1848. A panther was killed in McKean County by William Eastman and George Smith about 1858 or 1859. The last panther killed in Warren County was in Corydon Township, by Sylvester C. Williams, December 18, 1863, and the last wolf killed in Warren County was by James Irwin in Mead Township, March 17, 1866. The last panther killed in Tioga County was in 1841.

" JACK LONG"

Andrew Jackson Long, a son of William and Nancy Barlett Long, *née* Mason, was born in Jefferson County, Pennsylvania, in 1829, on what is known and now called the Horn farm. He moved with his father to the neighborhood of Falls Creek, in Clearfield County, when he was about twelve years old. I knew him from my boyhood, and visited with him in his home for two days in 1899, when he gave me the following facts in regard to his hunting career:

"I have killed six deer in a day, often four or five in a day. I have killed four panthers in a day, and twenty during my life. The last panther I killed was in 1872. It was the largest one, and measured eleven feet from

179

tip of nose to end of tail. I have killed about three hundred and fifty bears. In 1898 I killed nine bears. I have killed about fifteen hundred deer. I have killed about one hundred and fifty wolves. The last wolves—two in number—I killed in 1881. I have killed foxes, wild-cats, catamounts, etc., without number. I caught in traps twenty otter and one black fox.

"When hungry, wolves and bears will eat one another. A bear will fight for its cubs even to death; a panther will not. Wolves make some fight for their young but not a close one. A large bear will kill a panther in a fight. Bears have wallows, and have paths for miles to and from their dens. These paths are usually blazed on hemlock-trees. Each bear, big or little, travelling the same path, will bite the blazed trees. Wolves have their paths too. Wolves will kill a deer for their young, cut it up, and bury it along their paths. Panthers usually have from two to three cubs in September of each year. A panther will eat only fresh meat.

"I have tamed panthers until they were about two years old, when they became vicious and had to be killed. I have tamed wolves and used them for the same purposes as a dog. They would follow me as dogs, and hunted with me, but at the age of two years I generally had to kill them. For bear-traps, I used venison, groundhog, and beef, for bait. A bear will patiently dig a whole day for a groundhog. I have found many deer horns in the woods, that were locked by combat, each deer having died from this fight. In 1853 my father and I killed five grown panthers on Medix Run. In March of the same year Peter Smith and Erasmus Morey killed six full-grown panthers in the same neighborhood, making eleven in all."

Andrew Jackson Long died at his home, about two miles from Du Bois, June 18, 1900.

CHAPTER VIII

In 1791 and 1793 a State road through this wilderness to what is now called Waterford was incepted, agitated, and legalized; but, owing to the Indian troubles of 1791, '92, '93, and '94, all efforts had to be stopped and all legal proceedings annulled and repealed. The Indian troubles were settled in 1794 by war and purchases, and then legal steps were again taken to open up this great northwest in 1795 and 1796. The reader will please bear in mind that Le Bœuf is now Waterford, Pennsylvania, Presque Isle is now Erie City, Pennsylvania, and Bald Eagle's Nest is now Milesburg, Centre County, Pennsylvania.

EARLY ROADS AND TRAILS

In 1784-85 the old State Road from the east was opened through to Fort Pitt in the west over what had been previously a path, or what was called Forbes's Trail. This trail passed through Bedford, Westmoreland, and other counties. In those days the State surveyed and laid out county seats and sold the lots. The lots were generally sold at auction. All government stores, as well as groceries and goods of every description, were for a long time carried from the east to the west on pack-horses over trails. One man would sometimes drive a hundred horses.

Guards from the militia were a necessity for their trains. Guards were also a necessity for the road surveyors and road-makers. A body of about fifty militia was the usual number, and sometimes these soldiers would do some work as well as guard the road-makers. Transportation was also carried over Meade's Trail, which passed through West Reynoldsville, in the same way. In 1787 the only road from Fort Pitt to Le Bœuf (now Waterford) was a trail or path through what is now Butler County and up the Allegheny River. The turnpike over or across the old Forbes's Trail was finished to Pittsburg in 1819.

In 1794 the great problem was a thoroughfare from the east to the northwest. The defence of the western portion of the State from Indians required the State and the national authorities to be constantly on the alert. On the

28th of February, 1794, the Legislature passed an act for " raising soldiers for the defence of the western frontiers." Also at this time a combined effort of the nation and State was made to lay out a town at Presque Isle (now Erie) on Lake Erie.

WHY THE STATE ROAD WAS MADE

In order to protect these frontiers from the British and Indians a road through this wilderness seemed an absolute necessity, hence an act was passed through the Legislature previous to or in 1794, authorizing the surveying and making of a State road from Reading to Presque Isle (Erie City). Colonel William Irvine and Andrew Ellicott were the commissioners. These men were also commissioners to lay out the town of Erie (Presque Isle). The official instructions to the commissioners and Captain Denny were as follows:

" PHILADELPHIA, March 1, 1794.

" GENTLEMEN,—In providing for the general defence of the frontiers, the Legislature has authorized me to form a detachment of troops, for carrying into effect the act directing a town to be laid out at or near Presque Isle; and as the subject of the commission to survey and lay out a road from Reading to Presque Isle may be promoted by the same measure, I have instructed Captain Denny, the commanding officer of the detachment, to grant to you as commissioners all the aid and protection that is compatible with a due attention to the particular charge which is confided to him. ·Under these circumstances, I trust you will find it convenient to proceed immediately in the execution of your work.

" I am, gentlemen,
" Your most obedient servant,
" THOMAS MIFFLIN.

" To WILLIAM IRVINE and ANDREW ELLICOTT, Commissioners for laying out a road from Reading to Presque Isle."

" PHILADELPHIA, March 1, 1794.

" The Legislature having made provision for surveying and opening two roads,—one from Reading and the other from French Creek to Presque Isle, —it is obvious that the establishment of the town is intimately connected with those objects; and, therefore, you shall deem it your duty to grant all the aid and protection to the respective commissioners and contractors employed in surveying and opening those roads that is compatible with due attention to the particular charge confided in you.

" Your most obedient servant, ·
" THOMAS MIFFLIN.

" To EBENEZER DENNY, ESQ., Captain of the Allegheny Company, &c."

Captain Ebenezer Denny, with a detachment of soldiers, was ordered by the government to accompany these men. On the arrival of Denny and the soldiers at what is now Franklin, Venango County, he discovered that the Indians were cross and ugly, and General Wilkins, in talking to Mr. Dallas, said, "The English are fixed in their opposition to the opening of the road to Presque Isle, and are determined to prevent it by the English and Indians." Orders were then given to Captain Denny to go no farther than Le Bœuf (now Waterford), and occupy two small block-houses, which had been erected for Commissioners Irvine and Ellicott.

This was the first attempt to open up an east and west road through this wilderness. Governor Mifflin applied to the President for a thousand militia soldiers to enforce this work; but the President counselled peace. Work was suspended at Presque Isle, and it was not until in April, 1795, that all difficulties were removed and Colonel William Irvine and Andrew Ellicott resumed work. At this time Irvine commanded the troops and Ellicott had charge of the surveyors.

"'An Act to provide for opening a road from near the Bald Eagle's Nest, in Mifflin County, to Le Bœuf, in the county of Allegheny,' passed April 10, 1790, published in full in Bioren's 'Laws of Pennsylvania,' vol. vi. p. 24. The reference in the preamble of this act to a road 'in part laid out from Reading to Presque Isle,' is probably to an act passed April 11, 1793, appropriating certain sums of money for laying out a large number of roads within the State. The following appropriation is made in the first section: 'For viewing and laying out a road from Reading to Presque Isle, one thousand three hundred and thirty-three dollars.' This act appears in Bioren's 'Laws,' vol. iv. p. 277 *et seq.* It is possible, however, that the reference was intended to apply to a road from the Bald Eagle's Nest to the Allegheny River, which was surveyed and laid out under an act passed April 4, 1796, entitled 'An Act for laying out and opening sundry roads within this Commonwealth, and for other purposes.' This act will be found in full in Bioren's 'Laws,' vol. v. p. 187. By this act the governor was authorized and empowered to appoint 'three skilful persons to view the ground, and estimate the expense of opening and making a good wagon road from the Bald Eagle's Nest, or the end of the Nittany Mountain, to the town of Erie at Presque Isle.'

"Under this last act the governor, on the 13th day of April, 1796, appointed William Irvine, Andrew Ellicott, and George Wilson commissioners to make the survey. Andrew Ellicott declined the appointment, and Joseph Ellicott was appointed in his place. These men met to examine the situation of the country at the Bald Eagle's Nest and at the end of Nittany Mountain, and determined to start at the Bald Eagle's Nest, now Milesburg, Centre County. It appears, however, that William Irvine returned home, and George Wilson and Joseph Ellicott proceeded to make the survey. Their draft and report are among the records of the department, at Harrisburg, and show their work from the Bald Eagle's Nest to the Allegheny River, a distance of one hundred and sixteen miles by their measurement. After reaching the Allegheny River, they say that in consequence of the failure of horses [gnats and flies killed them], the scarcity of provisions, the advanced season of the year, and various other obstacles which retarded the prosecution of the business, they were compelled to relinquish the object of their mission, and have left above thirty-six miles of the road unfinished.'"

THE SURVEY

The point on the Allegheny River where these surveyors stopped in the fall of 1796 was on the land where Eli Holeman settled in 1800. It is three miles below Tionesta borough, Forest County, Pennsylvania. For the twenty years of travel and traffic of emigrants and others over this old State Road each and all had to ford or cross this ferry. The old State Road never passed through where Clarion now is, or through Franklin or Meadville. It passed through the wilderness away north of these towns, but connected with other State roads running through them. All of the county histories which have been written prior to this one confound this road with the turnpike, which was not finished or opened for traffic until November, 1824. At Brookville the turnpike survey in 1818 took a separate and distinct southerly course from the old State Road, and passed through Franklin, Meadville, and so forth.

THE ROAD COMPLETED

The road was officially taken from the contractors and a quietus entered as to the contract April 2, 1804. The course of the road through what is now Winslow Township was through Rathmel, down Sandy Lick to the south side, crossing the creek between Sandy Valley and near where West Reynoldsville now is, where it deflected to the right over the hill, through the farm now occupied by Robert Waite. This State Road was the great public thoroughfare for emigrants from the east to the northwest for a period of twenty years, until the turnpike was finished in 1824. A portion of about seven miles is still in use from Brookville to the Clarion County line, parallel with but north of that part of the turnpike which extends from Brookville to Corsica.

SANCTIONED BY THE LEGISLATURE

The following is the act which authorized the building of the State Road, of which this article is a history:

"AN ACT FOR LAYING OUT AND OPENING SUNDRY ROADS WITHIN THIS COM-
MONWEALTH, AND FOR OTHER PURPOSES

" WHEREAS, From the increasing population of the northern and northwestern parts of this State, it becomes expedient at this time to provide for
the laying out and opening the necessary roads, for the accommodation of
the same; therefore,

" SECTION 1. *Be it enacted by the Senate and House of Representatives,*
etc., That the governor be, and he is hereby, authorized and empowered to
appoint three skilful persons to view the ground and estimate the expense of
opening and making a good wagon road from the town of Northampton,
in the county of Northampton, to the mouth of Tioga, in the county of
Luzerne, and from thence, by the most practical route, to the northern
line of this State; and three skilful persons to view the ground and estimate
the expense of opening and making a good wagon road from the Bald
Eagle's Nest, or the end of the Nittany Mountain, to the town of Erie, at
Presque Isle; and to cause the said roads to be surveyed and staked out by
the most practicable routes; and also to cause drafts of the roads to be made
in profile, and report to the Legislature the proportional parts of the expense
that will be incurred in each county through which the said road will pass;
provided that the commissioners thus appointed shall not stake out any part
of the said roads when they may be carried on roads heretofore laid out and
opened agreeably to the provisions of former laws of this State.

" SECTION 2. *And be it further enacted by the authority aforesaid,* That
the governor be, and he is hereby, empowered to contract, either with individuals, or with companies, for opening a road from Pittsburg, by the way of
Fort Franklin, to Le Bœuf, and to draw his warrant on the State Treasurer
for a sum not exceeding two thousand dollars, to defray the expense of
laying out the roads to Tioga and Erie; a sum not exceeding four thousand
dollars, to defray the expense of opening the road from Pittsburg, by Fort
Franklin, to Le Bœuff. *Provided always,* That all contracts to be made by
virtue of this act shall be registered by the governor, according to the
directions of the eighth section of the act, entitled ' An Act to provide for
the opening and improving sundry navigable waters and roads within the
Commonwealth,' passed the thirteenth day of April, one thousand seven
hundred and ninety-one.*

" SECTION 3. *And be it further enacted, etc.,* That the governor be, and
he is hereby, empowered to draw his warrant in favor of Joseph Horsefield
for any sum not exceeding five hundred dollars, to be applied toward removing the fallen timber and other obstructions in the road leading from Jacob
Heller's tavern, in Northampton County, to Wilkesbarre, in Luzerne County.

" Passed 4th April, 1796."

---

* For the act referred to in this section, see vol. iv. chap. 1558.

CONTRACT AND REPORTS

Here is a copy of the contract and the reports of John Fleming relating to the road from Bald Eagle's Nest to Le Bœuff:

"ARTICLES OF AGREEMENT made and entered into this third day of July, in the year of our Lord one thousand seven hundred and ninety-nine, between Thomas Mifflin, Governor of the Commonwealth of Pennsylvania, of the one part, and Samuel Miles and Roger Alden, of the City of Philadelphia, Esquires, of the other part.

"WHEREAS, In and by an Act of the General Assembly, entitled ' An Act to provide for opening a Road from near the Bald Eagle's Nest, in Mifflin county, to Le Bœuff, in the county of Allegheny,' passed the tenth day of April, in the year one thousand seven hundred and ninety-nine, the Governor is empowered to contract for opening and improving the said road in the manner and on the terms in the said act prescribed: AND WHEREAS, The said Samuel Miles and Roger Alden have made proposals for entering into the said contract upon principles which appear to the Governor most likely to accomplish the good purposes by the Legislature intended: Now THESE ARTICLES WITNESS, That the said Samuel Miles and Roger Alden, jointly and severally for themselves, their Heirs, Executors, and Administrators, covenant, promise, and agree to and with the said Thomas Mifflin and his successors, Governors of the Commonwealth of Pennsylvania, in consideration of the Covenant on behalf of the said Commonwealth hereinafter made, That they, the said Samuel Miles and Roger Alden, their Heirs, Executors, and Administrators, shall and will, well and faithfully, and with all convenient diligence, open, extend, and improve the said Road in manner following,—that is to say: That the Road shall be opened generally of such width as to enable and admit two waggons to pass each other, except only in such place or places as from great natural difficulty of Mountains, Hills, Rocks, and Morasses shall render such an undertaking impracticable or unreasonably laborious and expensive, considering the public consideration therefor given. But in all such place or places there shall be a good passage of at least ten feet wide, with proper and convenient passing places in view: And that the said Contractors will advance by anticipation (if necessary) the sums of money requisite to open the said Road in the manner aforesaid. And the said Thomas Mifflin, in consideration of the Covenants and undertaking of the said Contractors, and by virtue of the power in the said Act of Assembly to him given, covenants, promises, and agrees to and with the said Samuel Miles and Roger Alden, their Executors, Administrators, and Assigns, that they shall have and receive the sum of Five Thousand Dollars, to be paid out of the first money arising from the sale of the reserved Lands & Lots at the Towns of Erie, Franklin, Warren, and Waterford: And for which sum of Five Thousand Dollars, the said Thomas Mifflin covenants, promises, and agrees to draw his Warrant or Warrants on the State Treasurer in favor of the said Contractors. In Witness whereof the parties have hereunto set their respective hands & seals the day and year first above written.

(Signed)   " SAMUEL MILES, [SEAL]

ROGER ALDEN, [SEAL]

THOS. MIFFLIN. [SEAL]

" Sealed and Delivered
in the presence of
    A. W. FOSTER,
    JNO. MILES."

To the above contract appear the names of George Fox, James Phillips, and Tench Coxe as sureties for its " true, faithful, perfect, and diligent performance," and also the following endorsement on the back of the same:

" The Governor, being satisfied, from three several reports of John Fleming, Esquire, (the two first dated on the 16th of December, 1801, & the 10th of January, 1803, respectively; & the last without date, but delivered into the Secretary's Office in the month of January last,) that Samuel Miles & Roger Alden, Esquires, have completed their contract for opening a road from near the Bald Eagle's Nest to Le Bœuff, by opening and improving the same agreeably to the terms of said contract, as far as could reasonably be expected from the situation and nature of the country through which said road passes, & the public consideration given therefor, this day directed a quietus to be entered upon the contract.

(Signed)   " T. M. THOMPSON, Sec.

" April the 2nd, 1804."

" TO HIS EXCELLENCY THOMAS MCKEAN, ESQUIRE, Governor of the State of Pennsylvania:

" SIR,—In pursuance of your Excellency's letter appointing me a Commissioner to view and report on that part of the State Road from Milesburg to Le Bœuff, which was undertaken to be opened by Col. Samuel Miles, I proceeded to Milesburg and viewed the said Road as shewn to me by Mr. Richard Miles, and beg leave to submit the following Report:

" Beginning at Milesburg the road crosses Bald Eagle creek, over which is a sufficient wooden Bridge, thence up the said creek on the north side of it for five miles; the road passable for waggons. Within these five miles, on the west side of Wallis's run, there is some wet ground a little swampy.

" Leaving the Bald Eagle creek and thence to the foot of the Allegheny mountain, five miles, the Road is good excepting some trees that have fallen across it since it was opened.

" Across the mountain is three miles. The ascent is one mile, of which 240 perches are dug, in some places, nine feet wide. Toward the top it is too steep for carriages. The descent of the mountain is about two miles and gradual.

" About one mile from the foot of the mountain is a small run difficult to pass.

" Here I must beg leave to remark, as applicable to this as well as to other small runs that may be mentioned in this Report, that many very small streams in the country over which this road passes run in narrow channels, the bottoms of which lie from one to three feet below the surface of the earth. A footman can step over many of them, where, from the nature of the soil at the bottom, a horse is in great danger of being mired.

" After crossing the last-mentioned run there is a hill which in ascent there are thirty perches, and in descent twelve perches not passable for waggons for want of digging. Near this are two small runs, both difficult to pass.

" To Phillipsburg from thence, a distance of more than eight miles, the Road is good, excepting some very swampy ground on the east of what is called the five mile run, and some miry ground at Coldstream, one mile from Phillipsburg. Some more work is necessary on the hill west of the five mile run. The whole distance from Milesburg to Phillipsburg is twenty-six miles.

" Passing Phillipsburg one mile is Moshannon creek. It is not bridged nor is it fordable at the place where the Road crosses it at any season. There is some timber prepared at the place for a bridge. It is about six perches wide with steep banks. There is a Fording about half a mile below. Three miles further the road is good excepting a few wet places. Within two miles further there are two runs, the banks of which are dug, and the road is good.

"Thence to Clearfield creek, four miles, some digging done in two places, and on the hill descending to Clearfield forty perches are well dug; the road is good.

" Thence to the Susquehanna river, five miles, the road good. The breadth of the river is twelve perches.

" Thence to Anderson's creek, nearly three miles, some digging done on Hogback hill. The road in general good.

" Thence to a branch of Anderson's creek, about eight miles, several places dug and some bridges made: the road is tolerably good. More digging and bridges wanted.

" Thence to the waters of Stump creek, about three miles, several bridges made and digging done in some places; the road good.

" Thence five miles, crossing two ridges on each of which there is digging done, and several runs, two of which are bridged. In the latter part of these five miles are two runs necessary to be bridged. With this exception the road is tolerably good.

" Thence to a branch of Sandy Lick creek, about six miles, in several places the road is dug and some bridges made. The road tolerably good.

" Thence about three miles; several steep banks, deep runs and wet places; road not passable.

HISTORY OF NORTHWESTERN PENNSYLVANIA

" Thence to the end of Col. Miles' opening is four miles. The road good.

" From Milesburg until the road crosses the Susquehanna the road is opened from sixteen to twenty feet wide, and from thence to the end it is opened from twelve to sixteen feet wide. The whole length of the road opened as aforesaid by Col. Miles is seventy-four miles and eighty-six perches.

(Signed)   " J<small>NO</small>. F<small>LEMING</small>.

" December 16, 1801."

Only the commonest goods were hauled into this county from Philadelphia over the old State Road. The freightage from Philadelphia to Port Barnett was about six dollars per one hundred pounds, and it took four weeks to come from Philadelphia. In 1800 wheat brought one dollar and a half a bushel, wheat flour four and five dollars per one hundred pounds, corn one dollar per bushel, oats seventy-five cents, potatoes sixty-five cents. Tobacco was sold by the yard at four cents per yard, common sugar thirty-three cents, and loaf (white sugar) fifty cents per pound. A hunter's rifle cost twenty-five dollars, a yoke of oxen eighty dollars, boots from one to three dollars, a pair of moccasins about three or four shillings.

S. B. Rowe, in his " Pioneer History of Clearfield County," says, " The State, in order to connect the western frontier with the eastern settlements, had laid out several roads, among others one leading from Milesburg to Erie. This road was opened in the year 1803. It crossed the Susquehanna River near the residence of Benjamin Jordan.

" The Milesburg and Le Bœuff road became subsequently an important and leading thoroughfare. It was a road of the worst kind, laid out with very little skill, and made with a great deal of dishonesty. It had but one bridge— at Moshannon—between Bellefonte and Anderson's Creek, and to avoid digging the hill-side, Anderson's Creek was crossed three times in less than two miles. Large quantities of merchandise passed over it, principally upon pack-horses, companies of which, exceeding a score in number, might often be seen traversing it. Until the place of this road was supplied by an artificial road, located on or near its bed, it was the principal road leading to Erie and the great West. About the time the State Road was supplanted by the turnpike the now almost forgotten Conestoga wagon, with its heavy horses, walking leisurely along, their tread measured by the jingling of bells, afforded cheaper and better mode of transportation for goods. A trip to Philadelphia to purchase goods or to ' see the sights' of that village was then quite an undertaking, and called for weeks of preparation."

" T<small>O</small> <small>HIS</small> E<small>XCELLENCY</small> T<small>HOMAS</small> M<small>C</small>K<small>EAN</small>, E<small>SQUIRE</small>, *Governor of the Commonwealth of Pennsylvania:*

 " Agreeably to your Instructions received through the Secretary of the Commonwealth, I proceeded to review that part of the road leading from

Milesburg to Le Bœuff, opened by Major Roger Alden, and beg leave to submit the following report:

"Beginning at the west end of Col. Samuel Miles' opening,

"2 miles, a hill with some digging; the road good.

"1½ miles to the crossing of the north branch of Sandy Lick creek. The road good.

"9 m farther. The road good.

"4 m of rough road. There is in this distance four streams of water crossing it, with bad hills on each side of each of them. They are generally all dug that carriages may pass.

"4 m farther to Toby's creek [Clarion River]: some digging done on the descent of the hill going down to the creek—the road tolerably good.

"2 m farther to the hill descending to Little Toby creek [Venango County]. The road good. When I reported before, this descent to the creek was impassable with waggons; since that time the road has been changed, and laid on better ground, and the road dug. The road good. West of the creek the road is somewhat difficult for carriages.

"4 m. The road passable for carriages.

"1 m. A hill descending to Licking creek, bad, as is also the hill on the west side of the creek. There is some digging done here. These hills comprehend a distance exceeding a mile.

"10 m. Road good, lying on chestnut ridges. In this distance there is little difference in the road.

"4 m to the Allegheny river, lying over pine ridges, some of them steep. The hill to the river near a mile long. Since my last report some bridging and digging has been done. Passable for carriages.

"6 m from the crossing of the Allegheny river to Pithole creek. The road crosses several ridges, one of which is dug.

"2 m of good road.

"2 m of very swampy ground, principally bridged and causewayed. Passable with carriages.

"3 m to the crossing of the south-east branch of Oil creek. There are several bridges made in this distance. There is a good one across the creek. The road good.

"7 m to the crossing of the N. W. branch Oil creek. There are several bridges made in this distance. Since my last report the fording of the creek is changed for the better.

"1 m. West of the creek for near a mile the road is altered, making the ascent of the hills that I noticed easier. They are still difficult for carriages.

"7 m to where this road intersects the public road from Pittsburg to Le Bœuff by the way of Franklin. In this distance the road in general is good. A number of bridges are made on it.

"3 m to the crossing of Muddy creek—several bridges made. The road something wet.

"12 m to the crossing of French creek—a number of bridges made.

"3 m to Le Bœuff—a number of bridges made, and the road good. From the intersection of the Franklin road to Le Bœuff the soil is generally wet.

"I would generally observe that a considerable quantity of timber is fallen across the road, and the sprouts in such quantities grown up in many places, since the road was opened, as to render travelling difficult. There has not been any cutting done since I reported, unless where the road is changed in the two places before mentioned.

"I am Sir,

"Your Excellency's very humble servant,

"JOHN FLEMING."

An act making appropriation for certain improvements on this road in Erie, Crawford, Venango, Jefferson, and Armstrong Counties was passed in 1811, and appropriating two thousand four hundred dollars therefor.

In 1749 the governor-general of Canada sent an expedition under Celeron de Bienville down what is now known as the Allegheny and Ohio Rivers, to take possession of the country in the name of the king of France. The command embraced two hundred and fifteen French and Canadian soldiers and fifty-five Indians. Father Bonnecamp, a chaplain of this expedition, drew a map of the route, locating the tribes of Indians, and giving the Indian names of the tributaries of these rivers and also the names of the Indian villages. This manuscript map was deposited and is still in the archives of the Department de la Farine in Paris, and is styled "Map of a Voyage made on the Beautiful River in New Flanders, 1749, by Rev. Father Bonnecamp, Jesuit Mathematician." The map is very correct, considering all the circumstances. It has been reproduced on a smaller scale by George Dallas Albert and published in "The Frontier Forts of Pennsylvania," in vol. ii., with an explanation of the map, French names, and their corresponding American designations. In this map I find Rivière au Vermillon emptying into the Allegheny River, corresponding to the exact location of what is now called Red Bank Creek, and unfortunately translated by Mr. Albert as Mahoning Creek. On the Allegheny River going downward I find Rivière aux Bœuf, Beef, or Buffalo River, now called French Creek: then Rivière au Fiel,—Gall River or Clarion River; third, Riviére au Vermillon or Red Bank Creek; fourth, a stream not named, which must have been Mahoning; and then Attique, a village, or what is now Kittanning. Mr. Albert should have named the undesignated stream Mahoning and the Vermilion River Red Bank.

In 1798 this stream was designated by legal statute as Sandy Lick or Red Bank Creek, but later by common acceptance the name Sandy Lick was applied to that portion above where the North Fork unites, and Red Bank from Brookville to the mouth.

"The first lot of lumber which Barnett and Scott sent down the Red Bank was a small platform of timber, with poles instead of oars as the propelling power. There was a flood in this stream in 1806 which reached eight or ten feet up the trees on the flats.

"One thousand dollars was appropriated by the act of Assembly ' making appropriations for certain internal improvements,' approved March 24, 1817, for the purpose of improving this creek, and Levi Gibson and Samuel C. Orr were appointed commissioners to superintend the application of the money. By the act of April 4, 1826, ' Sandy Lick, or Red Bank Creek,' was declared

Driving logs

a public highway only for the passage of boats, rafts, etc., descending it. That act also made it lawful for all persons owning lands adjoining this stream to erect mill-dams across it, and other water-works along it, to keep them in good repair, and draw off enough water to operate them on their own land, but required them ' to make a slope from the top, descending fifteen feet for every foot the dam is high, and not less than forty feet in breadth,' so as to afford a good navigation, and not to infringe the rights and privileges of any owner of private property.

"The first flat-boat that descended this stream was piloted by Samuel Knapp, in full Indian costume. In 1832 or 1833 two boats loaded with sawed lumber owned by Uriah Matson, which found a good market in Cincinnati, with the proceeds of which Matson purchased the goods with which he opened his store at Brookville."—*History of Armstrong County.*

An act declaring the rivers Ohio and Allegheny, and certain branches thereof, public highways,—

"SECTION 1. *Be it enacted, etc.*, That from and after the passing of this act, the river Ohio, from the western boundary of the State up to the mouth of the Monongahela, Big Beaver Creek, from the mouth of the first fork in the seventh district of donation land, Allegheny River, from the mouth to the northern boundary of the State, French Creek to the town of Le Bœuf, and Conewango Creek, from the mouth thereof to the State line, Cussawago Creek, from the mouth of the main forks, Little Coniate Creek, from the mouth up to the inlet of the little Coniate Lake, Toby's Creek, from the mouth up to the second fork (now Clarion River, and Johnsonburg was the second fork), Oil Creek, from the mouth up to the main fork, Broken Straw Creek, from the mouth up to the second fork, Sandy Lick, or Red Bank Creek, from the mouth up to the second great fork, be, and the same are hereby declared to be public streams and highways for the passage of boats and rafts; and it shall and may be lawful for the inhabitants or others desirous of using the navigation of the said river and branches thereof to remove all natural obstructions in the said river and branches aforesaid."

Passed March 21, 1798. Recorded in Law Book No. VI., page 245.

The first fork was at Brookville's site, the second great fork was at Port Barnett.

An act, No. 189, declaring Little Toby's Creek, Black Lick Creek, Little Oil Creek, and Clark's Creek public highways,—

"SECTION 1. *Be it enacted, etc.*, That from and after the passage of this act Little Toby's Creek, in the counties of Clearfield and Jefferson, from the mouth of John Shaffer's mill run, on the main branch of Toby's Creek, and from the forks of Brandy Camp (or Kersey Creek) to the Clarion River,

*   *   *   *   *   *   *   *   *

be, and the same are hereby declared public highways for the passage of rafts, boats, and other craft, and it shall and may be lawful for, etc. (The same provisions follow here as in No. 129.)

"Approved—the fourteenth day of April, A.D. one thousand eight hundred and twenty-eight.

"J. ANDW. SHULTZ,
"*Governor.*"

CHAPTER IX

"AN ACT TO PROVIDE FOR OPENING A ROAD FROM NEAR THE BALD EAGLE'S NEST, IN MIFFLIN COUNTY, TO LE BŒUF, IN THE COUNTY OF ALLEGHENY

"WHEREAS, A road has, under the direction of the Legislature, been in part laid out from Reading and Presque Isle [a peninsula], AND WHEREAS, It is considered that opening and improving said road would be greatly conducive to the interests of the community by opening a communication with the northwest part of the State, and would much facilitate an intercourse with Lake Erie;

"SECTION 1. *Therefore be it enacted, etc.*, That the governor be empowered to contract for the opening and improving of the road between the Bald Eagle's Nest and the Allegheny River to Le Bœuf.

"SECTION 2. *And be it further enacted by the authority aforesaid*, That when it shall appear to the persons who may contract for the opening of said road that deviations from such parts of the road as laid out are essentially necessary, he or they shall be authorized to make such deviations, provided that such deviations do not depart materially from the survey already made.

"SECTION 3. *And be it further enacted by the authority aforesaid*, That in order to carry this into effect the governor is empowered to draw his warrant on the State Treasurer for five thousand dollars, to be paid out of the sale of reserved lands and lots in the towns of Erie, Franklin, Warren, and Waterford."

Passed April 10, 1799. Recorded in Law Book No. VI., p. 443.

The Bald Eagle's Nest referred to above was Milesburg. The nest was not that of a bird, but that of an Indian warrior of that name, who built his wigwam there between two large white oaks. The western terminus of the road, then called Le Bœuf, is now known as Waterford, Erie County, Pennsylvania. On the completion of the turnpike most of this road was abandoned in this county. It is still in use from Brookville, about seven or eight miles of it, to the Olean road north of Corsica. It passed through where Brookville now is, near or on what is now Coal Alley. It was a great thoroughfare for the pioneers going to the West and Northwest.

HISTORY OF NORTHWESTERN PENNSYLVANIA

"WHEREAS, In and by an Act of the General Assembly entitled 'An Act for laying out and opening sundry Roads within this Commonwealth and for other purposes,' it is among other things provided and declared, that your Excellency shall be empowered and required to appoint three persons as Commissioners, ' to view the ground and estimate the expense of opening and making a good Waggon Road from the Bald Eagle's Nest, or the end of Nittany Mountain, to the Town of Erie at Presque-isle, and to cause the said

Conestoga wagon

Road to be Surveyed and staked out, by the most practicable Route, and also cause a draft of the survey to be made out in Profile, and to report to the Legislature the several parts of the expense that will be incurred in each County through which the said Road will pass: *Provided*, That the Commissioners thus appointed shall not stake out any part of the said Road when it may be carried on Roads heretofore laid out and opened, agreeably to the Provisions of former laws of this State.'

" AND WHEREAS, In pursuance of the power and authority given and granted in and by the said recited Act of Assembly, William Irvine, Andrew Ellicott, and George Wilson, Esquires, were by Letters Patent under your Excellency's hand, and the great Seal of the State, bearing date the thirteenth day of April, in the year of our Lord one thousand seven hundred and ninety-six, appointed Commissioners for the purposes aforesaid; but the said Andrew Ellicott, Esq., hath since resigned the said appointment, and his resignation hath been duly accepted.

" AND WHEREAS, In pursuance of the power and authority given and granted in and by the said recited Act of Assembly, Joseph Ellicott was, by Letters Patent, under your Excellency's Hand and the great Seal of the State, bearing date the nineteenth day of August, in the year of our Lord one thousand seven hundred and ninety-six, appointed a Commissioner in the lieu and stead of the said Andrew Ellicott, Esq., who had resigned as aforesaid, and in conjunction with the said William Irvine and George Wilson, Esquires, the two other Commissioners for the purpose of viewing and laying out the said Road in manner as stated in and by the above recited Act of Assembly.

" Now THEREFORE, The said George Wilson and Joseph Ellicott, two of the Commissioners appointed as aforesaid for the purposes aforesaid, beg leave to report:

" I. That the said William Irvine, George Wilson, and Joseph Ellicott, the Commissioners appointed as aforesaid, in conformity to your Excellency's Instructions in pursuance of the above recited Act of Assembly, with all convenient dispatch, in the execution of the trust reposed in them, proceeded to examine the situation of the Country at the Bald Eagle's Nest and to the end of Nittany Mountain, and having viewed the respective *scites*, they unanimously agreed to take their departure from the Bald Eagle's Nest. As soon as this decision took place the said William Irvine left the other Commissioners and returned home.

" II. That the said George Wilson and Joseph Ellicott then proceeded to view, survey, and stake out by a route, in their opinion, deemed the most practicable, a Road from the Bald Eagle's Nest toward the town of Erie at Presque-isle, and that they have ascertained the various courses and distances, the topographical situation, &c., of the said Road for the length of one hundred and sixteen miles, as represented in and by the Draft in profile hereunto annexed.

" III. That in consequence of the failure of Horses, the scarcity of Provisions, the advanced season of the year, and various other obstacles which retarded the prosecution of the business, they were compelled to relinquish the object of their mission, and have left above thirty-six miles of the Road unfinished.

" IV. That they have used their utmost diligence and attention to direct the course of the said Road over firm and level ground; but that frequently became totally impracticable, and where the ascent and descent of hills and mountains became unavoidable they made use of an altitude level, and have so adjusted its course that in its greatest elevation or depression it never exceeds an angle of six degrees with the horizon: Hence it may easily be inferred that considerable deviations from a straight line have necessarily occurred.

"V. That the land in that part of Mifflin County through which the Road passes is generally of an indifferent quality. For a part of this distance the Road passes over the declivities of the Allegheny Mountain and the Mushanon Hills. The country, however, for several miles between the summit of the Allegheny Mountain and the Mushanon hills, and also that part of Huntingdon County which the Road intersects, is generally level and free from stones, well timbered with Hickory, White and Black Oak, Dogwood, Ash, Chestnut, Poplar, White Pine, &c., and upon the whole well calculated for settlements. The soil of that part of Lycoming County which is intersected by the Road is generally of a luxuriant quality, abounding in many places with Stone coal, well timbered with various species of wood, and adapted to the production of all kinds of grain, &c., peculiar to the climate.

"VI. Your Commissioners with pleasure remark that from the Susquehanna River at Anderson's Creek to the first navigable stream of Sandy Lick Creek (a branch of Allegheny River) the portage along the said road is but twenty-two Miles. The road crosses Sandy Lick Creek about fifty miles from its junction with the Allegheny River, and from the Susquehanna to the North-Western branch of Sandy Lick Creek [Brookville] the portage is thirty-three miles. The North-Western branch discharges its waters into Sandy Lick Creek, about sixty perches below the place where it is intersected by the Road at the junction of the North-Western branch. The Sandy Lick Creek is as large as the Susquehanna River at Anderson's Creek, and the distance of the said Creek from the Allegheny River is about thirty-five miles. The Portage from the Susquehanna at Anderson's to Toby's Creek is forty-nine miles. Toby's Creek is twenty-two perches wide, and its distance from the intersection of the Road to the Allegheny River is about forty miles. It is navigable for boats, rafts, &c., from the intersection of the Road to the Allegheny River and about fifty or sixty miles above the place of intersection. The portage from the Susquehanna to the Allegheny River at Sussunadohtaw is seventy-two miles, and for the greater part of the distance of these portages the Road passes through a rich and fertile country.

"VII. That your Commissioners have formed their estimate of expenses upon the supposition that the said Road, as far as it has been surveyed, will be opened thirty feet in width; sixteen feet in the middle to be cut and cleared as nearly level with the surface of the earth as practicable, but where digging and levelling on the sides of Hills and Mountains shall become necessary that a passage will be dug twelve feet wide, and that Bridges and causeways will be erected and formed over all miry places to enable Waggons to pass.

"A general estimate of expenditures requisite in opening, clearing, digging, levelling, erecting Bridges and forming causeways over the said Road.

"The expenses in opening the Road through the County of Mifflin, commencing at the Bald Eagle's Nest and ending at the Big Mushanon Creek, nineteen miles & sixteen perches.

"For opening, cleaning, digging, levelling, forming causeways on the said Road and erecting a Bridge over the Little Mushanon in the said County. } Dolls. 3316.74.

"The expenses in opening the Road through the County of Huntingdon, commencing at the Big Mushanon Creek and ending at the West branch of the Susquehanna River, twenty-one miles one hundred and fifty-seven perches.

"For opening, clearing, digging, levelling, forming causeways on the said Road and erecting a Bridge over Alder Run in said County. } 2643.37.

"The expenses in opening the Road through the County of Lycoming commencing at the West branch of Susquehanna and ending at the Allegheny River, seventy-two miles & 193 perches.

"For opening, clearing, digging, levelling, and forming Causeways on the said Road. } 7215.20.

"VIII. That the said Road in its whole length passes through one entire and uninterrupted Wilderness, and the expenses already incurred in the execution of the business have considerably exceeded the legal appropriation intended for its completion.

"GEO. WILSON.
JOSEPH ELLICOTT."

CHAPTER X

" WESTERN PENNSYLVANIA was untrodden by the foot of the white man
before the year 1700. As early as 1715 and 1720 occasionally a trader would
venture west of the Allegheny Mountain, and of these the first was James
Le Tort, who resided in 1700 east of the Susquehanna, but took up his residence west of it, at Le Tort Spring, Carlisle, in 1720. Peter Chever, John
Evans, Henry DeVoy, Owen Nicholson, Alexander Magenty, Patrick Burns,
George Hutchison, all of Cumberland County; Barnaby Currin, John Mc-
Guire, a Mr. Frazier, the latter of whom had at an early day a trading-house
at Venango, but afterwards at the Monongahela, at the mouth of Turtle
Creek, were all traders among the Indians. But no attempt had been made
by the whites at settlements in the region now occupied by the several counties west of the Alleghenies before 1748, when the Ohio Company was
formed. This company sent out the undaunted Christopher Gist, in 1750, to
explore the country and make report. He, it is said, explored the country
' from the South Branch of the Potomac northward to the heads of the
Juniata River, crossed the mountains, and reached the Allegheny by the
valley of Kiskiminitas. He crossed the Allegheny about four miles above
the forks, where Pittsburg now stands, thence went down the Ohio to some
point below Beaver River, and thence over to the Muskingum valley.' The
first actual settlement made was within the present limits of Fayette County,
in 1752, by Mr. Gist himself, on a tract of land, now well known there as
Mount Braddock, west of the Youghiogheny River. Mr. Gist induced eleven
families to settle around him on lands presumed to be within the Ohio
Company's grant.

" The more southern part of Western Pennsylvania (Greene, Washington, Fayette. and part of Somerset), which was supposed to be within the

boundaries of Virginia, was visited by adventurers from Maryland prior to 1754. Among these were Wendel Brown and his two sons and Frederick Waltzer, who lived four miles west of Uniontown. David Tygart had settled in the valley which still bears his name in Northwestern Virginia; several other families came here a few years afterwards. These were the only settlements attempted prior to Braddock's defeat, and those made immediately afterwards, or prior to 1760, were repeatedly molested, families murdered, cabins burnt, and, for a time, broken up, alternately abandoned and again occupied.

"The treaty of 1762 brought quiet and repose to some extent to the English colonies, and the first settlers on the frontiers returned to their abandoned farms, but they were soon again obliged to leave their homes and retire for safety to the more densely settled parts. Bouquet prosecuted his campaign with success against the Indians, and in November, 1764, compelled the turbulent and restless Kyashuta to sue for peace and bury the hatchet on the plains of Muskingum, and finally humbled the Delawares and Shawnees. Soon after, the refugee settlers returned to their cabins and clearings, resumed their labors, extended their improvements, and cultivated their lands. From this time forth the prosperity of Pennsylvania increased rapidly, and the tide of immigration with consequent settlements rolled westward, though the pioneer settlers were afterwards greatly exposed.

"Previous to 1758, Westmoreland was a wilderness trodden by the wild beast, the savage, and, like other portions of Western Pennsylvania, by an occasional white trader or frontiersman. No settlements were attempted prior to this date, when Fort Duquesne, afterwards Fort Pitt, was abandoned by the French, became an English military post, and formed a nucleus for an English settlement, and two years afterwards (1760) a small town was built near Fort Pitt, which contained nearly two hundred souls, but on the breaking out of the Indian war, in 1763, the inhabitants retired into the fort, and their dwellings were suffered to fall into decay. In 1765, Pittsburg was laid out."—*History of Western Pennsylvania.*

This southern exploration was through what is now Somerset, Fayette, Westmoreland, and Allegheny Counties. In 1754 Lieutenant-Colonel George Washington, then twenty-one years old, penetrated this wilderness and improved this road. In 1755 General Braddock, accompanied by Washington, marched his army over this road. Hence the road has always been called Braddock's road.

The pioneer road from east to west was opened up in September, 1758, by General John Forbes. He commanded an army of about eight thousand men. General Forbes marched in the spring from Philadelphia with his troops to Raystown (now Bedford), but on account of the smallpox in his army he was detained at Carlisle, and failed to reach what is now Bedford until the middle of September. At a consultation of his officers at this point it was decided to cut out a new road over the mountains from Raystown to Loyalhanna, now in Westmoreland County, a distance of forty-five miles.

This new road passed through what is now Bedford, Somerset, and Westmoreland Counties. Colonel Bouquet, with twenty-five hundred men, cut out the road in September and October of that year.

Colonel Washington was at this consultation, and was opposed to the new road. Washington's arguments in favor of the southern route were as follows:

"CAMP AT FORT CUMBERLAND, August 2, 1758.

" SIR,—The matters of which we spoke relative to the roads have, since our parting, been the subject of my closest reflection, and so far am I from altering my opinion that the more time and attention I bestow the more I am confirmed in it, and the reasons for taking Braddock's road appear in a stronger point of view. To enumerate the whole of these reasons would be tedious, and to you, who are become so much master of the subject, unnecessary. I shall, therefore, briefly mention a few only, which I think so obvious in themselves, that they must effectually remove objections.

" Several years ago the Virginians and Pennsylvanians commenced a trade with the Indians settled on the Ohio, and, to obviate the many inconveniences of a bad road, they, after reiterated and ineffectual efforts to discover where a good one might be made, employed for the purpose several of the most intelligent Indians, who, in the course of many years' hunting, had acquired a perfect knowledge on these mountains. The Indians, having taken the greatest pains to gain the rewards offered for this discovery, declared that the path leading from Will's Creek was infinitely preferable to any that could be made at any other place. Time and experience so clearly demonstrated this truth that the Pennsylvania traders commonly carried out their goods by Will's Creek. Therefore the Ohio Company, in 1753, at a considerable expense, opened the road. In 1754 the troops whom I had the honor to command greatly repaired it, as far as Gist's plantation, and in 1755 it was widened and completed by General Braddock to within six miles of Fort Duquesne. A road that has so long been opened and so well and so often repaired must be much firmer and better than a new one. allowing the ground to be equally good.

" But supposing it were practicable to make a road from Raystown quite as good as General Braddock's, I ask, have we time to do it? Certainly not. To surmount the difficulties to be encountered in making it over such mountains, covered with woods and rocks, would require so much time as to blast our otherwise well-grounded hopes of striking the important stroke this season.

" The favorable accounts that some give of the forage on the Raystown road, as being so much better than that on the other, are certainly exaggerated. It is well known that on both routes the rich valleys between the mountains

abound with good forage, and that those which are stony and bushy are destitute of it. Colonel Byrd and the engineer who accompanied him confirm this
fact. Surely the meadows on Braddock's road would greatly overbalance
the advantage of having grass to the foot of the ridge, on the Raystown road;
and all agree that a more barren road is nowhere to be found than that from
Raystown to the inhabitants, which is likewise to be considered.

"Another principal objection made to General Braddock's road is in
regard to the waters. But these seldom swell so much as to obstruct the
passage. The Youghiogheny River, which is the most rapid and soonest
filled, I have crossed with a body of troops after more than thirty days almost
continued rain. In fine, any difficulties on this score are so trivial that they
really are not worth mentioning. The Monongahela, the largest of all these
rivers, may, if necessary, easily be avoided, as Mr. Frazier, the principal guide,
informs me, by passing a defile, and even that, he says, may be shunned.

"Again, it is said there are many defiles on this road. I grant that there
are some, but I know of none that may not be traversed, and I should be glad
to be informed where a road can be had over these mountains not subject to
the same inconvenience. The shortness of the distance between Raystown
and Loyal Hanna is used as an argument against this road, which bears in
it something unaccountable to me, for I must beg leave to ask whether it
requires more time or is more difficult and expensive to go one hundred and
forty-five miles on a good road already made to our hands than to cut one
hundred miles anew, and a great part of the way over impassable mountains.

"That the old road is many miles nearer Winchester in Virginia and
Fort Frederick in Maryland than the contemplated one is incontestable, and
I will here show the distance from Carlisle by the two routes, fixing the
different stages, some of which I have from information only, but others I
believe to be exact: From Carlisle to Fort Duquesne by way of Raystown,
193 miles; from Carlisle to Fort Duquesne by way of Fort Frederic and
Cumberland, 212 miles.

"From this computation there appears to be a difference of nineteen
miles only. Were all the supplies necessarily to come from Carlisle, it is
well known that the goodness of the old road is a sufficient compensation for
the shortness of the other, as the wrecked and broken wagons there clearly
demonstrate."—*The Olden Time*, vol. i.

For many years all government supplies for western forts, groceries,
salt, and goods of every kind, were carried from the East on pack-horses over
this Forbes road. One man would sometimes have under his control from
fifty to one hundred pack-horses. A panel pack-saddle was on each horse.
and the load for a horse was about two hundred pounds. Forts were established along the line of the road, and guards from the militia accompanied
these horse-trains, guarding them by night in their "encampments" and
protecting them by day through and over the mountains.

HISTORY OF NORTHWESTERN PENNSYLVANIA

This Braddock's road and the Raystown road were nothing more than trails or military roads, and it was not until 1784 or 1785 that the State opened a road from the east to the west over Forbes's military trail.

General John Forbes died in Philadelphia, Pennsylvania, on March 15, 1759.

One hundred years ago this pioneer road was crowded by carriers with their pack-horses going westward, laden with people, salt, iron, and merchandise. In fact, the pioneers of Lawrence, Mercer, Butler, Crawford, and Venango came mostly over this road.

" The pack-horses then travelled in divisions of twelve or fifteen, going single-file, each horse carrying about two hundred-weight; one man preceded and one brought up the rear of the file. Later on the carriers, to their bitter indignation, were supplanted by the Conestoga wagons [see p. 195], with their proud six-horse teams, with huge belled collars, the wagon stored with groceries, linens, calico, rum, molasses, and hams, four to five tons of load; by law none of these wagons had less than four-inch tires on its wheels."

From 1784 to 1834 was the stage-coach era in this country. In the year 1802 the government started a line of coaches between Philadelphia and New York, carrying their own mail. The fare of each passenger, all through, was four dollars. Four pence per mile was charged for way passengers. One hundred and fifty pounds of baggage, equal to one passenger, was sent at the risk of persons who forwarded the same. This was continued for three years, clearing an average yearly profit of four thousand dollars. In 1834 the Postmaster-General and the government preferred railroad transportation where it could be had. The government required from the railroads a schedule time of thirteen miles an hour for the mails. I give, as near as I can learn, the pioneer, individual stage-coach mail-lines :

" PHILADELPHIA AND PITTSBURGH MAIL STAGES

" A line of stages being established and now in operation to and from each of the above places. This line will start from John Tomlinson's Market-street, Philadelphia, every Friday morning, *via* Harrisburgh and Chambersburgh, to Pittsburgh, and perform the trip in 7 days. It will also start from THOMAS FERREE's the Fountain Inn, Water-street, Pittsburgh, every Wednesday morning, same rout to Philadelphia, and perform the trip in 7 days; Fare—Passengers 20 dollars and 20 lb. baggage free; all extra baggage or packages, if of dimentions such as to be admitted for transportation by this line, to pay 12 dollars per 100 lb. the baggage or the packages to be at the owner's own proper risque unless especially receipted for by one of the proprietors, which cannot be done if the owner is a passenger in the stage, same trip. These stages are constructed to carry three passengers on a seat, and more never shall be admitted.

" This line will also leave John Tomlinson's as above every Tuesday

203

morning for Chambersburgh, making the trip in 2½ days, and leave Mr. Hetrick's tavern in Chambersburgh, every Wednesday at noon, for Philadelphia, and make the trip in 2½ days; fare 9 dollars and 50 cents, under the same regulations as above.

"The public will perceive by this establishment, that they have a direct conveyance from Philadelphia and Pittsburgh once a week, and from Philadelphia and Chambersburgh twice a week.

"The proprietors being determined that their conduct shall be such as to merit support in their line.

"JOHN TOMLINSON & CO.

"July 3rd, 1804."

"PHILADELPHIA AND PITTSBURGH MAIL STAGES

"*The Proprietors*

"With pleasure now inform the public that they run their line of stages twice in the week to and from the above places.

"They leave John Tomlinson's Spread Eagle, Market-street, Philadelphia, every Tuesday and Friday morning, at 4 o'clock, and Thomas Ferry's Fountain Inn, Water-street, Pittsburgh, every Wednesday and Saturday morning, perform the trip in seven days. Fare each passenger 20 dollars; 14 lbs. of baggage free; extra baggage to pay 12½ cents per lb. This line runs through Lancaster, Elizabeth Town, Middle Town, Harrisburgh, Carlisle, Shippensburgh, Chambersburgh, McConnell's-town, Bedford, Somerset, Greensburgh, &c.

"JOHN TOMLINSON & CO.

"Nov. 9th, 1804."

The first cab was used in Paris in 1823; the first omnibus in 1827. From Philadelphia *via* Harrisburg by road was two hundred and ninety miles; *via* Yorktown, two hundred and eighty-eight miles.

In the summer of 1835, the usual trip from Philadelphia to Pittsburg, by canal and the portage railroad, was made in three and one-half days.

PIONEER MAIL-ROUTES AND POST-OFFICES—EARLY MAIL-ROUTES AND POST-OFFICES—TRANSMISSION OF MONEY THROUGH MAILS AND OTHERWISE

The pioneer post-office was established in this State under an act of Assembly, November 27, 1700,—viz.:

"AN ACT FOR ERECTING AND ESTABLISHING A POST OFFICE

"*Whereas*, The King and the late Queen Mary, by their royal letters patent under the great seal of England, bearing date the seventeenth of February, which was in the year one thousand and six hundred and ninety-and-one, did grant to Thomas Neal, Esquire, his executors, administrators and assigns, full power and authority to erect, settle and establish within the King's colonies and plantations in America, one or more office or offices for receiving and dispatching of letters and packets by post, and to receive, send and deliver the same, under such rates and sums of money as shall be agreeable to the rates established by act of parliament in England, or as the planters and others should agree to give on the first settlement, to have, hold and enjoy the same for a term of twenty-one years, with and under such powers, limitations and conditions as in and by the said letters patent may more fully appear;

"*And whereas*, The King's Postmaster General of England, at the request, desire and nomination of the said Thomas Neale, hath deputed Andrew Hamilton, Esquire, for such time and under such conditions as in his deputation is for that purpose mentioned, to govern and manage the said General Post Office for and throughout all the King's plantations and colonies in the main land or continent of America and the islands adjacent thereto, and in and by the said deputation may more fully appear:

"*And whereas*, The said Andrew Hamilton hath, by and with the good liking and approbation of the Postmaster General of England, made application to the proprietary and governor of this province and territories and freemen thereof convened in general assembly, that they would ascertain and establish such rates and sums of money upon letters and packets going by post as may be an effectual encouragement for carrying on and maintaining a general post, and the proprietary and governor and freemen in general assembly met, considering that the maintaining of mutual and speedy correspondencies is very beneficial to the King and his subjects, and a great encouragement to the trade, and that the same is best carried on and managed by public post, as well as for the preventing of inconveniences which heretofore have happened for want thereof, as for a certain, safe and speedy dispatch, carrying and recarrying of all letters and packets of letters by post to and from all parts and places within the continent of America and several parts of Europe, and that the well ordering thereof is matter of general concernment and of great advantage, and being willing to encourage such a public benefit:

" (SECTION I.) *Have therefore enacted, and be it enacted, etc.*, That there be from henceforth one general letter office erected and established within the town of Philadelphia, from whence all letters and packets whatsoever may be with speed and expedition sent into any part of the neighboring colonies and plantations on the mainland and continent of America, or into any other of the King's kingdoms or dominions, or unto any kingdom or country beyond the seas; at which said office all returns and answers may likewise be received, etc., etc."

The pioneer mail-route through this wilderness was over the old State Road; it was established in 1805. It was carried on horseback from Bellefonte to Meadville. The law declared then that " No other than a free white person shall be employed to convey the mail. Fifteen minutes shall be allowed for opening and closing the mails at all offices where no particular time is specified. For every thirty minutes' delay (unavoidable accidents excepted) in arriving after the time specified in the contract, the contractor shall forfeit one dollar; and if the delay continues until the departure of any depending mail, whereby the mails destined for each depending mail lose a trip, an additional forfeiture of five dollars shall be incurred."

The route was over the State Road to what is now the Clarion line; from there over a new road to the Allegheny River or Parker's Ferry, now Parker's City; up the river to Franklin, and from there to Meadville. The pioneer contractor's name was James Randolph, from Meadville. The next contractor was Hamilton, from Bellefonte; then by Benjamin Haitshour and others, until the turnpike was completed, when the first stage contract was taken by Clark, of Perry County. He sent on his coaches by John O'Neal, and from that time until the present the mail has been carried through this wilderness; and in 1812 we got our news from a Meadville paper, edited by Thomas Atkinson, called the *Crawford Weekly Messenger*. The nearest post-office west was Franklin, and east was Curwinsville. All papers were carried outside the mail and delivered by the mail-carrier. Our nearest post-office south was at Kittanning, Armstrong County, and when any one in the neighborhood would go there they would bring the news for all and distribute the same.

I cannot give the pioneer contractor (route, service, and compensation) for mail service through Butler, Mercer, Crawford, Venango, and Warren Counties, Pennsylvania, because the records of the United States Post-Office were almost entirely destroyed by fire in the year 1836, and the earliest trace of the above service is found in a printed advertisement for proposals for carrying the mails on route No. 161, Pittsburg, by Butler, Mercer, Meadville, Crawford, and Le Bœuf, to Presque Isle, once a week, from April 1, 1809, to March 31, 1811, the advertisement being dated October 31, 1808. In a subsequent advertisement this route is shown as having been changed to end at Erie instead of Presque Isle. It is assumed that contracts were awarded for the above service, but owing to the destruction of the records the facts are not known nor can the names of the contractors be given.

The earliest permanent records of the Department show that a contract was made with J. B. Curtis & Co., of Mercer, for service from 1832 to 1836, on route No. 1169, Pittsburg to Erie, one hundred and twenty-eight miles, daily, in four-horse post-chaise, and route No. 1174, Pittsburg to Mercer, fifty-five miles, twice a week, the compensation being two thousand seven hundred dollars per annum for both routes, and that a contract was made for the same period with Bradley Winton, of Meadville, for service on route No. 1190, Meadville to Warren, sixty-one miles, once a week, compensation two hundred and thirty dollars per annum.

In 1815 the United States had three thousand post-offices. The postage for a single letter, composed of one piece of paper, under forty miles, eight cents; over forty and under ninety miles, ten cents; under one hundred and fifty miles, twelve and one-half cents; under three hundred miles, seventeen cents; under five hundred miles, twenty cents; over five hundred miles, twenty-five cents. The law was remodelled in 1816 and continued until 1845, as follows,—viz.: Letters, thirty miles, six and one-quarter cents; over thirty and under eighty miles, ten cents; over eighty and under one hundred and fifty miles, twelve and one-half cents; over one hundred and fifty and under four hundred miles, eighteen and three-quarter cents; over four hundred miles, twenty-five cents. If the letter weighed an ounce, four times these rates were charged. Newspaper rates, in the State or under one hundred miles, one cent; over one hundred miles or out of the State, one and one-half cents. Periodicals, from one and one-half to two, four, and six cents. A portion of the records of the Postmaster-General's office at Washington were destroyed by fire in the year 1836; but it has been ascertained that an advertisement was issued May 20, 1814, for once-a-week service on route No. 51, Bellefonte to Franklin, Pennsylvania, from January 1, 1815, to December 31, 1817, Jefferson Court-House being mentioned as an intermediate point; that on May 26, 1817, an advertisement was issued for service between the same points from January 1, 1818, to December 31, 1819; and on May 26, 1819, service as above was again advertised from January 1, 1820, to December 31, 1823; the service during these years connecting at Franklin with another route to Meadville.

Owing to the incompleteness of the records of the office at Washington, for the reason above stated, the names of all the contractors prior to 1824 cannot be given; but under advertisement of June 10, 1823, for once-a-week service on route No. 158, Bellefonte to Meadville, from January 1, 1824, to December 31, 1827, contract was made with Messrs. Hayes and Bennett, of Franklin, Pennsylvania, at the rate of sixteen hundred dollars per annum.

From the best information at hand, it appears that a post-office was established at Port Barnett, Pennsylvania, January 4, 1826, the name changed to Brookville, September 10, 1830; that from the date of the establishment of the post-office to December 31, 1839, the office was supplied by star route from Bellefonte to Meadville, Pennsylvania, Messrs. Bennett and Hayes being the contractors to December 31, 1831, Messrs. J. and B. Bennett to December 31, 1835, and Mr. Benjamin Bennett to December 31, 1839.

From January 1, 1840, Brookville was supplied by route from Curwensville to Meadville, Pennsylvania (the service having been divided on Curwensville, the eastern route being from Lewistown *via* Bellefonte and other offices to Curwensville), Mr. Jesse Rupp being the contractor to June 30, 1844, and Mr. John Wightman to June 30, 1848.

Prior to 1826, or the completion of the turnpike, there was no post-office in Jefferson County. Not until Jefferson County had been created for twenty-two and the pioneers had been here for twenty-five years was a post-office opened. The second mail-route in Jefferson County commenced at Kittanning, Pennsylvania, and ended in Olean, New York. The route was one hundred and ten miles long. It was established in 1826. Roswell P. Alford, of Wellsville, Ohio, was the contractor and proprietor. The mail was to be carried through once a week, and this was done on horseback, and the pay for this service was four hundred dollars a year. The following-named post-offices were created in this county to be supplied by the carrier on his route:

Port Barnett, Pine Creek Township, January 4, 1826; Joseph Barnett, postmaster.

Montmorenci (now Elk County), Ridgway Township, February 14, 1826; Reuben A. Aylesworth, postmaster.

Punxsutawney, Young Township, February 14, 1826; Charles R. Barclay, postmaster.

Hellen (now Elk County), Ridgway Township, April, 1828; Philetus Clarke, postmaster.

Brockwayville, Pine Creek Township, April 13, 1829, Alonzo Brockway, postmaster.

From the information at hand it appears that an advertisement was issued in the year of 1825 for proposals carrying the mails on star route No. 79, from Bellefonte, by Karthaus, Bennett's Creek, Brockway, Gillett's, and Scull's, to Smithport, Pennsylvania, once in two weeks, from January 1, 1826, to December 31, 1827; and that in 1827 an advertisement was issued for service on route No. 219, from Bellefonte, by Karthaus, Fox, Bennett's Branch, Ridgway, Gillett's, Scull's, Montmorenci, Sergeant, and Smithport, Pennsylvania, to Olean, New York, once a week, from January 1, 1828, to December 31, 1831.

There is no record showing the contractors during the above terms.

In the year 1831 an advertisement was issued for star route No. 1127, from Bellefonte, by Milesburg, Karthaus, Bennett's Branch, Fox, Kersey, Ridgway, Montmorenci, Clermontville, Smithport, Allegheny Bridge, Pennsylvania, and Mill Grove, New York, to Olean, New York, once a week, from January 1, 1832, to December 31, 1835, and the contract was awarded to Mr. James L. Gillis, of Montmorenci, with pay at the rate of six hundred and seventy-four dollars per annum.

In 1835 an advertisement was issued for service on route No. 1206, from Bellefonte, by Milesburg, Karthaus, Bennett's Branch, Caledonia, Fox, Kersey, Ridgway, Williamsville, Clermontville, Smithport, Farmers Valley, Allegheny Bridge, Pennsylvania, and Mill Grove, New York, to Olean, New York, once a week, from January 1, 1836, to December 31, 1839, and the contract was awarded to Mr. Bernard Duffey (address not given) at six hundred and twenty-eight dollars per annum.

In 1839 an advertisement was issued for service on route No. 1593, from

Bellefonte, by Milesburg, Karthaus, Caledonia, Fox, Kersey, Ridgway, Williamsville, Clermontville, Smithport, Farmers Valley, Allegheny Bridge, Pennsylvania, and Mill Grove, New York, to Olean, New York, once a week between Bellefonte and Smithport, and twice a week the residue of route, from January 1, 1840, to June 30, 1844, and the contract was awarded to Mr. Gideon Ions (address not given) at eight hundred and forty-five dollars per annum.

Like every other business in those days, the postmaster trusted his patrons, as the following advertisement exhibits,—viz.:

"All persons indebted to C. J. Dunham for postage on letters or newspapers are notified to call and pay off their bills to James M. Steedman, or they may look for John Smith, as no longer indulgence can or will be given.

"February 18, 1834."

Barter was taken in exchange for postage. In those days uncalled-for letters were advertised in the papers. The pioneer advertisement of letters was in the *Philadelphia Gazette*, March 26, 1783.

In the thirties distance governed the postage on letters up to four hundred miles and more. The price of such a letter was twenty-five cents. The postmaster, who was also a merchant, took produce for letters the same as for goods, and for postage on such a letter as named would receive two bushels of oats, two bushels of potatoes, four pounds of butter, or five dozen eggs. To pay the postage on thirty-two letters, such as named, the farmer would have to sell a good cow. "In early times it was death by the law to rob the United States mails."

In the pioneer days, or previous to about 1860, there was no bank in Jefferson County. There was no way to transmit funds except sending them with a direct messenger or by some neighbor who had business in the locality where you desired to send your money. An adroit way was to secure a ten-, fifty-, or one-hundred-dollar bill, cut it in two, send the first half in a letter, wait for a reply, and then enclose the other half in a letter also. The party receiving the halves could paste them together. The pioneer merchants, when going to Philadelphia for goods, put their silver Spanish dollars in belts in undershirts and on other parts of their persons, wherever they thought it could be best concealed. In this way on horseback they made journeys. Every horseback rider (tourist) carried a pair of leather saddle-bags.

In the United States, July 1, 1837, the post-roads were about 118,264 miles in extent, and the annual transportation of the mails was at the rate of 27,578,621 miles,—viz.:

On horseback and in sulkies, 8,291,504; in stages, 17,408,820; in steamboats and railroad cars, 1,878,297.

The number of post-offices in the United States on July 1, 1835, was 10,770; on July 1, 1836, 11,091; and on December 1, 1837, 11,100.

In the year 1837 the Postmaster-General recommended a revision of the present rates of postage, making a reduction of about twenty per cent., to take effect on July 1, next. To this end he suggested the following letter postage:

75 miles and under	5 cents.
150 miles and over 75 miles	10 "
300 miles and over 150 miles	15 "
600 miles and over 300 miles............................	20 "
Over 600 miles	25 "

Postage stamps were invented by James Chalmers, an Englishman, and first used May 6, 1840, in London.

The first issue of the United States stamps took place in 1845, but the postmasters of several places had issued stamps for their own convenience a few years before this. These "Postmasters'," or provisional stamps, of course, were not good for postage after the government issue took place.

The first stamp sold of this issue was bought by the Hon. Henry Shaw. This issue consisted of but two denominations, the five- and ten-cent ones, and were unperforated, as were the stamps of the next series, issued in 1851–56.

The pioneer post-office was established in this State under an act of Assembly, November 27, 1700.

CHAPTER XI

In 1792 the first stone turnpike in the United States was chartered. It was constructed in Pennsylvania, in 1794, from Lancaster to Philadelphia. In this year, also, began the agitation in Pennsylvania for internal improvement. An agitation that resulted in a great era of State road, canal, and turnpike construction, encouraged and assisted by the State government. From 1792 until 1832 the Legislature granted two hundred and twenty charters for turnpikes alone.

These pikes were not all made, but there was completed within that time, as a result of these grants, three thousand miles of passable roads. The pioneer turnpike through our wilderness was the Susquehanna and Waterford turnpike. On February 22, 1812, a law was enacted by the Pennsylvania Legislature enabling the governor to incorporate a company to build a turnpike from the Susquehanna River, near the mouth of Anderson Creek, in Clearfield County, through Jefferson County and what is now Brookville, and through the town of Franklin and Meadville, to Waterford, in Erie County. The governor was authorized to subscribe twelve thousand dollars in shares toward building the road. Joseph Barnett and Peter Jones, of Jefferson County, and two from each of the following counties, Erie, Crawford, Mercer, Clearfield, Venango, and Philadelphia, and two from the city of Philadelphia, were appointed commissioners to receive stock. Each of the counties just named was required to take a specified number of shares, and the shares were placed at twenty-five dollars each. Jefferson County was required to take fifty shares.

The war of 1812 so depressed business in this part of the State that all work was delayed on this thoroughfare for six years. The company commenced work in 1818, and the survey was completed in October of that year. In November, 1818, the sections were offered for sale, and in November, 1820, the road was completed to Bellefonte.

The commissioners employed John Sloan, Esq., to make the survey and grade the road. They began the survey in the spring and finished it in the fall of 1818, a distance of one hundred and four miles. The State took one-third of the stock. James Harriet, of Meadville, Pennsylvania, took the contract to build the road, and he gave it out to sub-contractors. Some took five miles, some ten, and so on. The bridge over the Clarion River was built in 1821, by Moore, from Northumberland County; it was built with a single arch.

In March, 1821, an act was passed by the Legislature appropriating two thousand five hundred dollars for improving the road. Appointments were made in each county through which the road passed of people whose duty it was to receive the money for each county and to pay it out. Charles C. Gaskill and Carpenter Winslow represented Jefferson County.

Early barn

Andrew Ellicott never surveyed or brushed out this turnpike. He was one of the commissioners for the old State Road.

Our turnpike was one hundred and twenty-six miles long. The individual subscriptions to its construction were in total fifty thousand dollars, the State aid giving one hundred and forty thousand dollars. This was up to March, 1822. The finishing of our link in November, 1824, completed and opened one continuous turnpike road from Philadelphia to Erie. Our part of this thoroughfare was called a " clay turnpike," and in that day was boasted of by the early settlers as the most convenient and easy-travelling road in the

United States. That, in fact, anywhere along the route over the mountain the horses could be treated to the finest water, and that anywhere along the route, too, the traveller, as well as the driver, could regale himself " with the choicest Monongahela whiskey bitters," clear as amber, sweet as musk, and smooth as oil.

" Immediately after the completion of the turnpike mile-stones were set up. They were on the right-hand side of the road as one travelled east. The stones when first erected were white, neat, square, and well finished. On each stone was inscribed, ' To S. oo miles. To F. oo miles.' Of course, figures appeared on the stones where ciphers have been placed above. S. stood for Susquehanna, which is east, and F. for Franklin, which is west."

Only the commonest goods were hauled into this country over the old State Road, and in the early days of the turnpike, Oliver Gregg, with his six horses, and Joseph Morrow, with his outfit of two teams, were regularly employed for many years in carrying freight from Philadelphia to this section. It took four weeks to reach here from Philadelphia, and the charge for freight was about six dollars per hundred pounds. A man by the name of Potter in latter years drove an outfit of five roan horses. Each team had a Conestoga wagon and carried from three to four tons of goods.

THE TOLL-GATE

With the completion of the turnpike came the toll-gate. One was erected every five or ten miles.

Gangs of men were kept busy constantly repairing the pike, and they were individually paid at these gates. The road was then kept in good condition.

" AN ACT TO ENABLE THE GOVERNOR OF THE COMMONWEALTH TO INCORPORATE A COMPANY FOR MAKING AN ARTIFICIAL ROAD, BY THE BEST AND NEAREST ROUTE, FROM WATERFORD, IN THE COUNTY OF ERIE, THROUGH MEADVILLE AND FRANKLIN TO THE RIVER SUSQUEHANNA, AT OR NEAR THE MOUTH OF ANDERSON'S CREEK, IN CLEARFIELD COUNTY

" SECTION 13. *And be it further enacted by the authority aforesaid*, That the said company, having perfected the said road, or such part thereof, from time to time as aforesaid, and the same being examined, approved, and licensed as aforesaid, it shall and may be lawful for them to appoint such and so many toll-gatherers as they shall think proper, to collect and receive of and from all and every person and persons using the said road the tolls and rates hereinafter mentioned; and to stop any person riding, leading, or driving any horse or mule, or driving any cattle, hogs, sheep, sulkey, chair, chaise, phaeton, cart, wagon, wain, sleigh, sled, or other carriage of burden or pleasure from passing through the said gates or turnpikes until they shall have respectfully paid the same,—that is to say, for every space of five miles in length of the said road the following sum of money, and so in proportion for any greater or less distance, or for any greater or less number of hogs, sheep, or cattle, to wit: For every score of sheep, four cents; for every score of hogs, six cents; for every score of cattle, twelve cents; for every horse or mule, laden or unladen, with his rider or leader, three cents; for every sulkey, chair, chaise, with one horse and two wheels, six cents; and with two horses, nine cents; for every chair, coach, phaeton, chaise, stage-wagon, coachee, or light wagon, with two horses and four wheels, twelve cents; for either of the carriages last mentioned, with four horses, twenty cents; for every other carriage of pleasure, under whatever name it may go, the like sum, according

Port Barnett

to the number of wheels and of horses drawing the same; for every sleigh or sled, two cents for each horse drawing the same; for every cart or wagon, or other carriage of burden, the wheels of which do not in breadth exceed four inches, four cents for each horse drawing the same; for every cart or wagon, the wheels of which shall exceed in breadth four inches, and shall not exceed seven inches, three cents for each horse drawing the same; and when any such carriages as aforesaid shall be drawn by oxen or mules, in the whole or in part, two oxen shall be estimated as equal to one horse; and every ass or mule as equal to one horse, in charging the aforesaid tolls."

COMPLETION OF THE TURNPIKE

The first stage line was established over the Waterford and Susquehanna turnpike from Bellefonte to Erie by Robert Clark, of Clark's Ferry, Pennsylvania, in November, 1824. It was called a Concord line, and at first was a tri-weekly. The first stage-coach passed through where Brookville now is about November 6, 1824. In 1824 the route was completed to Philadelphia, through Harrisburg, and was a daily line.

" The arrival of the stages in old times was a much more important event than that of the railroad trains to-day. Crowds invariably gathered at the public houses where the coaches stopped to obtain the latest news, and the passengers were of decided account for the time being. Money was so scarce that few persons could afford to patronize the stages, and those who did

1824-50

were looked upon as fortunate beings. A short trip on the stage was as formidable an affair as one to Chicago or Washington is now by railroad. The stage-drivers were men of considerable consequence, especially in the villages through which they passed. They were intrusted with many delicate missives and valuable packages, and seldom betrayed the confidence reposed in them. They had great skill in handling their horses, and were the admiration and envy of the boys.

" The traffic on the turnpike began, of course, at its completion in November, 1824. It increased gradually until it reached enormous proportions. A quarter of a century after the road had been built it arrived at the zenith of its glory."

Pedlers of all kinds, on foot and in covered wagons, travelled the pike. From Crawford County came the cheese and white-fish pedler. Several people, including the hotel-men, would each buy a whole cheese.

The pioneer inns or taverns in Jefferson County along this highway were about six in number. Five of the six were built of hewed logs,—viz.: one where Reynoldsville is; the Packer Inn, near Peter Baum's; one near Campbell Run (Ghost Hollow); the William Vastbinder Inn; James Winter's tavern, at Roseville; and John McAnulty's inn, kept by Alexander Powers, where Corsica is now located. The Port Barnett Inn at this time was a "frame structure," as its picture represents.

The old State Road was opened and finished to Holeman's Ferry, on the Allegheny River, in 1804. This point is now in Forest County. There was no provision made to complete the road from there to Waterford by the Legislature until 1810. At that time Clarion County was not organized, and the part of the State Road that now lies in Clarion County was then in Venango County.

CHAPTER XII

FOR convenience in description I may here state that the soil of North-western Pennsylvania was covered in sections with two different growths of timber,—viz.: sections of oak and other hard-wood timber, with underbrush and saplings. Some of these sections were called the barrens. The other sections were covered with a dense and heavy growth of pine, hemlock, poplar, cucumber, bass, ash, sugar, and beech, with saplings, down timber, and under-brush in great profusion. The mode of clearing in these different sections was not the same. In the first-mentioned or sparsely covered section the pre-liminary work was grubbing. The saplings and underbrush had to be grubbed up and out with a mattock and piled in brush-piles. One man could usually grub an acre in four days, or you could let this at a job for two dollars per acre and board. The standing timber then was usually girdled or deadened, and allowed to fall down in the crops from year to year, to be chopped and rolled in heaps every spring. In the dense or heavy-growth timber the preliminary work was underbrushing, cutting the saplings close to the ground, piling the brush or not, as the necessity of the case seemed to require. The second step was the cutting of all down timber into lengths of ten or fifteen feet. After this came the cutting of all standing timber, which, too, had to be brushed and cut into twelve- or fifteen-foot lengths. This latter work was always a winter's job for the farmer, and the buds on these falling trees made excellent browsing feed for his cattle. In the spring-time, after the brush had become thoroughly dry, and in a dry time, a good burn of the brush, if possible, was obtained. The next part of the process was logging, usually after harvest. This required the labor of five men and a team of oxen,—one driver for the oxen and two men at each end of the log-heap. Neighbors would "morrow" with each other, and on such occasions each neighbor usually brought his own handspike. This was a round pole, usually made of beech-, dog-, or iron-wood, without any iron on or in it, about six feet long, and sharpened at the large end. Logs were rolled on the pile over skids. Sometimes the cattle were made to draw or roll the logs on the heap. These piles were then burned, and the soil was ready for the drag or the triangular harrow. I have looked like a negro many a time while working at this logging. Then money was scarce, labor plenty and cheap, and amusements few, hence grubbing, chopping, and logging " frolics" were frequent and popular. For each frolic one or more two-gallon jugs of whiskey were indispensable. A jolly good time was had, as well as a good dinner and supper, and every one in the neighborhood expected an invitation.

As there was a fence law then, the ground had to be fenced, according to this law, " horse-high, bull-strong, and hog-tight." The effort made by the pioneer to obey this law was in four ways,—viz.: First, by slashing trees and placing brush upon the trees; second, by using the logs from the clearing for the purpose of a fence; third, by a post- and rail-fence, built straight, and the end of each rail sharpened and fastened in a mortised post; fourth, by the common rail- or worm-fence. These rails were made of ash, hickory, chestnut, linn, and pine. The usual price for making rails per hundred was fifty cents with board. I have made them by contract at that price myself.

> " I seem to see the low rail-fence,
>   That worming onward mile on mile,
> Was redolent with pungent scents
>   Of sassafras and camomile.
> Within a fence-rail tall and bare,
> The saucy bluebird nested there;
> 'Twas there the largest berries grew,
> As every barefoot urchin knew!
> And swiftly, shyly creeping through
>   The tangled vine and the bramble dense,
> The mingled sunshine and the dew,
>   The Bob-White perched atop the fence;
> And, flinging toil and care away,
> He piped and lilted all the day."

In 1799, when Joseph Hutchison lived in what is now Jefferson County, wheat sold in this section of the State for two dollars and fifty cents per bushel, flour for eighteen dollars per barrel, corn two dollars, oats one dollar and fifty cents, and potatoes one dollar and fifty cents per bushel.

Wheat was brought into Massachusetts by the first settlers. Rye was also brought by them and cultivated. Our Indian corn was first successfully raised in 1608, on the James River, Virginia. Oats were brought by the first settlers and sown in 1602. Buckwheat, a native of Asia, was taken to Europe in the twelfth century, and was grown in Pennsylvania in 1702. Barley was introduced by permanent settlers and is a native of Egypt.

Columbus brought domestic animals in his second voyage, in 1493. He brought a bull, several cows, and an assortment of horses. In 1609, sheep, goats, swine, and fowls were brought.

The early axes were called pole-axes. They were rude, clumsy, and heavy, with a single bit. About 1815 an improved Yankee single-bit axe was introduced, but it, too, was heavy and clumsy. In about 1825 the present double-bitted axe came to be occasionally used.

I have never seen the wooden plough, but I have seen them with the iron shoe point and coulter. These were still in use in the late twenties. I have driven an ox-team to the drag or triangular harrow. This was the principal implement used in seeding ground, both before and after the introduction of the shovel-plough in 1843.

" The greatest improvement ever made on ploughs, in this or any other country, was made by Charles Newbold, of Burlington, New Jersey, and patented in 1797. The mould-board, share, landslide, and point were all cast together in one solid piece. The plough was all cast iron except the beam and handles. The importance of this invention was so great that it attracted the

Clearing land

attention of plough-makers and scientific men all over the country. Thomas Jefferson (afterwards President of the United States) wrote a treatise on ploughs, with a particular reference to the Newbold plough. He described the requisite form of the mould-board, according to scientific principles, and calculated the proper form and curvature of the mould-board to lessen the friction and lighten the draught.

" The Newbold plough would have been nearly perfect had it not been for one serious defect. When the point, for instance, was worn out, which would soon be accomplished, the plough was ruined and had to be thrown aside. This defect, however, was happily remedied by Jethro Wood, who was the first to cast the plough in sections, so that the parts most exposed to wear could be replaced from the same pattern, by which means the cast-iron plough became a complete success. His plough was patented in 1819, twenty-two years after Newbold's patent. It is a wonder that so long a time should have elapsed before any one thought of this improvement. These two men did more for the farmers in relation to ploughs than any others before their time or since."

In harvest-time the grain was first reaped with a sickle; then came the cradle. In my boyhood all the lying grain thrown down by storms was still reaped with a sickle. I carry the evidence of this on my fingers. A day's work was about two acres. McCormick perfected his reaper in 1848. Grain was usually thrashed by a flail, though some tramped it out with horses. By the flail ten bushels of wheat or twenty bushels of oats was a good day's work. Men who travelled around thrashing on shares with the flail charged every tenth bushel, including board. The tramping was done by horses and by farmers who had good or extra barn floors. The sheaves were laid in a circle, a man stood in the middle of the circle to turn up and over the straw as needed, and then, with a boy to ride one horse and lead another, the "tramping" in this circuit commenced. This was hard work for the boy; it made him tired and sore *where* he sat down. To prevent dizziness, the travel on the circuit was frequently reversed. One man, a boy, and two horses could tramp out in this way in a day about fifteen bushels of wheat or thirty-five bushels of oats. Grain was cleaned by means of two hand-riddles, one coarse and one fine. These riddles had no iron or steel about them, the bottom of each being made of wooden splints woven in. The riddles were two and one-half feet in diameter and the rings about four inches wide. Three men were required to clean the grain,—one to shake the riddle, while two others, one at each end of a tow sheet, doubled, swayed the sheet to and fro in front of the man shaking the riddle. These three men in this way could clean about ten or fifteen bushels of wheat in a day. This process was practised in the twenties. Windmills came into use about 1825. For many years there were extremely few wagons and but poor roads on which to use them. The early vehicles were the prongs of a tree, a sled made of saplings, called a "pung," and ox-carts. In fact, about all the work was done with oxen, and in driving his cattle the old settler would halloo with all his might and swear profusely. This profanity and hallooing was thought to be necessary. The pioneer sled was made with heavy single runners, the "bob"-sled being a later innovation. It might be proper to say here that the first agricultural society in America was organized in Pennsylvania in 1784.

" HAYING IN THE OLDEN TIME

" Haying in the old days was a much more formidable yearly undertaking than it is to modern farmers. Before the era of labor-saving haying implements farmers began the work of haying early in the day and season, and toiled hard until both were far spent. Human muscle was strained to exert a force equal to the then unused horse-power. On large farms many 'hands' were required. Haying was an event of importance in the farmer's year. It made great demands upon his time, strength, and pocket-book. His best helpers were engaged long in advance, sometimes a whole season. Ability to handle a scythe well entitled a man to respect while haying lasted. Experts took as much pains with a scythe as with a razor. Boys of to-day have never seen such a sight as a dozen stalwart men mowing a dozen-acre field.

"On the first day of haying, almost before the sun was up, the men would be at the field ready to begin. The question to be settled at the very outset was as to which man should cut the 'double.' This was the first swath to be cut down and back through the centre of the field.

"The boys brought up the rear in the line of mowers. Their scythes were hung well 'in,' to cut a narrow swath. They were told to stand up straight when mowing, point in, keep the heel of the scythe down, and point out evenly, so as not to leave 'hog-troughs' on the meadow when the hay was raked up. Impatient of these admonitions, they thought they could mow pretty well, and looked ambitiously forward to a time when they might cut the 'double.'"

HOW THE PIONEER BOUGHT HIS LAND

In 1825 Charles C. Gaskill, who lived in Punxsutawney and was agent for the Holland Land Company, advertised one hundred and fifty thousand acres of land for sale, in lots to suit purchasers, and on the following terms,— viz.: All purchasing land for two dollars per acre must pay ten dollars down, the balance in eight annual payments, with interest on and after the third year. Those buying at one dollar and seventy-five cents per acre, one-fourth in hand, the balance in eight annual payments, with interest on and after third payment. Those paying one dollar and fifty cents per acre, one-half down, and the remainder in payments as above stated. All land was bought and sold on a simple article of agreement.

DRESS OF MEN

Moccasin shoes, buckskin breeches, blue broadcloth coats and brass buttons, fawn-skin vests, roundabouts, and woollen warmuses, leather or woollen gallowses, coon- or seal-skin caps in winter with chip or oat-straw hats for summer. Every neighborhood had then usually one itinerant shoemaker and tailor, who periodically visited cabins and made up shoes or clothes as required. All material had to be furnished, and these itinerant mechanics worked for fifty cents a day and board. Corduroy pants and corduroy overalls were common.

The old pioneer in winter often wore a coon-skin cap, coon-skin gloves, buckskin breeches, leggins, and a wolf-skin hunting-shirt.

The warmuses, breeches, and hunting-shirts of the men, the linsey petticoats, dresses, and bed-gowns of the women, were all hung in some corner of the cabin on wooden pegs. To some extent this was a display of pioneer wealth.

221

DRESS OF WOMEN

Home-made woollen cloth, tow, linen, linsey-woolsey, etc. I have seen "barefoot girls with cheek of tan" walk three or four miles to church, when, on nearing the church, they would step into the woods to put on a pair of shoes they carried with them. I could name some of these who are living to-day. A woman who could buy eight or ten yards of calico for a dress at a dollar a yard put on queenly airs. Every married woman of any refinement then wore day-caps and night-caps. The bonnets were beaver, gimp, leghorn, and sun-bonnets. For shoes, women usually went barefoot in the summer, and in the winter covered their feet with moccasins, calf-skin shoes, buffalo overshoes, and shoe-packs.

Large spinning-wheel

Linen and tow cloth were made from flax. The seed was sown in the early spring and ripened about August. It was harvested by "pulling." This was generally done by a "pulling frolic" of young people pulling it out by the root. It was then tied in little sheaves and permitted to dry, hauled in, and thrashed for the seed. Then the straw was watered and rotted by laying it on the ground out of doors. Then the straw was again dried and "broken in the flax-break," after which it was again tied up in little bundles and then scutched with a wooden knife. This scutching was a frolic job too, and a dirty one. Then it was hackled. This hackling process separated the linen part from the tow. The rest of the process consisted of spinning, weaving, and dyeing. Linen cloth sold for about twenty-four cents a yard, tow cloth for about twenty cents a yard. Weaving originated with the Chinese. It took a thousand years for the art to reach Europe.

In the State Constitutional Convention of 1837 to amend the constitution I find the occupation of the members elected to that body to be as follows, —viz.: Farmers, 51; iron-masters, 3; manufacturer, 1; mechanics, 2; house-carpenters, 2; brick-maker, 1; paper-maker, 1; printers, 2; potter, 1; judge, 1; attorneys, 41; doctors, 12; editor, 1; merchants, 9; surveyors, 4; clerks, 4; total membership, 136. From this it will be seen that farmers received proper recognition in the earlier elections.

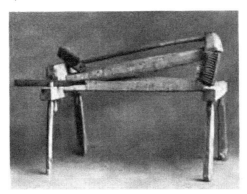

Flax-brake

THE PIONEER HOMES OF NORTHWESTERN PENNSYLVANIA

" This is the land our fathers loved,
The homestead which they toiled to win.
This is the ground whereon they moved,
And here are the graves they slumber in."

The home of the pioneer was a log cabin, one story high, chinked and daubed, having a fireplace in one end, with a chimney built of sticks and mud, and in one corner always stood a big wooden poker to turn back-logs or punch the fire. These cabins were usually small, but some were perhaps twenty by thirty feet, with a hole cut in two logs for a single window,—oiled paper being used for glass. For Brussels carpet they had puncheon floors, and a clapboard roof held down by weight poles to protect them from the storm. Wooden pegs were driven in the logs for the wardrobe, the rifle, and the powder-horn. Wooden benches and stools were a luxury upon which to rest or sit while feasting on mush and milk, buckwheat cakes, hog and hominy.

Hospitality in this log cabin was simple, hearty, and unbounded. Whiskey was pure, cheap, and plenty, and was lavished bountifully on each and all social occasions. Every settler had his jug or barrel. It was the drink of drinks at all merry-makings, grubbings, loggings, choppings, house-warmings, and weddings. A drink of whiskey was always proffered to the visitor or traveller who chanced to call or spend a night in these log cabins.

Puncheon boards or planks were made from a log of straight grain and clear of knots, and of the proper length, which was split into parts and the face of each part smoothed with a broadaxe. The split parts had to be all started at the same time, with wedges at the end of the log, each wedge being struck alternately with a maul until all the parts were separated.

The furniture for the table of the pioneer log cabins consisted of pewter dishes, plates, and spoons, or wooden bowls, plates, and noggins. If noggins were scarce, gourds and hard-shelled squashes answered for drinking-cups.

Spinning-wheel, reel, and bed-warmer

The iron pots, knives and forks, along with the salt and iron, were brought to the wilderness on pack-horses over Meade's trail or over the Milesburg and Le Bœuf State road.

Some of these log cabins near Brookville were still occupied in the forties. I have been in many of them in my childhood. In proof of the smallness of the early cabin I reproduce the testimony on oath of Thomas Lucas, Esq., in the following celebrated ejectment case,—viz.:

" EJECTMENT

" In the Court of Common Pleas of Jefferson County. Ejectment for sixteen hundred acres of land in Pine Creek township. Elijah Heath *vs.* Joshua Knap, *et al.*

" 16th September, 1841, a jury was called *per minets*. The plaintiff after having opened his case in support of the issue, gave in evidence as follows:

" Thomas Lucas.—Masons have in the surveys about twelve acres of land, a cabin house, and stable thereon. They live near the line of the town tract, the town tract takes in the apple-trees; think they claim on some improvement. Some of this improvement I think is thirty-five years old,—this was the Mason claim. The first improvement was made in 1802; I call it the Pickering survey, only an interference. Jacob Mason has been living off and on since 1802,—two small cabin houses on the interference, one fifteen or sixteen feet square, the other very small, twelve or fifteen feet,—a log stable."

At this time and before it many of these cabins were lighted by means of a half window,—viz.: one window-sash, containing from four to six panes of seven by nine glass. Up to and even at this date (1841) the usual light

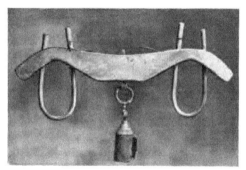

Ox-yoke and tin lantern

at night in these cabins was the old iron lamp, something like the miner wears in his hat, or else a dish containing refuse grease, with a rag in it. Each smoked and gave a dismal light, yet women cooked, spun, and sewed, and men read the few books they had as best they could. The aroma from this refuse grease was simply horrible. The cabin was daily swept with a split broom made of hickory. The hinges and latches of these cabins were made of wood. The latch on the door was raised from without by means of a buckskin string. At night, as a means of safety, the string was " pulled in," and this locked the door. As a further mark of refinement each cabin was generally guarded by from two to six worthless dogs. Cabins, as a rule, were built one story and a half high, and the space between the loose floor and roof of the half-story was used as a sleeping room. I have many a time climbed up an outside ladder, fastened to and near the chimney, to a half-story in a cabin, and slept on a bed of straw on the floor.

15   225

Of pests in and around the old cabin, the house-fly, the bed-bug, and the louse were the most common on the inside; the gnat, the wood-tick, and the horse-fly on the outside. The horse-fly is the most cruel and bloodthirsty of the entire family. He is armed with a most formidable weapon, which consists of four lancets, so sharp and strong that they will penetrate leather. He makes his appearance in June. The female is armed with six lancets, with which she bleeds both cattle and horses, and even human beings. It was a constant fight for life with man, cattle, and horses against the gnat, the tick, and the horse-fly, and if it had not been for the protection of what were called "gnat-fires," life could not have been sustained, or at least it would have been unendurable. The only thing to dispel these outside pests was to clear land and let in the sunshine. As an all-around pest in the cabin and out, day and night, there was the flea.

PIONEER FOOD—WHAT THE PIONEER COULD HAVE, OR DID HAVE, TO EAT

Buckwheat cakes, mush, and souens, corn-mush and milk, rye-mush and bread, hominy, potatoes, turnips, wild onions or wramps, wild meats, wild birds, fish, and wild fruits.

In and before 1830 flour was three dollars per barrel; beef, three cents a pound; venison ham, one and one-half cents a pound; chickens, six cents a piece; butter, six and eight cents a pound; and eggs, six cents a dozen.

In the early cooking everything was boiled and baked; this was healthy. There was no "rare fad," with its injurious results. The common dishes served were wheat- and rye-bread, wheat- and rye-mush, Indian corn-pone, cakes, and mush, sweet and buttermilk boiled and thickened, doughnuts, and baked pot-pies. Soda was made by burning corncobs. We are indebted to the heathen Chinese for the art of bread-making from wheat, 1998 B.C.

Buckwheat souens was a great pioneer dish. It was made in this wise: Mix your buckwheat flour and water in the morning; add to this enough yeast to make the batter light; then let it stand until evening, or until the batter is real sour. Now stir this batter into boiling water and boil until it is thoroughly cooked, like corn-mush. Eat hot or cold with milk or cream. Buckwheat is a native of Asia.

MEATS

Hogs, bears, elks, deer, rabbits, squirrels, and woodchucks.

The saddles or hams of the deer were salted by the pioneer, then smoked and dried. This was a great luxury, and could be kept all the year through.

The late Dr. Clarke wrote, " Wild game, such as elks, deer, bears, turkeys, and partridges, were numerous, and for many years constituted an important part of the animal food of the early settlers in this wilderness. Wolves and panthers came in for a share of this game, until they, too, became game for the hunters by the public and legal offer of bounties to be paid for their scalps, or rather for their ears, for a perfect pair of ears was required to secure the bounty. All these have become nearly extinct. The sturdy elk no longer roves over the hills or sips 'salty sweetness' from the licks. The peculiar voice of the stately strutting wild turkey is heard no more. The howl of the wolf and the panther's cry no longer alarm the traveller as he winds his way over the hills or through the valleys, and the flocks are now permitted to rest in peace. Even the wild deer is now seldom seen, and a nice venison steak rarely gives its delicious aroma among the shining plate of modern well-set tables."

FISH

Pike, bass, catfish, suckers, sunfish, horn-chubs, mountain trout, and eels.

The old settler shot, seined, hooked with a line, and gigged his fish. Gigging was done at night by means of a light made from burning fagots of pitch-pine. It usually required three to do this gigging, whether "wading" or in a canoe,—one to carry the light ahead, one to gig, and one to care for the fish.

BIRDS

Pheasants were plentiful, and enlivened the forests with their drumming. The waters and woods were full of wild ducks, geese, pigeons, and turkeys.

The most remarkable bird in America was the wild turkey. It is the original turkey, and is the stock from which the tame turkeys sprung. In the wild state it was to be found in the wooded lands east of the Rocky Mountains. In pioneer times it was called gobbler or Bubly Jock by the whites, and Oo-coo-coo by the Indians. Our pioneer hunters could mimic or imitate the gobbling of a turkey, and this deceptive ruse was greatly practised to excite the curiosity and bring the bird within shooting distance. The last wild turkey in Jefferson County was killed in the seventies near the town of False Creek.

To obtain a turkey roast when needed, the pioneer sometimes built in the woods a pen of round logs and covered it with brush. Whole flocks of turkeys were sometimes caught in these pens, built in this wise:

" First, a narrow ditch, about six feet long and two feet deep, was dug. Over this trench the pen was built, leaving a few feet of the channel outside of the enclosure. The end of the part of the trench enclosed was usually about the middle of the pen. Over the ditch, near the wall of the pen, boards were laid. The pen was made tight enough to hold a turkey and covered with poles. Then corn was scattered about on the inside, and the ditch outside baited with the same grain. Sometimes straw was also scattered about in the pen. Then the trap was ready for its victims. The turkeys came to the pen, began to pick up the corn, and followed the trench within. When they had eaten enough, the birds tried to get out by walking around the pen, looking up all the time. They would cross the ditch on the boards, and never think of going to the opening in the ground at the centre of the pen. When the

227

hunter found his game he had only to crawl into the pen through the trench and kill the birds."

In the fall turkeys became very fat, and gobblers were sometimes captured for Christmas in this way weighing over twenty pounds.

FRUITS

Apples, crab-apples, wild, red, and yellow plums, blackberries, huckle-berries, elderberries, wild strawberries, choke-cherries, and wild gooseberries; and there were

SWEETS

Domestic and wild honey, maple-sugar, maple-molasses, and corn-cob molasses. Bee-trees were numerous, and would frequently yield from eight to twelve gallons of excellent honey. These trees had to be cut in the night by the light of pitch-pine fagots.

DRINK

Metheglin, a drink made from honey; whiskey, small beer, rye coffee, buttermilk, and fern, sassafras, sage, and mint teas.

Distilled liquor was discovered in India and introduced into Europe in 1150. The name whiskey was given to it by the Scotch, who made it from barley.

To fully illustrate the pioneer days I quote from the "History of Crawford County, Pennsylvania,"—viz.:

"The habits of the pioneers were of a simplicity and purity in conformance to their surroundings and belongings. The men were engaged in the herculean labor, day after day, of enlarging the little patch of sunshine about their homes, cutting away the forest, burning off the brush and débris, preparing the soil, planting, tending, harvesting, caring for the few animals which they brought with them or soon procured, and in hunting. While they were engaged in the heavy labor of the field and forest, or following the deer, or seeking other game, their helpmeets were busied with their household duties, providing for the day and for the winter coming on, cooking, making clothes, spinning, and weaving. They were fitted by nature and experience to be the consorts of the brave men who first came into the western wilderness. They were heroic in their endurance of hardship and privation and loneliness.

"Their industry was well directed and unceasing. Woman's work then, like man's, was performed under disadvantages, which have been removed in later years. She had not only the common household duties to perform, but many others. She not only made the clothing, but the fabric for it. That old, old occupation of spinning and weaving, with which woman's name has been associated in all history, and of which the modern world knows nothing, except through the stories of those who are great-grandmothers now,—that

228

old occupation of spinning and weaving which seems surrounded with a glamour of romance as we look back to it through tradition and poetry, and which always conjures up thoughts of the graces and virtues of the dames and damsels of a generation that is gone,—that old, old occupation of spinning and weaving was the chief industry of the pioneer woman. Every cabin sounded with the softly whirring wheel and the rhythmic thud of the loom. The woman of pioneer times was like the woman described by Solomon: ' She seeketh wool and flax, and worketh willingly with her hands; she layeth her hands to the spindle, and her hands hold the distaff.'

" Almost every article of clothing, all of the cloth in use in the old log cabins, was the product of the patient woman-weaver's toil. She spun the flax and wove the cloth for shirts, pantaloons, frocks, sheets, and blankets. The linen and the wool, the ' linsey-woolsey' woven by the housewife, formed all of the material for the clothing of both men and women, except such articles as were made of skins. The men commonly wore the hunting-shirt, a kind of loose frock reaching half-way down the figure, open before, and so wide as to lap over a foot or more upon the chest. This generally had a cape, which was often fringed with a ravelled piece of cloth of a different color from that which composed the garment. The bosom of the hunting-shirt answered as a pouch, in which could be carried the various articles that the hunter or woodsman would need. It was always worn belted, and made out of coarse linen, or linsey, or of dressed deer-skin, according to the fancy of the wearer. Breeches were made of heavy cloth or of deer-skin, and were often worn with leggings of the same material or of some kind of leather, while the feet were most usually encased in moccasins, which were easily and quickly made, though they needed frequent mending. The deer-skin breeches or drawers were very comfortable when dry, but when they became wet were very cold to the limbs, and the next time they were put on were almost as stiff as if made of wood. Hats or caps were made of the various native furs. The women were clothed in linsey petticoats, coarse shoes and stockings, and wore buckskin gloves or mittens when any protection was required for the hands. All of the wearing apparel, like that of the men, was made with a view to being serviceable and comfortable, and all was of home manufacture. Other articles and finer ones were sometimes worn, but they had been brought from former homes, and were usually relics handed down from parents to children. Jewelry was not common, but occasionally some ornament was displayed. In the cabins of the more cultivated pioneers were usually a few books, and the long winter evenings were spent in poring over these well-thumbed volumes by the light of the great log-fire, in knitting, mending, curing furs, or some similar occupation.

"As the settlement increased, the sense of loneliness and isolation was dispelled, the asperities of life were softened and its amenities multiplied; social gatherings became more numerous and more enjoyable. The log-rollings, harvestings, and husking-frolics for the men, and apple-butter-making and the quilting-parties for the women, furnished frequent occasions for social intercourse. The early settlers took much pleasure and pride in rifle-shooting, and as they were accustomed to the use of the gun as a means often of obtaining a subsistence, and relied upon it as a weapon of defence, they exhibited considerable skill.

" Foot-racing, wrestling, and jumping matches were common. The jumping matches consisted of the ' single jump,' backward jump, high jump, three jumps, and the running hop, step, and jump.

"A wedding was the event of most importance in the sparsely settled new country. The young people had every inducement to marry, and generally did so as soon as able to provide for themselves. When a marriage was to be celebrated, all the neighborhood turned out. It was customary to have the ceremony performed before dinner, and in order to be in time, the groom and his attendants usually started from his father's house in the morning for that of the bride. All went on horseback, riding in single file along the narrow trail. Arriving at the cabin of the bride's parents, the ceremony would be performed, and after that dinner served. This would be a substantial back-woods feast, of beef, pork, fowls, and bear- or deer-meat, with such vegetables as could be procured. The greatest hilarity prevailed during the meal. After it was over, the dancing began, and was usually kept up till the next morning, though the newly made husband and wife were, as a general thing, put to bed in the most approved fashion and with considerable formality in the middle of the evening's hilarity. The tall young men, when they went on the floor to dance, had to take their places with care between the logs that supported the loft-floor, or they were in danger of bumping their heads. The figures of the dances were three- and four-hand reels, or square sets and jigs. The commencement was always a square four, which was followed by ' jigging it off,' or what is sometimes called a ' cut-out jig.' The ' settlement' of a young couple was thought to be thoroughly and generously made when the neighbors assembled and raised a cabin for them."

PIONEER PRICES FOR SKILLED AND UNSKILLED LABOR

For Carpenters.	For Day Laborers.
1800....................70 cents per day	1800.....................62 cents per day
1810..................... ..$1.09 per day	1810......... ....82 cents per day
1820...;................... 1.13 per day	1820......................90 cents per day
1830–1840.................. 1.40 per day	1840–1860..........$1.00 (about) per day
1850–1860................... 1.50 per day	

Previous to 1840, a day's work was not limited by hours. It was by law and custom from " sunrise to sunset," or whatever the employer exacted. In 1840, however, President Van Buren signed the pioneer executive order fixing a day's work in the Washington Navy-Yard at ten hours per day. It took a great and protracted struggle for years and years to secure the general adoption of the ten-hour system.

PIONEER EVENING FROLICS, SOCIAL PARTIES, PLAYS, AND AMUSEMENTS—HOW
   THE PIONEER AND EARLY SETTLERS MADE THEIR LOG CABINS MERRY WITH
   SIMPLE, PRIMITIVE ENJOYMENTS

In the pioneer days newspapers were few, dear, printed on coarse paper, and small. Books were scarce, only occasional preaching, no public lectures, and but few public meetings, excepting the annual Fourth of July celebration, when all the patriots assembled to hear the Declaration of Independence read. The pioneer and his family had to have fun. The common saying of that day was that "all work and no play makes Jack a dull boy." As a rule, outside of the villages, everybody lived in log cabins, and were bound together by mutual dependence and acts of neighborly kindness. At every cabin the latch-string was always out. The young ladies of the "upper ten" learned music, but it was the humming of to "knit and spin;" their piano was a loom, their sunshade a broom, and their novel a Bible. A young gentleman or lady was then as proud of his or her new suit, woven by a sister or a mother on her own loom, as proud could be, and these new suits or "best clothes" were always worn to evening frolics. Social parties among the young were called "kissing parties," because in all the plays, either as a penalty or as part of the play, all the girls who joined in the amusement had to be kissed by some one of the boys. The girls, of course, objected to the kissing; but then they were gentle, pretty, and witty, and the sweetest and best girls the world ever knew. This was true, for I attended these parties and kissed some girls myself. To the boys and girls of that period—

> " The earth was like a garden then,
>   And life seemed like a show,
>   For the air was rife with fragrance,
>   The sky was all rainbow,
>   And the heart was warm and joyous;
>   Each lad had native grace,
>   Sly Cupid planted blushes then
>   On every virgin's face."

The plays were nearly all musical and vocal, and the boys lived and played them in the "pleasures of hope," while usually there sat in the corner of the cabin fireplace a grandad or a grandma smoking a stone or clay pipe, lighted with a live coal from the wood-fire, living and smoking in the "pleasures of memory."

The plays were conducted somewhat in this way:

A popular play was for all the persons present to join hands and form a ring, with a dude of that time, in shirt of check and bear-greased hair, in the centre. Then they circled round and round the centre person, singing,—

> " King William was King James's son,
> And of that royal race he sprung;
> He wore a star upon his breast,
> To show that he was royal best.
> Go choose your east, go choose your west,
> Go choose the one that you like best;
> If he's not here to take your part,
> Go choose another with all your heart."

The boy in the centre then chose a lady from the circle, and she stepped into the ring with him. Then the circling was resumed, and all sang to the parties inside,—

> " Down on this carpet you must kneel,
> Just as the grass grows in the field;
> Salute your bride with kisses sweet,
> And then rise up upon your feet."

The play went on in this manner until all the girls present were kissed.

Another popular play was to form a ring. A young lady would step into the circle, and all parties would join hands and sing,—

> " There's a lily in the garden
> For you, young man;
> There's a lily in the garden,
> Go pluck it if you can," etc.

The lady then selects a boy from the circle, who walks into the ring with her. He then kisses her and she goes out, when the rest all sing,—

> " There he stands, that great big booby,
> Who he is I do not know;
> Who will take him for his beauty?
> Let her answer, yes or no."

This play goes on in this way until all the girls have been kissed.

Another favorite play was:

> " Oats, peas, beans, and barley grows;
> None so well as the farmer knows
> How oats, peas, beans, and barley grows;
> Thus the farmer sows his seed,
> Thus he stands to take his ease;
> He stamps his foot and claps his hands,
> And turns around to view his lands," etc.

Another great favorite was:

> "Oh, sister Phœbe, how merry were we
> The night we sat under the juniper-tree,
>   The juniper-tree, I, oh.
> Take this hat on your head, keep your head warm,
> And take a sweet kiss, it will do you no harm,
>   But a great deal of good, I know," etc.

Another was:

> "If I had as many lives
>   As Solomon had wives,
>   I'd be as old as Adam;
>   So rise to your feet
>   And kiss the first you meet,
>   Your humble servant, madam."

Another was:

> "It's raining, it's hailing, it's cold, stormy weather;
> In comes the farmer drinking of his cider.
> He's going a-reaping, he wants a binder,
> I've lost my true love, where shall I find her."

A live play was called " hurly-burly." " Two went round and gave each one, secretly, something to do. The girl was to pull a young man's hair; another to tweak an ear or nose, or trip some one, etc. When all had been told what to do, the master of ceremonies cried out, ' Hurly-burly.' Every one sprang up and hastened to do as instructed. This created a mixed scene of a ludicrous character, and was most properly named 'hurly-burly.' "

TREES, SNAKES, AND REPTILES

Our forests were originally covered by a heavy growth of timber-trees of various kinds. Pine and hemlock predominated. Chestnut and oak grew in some localities. Birch, sugar-maple, ash, and hickory occupied a wide range. Birch- and cherry-trees were numerous, and linnwood-, cucumber-, and poplar-trees grew on many of the hill-sides, and butternut, sycamore, black ash, and elm on the low grounds.

In all, about one hundred varieties of trees grew here. These forests have become the prey of the woodman's axe. There has been no voice raised effectively to restrain the destruction, wanton as it has been, of the best specimens of the pine which the eye of man ever saw. The growth of hundreds of years felled to the ground, scarified, hauled to the streams, tumbled in, and floated away to the south and east and west for the paltry pittance of ten cents a foot! Oh, that there could have been some power to restrain the grasping, wasteful, avaricious cupidity of man, of some voice of thunder crying, " Woodman, woodman, spare that tree! That old familiar

233

forest-tree, whose glory and renown has spread over land and sea, and wouldst thou hack it down?"

But they are gone, all gone from the mountain's brow. The hands, also, that commenced the destruction are now mouldering into dust, thus exemplifying the law of nature, that growth is rapidly followed by decay, indicating a common destiny and bringing a uniform result. And such are we; it is our lot thus to die and be forgotten.

Reptiles and snakes were very numerous. The early pioneer had to contend against the non-poisonous and poisonous snakes. The non-poisonous were the spotted adder, blacksnake, the green-, the garter-, the water-, and

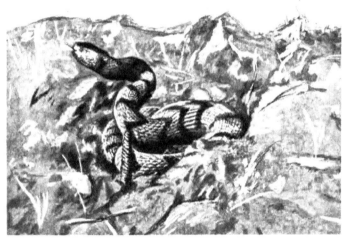

Banded rattlesnake (*Crotalus Horridus*)

the house-snake. The blacksnake sometimes attained a length of six and eight feet. But dens of vicious rattlesnakes existed in every locality. In the vicinity of Brookville there was one at Puckerty, several on the north fork, one at Iowa Mills, and legions of rattlers on Mill Creek. The dens had to be visited by bold, hardy men annually every spring to kill and destroy these reptiles as they emerged in the sun from their dens. Hundreds had to be destroyed at each den every spring. This was necessary as a means of safety for both man and beast. Of copperheads, there were but a few dens in Jefferson County, and these in the extreme south and southwest,—viz.: in Perry Township, in Beaver Township, on Beaver Run; and two or three dens in Porter Township, on the head-waters of Pine Run,—viz.: Nye's Branch and Lost Hill. Occasionally one was found in Brookville.

The copperhead is hazel-brown on the back and flesh-colored on the belly. On each side there are from fifteen to twenty-six chestnut blotches or bands, that somewhat resemble an inverted Y. His head is brighter and almost copper-colored on top, and everywhere over his back are found very fine dark points. The sides of his head are cream-colored. The dividing line between the flesh of the side and the copper of the top passes through the upper edge of the head, in front of the eye, and involves three-fourths of the orbit. The line is very distinct. He cannot climb, and lives on lizards,

Copperhead (*Ancistrodon Contortrix*)

mice, frogs, and small birds, summers mostly on low, moist ground, but winters on ridges.

He is commonly found wherever the rattler is, but he does not live quite so far north in our wilderness. He has a variety of names,—upland moccasin, chunkhead, deaf-adder, and pilot-snake among the rest. It is agreed that he is a much more vicious brute than the rattlesnake. He is more easily irritated and is quicker in his movements. It is said that he will even follow up a victim for a second blow. On the other hand, his bite is very much less dangerous for a variety of reasons. In the first place, he is no more than three feet long, and his fangs are considerably shorter than those of a rattler of the same size, while his strength is less, and the blow, therefore, less effective. So he cannot inflict as deep a wound nor inject so much venom. The chances of his getting the venom directly into a large vein are proportionately less.

Rattlesnakes, copperheads, and other large snakes do most of their travelling in the night. " Snakes, it appears, are extremely fastidious, every species being limited to one or two articles of diet, and preferring to starve rather than eat anything else apparently quite as toothsome and suitable. Individual snakes, too, show strange prejudices in the matter of diet, so that it is necessary in every case to find out what the snake's peculiarities are before feeding him."

Rattlesnakes eat rabbits, birds, mice, rats, etc., and live on barren, rocky, or on huckleberry land. They like to bathe, drink, and live in the sunshine. This, too, makes them avoid ridgy, heavily timbered land. They can live a year without food.

The bigger the reptile, of course, the more poison it has. Furthermore, it is to be remembered that of all American serpents the rattlesnake is the most dangerous, the copperhead less so, and the water-moccasin least. It is a fact that the poisonous snakes are proof against their own venom. That this is true has been demonstrated repeatedly by inoculating such serpents with the poisonous secretion from their salivary glands. It is believed that there exists in the blood of the venomous snake some agent similar to the poison itself, and that the presence of this toxic principle is accountable for the immunity exhibited.

One safety from the snakes to the pioneer and his family was the great number of razor-back hogs. These animals were great snake-hunters, being very fond of them.

RATTLESNAKES FIRST KILL THEIR PREY, THEN SWALLOW IT WHOLE

The rattlesnake and copperhead are not found anywhere but in America. The rattler belongs to the viper family. There are twelve species and thirteen varieties. They vary in size and color, one variety being red, white, and green spotted and black. A rattle is formed at each renewal of the skin, and as the skin may be renewed more than once a year, rattles do not indicate the exact age. They live to a ripe old age, and have sometimes as many as thirty rattles. In the natural state the rattler sheds his skin but once a year, but in confinement he can be forced to shed the skin two or three times annually by giving him warm baths and keeping him in a warm place. Rattlers feed two or three times a year, but drink water freely and often, and like a horse. Rattlers are indifferent climbers of trees, are fond of music, and do not chase a retreating animal that has escaped their " strike."

The rattlesnake of Northwestern Pennsylvania is the *Crotalus horridus*, or North American species, and is black and yellow spotted, called banded or timber. They have no feet or legs, but have double reproductive organs, both the male and female. Their scent is very acute, and by scent they find food and their mates. Our snake attains the length of five feet, but usually only four and one-half feet, and they inhabit the barren, rocky portions of the northwest, formerly in immense numbers, but of late years they are not so plentiful.

Dr. Ferd. Hoffman, of our town, celebrated as a snake-charmer, brought a rattlesnake into our store one day, in a little box covered with wire screen. The snake was small, being only thirty inches long and having seven rattles. Desiring to see the reptile eat, and knowing that they will not eat anything but what they kill themselves, we conceived the idea of furnishing his king-

Rattlesnake Pete catching banded rattlers in Venango County

ship a repast. Mr. Robert Scofield went out and captured a large field-mouse (not mole) and brought it in, and, in the presence of myself, Scofield, Albert Gooder, 'Squire McLaughlin and brother, and Frank Arthurs, dropped it into the box under the screen. The box was fourteen inches long and seven inches wide. The snake, being lively, immediately struck the mouse back of the head. The mouse gave a little squeak of terror and ran fourteen inches, then staggered fourteen inches, the length of the box, then was apparently seized with spinal paralysis, for it had to draw its hind limbs with its front feet to a corner of the box. It then raised up and fell dead on its back. After

237

striking the mouse, the snake paid no attention to anything until the mouse dropped over dead, then his snakeship wakened up and apparently smelled (examined) the mouse all over. Satisfied it was healthy and good food, the snake caught the mouse by the nose and pulled it out of the corner. After

Dr. Ferd. Hoffman, of Brookville

this was done, the snake commenced the process of swallowing in this manner, —viz.: He opened his jaws and took the head of the mouse in one swallow, pulling alternately by the hooks in the upper and lower jaw, thus forcing the mouse downward, taking an occasional rest, swallowing and resting six times in the process. He rattled vigorously three times during this procedure. It is said they rattle only when in fear or in danger. This rattling of his must

238

have been a notice to us that he was dining, and to stand back. The rattler is the most intelligent of all snake kind.

I am informed by my friend Dr. Hoffman, of Brookville, Pennsylvania, that the rattlesnake is possessed of both intelligence and a memory; that he can be domesticated, and in that state become quite affectionate and fond of his master, and that snakes thus domesticated will vie and dispute with each other in manifestations of affection to and for their master. They have their dislikes also. He also informs me that rattlesnakes are unlike in disposition,— some are cross and ugly, while others are docile and pleasant.

He also informs me that the rattlesnake can be trained to perform tricks, as he has thus trained them himself and made them proficient in numerous acrobatic tricks, such as suspending a number by the head of one on his thumb, the forming of a suspension chain or bridge, and many other tricks too numerous to relate.

To my personal knowledge, he has educated or trained the rattlers in numbers to perform in the manner indicated here, and without removing, in a single instance, any poisonous tooth or sac. These trained rattlers will fight any stranger the moment he presents himself; but if the master or their acquaintance presents himself, the rattlers will at once recognize him, and to him be kind, docile, and affectionate. A rattler matures at the age of two years, and at three is full grown.

"All the different species of rattlesnakes are provided with two small sacs, each of which contains a minute quantity of poison, and communicates, by means of a short excretory duct, with the canal in the fang on each side of the upper jaw. It is enclosed by a bony framework, situated external to the proper jaw, and is under the control of appropriate muscles, the action of which aids materially in expelling its contents. The fangs, situated just at the verge of the mouth, are very long, sharp, and crooked, like the claws of a cat, and are naturally retracted and concealed in a fold of integument; but, when the animal is irritated, are capable of being instantly raised, and darted forward with great force into the skin, followed by an emission of poison. The snake, then, does not bite, but strikes, making a punctured wound.

" The poison of the rattlesnake is a thin, semi-transparent, albuminous fluid, of a yellowish color, with, occasionally, a tinge of green, and is deadly. When a bite is not fatal it is because of no poison in sack, broken teeth, or failure to puncture the skin or clothing. It is fatal in from ten minutes to two hours.

" The quantity of venom contained in the poison-bag does not generally exceed a teaspoonful; but it accumulates when the animal is inactive, and Dr. Mitchell had a snake which, on one occasion, ejected fifteen drops, its fang not having been used for several weeks. It is peculiarly acrid and deadly in hot weather and during the procreating season. In winter and early spring the reptile is in a torpid condition, and the poison is then diminished in quantity, and unusually thick, although not less virulent."

Nearly every variety of the snake family is oviparous. The eggs are oblong. The blacksnake lays a large number of eggs, about the size of your thumb, in July or August. During this breeding season blacksnakes are bold, and will attack persons with great courage if their nests are approached. The attack is with activity and by direct assault. Their bite is harmless, and the blacksnake is a great tree-climber. The rattlesnake is viviparous, and

Peter Gruber, now of Rochester, New York, late of Oil City. Pennsylvania, taking the poison from a diamond-back rattler for the author

has from five to twenty young in July or August, each eight to fourteen inches long and as thick as a lead-pencil. They are ready to fight, and eat a mouse or young squirrel every fifth day. The male is the slimmest. The blacksnake and rattlesnake are mortal enemies. They always fight when they meet, the blacksnake usually kills the other, his activity enabling him to tear the rattler to pieces. He coils himself around the head and tail of the rattler, and then pulls him in two. Snakes have what phrenologists call love of home. A rattler will travel forty miles to winter in his ancestral den. Snakes have ears, but no apparent external opening, the orifice being covered with a scale. They usually travel in mated pairs; if you kill one there is another near by. Usually when one snake rattles in a den they all commence. The sickening odor of the den is due to urination when excited. Rattlesnake oil is in great repute as a medicine for external application.

The copperheads have their young alive, and never more than seven at a birth. The young are ready to fight from birth.

" Rattlesnake Pete," * of Rochester, New York, has been bitten by rattlers over eighteen times, and, as a result, has passed a good deal of his time in hospitals, swathed in bandages, and enduring the most agonizing pains.

Blacksnake

" Whenever I am bitten now," he remarked to me, " I never suck the wound. If there were any slight superficial wound in the mouth, such as a scratch, the venom would thus get into the system and would perhaps prove fatal. Directly I have been bitten I cut the flesh around the puncture and make another wound between the injured spot and the heart with a sharp knife, which I always carry with me in case of such an emergency. Into these two self-inflicted wounds I then inject permanganate of potash, which has the effect of nullifying the serpent's venom."

The snapping-turtle, the mud-turtle, and the diamond-back terrapin existed in countless numbers in the swamps and around the streams, and formed a part of the Indian's food. The tree-toad, the common toad, common frog,

* Peter Gruber, who was born and raised near Oil City, Pennsylvania.

lizard, and water-lizard lived here before the pioneers took possession of the land.

The tools of the pioneer were the axe, six-inch auger, the drawing-knife, the shaving-knife, a broadaxe, and a cross-cut saw. These were "all used in the erecting of his shelters." The dexterity of the pioneer in the "sleight" and use of the axe was remarkable, indeed marvellous. He used it in clearing land, making fences, chopping firewood, cutting paths and roads, building cabins, bridges, and corduroy. In fact, in all work and hunting, in travelling by land, in canoeing and rafting on the water, the axe was ever the friend and companion of the pioneer.

The civilized man in his first undertakings was farmer, carpenter, mason, merchant, and manufacturer—complete, though primitive, in the individual. But he was a farmer first and foremost, and used the other avocations merely as incidentals to the first and chief employment. Less than half a century has elapsed since the spinning-wheel and the loom were common and necessary in the home.

SOLDIERS OF 1812 WHO PASSED THROUGH THIS WILDERNESS TO FIGHT GREAT BRITAIN—AN INTERESTING ACCOUNT OF THE PENNSYLVANIA MILITIA WHICH MARCHED OVER THE OLD STATE ROAD THROUGH BROOKVILLE AND WITHIN TWO MILES OF WHERE REYNOLDSVILLE NOW STANDS, NEAR WHERE CLARION BOROUGH NOW IS, WHILE ON ITS WAY TO ERIE

George Washington never passed through any portion of Jefferson County with soldiers; neither did Colonel Bird, who was stationed at Fort Augusta in 1756; neither was there a "road brushed out for the purpose of transferring troops to Erie." In 1814, early in the spring, a detachment of soldiers, under command of Major William McClelland, travelled through our county, over the old State Road (Bald Eagle's Nest and Le Bœuf Road) to Erie. They encamped at Soldiers' Run, in what is now Winslow Township, rested at Port Barnett for four days, and encamped over night at the "four-mile" spring, on what is now the Afton farm. Elijah M. Graham was impressed with his two "pack-horses" into their service, and was taken as far as French Creek, now in Venango County.

Joseph B. Graham gave me these facts in regard to McClelland.

These soldiers were Pennsylvania volunteers and drafted men, and were from Franklin County. Major McClelland, with his officers and men, passed through where Brookville now is, over the old Milesburg and Waterford Road. Three detachments of troops left Franklin County during the years 1812–14 at three different times,—one by way of Pittsburg, one by way of Baltimore, and the last one through this wilderness. All of these troops in these three detachments were under the supervision of the brigade inspector, Major McClelland.

I quote from an early history of Franklin County, Pennsylvania:

" In the early part of the year 1814, the general government having made a call upon the State of Pennsylvania for more troops, Governor Simon Snyder, about the beginning of February of that year, ordered a draft for one thousand men from the counties of York, Adams, Franklin, and Cumberland, Cumberland County to raise five hundred men and the other counties the balance. The quota of Franklin County was ordered to assemble at Loudon on the 1st of March, 1814. What was its exact number I have not been able to ascertain.

"At that time Captain Samuel Dunn, of Path Valley, had a small volunteer company under his command, numbering about forty men. These, I am informed, volunteered to go as part of the quota of the county, and were accepted. Drafts were then made to furnish the balance of the quota, and one full company of drafted men, under the command of Captain Samuel Gordon, of Waynesburg, and one partial company, under command of Captain Jacob Stake, of Lurgan Township, were organized, and assembled at Loudon in pursuance of the orders of the governor. There the command of the detachment was assumed by Major William McClelland, brigade inspector of the county, who conducted it to Erie. It moved from Loudon on the 4th of March, and was twenty-eight days in reaching Erie. According to Major McClelland's report on file in the auditor-general's office at Harrisburg, it was composed of one major, three captains, five lieutenants, two ensigns, and two hundred and twenty-one privates.

" Captain Jacob Stake lived along the foot of the mountains, between Roxbury and Strasburg. He went as captain of a company of drafted men as far as Erie, at which place his company was merged into those of Captains Dunn and Gordon, as the commissions of those officers antedated his commission, and there were not men enough in their companies to fill them up to the required complement."

Upon the arrival of these troops at Erie, and after their organization into companies, they were put into the Fifth Regiment of the Pennsylvania troops, commanded by Colonel James Fenton, of that regiment. James Wood, of Greencastle, was major, and Thomas Poe, of Antrim Township, adjutant. the whole army being under the command of Major General Jacob Brown, a gallant soldier.

Adjutant Poe is reputed to have been a gallant officer, one to whom fear was unknown. On one occasion he quelled a mutiny among the men in camp, unaided by any other person. The mutineers afterwards declared that they saw death in his eyes when he gave them the command to " return to quarters." He fell mortally wounded at the battle of Chippewa, July 5, 1814, and died shortly afterwards.

These soldiers did valiant service against the British. They fought in the desperate battles of Chippewa and Lundy's Lane, on July 5 and 25 of the year 1814.

WARS OF THE UNITED STATES—1775–1865

War of the Revolution.—April 19, 1775, to April 11, 1783. Regulars, 130,711; militia and volunteers, 164,080; total, 309,781. Number of Americans killed, wounded, and missing, 12,861. Navy, vessels, 4; Americans killed, 912.

Daniel F. Bakeman, the last survivor of the war of the Revolution, died in Freedom, Cattaraugus County, New York, April 5, 1869, aged one hundred and nine years.

War with France.—July 9, 1798, to September 30, 1800. Entirely naval. Men, 4593. Americans won every battle.

War with Tripoli.—June 10, 1801, to June 4, 1805. Naval. Men, 3330. Americans won every battle.

War of 1812.—June 18, 1812, to February 17, 1815. Regulars, 85,000; militia and volunteers, 471,622; total, 576,622. Americans killed, wounded, and missing, 5614. American navy had twelve vessels at outbreak of war. England, one thousand. Fifteen battles were fought on the sea. Americans victorious in twelve. Americans killed, 1233.

War with Mexico.—April 12, 1846, to July 4, 1848: Regulars, 30,954; militia and volunteers, 73,776; total, 112,230.

Americans killed, 4,197; Americans killed in navy, 140; killed from Jefferson County, 1.

The United States has always been successful in every war, on land or sea.

A British statesman made the declaration at the commencement of hostilities in 1812, " that the assembled navy of America could not lay siege to an English sloop of war." I guess the siege was pretty well laid.

The aggregate number of men raised by the government for the Union armies from 1861 to 1865 reached over two million six hundred and eighty-eight thousand soldiers, and if you add to this the Confederate forces, you will have a grand aggregate of four million of men, at once the largest force ever put on a war footing in any one country in any age of the world.

The United States paid during the Mexican War, to privates in infantry, seven dollars per month, and to privates in cavalry, eight dollars per month.

In the war of the Rebellion the United States government paid, until August, 1861, to privates of cavalry, twelve dollars per month, and to privates of infantry, eleven dollars per month. From August 6, 1861, until January 1, 1862, the pay of privates was thirteen dollars per month. Specie payment was suspended by the nation, January 1, 1862, and all payments to soldiers after that were in depreciated currency. From January 1, 1862, the pay of all privates in currency was thirteen dollars per month, until May 1, 1864, equal to about eight dollars in gold. From May 1, 1864, to the close of the war in 1865, the pay of all private soldiers was sixteen dollars per month in currency, equal to about ten dollars per month in gold.

Over fourteen million lives were lost from 1800 to 1900 in war.

COST OF PENSIONS

" Of the amount that has been expended for pensions since the foundation of the government, $70,000,000 was on account of the war of the Revolution, $45,326,774.16 on account of service in the war of 1812, $6,980,896.93 on account of service in the Indian wars, $35,162,130.35 on account of service in the Mexican war, $8,586,200.09 on account of the war with Spain, $2,287,924.99 on account of the regular establishment, and $3,011,373,235.13 on account of the War of the Rebellion."

AN OUTLINE OF THE PIONEER LEGAL RELATIONS OF MAN AND WIFE

Up to and later than 1843, Pennsylvania was under the common law system of England. Under this law the wife had no legal separate existence. The husband had the right to whip her, and only in the event of her committing crimes had she a separate existence from her husband. But if the crime was committed in her husband's presence, she was then presumed not guilty. Her condition was legally little, if any, better than that of a slave.

Under the common law, husband and wife were considered as *one person*, and on this principle all their civil duties and relations rested.

The wife could not sue in her own name, but only through her husband. If she suffered wrong in her person or property, she could, with her husband's aid and assistance, prosecute, but the husband had to be the plaintiff. For crimes without any presumed coercion of her husband, the wife could be prosecuted and punished, and for these misdemeanors the punishments were severe.

The wife could make no contract with her husband. The husband and she could make a contract through the agency of trustees for the wife, the wife, though, being still under the protection of her husband.

All contracts made between husband and wife before marriage were void after the ceremony. The husband could in no wise convey lands or realty to his wife, only and except through a trustee. A husband at death could bequeath real estate to his wife.

Marriage gave the husband all right and title to his wife's property, whether real or personal, but he then became liable for all her debts and contracts, even those that were made before marriage, and after marriage he was so liable, except for " superfluities and extravagances."

If the wife died before the husband and left no children, the husband and his heirs inherited her real estate. But if there were children, the husband remained in possession of her land during the lifetime of the wife, and at his death the land went to the wife's heirs.

All debts due to the wife became after marriage the property of the husband, who became invested with power to sue on bond, note, or any other obligation, to his own and exclusive use. The powers of discharge and assignment and change of securities were, of course, involved in the leading principle. If the husband died before the recovery of the money, or any change in the securities, the wife became entitled to these debts, etc., in her own right. All personal property of the wife, such as money, goods, movables, and stocks, became absolutely the property of the husband upon marriage, and at his death went to his heirs.

Property could be given to a wife by deed of marriage settlement.

Property could be settled on the wife after marriage by the husband, provided he was solvent at the time and the transfer not made with a view to defraud.

The wife could not sell her land, but any real estate settled upon her to a trustee she could bequeath.

The husband and wife could not be witnesses against each other in civil or criminal cases where the testimony could in the least favor or criminate either. One exception only existed to this rule, and that was that "the personal safety or the life of the wife gave her permission to testify for her protection." For further information, see my "Recollections."

A PIONEER SONG THAT WAS SUNG IN EVERY FAMILY

"Old Grimes is dead, that good old man,
    We ne'er shall see him more;
He used to wear a long black coat
    All buttoned down before.

"His heart was open as the day,
    His feelings all were true;
His hair was some inclined to gray,
    He wore it in a queue.

"Whene'er he heard the voice of pain
    His breast with pity burned;
The large round head upon his cane
    From ivory was turned.

"Kind words he ever had for all;
    He knew no base design;
His eyes were dark and rather small,
    His nose was aquiline.

"He lived in peace with all mankind,
    In friendship he was true;
His coat had pocket-holes behind,
    His pantaloons were blue.

246

" Unharmed, the sin which earth pollutes
    He passed securely o'er,
And never wore a pair of boots
    For thirty years or more.

" But good Old Grimes is now at rest,
    Nor fears misfortune's frown;
He wore a double-breasted vest,
    The stripes ran up and down.

" He modest merit sought to find,
    And pay it its desert:
He had no malice in his mind,
    No ruffles on his shirt.

" His neighbors he did not abuse,
    Was sociable and gay;
He wore large buckles on his shoes,
    And changed them every day.

" His knowledge hid from public gaze
    He did not bring to view,
Nor make a noise town-meeting days,
    As many people do.

" His worldly goods he never threw
    In trust to fortune's chances,
But lived (as all his brothers do)
    In easy circumstances.

" Thus undisturbed by anxious cares
    His peaceful moments ran;
And everybody said he was
    A fine old gentleman."

                                    —ALBERT G. GREENE.

EARLY AND PIONEER MUSIC—PIONEER MUSIC-SCHOOLS AND PIONEER SINGING-
                MASTERS IN JEFFERSON COUNTY

" Oh, tell me the tales I delighted to hear,
    Long, long ago, long, long ago;
Oh, sing me the old songs so full of cheer,
    Long, long ago, long, long ago."

I. D. Hughes, of Punxsutawney, informs me that the first music-book he bought was Wyeth's " Repository of Sacred Music," second edition. I have seen this book myself, but a later edition (the fifth), published in 1820. Mr. Hughes says that Joseph Thompson, of Dowlingville, was the pioneer " singing-master" in Jefferson County, and that he sang from Wakefield's " Harp," second edition. He used a tuning-fork to sound the pitches, and accompanied his vocal instruction with violin music.

George James was an early " master," and used the same book as Thompson. These two taught in the early thirties. I. D. Hughes taught in 1840 and used the " Missouri Harmony." This was a collection of psalm and hymn tunes and anthems, and was published by Morgan & Co., Cincinnati, Ohio. The first tune in this old " Harmony," or " buckwheat" note-book, was " Primrose":

> " Salvation, oh, the joyful sound,
> 'Tis pleasure to our ears,
> A sovereign balm for every wound,
> A cordial for our fears."

On the second page was " Old Hundred," and on the same page " Canaan":

> " On Jordan's stormy banks I stand,
> And cast a wishful eye
> To Canaan's fair and happy land,
> Where my possessions lie."

The dear old pioneers who used to delight in these sweet melodies have nearly all crossed this Jordan, and are now doubtless singing " Harwell":

> " Hark! ten thousand harps and voices
> Sound the note of praise above;
> Jesus reigns, and heaven rejoices;
> Jesus reigns, the God of love."

Rev. George M. Slaysman, of Punxsutawney, was the pioneer teacher of round notes—the *do ra me's*—in the county. Judge William P. Jenks was also an early instructor in these notes.

We talk about progress, rapid transit, and electricity, but modern music-teachers have failed to improve on the melody of those old pioneer tunes, " that seemed like echoes from a heavenly choir; echoes that seemed to have increased power every time the pearly gates opened to admit some sainted father or mother."

> " God sent these singers upon earth
> With songs of sadness and of mirth,
> That they might touch the hearts of men
> And bring them back to Heaven again."

The pioneer organ used in church music was in Boston in 1714.

A PIONEER SONG FOR THE SUGAR-TROUGH CRADLE

DR. WATTS' CRADLE HYMN

> " Hush, my babe, lie still and slumber,
> Holy angels guard thy bed;
> Heavenly blessings, without number,
> Gently falling on thy head.

"Sleep, my babe, thy food and raiment,
  House and home thy friends provide,
All without thy care or payment,
  All thy wants are well supplied.

"How much better thou'rt attended
  Than the Son of God could be,
When from heaven He descended
  And became a child like thee.

"Soft and easy is thy cradle,
  Coarse and hard thy Saviour lay,
When His birthplace was a stable,
  And his softest bed was hay.

"Blessed babe! what glorious features.
  Spotless, fair, divinely bright!
Must He dwell with brutal creatures?
  How could angels bear the sight?

"Was there nothing but a manger
  Wicked sinners could afford
To receive the heavenly stranger?
  Did they thus affront the Lord?

"Soft, my child, I did not chide thee,
  Though my song may sound too hard:
'Tis thy mother sits beside thee,
  And her arms shall be thy guard.

"Yet, to read the shameful story,
  How the Jews abused their King;
How they served the Lord of Glory,
  Makes me angry while I sing.

"See the kinder shepherds round Him,
  Telling wonders from the sky;
There they sought Him, there they found Him,
  With his virgin mother by.

"See the lovely babe a-dressing,
  Lovely infant! how He smiled!
When He wept, His mother's blessing
  Soothed and hushed the holy child.

"Lo! He slumbers in a manger
  Where the horned oxen fed!
Peace, my darling, here's no danger,
  Here's no ox about thy bed.

"'Twas to save thee, child, from dying,
  Save my dear from burning flame,
Bitter groans, and endless crying,
  That thy blest Redeemer came.

" May'st thou live to know and fear Him,
   Trust and love Him all thy days!
Then go dwell forever near Him,
   See His face and sing His praise.

" I could give thee thousand kisses
   Hoping what I most desire;
Not a mother's fondest wishes
   Can to greater joys aspire."

MAPLE-SUGAR INDUSTRY

One of the pioneer industries in this wilderness was maple-sugar-making. The sugar season commenced either in the last of February or the first of March. In any event, at this time the manufacturer always visited his camp to see or set things in order. The camp was a small cabin made of logs, covered usually with clapboards, and open at one end. The fireplace or crane and hooks were made in this way: Before the opening in the cabin four wooden forks were deeply set in the ground, and on these forks was suspended a strong pole. On this pole was hung the hook of a limb, with a pin in the lower end to hang the kettle on. An average camp had about three hundred trees, and it required six kettles, averaging about twenty-two gallons each, to boil the water from that many trees. The trees were tapped in various ways,—viz.: First, with a three-quarter-inch auger, one or two inches deep. In this hole was put a round spile about eighteen inches long, made of sumach or whittled pine, two spiles to a tree. The later way was by cutting a hollow notch in the tree and putting the spile below with a gouge. This spile was made of pine or some soft wood. When a boy I lived about five years with Joseph and James McCurdy, in what is now Washington Township, and the latter method of opening trees was practised by them. Indeed, all I say here about this industry I learned from and while with them. At the camp there were always from one to three storage-troughs made of cucumber or poplar, and each trough held from ten barrels upward. Three hundred trees required a storage of thirty barrels and steady boiling with six kettles. The small troughs under the trees were made of pine and cucumber and held from three to six gallons. We hauled the water to the storage-troughs with one horse and a kind of "pung," the barrel being kept in its place by plank just far enough apart to hold it tight. In the fireplace there was a large back log and one a little smaller in front. The fire was kept up late and early with smaller wood split in lengths of about three feet. We boiled the water into a thick syrup, then strained it through a woollen cloth while hot into the syrup-barrel. When it had settled, and before putting it on to "sugar off," we strained it the second time. During this sugaring we skimmed the scum off with a tin skimmer and clarified the syrup in the kettle with eggs well beaten in sweet milk. This "sugaring off" was always done in cloudy or cold days, when the trees wouldn't run "sap." One barrel of sugar-water from a sugar-

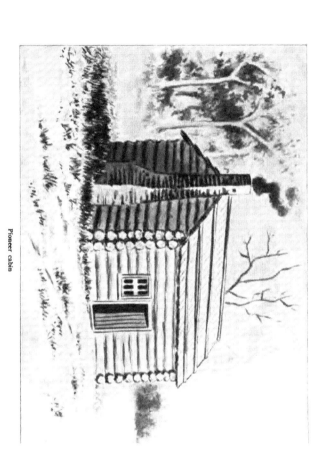

Pioneer cabin

tree, in the beginning of the season, would make from five to seven pounds of sugar. The sugar was always made during the first of the season. The molasses was made at the last of the season, or else it would turn to sugar in a very few days. The sugar was made in cakes, or " stirred off" in a granulated condition, and sold in the market for from six and a quarter to twelve and a half cents a pound. In " sugaring off," the syrup had to be frequently sampled by dropping some of it in a tin of cold water, and if the molasses formed a "thread" that was brittle like glass, it was fit to stir. I was good at sampling, and always anxious to try the syrup, as James

James McCurdy. Born January, 1816; died October, 1902

McCurdy, if he were living, could substantiate. In truth, I was never very hungry during sugar-making, as I had a continual feast during this season of hot syrup, treacle, and sugar.

Skill and attention were both necessary in " sugaring off," for if the syrup was taken off too soon the sugar was wet and tough, and if left on too long, the sugar was burnt and bitter. Time has evoluted this industry from Northwestern Pennsylvania.

Sugar is supposed to have been first used by the Hebrews.

Joseph McCurdy came to Beechwoods, Jefferson County, from Indiana County in the year 1834. He was accompanied by his mother, two brothers, Robert and James, and three sisters, Martha, Margaret, who married John Millen, and Betsy, who married Andrew Hunter. They settled where James McCurdy lived before his recent death. As a man, he was very quiet and unassuming, without show or pretence. He was faithful as a Christian, firm and decided as an elder in maintaining discipline in the church, and mild in enforcing the same; a firm believer in the doctrines of the Presbyterian Church as being the truths taught by the Word of God. These truths he unflinchingly maintained and defended through life. He did much for the church, and after his death his mantle fell upon his brother James.

HOW THE PIONEER BUILT HIS CABIN

" On the first day the material was gathered at the point for erection, the clapboards for the roof and the puncheons for the floors were made. The puncheons were made from trees eighteen inches in diameter, and had the face hewed by a broad-axe. They were in length one-half that of the floor.

" In the morning of the next day the neighbors collected for the raising. The first thing to be done was the election of four corner-men, whose business it was to notch and place the logs. The rest of the company furnished them with the timbers. In the mean time the boards and puncheons were collecting for the floor and roof, so that by the time the cabin was a few rounds high, the sleepers and floor began to be laid. The door was made by sawing or cutting the logs in one side, so as to make an opening about three feet wide. This opening was secured by upright pieces of timber, about three inches thick, through which holes were bored into the ends of the logs, for the purpose of pinning them fast. A similar opening, but wider, was made at the end for the chimney. This was built of logs, and made large, to admit of a back and jambs of stone. At the square, two end logs projected a foot or eighteen inches beyond the wall, to receive the butting poles, as they were called, against which the first row of clapboards was supported. The roof was formed by making the end logs shorter, until a single log formed the comb of the roof. On these logs the clapboards were placed, the ranges of them lapping some distance over those next below them, and kept in their places by logs placed at proper distances upon them.

" The roof, and sometimes the floor, were finished on the same day of the raising. A third day was commonly spent by a few carpenters in levelling off the floor, making a clapboard door and a table. This last was made of a split slab, and supported by four round logs set in auger-holes. Some three-legged stools were made in the same manner. Some pins stuck in the logs at the back of the house supported some clapboards, which served for shelves for the table furniture. A single fork, placed with its lower end in a hole in the floor, and the upper end fastened to a joist, served for a bedstead, by placing a pole in the fork, with one end through a crack between the logs of the wall. This front pole was crossed by a shorter one within the fork, with its outer end through another crack. From the front pole, through a crack between the logs of the end of the house, the boards were put on which formed the bottom of the bed. Sometimes other poles were pinned to the fork a little distance above these, for the purpose of supporting the front and foot of the bed, while the walls were the supports of its back and head. A few pegs around the walls, for a display of the coats of the women and

Cabin barn

hunting-shirts of the men, and two small forks or buck's horns fastened to a joist for the rifle and shot-pouch, completed the carpenter work.

"In the mean time the masons were at work. With the heart pieces of timber of which the clapboards were made, they made billets for chunking up the cracks between the logs of the cabin and chimney. A large bed of mortar was made for daubing up these cracks. A few stones formed the back and jambs of the chimney."

CHAPTER XIII

> "It is religion that will give
> Sweetest comfort while we live."

THE pioneer minister to travel through this wilderness was a Moravian missionary, or a preacher of the United Brethren Church, the Rev. Christian Frederic Post. He travelled from Philadelphia to the Ohio (Allegheny) River in 1758, on a mission from the government of Pennsylvania to the Delaware, Shawnee, and Mingo Indians. These Indians were then in alliance with the French, and Rev. Post's mission was to prevail on them to withdraw from that alliance. Post passed through what is now Jefferson County, from Clearfield, over Boone's Mountain, crossed Little Tobec (Little Toby), and then over Big Tobec (Big Toby) Creek.

From Post's journal I quote the following extract:

"*August 2nd*—We came across several places where two poles, painted red, were stuck in the ground by the Indians, to which they tye the prisoners, when they stop at night, in their return from their incursions. We arrived this night at Shinglimuce, where was another of the same posts. It is a disagreeable and melancholy sight, to see the means they make use of, according to their savage way, to distress others.

" *3rd*—We came to a part of a river called Tobeco, over the mountains, a very bad road.

" *4th*—We lost one of our horses and with much difficulty found him, but were detained a whole day on that account [at what is now Brockwayville]. I had much conversation with Pisquetumen [an Indian chief that travelled with him]; of which I think to inform myself further when I get to my journey's end.

" *5th*—We set out early this day, and made a good long stretch, crossing the big river Tobeco, and lodged between two mountains [at Cooksburgh]. I had the misfortune to lose my pocket-book with three pounds five shillings, and sundry other things. What writings it contained were illegible to anybody but myself.

" *6th*—We passed all the mountains, and the big river, Weshawaucks, and crossed a fine meadow two miles in length, where we slept that night, having nothing to eat.

" *7th*—We came in sight of Fort Venango [now Franklin], belonging to the French, situate between two mountains, in a fork of the Ohio [Allegheny] river. When we arrived, the fort being on the other side of the river, we hallooed, and desired them to fetch us over: which they were afraid to do; but showed us a place where we might ford. We slept that night within half gun shot of the fort."

*   *   *   *   *   *   *   *   *

"Christian Frederic Post accompanied by several friendly Indians, set out from Bethlehem on the 19th of July, for Fort Augusta (Sunbury). There he took the path along the right bank of the West Branch, leading over the Chillisquaque, over Muncy, Loyalsock, and Pine Creeks, crossed the Susquehanna at the Great Island, and then struck one of the main Indian thoroughfares to the West. On the 30th of July he forded Beech Creek, on whose left bank he came to the forks of the road. One branch led southwest along the Bald Eagle, past the Nest to Frankstown, and thence to the Ohio country; the other due west to Chinklacamoose. Post took the latter. It led over the Moshannon, which he crossed on the 1st of August. Next day he arrived at the village of Chinklacamoose in the ' Clear Fields.' Hence the travellers struck a trail to the northwest, crossed Toby's Creek (Clarion River), and on the 7th of August reached Fort Venango, built by the French in 1753, in the forks of the Allegheny. ' I prayed the Lord,' writes Post, ' to blind the French, as he did the enemies of Lot and Elisha, that I might pass unknown.'

"Leaving Venango, Post and his companions turned their horses' heads to the southwest, struck the Conequenessing [now in Butler County] on the 12th of August, crossed the Big Beaver, and next day arrived at Kaskadkie, the terminus of their journey and the head-quarters of ' the Beavers' and ' Shingas,' war-chiefs of the western Delawares." Post was, therefore, the first Moravian west of the Alleghenies. He closes his interesting journal with these words:

"Thirty-two days that I lay in the woods, the heavens were my covering, and the dew fell so hard sometimes that it pricked close to the skin. During this time nothing lay so heavily on my heart as the man who went along with me [Shamokin Daniel], for he thwarted me in everything I said or did; not that he did it against me, but against the country on whose business I was sent. When he was with the French he would speak against the English, and when he was with the English he would speak against the French. The Indians observed that he was unreliable, and desired me not to bring him any more to transact business between them and the prisoners. But praise and glory be to the Lamb that was slain, who brought me through a country of dreadful jealousy and mistrust, where the Prince of this world holds rule and government over the children of disobedience. It was my Lord who preserved me amid all difficulties and dangers, and his Holy Spirit directed me. I had no one to commune with, but Him; and it was He who brought me from under a thick, heavy, and dark cloud into the open air, for which

I adore, and praise and worship Him. I know and confess that He, the Lord my God, the same who forgave my sins and washed my heart in his most precious blood, grasped me in his Almighty hand and held me safe,—and hence I live no longer for myself, but for Him, whose holy will to do is my chiefest pleasure."

" Christian Frederic Post, the most adventurous of Moravian missionaries employed among the North American Indians, was born at Conitz, Polish Prussia, in 1710. He immigrated to this country in June, 1742. Between 1743 and 1749 he was a missionary to the Moravian Indians in New York and Connecticut. He first married Rachel, a Wampanoag, and after her death, Agnes, a Delaware. Having become a widower a second time, he, in 1751, returned to Europe: hence he sailed for Labrador in 1752, engaging in an unsuccessful attempt to bring the gospel to the Esquimaux. Having returned to Bethlehem in 1754, he was sent to Wyoming, where he preached to the Indians until in November of 1755. In the summer of 1758 Post undertook an embassy in behalf of government to the Delawares and Shawnees of the Ohio country, which resulted in the evacuation of Fort Duquesne by the French and the restoration of peace. In September of 1761 he engaged in an independent mission to the Indians of that distant region, and built him a hut on the Tuscarawas, near Bolivar, in Stark County, Ohio. John Heckewelder joined him in the spring of 1762. But the Pontiac war drove the missionaries back to the settlements, and the project was abandoned. Impelled by his ruling passion, Post now sought a new field of activity in the southern part of the continent, and in January of 1764 sailed from Charleston, *via* Jamaica, for the Mosquito coast. Here he preached to the natives for upward of two years. He visited Bethlehem in July of 1767, returned to Mosquito, and was in Bethlehem, for the last time, in 1784. At this date he was residing with his third wife, who was an Episcopalian, in Germantown, Philadelphia. Here he deceased April 29, 1785. On the 5th of May his remains were interred in the Lower Graveyard of that place, Rev. William White, of Christ Church, conducting the funeral service. A marble slab, bearing an appropriate obituary record, was placed, some thirty years ago, upon the veteran missionary's grave."—*Transactions of the Moravian Historical Society*, vol. i.

The second minister to cry aloud in this wilderness was the Rev. John Heckewelder in 1762. He came from Bethlehem over the Chinklacamoose trail to Punxsutawney. He was a Moravian missionary, and travelled thirty thousand miles in Indian missionary work between the years 1762 and 1814.

The third preacher to penetrate this wilderness was a Moravian minister, the Rev. David Zeisberger, and he passed through or near Brockwayville over the northwest trail to what was then the Ohio, now the Allegheny (in what is now Forest County) River.

I quote as follows from " Day's Collections":

" In the year 1767 an unarmed man of short stature, remarkably plain in his dress, and humble and peaceable in his demeanor, emerged from the thick forest upon the Allegheny River, in the neighborhood of the Seneca towns. This was the Moravian missionary, Rev. David Zeisberger, who, led by Anthony and John Papanhunk, Indian guides and assistants in his pious labors, had penetrated the dense wilderness of Northern Pennsylvania, from Wyalusing, on the Susquehanna, to preach the gospel to the Indians in this region. His intended station was at Goshgoshunk, which appears to have been on the left bank of the Allegheny, not far from the mouth of the Tionesta. Possibly Goshgoshunk was the same as the Indian name Cush-cush.

" The Seneca chief, believing Brother Zeisberger to be a spy, received him roughly at first; but, softened by his mild demeanor, or perhaps by the holy truths which he declared to the chief, he at length bade him welcome, and permitted him to go to Goshgoshunk. He warned him, however, not to trust the people there, for they had not their equals in wickedness and thirst for blood. This was but another incentive to him who came to preach ' not to the righteous, but to sinners.' However, on his arrival he was well received, and shared the hospitality of a relative of one of his guides. Goshgoshunk, a town of the Delawares, consisted of three villages on the banks of the Ohio [Allegheny]. The whole town seemed to rejoice at the novelty of this visit.

" The missionary found, however, that the Seneca chief had told him truly. He was shocked at their heathenish and diabolical rites, and especially by their abuse of the holy name of God. An Indian preacher, called Wangomen, strenuously resisted the new doctrines of the missionaries, especially that of the incarnation of the Deity, and instigated the jealousy of his people; but the truth, preached in its simplicity and power, by the missionaries, overcame him, and he yielded his opposition so far as to join the other Indians in an invitation to the missionaries to settle among them. The old blind chief, Allemewi, was awakened, and afterwards baptized, with the Christian name of Solomon. The missionary went home to report his progress to his friends in Bethlehem. The following year Zeisberger returned, accompanied by Brother Gottlob Senseman and several Moravian Indian families from the Susquehanna, to establish a regular mission at Goshgoshunk. They built a block-house, planted corn, and, gathering round their block-house several huts of believing Indians, they formed a small hamlet, a little separated from the other towns. ' To this a great number resorted, and there the brethren ceased not, by day and night, to teach and preach Jesus, and God in Christ, reconciling the world unto himself.' These meetings were fully attended, ' and it was curious to see so many of the audience with their faces painted black and vermilion and heads decorated with clusters of feathers and fox-tails.' A violent opposition, however, succeeded, occasioned by the malicious lies of the magicians and old women,—' the corn was blasted, the deer and game began to retire from the woods, no chestnuts nor bilberries would grow any more, merely because the missionaries preached a strange doctrine, and the Indians were changing their way of life.' Added to this, the grand council at Onondaga and Zeneschio (Ischua) looked with extreme jealousy upon this new encroachment of white men upon their territories and discountenanced the establishment. In consequence of these things the missionaries left Goshgoshunk, and retired fifteen miles farther up the river, to a place called Lawanakanuck, on the opposite bank, probably near Hickory-town. Here they again started a new settlement, built at first a hunting-den, and afterwards a chapel and a dwelling-house, 'and a bell, which they received from Bethlehem, was hung in a convenient place.'

"About the year 1765 the Moravian missionary David Zeisberger established the mission of Friedenschnetten, near the present town of Wyalusing, in Bradford County. This town, the name of which signifies 'tents of peace,' contained 'thirteen Indian huts, and upward of forty frame houses, shingled, and provided with chimneys and windows.' There was another mission about thirty miles above Friedenschnetten,—'Tschechsehequanink,' or, as it was translated, 'where a great awakening had taken place.' This latter mission was under the charge of Brother Roth.

"These missions prospered greatly, and much good was done among the Indians, until 1768, when the Six Nations, by the treaty made that year, 'sold the land from under their feet,' and the missionaries encountered so much trouble from both the Indians and whites, that in 1772 the brethren decided to abandon these missions and remove to the new field which had been planted by the indefatigable Zeisberger on the banks of the Ohio. They therefore started from Wyalusing on the 12th day of June, 1772, in number two hundred and forty-one souls, mostly Indians, of all ages, with their cattle and horses. Their destination was Friedenstadt,* near the present site of Beaver, Pennsylvania. They were under the guidance of Brothers Roth and Ettewein, and their course was from the North Branch across the Allegheny Mountains, by way of Bald Eagle, to the Ohio River. Brother Roth conducted those who went by water and Brother Ettewein those who travelled by land. In 1886 the *Moravian*, published at Bethlehem, gave the journal of Rev. John Ettewein, and we give the extracts from it of the progress of the party, with the explanatory foot-notes in the *Moravian*, translated by Mr. Jordan:

" ' *1772*

"' *Tuesday, July 14.*—Reached Clearfield Creek, where the buffaloes formerly cleared large tracts of undergrowth, so as to give the appearance of cleared fields. Hence, the Indians called the creek "Clearfield." Here

* "The Annals of Friedenschnetten, on the Susquehanna, with John Ettewein's Journal of the Removal of the Mission to Friedenstadt, 1765 and 1772, by John W. Jordan."

at night and next morning, to the great joy of the hungry, nine deer were shot. Whoever shoots a deer has for his private portion, the skin and inside; the meat he must bring into camp and deliver to the distributors. John and Cornelius acted in this capacity in our division. It proved advantageous for us not to keep so closely together, as we had at first designed; for if the number of families in a camp be large, one or two deer, when cut up, afford but a scanty meal to each individual. So it happened that scarce a day passed without there being a distribution of venison in the advance, the centre, and the rear camp. (On the route there were one hundred and fifty deer and but three bears shot.) In this way our Heavenly Father provided for us; and I often prayed for our hunters, and returned thanks for their success.

"' Thursday, July 16.— . . . I journeyed on, with a few of the brethren, two miles in a falling rain, to the site of Chinklacamoose [Clearfield town], where we found but three huts, and a few patches of Indian corn. The name signifies " No one tarries here willingly." It may, perhaps, be traced to the circumstance that some thirty years ago an Indian resided here as a hermit, upon a rock, who was wont to appear to the Indian hunters, in frightful shapes. Some of these, too, he killed, others he robbed of their skins; and this he did for many years. We moved on four miles, and were obliged to wade the West Branch three times, which is here like the Lehigh at Bethlehem, between the island and the mountain, rapid and full of ripples.

"' Friday, July 17.—Advanced only four miles to a creek that comes down from the northwest.* Had a narrow and stony spot for our camp.

"' Saturday, July 18.—Moved on without awaiting Roth and his division, who on account of the rain had remained in camp. To-day Shebosch lost a colt from the bite of a rattlesnake. Here we left the West Branch three miles to the Northwest, up the creek, crossing it five times. Here, too, the path went precipitately up the mountain, and four or five miles up and up to the summit—to a spring the head-waters of the Ohio. † Here I lifted up my heart in prayer as I looked westward, that the Son of Grace might rise over the heathen nations that dwell beyond the distant horizon.

"' Sunday, July 19.—As yesterday, but two families kept with me, because of the rain, we had a quiet Sunday, but enough to do drying our effects. In the evening all joined me, but we could hold no service as the Ponkis [gnats] were so excessively annoying that the cattle pressed toward and into our camp, to escape their persecutors in the smoke of the fires. This vermin is a plague to man and beast, both by day and night. But in the swamp through which we are now passing, their name is legion. Hence the Indians

---

* " Anderson's Creek, in Clearfield County, which they struck at a point near the present Curwensville."

† " Probably the source of the North Branch of the Mahoning, which rises in Brady Township, Clearfield County, and empties into the Allegheny, in Armstrong County, ten miles above Kittanning."

call it the Ponksutenink,—*i.e.*, the town of the Ponkis.* The word is equivalent to living dust and ashes, the vermin being so small as not to be seen, and their bite being hot as sparks of fire. or hot ashes. The brethren here related an Indian myth, to wit: That the aforecited Indian hermit and sorcerer, after having been for so many years a terror to all Indians, had been killed by one who had burned his bones, but the ashes he blew into the swamp, and they became living things, and hence the Ponkis.

" ' *Monday, July 20.*—After discoursing on the daily word—" The Lord our God be with us, may he not forsake us"—we travelled on through the swamp, and after five miles crossed the path that leads from Frankstown † to Goshgoshunk, and two miles from that point encamped at a run. At 5 P.M., came Brethren Peter, Boaz, and Michael, with fourteen unbaptized Indians, from Lagundontenink, to meet us with four horses, and five bushels of Indian corn. also Nathaniel's wife from Sheninga ‡ with a letter from Brother Jungman. I thought had I but milk or meat, I would add rice, and prepare a supper for the new-comers. But two of them went to hunt, and in half an hour Michael brought in a deer to my fire. My eyes moistened with tears. Sister Esther hunted up the large camp kettle, and all had their fill of rice and venison, and were much pleased. That night and the following morning there were four deer shot by the company.

" ' *Tuesday, July 21.*—The rear division came up, and the destitute—viz., such as had lived solely upon meat and milk—were supplied each with one pint of Indian corn. We proceeded six miles to the first creek. In the evening a number of the brethren came to my fire, and we sat together right cheerful until midnight. Once when asleep I was awakened by the singing of the brethren who had gathered around the fire of the friends from Lagundontenink. It refreshed my inmost soul.

" ' *Wednesday, July 22.*—We journeyed on four miles, to the first fork § where a small creek comes down from the mouth.

" ' *Thursday, July 23.*—Also four miles to the second fork, to the creek, coming in from the south-east. ‖ As a number of us met here in good time we had a meeting. Cornelius's brother-in-law stated that he was desirous of being the Lord's; therefore he had left his friends so as to live with the brethren, and to hear of the Saviour.

" ' *Friday, July 24.*—The path soon left the creek, over valleys and heights to a spring. Now we were out of the swamp, and free from the

* " Kept down the valley of the Mahoning, into Jefferson County. Punxsutawney is a village in Young Township, Jefferson County. The swamp lies in Gaskill and Young Townships, Jefferson County."

† " Near Hollidaysburg. See Scull's map of 1759 for this path."

‡ " Sheninga is a township in Lawrence County, just above Friedenstadt."

§ " A branch of the Mahoning."

‖ " *Query.*—The creek that comes in and up below Punxsutawney."

plague of the Ponkis. Also found huckleberries, which were very grateful. Our to-day's station was five miles, and about so far we advanced on.

. " ' *Saturday, July 25.*—On which day we encamped at a Salt Lick, and kept Sunday some three miles from the large creek, which has so many curves, like a horseshoe, so that if one goes per canoe, when the water is high, four days are consumed in reaching the Ohio, whereas, by land, the point can be reached in one day.* Our youngsters went to the creek to fish, and others to hunt; and at sunset they came in with two deer, and four strings of fish.' "

" John Roth was born in Brandenburg, February 3, 1726, of Catholic parents, and was brought up a locksmith. In 1748 he united with the Moravians and emigrated to America, arriving at Bethlehem in June of 1756. He deceased at York, Pennsylvania, July 22, 1791.

" John Ettewein was born 29th of June, 1721, in Freudenstadt, Würtemberg. He united with the Moravians in 1740, and came to Bethlehem in April of 1754. Here he was set apart for service in the schools of his adopted church, when, in 1758, a new field of labor was assigned him at the Brethren's settlements in Western North Carolina (Forsyth and adjacent counties). During his residence in Wachovia he itinerated among the spiritually destitute Germans of South Carolina (1762), and visited the Salburgers and Swiss of Ebenezer (in Georgia) in 1765. The following year he was recalled to Bethlehem. This place was the scene of his greatest activity, as here, under God, he led the Moravian Church in safety through the stormy times of the Revolution. He was ordained a bishop in 1784. In 1789 he sailed for Europe, and attended a general synod convened at Herrnhut. John Ettewein was one of the remarkable men of the Brethren's Church in North America. He deceased at Bethlehem, 2d of January, 1802."

ASSOCIATE REFORMED, SECEDER, OR THE UNITED PRESBYTERIAN CHURCH

This church is one of the youngest of the Presbyterian bodies in America, but the history of its antecedents extends back more than a century. Its original antecedents were the Associate and Reformed Presbyterian bodies. The former body was composed of Presbyterians who seceded from the General Assembly of Scotland in 1733 and formed themselves into what was known as the "Associate Presbytery," or, as the masses knew them, " the Seceders." The first minister of that denomination to arrive in America was Rev. Alexander Gellatly, who settled at Octorara, Pennsylvania, in 1753,

---

* " The Mahoning, formed by the junction of the East and South Branch, which meets at Nicholsburg, in Indiana County. This route to the Allegheny was the same path taken by Post in 1758, when returning from his second visit to the Ohio Indians in that year, and between Chinklacamoose and the Allegheny, over the same path travelled by Barbara Leininger in 1755, when Chinklacamoose and Punxsutawney were villages.

where he labored for eight years. Many members of the body had preceded him to this country, settling along the seaboard, and some of them going as far south as the Carolinas. The church was largely increased by immigration from year to year, and the Presbytery of Pennsylvania was organized in 1758.

The first minister of the Reformed Presbyterian or Covenanter Church to arrive in America was Rev. John Cuthbertson, who came in 1752.

I here reproduce an extract from Rev. David X. Junkins's centennial sermon delivered at New Castle, Pennsylvania, in July, 1876:

"One hundred and nine years ago there came to the Indian town of Gosch-gosch-kunk, at the mouth of the Tionesta Creek, where it debouches into the Allegheny River, in what is now Forest County, Pennsylvania, a solitary German, a minister of the gospel in the Unitas Fratrum Church, usually called Moravians. Accompanied by two converted Indians, he had set out from the Christian Indian town of Friedenshutten, on the north branch of the Susquehanna, which stood near to the present town of Wyalusing (Bradford County). Traversing the unbroken and dense forests of Northern Pennsylvania and Southern New York on foot, with but a single pack-horse to carry their baggage, after many dangers and hardships they arrived at Gosch-gosch-kunk, at the mouth of the Tionesta, on the 16th day of October, 1767. This village was only two years old, having been founded after the close of Pontiac's war.

"Soon after, this missionary was joined by his wife, and by John Senseman and his wife, and a band of Christian Indians from the Susquehanna, and they attempted to establish a mission at that point. But they found much opposition from the chiefs and others, and although they were blest in winning a few converts, the roughness of the country, the leanness of the land, and the opposition of the natives proved so discouraging that they soon began to contemplate a change of locality. God prepared the way for this in a most remarkable manner.

"The tribes of Indians which roamed along the Allegheny and the Beaver at that day were chiefly of the Lenni Lenape or Delaware nation, a branch of which was at Gosch-gosch-kunk, called Munseys, but there were mingled with them Senecas, Shawnees, and some Mohicans. The Senecas claimed the soil on the Allegheny, and their chief, Wangomen, took violent ground against the missionaries, and objected to the Munseys, who had built their town by permission of the former tribe, permitting the missionaries to build houses and a church upon it. Failing to obtain by negotiation the necessary privileges, the necessity for a change of locality became imminent. They accordingly moved across the Allegheny River, and built a mission town in what is now the heart of the Oil Creek oil region. The oil was gathered even then, and used by both Indians and missionaries for medicinal purposes.

" At that time there were two villages of the Lenni Lenape in this vicinity, —one near the mouth of the Mahoning, called Kas-kas-kunk. The name of the chief who held sway in this valley at that day was Pack-an-ke. His principal sub-chief, counsellor, and warrior was named Glik-kik-an. He was a man of great natural powers. His fame as a warrior was only eclipsed by his reputation for eloquence. He had fought many battles, both in the wars between the tribes and in the wars of the French against the English, and he possessed a glowing eloquence which carried all before it at the council-fire. He had disputed with Christian Frederick Post at Tuscarawas; he had silenced the Jesuit priests in argument at Venango; and he came up to the mission town in the oil region to dispute with and overcome Zeisberger and Senseman. Escorted to Lawunack-han-nek by Wangomen and a procession of Indians, he entered the mission-house to challenge the missionaries to theological combat. Zeisberger being absent, Glik-kik-an was received by Anthony, a converted Indian, who, as Zeisberger remarked, ' was as eager to bring souls to Christ as a hunter's hound is eager to chase the deer.'

" Placing food before his guests, he at once introduced the subject of religion. ' My friends,' said he, ' I will tell you a great thing. God made the heavens and the earth and all things that in them are. Nothing exists that God did not make.' Pausing, he added: ' God has created us. But who of us knows his Creator? not one! I tell you the truth—not one! For we have fallen away from God—we are polluted creatures; our minds are darkened by sin.'

" Here he sat down and was silent a long time. Suddenly rising again, he exclaimed, ' God who made all things and created us came into the world in the form and fashion of a man. Why did he thus come into the world? Think of this!' He paused, and then answered, ' God took upon him flesh and blood in order that, as man, he might reconcile the world unto himself. By his bitter death on the cross he procured for us life and eternal salvation, redeeming us from sin, from death, and from the power of the devil.' In such apothegms he unfolded the whole gospel. When he ceased, Zeisberger, who had in the mean time entered, briefly corroborated his words, and exhorted Glik-kik-an to lay them to heart.

" ' Glik-kik-an,' says De Schweinitz, ' was an honest man and open to conviction. He had upheld the superstitions of his fathers because he had not been convinced that the Christian faith was true.' But now the truth began to dawn upon his mind. In the place of his elaborate speech he merely replied, ' I have nothing to say; I believe your words.' And when he returned to Gosch-gosch-kunk, instead of boasting of a victory over the teachers, he urged the people to go and hear the gospel. He had been hired, like Balaam, to curse God's own, but, like Balaam, he was constrained to bless them. Not long after this first visit of the warrior of the Mahoning, Zeisberger was constrained to go to Fort Pitt (Pittsburg) to obtain provisions.

Senseman accompanied him, and they were instrumental in saving the country from the horrors of another war.

" They passed Fort Venango (Franklin) on their return. Soon after this they received a second visit from Glik-kik-an. He came to tell them that he had determined to embrace Christianity, and he brought an invitation from Pack-an-ke to settle on the banks of the Beaver, on a tract of land which should be reserved for the exclusive use of the mission. Zeisberger saw the advantages of the offer, but not feeling authorized to accept it without consent of the board at Bethlehem, he sent two runners to that town in Northampton county, for instructions. The board gave him plenary power, and he accepted the offer of a home in our beautiful valley. It took time. however. for the runners to go and come through that vast stretch of wilderness, and the migration was not effected until the next April.

" But before they left the oil region the Lord cheered them with some fruits of their toil. Early in December, 1769, the first Protestant baptism in the valley of the Allegheny took place at Lawunakhannek. Luke and Paulina were then baptized; and Allemewi at Christmas; and in the beginning of 1770 several other converts were added.

" On the 17th day of April, 1770, after a friendly parting with Wangomen and their other opponents, who now began to regret their removal, Zeisberger. Sensemen, and their families with the Christian Indians, left Lawunakhannek in fifteen canoes. They swept past Gosch-gosch-kunk and bore down the Allegheny. and reached Fort Pitt on the 20th of April.

" It was a novel sight presented to the traders and the garrison at that point, to see a colony of Protestant Christian Indians, who from savages had been transformed into mild and consistent followers of Jesus.

" Leaving Fort Pitt, they descended the Ohio to the mouth of the Beaver. That now populous locality was then a deep solitude. Not even a wigwam was to be seen where Beaver, Rochester, New Brighton, Bridgewater, Fallston, and Beaver Falls now throng with population.

"Ascending the Beaver, they carry their canoes and goods around the falls, and arrive at a town on the west bank of that river a little north of where Newport now stands. This Indian town was inhabited by a community of women, all single, and all pledged never to marry. An uncloistered nunnery! I do not wonder that Indian women, who were doomed to do the drudgery of the family, both in the wigwam and the cornfield, should resolve to lead a life of single-blessedness. It is less excusable in civilized society, in which Christianity has emancipated woman from such hardships.

"A little more than a mile above this town of maidens, on the east bank of the Beaver. and below the afflux of the Mahoning, they found a broad plain, or bottom-land, as we would call it, upon which they made an encampment, putting up log huts.

" ' The first business,' says De Schweinitz, ' undertaken was an embassy
266

to Pack-an-ke, whose capital stood near, or, perhaps, upon the site of New Castle, and was called New Kas-kas-kunk. Old Kas-kas-kunk, the former capital, was at the confluence of the Shenango and Mahoning Rivers.

" ' Pack-an-ke, a venerable, gray-haired chief, but active as in youth, received the deputation at his own house.

" ' In response to the speeches of Abram (a converted Indian) and Zeisberger, he said they were welcome to his country, and should be undisturbed in the worship of their God.

" ' A great feast was in preparation. Indians were flocking in in great numbers. Native etiquette required that the deputies should grace the occasion with their presence; but after Abram's exposition of their views, Pack-an-ke made no attempt to detain them.

" ' Thus one hundred and six years ago, on this soil, and probably about the place where our Second Ward school-house (New Castle) now stands, was exhibited by a pagan savage chief, or king, a measure of hospitality and religious toleration, such as nominally Christian Rome denies, and such as even Protestant Christians are slow to extend to their fellow-men.'

" A village of cabins was soon built upon the site of the encampment, to which Zeisberger gave the name of Langunton-temunk in the Delaware language; in German, Friedenstadt; and in English, City of Peace. It soon began to attract the Indians. Some Munseys from Gosch-gosch-kunk were the first to come and join the mission; soon after, Glik-kik-kan from Kas-kas-kunk. He was the first convert to Christianity in the valley of the Shenango.

" Zeisberger had warned this brave warrior that persecution would follow his embracing Christianity, but it did not deter him. King Pack-an-ke reproached him. ' And have you gone to the Christian teachers from our very councils?' said he. ' What do you want of them? Do you hope to get a white skin? Not so much as one of your feet would turn white. How then can your whole skin be changed? Were you not a brave man? Were you not an honorable counsellor? Did you not sit at my side in this house, with a blanket before you, and a pile of wampum belts upon it, and help me to direct the affairs of our nation? And now you despise all this! You think you have found something better! Wait! in good time you will see how miserably you have been deceived!'

" To this burst of passion Glik-kik-kan replied, ' You are right; I have joined the brethren. Where they go, I will go; where they lodge, I will lodge; nothing shall separate me from them; their people shall be my people, and their God, my God.' Attending church a few days after this, a sermon on the heinousness of sin so moved him that he walked through the village to his tent sobbing aloud. 'A haughty war-captain,' wrote Zeisberger, ' weeps publicly in the presence of his former associates. This is marvellous. Thus the Saviour, by his word, breaks the hard hearts and humbles the proud minds of the Indians.'

" Finding their locality, which was on or near the present site of the hamlet of Moravia, too low and unhealthy, Zeisberger, toward the end of July, laid out a new and larger town, with a church on a hill, on the west side of the river opposite the first. This town was located on the ridge to the west of the railroad, and extending north from the Spring run this side (north) of Moravia station. Thus one hundred and six years ago, this month (July, 1876), was founded the first Christian village and community in this beautiful valley—yes, the first west of the Allegheny Mountains! We cannot pursue the details of its history farther in this discourse except to say that upon that spot, consecrated by the prayers and tears and the toils of David Zeisberger, John Senseman, George Youngman, and their wives, and of Abraham, Glik-kik-kan, and other red men who had given their hearts to Jesus, a Christian town of five hundred souls grew rapidly up. The number of converts increased until, before they migrated to the Tuscarawas, it reached two hundred. The town and church were built of hewn logs, and were occupied by an industrious and orderly community. It continued to prosper until, from various considerations, they were induced to emigrate to the valley of the Muskingum, in what is now the State of Ohio.

" The considerations which led to this change grew out of various circumstances; partly from the necessity of the removal of the Christian Indians on the Susquehanna to a place where they would be more exempt from the encroachments of the white settlers, and partly from untoward influences gathering round them in this vicinity.

" Traders had early established posts along the Allegheny and Ohio. Whiskey was introduced by them, and habits of intemperance grew rapidly among the pagan Indians. It not unfrequently happened that the wild Indians, when drunk, would come to the peaceable Christian town, and whoop and shriek along the streets, insult the women, and sometimes disturb even the meetings for worship. Thus early were the atrocities that inevitably spring from the rum-traffic perpetrated in our loved valley, and down to the present day those atrocities have never ceased.

" Early in the spring of 1772, accompanied by Glik-kik-an and several others of the Indians, Zeisberger proceeded to the Tuscarawas to announce the coming of the Susquehanna Indians, and prepare for their reception. The work still went on at Friedenstadt until the spring of 1773, when the missionaries and their Christian Indians took a sad farewell of their beautiful home on the banks of the Beaver; levelled their beautiful sanctuary with the ground, to prevent its desecration, and bent their faces toward the banks of the Tuscarawas, where, at the beautiful locality of the ' Big Spring,' a few miles from it, they built two towns,—Gnattenhutten and Schoenbrun,—in which they lived happily and labored faithfully for Christ, until the wars came on which resulted in so many disasters and so much bloodshed, and they were cruelly murdered. Glik-kik-an among them, by a body of frontiersmen from

268

Washington and Green Counties, Pennsylvania, and from West Virginia, under the command of Colonel David Williamson. These men had marched to avenge some atrocious murders which had been committed by wild Indians in those counties, and, failing to discriminate between the harmless Moravian Indians and the real authors of the murders, they cruelly slaughtered nearly one hundred old men, women, and children! It was a terrible tragedy, illustrative of the fearful nature of unbridled and undiscriminating vengeance.

" Although not directly connected with the history of our congregation, I have deemed it proper to give this brief and imperfect sketch of the interesting congregation of Christian Indians, which one hundred and six years ago was established in our immediate vicinity, and as our own was established near the same site, and once extended its borders almost, or quite, to Friedenstadt (Moravia), it may be considered the first successor of that interesting congregation.

" The tawny Delawares and Senecas and Shawnees still lingered along the banks of the Shenango and Neshannock for some years after this church was organized. After the decisive victory of General Wayne, in August, 1794, a treaty was formed with the Indians, by which the peace of the border was for a time secured; and, shortly after, white inhabitants began to cross the Ohio and Allegheny, and settle the country lying between those rivers and Lake Erie. Gradually the tide of population flowed north and west, and, by 1798, there was a considerable population scattered through what is now the counties of Beaver, Butler, Lawrence, Mercer, Venango, Crawford, and Erie.

" As in the entire process of settling Pennsylvania, the sturdy and intelligent Scotch-Irish race were the pioneers. They had at an early period settled in Bucks, Chester, Lancaster, and Cumberland Counties. They were the first to cross the Alleghenies and occupy the counties east of the Allegheny River and south of the Ohio; and when the broad, fertile, and forest-clad region north of that river was opened to them, they were prompt to enter it.

" An herculean task lay before them. A massive forest was to fell, fields were to clear and reclaim, and bread was to be wrung from the soil—rich, indeed, but rugged and untamed. But the very hardships of their condition developed energy and self-reliance. Trained in their former homes in the Bible and the Shorter Catechism, and most of them in the Psalms of David, they brought with them a piety, if rude, yet sturdy and sincere. They made their cabins and the surrounding forest vocal with their voice of unsophisticated praise and prayer. Loving the preached gospel, and reverencing the ministers whom they left behind in the older settlements, they had a natural desire to receive visits from them, and, at their request, some of the godly pastors from over the rivers made occasional visits. The venerable Elisha McCurdy and Thomas Marquis were the first ministers of our order who traversed the hills and valleys, gathering the scattered settlers in little assemblies to worship God and hear the precious gospel. They went as far north as Erie County, and visited many settlements, dispensing the word and ordinances. It is impossible in our day to appreciate the difficulties of such missionary tours. There was not a bridge from the Ohio to the lake, over any stream. The creeks were often swollen so that they were compelled to swim their horses across the angry current; and sometimes even this was impracticable, and the missionary would be prevented by such insurmountable obstacles from fulfilling his appointment."

Among the first ministers of the gospel who visited this region, some of whom remained permanently, was Thomas Edgar Hughes, who settled at Greensburg, now called Darlington. He was a man of mark, and the first settled pastor north of the Ohio. He was of Welch origin, his grandfather having come from Wales. He was born in York County, Pennsylvania, April 7, 1769. Licensed by the Presbytery of Ohio, now Pittsburg, in 1798, he was ordained and installed over the churches of New Salem and Mount Pleasant, August 28, 1796.

Soon after he was joined by two other ministers from the Reformed Presbyterian Church of Ireland.

A Presbytery was formed in 1774, and the church, as a body, obtained a foothold in the New World. The subject of union between these bodies was agitated before either was many years old, the leading ministers believing that such an alliance would add to the efficiency of both. During the Revolutionary War several meetings of ministers of the two denominations were held, at which the matter was thoroughly discussed. In 1782 three Presbyteries met in Philadelphia, and a union was consummated. The new organization took the name of the "Associate Reformed Synod of North America." A few of the ministers of both bodies refused to enter into the alliance, and the original bodies maintained a separate existence.

The Associate Reformed Church flourished. It spread rapidly to the westward, and was largely and steadily increased by immigration. In 1793 it had a firm hold on the territory now known as Western Pennsylvania. In that year the original Presbytery of Pennsylvania was divided into two,—the First and Second Associate Reformed Presbyteries of Pennsylvania. The Second, by order of the Synod, took the name of the Monongahela. It was composed of four ministers,—Revs. John Jamieson, Henderson, Warwick, and Rankin, with their elders. This was the first Presbytery organized in connection with any of the Reformed Churches west of the Allegheny Mountains. Its boundary lines were the Allegheny Mountains on the east and the Pacific Ocean on the west.

The prosperity of the new body in Western Pennsylvania was remarkable. Soon it became necessary to form new Presbyteries in the territory originally covered by the Presbytery of the Monongahela, and the church commanded the attention of the entire country.

HISTORY OF NORTHWESTERN PENNSYLVANIA

A union of the Associate with the Associate Reformed Churches of North America had been for a long time considered desirable by the leading ministers of both denominations, and it was accomplished in 1858. The consummation took place in Old City Hall, Pittsburg, and was the occasion of general rejoicing among the ministers and members of both bodies. It was in this city of ecclesiastical reunions that the United Presbyterian Church as a distinct Presbyterian body was born.

I give a sketch of one of these ministers, written by myself for the *United Presbyterian*, of Pittsburg, Pennsylvania:

"Rev. John Jamieson was born in Thornhill farm, Scotland, about eight miles south of Glasgow, in 1747. His father was Allan Jamieson, a descendant from the noble family of Bruce. One of Allan Jamieson's ancestors was steward to Mary, Queen of Scotland. This ancestry turned Protestant, left the court, and returned to Thornhill farm. Rev. John Jamieson's mother, according to the family tradition, was a descendant of Sir William Wallace, who left a natural daughter.

"Rev. John Jamieson enjoyed the advantages of wealth. He graduated from St. Andrew's University, and studied theology with Rev. John Brown, of Haddington, who formulated the Westminster Catechism. Rev. John Jamieson was licensed and ordained by a Burgher presbytery, of Scotland, in about his twenty-fifth year. He preached from the Hebrew or Greek Bible, translated his own texts, and was an expert shorthand writer. According to his diary, he preached at Bathgate, Scotland, in 1776. Rev. John Jamieson's early life embraced a stormy period in Scotland between the Scotch and English. His adult life was surrounded by a period of literary activity. The poems of Ramsay, Thompson, Burns, Scott, Holmes, and others were written and published from 1730 to 1785. The known Scottish poets then exceeded two thousand. In 1775 Rev. John Jamieson married Agnes (Nancy) Gibbs, daughter of John Gibbs, of Paisley. Gibbs's wife was a Miss Jackson. The young couple set up housekeeping in Edinburgh, Scotland, where they resided seven years. Three children were born to them in this city,—viz., Jeannette, John, and Agnes, otherwise called Nancy. Rev. John Jamieson, considering himself prepared for thorough gospel labor, determined to migrate to America and devote his life to missionary work in the New World. On August 27, 1783, he sold the Thornhill farm to a Mr. Wilson. It might be well to state here that Pollock, author of "The Course of Time," was born on the adjoining farm, and that these two farms are now literally covered with houses and form a part of greater Glasgow. At the age of thirty-six, with his wife and three children, Rev. John Jamieson started from Edinburgh, Scotland, for America, and in the latter part of November, 1783, landed in Philadelphia, Pennsylvania, where he immediately connected himself with the Associate Reformed Church.

"He resided here and went on missionary journeys through the wilderness on horseback as far south and west as the Carolinas and Georgia, until September 22, 1784, when he located at Big Spring, Cumberland County, Pennsylvania, at which place he preached in a log church for eight years, also at Stony Ridge, Shippensburg, Marsh Creek, Conococheague, and other points, in barns and houses. He also purchased six hundred acres of land and erected a grist-mill at or near Big Spring, and his son John, Jr., resided here until after 1809.

" Three children were born to Mr. Jamieson while living at Big Spring, —viz., William, Isabelle, and Margaret.

" In the early spring of 1792 Mr. Jamieson resigned his charges in Cumberland County and crossed the Allegheny Mountains with his wife and three children, with their effects all on horseback, or pack-horses, and located in Hannahstown, Westmoreland County, leaving John Jamieson, Jr., and two other children on the homestead at Big Spring. In 1794 he removed to Derry, and in 1796 to Altman's Run, where he erected his log cabin in what is now Conemaugh or Blacklick Township, Indiana County, Pennsylvania.

" In the year 1792 he and Rev. Matthew Henderson, Sr., were appointed by the synod to missionate in Virginia and Kentucky for one year. In 1794 he dropped Hannahstown and made frequent missionary tours through what is now Indiana and Armstrong Counties, and was the first pastor to have a charge north of the Conemaugh River and west of Blacklick in Indiana and Armstrong Counties. In 1793 the second presbytery of Pennsylvania was formed, and at a later time by order of the synod was called ' Monongahela.'

" This presbytery was composed of four ministers,—viz., Rev. John Jamieson, Rev. Matthew Henderson, Sr., Rev. Robert Warwick, and Rev. Adam Rankin, with their elders. Its boundary lines were the Allegheny Mountains on the east, and the Pacific Ocean on the west. Rev. John Jamieson's pioneer preaching in Western Pennsylvania was at the installation of Rev. Robert Warwick at Laurel Hill, Dunlap's Creek, and Spring Hill. These points are in Westmoreland and Fayette Counties.

" In 1794 Rev. John Jamieson organized the Crete church, in Indiana County, preaching to the people first from a small platform, five by eight feet, supported by wooden brackets between two large oak-trees, the congregation, of course, being seated on logs on the ground. His mode of preaching was to lecture or expound the Scripture in the morning, and to preach a sermon divided into firstly, secondly, etc., in the afternoon. At Crete a tent was secured for a while, and then, in 1815, a log church, twenty-four by thirty, was erected. He preached at this point until near 1820. From his diary I find that he also preached at Conemaugh, Crooked Creek, Bethel (Indiana County), Plum Creek, and Kittanning, and that he held services in cabins and log barns. The names of these places, dates, etc., are recorded in his diary, as well as notes of texts and sermons, many of these in shorthand.

" In 1790 the Presbytery of Pennsylvania was directed to deal with him

272

[Rev. John Jamieson] for not attending synod. In 1791 he was present, but was disgusted, as he tells us in his published account of his subsequent trial, so that he resolved to terminate his connection with the body. This threat he did not carry out, although he soon afterwards resigned his charge at Big Spring. Having finished his mission to Kentucky, he arrived during the winter of 1792–93, in Western Pennsylvania, and was very soon settled in Brush Creek, now Bethel, Westmoreland County, Hannahstown, near the present New Alexandria, and Conemaugh, Indiana County. He was released from Brush Creek and also from Hannahstown (which he had informally dropped), and his time was given to Loyalhanna in connection with Conemaugh, but he continued to visit and preach to groups of families in a·very large district. In May, 1794, he attended the meeting of the synod at Marsh Creek, Adams County, Pennsylvania. It was the custom of the synod then to make the next minister in seniority the moderator, and it happened to be Mr. Jamieson's turn. He took the chair, protesting, however, that he would not stay there long.

"At an early stage of the meeting he presented 'An Overture' for the consideration and adoption of the synod. This overture maintained that a strict and rigid uniformity in all things was essential to the government and discipline of the Church; and that the synod should adopt a confession and covenant to secure such uniformity in praise, public and private, in the administration of the Supper, in the solemnization of marriage, etc. The language of the overture was by no means soft and persuasive, and its personal thrusts were well understood. After debate, more plain than courteous, the overture found no friend but its author, and was emphatically rejected. Mr. Jamieson immediately left the chair, protesting that he could not preside over any body that would thus ignore 'the attainments' of the Church in Reformation days. Another moderator was elected, although Mr. Jamieson retained his seat in synod, and thus avoided the obligation of signing as moderator the minutes of a backsliding synod. He returned home filled with great indignation, and in his published defence takes great credit to himself that it was not until the second Sabbath after his arrival home that he commenced his public condemnation and protest. By his own confession he spared neither synod as a whole, nor the leading members individually; and he spoke equally severely of the Red Stone Presbytery of the Presbyterian Church, in the midst of which he lived. Complaint was made to synod in 1795 of his course by William Findley, one of his elders; and Messrs. Dobbins and Young were appointed a committee to go west and help the second Presbytery of Pennsylvania investigate these charges, together with other charges of heretical teaching. This was done in the autumn of the same year, and resulted in the tabling of a libel containing eleven specifications. This libel and all the testimony relating thereto was referred to the next synod. The gravamen of the whole may be reduced to two points,—viz., a false and injurious abuse

18   273

of the synod and particularly of Dr. Annan and of John M. Mason, ' who inherited his father's odiousness, and error in doctrine in reference to faith and the offer of the gospel to the reprobate.' There was no difficulty in the matter of proof, for he admitted that he had denounced the unfaithfulness of synod, because it ' made an act allowing or approving the singing of Watts's Psalms, Sternold and Hopkins, or anything that families pleased in family worship,' and that it did so at Dr. Annan's dictation, because Mr. Nourse, his wealthiest member and elder, claimed this privilege; also another act setting aside the fast-days and thanksgiving days usually observed in connection with the Lord's Supper; and that this was to favor the rich merchants in Dr. Mason's charge; and finally that they were about setting aside the publication of the banns of marriage, so that the clergy might not lose their marriage fees; ' that thus the worship, government, and discipline of the Church are nearly given up for a price or a loaf of bread.'

" Rev. John Jamieson ' was found guilty by synod at its meeting in 1796,' and ' suspended from the office of the ministry and prohibited from teaching students of divinity until next meeting of synod.' At the next meeting, in 1797, he refused to give any satisfaction, but read a protest, declined the authority of the synod, and withdrew. Synod forthwith deposed and excommunicated him, and this action was never reversed or modified. A large portion of his church at Hannahstown joined with him in his declinature, and he continued to minister to them ' for a season,'—viz., nine years, or until 1805.

" Mr. Jamieson was a man of decided abilities, and of some theological attainments; so that his presbytery placed their theological students under his care, and Alexander Porter, Alexander McCoy, and David Proudfit were at this time pursuing their studies with him."—*Big Spring Church History*.

" Nothing daunted, the Rev. John Jamieson wrote a book defending his views and the old-time customs of his Church. Also he continued to preach as an independent till near the day of his death. The country being new, he preached from settlement to settlement. For roads he had forest paths; bridges there were none, and in devotion to duty he braved alike the beasts of the forest, the summer's heat, and the winter's cold. Truly his was the ' voice of one crying in the wilderness;' in the wilderness, crying almost daily somewhere for thirty-six years, either in the open air, in the cabin, in the woods, in the log barn, or in the log church.

" From 1783 to at least 1816 he went about his Master's business. Money he did not need, for every cabin door was opened wide to him, while his wife and family were busy at his own cabin raising food, scutching, spinning, weaving, knitting, and making the family home-spun clothing.

" Of the twenty-six religious bodies in Pennsylvania that Rev. John Jamieson organized through his personality, twenty-four of them are to-day strong, wealthy United Presbyterian churches, and are under the jurisdiction of one of the following presbyteries,—viz., Big Spring, Westmoreland, Conemaugh, or Monongahela. Of the two remaining organizations, one is a Covenanter church at Alexandria, Westmoreland County, and the other is the Covenanter church at Clarksburg, Indiana County.

"Rev. John Jamieson was six feet three inches high, and dignified in bearing. Mentally he was able, thoroughly educated, and possessed wonderful vigor, energy, and endurance. His voice was strong, clear, and far reaching; his oratory magnetic, holding the attention of his hearers as well through a long service as a short one. He was courteous, imperious, self-willed, quick-tempered, ultra-conservative, and hyper-Calvinistic.

"Although by inheritance possessing considerable wealth, he gave himself incessantly to ministerial duties. By his commanding presence, by his ingenuous and fearless honesty, and by his ability, he became the leader generally of all clear-headed and honest people in the fields of labor; and was dreaded by all dishonest and time-serving persons whether in business, church, or state. He was characterized by his abhorrence of all shams and carnal policy, and by morality and kindness to the poor. He was frugal and temperate. He labored for the good of the community. He was a prominent leader in the formation of Indiana County. To aid in the civil interests of Indiana County, he contracted for the erection of the first county jail.

"He served as county commissioner for Indiana County for the years 1809, 1810, and 1811. He was actively engaged in educational matters, and was one of the pioneer trustees for the Indiana Academy, incorporated March 28, 1814. I find in his diary that he was actively and regularly preaching in and around Kittanning from 1813 to January 8, 1815; in Freeport region, in 1813–14; and what is now West Union, and in Conemaugh, Plumville, and Crete, up to 1816. His services in these years were held in cabins and barns and log churches. His pioneer home farm in Conemaugh Township, Indiana County, was first assessed to him in Indiana County, in 1805, along with two horses and three cows, valued at seven hundred and fifty-nine dollars. This homestead of two hundred and seventy-six acres continued to be occupied by and assessed to him until 1818, when he removed to within a mile of Crete, where he lived until he died, March 12, 1821, at the age of seventy-four years, and was buried at Crete church, Indiana County, Pennsylvania. His Conemaugh property, after 1818, became the Archibald Coleman homestead, and is now owned by William Irwin and occupied by a tenant."

This church originated in a religious camp-meeting held in Kentucky and Tennessee in 1801–03. In 1810 these religious enthusiasts organized themselves into a distinct and separate body. In 1860 they had seventeen synods, forty-eight presbyteries, one thousand churches, three hundred ministers, and one hundred thousand members.

The pioneer Presbyterian preaching in America was in Philadelphia, in 1698. In 1704 they erected a frame church on Market Street, and called it Buttonwood. The pioneer presbytery was in Philadelphia about the year 1705. In 1716 the pioneer synod was held, with the representation of twenty-five churches. In 1729 the Westminster Confession and Catechisms were formally adopted. In 1741 a schism on educational questions took place, but was healed in 1758. The first General Assembly met in 1789, and the confession and catechisms were again adopted, with some slight changes.

Presbyterianism, David's Psalms, and the Catechism was the pioneer service and creed in all this wilderness. The usual salary of a minister in pioneer days was four hundred dollars a year for full time. This was generally divided among two or more churches.

PIONEER BAPTIST CHURCH IN NORTHWESTERN PENNSYLVANIA, 1780–1850

" In most of the colonies the Baptists were persecuted. In Rhode Island they were especially numerous. They had much to do with that agitation for religious liberty which culminated in the passage of the first amendment to the Constitution of the United States. In 1762 there were fifty-six Baptist churches in the region now occupied by the United States; in 1792, 1000; in 1812, 2433; in 1832, 5322; in 1852, 9500."

The pioneer Baptist preaching in Pennsylvania was at Cold Spring, Bucks County, in 1684, by Rev. Thomas Dungan. This church died in 1702.

The pioneer Baptist preacher to have services in what is now Cameron, Elk, Forest, and Jefferson Counties was the Rev. Jonathan Nichols, who settled on the Turley farm, above Weedville, in 1817, then Clearfield County. In 1821 he moved to Brandycamp, now Elk County. As a clergyman his ministrations were generally well accepted, and his meetings were as well attended as could be in a country so sparsely settled; people frequently went six or eight miles to meeting. In the winter their carriages were sleds drawn by oxen; in the summer men, women, and children could walk nine or ten miles and home again the same day. Rev. Jonathan Nichols was a regularly ordained Baptist minister, and an educated physician. He migrated to what is now Elk County from Connecticut. He died in 1846, aged seventy-one years. His wife Hannah died in 1859, aged eighty-two years. His home was the late P. B. Little farm on Brandycamp. As a physician his labors were extended, and his ministry was well received by the scattered people of all beliefs. For a while he clung to the close communion, but, owing to the different beliefs adhered to by his hearers, he, after a few years, invited all Christian people who attended his services to the " Lord's table." His daughter told me his heart would not let him do otherwise. One who knew him well wrote of him: " He was a generous, kind-hearted gentleman, genial and urbane in his manners, with a helping hand ready to assist the needy.

and had kind words to comfort the sorrowing." Winter's snow never deterred him from pastoral work or visits to the sick.

PIONEER ORGANIZATION OF THE CLARION BAPTIST ASSOCIATION, HELD AT
BROOKVILLE, PENNSYLVANIA, JUNE 1 AND 2, 1838

On Friday, June 1, 1838, pursuant to adjournment, the Association convened in Brookville, Jefferson County, Pennsylvania. Rev. Thomas Wilson preached the introductory sermon, from Job thirty-third chapter and twenty-fourth verse. The moderator and clerk of the preparatory meeting of 1837 took their seats, and, after prayer by Rev. Samuel D. Morris, of Brookville, the letters from churches were read, and the names of the ministers and messengers present were enrolled. Each church was entitled to four messengers.

The following churches were represented: Zion church, Armstrong County (constituted June 21, 1821), by Rev. Thomas E. Thomas and Rev. S. Messenger, ordained ministers; messengers, or lay delegates, Amos Williams, William Corbet, and William Frampton; post-office, Strattonville, Pennsylvania. Red Bank church, Armstrong County (constituted May, 1837), by Rev. Thomas Wilson, ordained minister; messengers, I. Moorhead, T. Buzard, J. Putney; post-office, Red Bank, Pennsylvania. Mahoning church, Indiana County (constituted April, 1830), by Rev. Thomas Wilson, ordained minister; messengers, Jacob Keel, Thompson Hays; post-office, Smicksburg, Pennsylvania. Brookville church, Jefferson County (constituted May, 1837), by Rev. Samuel D. Morris, licensed minister; messengers, Michael Troy, James M. Craig, William Humphrey; post-office, Brookville, Pennsylvania. Gethsemane church, now Allens Mills, Jefferson County (constituted June, 1834), by Rev. Samuel Miles, ordained minister; messenger, G. Wilson; post-office, Brookville, Pennsylvania. Curwensville church, Clearfield County (constituted August, 1836), by no minister; messenger, N. Lawhead; post-office, Curwensville, Pennsylvania.

Brother Amos Williams was then chosen moderator, and Samuel D. Morris, of Brookville, clerk. Brothers Miles, Wilson, Williams, and Morris were appointed a committee to arrange the business and preaching for this session.

The Association was called Clarion, I suppose because " Clarion" means " a trumpet of a clear, shrill tone." Clarion *County* was not formed until March 11, 1839.

A constitution for the Association was adopted, Articles of Faith announced and promulgated, and Rules of Decorum for the Association adopted, " and to be read at the opening of every session and left on the table for the perusal of the members." It was further agreed, that " the next meeting of the Association be held with Zion church, Armstrong (now Clarion) County, on Friday preceding the first Lord's day in October, 1839," Rev. Samuel

Miles to preach the introductory sermon at that time, and Rev. Thomas Wilson to write the circular letter.

The following sums were received for printing minutes,—viz., Zion church, two dollars and fifty cents; Red Bank church, one dollar and fifty cents; Mahoning church, one dollar and seventy-five cents; Brookville church, one dollar; Gethsemane, one dollar and fifty cents; and Curwensville, one dollar. William Frampton was appointed treasurer; William King, Jr., to be stated clerk for the Association, post-office, Greenville, Armstrong County, Pennsylvania (now Limestone, Clarion County, Pennsylvania). Brother James M. Craig was authorized to have three hundred copies of the minutes printed, and to distribute them. Several resolutions in regard to missionary work, religious periodicals, etc., were read and adopted.

PIONEER LUTHERAN EVANGELICAL CHURCH IN NORTHWESTERN PENNSYL-
VANIA, 1780-1850

The pioneer Lutheran preaching in North America was in what is now New York (then New Amsterdam), in 1624. This service had to be held in a private house, and, as there was no religious liberty in that colony then, some of these early Lutherans who attended this service were imprisoned, and the pastor sent back to Holland. In 1638 a colony of Swedes settled at what is now Wilmington, Delaware. They erected a fort, called it Christina, and in the chapel of that fort celebrated their religious services in 1639, the Rev. Reorus Torkillus being the pastor. It was not, however, until 1742 that the church was really organized in America. On September 25, 1742, the Rev. Henry Melchior Muhlenberg located in Philadelphia, Pennsylvania, as a missionary, and commenced his work. He is considered the patriarch of the church in North America. The pioneer synod was held in Philadelphia in 1748.

PIONEER METHODISM

" This denomination first assumed its present name at the conference held in 1784. Previous to that time the scattered followers of this belief had met in societies, like those established in Great Britain by Rev. John Wesley. At the same conference the church was organized for missionary and pioneer work under charge of bishops sent to this country by Mr. Wesley, who was recognized as the spiritual father of the denomination. Its success during the next few years was remarkable. The zeal and energy of its preachers and the work of the lay members brought about within sixteen years an increase of membership and preachers almost fourfold. This church was the first officially to acknowledge the United States Constitution, and was very active in every antislavery movement. The first session of its General Conference was held in 1792, at which time the membership was about one hundred and ninety-five thousand. In 1843 the abolitionist party in the

278

church withdrew in dissatisfaction and founded the Wesleyan Methodist connection. Two years later the Southern Methodists, dissatisfied in their turn, separated and formed the Methodist Episcopal Church South."—*Dictionary United States History.*

On March 7, 1736, John Wesley preached the pioneer Methodist sermon in America, in Savannah, Georgia. Another early Methodist service in the United States was conducted in New York city by a Mr. Embury, aided and assisted by Barbara Heck. Barbara Heck emigrated from Ireland to New York in 1765. From her zeal, activity, and pious work as a Christian she is called the mother of American Methodism. Methodism was introduced into Pennsylvania in 1767 by Captain Thomas Webb, a soldier in the British army. Web was a preacher, and is called the apostle of American Methodism. In 1767 he visited Philadelphia, preached, and formed a class of seven persons. The first Annual Conferences of the Methodist Church held in America were in Philadelphia,—viz., in the years 1773, 1774, and 1775. After this year all Conferences were held in Baltimore, Maryland, until the organization of the Church in the New World.

The pioneer Methodist preaching in Pennsylvania was in Philadelphia, in a sail-loft near Second and Dock Streets. St. John's Church was established in 1769. Methodism was to be found in Philadelphia in 1772, York in 1781, Wilkesbarre in 1778, Williamsport in 1791, and in Pittsburg in 1801.

The pioneer Sunday-school in the world was opened at Glencastle, in England, in 1781, by Robert Raikes. The idea was suggested to him by a young woman, who afterwards became Sophia Bradburn. This lady assisted him in the opening of the first school. The pioneer Sunday-schools were started in the New World in 1790 by an official ordinance of the Methodist Conference establishing Sunday-schools to instruct poor children, white and black: "Let persons be appointed by the bishops, elders, deacons, or preachers to teach (gratis) all that will attend and have a capacity to learn, from six o'clock in the morning till ten, and from two o'clock in the afternoon until six, when it does not interfere with public worship."

The Methodist Church was really the first temperance organization in America. The general rules of the society prohibited the use of liquor as a beverage. Other modern temperance organizations are supposed to have their beginning about 1811. But little was done after this period outside of the churches for about twenty-five years.

Rev. William Watters was the pioneer American, itinerant, Methodist preacher. He was born in Baltimore County, Maryland, October 16, 1751.

Until 1824 Western Pennsylvania, or "all west of the Susquehanna River, except the extreme northern part, was in the Baltimore Conference." In 1824 the Pittsburg Conference was organized, and our wilderness came under its jurisdiction. In 1833 the first Methodist paper under the authority of the church was started. It was in Pittsburg, Pennsylvania, and the paper is now called the *Pittsburg Christian Advocate*. In 1836 the Erie Conference was formed.

Methodism in Northwestern Pennsylvania has been, first, in the Baltimore Conference; second, in the Pittsburg Conference; and is now in the Erie Conference.

The Methodists were slow in making an inroad in the northwest. The ground had been occupied by other denominations, and a hostile and bitter prejudice existed against the new " sect."

The pay of the pioneer Methodist ministers and preachers, and for their wives and children, was as follows:

" *1800.*—' 1. The annual salary of the travelling preachers shall be eighty dollars and their travelling expenses.

" ' 2. The annual allowance of the wives of travelling preachers shall be eighty dollars.

" ' 3. Each child of a travelling preacher shall be allowed sixteen dollars annually to the age of seven years, and twenty-four dollars annually from the age of seven to fourteen years; nevertheless, this rule shall not apply to the children of preachers whose families are provided for by other means in their circuits respectively.

" ' 4. The salary of the superannuated, worn-out, and supernumerary preachers shall be eighty dollars annually.

" ' 5. The annual allowance of the wives of superannuated, worn-out, and supernumerary preachers shall be eighty dollars.

" ' 6. The annual allowance of the widows of travelling, superannuated, worn-out, and supernumerary preachers shall be eighty dollars.

" ' 7. The orphans of travelling, superannuated, worn-out, and supernumerary preachers shall be allowed by the Annual Conference, if possible, by such means as they can devise, sixteen dollars annually.'

" *1804.*—The following inserted in clause 3, before ' nevertheless': ' and those preachers whose wives are dead shall be allowed for each child annually a sum sufficient to pay the board of such child or children during the above term of years.'

" The following added at the close of the section:

" ' 8. Local preachers shall be allowed a salary in certain cases as mentioned.'

" *1816.*—' The allowance of all preachers and their wives raised to one hundred dollars.'

" *1824.*—Under clause 2 (allowance to wives) it is added, ' But this provision shall not apply to the wives of those preachers who were single when they were received for trial, and marry under four years, until the expiration of said four years.'

" *1828.*—The seventh clause (relating to orphans) was altered so as to read as follows:

"'7. The orphans of travelling, supernumerary, superannuated, and worn-out preachers shall be allowed by the Annual Conferences the same sums respectively which are allowed to the children of living preachers. And on the death of a preacher, leaving a child or children without so much of worldly goods as should be necessary to his or her or their support, the Annual Conference of which he was a member shall raise, in such manner as may be deemed best, a yearly sum for the subsistence and education of such orphan child or children, until he, she, or they shall have arrived at fourteen years of age, the amount of which yearly sum shall be fixed by the committee of the Conference at each session in advance.'

"*1832.*—The following new clause was inserted:

"'8. The more effectually to raise the amount necessary to meet the above-mentioned allowance, let there be made weekly class collections in all our societies where it is practicable; and also for the support of missions and missionary schools under our care.'

"*1836.*—The regulation respecting those who marry 'under four years' was struck out, and bishops mentioned by name as standing on the same footing as other travelling preachers. Clauses 1, 2, 4, and 5 thrown into two, as follows:

"'1. The annual allowance of the married travelling supernumerary, and superannuated preachers and the bishops shall be two hundred dollars and their travelling expenses.

"'2. The annual allowance of the unmarried travelling, supernumerary, and superannuated preachers and the bishops shall be one hundred dollars and their travelling expenses.'

"The pioneer members were prohibited from wearing 'needless ornaments, such as rings, earrings, lace, necklace, and ruffles.'"—*Strickland's History of Discipline.*

PIONEER AND EARLY CAMP-MEETINGS

The pioneer camp-meeting in this wilderness was held at Meadville, in the fall of 1826.

The pioneer camp-meeting in the United States was held, between 1800 and 1801, at Cane Ridge, in Kentucky. It was under the auspices of several different denominational ministers. The meeting was kept up day and night. It was supposed that there were in attendance during the meetings from twelve to twenty thousand people. Stands were erected through the woods, from which one, two, three, and four preachers would be addressing the thousands at the same time. It was at this place and from this time that our camp-meetings took their rise.

Evans, the Shaker historian, who is strong in the gift of faith, tells us that "the subjects of this work were greatly exercised in dreams, visions, revelations, and the spirit of the prophecy. In these gifts of the Spirit they saw and testified that the great day of God was at hand, that Christ was about to set up his kingdom on earth, and that this very work would terminate in the full manifestation of the latter day of glory."

From another authority, endowed perhaps with less fervor but with more of common sense, we get a description of these "exercises," which has a familiar ring that seems to bring it very near home. "The people remained on the ground day and night, listening to the most exciting sermons, and engaging in a mode of worship which consisted in alternate crying, laughing, singing, and shouting, accompanied with gesticulations of a most extraordinary character. Often there would be an unusual outcry, some bursting forth into loud ejaculations of thanksgiving, others exhorting their careless friends to 'turn to the Lord,' some struck with terror and hastening to escape, others trembling, weeping, and swooning away, till every appearance of life was gone and the extremities of the body assumed the coldness of a corpse. At one meeting not less than a thousand persons fell to the ground, apparently without sense or motion. It was common to see them shed tears plentifully about an hour before they fell. They were then seized with a general tremor, and sometimes they uttered one or two piercing shrieks in the moment of falling. This latter phenomenon was common to both sexes, to all ages, and to all sorts of characters.

"After a time these crazy performances in the sacred name of religion became so much a matter of course that they were regularly classified in categories as the rolls, the jerks, the barks, etc. The rolling exercise was effected by doubling themselves up, then rolling from one side to the other like a hoop, or in extending the body horizontally and rolling over and over in the filth like so many swine. The jerk consisted in violent spasms and twistings of every part of the body. Sometimes the head was twisted round so that the face was turned to the back, and the countenance so much distorted that not one of its features was to be recognized. When attacked by the jerks they sometimes hopped like frogs, and the face and limbs underwent the most hideous contortions. The bark consisted in throwing themselves on all-fours, growling, showing their teeth, and barking like dogs. Sometimes a number of people crouching down in front of the minister continued to bark as long as he preached. These last were supposed to be more especially endowed with the gifts of prophecy, dreams, rhapsodies, and visions of angels."

Exactly when the pioneer camp-meeting was held in Jefferson County is unknown to me. Darius Carrier advertised one in the *Jeffersonian* as early as 1836, to be held near Summerville. The first one I remember was near Brookville, on the North Fork, on land now owned by F. Swartzlander. Others were held near Roseville, and in Perry Township and kindred points. The rowdy element attended these services, and there was usually a good deal of disturbance from whiskey and fights, which, of course, greatly annoyed the good people. The first "Dutch camp-meeting" was held in what is now Ringgold Township. In fact, these German meetings were only abandoned a few years ago. I reproduce a "Dutch camp-meeting hymn":

"CAMP-MEETING HYMN

"Satan and I we can't agree,
  Halleo, halleolujah!
For I hate him and he hates me,
  Halleo, halleolujah!

"I do believe without a doubt,
  Halleo, halleolujah!
The Christian has a right to shout,
  Halleo, halleolujah!

"We'll whip the devil round the stump,
  Halleo, halleolujah!
And hit him a kick at every jump,
  Halleo, halleolujah."

The mode of conducting our wood-meetings was patterned after the original in Kentucky. The manner of worship and conversions were the same, and while a great deal of harsh criticism has been made against this mode of religious worship, there is one thing that must be admitted,—many bad, wicked persons were changed into good religious people. Pitch-pine fagots were burned at night to light the grounds.

ROMAN CATHOLIC CHURCH

'The pioneer Catholic service in Pennsylvania was in Philadelphia, in 1780. The pioneer priest was either Polycarp Wickstead, or James Haddock. The pioneer church erected in Pennsylvania was St. Joseph's, in Philadelphia.

CHAPTER XIV

PIONEER CIRCUIT COURTS—PIONEER CIRCUIT JUDGES—PRESIDENT AND ASSO-
CIATES—PIONEER BAR AND EARLY LAWYERS

THE first legislation creating a judiciary in this State was called the provincial act of March 22, 1722. This court was styled " The Court of Quarter Sessions of the Peace and Gaol Delivery." The Orphans' Court was established in 1713. The constitution of 1776 provided for the continuance of these courts. By the constitution adopted in 1790 the judicial power of the State was vested in a Supreme Court, in a Court of Oyer and Terminer and General Jail Delivery, Common Pleas, Quarter Sessions, Orphans' Court, and Register Court for each county, and for justices of the peace for boroughs and townships. The early judges were appointed by the governor.

In 1806, for the more convenient establishment of the Supreme Court, the State was made into two districts,—viz., the Eastern and Western. The salary of a county associate judge was one hundred and fifty dollars per year.

Both the president judge of a district and the associate judges for a county were appointed in this State until 1850, when the State constitution was changed to make them elective. The term of the president judge ran ten years, but the term of the associates was for five. The president circuit judge's salary was sixteen hundred dollars a year and mileage.

Pennsylvania has had four constitutions. The first one, September 28, 1776. Under this constitution the General Assembly consisted of but one house. The members were elected yearly. The laws were called " Acts of Assembly." A new constitution was formed in 1790, when the Senate body of the Legislature was created. Under this constitution a free colored man could vote at any election in the State, hence all public notices were addressed to the freemen of the locality.

The third revision was in 1838. Under this constitution the free colored man was denied his vote. All life offices were abolished,

In 1838 the amended constitution as adopted limited the rights of any one man to serve in the office of governor to six years out of nine. Under the first constitution of 1790 the limit of service in this office was nine years out of twelve. It was customary then in Pennsylvania to publish laws and public documents in separate books, in English and German. The debates of the 1838 convention were so published.

284

Up to 1840 the judges were all appointed by the governor with the advice and consent of the Senate. Supreme Court judges were appointed for fifteen years, district judges of the Court of Common Pleas were appointed for ten years, and the associate judges were appointed for five.

The fourth revision was in 1873. One of the principal points in this constitution was to restrict local legislation, and under it the colored man was again given his right to vote. From 1843 to 1850 members of the Legislature received one dollar and fifty cents per day; in 1850 their pay was increased to three dollars per day for one hundred days, and one dollar and fifty cents per day for every day after that in session.

By an act of the General Assembly of April 13, 1791, the counties of Westmoreland, Fayette, Washington, and Allegheny constituted the Fifth Judicial District, and on March 26, 1804, Jefferson County was attached to Westmoreland for judicial purposes. On June 2, 1803, Samuel Roberts was commissioned President Judge for the Fifth Judicial District, by Governor McKean. This Samuel Roberts was Jefferson's pioneer territorial judge until March 10, 1806. Judge Roberts was an able jurist and a literary man of note. He compiled and published, in 1817, a text-work on law, a digest of the British statutes, with notes and illustrations. Samuel Roberts was born in Philadelphia, September 10, 1761, and as judge he continued to preside in Allegheny County until his death, in 1820.

By an act of Assembly of February, 24, 1806, the counties of Somerset, Cambria, Indiana, Armstrong, and Westmoreland were made into the Tenth Judicial District, and John Young, of Westmoreland, was commissioned Judge for that district March 1, 1806.

By an act of Assembly of March 10, 1806, the county of Indiana was organized for judicial purposes, to take effect the first Monday in November, 1806.

.By an act of Assembly of March 10, 1806, Jefferson County was annexed to the county of Indiana, and the authority of the county commissioners and other county officers of said Indiana County was extended over and within the county of Jefferson. Jefferson remained annexed to Indiana County until 1824, and for judicial purposes alone until, by act of Assembly, April 2, 1830, to organize the provisional county of Jefferson for judicial purposes, it was stipulated in Section 2 that the county should be attached to and form part of the Fourth Judicial District, and that the president judge of the Fourth Judicial District, and the associates to be appointed, shall have like power as other counties, etc., on and after the first Monday in October, to do and perform all duties, etc. Hon. Thomas Burnside, of Bellefonte, Centre County, was then the president judge of this Fourth Judicial District, composed of Mifflin, Center, Huntingdon, and Bedford Counties, and by this act of the Legislature he was made the pioneer judge to hold court in and for Jefferson County. Hon. Thomas Burnside was born in the county of .

Tyrone, Ireland, July 28, 1782. His father emigrated to Philadelphia, Pennsylvania, in 1792.

In 1800 Burnside read law with Hon. Robert Porter, of Philadelphia, who died suddenly in Brookville in 1842, being found dead in his bed in the morning at the Red Lion Tavern, kept by John Smith. Judge Porter stopped off the stage to rest over night while travelling through this wilderness. Porter is buried in the old cemetery. On February 13, 1804, Hon. Thomas Burnside was admitted to the Philadelphia bar. In the month of March of that year he moved to and settled in Bellefonte, Center County, Pennsylvania. In 1811 he was elected to the State Senate. In 1815 he was sent to Congress. In 1816 he was appointed a president judge. In 1823 he was again elected a State Senator and made Speaker. In 1826 he was again appointed president judge, and in 1845 he was commissioned judge for the Supreme Court of Pennsylvania.

In stature Judge Burnside was of medium height, dark complexioned, and very homely. He was a learned lawyer, an able jurist, and a kind, honest, open-hearted gentleman. He served as judge in Jefferson County until September 1, 1835, when the Eighteenth Judicial District was organized. Like other judges of his period, he could get " drunk through and through" every court week.

THE EIGHTEENTH DISTRICT

By an act passed April 8, 1833, the counties of Potter, McKean, Warren, and Jefferson were made the Eighteenth Judicial District, from and after September 1, 1835, and the governor was required to appoint a president judge for the district, and Nathaniel B. Eldred, of McKean County, was appointed judge November 10, 1835. Judge Eldred resigned in 1839. He died January 27, 1867.

COURTS WITHIN THE EIGHTEENTH JUDICIAL DISTRICT IN 1837

Warren County.—The court at Warren, for Warren County, will be held on the first Mondays of March, June, September, and December.

Jefferson County.—At Brookville, for Jefferson County, the second Mondays of February, May, September, and December.

McKean County.—At Smethport, for McKean County, the Mondays immediately after the courts in Brookville.

Potter County.—At Coudersport, for Potter County, on the Mondays immediately after the courts in McKean County.

HON. NATHANIEL B. ELDRED, *President Judge of said courts.*

Alexander McCalmont, of Franklin, Venango County, was appointed judge May 31, 1839, and served until 1849. As an illustration of the man, and his manner of holding court, I give an incident that occurred in Ridgway, Elk County, in 1844, while he was holding the pioneer court there.

The pioneer court crier was Nathaniel Hyatt, of Kersey, and he, like everybody else in those days, was fond of attending court for the sake of visiting, seeing the judge, telling stories, and " smiling with his neighbors."

Mr. Hyatt was a large man, peculiar, and had a coarse voice. Judge Alexander McCalmont, of Venango, was on the bench, a very easy-going, mild-mannered man.

One day while the court was in session Mr. Hyatt was busy telling a bevy of neighbors some stories in the court-room and talking loud. The judge thought there was a little too much noise in court, and, to personally reprimand Mr. Hyatt, he commenced " a rapping, gently tapping, tapping," three times on the desk and addressing Mr. Hyatt thus: " Crier, there is a little too much noise in court."

Promptly Mr. Hyatt responded by stamping his right foot violently on the floor, and in his loud, coarse voice exclaimed, " Let there be silence in court. What the hell are you about?"

Joseph Buffington, of Kittanning, Armstrong County, was appointed judge June 1, 1849, to serve until the end of the next session of the State Senate. He was reappointed January 15, 1850. Under the amended constitution of the State the president judge was made elective for ten years, and the associates for five.

Eminent lawyers then attended all courts in the district They rode in the stage or on horseback, wore green leggings, and carried their papers, books, etc., in large leather saddle-bags. Most of these circuit lawyers were very polite gentlemen, and particular not to refuse a " drink."

CRIME

From 1778 to 1855, inclusive, three hundred and twenty-eight persons were hanged in Pennsylvania. Of these, five suffered the penalty of death for high treason, eight for robbery, fourteen for burglary, three for assault, one for arson, four for counterfeiting, and seven for unknown offences. On April 22, 1794, the death penalty was abolished except for murder in the first degree. Before 1834 hangings took place in public, and since then in jail-yards or corridors.

I will here give a sample of justice in 1784. Joe Disbury was tried in Sunbury for thievery, etc., found guilty, and sentenced to receive thirty-nine lashes, stand in the pillory one hour, have his ears cut off and nailed to the post, and be imprisoned three months and pay a fine of thirty pounds.

CHAPTER XV

THE PIONEER DOCTOR IN NORTHWESTERN PENNSYLVANIA—BROOKVILLE'S
PIONEER RESURRECTION; OR, " WHO SKINNED THE NIGGER?"—THE TRUE
STORY OF THE ORIGIN OF THE STATE ANATOMICAL LAW

MEDICINE was practised by the Egyptian priests. Moses, the Law-giver, was a doctor and learned in all the arts of the Egyptians.

The pioneer and early doctor was a useful citizen, and his visits to the early settlers when afflicted was a great comfort. How we all long now to see the doctor when we are sick! These isolated people longed just the same for the coming of their doctor. The science of medicine then was very crude, and the art of it very imperfect, hence the early practitioner had but limited skill; yet, while exercising whatever he professed for the relief of suffering, his privations and labor while travelling by night or day on horseback with his "old pill-bags" were hard and severe in the extreme. The extent of his circuit was usually from fifty to one hundred miles over poor roads and paths, swimming his horse through creeks and rivers as best he could. I have travelled a circuit of one hundred miles in my day. In those days every one had respect for the doctor, and every family along his circuit was delighted with an opportunity to extend *free* hospitality to the doctor and his horse.

When I commenced the practice of medicine, I had to ride on horseback. My field extended all through and over Jefferson, Forest, Elk, as well as the western part of Clearfield County. My rides were long, day and night, through rain, mud, sleet, cold, snow, and darkness, with no rubber garments to protect me from storms. I have travelled the creek beds, forded and swam my horse when the rivers were in rafting stage, rode over paths, and ridden many a time from dark until daylight all alone through the wilderness, twenty, thirty, or forty miles, stopping about midnight at some cabin to give my horse a little feed.

In those days there was no telegraph, telephone, or daily mail through which to summon a doctor, but a neighbor had to be sent on foot or on horseback to find a physician, and not to come back without him. I was a good practical botanist, and used mostly herbs and roots; these I gathered in the spring, summer, and fall. Recipes were the fad then. One of my preceptors had a book of these, which I carefully copied, and any others I could find. Medical colleges were few, and medical literature was scarce. As doctors

288

we knew but little, and had to rely on what common-sense we possessed. My partner, Dr. Niver, made what he called "devil's broth." It was a mixed decoction of about all our roots and herbs, to be administered, as he said, "with the hope that some one of the ingredients would hit the disease."

Medicine and its practice was about all theory; remedies were crude and drastic; instruments few, imperfect, and clumsy. I feel amazed when I think how ignorant I was, yet I tied arteries, set broken bones, amputated limbs, saved lives! The pioneer doctor unselfishly responded to all calls, asking no questions as to pay, and performing more free labor for humanity than all other classes of men combined.

In learning the art I rode with my preceptor. In some of my long rides I have become so tired about midnight that I felt I could not go a step farther, when I would dismount from my horse, hitch him to a log on the outside of a log-barn, slip the bridle around his neck, climb into the mow, throw the horse an armful of hay, and then fall asleep in the hay, only to awaken when the sun was an hour or two high. The pioneer doctor carried his pill-bags well stocked with calomel, Dover's powder, tartar emetic, blistering salve, a pair of old turnkeys for extracting teeth, and spring- and thumb-lancets for bleeding purposes, as everybody had to be bled, sick or well. Twenty-five cents was the fee for bleeding, and the amount of blood drawn from the arm was from half a pint to a quart. The custom of bleeding sick or well fell into disrepute about 1850. A town visit was from twenty-five to fifty cents, a visit in the country twenty-five cents a mile, an obstetric fee five dollars. The pioneer doctor always wore green leggings or corduroy overalls. I was no exception to this rule. Sanitary science was unknown fifty years ago.

THE OLD-FASHIONED DOCTOR, BY H. C. DODGE

"He'd stalk to our crib-side and order us gruffly
    To stick out our tongue, which we'd do with such dread,
And give, while he handled our pulses so roughly,
    An ominous shake of his solemn old head.

"And then, while he listened to mother's description
    Of things we had eaten and what we had done,
He grimly would write his old Latin prescription
    For nastiest medicines under the sun.

"Those horrible doses. How mother would scold us,
    And beg us and buy us to take 'em in vain;
And oh, how we'd struggle when father would hold us
    And squeeze shut our noses regardless of pain.

"And, when forced to open our mouths, quickly mother
    Would shove in a spoonful that strangled us till
We spluttered it out—just in time for another.
    Its vile, deathly taste's in our memory still."

"BROOKVILLE'S PIONEER RESURRECTION; OR, 'WHO SKINNED THE NIGGER?'
—THE TRUTH TOLD FOR THE FIRST TIME, BY THE ONLY ONE NOW LIVING
OF THE SEVEN WHO WERE ENGAGED IN IT—THE TRUE STORY OF THE
ORIGIN OF THE STATE ANATOMICAL LAW

"To everything there is a time and a season."

"On Sunday morning, November 8, 1857, Brookville was thrown into
a state of the greatest commotion and excitement, occasioned by the discovery by W. C. Smith (then a lad of fifteen) of the mutilated remains of a
human being in an ice-house belonging to K. L. Blood, on the corner of
Pickering Street and Coal Alley, or where Mrs. Banks now lives. When
discovered by Smith, the door was broken open, having been forced during
the night, and the body was found lying on the ice, with a board under the
shoulders and head, the legs and arms spread apart, the intestines taken out,
a lump of ice placed in the abdominal cavity, and the body literally skinned,
the cuticle having been removed entirely from the crown of the head to the
soles of the feet.

"Filled with terror, young Smith ran from the spot, telling his discovery
to all he met. Men, women, and children rushed *en masse* to the ice-house.
Thoughts of savage butchery, suicide, and horror took hold of the people.
Women cried, and men turned pale with indignation. The news of Smith's
discovery spread like wildfire, and the excitement and indignation became
more and more intense as hundreds of men, women, and children from the
town and vicinity gathered around the lonely ice-house. It was at first
supposed to be murder most foul; but, on a closer inspection of the 'remains'
by Henry R. Fullerton, a little 'curly hair,' resembling 'negro wool,' was
found lying loose near the body. This was a clue. Fullerton then declared
it was the mutilated corpse of one Henry Southerland, who had died about
ten days before and been buried in the old graveyard. Tools were at once
procured by the excited mob, led by Henry R. Fullerton, Cyrus Butler, Sr.,
Richard Arthurs, Esq., and others, and a rush was made for Southerland's
grave. Arriving there, and upon the removal of a few shovelfuls of dirt, a
loose slipper was found, and farther on its mate. When the coffin was
reached, the body was found to be gone, and only the clothes, torn off, and
lying inside, were to be seen. What was this desecration for? Cyrus Butler,
Sr., a gruff old man, said, 'For money.' He boldly asserted that men nowadays would do anything for money. 'Yes,' he said, 'skin human excrement
and eat the little end on't.' Soon, in the absence of any better theory, everybody seemed to accept his belief, and it was positively asserted from one
to another that 'a negro hide would sell for five hundred dollars, to make
razor-strops,' etc.

"During the entire day the mob were at sea. The officials permitted the body to remain exposed,—a revolting spectacle to men, women, and children. To all of this I was an interested spectator.

"At nightfall an inquest was summoned of twelve men by Justices John Smith and A. J. Brady.

"CORONER'S INQUEST

"'Proceedings of the coroner's inquest, held in the borough of Brookville, upon the body of a man found in the ice-house belonging to K. L. Blood, on the corner of Pickering Street and Spring [Coal] Alley, on the morning of Sunday, November 8, 1857.

"'In pursuance of the summons issued by Justices John Smith and A. J. Brady, the following persons were called and sworn,—to wit: E. R. Brady, J. J. Y. Thompson, Andrew Craig, John Boucher, Levi A. Dodd, Christopher Smathers, Henry R. Fullerton, G. W. Andrews, S. C. Arthurs, John E. Carroll, John Ramsey, Daniel Smith, who repaired to the ice-house and made an examination of the body there deposited, and found the remains of a male human being, with the breast sawed open, the bowels and entrails removed, the toe- and finger-nails cut off at the first joint, and the skin of the entire body removed.

"'The grave in which Henry Southerland (colored), of Pine Creek Township, had been buried having been opened in the presence of a number of the jurors and other persons, and it being found that the body of said deceased had been removed from the said grave, the following witnesses were called and sworn:

"'David Banks, sworn: I helped open the grave in which the body of Henry Southerland (colored) had been buried; found no body in the coffin; found the burial clothes rolled up in a bundle and placed in the head of the coffin; found one of the slippers in which deceased was buried in the clay about a foot above and before coming to the coffin; the body had evidently been removed.

"'F. C. Coryell, sworn: Was present at the opening of the grave to-day; saw the coffin opened and no body there; found the clothes thrown in carelessly in a heap; one slipper with the clothes in the coffin and another in the clay some distance above the coffin; these slippers had my cost mark on, and are the same as purchased from me by the friends of Henry Southerland for his funeral.

"'A. R. Marlin, sworn: Henry Southerland was buried in the graveyard at Brookville on Wednesday or Thursday last; helped to bury him; the grave opened to-day is the one in which deceased was placed; no body in the coffin when opened to-day.

"'Richard Arthurs, sworn: I examined the body in the ice-house this day; looked at the mouth and tongue; they resembled those of a person who had died of a disease; two double teeth out; seemed as if they had recently been drawn: found some hair about the back of the neck, which was

291

HISTORY OF NORTHWESTERN PENNSYLVANIA

black and curly; think it was the hair of a negro, or whiskers; think this is the body of Henry Southerland; toes, fingers, and skin taken off.

" ' After making these enquiries and believing the body found in the ice-house to be that of Henry Southerland, which had been removed from the graveyard in the borough of Brookville, the jury caused the same to be taken up and deposited in the coffin, and placed in the grave from which the body of said Southerland had been removed, and the same filled up in their presence; then returning to the office of John Smith, Esq., a justice of the peace, adjourned, to meet at nine o'clock to-morrow (Monday) morning.

" ' The jury render their verdict as follows: That the body found in the ice-house is, to the best of their knowledge and belief, the body of Henry Southerland, stolen from the grave in which the same had been deposited; and that the skin, bowels, and toe- and finger-nails had been removed by some person or persons to the jury unknown.

" ' E. R. BRADY, *Foreman.*

" ' December 17, 1857. It is adjudged that there was probable cause for holding the inquest.

" ' By the Court,

" ' J. S. McCALMONT.'

" This coroner's verdict was supposed to have been manipulated by the ' Masons.' It was the custom then to charge all unpopular verdicts on ' the Masons.'

" After the inquest jurors viewed the body and ice-house on Sunday evening, a rope was tied around Southerland's neck, he was dragged into Coal Alley, thrown into his coffin, and reburied in the old graveyard, where lie

" ' Hearts once pregnant with celestial fire,
Hearts that the rod of empire might have swayed,
Or waked to ecstasy the living lyre.'

" Who were the ghouls? As usual, stupidity and prejudice came to the front, and picked out for vengeance two innocent and inoffensive colored men living in the suburbs of the town. ' The law ordained in reverence we must hold,' and so on Sunday evening Theresa Sweeney, a sister of Southerland's, was sent for, and she made information against Charles Anderson and John Lewis. Cyrus Butler, Jr., a constable then in Pine Creek Township, arrested forthwith these two harmless colored men and thrust them into jail. On Monday morning, the 9th, Anderson and Lewis had a hearing before Justices Smith and Brady. George W. Ziegler, an able lawyer, represented the Commonwealth; but the poor negroes were without friends or a lawyer. However, as there was no evidence against them, they were discharged. The excitement was now so intense that several newly made graves were opened to see if friends had been disturbed. A few timid people placed night-guards in the cemetery.

"In commenting on this atrocity, the *Jeffersonian* said, 'Taking everything into consideration, it was one of the most inhuman and barbarous acts ever committed in a civilized community; and although the instigators and perpetrators may escape the punishment which their brutality demands, they cannot fail to receive the indignant frowns of an insulted community. They may evade a prosecution through the technicalities of the law, and they may laugh it off, and when we have no assurance but that our bodies, or those of our friends, may be treated in the same manner, cold and hardened must be the wretch who does not feel the flame of indignation rise in his breast at the perpetration of such an offence.

*   *   *   *   *   *   *   *   *

"'Since the above was in type and the excitement somewhat allayed, it is now believed by every person that the body was placed in the ice-house for dissection, and it is supposed that those who had the matter in charge had the key to the door and left everything safe and secure on Saturday night, and that some thief, knowing that during the warm weather butter had been placed there for protection, broke open the door and entered the place for the purpose of stealing, and on striking a light or groping around in search of butter, he came across the "dead darky," and, in his haste to get away, forgot to shut the door, and we have no doubt that the fellow who broke open the door left in a hurry. This is, no doubt, the true state of the case.'

"All this confusion was a good thing for us guilty parties, as it gave time for the angry populace to cool off.

"Who was this Henry Southerland? He was a stout, perfect specimen of physical manhood. He was a son of Charles and Susan Southerland, *née* Van Camp. Charles Southerland came here in 1812,—a run-away slave. Miss Van Camp came to Port Barnett with her father, Fudge Van Camp, in 1801. Henry Southerland was born on the farm now owned by John Hoffman. He was a North Forker, and, like the other 'North Fork' boys, could drink, swear, wrestle, shoot, jump, 'pull square,' and raft. In the latter part of October, 1857, he took the fever and died in a few days, aged about thirty years. He lived then on what is called the Charles Horn farm. He was married and had one child. His widow and daughter now reside in the county, highly respectable people.

"Dr. J. C. Simons was then living in Brookville, practising medicine under his father-in-law, Dr. James Dowling. Simons was ambitious to become a surgeon. He believed, like all intelligent doctors then, that a knowledge of anatomy was the foundation of the healing art. Dissection of human bodies then in Pennsylvania was a crime. You could dissect mules and monkeys, but not men. It was legal in New York State, and was made so in 1789, to dissect the bodies of executed criminals, and this law in New York was greatly improved in 1854. New York was the first State in the New World to legalize ' the use of the dead to the living.' Massachusetts in 1860 passed a local law.

" The first legislation in Pennsylvania looking toward legalized dissection locally was in 1867. A member of the House introduced a local law to apply to the counties of Philadelphia and Allegheny,—viz., No. 482, ' An Act for the promotion of medical science, and to prevent the traffic in human bodies, in the city of Philadelphia and the county of Allegheny.' This law passed finally and was approved by John W. Geary on the 18th day of March, 1867."

This law of 1867 was incepted by the Philadelphia College of Physicians, manipulated and pushed in and through the Legislature by a committee of that body consisting of Drs. D. Hayes Agnew, S. D. Gross, Henry Hartshorn, and others.

Of the members and senators at that time who deserve a special notice for services rendered, I mention Dr. Wilmer Worthington, then a senator from Chester County.

" The first human body dissected was in Alexandria, Egypt, the cradle of anatomy. England legalized dissection in 1832. The first subject dissected in Jefferson County was in Brookville, in the winter of 1854–55, by Dr. George Watt, Dr. McClay, Samuel C. Arthurs, and a student, G. W. Burkett, now a doctor in Tyrone City, Pennsylvania. This subject was stolen from a graveyard in Clarion County, Pennsylvania. He was an Irishman who froze to death. He drank too much water in his whiskey.

" Ambition is something like love,—laughs at law and takes fearful risks. The death of Southerland, Simons thought, was a good chance for a subject and a surgical school to advance himself and assist the rest of us. On the day of Southerland's death Dr. Simons visited separately each of the following doctors in the town, and appointed a meeting to be held on Saturday night, October 31, at ten o'clock, in K. L. Blood's drug-store, for the purpose of organizing and resurrecting the dead negro: Drs. J. G. Simons, John Dowling, Hugh Dowling, A. P. Heichhold, and W. J. McKnight. By request, I secured, on Friday, October 30, permission from Dr. Clarke to use for our school the empty house then owned by him, and where John Means now lives. Augustus Bell, an educated gentleman from Philadelphia, who lived and died here, and K. L. Blood, both medically inclined, were taken in as friends. Promptly at ten o'clock, Saturday night, October 31, 1857, all these parties met in council in the drug-store. Simons, the two Dowlings, and ' Little Bell' filled themselves full to the brim with Monongahela whiskey. Blood, Heichhold, and McKnight remained dry and took not a drop. At about eleven o'clock P.M. we all marched up Pickering Street, with a mattock, shovel, and rope. John Dowling and I were quite young men, and were stationed as watchers, or guards. The others were to resurrect. Simons and

'Little Bell' worked like 'bees,' and were as brave as lions as long as the whiskey stimulated them; but when that died out they kicked and balked badly. Mr. Blood then took hold like a hero. He dug, shovelled, broke open the coffin, and 'there, down there in the earth's cold breast,' placed the rope around the subject and assisted in the resurrection of Southerland. Remember this:

> "'It was a calm, still night,
> And the moon's pale light
> Shone soft o'er hill and dale,'

when we, seven ghouls, stood around the empty tomb of Henry Southerland. The grave was then hastily filled, and carefully too. The naked corpse was now placed on a 'bier.' John Dowling and I took one side, K. L. Blood and Simons the other, and under the autumn's full moon we left the graveyard; down Barnett Street, across Coal Alley, across Jefferson Street, down to Cherry Alley, at the rear of Judge Clark's property now, and up Cherry Alley to the rear of the lot now owned by John Means, and down that lot to the kitchen part of the house, into which the body was carried and placed in a little bedroom west and south of the kitchen. This was done between the hours of one and two A.M., unobserved. Tired and weary, we all went home to rest, and expected to open the school on Monday night, the 2d, but for reasons I will give you farther on this was not done.

"On the evening of the 2d of November, 1857, my mother called me to one side and said, ' You have gotten yourself into trouble. You have been out nights. Don't say a word to me, just listen. You have been helping the other doctors to dig up Henry Southerland. Dr. Heichhold told Captain Wise all about it, Wise told his wife, she told Mrs. Samuel C. Arthurs, she told Mrs. Richard Arthurs, and Mrs. Richard Arthurs told me this afternoon. Now take care of yourself. As you are poor, you will have to suffer; the others are all rich and influential.'

"This was a nitroglycerin explosion to me. I made no reply to my dear mother, but left for Blood's drug-store, and repeated to him what mother had told me. His left hand went up as if struck by a Niagara electric current. I said to him, ' I want Dr. Clarke protected now; Southerland must be removed from his house.' Blood agreed with me. A caucus was then called for that night at the store, when it was decided to remove the body from the house down through the cellar and secrete it under those present front steps of John Means's house, and there it lay naked from Monday night until Wednesday night, when the cadaver was removed from there to Blood's ice-house, in a large coffee-sack, about nine P.M., as follows: McElhose had his printing-office in a little building east and on the same lot. It was on that vacant piece next to where Corbet's house is now. It was built for and used as a drug-store. There was a door upon the west side that opened into the under part of the porch and the front steps. If McElhose or any of his imps had ever opened that door, ' a dreadful sight would have met their startled view.' I was a printer and had learned the art in part with McElhose, and I was detailed to go into his office and make all kinds of noises and detract the attention of the printers from any sounds under the porch. This I did by dancing, kicking over furniture, etc. I could hear the other parties at times; but McElhose thought I was drunk, or such a fool that he only watched and heard me. Everything worked favorably, and ' Black Hen' was successfully removed to a house whose inside walls were frigid and white. ' In the icy air of night' the school for dissection was opened on Wednesday and closed on Saturday morning. As our secret was known to so many, and realizing that we could not dissect in Brookville without being caught up, we only skinned the cadaver to prevent identification and for our personal safety.

"At this time Brookville was full of burglars, thieves, and house-breakers. On Friday night, the 6th, A. B. McLain was patrolling for robbers in Coal Alley, and under the ' ebon vault of heaven, studded with stars un-utterably bright,' he espied what he thought to be three suspicious persons, and pounced down on them like a hawk on a chicken. The suspects proved to be Drs. Hugh Dowling, Heichhold, and ' Little Bell' (Augustus Bell). Mc-Lain was then taken a prisoner by the suspects, dumped into the ice-house, and for the first time in his life saw ' a man skinned.' The job was completed that night, and the cuticle, toes, fingers, and bowels were buried under a large rock in the ' Dark Hollow,' on Saturday forenoon, by Drs. Heichhold and John Dowling.

" For dissection the cadaver is divided into five parts: the head is given to one party, the right arm and side to another, the left arm and side to a third person, the right leg to a fourth, and the left leg to a fifth. In this way Dr. Simons and the four doctors skinned Henry Southerland. For us to dissect Southerland would have required about fifteen to twenty days.

" As dissection is a slow and intricate work, and to avoid discovery and arrest, efforts were made to remove as early as possible the subject from town. Dr. David Ralston, then practising medicine in Reynoldsville, was seen, and he agreed to come after the cadaver and take it home on Saturday night, the 7th. Dr. W. H. Reynolds, who resides now (1898) at Prescott-ville, this county, was then a young man, living on a farm near Rathmel, and Dr. Ralston secured his co-operation. On Saturday these two gentlemen came to Brookville with two mules in a wagon, and stopped at the American Hotel, J. J. Y. Thompson, proprietor. At a conference of all parties, it was arranged that Ralston and Reynolds should drive to the ice-house from the west end of Coal Alley about eleven o'clock P.M. They had a large store-box in the wagon to carry the corpse. The night was black dark. At ten P.M. J. Y. said, ' I'll be danged to Harry, what are so many doctors loafing here to-night for?' A little later, when Ralston ordered out the mules and wagon, Thomp-son was perfectly astonished, and exclaimed ' I'll be dod danged to Harry and dangnation, if you men will leave my house at this late hour and this kind of a night for Reynoldsville.' But his objections were futile. We ghouls were detailed as follows: Blood and Bell as watchers, Heichhold and Hugh Dowling to open the ice-house door, and John Dowling and myself to hand the 'cadaver' out of the house to the men in the wagon. Explicit directions were given to avoid meeting there and forming a crowd.

"Dr. John Dowling and I were there at our appointed time, but the door was unopened, and so we left as instructed. Dr. Heichhold in some way lost the key at or near the ice-house, and had to go and find a hatchet to open the door. This he did, and the wagon came along, and, finding no one there, stopped a moment and left without the subject. On the North Fork bridge they pushed their box into the creek. I always felt that Dowling and myself were somewhat to blame; but we were young and had received orders not to loiter around, and if the door was not opened to leave.

"About eight or nine o'clock on Sunday morning I went up to Dowling's and told John we had better go up and 'view the land.' When we arrived on the tragic scene we found the door open and broken. We peeped in, and while doing so we observed a boy—William C. Smith—on Pickering Street watching us. We walked briskly away up Coal Alley; but our actions and the 'broken door' excited Will's curiosity, and, hurrying over to the ice-house, he looked in, only to be horrified, and with arms extended toward heaven, pale as death, he ran home, exclaiming excitedly to those he met, that a man had been 'skinned alive' in Blood's ice-house. He had seen the man, and also saw Dr. John Dowling and Tom Espy looking at the man in the ice-house. William C. Smith has told his version of the discovery to me many times, and always put 'Tom Espy' in my place. He never knew otherwise until he read this article.

"In the evening of Sunday, the 8th, loud mutterings against the doctors were heard, and we all hid. I hid in the loft above our old kitchen. At midnight, 'in the starlight,' I left for McCurdy's, in the Beechwoods. Monday morning, Blood had business in Pittsburg. David Barclay, a very able man and lawyer, was then our member of Congress, and he took charge of the prosecution. He and Blood had a political feud, and Barclay thought now was his time to annihilate Blood. Hearing of Barclay's activity, my brother, the late Colonel A. A. McKnight, then a young lawyer, made information against me before Esquire Smith, under the act of 1849, to protect graveyards. I returned on Tuesday night, and was arrested, taken before Smith, pleaded guilty, and was fined twenty-five dollars and costs, which I paid in full to the county commissioners, and I was the only one who had to pay a penalty. Under the above act the penalty was fine or imprisonment, or both. My conviction before Smith was to give me the benefit in court of that clause in the constitution which says, 'No person for the same offence shall be twice put in jeopardy of life or limb.' Barclay was a Republican, Blood was a Democrat. I was a Republican, without money or friends, therefore Barclay commenced his prosecution against Blood and me, leaving the others all out for witnesses. The criminal records of Justices Smith and Brady for some reason have been destroyed, therefore I cannot give them. Barclay kept up his prosecution until 1859, as the following legal records of the court show.

(Copy.)
" 'No. 14 Feby. 1859. Q. S.
" ' Commonwealth vs. Kennedy L. Blood and William J. McKnight.
" ' Indictment for removing a dead body from burial-ground. Prosecutrix, Tracy Sweeney.
" ' Witnesses, Charles Anderson, F. C. Coryell, L. A. Dodd, John Mc-Given, A. P. Heichhold, Richard Arthurs, John Dowling, John Carroll, William Smith, Thomas Espy, Myron Pearsall, Hugh Dowling, Aug. Beyle, William Reynolds, Henry Fullerton, Matthew Dowling, William Russell, Sinthy Southerland, Zibion Wilber, James Dowling, A. M. Clarke, George Andrews, A. B. McLain, William Lansendoffer, I. D. N. Ralston, Charles McLain, James McCracken, Charles Matson. In the Court of Quarter Sessions for the County of Jefferson, February Session, 1859.

" ' The grand inquest of the Commonwealth of Pennsylvania, inquiring for the body of the county, upon their oaths and affirmations respectfully do present, that Kennedy L. Blood and William J. McKnight, late of the County of Jefferson, on the fifth day of November, in the year of our Lord one thousand eight hundred and fifty-seven, with force and arms, at the County of Jefferson, the burial-ground of and in the borough of Brookville there situate, unlawfully did enter and the grave there in which the body of one Henry Southerland deceased had lately before then been interred; and these two, with force and arms, unlawfully, wantonly, wilfully, and indecently, did dig open, and afterwards,—to wit, on the same day and year aforesaid,—with force and arms, at the county aforesaid, the body of him, the said Henry Southerland, out of the grave aforesaid, unlawfully and indecently, did take and carry away, against the peace and dignity of the Commonwealth of Pennsylvania.

" ' And the grand inquest aforesaid, upon their oaths and affirmation, do further present, that Kennedy L. Blood and William J. McKnight, late of the County of Jefferson, on the fifth day of November, in the year of our Lord one thousand eight hundred and fifty-seven, with force and arms, at the County of Jefferson, the burial-ground of and in the borough of Brookville there situate, unlawfully and clandestinely, did enter, and the grave there in which the body of one Henry Southerland, deceased, had lately before then been interred; and these two, with force and arms clandestinely, did dig open, and afterwards,—to wit, on the same day and year aforesaid, with force and arms, at the county aforesaid, the body of him, the said Henry Southerland, out of the grave aforesaid, clandestinely and indecently, did take, remove, and carry away, against the peace and dignity of the Commonwealth of Pennsylvania, and contrary to the form of the statute in such case made and provided.

"'A. L. GORDON,
"'District Attorney.

"'Commonwealth vs. K. L. Blood and William J. McKnight.

"'In the Court of Quarter Sessions of Jefferson County.

"'No. 14 Feby. Session, 1859. Q. S. D. No. 2, page 87.

"'Indictment for removing a dead body. Not a true bill. County to pay costs.

"'WILLIAM M. JOHNSON,
"'Foreman.

"'Received of A. L. Gordon, my costs, Hugh Dowling, Charles Anderson, John E. Carroll, A. P. Heichhold, W. C. Smith, M. A. Dowling, A. B. McLain, H. R. Fullerton, M. M. Pearsall. Justice Brady, $4.52; attorney, $3.'

"This indictment was under the act of 1855, 'To protect burial-grounds,' the penalty of which was: 'If any person shall open a tomb or grave in any cemetery, graveyard, or any grounds set apart for burial purposes, either private or public, held by individuals for their own use, or in trust for others, or for any church, or institution, whether incorporated or not, without the consent of the owners or trustees of such grounds, and clandestinely or unlawfully remove, or attempt to remove, any human body, or part thereof, therefrom, such person, upon conviction thereof, shall be sentenced to undergo an imprisonment in the county jail or penitentiary for a term of not less than one year, nor more than three years, and pay a fine of not less than one hundred dollars, at the discretion of the proper court.'

"The witnesses before the grand jury were of two kinds,—those who knew and those who didn't know. Those who knew refused to testify, on the ground of incriminating themselves, and Judge McCalmont sustained them.

"The attorneys for the Commonwealth were A. L. Gordon, district attorney, and Hon. David Barclay. Our attorneys were Amor A. McKnight, Benjamin F. Lucas, and William P. Jenks.

"K. L. Blood and Dr. Heichhold, until the day of their death, were opposite political party leaders, and whenever either one addressed a political assembly some wag or opponent in ambush would always interrogate the speaker with 'Who skinned the nigger?'

"Before concluding this article it might be well to say that the 'ice-house' was never used for any purpose after November 8, 1857.

"About the 1st of December, 1882, when I was a State Senator, I was invited to dine with Professor W. H. Pancoast, of Philadelphia. The city, State, and nation was agitated over the robbing of 'Lebanon Cemetery,' in that city. It was thought that these subjects were for dissection in Jefferson Medical College. Dr. Pancoast was then professor of anatomy in that school. While at dinner the question was raised as to what effect this scandal would have upon the college. During this talk I broached the idea that now would be an opportune time to secure legal dissection for Pennsylvania. The wisdom of my suggestion was doubted and controverted. I defended my position in this wise: The people of the city and State are excited, alarmed, and angered, and I would frame the 'act to prevent the traffic in human bodies and to prevent the desecration of graveyards.' This would appeal to the good sense of the people, as an effort, at least, in the right direction. Dr. Pancoast soon coincided with me, and from that moment took an active interest in the matter. He met with opposition at first from those who ought to have supported him; but I assured the doctor if he would get the Philadelphia Anatomical Association of the city to draft a suitable law and send it to Senator Reyburn, of that city, I would support it from the country, and that we would rush it through the Senate. Dr. Pancoast deserves great praise for his energy in overcoming the timidity and fears of the college deans and others in the city, and in finally inducing the 'Association' to frame the present new and State act and send it to Senator Reyburn. The framing of the act was brought about in this wise,—viz.:

EXTRACTS FROM THE MINUTES OF THE ASSOCIATION

"'PHILADELPHIA, December 28, 1882.

"'The undersigned request the Distribution Committee of the Anatomist's Association to call a meeting of the Association at an early date to consider the propriety of attempting to modify the existing Anatomy Act, or to have a new act passed which will increase the legal supply of material.

"'JOHN B. ROBERTS.
JNO. B. DEAVER.
W. W. KEEN.'

"A special meeting of this Association was called for January 4, 1883, at 1118 Arch Street. There were present at this meeting Drs. Garretson, Hunter, Du Bois, Perkins, Mears, and Keen. A committee was appointed to draft a new Anatomy Act, consisting of the following: Drs. Mears, Hunter, and Keen. On Tuesday, January 9, 1883, this committee read the draft of their act, which was read and finally adopted.

"JOHN B. ROBERTS,
"Secretary.

" MEETING OF WEDNESDAY, JANUARY 24, 1883

" The meeting was called to order by the President, and the minutes of the previous meeting were read and approved.

" Present: Drs. Leidy, Forbes, A. R. Thomas, Pancoast, Brinton, Oliver, Stubbs, Janney, Hunter, Mears, Roberts, and Keen.

" The new Anatomy Act, which had been printed and distributed as ordered at last meeting, was discussed, and a number of amendments suggested by the committee of revision were adopted. The last sentence of Section VI. (old Section V.) was discussed, and, on motion, its adoption was postponed until the next meeting. It was resolved to meet again on Saturday, January 27, at same place and hour, because some of the colleges had not had time to consider the act in faculty meeting.

" It was resolved that the colleges and schools be requested to subscribe to a fund to meet the necessary expenses of preparing and presenting the Act to the Legislature; the sums apportioned to each were, University, Jefferson, and Hahnemann, each twenty-five dollars; Woman's, Pennsylvania Dental, Philadelphia Dental, Medico-Chirurgical, each ten dollars; Academy of Fine Arts, Pennsylvania School of Anatomy, Philadelphia School of Anatomy, each five dollars.

" Adjourned.   " JOHN B. ROBERTS,
                                                              " Secretary.

" MEETING OF SATURDAY, JANUARY 27, 1883

" The meeting was called to order by the President. On motion of Professor Pancoast, William Janney was appointed secretary *pro tempore*. The minutes of the meeting held January 24 were read and approved.

" Present: Drs. Leidy, A. R. Thomas, Pancoast, Brinton, Oliver, Stubbs, Hunter, Mears, Keen, Agnew, and Janney.

" Dr. Brinton moved to postpone action on the Act until the Faculty of Jefferson College had examined it. Motion debated by Drs. Brinton, Mears, Oliver, Stubbs, and Agnew. Motion withdrawn.

" Motion by Dr. Agnew, seconded by Dr. Mears, that this bill be referred back to the Committee, with direction to employ counsel. Adopted.

" Adjourned to meet at the call of the Committee.
                                              " WILLIAM S. JANNEY,
                                                              " Secretary.

" MEETING OF TUESDAY, FEBRUARY 6, 1883

" Called to order by the President.

" Present: Drs. Leidy, Mears, Hunter, Oliver, Brinton, A. R. Thomas, Stubbs, and Roberts.

" As the minutes of the previous meeting had not been sent by the temporary secretary, their reading was dispensed with. Dr. Mears reported that

301

a new form of bill had been prepared by the Committee under the legal advice of Mr. Gendel and Mr. Sheppard. This was accepted *in toto*. Moved that twenty copies of a petition prepared by Dr. Keen, to accompany the Act, be printed and signed by the members of the various faculties and schools. Carried.

"Adjourned to meet Friday at five P.M. at same place.

"JOHN B. ROBERTS,

"*Secretary.*

"At a meeting of the Association, February 9, 1883, it was resolved that a committee be appointed to present the bill (as then perfected) to the Legislature, to consist of one representative from each school,—viz., Agnew, Brinton, Thomas, Parish, Oliver, Mears, Garretson, Keen, Janney, and Roberts. By resolution of that committee, Dr. Leidy was made Chairman *ex officio*.

"Furman Sheppard, Esq., put the act in legal form and charged a fee of fifty dollars.

"This State law in Pennsylvania legalizing dissection was passed finally on June 4, 1883. Its passage met serious and able opposition in both Houses. I firmly believe that had I not been connected with and prosecuted in this pioneer resurrection case in Brookville, I would not have been impelled to propose such a law or to champion it in the Senate. As introduced by Senator Reyburn, the title was, ' Senate bill 117, entitled An Act for the promotion of medical science, by the distribution and use of unclaimed human bodies for scientific purposes. through a board created for that purpose, and to prevent unauthorized uses and traffic in human bodies.' This State law was incepted and originated in the late residence of Professor W. H. Pancoast, Eleventh and Walnut Streets."

The petition of Dr. Keen was addressed to senators and members, as follows :

"*To the Senate and House of Representatives of the Commonwealth of Pennsylvania.*

"The petition of the undersigned respectfully shows that they present herewith the draft of ' An Act for the Promotion of Medical Science by the Distribution and use of Unclaimed Human Bodies for Scientific Purposes, through a Board created for that Purpose, and to prevent Unauthorized Uses and Traffic in Human Bodies,' which they pray your honorable bodies to enact into a law for the following reasons :

"It will increase the necessary facilities for medical education within this State, and will materially aid in preventing desecration of burial-grounds. Your petitioners do not deem it necessary to argue the point that the repeated

302

dissection of the human body is necessary before any student of medicine should be allowed to take charge of the health and lives of the community. No woman in childbirth, no person the victim of accident, no sufferer from disease, is safe in the hands of men ignorant of the structure of the human body.

"The only proper method to supply this knowledge is to furnish by law the bodies of those who have no friends or relatives whose feelings could be wounded by their dissection. This was done by the Anatomy Act of 1867. But this Act is defective in that its application is limited to the counties of Philadelphia and Allegheny, and an adequate supply of unclaimed dead human bodies is not furnished, and it does not provide specifically the machinery for an equitable distribution of the dead bodies so given for dissection.

"In the Session of 1881-82 there were in the Dissecting and Operative Surgery Classes of the Philadelphia Medical and Dental Colleges 1493 students. Each student pursues his studies in anatomy during two years. If he be allowed to dissect one-half of one body a year—including also the practice of operations upon the same—this would require 746 dead bodies. The professors would need for their lectures about fifty more, making in all 796 'subjects.' But during that same session the number actually available for use from all sources was only 405. This is only one-half of the smallest number reasonable, to say nothing of the desirableness of a larger number to afford all the facilities a great Commonwealth should give its citizens, who can obtain their needful knowledge in no other way that is lawful.

"That it is 'needful' one will readily see when it is remembered that the want of such knowledge renders doctors liable to suits for malpractice, which suits are upon the calendar of well-nigh every court of the State. The scanty supply is due to the fact that the unclaimed dead of *one county* are the only ones that are given for dissection, although the students come from all parts of this State in large numbers, as well as from other parts of this and other countries. (The present law, it is true, applies to Allegheny County, but this is practically of no use to the Philadelphia Colleges.)

"During the ten years, 1873-1883, at the Jefferson Medical College and the University of Pennsylvania alone, out of a total number of over ten thousand students, there were 2686 from Pennsylvania; of this number, 1172 were from Philadelphia and 1514 from other parts of the State. In view of these important facts it would seem but just that the unclaimed and uncared-for dead who must be a burden upon the taxpayers of the several counties of the State for burial, should be given to the medical schools to supply this urgent need for dissecting material by students from every county in the State.

"And your petitioners will ever pray, etc."

This petition was signed by the following physicians:

UNIVERSITY OF PENNSYLVANIA

William Pepper, M.D., Joseph Leidy, M.D., James Tyson, M.D., Theodore G. Wormley, M.D., D. Hayes Agnew, M.D., William Goodell, M.D., John Ashhurst, Jr., M.D., H. C. Wood, M.D., R. A. F. Penrose, M.D., Alfred Stillé, M.D., Harrison Allen, M.D., Charles T. Hunter, M.D.

JEFFERSON MEDICAL COLLEGE

S. D. Gross, M.D., Ellerslie Wallace, M.D., J. M. DaCosta, M.D.. Wm. H. Pancoast, M.D., Robert E. Rogers, M.D., Roberts Bartholow, M.D., Henry C. Chapman, M.D., J. H. Brinton, M.D., S. W. Gross, M.D.

PENNSYLVANIA ACADEMY OF FINE ARTS

W. W. Keen, M.D.

MEDICO-CHIRURGICAL COLLEGE OF PHILADELPHIA

George P. Oliver, M.D., George E. Stubbs, M.D., Charles L. Mitchell, M.D., Abraham S. Gerhard, M.D., Wm. S. Stewart, M.D., Frank O. Nagle, M.D., Wm. F. Waugh, M.D.

HAHNEMANN MEDICAL COLLEGE

A. R. Thomas, M.D., Lemuel Stephens, M.D., O. B. Gause, M.D., E. A. Farrington, M.D., B. F. Betts, M.D., Pemberton Dudley, M.D., W. C. Goodno, M.D., Charles M. Thomas, M.D., John E. James, M.D., Charles Mohr, M.D., R. B. Weaver, M.D., J. N. Mitchell, M.D.. W. H. Keim, M.D.

PHILADELPHIA SCHOOL OF ANATOMY

John B. Roberts, M.D.

WOMAN'S MEDICAL COLLEGE OF PENNSYLVANIA

James B. Walker, M.D., Rachel L. Bodley, M.D., Benj. B. Wilson, M.D., William H. Parrish, M.D., Anna E. Broomall, M.D., Clara Marshall, M.D., Emilie B. Du Bois, M.D.

PENNSYLVANIA COLLEGE OF DENTAL SURGERY

T. L. Buckingham, D.D.S., J. Ewing Mears, M.D., C. N. Peirce, D.D.S., Henry C. Chapman, M.D., W. F. Litch, D.D.S.

R. J. Levis, M.D., Thos. G. Morton, M.D., J. Solis Cohen, M.D., George C. Harlan, M.D., Henry Leffman, M.D., Edward O. Shakespeare, M.D., James Cornelius Wilson, M.D., John B. Roberts, M.D., Charles H. Burnett, M.D., Arthur Van Harlingen, M.D., Charles K. Mills, M.D., Edward L. Duer, M.D., J. Henry C. Simes, M.D.

PHILADELPHIA COUNTY MEDICAL SOCIETY

" This petition was presented to the Philadelphia County Medical Society and unanimously ordered to be signed by the officers."

Resolutions endorsing the new law and petition were passed by the County Medical Societies throughout the State.

" The act as passed and approved reads as follows,—viz.:

" ' NO. 106. AN ACT FOR THE PROMOTION OF MEDICAL SCIENCE BY THE DIS-TRIBUTION AND USE OF UNCLAIMED HUMAN BODIES FOR SCIENTIFIC PURPOSES THROUGH A BOARD CREATED FOR THAT PURPOSE, AND TO PRE-VENT UNAUTHORIZED USES AND TRAFFIC IN HUMAN BODIES

" ' SECTION 1. *Be it enacted, etc.,* That the professors of anatomy, the professors of surgery, the demonstrators of anatomy, and the demonstrators of surgery of the medical and dental schools and colleges of this Common-wealth, which are now or may hereafter become incorporated, together with one representative from each of the unincorporated schools of anatomy or practical surgery, within this Commonwealth, in which there are from time to time, at the time of the appointment of such representatives, not less than five scholars, shall be and hereby are constituted a board for the distribu-tion and delivery of dead human bodies, hereinafter described, to and among such persons as, under the provisions of this act, are entitled thereto. The professor of anatomy in the University of Pennsylvania, at Philadelphia, shall call a meeting of said board for organization at a time and place to be fixed by him within thirty days after the passage of this act. The said board shall have full power to establish rules and regulations for its government, and to appoint and remove proper officers, and shall keep full and complete minutes of its transactions ; and records shall also be kept under its direction of all bodies received and distributed by said board, and of the persons to whom the same may be distributed, which minutes and records shall be open at all times to the inspection of each member of said board, and of any district attorney of any county within this Commonwealth.

" ' SECTION 2. All public officers, agents, and servants, and all officers, agents, and servants of any and every county, city, township, borough, dis-trict, and other municipality, and of any and every almshouse, prison, morgue, hospital, or other public institution having charge or control over dead human bodies, required to be buried at the public expense, are hereby required to notify the said board of distribution, or such person or persons as may, from time to time, be designated by said board as its duly authorized officer or agent, whenever any such body or bodies come into his or their possession, charge, or control; and shall, without fee or reward, deliver such body or bodies, and permit and suffer the said board and its agents, and the physicians and surgeons from time to time designated by them, who may comply with the provisions of this act, to take and remove all such bodies to be used within this State for the advancement of medical science; but no such notice need be given nor shall any such body be delivered if any person claiming to be and satisfying the authorities in charge of said body that he or she is of kindred or is related by marriage to the deceased, shall claim the said body for burial, but it shall be surrendered for interment, nor shall the notice be given or body delivered if such deceased person was a traveller who died suddenly, in which case the said body shall be buried.

" ' SECTION 3. The said board or their duly authorized agent may take and receive such bodies so delivered as aforesaid, and shall, upon receiving them, distribute and deliver them to and among the schools, colleges, physicians, and surgeons aforesaid, in manner following: Those bodies needed for lectures and demonstrations by the said schools and colleges incorporated and unincorporated shall first be supplied; the remaining bodies shall then be distributed proportionately and equitably, preference being given to said schools and colleges, the number assigned to each to be based upon the number of students in each dissecting or operative surgery class, which number shall be reported to the board at such times as it may direct. Instead of receiving and delivering said bodies themselves, or through their agents or servants, the board of distribution may, from time to time, either directly or by their authorized officer or agent, designate physicians and surgeons who shall receive them, and the number which each shall receive: *Provided always, however,* That schools and colleges incorporated and unincorporated, and physicians or surgeons of the county where the death of the person or persons described takes place, shall be preferred to all others: *And provided also,* That for this purpose such dead body shall be held subject to their order in the county where the death occurs for a period not less than twenty-four hours.

" ' SECTION 4. The said board may employ a carrier or carriers for the conveyance of said bodies, which shall be well enclosed within a suitable encasement, and carefully deposited free from public observation. Said carrier shall obtain receipts by name, or if the person be unknown by a description of each body delivered by him, and shall deposit said receipt with the secretary of the said board.

" ' SECTION 5. No school, college, physician, or surgeon shall be allowed or permitted to receive any such body or bodies until a bond shall have been given to the Commonwealth by such physician or surgeon, or by or in behalf of such school or college, to be approved by the prothonotary of the court of common pleas in and for the county in which such physician or surgeon shall reside, or in which such school or college may be situate, and to be filed in the office of said prothonotary, which bond shall be in the penal sum of one thousand dollars, conditioned that all such bodies which the said physician or surgeon, or the said school or college shall receive thereafter shall be used only for the promotion of medical science within this State; and whosoever shall sell or buy such body or bodies, or in any way traffic in the same, or shall transmit or convey or cause or procure to be transmitted or conveyed said body or bodies, to any place outside of this State, shall be deemed guilty of a misdemeanor, and shall, on conviction, be liable to a fine not exceeding two hundred dollars, or be imprisoned for a term not exceeding one year.

"' Section 6. Neither the Commonwealth nor any county or municipality, nor any officer, agent, or servant thereof, shall be at any expense by reason of the delivery or distribution of any such body; but all the expenses thereof and of said board of distribution shall be paid by those receiving the bodies, in such manner as may be specified by said board of distribution, or otherwise agreed upon.

"' Section 7. That any person having duties enjoined upon him by the provisions of this act who shall neglect, refuse, or omit to perform the same as hereby required, shall, on conviction thereof, be liable to fine of not less than one hundred nor more than five hundred dollars for each offence.

"' Section 8. That all acts or parts of acts inconsistent with this act be and the same are hereby repealed.

"' Approved—the 13th day of June, A.D. 1883.

"' Robert E. Pattison.'

" In debate in the Senate, the above law was ably opposed by Senators Laird, Lee, and Stewart, and its passage was advocated by Senators Reyburn, Grady, Patton, and McKnight.

" In closing this narrative I quote a paragraph from my remarks in the Senate in support of the passage of the law and in reply to the speeches of other senators:

"' Where would the humanity exist then, especially that kind of which so much is said in regard to the dead? Humanity, I think, should first be shown to the living, and the Great Physician, whom senators quote on this floor as having had a regard for humanity, said, " Let the dead bury the dead." He took the same practical view that humanity should be practised for the living. We take a harsh view as medical men in regard to the dissection of dead bodies. We consider subjects just as clay. I know this is repugnant to the common idea of mankind, but it is the true idea. It is the idea that will enable a medical man to be of sound, practical good, professionally, in the world. For the crushed, relief in life is the great object, not relief after death. We have nothing to do with that. Beautiful poetry and nice homilies can be delivered here by senators about death, but it is the living that we want to be humane to and not the dead, and if it requires the dissection of ninety-nine dead persons to relieve one living sufferer, I would dissect the ninety-nine dead persons and relieve the one living person. Other senators here would have us do just the reverse of that. I repeat, Mr. President, this measure is in the interest of the laboring man; it is in the interest of the mechanic; it is in the interest of science; it is in the interest of the poor the world over; it is in the interest of the man who gets torn and lacerated in our mines and workshops, and who is too poor to travel to Philadelphia for his surgical aid. Enact this law, and the young man can go from Allegheny, from Jefferson, and from Armstrong Counties to Philadelphia, and he can legally take the human body, which is the A B C of all medical knowledge, and he can dissect it there, and learn by that means just where each artery is, and where each vein is, and where the different muscles lie and the different relations they sustain to one another, and then he is qualified to return to Allegheny or Jefferson County, locate at the cross-roads or in the village, and perform the operations that are so much needed there for the relief of suffering humanity and the suffering poor.

" ' You all know that the surgeons of Philadelphia are famous, not only in Philadelphia, but throughout the world, and why? It is because they have studied the anatomy of the human body so thoroughly and so perfectly.

" ' We must have anatomical dissections. No man learns anatomy in any other way in the world than through anatomical dissections. Pictures, models, and manikins won't do. He must not only dissect one body, but he must dissect a large number of bodies. He cannot dissect too many, neither can he dissect too often; therefore humanity requires that this dissection be legalized and go on.

" ' Of course, we must have some regard for the sentiment of the living, and to respect that, we, in this bill, only ask that the unclaimed bodies of paupers be given to the medical colleges, not the bodies of those having friends. No body can be taken if any one objects.' "

For the law the yeas were, in the Senate: Adams, Arnholt, Biddis, Cooper, Coxe, Davies, Grady, Hall, Hess, Humes, Keefer, Lantz, Longenecker, McCracken, MacFarlane, McKnight, Patton, Reyburn, Shearer, Sill, Smith, Sutton, Vandegrift, Upperman, Wagner, Wallace, Watres, and Wolverton—28.

Nays: Agnew, Herr, Laird, Lee, Ross, Stehman, and Stewart—7.

We have now, in 1904, legalized dissection of the human body in nearly every State of the Union, and, as a result, the skill of the physician in the future " shall lift up his head, and in the sight of great men he shall stand in admiration."

POPULATION OF THE STATE OF PENNSYLVANIA AND OF THE UNITED STATES
FROM 1790 TO 1850 INCLUSIVE

Year	Whites	Free Colored	Negro Slaves	Total in Pennsylvania	Population in the United States
1790	424,099	6,537	3,737	434,373	3,929,827
1800	586,098	14,561	1,706	602,365	5,305,941
1810	786,704	22,492	795	810,091	7,239,814
1820	1,017,094	32,153	211	1,049,458	9,638,191
1830	1,309,900	37,930	403	1,348,233	12,866,020
1840	1,676,115	47,854	64	1,724,033	17,069,453
1850	2,258,160	53,626	..	2,311,786	23,191,876

RATIO OF REPRESENTATION IN THE UNITED STATES HOUSE OF REPRESENTATIVES

From 1789 to 1793 as provided by the United States Constitution 30,000
"   1793 " 1803 based on the United States Census of 1790 33,000
"   1803 " 1813   "   "   "   "   1800 33,000
"   1813 " 1823   "   "   "   "   1810 35,000
"   1823 " 1833   "   "   "   "   1820 40,000
"   1833 " 1843   "   "   "   "   1830 47,700
"   1843 " 1853   "   "   "   "   1840 70,680
"   1853 " 1863   "   "   "   "   1850 93,420
"   1863 " 1873   "   "   "   "   1860 127,381

" From the first Congress, in 1789, inclusive, until March 4, 1795, Senators and Representatives received each six dollars per diem, and six dollars for every twenty miles' travel. From March 4, 1795, to March 4, 1796, Senators received seven dollars, and Representatives six dollars per diem. From March 4, 1796, until December 4, 1815, the per diem was six dollars, and the mileage six dollars, to Senators and Representatives. From December 4, 1815, until March 4, 1817, each Senator and Representative received one thousand five hundred dollars per annum, with a proportional deduction for absence, from any cause but sickness. The President of the Senate *pro tempore,* and Speaker of the House, three thousand dollars per annum, each. From March 4, 1817, the compensation to members of both Houses has been eight dollars per diem, and eight dollars for every twenty miles' travel; and to the President of the Senate *pro tempore,* and Speaker of the House, sixteen dollars per diem, until 1860."

CHAPTER XVI

WHITE slavery is older than history. Its origin is supposed to have been from kidnapping, piracy, and in captives taken in war. Christians enslaved all barbarians and barbarians enslaved Christians. Early history tells us that Rome and Greece were great markets for all kinds of slaves, slave-traders, slave-owners, etc. The white slaves of Europe were mostly obtained in Russia and Poland in times of peace. All fathers could sell children. The poor could be sold for debt. The poor could sell themselves. But slavery did not exist in the poor and ignorant alone. The most learned in science, art, and mechanism were bought and sold at prices ranging in our money from one hundred to three hundred dollars. Once sold, whether kidnapped or not, there was no redress, except as to the will of the master. At one time in the history of Rome white slaves sold for sixty-two and a half cents apiece in our money. These were captives taken in battle. By law the minimum price was eighty dollars. A good actress would sell for four thousand and a good physician for eleven thousand dollars. The state, the church, and individuals all owned slaves. Every wicked device that might and power could practise was used to enslave men and women without regard to nationality or color. And when enslaved, no matter how well educated, the slaves possessed no right in law and were not deemed persons in law, and had no right in and to their children. Slavery as it existed among the Jews was a milder form than that which existed in any other nation. The ancients regarded black slaves as luxuries, because there was but little traffic in them until about the year 1441, and it was at that date that the modern African slave-trade was commenced by the Portuguese. The pioneer English African slave-trader was Sir John Hawkins. Great companies were formed in London to carry on African traffic, of which Charles II. and James II. were members. It was money and the large profits in slavery, whether white or black, that gave it such a hold on church and state. The English were the most cruel African slave-traders. Genuine white slavery never survived in what is now the United States. In the year A.D. 1620 the pioneer African slaves were landed at Hampton Roads in Virginia, and nineteen slaves were sold. In

310

1790 there were six hundred and ninety-seven thousand six hundred and eighty-one African slaves in the Middle States.

Slavery was introduced in Pennsylvania in 1681, and was in full force until the act quoted below for its gradual abolition was enacted in 1780, by which, as will be seen, adult slaves were liberated on July 4, 1827, and the children born before that date were to become free as they reached their majority. This made the last slave in the State become a free person about 1860.

In 1790 Pennsylvania had slaves			....	3737
In 1800	"	"	"	....	1706
In 1810	"	"	"	....	795
In 1820	"	"	"	....	211
In 1830	"	"	"	....	403
In 1840	"	"	"	....	64

On December 4, 1833, sixty persons met in Philadelphia, Pennsylvania, and organized the American Anti-Slavery Society.

NEGRO SLAVERY

" He found his fellow guilty—of a skin not colored like his own; for such a cause dooms him as his lawful prey."

Negro slaves were held in each of the thirteen original States.

NUMBER OF SLAVES IN THE ORIGINAL THIRTEEN STATES IN 1776

Massachusetts	3,500	Maryland	80,000
Rhode Island	4,337	Virginia	165,000
Connecticut	6,000	North Carolina	75,000
New Hampshire	629	South Carolina	110,000
New York.	10,000	Georgia	16,000
Pennsylvania	10,000		
New Jersey	7,600	Total	497,066
Delaware	9,000		

In March, 1780, Pennsylvania enacted her gradual abolition law. Massachusetts, by constitutional enactment in 1780, abolished slavery. Rhode Island and Connecticut were made free States in 1784, New Jersey in 1804, New York in 1817, and New Hampshire about 1808 or 1810. The remaining States of the thirteen—viz., Maryland, Delaware, Virginia, North and South Carolina, and Georgia—each retained their human chattels until the close of the Civil War. In one hundred years, from 1676 until 1776, it is estimated that three million people were imported and sold as slaves in the United States.

As late as 1860 there was still one slave in Pennsylvania; his name was Lawson Lee Taylor, and he belonged to James Clark, of Donegal Township, Lancaster County.

SLAVERY AUGUST 1, 1790.	Slaves.	AUGUST 1, 1810.	Slaves.
Free States	40,850	Free States	27,510
Southern States	645,047	Southern States	1,063,854
	685,897		1,091,364

AUGUST 1, 1800.		AUGUST 1, 1820.	
Free States	35,946	Free States	19,108
Southern States	857,095	Southern States	1,524,580
	893,941		1,543,688

JUNE 1, 1830.	Slaves.
Free States	3,568
Southern States	2,005,475
	2,009,043

FREE STATES JUNE 1, 1840.

Maine, no slaves.		Ohio	3
New Hampshire	1	Indiana	3
Vermont, none.		Illinois	331
Massachusetts, none.		Michigan, none.	
Rhode Island	5	Wisconsin	11
Connecticut	17	Iowa	16
New York	4		
New Jersey	674	Total in Free States	1,129
Pennsylvania	64	Total in Southern States	2,486,226

The first man who died in the Revolution was a colored man, and Peter Salem, a negro, decided the battle of Bunker Hill; clinging to the Stars and Stripes, he cried, " I'll bring back the colors or answer to God the reason why !" His example fired the hearts of the soldiers to greater valor, and the great battle was won by our men.

" It was on the soil of Pennsylvania in 1682 that the English penalty of death on over two hundred crimes was negatived by statute law, and the penalty of death retained on only one crime,—viz., wilful murder. It was in the province of Pennsylvania that the law of primogeniture was abolished. It was on the soil of Pennsylvania that the first mint to coin money in the United States was established. It was on the soil of Pennsylvania in 1829, and between Honesdale and Carbondale, that the pioneer railroad train, propelled by a locomotive, was run in the New World. It was on the soil of Pennsylvania that the first Continental Congress met. It was on the soil of Pennsylvania that the great *Magna Charta* of our liberties was written, signed, sealed, and delivered to the world. It was on the soil of Pennsylvania that the fathers declared ' that all men are born free and equal, and are alike entitled to life, liberty, and the pursuit of happiness.' It was on the soil of Pennsylvania that the grand old Republican party was organized, and the declarations of our fathers reaffirmed and proclaimed anew to the world. It was on the soil of Pennsylvania that Congress created our national emblem,

Branding slaves

the Stars and Stripes; and it was upon the soil of Pennsylvania that fair women made that flag in accordance with the resolution of Congress. It was upon the soil of Pennsylvania that our flag was first unfurled to the breeze, and from that day to this that grand old flag has never been disgraced nor defeated. It was upon the Delaware River of Pennsylvania that the first steamer was launched. It was in Philadelphia that the first national bank opened its vaults to commerce. It was upon the soil of Pennsylvania that Colonel Drake first drilled into the bowels of the earth and obtained the oil that now makes the 'bright light' of every fireside 'from Greenland's icy mountains to India's coral strand.' It was on the soil of Pennsylvania that the first Christian Bible Society in the New World was organized. It was on the soil of Pennsylvania that the first school for the education and maintenance of soldiers' orphans was erected. It was on the soil of Pennsylvania that the first medical college for the New World was established.

"And now, Mr. President, I say to you that it was permitted to Pennsylvania intelligence, to Pennsylvania charity, to Pennsylvania people, to erect on Pennsylvania soil, with Pennsylvania money, the first insane institution, aided and encouraged by a State, in the history of the world."

The above is an extract from a speech made by me when Senator in the Senate of Pennsylvania in 1881. I reproduce it here only to reassert it and crown it with the fact that Pennsylvania was the first of the united colonies to acknowledge before God and the nations of the earth, by legal enactment, the Fatherhood of God and the brotherhood of man. Pennsylvania was the first State or nation in the New World to enact a law for the abolition of human slavery. This act of justice was passed, too, when the struggle for independence was still undetermined. The British were pressing us on the east, and the savages on the west were torturing and killing the patriot fathers and mothers of the Revolution.

George Bryan originated, prepared, offered, and carried this measure successfully through the Legislature. I quote from his remarks on this measure: "Honored will that State be in the annals of mankind which shall first abolish this violation of the rights of mankind; and the memories of those will be held in grateful and everlasting remembrance who shall pass the law to restore and establish the rights of human nature in Pennsylvania." George Bryan did this. He was born in Dublin, Ireland, in 1732, died in Philadelphia, Pennsylvania, in 1791. To exhibit the advanced sentiment of George Bryan, I republish his touching and beautiful preamble to his law, and a section or two of the law which will explain its work:

"AN ACT FOR THE GENERAL ABOLITION OF SLAVERY

"When we contemplate our abhorrence of that condition to which the arms and tyranny of Great Britain were exerted to reduce us, when we look back on the variety of dangers to which we have been exposed, and how

miraculously our wants in many instances have been supplied, and our de-
liverances wrought, when even hope and human fortitude have become unequal
to the conflict, we are unavoidably led to a serious and grateful sense of the
manifold blessings which we have undeservedly received from the hand of
that Being from whom every good and perfect gift cometh. Impressed with
these ideas, we conceive that it is our duty, and we rejoice that it is in our
power, to extend a portion of that freedom to others which hath been extended
to us, and release from that state of thraldom to which we ourselves were
tyrannically doomed, and from which we have now every prospect of being
delivered. It is not for us to inquire why, in the creation of mankind, the
inhabitants of the several parts of the earth were distinguished by a difference
in feature or complexion. It is sufficient to know that all are the work of an
Almighty hand. We find, in the distribution of the human species, that the
most fertile as well as the most barren parts of the earth are inhabited by men
of complexions different from ours, and from each other; from whence we
may reasonably, as well as religiously, infer that He who placed them in their
various situations hath extended equally His care and protection to all, and
that it becometh not us to counteract His mercies. We esteem it a peculiar
blessing granted to us that we are enabled this day to add one more step to
universal civilization, by removing, as much as possible, the sorrows of those
who have lived in undeserved bondage, and from which, by the assumed
authority of the kings of Great Britain, no effectual legal relief could be
obtained. Weaned, by a long course of experience, from those narrow prejudices and partialities we had imbibed, we find our hearts enlarged with kindness and benevolence towards men of all conditions and nations; and we conceive ourselves at this particular period extraordinarily called upon, by the
blessings which we have received, to manifest the sincerity of our profession
and to give a substantial proof of our gratitude.

"II. And whereas the condition of those persons, who have heretofore
been denominated Negro and Mulatto slaves, has been attended with circumstances which not only deprived them of the common blessings that they were
by nature entitled to, but has cast them into the deepest afflictions, by an
unnatural separation and sale of husband and wife from each other and from
their children, an injury the greatness of which can only be conceived by
supposing that we were in the same unhappy case. In justice, therefore,
to persons so unhappily circumstanced, and who, having no prospect before
them whereon they may rest their sorrows and their hopes, have no reasonable
inducement to render their service to society, which they otherwise might, and
also in grateful commemoration of our own happy deliverance from that state
of unconditional submission to which we were doomed by the tyranny of
Britain—

"III. *Be it enacted, and it is hereby enacted,* That all persons, as well
Negroes and Mulattoes as others, who shall be born within this State from

and after the passage of this act, shall not be deemed and considered as servants for life, or slaves; and that all servitude for life, or slavery of children, in consequence of the slavery of their mothers, in the case of all children born within this State from and after the passing of this act as aforesaid, shall be, and hereby is, utterly taken away, extinguished, and forever abolished.

" IV. *Provided always, and be it further enacted,* That every Negro and Mulatto child born within this State after the passing of this act as aforesaid (who would, in case this act had not been made, have been born a servant for years, or life, or a slave) shall be deemed to be, and shall be, by virtue of this act, the servant of such person, or his or her assigns, who would in such case have been entitled to the service of such child, until such child shall attain unto the age of twenty-eight years, in the manner and on the conditions whereon servants bound by indenture for four years are or may be retained and holden; and shall be liable to like correction and punishment, and entitled to like relief, in case he or she be evilly treated by his or her master or mistress, and to like freedom, dues, and other privileges, as servants bound by indenture for four years are or may be entitled, unless the person to whom the service of such child shall belong, shall abandon his or her claim to the same; in which case the overseers of the poor of the city, township, or district, respectively, where such child shall be so abandoned, shall by indenture bind out every child so abandoned as an apprentice, for a time not exceeding the age herein before limited for the service of such children."

Passed March 1, 1780.

THE " UNDERGROUND RAILROAD" IN NORTHWESTERN PENNSYLVANIA

" My ear is pained,
My soul is sick with every day's report
Of wrong and outrage with which this earth is filled."

The origin of the system to aid runaway slaves in these United States was in Columbia, Lancaster County, Pennsylvania. In 1787 Samuel Wright laid out that town, and he set apart the northeastern portion for colored people, and to many of whom he presented lots. Under these circumstances this section was settled rapidly by colored people. Hundreds of manumitted slaves from Maryland and Virginia migrated there and built homes. This soon created a little city of colored people, and in due time formed a good hiding-place for escaped slaves. The term " underground railroad" originated there, and in this way: At Columbia the runaway slave would be so thoroughly and completely lost to the pursuer, that the slave-hunter, in perfect astonishment, would frequently exclaim, " There must be an underground railroad somewhere." Of course, there was no railroad. There was only at this place an organized system by white abolitionists to assist, clothe, feed, and conduct fugitive slaves to Canada. This system consisted in changing the clothing, secreting and hiding the fugitive in daytime, and then carrying or directing him how to travel in the night-time to the next abolition station, where he would be cared for. These stations existed from the Maryland line clear through to Canada. In those days the North was as a whole for slavery, and to be an abolitionist was to be reviled and persecuted, even by churches of nearly all denominations. Abolition meetings were broken up by mobs, the speakers rotten-egged and murdered; indeed, but few preachers would read from their pulpit a notice for an anti-slavery meeting. Space will not permit me to depict the degraded state of public morals at that time, or the low ebb of true Christianity in that day, excepting, of course, that exhibited by a small handful of abolitionists in the land. I can only say, that to clothe, feed, secrete, and to convey in the darkness of night, poor, wretched human

Charles Brown handcuffed and shackled in Brookville jail, 1834

" The shackles never again shall bind this arm, which now is free."

" My world is dead,
A new world rises, and new manners reign."

beings fleeing for liberty, to suffer social ostracism, and to run the risk of the heavy penalties prescribed by unholy laws for so doing, required the highest type of Christian men and women,—men and women of sagacity, coolness, firmness, courage, and benevolence; rocks of adamant, to whom the down-trodden could flock for relief and refuge. A great aid to the ignorant fugitive was that every slave knew the " north star," and, further, that if he followed it he would eventually reach the land of freedom. This knowledge enabled thousands to reach Canada. All slave-holders despised this " star."

To William Wright, of Columbia, Pennsylvania, is due the credit of putting into practice the first " underground railroad" for the freedom of slaves. There was no State organization effected until about 1838, when, in Philadelphia, Robert Purvis was made president and Jacob C. White secretary. Then the system grew, and before the war of the Rebellion our whole State became interlaced with roads. We had a route, too, in this wilderness. It was not as prominent as the routes in the more populous counties of the State. I am sorry that I am unable to write a complete history of the pure, lofty, generous men and women of the northwest and in our county who worked these roads. They were Quakers and Methodists, and the only ones that I can now recall in Jefferson County were Elijah Heath and wife, Arad Pearsall and wife, James Steadman and wife, and the Rev. Christopher Fogle and his first and second wife, of Brookville (Rev. Fogle was an agent and conductor in Troy), Isaac P. Carmalt and his wife, of near Clayville, James A. Minish, of Punxsutawney, and William Coon and his wife, in Clarington, now Forest County. Others, no doubt, were connected, but the history is lost. Jefferson's route started from Baltimore, Maryland, and extended, *via* Bellefonte, Grampian Hills, Punxsutawney, Brookville, Clarington, and Warren, to Lake Erie and Canada. A branch road came from Indiana, Pennsylvania, to Clayville. At Indiana, Pennsylvania, Dr. Mitchell, James Moorhead, James Hamilton, William Banks, and a few others were agents in the cause.

In an estimate based on forty years, there escaped annually from the slave States fifteen hundred slaves; but still the slave population doubled in these States every twenty years. Fugitives travelled north usually in twos, but in two or three instances they went over our wilderness route in a small army, as an early paper of Brookville says, editorially, " Twenty-five fugitive slaves passed through Brookville Monday morning on their way to Canada." Again: " On Monday morning, October 14, 1850, forty armed fugitive slaves passed through Brookville to Canada."

Smedley's " Underground Railroad" says, " Heroes have had their deeds of bravery upon battle-fields emblazoned in history, and their countrymen have delighted to do them honor; statesmen have been renowned, and their names have been engraved upon the enduring tablets of fame; philanthropists have had their acts of benevolence and charity proclaimed to an appreciating world; ministers, pure and sincere in their gospel labors, have had their teachings collected in religious books that generations might profit by the reading; but these moral heroes, out of the fulness of their hearts, with neither expectations of reward nor hope of remembrance, have, within the privacy of their own homes, at an hour when the outside world was locked in slumber, clothed, fed, and in the darkness of night, whether in calm or in storms, assisted poor degraded, hunted human beings on their way to liberty.

*   *   *   *   *   *   *   *   *

" When, too, newspapers refused to publish antislavery speeches, but poured forth such denunciations as, ' The people will hereafter consider abolitionists as out of the pale of legal and conventional protection which society affords its honest and well-meaning members,' that ' they will be treated as robbers and pirates, and as the enemies of mankind;' when Northern merchants extensively engaged in Southern trade told abolitionists that, as their pecuniary interests were largely connected with those of the South, they could not afford to allow them to succeed in their efforts to overthrow slavery, that millions upon millions of dollars were due them from Southern merchants, the payment of which would be jeopardized, and that they would put them down by fair means if they could, by foul means if they must, we must concede that it required the manhood of a man and the unflinching fortitude of a woman, upheld by a full and firm Christian faith, to be an abolitionist in those days, and especially an ' underground railroad' agent."

SLAVE TRAFFIC AND TRADE

"And he that stealeth a man, and selleth him, or if he be found in his hand, he shall surely be put to death."—*Exod.* xxi. 16.

In the United States Constitutional Convention of 1787 the Carolinas, Georgia, and New York wanted the slave-trade continued and more slave *property.* To the credit of all the other colonies, they wanted the foreign slave traffic stopped. After much wrangling and discussion a compromise was effected by which no enactment was to restrain the slave-trade before the year 1808. By this compromise the slave-trade was to continue twenty-one years. On March 2, 1807, Congress passed an act to prohibit the importation of any more slaves after the close of that year. But the profits from slave-trading were enormous, and the foreign traffic continued in spite of all law. It was found that if one ship out of every three was captured, the profits still would be large. Out of every ten negroes stolen in Africa, seven died before they reached this *market.* A negro cost in Africa twenty dollars in gunpowder, old clothes, etc., and readily brought five hundred dollars in the United States. Everything connected with the trade was brutal. The daily ration of a captive on a vessel was a pint of water and a half-pint of rice. Sick negroes were simply thrown overboard. This traffic " for revolting, heartless atrocity would make the devil wonder." The profits were so large that no slave-trader was ever convicted in this country until 1861, when Nathaniel Gordon, of the slaver " Erie," was convicted in New York City and executed. It was estimated that from thirty to sixty thousand slaves were carried to the Southern States every year by New York vessels alone. A wicked practice was carried on between the slave and free States in this way. A complete description of a free colored man or woman would be sent from a free State to parties living in a slave State. This description would then be published in hand-bills, etc., as that of a runaway slave. These bills would be widely circulated. In a short time the person so described would be arrested, kidnapped in the night, overpowered, manacled, carried away, and sold. He had no legal right, no friends, and was only a " nigger." Free colored men on the borders of Pennsylvania have left home to visit a neighbor and been kidnapped in broad daylight, and never heard of after. A negro man or woman would sell for from one to two thousand dollars, and this was more profitable than horse-stealing or highway robbery, and attended with but little danger. A report in this or any other neighborhood that kidnappers were around struck terror to the heart of every free colored man and woman. Negroes of my acquaintance in Brookville have left their shanty homes to sleep in the stables of friends when such rumors were afloat.

Before giving any official records in this history, I must pause to present the fact that one Butler B. Amos, an all-around thief, then in Jefferson County, was, in 1834, in jail, sentenced to "hard labor" under the law, and to be fed in the manner directed by law,—viz., on bread and water.

Early convicts were sentenced to hard labor in the county jail, and had to make split-brooms from hickory-wood, as will be seen from this agreement, between the commissioners and the jailer:

"Received, Brookville, Sept. 29th, 1834, of the commissioners of Jefferson county, thirty-seven broomsticks, which I am to have made into brooms by Butler B. Amos, lately convicted in the Court of Quarter Sessions of said county for larceny and sentenced to hard labour in the gaol of said county for six months, and I am also to dispose of said brooms when made as the said commissioners may direct, and account to them for the proceeds thereof as the law directs. Received also one shaving horse, one hand saw, one drawing knife and one jack knife to enable him to work the above brooms, which I am to return to the said commissioners at the expiration of said term of servitude of the said Butler B. Amos, with reasonable wear and tear.

"ARAD PEARSALL, *Gaoler.*"

Amos had been arrested for theft, as per the following advertisement in the *Jeffersonian* of the annexed date:

"Commonwealth *vs.* Butler B. Amos. Defendant committed to September term, 1834. Charge of Larceny. And whereas the act of General Assembly requires that notice be given, I therefore hereby give notice that the following is an inventory of articles found in the possession of the said Butler B. Amos and supposed to have been stolen, viz.: 1 canal shovel, 1 grubbing hoe, 2 hand saws, 2 bake kettles, 1 curry comb, 2 wolf traps, 1 iron bound bucket, 1 frow, 3 log chains, 1 piece of log chain, 2 drawing chains, 1 piece of drawing chain, 1 set of breast chains, 1 hand ax, &c. The above mentioned articles are now in possession of the subscriber, where those interested can see and examine for themselves.

"ALX. M'KNIGHT, *J. P.*

"BROOKVILLE, August 25th, 1834."

A few years after this sentence was complied with Amos left Brookville on a flat-boat for Kentucky, where he was dirked in a row and killed. Although Amos was a thief, he had a " warm heart" in him, as will be seen farther on. In the year 1829 seventy thousand persons were imprisoned in Pennsylvania for debt.

The earliest official record I can find of Jefferson's underground road is in the *Jeffersonian* of September 15, 1834, which contained these advertisements,—viz.:

" $150 REWARD

" ESCAPED from the jail of Jefferson county, Pennsylvania, last night —a black man, called *Charles Brown*, a slave to the infant heirs of *Richard Baylor*, deceased, late of Jefferson county, Virginia; he is about 5 feet 7 inches high, and 24 years of age, of a dark complexion—pleasant look, with his upper teeth a little open before. I was removing him to the State of Virginia, by virtue of a certificate from Judges' *Shippen, Irvin & M'Kee*, of the Court of Common Pleas of the county of Venango, as my warrant, to return him to the place from which he fled. I will give a reward of $150 to any person who will deliver him to the Jailor of Jefferson county Virginia, and if that sum should appear to be inadequate to the expense and trouble, it shall be suitably increased.

" JOHN YATES,
" Sept. 15, 1834."   *" Guardian of the said heirs.*

" $150 REWARD!!

" ESCAPED from the Jail of Jefferson county; Pennsylvania last night, a black man, nam'd WILLIAM PARKER alias ROBINSON a slave, belonging to the undersigned: aged about 26 years, and about 5 feet 6 inches high; broad shoulders; full round face, rather a grave countenance, and thick lips, particularly his upper lip, stammers a little, and rather slow in speech.—I was removing him to the State of Virginia, by virtue of a certificate, from Judges *Shippen and Irvin*, of the Court of Common Pleas, of Venango county; as my warrant to return him to the place, from which he fled. I will give a reward of $150, to any person, who will deliver him to the Jailor of Jefferson county Virginia; and if that sum should appear to be inadequate to the expense and trouble, it shall be suitably increased.

" STEPHEN DELGARN.
" September 15, 1834."

These slaves were very intelligent and good-looking.

Arad Pearsall was then our jailer, and he was a Methodist and an abolitionist.

Jefferson's pioneer jail, as I remember it, was constructed from stone

322

spawls, with wooden doors and big iron locks. For safety, the prisoners were usually shackled and handcuffed, and they were fed on "bread and water." When recaptured, escaped slaves were lodged in county jails and shackled for safety. These slaves had been so lodged, while their captors slept on beds "as soft as downy pillows are." Charles Brown and William Parker reached Canada. Heath and Steadman furnished augers and files to the thief Amos, who filed the shackles loose from these human beings, and with the augers he bored the locks off the doors. Pearsall, Heath, and Steadman did the rest. In addition, Steadman had Yates and Delgarn arrested for travelling on Sunday, and this trial, before a justice of the peace, gave the two slaves time to get a good start through the woods for Canada. Some person or persons in Brookville were mean enough to inform, by letter or otherwise, Delgarn and Yates that Judge Heath, Arad Pearsall, and James Steadman had liberated and run off their slaves, whereupon legal steps were taken by these men to recover damages for the loss of property in the United States Court at Pittsburg, the minutes of which I here reproduce: .

" At No. 4 of October Term, 1835, in the District Court of the United States for the Western District of Pennsylvania, suit in trespass, brought July 10, 1835, by Thomas G. Baylor and Anna Maria Baylor, minors, by John Yates, Esq., their guardian, all citizens of Virginia, against Elijah Heath, James M. Steadman, and Arad Pearsall.

" At No. 5, October Term, 1835, suit in trespass by Stephen Delgarn, a citizen of Virginia, against same defendants as in No. 4, brought at same time. Burke and Metcalf, Esqs., were attorneys for the plaintiffs in each case, and Alexander M. Foster for the defendants.

" Suit, as No. 4, was tried on May 3, 4, and 5, 1836, and on May 6, 1836, verdict rendered for plaintiff for six hundred dollars.

" Suit No. 5 was tried May 6 and 7, 1836, and verdict rendered May 7, 1836, for eight hundred and forty dollars. November 24, 1836, judgments and costs collected upon execution and paid to plaintiffs' attorneys.

" In suit No. 4 the allegations as set forth in the declarations filed are: That plaintiffs, citizens of Virginia, were the owners of 'a certain negro man' named Charles Brown, otherwise 'Charles,' of great value,—to wit, of the value of one thousand dollars,—to which said negro they were lawfully entitled as a servant or slave, and to his labor and service as such, according to the laws of the State of Virginia. That on or about the 1st day of August, 1834, the said negro man absconded, and went away from and out of the custody of said plaintiffs, and afterwards went and came into the Western District of Pennsylvania; and the said plaintiffs, by their guardian, did, on or about the 13th day of September, 1834, pursue the said servant or slave into the said Western District of Pennsylvania, and finding the said servant or slave in said district, and there and then claimed him as a fugitive from labor, and caused him to be arrested and brought before the judges of the Court of Common Pleas of Venango County, in said Western District of Pennsylvania; and it appearing upon sufficient evidence before them produced in due and legal form, that the said negro man did, under the laws of Virginia, owe service and labor unto said plaintiffs, and that the said negro man had fled from the service of his said master in Virginia into Venango County, Pennsylvania, aforesaid; and the said plaintiffs, by their guardian, did, on the said 13th day of September, 1834, obtain from the said judges of the Court of Common Pleas of Venango County aforesaid a warrant for the removal of the said negro man to Virginia aforesaid; and the said guardian was returning and taking with him, under and by virtue of the said warrant, said servant or slave to the said plaintiffs' residence in Virginia; and while so returning—to wit, on or about the day and year last aforesaid—the said guardian at Jefferson County, in the Western District of Pennsylvania aforesaid, did, with the assent and by the permission of the person or persons having charge of the public jail or prison in and for said County of Jefferson, place the said servant or slave in said jail or prison for safe-keeping, until he, the said guardian, could reasonably proceed on his journey with the said aforesaid servant or slave to Virginia aforesaid. Yet the said defendants, well knowing the said negro man to be the servant or slave of the plaintiffs and to be their lawful property, and that they, the said plaintiffs, by their guardian aforesaid, were entitled to have the possession and custody of him, and to have and enjoy the profit and advantage of his labor and services; but contriving and unlawfully intending to injure the said plaintiffs, and to deprive them of all benefits, profits, and advantages of and which would accrue to these said plaintiffs from said services, then and there, on or about the day and year aforesaid at Jefferson County aforesaid, did secretly and in the night-time unlawfully, wrongfully, and *unjustly* release, take, and assist in releasing and taking, or procure to be released or taken, the said negro man, then being as aforesaid the servant or slave of the said plaintiffs, from and out of the said prison or jail, where said servant or slave was placed for safe-keeping by said guardian as aforesaid; whereby said servant or slave escaped, ran off, and was and is wholly lost to said plaintiffs, and said plaintiffs deprived of all the profits, benefits, and advantages which might and otherwise would have arisen and accrued to said plaintiffs from the said services of said servant or slave.

"The allegations and declarations in No. 5 were materially the same as in No. 4."

Isaac P. Carmalt was co-operating with Heath and others at this time. Heath was a Methodist, and so was Pearsall. Heath moved away about 1846, and Pearsall died in Brookville about 1857.

Isaac P. Carmalt was a Quaker, a relative of William Penn, and was born in Philadelphia, Pennsylvania, in 1794. He learned the carpenter trade.

In 1818 he left his native city with two horses and a Dearborn wagon, and in three weeks he crossed the Allegheny Mountains and located in Indiana County, Pennsylvania. In 1821 he moved to Punxsutawney. In 1822 he bought a farm near Clayville. In 1823 he married Miss Hannah A. Gaskill, a Quakeress, in Philadelphia, Pennsylvania. But little can be given of his great work in this direction owing to his death. His daughter, Mrs. Lowry, writes me as follows:

"The last slave that came to our house was after the insurrection at Harper's Ferry. He claimed to have been in the insurrection. He came with a colored man who lived near Grampian Hills, whose name was George Hartshorn. This one was a mulatto, and claimed to be the son of Judge Crittenden, who, I think, held some important office at Washington,—Senator or Congressman. The slave was very nervous when he came, and asked for a raw onion, which, he said, was good to quiet the nerves. He was also quite suspicious of Joe Walkup, who was working at our house at the time. He called him out and gave him his revolver, and told him he would rather he would blow his brains out than to inform on him, for if he was taken he would certainly be hung. He left during the night for Brookville. Most of the fugitives came through Centre and Clearfield Counties. One of the underground railroad stations was in Centre County, near Bellefonte, kept by a friend by the name of Iddings, who sent them to the next station, which was Grampian Hills, from thence to our house, and from here to Brookville. I remember well one Sabbath when I was coming home from church; Lib Wilson was coming part way with me. We noticed a colored man ahead of us. I paid but little attention, but she said, 'I know that is a slave.' I knew Wilson's pro-slavery sentiments, and replied very carelessly that 'there was a colored family living near Grampian Hills. I supposed he was going to our house, as we had been there a short time before, wanting to trade horses for oxen to haul timber with.' But as soon as she left me I quickened my pace and tried to overtake him. I was afraid he might go through Clayville, where I knew there was a perfect nest of pro-slavery men, who had made their threats of what they would do if father assisted any more slaves to gain their freedom. Among them were the Gillespies, who boasted of being overseers or slave-drivers while they were in the South. He kept ahead of me and stopped at James Minish's, and I thought it was all over with him, as they and the Gillespies were connected, and most likely were of the same sentiment in regard to slavery. But imagine my surprise when I came up, Mr. Minish handed me a slip of paper with the name of 'Carmalt' on it, and remarked that I was one of the Carmalt girls. (I suppose it was the name of a station.) But he hurried the fugitive on, and I directed him to go up over the hill through the woods. I then hurried home for father to go and meet him. But when I got home, father was not there, so I put on my sun-bonnet and went but a short distance, when I met him. There were several persons in the house, so I slipped him in the back way. He seemed to be in great misery and could not eat anything, but asked for something to bathe his foot in. Then he gave a short account of his escape from slavery three years previous. After escaping he stopped with a man near Harrisburg, at what he called Yellow Breeches Creek, and worked for him, during which time he married and had a little home of his own. One day when ploughing in the field he discovered his old master from whom he had escaped and two other men coming toward him. He dropped everything and ran to his benefactor's house, and told him who he had seen. His benefactor then pulled off his coat and boots and directed him to put them on, as he was in his bare feet, having left his own coat and boots in the field. Being closely pursued, he ran to the barn, and the men followed him. He was then compelled to jump from a high window, and, striking a sharp stone, he received a severe cut in one heel, not having had time to put on the boots given him by his benefactor. When he came to our house he was suffering terribly, not having had an opportunity to get the wound dressed. His benefactor had charged him not to tarry on the road. But father, seeing the seriousness of his wound, persuaded him to go to bed until midnight. But the poor fellow could not sleep, but moaned with pain. We gave him his breakfast, and then father had him get on a horse, while he walked, and it was just breaking day when they arrived at Brookville. A gentleman by the name of Christopher Fogle was waiting to receive them. We heard afterwards that the poor slave succeeded in reaching Canada, but returned for his wife, and was captured and taken back to slavery.

" There is just one more incident that I will mention, which occurred at an earlier date. One morning I went to the door and saw four large colored men hurrying to the barn. I told father, and he went out and brought them in. Our breakfast was just ready. We had them sit down and eat as fast as they could, taking the precaution to lock the door, for several persons came along while they were eating. Father noticed that one of the slaves looked dull and stupid, and inquired if he was sick. One of the others replied that he was only a little donsey. When they were through eating, father hurried them to the woods and hid them somewhere near the old schoolhouse then on the farm. When father went to take their dinner to them, the one said he was still a little donsey, and then showed father his back. His shirt was sticking to his back. He had been terribly whipped, and they had rubbed salt in the gashes. They then gave a short history of their escape. They said they had a good master and mistress, but their master had died and the estate was sold. The master's two sons then sold them, and they were to be taken to the rice-swamps to toil their lives away. They were determined to make their escape, but the one who had been so terribly whipped was captured and taken back. Their old mistress planned and assisted him to make his escape by dressing him as a coachman, and with her assistance he found his way to Washington, where he met his companions and friends. From Washington they were guided by the north star, travelling only by night.

"I think but few fugitives came by the way of Indiana, though I remember of hearing father tell of one or two that he brought with him when he first came from Indiana who had escaped by way of Philadelphia. I think most came through Baltimore, where a Quaker friend by the name of Needles assisted the runaways through this branch of the underground railroad. From Baltimore they came through the Quaker settlements in Centre and Clearfield Counties. Father was the only one who conveyed them from our house near Clayville to Brookville. This he generally did by going himself or by sending some reliable person with them. Father concealed a man from Baltimore, a German, who used to smuggle slaves through. He had a furniture wagon, in which he concealed them, but was discovered and put in jail at York, Pennsylvania, but he escaped to Iddings, near Bellefonte, thence to Grampian Hills, and from there to father's, where he worked five years. He then left, and moved to Ohio. He became afraid to stay, for there were a few who had an inkling of his history and knew there was a reward of three thousand dollars for his arrest. One day in going to his work he met the sheriff from Baltimore, who knew him well, and told him to keep out of his sight, that there was a big reward offered for him. When he was first arrested he had a colored girl concealed in a bureau which he was hauling on his wagon."

Christopher Fogle was born in Baden, Germany, in 1800. His father came with his family to Philadelphia, Pennsylvania, in 1817, and Christopher learned the tanning trade in Germantown. On June 26, 1826, he was married in Dauphin County, Pennsylvania. About this time he joined the Methodist Church. In 1835 he migrated to Heathville, Jefferson County, Pennsylvania, and built a tannery. In 1843 he moved to Troy and had a tannery. This he afterwards sold out to Hulett Smith, when he moved to Brookville and purchased from Elijah Heath and A. Colwell what was called the David Henry tannery. Rev. Fogle was in the underground railroad business in Heathville, and Mrs. Jane Fogle, his second wife, who still survives him, informs me that he continued in that business until the war for the Union, and she assisted him. The points in and around Brookville where the Rev. Fogle lived and secreted fugitives were, first the old tannery; second, the K. L. Blood farm; third, the little yellow house where Benscotter's residence now is; and, fourth, the old house formerly owned by John J. Thompson, opposite the United Presbyterian church. Officers frequently were close after these fugitives, and sometimes were in Brookville, while the agents had the colored people hid in the woods. The next station on this road to Canada was at the house of William Coon, in Clarington, Pennsylvania. Coon would ferry the slaves over the Clarion, feed, refresh, and start them through the wilderness for Warren, Pennsylvania, and when Canada was finally reached, the poor fugitive could sing, with a broken heart at times, thinking of his wife, children, and parents yet in bonds,—

> " No more master's call for me,
>   No more, no more.
> No more driver's lash for me,
>   No more, no more.
> No more auction-block for me,
>   No more, no more.
> No more bloodhounds hunt for me,
>   No more, no more.
> I'm free, I'm free at last; at last,
>   Thank God, I'm free !"

The following census tables are taken from Williams's " Memoirs and Administration," published in 1850:

PROGRESS OF POPULATION IN THE UNITED STATES FOR FIFTY YEARS, FROM 1790 TO 1840

First Census, August 1, 1790.

	Whites.	Free Colored.	Slaves.	Total.
Free States	1,900,772	26,831	40,850	1,968,453
Slave States	1,271,692	32,635	645,047	1,961,374
Total	3,172,464	59,446	697,897	3,929,827

Second Census, August 1, 1800.

	Whites.	Free Colored.	Slaves.	Total.
Free States	2,601,509	47,154	35,946	2,684,609
Slave States	1,702,980	61,241	857,095	2,621,316
Total	4,304,489	108,395	893,041	5,305,925

Third Census, August 1, 1810.

	Whites.	Free Colored.	Slaves.	Total.
Free States	3,653,219	78,181	27,510	3,758,910
Slave States	2,208,785	108,265	1,163,854	3,480,904
Total	5,862,004	186,446	1,191,364	7,239,814

Fourth Census, August 1, 1820.

	Whites.	Free Colored.	Slaves.	Total.
Free States	5,030,371	102,893	19,108	5,152,372
Slave States	2,842,340	135,434	1,524,580	4,502,224
Total	7,872,711	238,197	1,543,688	9,654,596

Fifth Census, June 1, 1830.

	Whites.	Free Colored.	Slaves.	Total.
Free States	6,876,620	137,529	3,568	7,017,717
Slave States	3,660,758	182,070	2,005,475	5,848,303
Total	10,537,378	319,599	2,009,043	12,866,020

Sixth Census, June 1, 1840.

	Whites.	Free Colored.	Slaves.	Total.
Free States	9,557,065	170,727	1,129	9,723,921
Slave States	4,632,640	215,568	2,486,226	7,334,434
Total	14,189,705	386,295	2,487,355	17,063,355

SUMMARY OF THE CENSUS OF THE UNITED STATES, JUNE 1, 1840

Free or Non-Slaveholding States.

States and Territories.	Whites.	Free Colored.	Slaves.	Total.
Maine	500,438	1,355	..	501,793
New Hampshire	284,036	537	1	284,574
Vermont	291,218	730	..	291,948
Massachusetts	729,030	8,668	..	737,698
Rhode Island	105,587	3,238	5	108,830
Connecticut	301,856	8,105	17	300,978
Total, New England........	2,212,165	22,633	23	2,234,821
New York	2,378,890	50,027	..	2,428,921
New Jersey	351,588	21,044	674	373,306
Pennsylvania	1,676,115	47,854	64	1,724,033
Ohio	1,502,122	17,342	3	1,519,467
Indiana	678,698	7,165	3	685,866
Illinois	472,254	3,598	331	476,183
Michigan	211,560	707	..	212,267
Wisconsin	30,749	185	11	43,112
Iowa	42,924	172	16	30,945
Total, Free States	9,557,065	170,727	1,129	9,728,921

Slaveholding States.

Delaware	58,561	16,919	2,605	78,085
Maryland	318,204	62,078	89,737	470,019
District of Columbia	30,657	8,361	4,694	43,712
Virginia	740,968	49,842	448,987	1,239,797
North Carolina	484,870	22,732	255,817	753,419
South Carolina	259,084	8,276	327,038	494,398
Georgia	407,695	2,753	280,944	691,392
Florida	27,943	817	25,717	54,477
Alabama	335,185	2,039	253,532	590,756
Mississippi	179,074	1,369	195,211	375,654
Louisiana	158,457	25,502	168,451	352,411
Arkansas	77,174	465	19,935	97,574
Tennessee	640,627	5,524	183,059	829,210
Kentucky	590,253	7,317	182,258	779,828
Missouri	323,888	1,574	58,240	383,702
Total, Slave States	4,632,640	215,568	2,486,226	7,334,434
Total, United States	14,189,705	386,295	2,487,355	17,063,355

INDENTURED APPRENTICES, WHITE SLAVERY, AND REDEMPTIONERS

Colored people were not the only class held in servitude by Pennsylvanians. Another form of slavery was carried on by speculators called Newlanders. These traders in "white people" were protected by custom and legal statutes. They ran vessels regularly to European seaports, and induced people to emigrate to Pennsylvania. By delay and expensive formalities these emigrants were systematically robbed during the trip of any money they might have, and upon their arrival at Philadelphia would be in a strange country, without money or friends to pay their passage or to lift their goods from the villanous captains and owners of these vessels which brought them to the wharves of Philadelphia. Imagine the destitute condition of these emigrants. Under the law of imprisonment for debt the captain or merchant either sold these people or imprisoned them.

The Newlanders were the first German emigrants to Pennsylvania. Actuated by sinister motives, the Newlander would return to Germany, and rely on his personal appearance and flattering tongue to mislead and induce all classes, from the minister down to the lowest strata of humanity, to migrate to the New World. The Newlanders would receive from the owner or captain of a vessel a stipulated sum per passenger. By arts and representations the Newlander ingratiated himself into the confidence of the emigrant, securing possession of his property, and before taking passage the emigrant had to subscribe to a written contract in English, which enabled the Newlander the more fully to pluck his victim, for when the vessel arrived at Philadelphia the list of passengers and their agreements were placed in the hands of merchants. The Newlander managed it so that the emigrant would be in his debt, and then the poor foreigners had to be sold for debt. The merchants advertised the cargo; the place of sale on the ship. The purchasers had to enter the ship, make the contract, take their purchase to the merchant and pay the price, and then legally bind the transaction before a magistrate. Unmarried people and young people, of course, were more readily sold, and brought better prices. Aged and decrepit persons were poor sale; but if they had healthy children, these children were sold at good prices for the combined debt, and to different masters and in different States, perhaps never to see each other in this world. The parents then were turned loose to beg. The time of sale was from two to seven years for about fifty dollars of our money. The poor people on board the ship were prisoners, and could neither go ashore themselves or send their baggage until they paid what they did not owe. These captains made more money out of the deaths of their passengers than they did from the living, as this gave them a chance to rob chests and sell children. This was a cruel, murdering trade. Every cruel device was resorted to in order to gain gold through the misfortune of these poor people. One John Stedman, in 1753, bought a license in Holland that no captain or merchant could load any passengers unless he had two thousand. He treated these deluded people so cruelly on ship-board that two thousand in less than one year were thrown overboard. This was monopoly.

As will be seen in this chapter, under the head of advertisements, many of the leading merchants in Philadelphia were engaged in this nefarious business. In answer to the daily advertisements of "Redemptioners for Sale," citizens from all parts of Pennsylvania and adjoining States visited Philadelphia and bought these poor white people, the same as sheep and oxen. Many of the best families and people in this State are descendants of these " white slaves." We have some such descendants in Jefferson County and through the northwest. I could name them.

Under this debasing system of indentured apprentices, the legal existence of African slavery, and the legalized sale of white emigrants in our State, is it any wonder that among the people intemperance, illiteracy, lottery schemes for churches, gambling, and profanity were the rule, or that to the poor, the weak, and the wretched the prisons were the only homes or hospitals for them, and that the " driver's lash" fell alike on the back of the old and young, black and white, minister, school-master, and layman?

> " I pity the mother, careworn and weary,
> As she thinks of her children about to be sold;
> You may picture the bounds of the rock-girdled ocean,
> But the grief of that mother can never be told."

ACT OF 1700

" AN ACT FOR THE BETTER REGULATION OF SERVANTS IN THIS PROVINCE AND TERRITORIES

" For the just encouragement of servants in the discharge of their duty, and the prevention of their deserting their masters' or owners' service, *Be it enacted,* That no servant, bound to serve his or her time in this province, or counties annexed, shall be sold or disposed of to any person residing in any other province or government, without the consent of the said servant, and two Justices of the Peace of the county wherein he lives or is sold, under the penalty of ten pounds; to be forfeited by the seller.

" II. *And be it further enacted,* That no servant shall be assigned over to another person by any in this province or territories, but in the presence of one Justice of the Peace of the county, under the penalty of ten pounds; which penalty, with all others in this act expressed, shall be levied by distress and sale of goods of the party offending.

" III. *And be it enacted,* That every servant that shall faithfully serve four years, or more, shall, at the expiration of their servitude, have a discharge, and shall be duly clothed with two complete suits of apparel, whereof one shall be new, and shall also be furnished with one new axe, one grubbing-hoe, and one weeding-hoe, at the charge of their master or mistress.

331

· " IV. And for prevention of servants quitting their masters' service, *Be it enacted,* That if any servant shall absent him or herself from the service of their master or owner for the space of one day or more, without leave first obtained for the same, every such servant shall, for every such day's absence, be obliged to serve five days, after the expiration of his or her time, and shall further make such satisfaction to his or her master or owner, for the damages and charges sustained by such absence, as the respective County Court shall see meet, who shall order as well the time to be served, as other recompense for damages sustained.

" V. And whosoever shall apprehend or take up any runaway servant, and shall bring him or her to the Sheriff of the county, such person shall, for every such servant, if taken up within ten miles of the servant's abode, receive ten shillings, and if ten miles or upwards, twenty shillings reward, of the said Sheriff, who is hereby required to pay the same, and forthwith to send notice to the master or owner, of whom he shall receive five shillings, prison fees, upon delivery of the said servant, together with all other disbursements and reasonable charges for and upon the same.

" VI. And to prevent the clandestine employing of other men's servants, *Be it enacted,* That whosoever shall conceal any servant of this province or territories, or entertain him or her twenty-four hours, without his or her master's or owner's knowledge and consent, and shall not within the said time give an account thereof to some Justice of the Peace of the county, every such person shall forfeit twenty shillings for every day's concealment. And in case the said Justice shall not, within twenty-four hours after complaint made to him, issue his warrant, directed to the next constable, for apprehending and seizing the said servant, and commit him or her to the custody of the Sheriff of the county, such Justice shall, for every such offence, forfeit five pounds. And the Sheriff shall by the first opportunity, after he has received the said servant, send notice thereof to his or her master or owner; and the said Sheriff, neglecting or omitting in any case to give notice to the master or owner of their servant being in his custody as aforesaid, shall forfeit five shillings for every day's neglect after an opportunity has offered, to be proved against him before the next County Court, and to be there adjudged.

" VII. And for the more effectual discouragement of servants imbezzling their masters' or owners' goods, *Be it enacted,* That whosoever shall clandestinely deal or traffic with any servant, white or black, for any kind of goods or merchandise, without leave or order from his or her master or owner, plainly signified or appearing, shall forfeit treble the value of such goods to the owner; and the servant if a white, shall make satisfaction to his or her master or owner by servitude, after the expiration of his or her time, to double the value of the said goods; And if the servant be a black, he or she shall be severely whipped, in the most public place of the township where the offence was committed."

332

ACT OF 1705

" SECTION 2. *Provided,* That no person shall be kept in prison for debt or fines, longer than the second day of the next session after his or her commitment, unless the plaintiff shall make it appear that the person imprisoned hath some estate that he will not produce, in which case the court shall examine all persons suspected to be privy to the concealing of such estate; and if no estate sufficient shall be found, the debtor shall make satisfaction by servitude to the judgment of the court where such action is tried (not exceeding seven years if a single person, and under the age of fifty and three years, or five years if a married man, and under the age of forty and six years) if the plaintiff require it; but if the plaintiff refuse such manner of satisfaction, according to the judgment of the court as aforesaid, then and in such case the prisoner shall be discharged in open court.

" SECTION 3. *Provided,* That nothing in this act contained shall be construed to subject any master of ship or other vessel, trading into this province from other parts, to make satisfaction for debt by servitude as above said."

Up to 1842 this law of Pennsylvania authorized the imprisonment of men for debt. The act of July 12 of that year abolished such imprisonment. Quite a number of men were committed to the old jail in Brookville because of their inability to pay their debts. Sometimes their friends paid the debt for them, and sometimes they came out under the insolvent debtor's law. Below I give an exact copy of an execution issued by 'Squire Corbet, a justice of the peace in Brookville:

" JEFFERSON COUNTY, *ss.*

" The Commonwealth of Pennsylvania to James Cochran, constable of borough, greeting: *Whereas* judgment against Stephen Tibbits for the sum of 5 dollars and 27 cents and the costs was had the 6th day of Jany, '39, before me, at the suit of Heath, Dunham & Co.: These are therefore in the name of the commonwealth, to command you to levy distress on the goods and chattles of the said Stephen Tibbits, and make sale thereof according to law to the amount of said debt and costs, and what may accrue thereon, and make return to me in twenty days from the date thereof; and for want of goods and chattels whereon to levy, you are commanded to convey the body of said Stephen Tibbits to the jail of the said county, the jailer whereof is hereby commanded to receive the same, in safe custody to keep until the said debt and costs are paid, or otherwise discharged by due course of law. Given under my hand and seal the 15 day of May, 1841.

" JAMES CORBET."

This execution was numbered 811. The debt was $5.27; interest, 60 cents; justice's costs, 25 cents; execution and return, 20½ cents; total, $6.32½. The whole sum was paid May 26, 1841.

By the act passed April 8, 1785, entitled "An Act for establishing the office of a register of all German passengers who shall arrive at the port of Philadelphia, and of all indentures by which any of them shall be bound servants for their freight, and of the assignments of such servants in the city of Philadelphia," it was provided that the register should understand and speak both German and English languages, and that he could have "all the powers and authorities of a justice of the peace, as far as the same shall be required for the support and efficiency of his office, and the laws respecting the importation of German passengers and binding them out servants." All indentures and assignments to be made and acknowledged before the register or his deputy, and he to register all indentures or assignments, as servants' indentures or assignments.

Under the act for regulating the importation of German and other passengers, passed February 7, 1818, the captain was compelled to give a bill of lading of merchandise to passengers, under a penalty of one hundred dollars. Passengers to be discharged on payment of freight. When passengers were sold for servitude, the indenture to be acknowledged before the mayor of the city of Philadelphia; "but no master, captain, owner, or consignee of any ship or vessel shall separate any husband and wife, who came passengers in any such ship or vessel, by disposing of them to different masters or mistresses, unless by mutual consent of such husband and wife; nor shall any passenger, without his or her consent, be disposed of to any person residing out of this Commonwealth, under the penalty of one hundred dollars." The goods of each passenger to be a pledge for freight.

AN ACT FOR THE RELIEF OF REDEMPTIONERS

"Section 1. *Be it enacted by the Senate and House of Representatives of the Commonwealth of Pennsylvania, in General Assembly met, and it is hereby enacted by the authority of the same,* That the several provisions of an act of Assembly of this Commonwealth, passed the twenty-ninth day of September, one thousand seven hundred and seventy, entitled 'An Act for the regulation of apprentices within this province,' and of an act passed the eleventh day of April, one thousand seven hundred and ninety-nine, entitled a supplement to the act entitled 'An Act for the regulation of apprentices,' be and the same are hereby extended to all Redemptioners bound to service for a term of years." Passed 9th February, 1820.

ACT OF SEPTEMBER 29, 1770

"Section 1. All and every person or persons that shall be bound by indenture to serve an apprentice in any art, mystery, labour, or occupation, with the assent of his or her parents, guardian or next friend, or with the assent of the overseers of the poor, and approbation of any two Justices, although such persons, or any of them, shall be within the age of twenty-one years at the time of making their several indentures, shall be bound to serve the time in their respective indentures contained, so as such time or term of years of such apprentice, if female, do expire at or before the age of eighteen years, and if a male, at or before the age of twenty-one years, as fully to all intents and purposes as if the same apprentices were of full age at the time of making the said indentures.

"SECTION 2. If any master or mistress shall misuse, abuse, or evilly treat, or shall not discharge his or her duty toward his or her apprentice, according to the covenants in the indentures between them made, or if the said apprentice shall abscond or absent him or herself from his or her master's or mistress's service without leave, or shall not do and discharge his or her duty to his or her master or mistress, according to his or her covenants aforesaid, the said master or mistress, or apprentice, being aggrieved in the premises, shall or may apply to any one Justice of the Peace, of any county or city, where the said master or mistress shall reside, who, after giving due notice to such master or mistress, or apprentice, if he or she shall neglect or refuse to appear, shall thereupon issue his warrant for bringing him or her, the said master, mistress, or apprentice, before him, and take such order and direction, between the said master or mistress and apprentice, as the equity and justice of the case shall require : And if the said Justice shall not be able to settle and accommodate the difference and dispute between the said master or mistress and apprentice, through a want of conformity in the master or mistress, then the said Justice shall take a recognizance of the said master or mistress, and bind him or her over, to appear and answer the complaint of his or her apprentice, at the next county court of Quarter Sessions, to be held for the said county or city, and take such order with respect to such apprentice as to him shall seem just ; and if through want of conformity in the said apprentice he shall, if the master or mistress or apprentice request it, take recognizance of him or her with one sufficient surety, for his or her appearance at the said sessions, and to answer the complaint of his or her master or mistress, or commit such apprentice for want of such surety, to the common gaol or work-house of the said county or city respectively ; and upon such appearance of the parties and hearing of their respective proofs and allegations, the said court shall, and they are hereby authorized and empowered, if they see cause, to discharge the said apprentice of and from his or her apprenticeship, and of and from all and every the articles, covenants, and agreements in his or her said indenture contained ; but if default shall be found in the said apprentice, then the said court is hereby authorized and empowered to cause, if they see sufficient occasion, such punishment by imprisonment of the body, and confinement at hard labour, to be inflicted on him or her, as to them, in their discretion, they shall think his or her offence or offences shall deserve."

ACT OF APRIL 11, 1799

" SECTION 1. If any apprentice shall absent himself or herself from the service of his or her master or mistress, before the time of his or her apprenticeship shall be expired, without leave first obtained, every such apprentice, at any time after he or she arrives at the age of twenty-one years, shall be liable to, and the master or mistress, their heirs, executors, or administrators, are hereby enabled to sustain all such actions, and other remedies against him or her, as if the said apprentice had been of full age at the time of executing his or her indenture of apprenticeship.

" SECTION 2. When any master or mistress shall die before the term of apprenticeship shall be expired, the executors or administrators of such master or mistress, provided the term of the indenture extended to executors and administrators, shall and may have a right to assign over the remainder of the term of such apprenticeship to such suitable person of the same trade or calling mentioned in the indenture, as shall be approved of by the court of Quarter Sessions of the county where the master or mistress lived, and the assignee to have the same right to the service of such apprentice as the master or mistress had at the time of his or her death; and also when any master or mistress shall assign over his or her apprentice to any person of the same trade or calling mentioned in the indenture, the said assignment shall be legal, provided the terms of the indenture extended to assigns, and provided the apprentice, or his or her parents, guardian or guardians, shall give his, her, or their consent to such assignment before some Justice of the Peace of the county where the master or mistress shall live."

These advertisements are selected from a large number of a similar kind that are found in Relf's *Philadelphia Gazette and Daily Advertiser* for the years 1804–05:

" GERMAN REDEMPTIONERS

" To be disposed of, the time of a number of German Redemptioners, consisting of Clerks, Shoemakers, Taylors, Cloth makers, Weavers, Stocking weavers, Blacksmiths, Watch makers, Miniature painters &c. on board the Ship Cato, Capt. Barden, from the river Jade, lying off Vine Street, apply to the captain on board Cato.

" SMITH RIDGWAY & CO.
" No. 50 n. front street.

" Nov. 3rd (1804)."

" TO BE DISPOSED OF

"The Time of a German Servant Girl, who has eight years to serve. She is strong and hearty, understands English, and can be well recommended. Enquire at No. 15 South Third Street.

" January 9th, 1805."

"GERMAN REDEMPTIONERS

" A number of German Redemptioners of different ages and professions, to be disposed of on board ship Venus from Amsterdam. For terms apply on board, opposite Callowhill street.

"Sept. 9th, 1805."

" SWISS AND GERMAN PASSENGERS

" The Time

" Of the following passengers mostly farmers and a few mechanics, viz : 17 men, 11 women, 13 boys and 14 girls now to be seen at the Spread Eagle Tavern, Callowhill street near the water, to be disposed of by their agents Winkleblick & Bund, at the Red Lion Tavern, Market Street, between 6 and 7 street, South from 9 in the morning till 6 o'clock in the evening. The payment to be made at the counting house of Mr. L. Huson, No. 19 South Wharves."

" GERMAN REDEMPTIONERS

" On board the ship Indostan laying in the stream above Vine street, consisting of carpenters, bakers, butchers, gardeners, blacksmiths, sugar refiners, glass makers, taylors, servants &c. &c. whose times are to be disposed of, by

" ISAAC HAZELHURST & SONS.

" April 16th 1804."

" 20 DOLLARS REWARD

" RAN AWAY on Saturday last from the subscriber, a German indentured servant man, named Tobias Schwenck, a weaver by trade, about 25 years of age, about 5 feet 6 inches high. When he speaks he has a fashion of swinging his arms in a very passionate manner, pale face, slender made, light straight hair, speaks a little English; took with him a tight body blue coat made in the German fashion, a blue surtout coat, two pair of Russia sheeting trousers, and a pair of blue velvet pantaloons, and a number of other clothing, a pair of new full boots broad round toed.

" Whoever secures the above run-away in any gaol, or delivers him to the subscriber, shall receive the above reward and reasonable charges paid by

" HENRY DOTTERER,

" Sign of the Buck, Second street, Philadelphia.

" Oct. 1804."

" $2 DOLLARS REWARD

" Ran away, an indentured Dutch servant girl, (the property of Richard Baily, near the 7 mile stone, Germantown) about 8 years of age, light complexion, named Maria, was dressed in a striped lindsey short gown and petticoat, blue worsted stockings, and speaks but little of her native language.

All persons are cautioned against detaining or harboring the said girl. In addition to the above reward, any reasonable expense will be allowed.

"Dec. 18th 1804."

"$10 DOLLARS REWARD

"Ran away from the subscriber living in the village of New-Holland, Lancaster County, on the evening of the 7th last, a German indentured servant Girl, named Anna Maria Wagner, she came from Germany last fall in the brig Newton, Capt. Reilly. She is about 19 or 20 years old, of a low stature, she hath short and sandy hair, freckled face, her arms, hands, and feet, very small. Had on when she went away, a blue and white striped petticoat of German manufacture, and a blue jacket, which is remarkable, being lined after the German manner with whalebone. It is said that she hath a sister living in the neighborhood of Kutz town, Berks county, bound to Mr. Lesher. Whoever will secure and deliver her in any gaol, and give notice to the subscriber thereof, so that he may get her again, shall have the above reward, and reasonable charges paid. All persons are hereby forewarned not to harbour her at their peril.

"JONATHAN ROLAND.

"NEW-HOLLAND, Jan. 3rd 1805."

"In law, this system was known as an apprenticeship, or service entered into by a free person, voluntary, by contract for a term of years on wages advanced before the service was entered. The servants, by performing the service, were redeeming themselves, and therefore called 'Redemptioners.' In practice, however, with a certain class of people, and in instances hereinafter related, this system was as revoltingly brutal and degenerating as the negro slavery abolished in our own time in its worst aspects.

"It was conceived and had its beginning in the harmless and in some respects benevolent idea to help a poor person in Europe who wished to emigrate to America and had not the money to pay for his passage across the ocean, by giving him credit for his passage-money, on condition that he should work for it after his arrival here, by hiring as a servant for a term of years to a person who would advance him his wages by paying his passage-money to the owner or master of the vessel.

"There are instances on record when school-teachers, and even ministers of the gospel, were in this manner bought by congregations to render their services in their respective offices. Laws were passed for the protection of the masters and of the servants. Whilst this is the bright side of the Redemptioners' life, it had also a very dark side. The Redemptioners on their arrival here were not allowed to choose their masters nor kind of service most suitable to them. They were often separated from their family, the wife from the husband, and children from their parents; were disposed of for the term of years, often at public sale, to masters living far apart, and always to the greatest

338

advantage of the shipper. I have read many reports of the barbarous treatment they received, how they were literally worked to death, receiving insufficient food, scanty clothing, and poor lodging. Cruel punishments were inflicted on them for slight offences when they were at the mercy of a hard and brutal master. Their fellow black slave was often treated better, for he was a slave for life, and it was in the interest of the master to treat him well to preserve him, whilst the poor Redemptioner was a slave for a number of years only, and all his vital force was worked out of him during the years of his service.

" No public records were kept of the contracts entered into abroad by the Redemptioners, nor of the time of the expiration of their service. The Redemptioners were not furnished with duplicates of their contracts. They were sometimes, and could be, mortgaged, hired out for a shorter period, sold, and transferred like chattel by their masters. The Redemptioners belonging to the poor and most of them to the ignorant class, it is apparent that under these conditions they were at a great disadvantage against a rapacious master, who kept them in servitude after the expiration of their true contract time, claiming their services for a longer period.

" For many years the Redemptioners in Maryland had come principally from England and Ireland. The abuses of the system having become known in England, rigorous laws and measures were adopted in England for their better protection, and letters and articles appeared in the newspapers warning the poor people from entering into these contracts. The first and early immigration of Germans came into Maryland from Pennsylvania. From Lancaster County it extended into Baltimore, Harford, Frederick, and the western counties of our State. As wages advanced, the trade of shipping Redemptioners to the colony became highly lucrative. Large profits were made in a successful voyage with a full cargo of human beings, who, on their arrival here, were sold to the highest bidder for a term of years.

" The Dutch, who, in 1620, had sent the first cargo of negro slaves to this country, and had amassed great wealth in the pursuit of the negro slave-trade from distant Africa, discovered that it was less troublesome and equally remunerative to engage in a sort of a white slave-trade, by shipping Redemptioners from their own country, Germany, Switzerland, and adjoining countries, to the American colonies. The shipping merchants of Holland would send regular agents, or drummers, as we now would call them, who received one-half of a doubloon for every Redemptioner shipped by them into these colonies. These agents generally appeared in gaudy dress, with flourish of trumpets, and in glowing language depicted the wealth and happiness of the people of this country, whereof all could partake if they only would come here; that they did not need any money for their passage, as all they had to do was to sign a contract that on their arrival here they would pay for the same out of their first earnings. In this manner these agents would travel from village to village, deluding the poorest and most ignorant to follow them to the New Eldorado.

"Whenever such an agent had collected a sufficient number, he would take them personally to the shipping harbor in Holland. It was a gay crowd which travelled in this manner in wagons across the country. The horses and wagons were decorated with gay ribbons, and joyous songs were heard from the emigrants, who believed they were leaving toil and poverty to go to the fabulously rich America to enjoy the ease and plenty of this world's goods. This spirit was artificially kept up by the liberality of the agent until they were safely aboard the ship. From thence such a life of suffering, privation, and hardship commenced, that it seems incredible that the Christian nations of Europe and America should have permitted such a trade to flourish up to nearly the end of the first quarter of the present century. I myself know several very old persons yet living in Baltimore who came to this country in this manner. The contracts which these Redemptioners had to sign in Holland, and which few of them then understood, contained the proviso that if any passenger died on the voyage, the surviving members of the family, or the surviving Redemptioner passengers, would make good his loss. Thereby a wife who had lost her husband during the sea-voyage, or her children, on her arrival here would be sold for five years for her own voyage and additional five more years for the passage-money of her dead husband or dead children, although they may have died in the very beginning of the voyage. If there were no members of the family surviving, the time of the dead was added to the time of service of the surviving fellow-passengers. The effects and property of the dead were confiscated and kept by the captain. By this the shipping merchant and the captain of the vessel would gain by the death of a part of the passengers, for the dead did not require any more food and provision. It seems that many acted on this principle. The ships were often so overcrowded that a part of the passengers had to sleep on deck. Christoph Saur, in his petition to the governor of Pennsylvania in 1775, asserts that at times there were not more than twelve inches room for each passenger (I presume he means sleeping room below deck), and but half sufficient bread and water. Casper Wister, of Philadelphia, in 1752, writes, 'Last year a ship was twenty-four weeks at sea, and of the one hundred and fifty passengers on board thereof more than one hundred died of hunger and privation, and the survivors were imprisoned and compelled to pay the entire passage-money for themselves and the deceased.' In this year ten ships arrived in Philadelphia with five thousand passengers. One ship was seventeen weeks at sea, and about sixty passengers thereof died. Christoph Saur, in 1758, estimates that two thousand of the passengers on the fifteen ships which arrived that year died during the voyage. Heinrich Keppele, the first president of the German Society of Pennsylvania, writes in his diary that of the three hundred and twelve passengers on board of the ship wherein he crossed the ocean, two hundred and fifty died during the voyage. In February, 1775, Christoph Saur relates in his newspaper, ' Another ship has arrived. Of the four hundred passengers, not more than fifty are reported alive. They received their bread every two weeks. Some ate their portion in four, five, and six days, which should have lasted fifteen days. If they received no cooked victuals in eight days, their bread gave out the sooner, and as they had to wait until the fifteen days were over, they starved, unless they had money with which to buy of the mate flour at three pence sterling a pound, and a bottle of wine for seven kopstick thalers.' Then he relates how a man and his wife, who had ate their bread within eight days, crawled to the captain and begged him to throw them overboard, to relieve them of their misery, as they could not survive till bread-day. The captain refused to do it, and the mate in mockery gave them a bag filled with sand and coals. The man and his wife died of hunger before the bread-day arrived. But, notwithstanding, the survivors had to pay for the bread which the dead ought to have had. Pennsylvania, in 1765, at the instigation of the German Society, passed rigorous laws for the protection of the Redemptioners, but Maryland remained inactive until more than fifty years later."—*Hennighausen.*

In Pennsylvania this traffic in white people continued until about 1831, when public sentiment compelled it to be discontinued.

Fifty thousand white people were thus sold in Virginia, and many of them bartered for tobacco.

CHAPTER XVII

" THE subject of a national mint for the United States was first intro-duced by Robert Morris, the patriot and financier of the Revolution. As head of the finance department, Mr. Morris was instructed by Congress to prepare a report on the foreign coins then in circulation in the United States. On the 15th of January, 1782, he laid before Congress an expo-sition of the whole subject. Accompanying this report was a plan for Ameri-can coinage. But it was mainly through his efforts, in connection with Thomas Jefferson and Alexander Hamilton, that a mint was established in the early history of the Union of the States. On the 15th of April, 1790, Congress instructed the Secretary of the Treasury, Alexander Hamilton, to prepare and report a proper plan for the establishment of a national mint, and Mr. Hamilton presented his report at the next session. An act was framed establishing the mint, which finally passed both houses and received President Washington's approval April 2, 1792.

" A lot of ground was purchased on Seventh Street near Arch, and appropriations were made for erecting the requisite buildings. An old still-house, which stood on the lot, had first to be removed. In an account-book of that time we find an entry on the 31st of July, 1792, of the sale of some old materials of the still-house for seven shillings and sixpence, which ' Mr. Rittenhouse directed *should be laid out for punch* in laying the foundation-stone.'

" The first building erected in the United States for public use under the authority of the federal government was a structure for the United States Mint. This was a plain brick edifice, on the east side of Seventh Street near Arch, Philadelphia, Pennsylvania, the corner-stone of which was laid by David Rittenhouse, director of the mint, on July 31, 1792. In the following October operations of coining commenced. It was occupied for about forty years. On the 19th of May, 1829, an act was passed by Congress locating the United States Mint on its present site.

" The first coinage of the United States was silver half-dimes, in Octo-ber, 1792, of which Washington makes mention in his address to Congress, on November 6, 1792, as follows: ' There has been a small beginning in the coinage of half-dimes, the want of small coins in circulation calling the first attention to them.' The first metal purchased for coinage was six pounds of old copper at one shilling and three pence per pound, which was coined and delivered to the treasurer in 1793. The first deposit of silver bullion was made on July 18, 1794, by the Bank of Maryland. It consisted of 'coins of France,' amounting to eighty thousand seven hundred and fifteen dollars and seventy-three and a half cents. The first returns of silver coins to the treasurer was made on October, 15, 1794. The first deposit of gold bullion for coinage was made by Moses Brown, merchant, of Boston, on February 12, 1705; it was of gold ingots, worth two thousand two hundred and seventy-six dollars and seventy-two cents, which was paid for in silver coins.

" The first return of gold coinage was on July 31, 1795, and consisted of seven hundred and forty-four half-eagles. The first delivery of eagles was on September 22, same year, and consisted of four hundred pieces.

" Previous to the coinage of silver dollars at the Philadelphia Mint, in 1794, the following amusing incidents occurred in Congress while the emblems and devices proposed for the reverse field of that coin were being discussed.

" A member of the House from the South bitterly opposed the choice of the eagle, on the ground of its being the 'king of birds,' and hence neither proper nor suitable to represent a nation whose institutions and interests were wholly inimical to monarchical forms of government. Judge Thatcher playfully, in reply, suggested that perhaps a goose might suit the gentleman, as it was a rather humble and republican bird, and would also be serviceable in other respects, as the goslings would answer to place upon the dimes. This answer created considerable merriment, and the irate Southerner, conceiving the humorous rejoinder as an insult, sent a challenge to the judge, who promptly declined it. The bearer, rather astonished, asked, ' Will you be branded as a coward?' ' Certainly, if he pleases,' replied Thatcher; ' I always was one, and he knew it, or he would never have risked a challenge.' The affair occasioned much mirth, and, in due time, former existing cordial relations were restored between the parties, the irritable Southerner concluding there was nothing to be gained in fighting with one who fired nothing but jokes.

" Previous to the passage of the law by the federal government for regulating the coins of the United States, much perplexity arose from the use of no less than four different currencies or rates, at which one species of coin was recoined, in the different parts of the Union. Thus, in New Hampshire, Massachusetts, Maine, Rhode Island, Connecticut, Vermont, Virginia, and Kentucky the dollar was recoined at six shillings; in New York and North Carolina at eight shillings; in New Jersey, Pennsylvania, and Maryland at seven shillings and six pence; in Georgia and South Carolina at four shillings and eight pence. The subject had engaged the attention of the Congress of the old confederation, and the present system of the coins is formed upon the principles laid down in their resolution of 1786, by which the denominations

343

of money of account were required to be dollars (the dollar to be the unit), dimes or tenths, cents or hundredths, and mills or thousandths of a dollar. Nothing can be more simple or convenient than this decimal subdivision. The terms are proper because they express the proportions which they are intended to designate. The dollar was wisely chosen, as it corresponded with the Spanish coin, with which we had been long familiar."—*G. G. Evans's History of the United States Mint.*

TABLE OF THE DENOMINATIONS OF UNITED STATES MONEY

Standard Weight as established by Law

	Dwt.	Gr.
½ cent	3	12
10 mills make 1 cent	7	00
½ dime	0	$20\frac{4}{10}$
10 cents make 1 dime	1	$17\frac{6}{10}$
¼ dollar	4	8
½ dollar	8	16
10 dimes make 1 dollar	17	8
¼ eagle	2	$16\frac{3}{10}$
½ eagle	5	9
10 dollars make 1 eagle	10	18

The mills were imaginary and never coined. The old cents were made of copper, round, and about one inch in diameter and one-sixth of an inch in thickness. Silver was first coined into money eight hundred and sixty-nine years before Christ.

PIONEER BANKS

The pioneer act of the Legislature of Pennsylvania regulating banks was passed March 21, 1813, but Governor Snyder vetoed the bill. On March 21, 1814, this bill was "log-rolled" through the Legislature and became a law over Governor Snyder's veto. Previous to that time banks were organized under articles of association.

CURRENCY

" The best currency of those times was New York bank-notes, and the poorest those of the Western banks. Pennsylvania bank-notes had only a small circulation in the country, and held a place in popular estimation intermediate between the above. There was a discount on all these, ranging from one to twenty per cent. It was for the interest of the private bankers to circulate the notes on which there was the largest discount, and as a consequence the county was flooded with the bills of banks the locations of which were hardly known. Every business man had to keep a ' Bank-Note Detector,' revised and published monthly or weekly, on hand, and was not sure then that the notes he accepted would not be pronounced worthless by the next mail.

There was hardly a week without a bank failure, and nearly every man had bills of broken banks in his possession. To add to the perplexities of the situation, there were innumerable counterfeits which could with difficulty be distinguished from the genuine. Granting that the bank was good, and that the discount was properly figured, there was no assurance that the bill was what it purported to be. All this was a terrible annoyance and loss to the people, but it was a regular bonanza to the 'shaving-shops.' Even of the uncertain bank-notes there was not enough to do the business of the community. Most of the buying and selling was done on long credit, and occasionally a manufacturing firm, to ease itself along and relieve the necessities of the public, would issue a mongrel coin, which went by the name of ' pewter-inctum.' "

Up to 1860 the business of the country was greatly carried on by a currency of State banks, orders, and county orders, and the more you had of this money sometimes the poorer you were. We have now (1901) three thousand eight hundred and twenty-eight millionaires in the United States. Up to about 1860 there were not more than six or seven millionaires in the country. Eighty-seven per cent. of our millionaires under our improved conditions, have built their own fortunes, and most of these from extreme poverty.

CHAPTER XVIII

SCOTCH-IRISH

THE term " Scotch-Irish" is so frequently used, particularly in Pennsylvania, and is so little understood, even by those who claim such relationship, that I consider it appropriate in this place to explain its derivation. In the time of James I. of England, the Irish earls of Tyrone and Tyrconnell conspired against his government, fled from Ireland, were proclaimed outlaws, and their estates, consisting of about five hundred thousand acres of land, were seized by the crown. The king divided these lands into small tracts, and gave tracts to persons from his own country (Scotland), on the sole condition that each individual securing a tract of land should cross over into Ireland within four years and reside upon the land permanently. A second insurrection soon after gave occasion for another large forfeiture, and nearly six counties in the province of Ulster were confiscated and taken possession of by the officers of the crown. King James was a zealous sectarian, and his primary object was to root out the native Irish, who were all Catholics, hostile to his government, and almost continually plotting against it, and to populate Ireland with those from his own country (Scotland), whom he knew would be loyal to him.

The distance from Scotland to County Antrim, in Ireland, was but twenty miles. The lands offered by James free of cost were among the best and most productive in the Emerald Isle, though they had been made barren by the strifes of the times and the indolence of a degraded peasantry. Having the power of the government to encourage and protect them, the inducements offered to the industrious Scotch could not be resisted. Thousands went over. Many of them, though not lords, were lairds, or those who held lands direct from the crown, and all were men of enterprise and energy, and above the average in intelligence. They went to work to restore the land to fruitfulness, and to show the superiority of their habits and belief compared with those of the natives among whom they settled. They soon made to blossom as a rose the counties of Antrim, Armagh, Caven, Donegal, Down, Fermanagh, Londonderry, Monaghan, and Tyrone,—all names familiar to Northwestern Pennsylvania settlers.

These were the first Protestants to settle in Ireland, and they at once secured the ascendency in the counties in which they settled, and their descendants have maintained that ascendency to the present time against the efforts of the Church of England on the one hand and the Roman Catholic Church on the other. These Scots refused to intermarry with the Irish who surrounded them. The Scotch were Saxon in blood and Presbyterian in religion, while the Irish were Celtic in blood and Roman Catholic in religion. These were elements that would not coalesce; hence the races are as distinct in Ireland to-day, after a lapse of more than two hundred and fifty years, as when the Scotch first crossed over. The term Scotch-Irish is purely American. It is not used in Ireland; in the United States it is given to the Protestant emigrants from the north of Ireland, simply because they were descendants of the Scots who had in former times taken up their residence in Ireland.

But few Scotch-Irish emigrants found their way to the Province of Pennsylvania prior to 1719. Those that came in that year came from the north of Ireland. Subsequently the descendants of the Scots in Ireland were bitterly persecuted by the English government; hence thousands of them migrated to and settled in Pennsylvania. In 1729, thousands of Scotch-Irish arrived in Philadelphia from Ireland, as well as some English, Welsh, and Scotch people, many of whom were sold in servitude for a term of from three to seven years, for about forty dollars each, to pay passage-money or for their goods. For a further description of this form of slavery, see chapter on German Redemptioners, p. 310.

In September, 1736, one thousand Scotch-Irish families sailed from Belfast because of an inability to renew their land leases upon satisfactory terms, and the most of these people settled in the eastern and middle counties of Pennsylvania. By a change of residence they hoped to find an unrestrained field for the exercise of industry and skill, and for the enjoyment of religious opinions. They brought with them a hatred of oppression and a love of freedom that served much to give that independent tone to the sentiments of the people of the province which prevailed in their controversies with the English government years before these Scots entertained a thought of American political independence.

The Scotch-Irish who settled in the Cumberland Valley of Pennsylvania brought its fair lands under cultivation. They fought the savages and stood as a wall of fire against savage forays eastward. It is said that between 1771 and 1773 over twenty-five thousand of these Scotch-Irish were driven from Ireland by the rapacity of Irish lairds or landlords, and located either in that rich valley or west of the Allegheny Mountains in Pennsylvania. This was just before the Revolutionary War, and while the angry controversies that preceded it were taking place between the colonists and the English government. Hence these Pennsylvanians were in just the right frame of mind to make them espouse to a man the side of the patriots. A Tory was unheard of among them. They were found as military leaders in all times of danger, and were among the most prominent law-makers through and after the seven years' struggle for freedom and human rights. The Scotch-Irish in the United States have furnished Presidents, United States Senators, Congressmen, judges, and many others in civil as well as in all stations of life.

The pioneers of Northwestern Pennsylvania were made up principally of these Scotch-Irish or their descendants. I am indebted to the " History of Franklin County, Pennsylvania," 1876, for the data and facts contained in this article.

CHAPTER XIX

THE COMMON SCHOOL SYSTEM—ITS INCEPTION—INTRODUCTION INTO AMERICA —STATE EFFORT—HISTORY OF EDUCATION IN THE STATE—PROGRESS OF EDUCATION, ETC.

As an introduction to this chapter, I cannot do better than reproduce an extract from a speech delivered by myself before a convention of Jefferson County school directors,—viz. :

" GENTLEMEN OF THE CONVENTION,—I thank you for this honor. I highly appreciate it. As the representatives of thirty-two school districts, two hundred and forty schools, and twelve thousand pupils, we have met this day to consider modes and methods by which we can best advance the cause of education. This is wise and patriotic. Perhaps it might be well as an introduction to our work to review a little history as to the origin and present status of our common schools. Martin Luther, a German, was the first to advocate the public school system. This he did in 1524, ably, vigorously, and boldly. He asserted that the ' government, as the natural guardian of all the young, has the right to compel the people to support schools.' He further said, ' Now, nothing is more necessary than the training of those who are to come after us and bear rule.' The education of the young of all classes in free schools was one of the objects nearest Luther's heart. Scotland is the only other country of Europe that took an early interest in public school education. In 1560, John Knox urged the necessity of schools for the poor. These grand humane impulses of John Knox and other Scotch fathers have spread abroad, ' wide as the waters be,' only to germinate, bud, and bloom into the grandest social, theological, and political conditions ever attained by man. But it remained for the Puritan fathers of New England (America) to completely develop the common school system of our time. In New England education early made great progress. Under the eaves of their church the Puritans always built a school-house. As early as 1635, Boston had a school for ' the teaching of all children with us.' In 1647, Massachusetts made the support of schools compulsory and education universal and free by the enactment of the following law,—viz. : ' It is therefore ordered that every township in this jurisdiction, after the Lord hath increased them to the number of fifty householders, shall then forthwith appoint one within the town to teach all such children as shall resort to him to write and read, whose wages shall be paid either by the parents or masters of such children, or by the inhabitants in general by way of supply, as the major part of those who ordered the prudentials of the town shall appoint, provided those that send their children be not oppressed by paying much more than they can have them taught for in other towns.' In Connecticut, in 1665, every town that did not keep a school for three months in the year was liable to a fine. On April 1, A.D. 1834, one hundred and eighty-seven years later than the enactment of the common school law of Massachusetts, the law creating the common school system of Pennsylvania was approved by George Wolf, governor. Our second State superin-

Thomas H. Burrows

tendent of public instruction was appointed under this law. His name was Thomas H. Burrows.

"The foundation of our common school system was built by the convention to form a State constitution in 1790. The article as incorporated in that document reads as follows:

"'SECTION 1. The Legislature shall, as soon as conveniently may be, provided by law for the establishment of schools throughout the State, in such a manner that the poor may be taught gratis.

"'SECTION 2. The arts and sciences shall be promoted in one or more seminaries of learning.'

"This educational article was also incorporated into the constitution of 1838. But little effort was made under the first constitution by legislative bodies to establish schools under the first section. Their only aim seemed to be to aid the churches and neighborhood schools to carry on the work they had been doing for a hundred years. The pioneer effort by the Legislature seems to have been in 1794, when, on December 8, 1794, a committee was appointed by the House to report a proper mode of carrying into effect that part of the governor's message in regard to schools. The committee reported as follows:

"'Resolved, That schools may be established throughout the State, in such a manner that the poor may be taught gratis.

"'Resolved, That one-fifth part of the expense necessary to support the masters of said schools be paid out of the general funds of the State.

"'Resolved, That the remaining four-fifths of the said expense be paid in each county, respectively, by means of a county tax.

"'Resolved, That the said schools be put under the direction of trustees in each county, subject to such limitations and regulations, as to the distribution of their funds, the appointment of masters, and their general arrangements, as shall be provided by law.

"'Resolved, That the schools thus established shall be free schools, and that at least spelling, reading, writing, and arithmetic shall be taught therein.

"'Resolved, That ten thousand dollars a year be appropriated out of the funds of this Commonwealth to encourage the establishment of academies, in which grammar, the elements of mathematics, geography, and history shall be taught.

"'Resolved, That the said sum be apportioned amongst the city and several counties of the State in proportion to their respective population.

"'Resolved, That whenever a sum sufficient, with the addition of the sums proposed to be given by the public, to support an academy for the purpose aforesaid shall have been subscribed, or contributed, the additional sum of one hundred dollars a year shall be given out of the public treasury in aid of such academy.

"'Resolved, That when the number of academies in any county shall be so great that the sum to which such county is entitled becomes insufficient to afford one hundred dollars to each, it shall be divided by the trustees aforesaid among the whole of such academies, in proportion to the number of masters employed and scholars taught, and the length of time in each during which each academy is so kept and supported.

"'Resolved, That whenever a sum is subscribed and contributed sufficient, if added to the income of any of the inferior schools, to procure the instruction contemplated to be given in the academies, such school shall become an academy and receive the additional bounty of one hundred dollars as aforesaid, subject to a reduction in the manner aforesaid.'

"A bill was prepared in accordance with these resolutions and passed both branches, but was lost in conference committee. This was forty years before the enactment of 1834."

THE PIONEER ACT

On March 1, 1802, Governor McKean approved the pioneer law of this State making a provision for the education of the poor, the title being "An Act to provide for the Education of Poor Children gratis."

It was found that the act of 1802 was unsatisfactory, and, in the hope of betterment, an act of 1804 was passed entitled "An Act to provide for the more Effectual Education of the Children of the Poor gratis."

Agitation and discussion over this law resulted in the act of 1809, better drawn, with the same title and aim.

THE LAW OF 1809

"AN ACT TO PROVIDE FOR THE EDUCATION OF THE POOR GRATIS

"SECTION 1. *Be it enacted by the Senate and House of Representatives of the Commonwealth of Pennsylvania in General Assembly met, and it is hereby enacted by the authority of the same,* That it shall be the duty of the Commissioners of the several counties within this Commonwealth, at the time of issuing their precepts to the assessors, annually to direct and require the assessor of each and every township, ward, and district to receive from the parents the names of all the children between the ages of five and twelve years who reside therein, and whose parents are unable to pay for their schooling; and the Commissioners when they hold appeals shall hear all persons who may apply for alterations or additions of names in the said list, and make all such alterations as to them shall appear just and reasonable, and agreeably to the true intent and meaning of this act; and after adjustment they shall transmit a correct copy thereof to the respective assessor, requiring him to inform the parents of the children therein contained that they are at liberty to send them to the most convenient school free of expense; and the said assessor, for any neglect of the above duty, shall forfeit and pay the sum of five dollars, to be sued for by any person, and recovered as debts of that amount are now recoverable, and to be paid into the county treasury, for county purposes: *Provided always,* That the names of no children whose education is otherwise provided for shall be received by the assessors of any township or district.

"SECTION 2. *And be it further enacted by the authority aforesaid,* That the said assessor shall send a list of the names of the children aforesaid to the teachers of schools within his township, ward, or district, whose duty it shall be to teach all such children as may come to their schools in the same manner as other children are taught, and each teacher shall keep a day-book, in which he shall enter the number of days each child entitled to the provisions of this act shall be taught, and he shall also enter in said book the amount of all stationery furnished for the use of said child, from which book he shall make out his account against the county, on oath or affirmation, agreeably to the

352

usual rates of charging for tuition in the said school, subject to the examination and revision of the trustees of the school where there are any; but where there are no trustees, to three reputable subscribers to the school; which account, after being so examined or revised, he shall present to the County Commissioners, who, if they approve thereof, shall draw their order on the county treasurer for the amount, which he is hereby authorized and directed to pay of any moneys in the treasury.

"Approved—the fourth day of April, one thousand eight hundred and nine.

"SIMON SNYDER."

Each of these acts compelled parents to publish to the world their poverty and to send their children to school as paupers.

Governor Joseph Ritner

The method of organizing schools and hiring masters under these laws was as follows: A school-meeting was called by a notice posted in the district. The inhabitants then met and elected in their own way three of their number to act as a committee or as trustees with power to hire a master or mistress, and this committee executed a supervision over the school. A rate bill was always made out by the master and handed to the committee, who collected the moneys and paid it to the master.

The pioneer and early modes of school discipline were the cat-o'-nine-tails and the rod, carrying the offender on the back of a pupil and then flogging him, setting the boys with the girls and the girls with the boys, fastening a split stick to the ear or the nose, laying the scholar over the knee and applying the ferule to the part on which he sat. These punishments lasted for years after the common schools came into use. For the benefit of young teachers I will give the mode of correction. The masters invariably kept what was called toms, or, more vulgarly, cat-o'nine-tails, all luck being in odd numbers. This instrument of torture was an oaken stick about twelve inches long to which was attached a piece of raw-hide cut into strips, twisted while wet, and then dried. It was freely used for correction, and those who were thus corrected did not soon forget it, and not a few carried the marks during life. Another and no less cruel instrument was a green cow-hide. Comment upon the above is useless, as the words cruelty and barbarity will suggest themselves to the minds of all who read it. For our text-books we had Dilworth's and the " United States Speller," and our readers were the good old Bible and Testament. The " Western Calculator" was all the arithmetic that was in use, and the one who got through the " rule of three" was called tolerably good in figures, and the lucky wight who got through the book was considered a graduate in mathematics. Grammar and geography were not taught in common schools, being considered higher branches.

Not one of the governors of the State during the time the law of 1809 was in force believed it met the requirements of the constitution, hence in 1824 an act was passed repealing it and another one substituted. The new act was violently opposed, never went into effect, was repealed in 1826, and the act of 1809 was re-enacted. The policy enforced in our State for fifty years after the Revolutionary War was the endowment of academies and the free instruction of poor children in church and neighborhood schools.

Governor Wolf, in 1833–34, made education the leading topic of his message. Among other things he said,—

" To provide by law ' for the establishment of schools throughout the State, and in such a manner that the poor may be taught gratis,' is one of the public measures to which I feel it to be my duty now to call your attention, and most solemnly to press upon your consideration. Our apathy and indifference in reference to this subject becomes the more conspicuous when we reflect that whilst we are expending millions for the physical condition of the State, we have not hitherto appropriated a single dollar that is available for the intellectual improvement of its youth, which, in a moral and political point of view, is of tenfold more consequence, either as respects the moral influence of the State or its political power and safety.

" According to the returns of the last census, we have in Pennsylvania five hundred and eighty-one thousand one hundred and eighty children under the age of fifteen years, and one hundred and forty-nine thousand and eighty-nine between the ages of fifteen and twenty years, forming an aggregate of seven hundred and thirty thousand two hundred and sixty-nine juvenile persons of both sexes under the age of twenty years, most of them requiring more or less instruction. And yet with all this numerous youthful population growing up around us, who, in a few years, are to be our rulers and our lawgivers, the defenders of our country and the pillars of the State, and upon whose education will depend in great measure the preservation of our liberties and the safety of the republic, we have neither schools established for their instruction nor provision made by law for establishing them as enjoined by the constitution."

In 1827 William Audenreid, then a senator from Schuylkill County, introduced a bill into the Senate, the title of which was, " To provide a Fund in support of a General System of Education in Pennsylvania." This bill

Governor George Wolf

passed the Senate that session, but was defeated in the House, but being urged and pressed every session it became a law on April 2, 1831. This law entitled Senator Audenreid to be called the author of our school system. The law read as follows:

" SECTION 1. That there shall be and there hereby is established a fund, to be denominated a Common School Fund, and the Secretary of the Commonwealth, the Auditor-General, and the Secretary of the Land-Office shall be Commissioners thereof, who, or a majority of them, in addition to the duties they now perform, shall receive and manage such moneys and other things as shall pertain to such fund, in the most advantageous manner, and shall receive and hold to the use of said fund all such gifts, grants, and donations as may be made; and that said Commissioners shall keep a correct record of their proceedings, which, together with all papers and documents relative to said fund, shall be kept and preserved in the office of the Auditor-General.

"Section 2. That from and after the passage of this act, all moneys due and owing this Commonwealth by the holders of all unpatented lands; also all moneys secured to the Commonwealth by mortgages or liens on land for the purchase money of the same; also all moneys paid to the State Treasurer on any application hereafter entered, or any warrant hereafter granted for land, as also fees received in the land-office, as well as all moneys received in pursuance of the provisions of the fourth section of an act entitled 'An Act to increase the County Rates and Levies for the Use of the Commonwealth,' approved the twenty-fifth day of March, 1831, be and the same are hereby transferred and assigned to the Common School Fund; and that at the expiration of twelve months after the passage of this act, and regularly at the expiration of every twelve months thereafter, the State Treasurer shall

Pioneer school-house

report to the said Commissioners the amount of money thus received by him during the twelve months last preceding, together with a certificate of the amount thereof, and that the same is held by the Commonwealth for the use of the Common School Fund, at an interest of five per cent.

"Section 3. That the interest of the moneys belonging to said fund shall be added to the principal as it becomes due, and the whole amount thereof shall be held by the Commonwealth, and remain subject to the provisions of an act entitled 'An Act relative to the Pennsylvania Canal and Railroad,' approved the twenty-second of April, 1829, until the interest thereof shall amount to the sum of one hundred thousand dollars annually, after which the interest shall be annually distributed and applied to the support of common schools throughout this Commonwealth, in such a manner as shall hereafter be provided by law."

In 1834 there were four thousand school-cabins like the accompanying illustration in Pennsylvania, built on the neighborhood plan under the law of 1809.

About those little school-houses were formed many ties which bound men and women together as friends in long succeeding years. Around those little temples of learning I have seen

> " The hoop, the bow and arrow,
>   The soaring of the kite and swing,
> The humming of the 'over-ball,'
>   And the marbles in the ring;
> The sleds, the rope, and sliding-boards,
>   The races down the yard,
> And the war of snow-ball armies,
>   The victors and the scarred."

The creation of the common schools in Pennsylvania was not the work of any one man or set of men, nor was it imported from any other State. It

Hon. Thaddeus Stevens

was the outgrowth of freedom. In a book like mine I cannot enumerate all the glorious workers in the fight. The Pennsylvania Society for the Promotion of Public Schools, organized in Philadelphia in 1827, was a great factor in the work. Senator Audenreid, Dr. Anderson, and Senator Smith, of Delaware County; N. B. Fetterman, of Bedford; Samuel Breck, a senator from Philadelphia; and Thaddeus Stevens, all deserve to be forever remembered for their able and untiring labor in this direction.

The pioneer school in the United States for the education of teachers was the model school of Philadelphia, established and opened in 1838. The finest and most costly educational structures in the world are the Girard College buildings in Philadelphia. The pioneer law enacted in the interest of female education was by New York State in 1818. The first female assistant in a seminary was in 1822.

In the session of 1834, Samuel Breck, a senator from Philadelphia, was made chairman of a joint committee on education. The members of this committee on the part of the Senate were Samuel Breck, Charles B. Penrose, William Jackson, Almon H. Read, and William Boyd; of the House, Samuel Anderson, William Patterson, James Thompson, James Clarke, John Wiegand, Thomas H. Crawford, and Wilmer Worthington. This committee secured all possible information on the subject from all sources. The author of the bill as passed was Samuel Breck. It was but little discussed and met with but little opposition in the Legislature.

COMMON SCHOOL NOTICE

" For the purpose of settling controversies, of collecting and imparting information connected with the Common School System, so as to produce harmony and vigor in every department of its operations, the Superintendent will be at the county towns mentioned in the following lists on the days therein designated at ten o'clock A.M.

" Directors, Teachers, and all others who may have business to transact with the Superintendent, under the 4th paragraph of 10th section of the school law, will meet him at their proper county towns on the days respectively named. As the chain of appointments now made will not admit of more than one day's delay at each place, early and punctual attendance is earnestly requested.

" Beaver, Wednesday, August 23. Butler, Friday, August 25. Mercer, Monday, August 28. Meadville, Wednesday, August 30. Erie, Saturday, September 2. Franklin, Monday, September 11. Brookville, Thursday, September 14.

" THOS. H. BURROWS,

" *Superintendent Common Schools.*

"SECRETARY'S OFFICE, HARRISBURG, July 18, 1837."

THE LAW OF 1834 AND ITS WORKINGS

" WHEREAS, It is enjoined by the constitution, as a solemn duty which cannot be neglected without a disregard of the moral and political safety of the people; and

" WHEREAS, The fund for the common school purposes, under the act of the 2d of April, 1831, will, on the 4th of April next, amount to the sum of $546,563.72, and will soon reach the sum of $2,000,000, when it will produce at five per cent an increase of $100,000, which, by said act, is to be paid for the support of common schools; and

"WHEREAS, Provisions should be made by law for the distribution of the benefits of this fund to the people of the respective counties of the Commonwealth; therefore,

"SECTION 1. *Be it enacted, etc.,* That the city and county of Philadelphia, and every other county in this Commonwealth, shall each form a school division, and that every ward, township, and borough, within the several school divisions, shall each form a school district.

"SECTION 2. It shall be the duty of the sheriff of each county, thirty days previous to the third Friday in September of the current year, 1834, to give notice, by proclamation, to the citizens of each school district to hold elections in their respective townships, wards, and boroughs at the places where they hold their elections for supervisors, town councils, and constables, to choose six citizens, of each school district, to serve as school directors of said districts respectively; which elections shall, on the said day, be conducted and held in the same manner as elections for supervisors and constables are by law held and conducted; and on the day of the next annual election of supervisors in the respective townships, and of constables in the respective cities of the Commonwealth, a new election for directors shall take place in the said townships, boroughs, and cities, at which election, and annually thereafter at that time, and in manner and form aforesaid, two directors shall be chosen, who shall serve for three years; the sheriff giving thirty days' notice previous to such election."

The law of 1831, of Senator Audenreid, is the foundation-stone, and that of 1834 and the act of 1837 completed our common school system, erroneously called "the free school system."

The pioneer and early State appropriations to the common schools were as follows: 1835 and 1836, each, $75,000; 1837, $700,000; 1838, 1839, 1840, each, $108,919; 1841, $330,000; 1842, $200,000; 1843, $250,000; 1844, 1845, 1846, 1847, 1848, 1849, 1850, 1851, 1852, 1853, each, $200,000; 1854, 1855, each, $230,000; 1856, $231,500; 1857, 1858, 1859, 1860, 1861, each, $280,000.

TEACHER'S INSTITUTE AND ACADEMIES

The pioneer Teachers' Institute in the United States was held in Connecticut in 1839; in New York in 1842; and in Massachusetts and Ohio in 1845.

The pioneer institute in Pennsylvania was in Lawrence County for one week, October 27, 1851.

In Crawford County a female seminary was incorporated at Meadville, in 1802. In 1806 the State gave one thousand dollars.

At New Castle, Lawrence County, a female seminary was chartered in 1838, and flourished for ten years.

The Tioga County Academy was incorporated in 1817, and received State aid.

Smethport Academy, in McKean County, was chartered in 1829, but not opened until 1837.

Mercer Academy was chartered in 1811.

Potter County Academy was incorporated in 1838.

Venango Academy was chartered in 1812; building erected in 1815.

Warren County Academy was chartered in 1822. The first building was one story. The second building was erected in 1834–35.

It was the rule in this wilderness for any boy who wished an education to attend the winter term of school at home until fit to teach a country school, then to teach in winter and work in summer until he could earn and save enough money to attend an academy. Well, but how did he get to the academy? Why he simply walked a hundred miles or more if necessary.

CHAPTER XX

IN 1840 there were in the northwest purchase but nine erected and complete counties,—to wit, Butler, Crawford, Jefferson, McKean, Mercer, Potter, Tioga, Venango, and Warren. Butler County had twenty-two thousand three hundred and seventy-one people, and the county contained fifteen towns, townships, and boroughs,—to wit, Buffalo, Clearfield, Donegal, Centre, Parker, Venango, Mercer, Middlesex, Cherry, Slippery Rock, Butler Borough, Butler, Muddy Creek, Conoquenessing, and Cranberry. In that year Butler County had three charcoal furnaces, with an output of six hundred and twenty-five tons. The amount of coal mined in the county was one hundred and two thousand three hundred bushels; number of miners employed, thirty-one. Retail stores in the county, fifty-five, with a capital of $172,850. Value of hats and caps manufactured in the county, $3750. Number of tanneries, twenty-two; number of men employed, thirty-one. Number of distilleries, thirteen. Number of breweries, two. Number of printing-offices, two. Number of oil-mills, four. Number of saw-mills, sixty-four. Number of grist-mills, fifty-four.

CRAWFORD COUNTY

In 1840 Crawford County had thirty-seven thousand seven hundred and twenty-four people, and the county contained twenty-seven towns, townships, and boroughs,—to wit, South Shenango, Greenwood, Venango, Fallowfield, Randolph, Woodcock, Vernon, Mead, Summerhill, Sadsbury, Meadville Borough, Sparta, Oil Creek, Richmond, Rome Cossawago, Beaver, Wayne, Bloomfield, Rockdale, Athens, Troy, Hayfield, Spring, Conneaut, Fairfield, and North Shenango. In that year Crawford County had two charcoal furnaces. The coal output was two thousand tons; number of miners employed, six. Retail stores in the county, sixty-two, with a capital of $196,200. Value of hats and caps manufactured, four thousand. Number of tanneries, fourteen; number of men employed twenty-six. Number of distilleries, fourteen. Number of breweries, one. Number of paper-mills, two. Number of printing-offices, two. Number of grist-mills, thirty-nine. Number of saw-mills, one hundred and twenty-nine. Number of oil-mills, two. These were flax-seed mills, making linseed oil. These mills were quite numerous in Northwestern Pennsylvania, and an industry of importance and profit.

HISTORY OF NORTHWESTERN PENNSYLVANIA

JEFFERSON COUNTY

In 1840 Jefferson County had seven thousand two hundred and fifty-three people, and the county contained thirteen towns, townships, and boroughs,—to wit, Brookville Borough, Rose, Washington, Snyder, Ridgway, Eldred, Tionesta, Barnett, Jenks, Pine Creek, Porter, Perry, and Young. The output of coal that year was two thousand five hundred tons; number of miners employed, two. The total sale of furs and pelts was $1029. Number of tanneries, six; number of men employed, seven. Number of distilleries, two. Number of grist-mills, fourteen. Number of saw-mills, sixty-eight. Number of stores, nineteen. Maple sugar, twenty seven thousand and sixty-seven pounds. Value of lumber output, $50,603.

M'KEAN COUNTY

In 1840 McKean County had two thousand nine hundred and seventy-five people, and the county contained nine towns, townships, and boroughs, —to wit, Keating, Ceres, Bradford, Corydon, Sergeant, Liberty, Norwich, Shippen, and Hamilton. The amount of coal mined that year was one thousand bushels; number of miners employed, two. Salt manufactured, one thousand bushels; number of men employed, two. Number of retail stores, ten; amount of capital invested, $28,100. Total value of lumber, $88,700. Sale of furs and pelts, $963. Number of tanneries, two; number of men employed, four. Number of grist-mills, nine. Number of saw-mills, thirty-three. Maple sugar manufactured, sixty-nine thousand seven hundred and fifty pounds.

MERCER COUNTY

In 1840 Mercer County had thirty-two thousand eight hundred and seventy-three people, and the county contained nineteen towns, townships, and boroughs,—to wit, Springfield, West Salem, Pymatuning, Delaware, Wolf Creek, Hickory, Slippery Rock, Salem, West Greenville, Mahoning, Neshannock, New Castle Borough, Shenango, Lackawannock, Cool Spring, Sandy Lake, French Creek, Dandy Creek, and Mercer Borough. In that year Mercer County had four charcoal furnaces; total output of iron, fifty-nine tons. Total output of coal mined, one hundred and forty-one thousand eight hundred and sixty tons; number of men employed, twenty-one. Maple sugar manufactured, one hundred and twenty-one thousand two hundred and fourteen pounds. Retail stores, ninety-three; capital invested, $214,893. Value of hats and caps manufactured, $6770. Number of tanneries, thirty-five; number of men employed, one hundred and thirty-one. Number of distilleries, twelve. Number of printing-offices, one. Number of grist-mills, seventy-three. Number of saw-mills, one hundred and twenty-eight. Number of oil-mills, two.

POTTER COUNTY

In 1840 Potter County had three thousand three hundred and seventy-one people, and the county contained fifteen towns, townships, and boroughs,— to wit, Eulalia, Harrison, Bingham, Ulysses, Alleghany, Genesee, Sharon, Hebron, Oswego, Clara, Sweden, Wharton, Roulette, Hector, and Pike. In that year the output of coal was one hundred bushels. Maple sugar manufactured, one hundred and three thousand one hundred and ninety-nine pounds. Retail stores, six; capital invested, $11,700. Value of lumber products, $25,038. Number of tanneries, one; number of men employed, two. Number of printing-offices, one. Number of grist-mills, eight. Number of saw-mills, thirty. Value of furs and pelts, $855.

TIOGA COUNTY

In 1840 Tioga County had fifteen thousand four hundred and ninety-eight people, and contained twenty-one towns, townships, and boroughs,—to wit, Jackson, Liberty, Union, Middlebury, Morris, Delmar, Tioga, Lawrence, Elkland, Farmington, Chatham, Westfield, Rutland, Sullivan, Richmond, Covington, Charleston, Shippen, Deerfield, Brookfield, and Gaines. In that year the output of coal was thirty-six thousand bushels; number of men employed, one hundred and four. Maple sugar manufactured, one hundred and eighty-one thousand and sixty-four pounds. Retail stores, fifty two; capital invested, $111,800. Value of lumber produced, $37,189. Number of tanneries, thirteen; number of men employed, thirty-three. Number of distilleries, two. Number of printing-offices, two. Number of grist-mills, twenty-six. Number of saw-mills, one hundred and forty-five. Number of oil-mills, one. Value of pelts and furs, $1415.

VENANGO COUNTY

In 1840 Venango County had seventeen thousand nine hundred people, and contained twenty towns, townships, and boroughs,—to wit, Scrubgrass, Irwin, Sandy Creek, Paint, Farmington, Tionesta, Corn Planter, French Creek, Cherry Tree, Richland, Beaver, Sugar Creek, Plum, Pine Grove. Alleghany, Canal, Rockland, Cranberry, Elk, and Franklin Borough. In that year Venango County had sixteen charcoal furnaces. One bloomary, with an output of cast-iron of six thousand five hundred and forty-six tons, and of bar iron of two hundred and eight tons. Coal mined, thirty thousand three hundred tons; number of men employed, fourteen. Maple sugar manufactured, seventeen thousand five hundred and sixty-one pounds. Retail stores, forty-three; capital invested, $120,000. Lumber products, $24,204. Value of hats and caps manufactured, $1200; number of people employed, five. Number of tanneries, seventeen; number of men employed, twenty. Number of distilleries, four; number of men employed, four. Number of printing-offices, one. Number of grist-mills, forty-nine. Number of saw-mills, fifty-nine. Number of oil-mills, two. Value of furs and pelts, $746.

In 1840 Warren County had nine thousand two hundred and seventy-eight people, and contained fifteen towns, townships, and boroughs,—to wit, Warren Borough, Connewango, Broken Straw, Columbus, Sugar Grove, Pine Grove, Freehold, Elk, Spring Creek, Deerfield, Kinzua, Pleasant, Southwest, Sheffield, and Limestone. In that year Warren County had three charcoal furnaces, with an output of thirty tons. Coal mined, seven hundred and fifty bushels; miners employed, one, in Elk Township. Maple sugar manufactured, ninety-one thousand three hundred and eighteen pounds. Retail stores, twenty-eight; capital invested, $65,750. Value of lumber produced, $88,062. Furs and pelts, $513. Hats, caps, and bonnets manufactured, $2200. Number of tanneries, six; number of men employed, ten. Number of printing-offices, two. Number of grist-mills, sixteen. Number of saw-mills, one hundred and twenty-three. Number of barrels of flour manufactured, five hundred.

NEGRO SLAVERY IN NORTHWESTERN PENNSYLVANIA. CENSUS RETURNS

County.	1810.	1820.	1830.
Butler	..	..	4
Crawford	2	..	..
Jefferson	..	..	1
McKean	1	..	..
Mercer	3	1	6
Potter	..	.	..
Tioga	..	..	..
Venango	..	..	3
Warren	..	..	..

In 1809 James G. Heron, who lived in Franklin, had two slaves, both negro girls.

In 1807 Collender Irvine had one slave, Black Tom, in Warren County.

In 1802 William Hillis Wells settled near Wellsboro, Tioga County, and brought with him four slaves.

William Ayers had one slave in Potter County from 1808 to 1814.

In 1808 there were six hundred and five negro slaves in Pennsylvania. The pioneer court records of Crawford County contained such items as the following: "William Davis, farmer, of Mead Township, Crawford County, returns to the Clerk of the Peace of Crawford County, one female mulatto child, Dinah, born on the 25th of April last, of his negro woman Vine, October 28, 1802."

The Crawford *Messenger*, of December 24, 1831, has an advertisement for the sale of a colored boy, who is twelve years old.

The negro slave in Jefferson County in 1830 was named Sam, and was a miller. He belonged to James Parks, whose mill was near where Christ's brewery now is. In 1824 Sam was assessed at fifty dollars. In 1829 he was assessed at one hundred dollars.

In 1833 one negro slave was assessed in Brookville to William Jack,—to wit, one boy of color, worth forty dollars.

In 1836 Rev. Jesse Smith, a Presbyterian minister, living one mile north from where Corsica, Jefferson County, now is, was assessed with one mulatto, valuation fifty dollars.

The pioneer slave in Mercer County was in Sandy Lake Township in 1801. The pioneer will recorded in Mercer County was that of John Calvin, in 1804, of Salem Township. In this will he bequeathed a mulatto to his wife. John Sheakley migrated from Gettysburg, Pennsylvania, to Sandy Creek Township, Mercer County, in 1804, bringing with him four negro slaves,—viz., Sam, Steve, Phœbe, and Hannah. Phœbe had two children born in slavery in Mercer County,—to wit, Ben and Rose. John Sheakley died in 1816, and in his will he bequeathed a mulatto girl to his wife; all of his other slaves were then free. John Young lived on Indian Run, in Springfield Township. He owned slaves; how many is not known. In his will of April 20, 1825, he says, " I do will that Peg, the old wench, is to be supported out of my farm, left to John and David." Peg had two children born in slavery in Mercer County,—to wit, Robert Johnson and Sallie Johnson. Robert worked at shoe-making after his freedom.

PIONEER ADVERTISEMENT IN PENNSYLVANIA IN SLAVERY DAYS

" 2 S. (SHILLINGS) REWARD

" Ran away on the 2d inst. negro man John, about 22; also negro girl named Flora, about 18, slender made, speaks bad English and a little French. Has a scar on her upper lip and letters branded on her breast. Whoever secures the runaways in any place where their master can get them shall have the above reward and reasonable charges paid by

" JOHN PATTON.

" CENTRE FURNACE, MIFFLIN COUNTY, July 26, 1799."

Thank God this cruel slavery, which existed once in Pennsylvania, is forever wiped out in these United States! There is now no master's call, no driver's lash, no auction-block on which to sell, and no bloodhounds to hunt men and women fugitives not from justice, but fugitives for justice. Thank God for John Brown, and may " his soul go marching on!"

John Brown was born in Torrington, Connecticut, May 9, 1800. He was found in this wilderness June 21, 1820, and settled in Richmond Township, Crawford County, in 1826, and engaged in tanning, farming, and sheep-raising avocations.

In 1832 he married Mary A. Day, of Meadville. He was a strict Presbyterian until the day of his execution. The year 1800 began with nine hundred thousand slaves in the United States. The year 1900 closed without one.

REVOLUTIONARY SOLDIERS

Patriots of the Revolutionary War settled in every county in Northwestern Pennsylvania. In the counties where the "donation lands" were located, they settled in quite large numbers. I deem it my duty to the descendants of these patriots to give the pay received by their ancestors for services in the Continental army.

The first pay schedule was set forth in the Act of April 12, 1785, which fixed the pay of an infantry private at four dollars a month. By the Act of April 30, 1790, the pay was reduced to three dollars a month. The Act of January 1, 1795, again made it four dollars, at which it remained for three years, but by the Act of July 17, 1798, when we were preparing for a war with France, it was raised to five dollars. It remained at this for fourteen years.

By the Act of December 12, 1812, when an army had to be raised for the second war with England, the pay was raised to eight dollars. It remained at this during the war, but as soon as peace came the Act of March 3, 1815, reduced it to five dollars again. It remained at this for eighteen years, when the Act of March 2, 1833, raised it to six dollars. The Act of July 7, 1838, raised it to seven dollars, where it remained for sixteen years, and all through the Mexican War.

In 1785 the pay of a lieutenant-colonel commanding—ranking with a colonel now—was only sixty dollars a month.

In 1785 a lieutenant-colonel received fifty dollars a month.

In 1785 a major received forty-five dollars a month.

In 1785 a captain was paid thirty-five dollars a month.

In 1785 a first lieutenant received twenty-six dollars a month.

In 1785 a second lieutenant received twenty dollars a month.

INCIDENTS AND ANECDOTES

On October 23, 1819, was the "dark day." Between nine and ten o'clock in the morning the darkness was so great that the pioneer had to light his old lamp or blaze his pitch-pine knot.

In January, 1828, there was a great flood; and also a great one on February 10, 1832.

In 1816, or the year without a summer, frost occurred in every month. Ice formed half an inch thick in May. Snow fell to the depth of three inches in June. Ice was formed to the thickness of a common window-glass on July 5. Indian corn was so frozen that the greater part was cut in August and dried for fodder; and the pioneers supplied from the corn of 1815 for the seeding of the spring of 1817.

In 1809 Fulton patented the steamboat.

The pioneer steam-vessels that made regular trips across the Atlantic Ocean were the "Sirius" and "Great Western" in the year 1830.

The pioneer use of gas for practical illumination was in 1802.

The pioneer mill to make finished cloth from raw cotton was erected in Waltham, Massachusetts, in 1813.

In 1807 wooden clocks were made by machinery.

The anthracite coal business was established about 1820.

In 1836 matches were patented.

"The first practical friction matches were made in 1827 by an English apothecary named Walker, who coated splints of card-board with sulphur and tipped them with a mixture of sulphate of antimony, chlorate of potash, and gum. A box of eighty-four matches sold for one cent, a piece of glass-paper being furnished with it for obtaining ignition. In 1830 a London man named Jones devised a species of match which was a little roll of paper soaked in chlorate of potash and sugar, with a thin glass globule filled with sulphuric acid attached to one end. The globule being broken, the acid acted upon the potash and sugar, producing fire. Phosphorus matches were first introduced on a commercial scale in 1833, and after that improvements were rapid.

"The modern lucifer match combines in one instrument arrangements for creating a spark, catching it on tinder, and starting a blaze,—steps requiring separate operations in primitive contrivances. It was in 1836 that the first United States patent for friction matches was issued. Splints for them were made by sawing or splitting blocks of wood into slivers slightly attached at the base. These were known as 'slab' or 'block' matches, and they are in use in parts of this country to-day."

The pioneer strike in America was that of the journeymen boot-makers of Philadelphia in 1796. The men struck, or "turned out," as they phrased it, for an increase of wages. After two weeks' suspension of trade their demands were granted, and this success gained them greater strength and popularity, so that when they "turned out" in 1798, and again in 1799, for further increases, they were still successful and escaped indictment.

Vulcanized rubber was patented in 1838.

In 1840 Daguerre first made his pictures.

The express business was started about 1840.

The pioneer telegram was sent in 1845.

The pioneer steamer to cross the Atlantic was built in New York in 1818 by Francis Picket. The vessel was called the "Savannah." In the trip she carried seventy-five tons of coal and twenty-five cords of wood. She left Savannah, Georgia, in May, 1819, and arrived at Liverpool in June, 1819. She used steam eighteen of the twenty-six days.

Before "stocks" were invented oxen had to be thrown and tied and the shoes nailed on while down.

In 1811 a furious tornado swept across this wilderness.

On March 9, 1828, an earthquake shock was felt in Northwestern Pennsylvania.

The earliest recorded tornado in the United States was in 1794. It passed north of Brookville, in what is now Heath and other townships, and extended to Northford, Connecticut.

In June, about the year 1818, a terrible hail-storm swept through this region and extended its ravages several miles, killing and destroying the largest pine-trees, leaving them standing as dead. The width of this storm was about half a mile.

On June 6, 1806, there was a total eclipse of the sun. Fowls went to roost and bees hastened to their hives. The pioneers and Indians were greatly alarmed.

Between the hours of three and seven o'clock in the morning of December 16, 1811, two distinct shocks of earthquake startled the pioneers of Northwestern Pennsylvania. The violence was such as to shake their log cabins.

PIONEER THANKSGIVING DAYS

The first recorded Thanksgiving was the Hebrew feast of the Tabernacles.

The New England Thanksgiving dates from 1633, when the Massachusetts Bay colony set apart a day for thanksgiving.

The first national Thanksgiving proclamations were by Congress during the Revolutionary War.

The first great American Thanksgiving day was in 1784, for the declaration of peace. There was one more national Thanksgiving in 1789, and no other till 1862, when President Lincoln issued a national proclamation for a day of thanksgiving.

The pioneer Thanksgiving day in Northwestern Pennsylvania, was on the last Thursday of November, 1819, by proclamation of Governor Findlay.

In 1803 the name Keystone was first applied to the State. This was in a printed political address to the people. Pennsylvania was the central State of the original thirteen.

The winter of 1842–43 was severe and bitter cold, with snow three feet deep all winter. In the fall thousands and thousands of black squirrels migrated through this wilderness.

RECORD OF BIG FLOODS

In 1806, the year of the big flood, Redbank had a rise of twenty-one feet. On September 27, 1861, twenty-two feet.

We had big floods on November 10, 1810; January, 1828; February 10, 1832; February 1, 1840.

September, 1844, a foot of snow fell, followed by a warm rain, which caused a great flood.

In 1816 Ludwig Long and his son William shot five wolves without changing position with single-barrelled, muzzle-loading guns.

In 1823 David Postlethwait, then living in Perry Township, found a rattlesnake den about a mile from his cabin, in what is now Porter Township, and killed forty or fifty of the reptiles. In 1824 he, Nathaniel Postlethwait, and James Stewart killed, in two hours, three hundred snakes at this den. John Goheen now owns (1901) this snake farm. It is in Jefferson County.

In 1850 " Jack Long" crept through the rocks sixty feet into a panther's den and shot a full grown panther by the light of the creature's eyes.

In 1840 the tolls received for that year on the pike were $4,109.10; costs of repairs and improvements, $3,338.17; amount paid gate-keepers, $784.33.

SHOOTING STARS IN 1833—A SHOWER OF FIRE—NATURAL PHENOMENON

"The heavens declare Thy glory, O Lord."

On Wednesday, November 13, 1833, about five o'clock A.M., the heavens presented a spectacle in this wilderness as has seldom been seen in the world. It struck terror to the hearts of those who saw it, and many ran away from home to their neighbors, declaring that the "day of judgment had arrived." The duration of the display was about an hour.

The theory of meteorites is that they are parts of comets. The greatest fall of meteorites in the history of the world was in 1833.

This shower was the result of the disappearance of a comet of which the meteorites were parts, and they are still falling. Though that was seventy years ago, stars still continue to shoot down the path, and astronomers say that they are the remaining pieces of the same vanished comet.

A RAILROAD COLLISION OF 1837

"FATAL RAILROAD ACCIDENT

"STEAMBOAT 'COLUMBUS,' August 12, 1837.

"The most serious accident has occurred in Eastern Virginia since my recollection happened on the Portsmouth and Roanoke Railroad, one and a half miles from Suffolk, yesterday, between nine and ten o'clock. A company, consisting of about one hundred and fifty ladies and gentlemen, from the counties of the Isle of Wight, Nansemond, and Southampton, came down on the railroad on Thursday, the 10th inst., with the view of visiting Portsmouth, Norfolk, Fortress Monroe, and returning the next day. On their return, at the time and place above mentioned, they met a locomotive and train of burden-cars, and, horrible to relate, the two ran

24   369

together while going at the rate of ten or twelve miles an hour."—*Brookville Republican*, August 31, 1837.

Archie Campbell married Mary Ann Kyle. Archie and his wife lived in the vicinity of what is now Reynoldsville, and one winter day they concluded to visit the Kyles. They hitched up their horse in a little jumper, and reached their destination, some four miles over the Ceres road, and remained over night with their relations. During the night there was a heavy snow-fall. On starting home in the morning the Kyles presented Mary Ann with a small crock of apple-butter. The crock was stored between Mrs. Campbell's feet when she took her seat in the jumper. The road-track was covered with fresh snow, and Archie could not, of course, discern it. After driving some distance he struck a trot, the jumper went over a stump, and threw Archie and Mary Ann violently into the snow. Archie scrambled up and cried, " Mary Ann, my dear, are you hurted?" " My thigh is broken, my thigh is broken, Archie!" Archie rushed to her aid, and running his hand up her limb to ascertain her injury, he exclaimed, " It's wurse than that, it's wurse than that, Mary Ann; your bowels are busted, your bowels are busted!" And it was only apple-butter.

Joseph Matson, Esq., lived in Eldred Township, Jefferson County, and in the early days he built an outside high brick chimney. He employed a pioneer stonemason by the name of Jacob Penrose to do the job. Penrose was a very rough mason, but had a high opinion of his own skill, and was quite confiding and bombastic in his way. After he finished the chimney, and before removing the scaffold, he came down to the ground to blow off a little steam about his work. Placing his arm around Matson's neck, he exclaimed, pointing to the chimney, " There, Matson, is a chimney that will last you your lifetime, and your children and your children's children." " Look out!" said Matson. " God, she's a coming!" True enough, the chimney fell, a complete wreck.

Archie Campbell and James Kyle were brothers-in-law and lived in Jefferson County. They were odd, eccentric, and stingy, but each prided himself on being very generous. A true story of them is told in the following verses:

" ARCHIE CAMPBELL AND JIMMIE KYLE

" Archibald Campbell and his friend Jimmy Kyle
Were sturdy old gents from the Emerald Isle.
Jimmy lived on a farm just below Prospect Hill
And Archie kept tavern in old Reynoldsville.
Now this was long since, perhaps during the war,
And possibly even a few years before.
Both were thrifty and close, and knew to the cent
Precisely the quantity of money they spent.
It happened one day, in the course of affairs,
That the old Prospect graveyard needed repairs.

370

It had grown up with briars, bushes and trees,
The fence was quite rotten and weak in the knees,
And tombstones that ought to be standing erect
Were prone from a true upright course to deflect.
Now this was a shame, the good citizens said,
For they ought to show more respect for the dead.
And so they agreed, to accomplish their ends,
To raise a subscription amongst their good friends.
Tom Dolan, Ed. Seeley, Ben Haugh, and Pete Brown
George Sprague and Wash Fuller all put their names down.
But still they were short, and to increase the pile
They handed the paper to old Jimmy Kyle.
For a ten dollar bill he put down his name,
And said he'd make Campbell contribute the same.
And forth with his paper friend Kyle did essay,
Talking loud to himself as he wended his way:
'Sure Archie is ruch; he sells whusky and ale,
An' a paltry tin dollars he never would fale,'
And thus with himself he debated the case
Till firmly convinced. When he reached Archie's place
He knocked at the door of the old Sandy Lick,
When Archie jumped up and opened it quick.
'Gud mornin',' said Jimmy, all wreathed in a smile,
'An how's Muster Cummel?' 'Quite wull, Muster Kyle,
Except for me legs, fer yez know how it is,
I'm bothered a gud but wuth ould rheumatiz.
In a general way me health's gud enough,
An' I'd be all right if I wasn't so stuff.'
'An how's Mary Ann?' 'She is gud—very gud;
She's out in the back yard splitting some wud.'
'Muster Cummel,' said Jimmy, 'I'll sthate what I want:
We're fixin' the cimetry over beyant—
I've a subscruption papur I want yez to sign:
Jist put down yer name for a tin below mine.'
'Egad!' exclaimed Archie, 'not a cint will I guv!
I won't be buried there as long as I luv!'
'We duffer on that pint,' said Kyle, 'be me s'ul!
If I luv and kape me health, Archie, I wull!'"
      —W. O. SMITH, in *Punxsutawney Spirit.*

As Americans we are proud of this blood. In our struggle for independence they were loyal. A Tory was unheard of among them. Pennsylvania and the nation owe very much of their greatness to this race. Natural-born leaders and orators, they have given us statesmen, teachers, professors, ministers, physicians, judges, Congressmen, and generals, even to our Sheridan and Grant. They have furnished the nation with seven Presidents and our State with seven governors. Brave, intelligent, warm hearted, and true, their influence must and always will be potent.

Rev. Alexander McCahon, a " Seceder" minister who preached in and near Brookville about 1850, and before that time, was a Scotch-Irishman, talented and well educated, but like many of that time, including preachers, was fond of " the gude crayther of God." He was accustomed to get his jug filled regularly at Judge Evan's store, and before leaving he would nearly always request William C., who still lives in Brookville (1899), to "jist open the molasses gate and let a little New Orleans drop on the cork." He must have been very fond of molasses. I remember him well. The town papers occasionally published one of his sermons.

SAW-MILLS

The earliest form of a saw-mill was a " saw-pit." In it lumber was sawed in this way: by two men at the saw, one man standing above the pit, the other man in the pit, the two men sawing the log on trestles above. Saws are prehistoric. The ancients used "bronzed saws." Saw-mills were first

Pioneer saw-mill

run by "individual power," and water-power was first used in Germany about 1322. The primitive water saw-mill consisted of a wooden pitman attached to the shaft of the wheel. The log to be sawed was placed on rollers, sustained by a framework over the wheel, and was fed forward on the rollers by means of levers worked by hand. The pioneer saw-mill erected in the United States was near or on the dividing line of Maine and New Hampshire. in 1634.

The early up-and-down saw-mills were built of frame timbers mortised and tenoned and pinned together with oak pins. In size these mills were from twenty to thirty feet wide and from fifty to sixty feet in length, and were roofed with clapboards, slabs, or boards. The running-gear was an undershot flutter-wheel, a gig-wheel to run the log-carriage back, and a bull-wheel with a rope or chain attached to haul the logs into the mill on and over the slide. The capacity of such a mill was about four thousand feet of boards in twenty-four hours. The total cost of one of these up-and-down saw-mills when completed was about three hundred dollars, one hundred dollars for iron used and two hundred dollars for the work and material.

In 1827 the pioneer planing-mill in the world was invented and used. The band saw was invented in 1815. The circular saw was invented in 1805. In 1815 a machine for turning hat blocks, shoe lasts, and wheel spokes was invented. In 1818 a machine to make wooden pegs for boots and shoes was invented.

HORSE-RACING

Horse-racing was practised as early as when Troy was besieged by the Greeks. In the plain before the city the besiegers celebrated holidays by sports and horse-races, and Homer says the walls of Troy were covered with sporting Trojans watching the result.

The trotting horse is an institution of the present century. Before 1800 running was the only method of racing.

Horse-racing as practised in the pioneer days of our country was a great sport. People came here from all the northwest.

THE ROSEVILLE PIONEER RACE-GROUND

"*Jefferson County Races.*—On Tuesday, the 14th of November, instant, will be run over the race-course on the Lewistown and Erie Turnpike, near the public house of Mrs. Mills, four miles west of Brookville, a *match race* of 600 yards between the celebrated racers *Robin* and *Zib*. The public and all others friendly are hereby invited to attend. By order of

"THE PROPRIETORS.

"November 2, 1837."

"Robin" was a Brookville horse, and won this race. He was a sorrel, and belonged to John Pierce and Major William Rodgers. These men purchased him from Ephraim Bushly for five hundred dollars, and they sold him to Benjamin Bennett, Sr., of Bellefonte, where he was taken and matched for a race. He had never been beaten in a race, but before this match took place in Centre County he was poisoned and ruined.

"Zib" was a dark bay horse, and was owned by a Mr. Chambers, of Crawford County, Pennsylvania. The "stake" in the above race was three hundred dollars. Great crowds attended these races. People came from Indiana, Armstrong, Crawford, Erie, Clearfield, and Centre. The stake was usually three hundred dollars, and the excitement and side-betting was lively.

Previous to 1793 there were no postal or post-office facilities in this wilderness. Letters and papers had to be sent with friends, neighbors, or by special carriers. The first newspaper started in the western part of the State was the *Pittsburg Gazette*. It was published by John Scull, and issued in 1786. It was distributed to patrons by special carriers.

In the forties, Peter Ricord, Sr., and his son Peter erected on their farm in what was then called " Jericho," and now Warsaw Post-Office, Jefferson County, a frame grist-mill structure thirty by thirty feet. This mill had one run of stones, and the motive power was one yoke of oxen. I cannot describe it. The capacity was about thirty bushels of corn or grain a day. Ephraim Bushly was the millwright; Peter Ricord, Jr., the miller. The scheme not proving a financial success, the running gear was removed in a few years, and the building utilized as a barn by the Ricords, and afterwards by John A. Fox.

The pioneer convention of national delegates to nominate a candidate for President was held at Baltimore, September 26, 1831. The anti-Masonic party then and there nominated William Wirt, of Maryland, for President, and Amos Ellmaker, of Pennsylvania, for Vice-President.

Previous to 1831 Presidential nominees were made by each party in this way,—viz., first, the Congressional caucus; second, the legislative caucus; third, the legislative mixed caucus; fourth, the legislative convention. From 1796 to 1824 the Congressional caucus was in power. The legislative caucus fell by its own weight. The legislative mixed caucus stood for a short time, and then died.

" Natural gas, we are informed, was first discovered in the United States in natural springs in Western New York and Pennsylvania by the Indians, who used to perform their semi-religious ceremonies in the light of the burning springs. The early history of it elsewhere dates back to the dawn of history itself.

" The first historical record of natural gas in the United States was in 1775, when General Washington visited the natural gas spring a few miles east of the present site of Charleston, when the sight of it so impressed him that he pre-empted an acre of ground surrounding it, dedicating it to the public forever. This feeling, however, at the first sight of this phenomenon was not an unusual one, as Humboldt is quoted as declaring it the " eighth wonder of the world."

" The first economical use of gas in the United States was at Fredonia, Chautauqua County, New York, when, in 1821, a well was drilled twenty-seven feet deep and one and one-half inches in diameter, that produced sufficient gas to illuminate the little village, which was lighted by thirty burners, these being made by drilling a hole the size of a small knitting-needle in the pipe. This gas was conveyed from the well to the place where it was used in wooden pipes.

"The first application of natural gas for fuel was in Erie, Pennsylvania, about 1868, and the first natural gas plant which supplied lights and heat in a large and permanent quantity by methods and appliances similar to those used at the present time was constructed in Titusville, Pennsylvania, in 1872, and the first natural gas line was built in 1875 from Butler County, Pennsylvania, to Pittsburg, which was seventeen miles long and six inches in diameter. Since that time its application has increased by leaps and bounds until reckless consumption and appalling waste depleted many of the original fields."—*Potter Journal.*

Snow fell in 1799 to the depth of five feet. Many wild animals starved to death. There was a great fall of snow in 1817.

Locusts swarmed through this wilderness in 1795, in 1812, in 1829, and in 1846. A big frost,—a regular freeze,—occurred in June, 1843.

CHAPTER XXI

"How dear to my heart are the scenes of my childhood,
When fond recollection presents them to view.
    . . . the deep tangled wildwood,
And every loved spot which my infancy knew."

I was born in Brookville when wolves howled almost nightly on what
is now known as our " Fair Ground ;" when the pine in its lofty pride leaned

Pioneer court house and jail, 1831

" Where gross misconduct met the lash,
    And there see the rock-built prison's dreadful face."

gloomily over every hill-side; when the shades of the forest were heavy
the whole day through; when the woods around our shanty town was the

376

home of many wild animals and birds, such as panthers, bears, wild-cats, foxes, deer, wolves, elks, rabbits, catamounts, coons, ground-hogs, porcupines, partridges, turkeys, and pheasants; when the clear sparkling waters of the North Fork, Sandy Lick, and Red Bank Creeks contained choice pike, many bass, sunfish, horned chubs, trout, and other fish; when the wild "bee trees" were quite numerous and full of luscious sweets for the woodman's axe. As you will see, choice meals for hunters could easily be obtained from the abundance of this game. All flesh-eating animals were either hunters, fishers, or both.

The conditions and circumstances of the county made every man a hunter, and each and every one had his gun, bullet-moulds, shot-pouch, and powder-horn for any and every emergency. It was frequently found necessary before going to church on Sunday to shoot a wild turkey or a deer to "keep them off the grass." The "mighty hunters," though, were " Mike," " Dan," John, and " Bill" Long. Dan was murdered on the Clarion River, near Raught's mill. John was the father of Hon. James E. Long. In winter these hunters wore a white garment, called a " hunting-shirt," buckskin breeches, and moccasin shoes. In their shirt belts each carried a flint-knocker, spunk, hunting-knives, and a tomahawk. Animals were ruthlessly killed for their skins. Deer were thus slaughtered, only the " saddles" or hind quarters being saved for food. If a history of these Longs could be truthfully written, —a full narration of their adventures, perils, coolness, and daring while on the trail of bears, wolves, and panthers,—it would, perhaps, make a book equally as interesting as the " Life of Daniel Boone and Simon Girty."

In the way of a preface to these imperfect reminiscences of Brookville and our dear fathers I simply ask of you this:

> "Let not ambition mock their useful toil,
>   Their homely joys and destiny obscure,
>   Nor grandeur hear with a disdainful smile
>   These short and simple annals of the poor."

My first clear and distinct recollections of our town and the people in it are in the years 1840 to 1843. The ground where the *Democrat* is now printed was then covered with pines. Then Brookville was a town of forty or fifty " shanties" and eight or ten business places, including the " old brick court-house" and the " old stone jail." The number of people in the town was three hundred and twenty-two. These " shanties" were principally on Main Street, and extended from where the Baptist church now is in the east to where Judge Clark now lives in the west. There were a few scattered shanties on Jefferson Street. A great deep gully crossed Main Street about where the Brookville National Bank now stands.

A common sight in those days was, " Cakes & Beer For Sale Here,"— a bottle of foaming beer in a glass in the corner. The first of these signs which I remember was one on John Brownlee's house, on the northeast corner of Main and Mill Streets, and one on John Showalter's house (the late gunsmith), now the property of John S. Moore. The cakes were made of New Orleans molasses, and were delicious, more so than any you can make or buy now. They were sold for a cent apiece. The beer was home-made, and called " small beer," and sold for three cents a glass. It was made of hops, ginger, spruce, sassafras-roots, wheat bran, molasses, yeast, and water. About every family made their own beer. Mrs. Showalter and other old ladies living in the town now (1898), I venture to say, have made "barrels" of it.

The taverns in the town then were four in number. First, the "Red Lion." This inn was kept by John Smith, the step-father of David Eason. The second was the "Jefferson House," then kept by Thomas Hastings, now occupied and kept by Phil. J. Allgeier. In this hotel the "light fantastic toe" was tripped to the airs of "Money Musk," "Virginia Reel," "French Four," and "Pine Creek Lady." The orchestra for these occasions was George Hayes, who came from Westmoreland County, a colored fiddler of the town, who could play the violin behind his back as well as before his face, with his left or right hand, and asleep or awake. I could name quite a number of ladies in the town now whom I used to see enjoying themselves in this way. The third was the "Franklin House," built by John Gelvin, and then kept by John Pierce. The Central Hotel, owned by S. B. Arthurs, has been erected on the ground occupied by the Franklin. The fourth was on the corner of Main and Barnett Streets, erected by John Dougherty. It swung the sign,—

"Peace and Poverty, by John Dougherty."

In 1840 it was occupied and kept by John Gallagher. Each of these hotels had license, and sold whiskey at three cents a drink, mostly on credit. You could have your whiskey straight, or have brown sugar or "tansy bitters" in it. The bars had to be opened regularly on Sunday for "morning bitters." Single meals were given for twenty-five cents, a "check" or cold meal for a "'leven-penny bit," and a bed for ten cents. You could stop over night, have supper, bed, morning bitters, and breakfast, all for fifty cents. There was but one table, one hour, one ringing of the bell.

The Susquehanna and Waterford turnpike was completed in 1824. It was a good road, and was kept in fair repair. In 1840 it passed from under State control, and the magnitude of the travel over it was great. The stage line was started in 1824. Morrow started his team then, and cattle and other droving commenced in 1835. All this I am told; but I know the stage was a big factor in 1840. Morrow was on time, and droving was im-mense. I have seen passing through Brookville on their way east from four to six droves of cattle in a day. The droves were generally divided into three

378

sections. At the head of the first would be a man leading a big ox, his extra clothing strapped on the ox's head, and the man would be crying out ever and anon, " K-o, b-o-s-s;" " Come, boss." I have seen two and three droves of sheep pass in a day, with occasionally a drove of hogs sandwiched between them. Horse droves were numerous, too. I have seen a few droves of colts, and a few flocks of turkeys. I could not give an estimate of the number of these droves I have seen passing our home in a day. The business of droving began in June of each year, and ended in November. There was no other way to take this merchandise east than to drive it.

But you must not think everybody was going east. A big lot of people were going west, including their cousins and their aunts. This turnpike was the shortest line west. We lived where T. L. Templeton now lives, and every few days all through the summer months I would see, nearly opposite the Baptist church, in the middle of the street, two men and a dog, and one of the men usually carrying a gun. They were the advance-guard for an " emigrant train." In a few minutes from one to six wagons would come in sight and stop,—all stopping here for a short rest. " Where are you going?" was the usual inquiry. " Going West; going to Ohio." The wagons were heavy, wide-tracked, covered with hoops and a white canvas, and had a stiff tongue and iron pole-chains. The horses wore heavy harness with iron trace-chains. An occasional emigrant would locate in our county, but the great majority generally struggled on for the far West,—Ohio.

The usual mode of travel for the people was on foot or on horseback; but the most interesting mode was the daily stage, which " brought" and " took" the mail and carried the passengers who were going east or west. This was the " limited mail," and the " day and night express" of these days, —a through train, only stopping thirty minutes for meals. Of course this " limited mail," this " day and night express," over this " short route," eclipsed and overshadowed every other line and mode of travel. It was " grand, startling, and stupendous." There were no through tickets sold, to be

" Punched, punched with care,
Punched in the presence of the passengaire."

The fare was six cents a mile in advance, and to be paid in " bimetallism." When the officials made their usual tour of inspection over this " road," they had extended to them the genuine hospitality of everybody, including that of the landlords, and free whiskey. The President of the great Pennsylvania line is a small potato to-day in contrast with the chief manager of our line in that day, for our line was then the vanguard of every improvement a passenger might desire or a traveller wish for.

The coaches were made in Concord, New Hampshire, and were called " rockaway coaches." Each coach had heavy leather belt-springs, and was a handsome vehicle, painted red, with gold stripes and letters, and was drawn by four horses. The coach was made to carry nine passengers, but I have often seen it with a dozen inside, two on the seat with the driver, and some on top. Trunks were carried on the top and in the "boot." Every driver carried a horn, and always took a "horn." When nearing a "relay" or a post-office, the valleys and hills were made to echo and re-echo to the "er-r-a-h, er-r-a-h, tat, tat, t-a-h, tat t-a-h" of the driver's horn, which was to attract the attention of the landlord or postmaster by night or by day. In later years the coaches were the most ordinary hacks, and the horses could be "seen through," whether sick or well, without the aid of any X-rays.

The roads in spring, summer, and fall were a succession of mud-holes, with an occasional corduroy. Don't mention bad roads now. The male passengers usually walked up the hills. All this in the blackness of darkness without a match, lantern, or light.

I take from an old paper the experience of one who rode in these stages:

> "Jolted, thumped, distracted,
>   Rocked, and quite forlorn.
> Oh! wise one, what duties
>   Now are laid on corn?
> Mad, disgusted, angry,
>   In a swearing rage,
> 'Tis the very d—l
>   Riding in this stage."

From 1832 to about 1840 the drivers were Henry Dull and Andrew Loux, father of Enoch Loux.

The prominent stage-drivers in 1840 were John S. Barr, S. P. Barr, Gabriel Vastbinder, Bill Adams, Joe Stratton, and others. Each driver carried a whip made as follows: a hickory stock, and a buckskin lash ten or twelve feet long, with a silk cracker on the end. These whips were handled with marvellous dexterity by drivers, and were made to crack over the horses' heads like pistols. The great pride of a driver then was to turn a "coach-and-four" with the horses on a "complete run." Bill Adams was good at this. A laughable incident occurred in one of these turns on Main Street. The driver was showing off in his usual style, and in making the turn with the horses on a complete run the coach struck a stone, which upset it. The weight of all the passengers coming against the coach-door burst it open, and the passengers, one and all, were thrown out and literally dumped into the hotel bar-room. This was a perfection in stage driving not easily attained.

In 1840 the Brookville merchant kept his own books,—or, as he would have said, his own accounts,—wrote all his letters with a quill, and when they were written let the ink dry or sprinkled it with sand. There were then no envelopes, no postage stamps, no letter-boxes in the streets, no collection of the mail. The letter written, the paper was carefully folded, sealed with wax or a wafer, addressed, and carried to the post-office, where postage was prepaid at rates which would now seem extortionate.

In 1840 Brookville merchants purchased their goods in Philadelphia. These purchases were made in the spring and fall. It took about two and a half days' continuous travelling in the "limited mail" day and night stage-coach to reach Lewistown, Pennsylvania, and required about one day and a half travelling over the canal and railroad to reach Philadelphia from that point. From Brookville to Philadelphia it required some four or five days' constant travelling. Our merchants carried their money on these trips as well as they could, mostly secreted in some way about their persons. After purchasing their goods in Philadelphia, they were ordered to be shipped to Brookville as "heavy freight," over the great corporation freight line of

Bennett's stage and Morrow's team

"Joe Morrow." Joe was a "bloated corporationist," a transportation mo-nopolist of that day. He was a whole "trust" in himself. He owned and managed the whole line, and had no opposition, on this end at least. His line consisted of two Conestoga wagons, the bed on each at least four feet high and sixteen feet long. Each wagon was painted blue, and each was covered with a white canvas, this covering supported by hoops. The wagon was always loaded and unloaded from the rear end. The tires on the wheels were six inches wide. Each wagon would carry over three tons of freight, and was drawn over good roads by six magnificent horses, and over bad roads by eight of such horses, and each horse weighed about fourteen hundred. The price of wagon carriage over this distance was five dollars and six dollars a hundredweight. This was the "fast" and heavy freight line from Philadelphia to Brookville until the canal was built to Lewistown, Pennsylvania, when Morrow changed his head-quarters from Philadelphia to Lewistown, and continued to run his semi-annual "freight train" from Lewistown to Brookville. Morrow's advent into town was always a great event. He always stopped his "train" in front of the Red Lion Hotel, then kept by John Smith. The horses were never stabled, but stood day and night in the street, three on each side of the stiff tongue of the wagon, and were fed in a box he carried with him, called his "feed-trough." The harness was broad and heavy, and nearly covered the horses; and they were "hitched up" to the wagon with iron "pole" and "trace-chains." The Brotherhood of Locomotive Engineers, the Switchmen's Union, the "American Railway Union," and all the Sovereigns and Debses put together, had no terrors for Joe, for he had but one employee, a "brakeman," for his second wagon. Joe was the employed and the employer. Like a "transportation king," like a "robber baron," he sat astride a wagon saddle on the hind near horse, driving the others with a single line and a blacksnake whip, to the words, "Gee," "Jep," and "Haw." He drove with one line, and when he wanted his horse to haw he would pull on the line; if he wanted him to gee he would jerk on the line. Morrow always remained in Brookville four or five days, to buy our products and load his train for the home trip. He bought and loaded clover, timothy, and flaxseed, feathers, old rags, tar, beeswax, wheat, rye, chestnuts, furs, and dried elderberries. The western terminus of his line was Shippenville, Clarion County, Pennsylvania, and on his return from there he bought up these products. Conestoga wagons came into use about 1760.

Morrow's last trip to Brookville with his train was about the year 1850. He was an Irishman, slim, wiry, industrious, and of business habits. He was killed by the kick of a horse, at Cross's tavern, Clearfield County, Pennsylvania,—kicked on the 11th day of September, 1855, and died on the 12th. I remember that he usually wore a spotted fawn-skin vest, made from the skin with the hair on. The merchants in Brookville of that day who are still living (1895), and for whom Morrow hauled goods, as far as I can recollect, are Uriah Matson, Harry Matson, Judge Henderson, Samuel Truby, Wm. Rodgers, and W. W. Corbet, who now resides in or near the town, Captain John Hastings, of Punxsutawney, W. F. Clark, of Maquoketa, Iowa, and S. M. Moore, of Minneapolis, Minnesota.

> "The past—the present race must tell
> Of deeds done by their friends of old,
> Who at their posts of duty fell,
> And left their acts and deeds untold."

The town was laid out in 1830. My father moved here in 1832. He taught the first term of school in the town, in the winter of 1832. He was lieutenant-colonel in the militia, a justice of the peace, and was county treasurer when he died, in 1837, at the early age of twenty-seven years, leaving my mother in this wilderness, a widow with three small children to support and rear. In 1840 my mother taught a summer term of school in what was then and is now called the Butler school-house. This school-house is on the Ridgway road, in Pine Creek Township, three miles from town. I was small, and had to go and come to and from this school with mother. We came home every Saturday to remain over Sunday, and to attend Presbyterian church, service being then held in the old brick court-house. The Presbyterians then called their church " Bethel." In 1842 it was changed to Brookville. We had no choir in the church then, but had a " clerk," who would stand in front of the pulpit, read out two lines, and then sing them, then read two more and sing them, and so on until the hymn or psalm was sung, the congregation joining in as best they could. Of these clerks, the only ones I can now recollect were Thomas Lucas, Samuel McQuiston, and John S. Lucas. I have no recollection of David's psalms being used other than is found in Watts' version, in combination with the hymns. I recollect two of the favorite hymns at that time with this church. The first verse of one hymn was as follows:

> " When I can read my title clear
> To mansions in the skies,
> I'll bid farewell to every fear,
> And wipe my weeping eyes."

The first verse of the second hymn was:

> " There is a land of pure delight,
> Where saints immortal reign ;
> Infinite day excludes the night,
> And pleasures banish pain."

One by one, these early pioneer Christians have left for this " land of pure delight !" to occupy these " mansions in the skies." I hope and pray that each one is now—

> " In seas of heavenly rest."

After returning home from the Butler school-house one Saturday, I remember I asked my mother for a " piece." She went to the cupboard, and when she got there the cupboard was not bare, for, lo! and behold, a great big snake was therein, coiled and ready for fight. My mother, in horror, ran to the door and called Mr. Lewis Dunham, a lawyer, who lived in the house now occupied by R. M. Matson, Esq. Mr. Dunham came on a run, and tried to catch or kill the snake with our " tongs," but it made good its escape through a rat-hole in the corner of the cupboard. Reptiles, such as black-, rattle-, house-, and other snakes were very plenty then in and around Brookville, and dangerous, too. These snakes fed and lived on birds, mice, etc., and were very fond of milk, which they drink after the manner of a horse.

In a former chapter I called Brookville a town of shanties. And so it was; but there was one exception, there was one solid building, a dwelling occupied by a man named Bliss, on Water Street, on or near the lot at present (1898) owned and occupied by Billy Barr. It was built of logs. The other shanties were solid enough, for they were built in a different manner from shanties now, being put together with " frame timbers," mortised

My mother

" Who ran to help me when I fell,
And would some pretty story tell,
Or kiss the place to make it well?
My mother !"

and tenoned, and fastened with oak pins, as iron and nails were scarce, people being poor and having little or no money. Every building had to have a " raising," and the neighbors had to be invited to help " raise." Cyrus Butler, a bluff, gruff Yankee, was the captain at all raisings. He would stand off by himself, crying out at the proper time, " All together, men, he-o-he! he-o-he !"

No dwelling in the town was then complete without having in the back-yard an " out-oven," an " ash-hopper," a " dye-kettle," and a rough box

384

fastened to the second story of the necessary, in which to raise early cabbage-plants. At the rear of each kitchen was a hop-vine with its pole, and each family raised its own catnip, peppermint, sage, and tansy.

> " The hand of the reaper
> Takes the leaves that are hoary,
> But the voice of the weeper
> Wails manhood in glory."

In 1840 there was a law requiring the enrolment of all able-bodied men between twenty-one and forty-five years of age in the militia. These were formed into companies and battalions, and organized into brigades, each brigade to meet once a year in " encampment," for a period of three days, two days for " muster and drill" and one day for " review." The encampments were held in May or June, and for some reason or other these soldiers were called the " cornstalk militia," because some of the soldiers carried cornstalks for guns. No uniforms were worn in most cases. The soldier wore his home-spun or store-clothes, and each one reported with his own pike, wooden gun, rifle, or musket, and, under the inspiring influence of his accoutrements, discipline, and drill,—

> " Each bosom felt the high alarms,
> And all their burning pulses beat to arms."

For non-attendance by a soldier at these encampments a fine of fifty cents was imposed for every day's absence. This fine had to be paid in cash, and was quite a severe penalty in those days of no money, county orders, and store barter.

The first encampment I remember was held on what is now called Granger (Jack) Heber's farm. Brigadier-General Mercer was the commander then. He rode a sorrel horse, with a silver mane and tail, and a curled moustache. His bridle was ornamented with fine leather straps, balls, and tassels, and the blue saddle-cloth was covered with stars and spangles, giving the horse the appearance of a " fiery dragon." The general would occasionally dismount, to make some inspection on foot, when the army was drawn up in line, and then a great race, and frequently a fight, would occur among the small boys for the possession of the horse. The reward for holding him at this time was a " fippenny-bit." The camp grounds were alive with whiskey-sellers, ginger-bread and small-beer dealers. Whiskey was to be had from barrels or jugs, in large or small quantities. When the army was in line it was dealt out to the soldiers from a bucket with a dipper. Anybody could sell whiskey and anybody could drink it. It was worth from twelve to twenty cents a gallon. The more brawls and fist-fights, the livelier, better, and greater was considered the muster. The bad blood between neighbors was always settled here. Each party always resolved to meet the other on review-day to fight it out, and after the fight to meet, drink together, and make up their difference. Pugilism was practised in that day, not on scientific principles, but by main strength. The terror of all public gatherings was a man called "Devil John Thompson." He lived in Indiana County, and came here always on reviews. Each military company had a fifer or drummer, seldom a complete band. I have seen the late Judge Taylor blowing his fife, the only musician of and for one of these companies. This occurred on Main Street, in front of our house; and when I look back on this soldier scene, it seems to me these soldiers, from their appearance, must have been composed of the rag-tag and bob-tail of creation. An odd and comic sight it really was. To be an officer or captain in one of these companies was considered a great honor, and something which the recipient was in duty bound to thank God for in his morning and evening prayers. I cannot do this subject justice. Such was the Pennsylvania militia as I saw it, and all that remains for me to say is, "Great the State and great her sons."

In 1840 we had two big men in the town,—Judge William Jack, who was sent to Congress, and who built and lived in the house on Pickering Street now owned and occupied by Joseph Darr, Esq., and General Levi G. Clover, who lived on Main Street, in a house that was burned down, which stood on the lot now owned by Mrs. Clarissa Clements, and is the place of business of Misses McLain and Fetzer. Clover was a big man physically, a big man in the militia, a big man in politics, and a big man in business. Like most big men in those days, he owned and ran a whiskey-still. This distillery was located on or near the property of Fred. Starr, in what is now Litchtown. I used to loaf occasionally in this distillery, and I have seen some of our old citizens take a pint tin cup and dip it full of whiskey from out of Clover's copper kettles, and then drink this whole pint of whiskey down apparently at one gulp. I might pause to say right here, that in drinking whiskey, racing, square pulling, swearing, and fighting the old settler was "right in it." The wrestling- and fighting-ground then for the men and boys was the ground now occupied by the Jenks machine-shop, and the highway to and from these grounds was down the alley between Ed. Snyder's blacksmith-shop and C. A. Carrier's store (1898). I have had business on that ground with some boys myself.

In the woods in and around Brookville in 1840 there were many sweet-singing birds and beautiful wild-flowers. I remember the laurel. We used to adorn our mantels and parlor fireplaces with these every spring. I remember the honeysuckle, the wild rose, the crab-apple tree, the thorn, and others. The aroma from many of these flowers was delightful. House-plants were unknown. The garden flowers of that day were the pink ("a flower most rare"), the lilac, the hollyhock, the sunflower, and the rose. Each garden had a little bed of "sweet-williams" and "johnny-jump ups."

The garden rose was a beautiful, sweet flower then, and it is a beautiful, sweet flower to-day, and it ever will be sweet and beautiful. My mother used to sing to me this hymn of Isaac Watts as a lullaby:

> "How fair is the rose, what a beautiful flower!
>   In summer so fragrant and gay;
>   But its leaves are beginning to fade in an hour;
>   And they wither and die in a day.
>
> " Yet the rose has one powerful virtue to boast
>   Above all the flowers of the field:
>   When its leaves are all dead and its fine colors lost,
>   Still how sweet a perfume it will yield.
>
> " So frail are the youth and the beauty of men,
>   Though they look gay and bloom like the rose,
>   Yet all our fond care to preserve them is vain,
>   Time kills them as fast as he goes.
>
> " Then I'll not be proud of my youth or my beauty,
>   Since both will soon wither and fade,
>   But gain a good name by performing my duty;
>   This will scent like the rose when I'm dead."

The rose is said to have been the first cultivated flower.

In 1840 there was no church building in the town. Our Presbyterian preacher in the town was the Rev. David Polk, a cousin to President Polk. The token was then given out on Saturday to all those who were adjudged worthy to sit at the Lord's table. These tokens were taken up on the following Sunday while seated at the table. Friday was " fast" or preparation day. We were not allowed to eat anything, or very little, until the sun went down. I can only remember that I used to get hungry and long for night to come. Rev. Polk preached half of his time in Corsica, the other half in Brookville. His salary was four hundred dollars per year,—two hundred dollars from Brookville and two hundred dollars from Corsica. He lived on the pike in the hollow beyond and west of Roseville. He preached in the court-house until the Presbyterians completed the first church building in the town, in 1843. It stood where the church now stands, and was then outside of the borough limits. The building was erected through the efforts of a lawyer then residing in Brookville, named C. A. Alexander. The ground for the church building was one acre; cost, fifty dollars; and the deed was obtained in 1848. The building was 40 by 60, and built by Phillip Schroeder for eleven hundred dollars. The ruling elders of the church then were Thomas Lucas, John Matson, Sr., Elijah Clark, John Lattimer, Joseph McCullough, and John Wilson.

Other preachers came to town occasionally in 1840, and held their services in the court-house. One jolly, aged Welshman was called Father Thomas. He was a Baptist, a dear old man, and a great singer. I always went to his church to hear him sing. I can sing some of his songs yet. I will repeat a stanza from one of his favorites:

> " Oh, then I shall be ever free,
> Happy in eternity,
> Eternity, eternity,
> Happy in eternity."

Dear old soul, he is in eternity, and I have no doubt is happy singing his favorite songs there.

A Methodist preacher named Elijah Coleman came here occasionally. Methodist head-quarters were at David Henry's and at Cyrus Butler's. The first Methodist prayer-meeting held in town was at Cyrus Butler's. It was held in the little yellow house occupied for years by Mrs. Rachel Dixon, and torn down by C. C. Benscoter, Esq., in 1887, in order to erect his present dwelling. In 1840 men and women were not permitted to sit on the same seat in church, or on the same side of the house.

The physicians in the town in 1840 were Dr. George Darling, father of the late Paul Darling, and Dr. Gara Bishop, father of Mrs. Edmund English. Dr. Bishop was also a Presbyterian preacher.

In 1840 Jefferson County contained a population of seven thousand two hundred and fifty-three people, and embraced nearly all of Forest and Elk Counties. Ridgway was then in the northeast corner of our county, and Punxsutawney was a village of about fifteen or twenty dwellings.

The politics of the county was divided into Whig and Democrat. The leading Whigs in Brookville, as I recollect them, were Thomas Lucas, Esq., James Corbet, father of Colonel Corbet, Benjamin McCreight, father of Mrs. Dr. Hunt, Thomas M. Barr, and Samuel H. Lucas. The leading Democrats were Hon. William Jack, General L. G. Clover, Judge Joseph Henderson, John Smith, Daniel Smith, Jesse G. Clark, father of Judge Clark, D. B. Jenks, John Dougherty, Richard Arthurs, and Thomas Hastings. Politics ran so high that year that each party had its own Fourth of July celebration. The Whigs celebrated at Port Barnett. Nicholas McQuiston, the miller who died at Langville a few years ago, had one of his legs broken at this celebration by the explosion of a log which he had filled with powder. The Democrats celebrated in Brookville, in front of the Franklin Hotel, now the Central. . I was big enough to have a full run and clear view of this table and celebration. The table was covered with small roasted pigs, roasted turkeys, venison, pies, gingerbread, "pound-cake," etc. I was not allowed to participate in the feast, although my father in his lifetime had been a Democrat. Boys and girls were then taught modesty, patience, and man-

388

ners by parents. Children were taught and compelled to respect age and to defer to the wishes of father and mother. Now the father and mother must defer to the wishes of children. There was more home and less public training of children, and, as a result, children had more modesty and patience and less impudence. In 1840 children slept in " trundle-beds," and were required by their mothers to repeat every night before going to sleep this little prayer:

> " Now I lay me down to sleep,
> I pray the Lord my soul to keep;
> If I should die before I wake,
> I pray the Lord my soul to take."

This home training was a constant building up of individual character, and I believe a much more effectual way for good than the present public way of building character collectively.

In 1840 our Congressman was Judge Jack, of Brookville, and our member of the Legislature was Hon. James L. Gillis, of Ridgway Township. The county officers were: Prothonotary, General Levi G. Clover; Sheriff, John Smith; Treasurer, Jesse G. Clark; Commissioners, Daniel Coder, Irwin Robinson, and Benjamin McCreight. The county was Democratic by one hundred and twenty-five majority.

The postmaster in Brookville was John Dougherty, and Joseph Henderson was deputy United States marshal for Jefferson County. He took the census of 1840 for our county.

Of the above-named politicians and officials, Judge Henderson is the only one now living (1895). Every day yet the judge can be found at his place of business, pleasant, cheerful, and intelligent,—a fine old gentleman. In his many political contests I always admired, defended, and supported him. One thing I begin to notice, " he is not as young as he used to be."

> " Oh, tell me the tales I delighted to hear,
> Long, long ago, long, long ago;
> Oh, sing me the old songs so full of cheer,
> Long, long ago, long, long ago."

In 1840 we boys amused ourselves in the winter months by catching rabbits in box-traps,—the woods were full of them,—skating on Geer's pond, a small lake then located where Allgeier's brewery now stands (this lake was destroyed by the building of Mabon's mill-race), skating on Barr's (now Litch's) dam, and coasting down the town or graveyard hill. In the summer and fall months the amusements were alley-ball behind the court-house, town-ball, over-ball, sock-ball, fishing in the streams and in Geer's pond, riding floats of slabs on the creek, swimming in the " deep hole," and gathering blackberries, crab-apples, wild plums, and black and yellow haws. But the amusement of all amusements, the one that was enjoyed every day in the year by the boys, was the cutting of fire-wood. The wood for heating and cooking was generally hauled in " drags" to the front door of each house on Main Street, and there cut on the " pile" by the boys of each house. The gathering of hazel-nuts, butternuts, hickory-nuts, and chestnuts was an agreeable and profitable recreation. My boy associates of those days—where are they? " Some sleep on battle fields and some beneath the sea." I can only recall the following, who are now living in Brookville (1898) : David Eason, W. C. Evans, Dr. C. M. Matson, Thomas E. Espy, Thomas P. McCrea, Daniel Burns, Clover Smith, W. C. Smith, and W. R. Ramsey. I understand John Craig, Frederick and Lewis Dunham, Elijah and Lorenzo Lowell,

Brookville kitchen, 1840

and Alexander Barr live in the State of Iowa, Richard Espy in Kentucky, and John L. and Anson Warren in Wisconsin.

In 1840 every housewife in Brookville cooked over a fireplace, in which a crane was fastened so as to swing in, out, off, on, and over the fire. Every fireplace had a wooden poker, a pair of tongs to handle burning wood, and a shovel to remove the ashes. The fuel used was wood,—pine, maple, oak, birch, and hickory. To every fire there had to be a " back log," and the smaller or front pieces were supported on " andirons" or common stones. Matches were not in use, hence fires were covered at night so as to preserve some live coals for the morning fire. Rich people had a little pair of bellows to blow these live coals into a blaze, but poor people had to do the best they

390

could with their mouths. After having nearly smoked my eyes out trying to blow coals into life, I have had to give it up and go to a neighbor to borrow a shovel of fire. Some old settlers used " spunk," a flint, and a barlow knife to start a fire in an emergency like this. Spunk—punk or touchwood—was obtained from the inside of a hollow white maple-tree. When matches were first brought around great fear was entertained that they might burn everybody out of house and home. My mother secured a tin box with a safe lid in which to keep hers. For some reason they were called locofoco matches.

The crane in the fireplace had a set of rods with hooks on each end, and they were graduated in length so as to hang the kettle at the proper height from the fire. In addition to the kettles we had the long-handled frying-pan, the handle of which had to be supported by some one's hand, or else on a box or a chair. Then there was the three-legged, short-handled spider. It could support itself. And I must not forget the griddle for buckwheat cakes. It had to be suspended by a rod on the crane. Then there was the old bake-kettle, or oven, with legs and a closely-fitted cover. In this was baked the " pone" for the family. I can say truthfully that pone was not used more than thirty days in the month.

This was a hard way to cook. Women would nearly break their backs lifting these heavy kettles on and off, burn their faces, smoke their eyes, singe their hair, blister their hands, and " scorch" their clothes.

Our spoons were pewter and iron; knives and forks were iron with bone handles. The chinaware was about as it is now.

The every-day bonnet of women then was the " sun-bonnet" for summer, and a quilted " hood" for winter. The dress bonnet was made of paper or leghorn, and was in shape something like our coal-scuttles.

In 1840 nearly every wife in Brookville milked a cow and churned butter. The cows were milked at the front door on Main Street. These cows were ornery, ill-looking, ill-fed, straw-stealing, and blue-milk giving creatures. The water with which to wash clothes and do the scrubbing was caught in barrels or tubs from the house-roof. Scrubbing the floors of a house had to be attended to regularly once a week. This scrubbing had to be done with powdered sand and a home-made " split broom." Every wife had to make her own soap, bake her own bread, sew and dye all the clothes for the family, spin the wool for and knit the mittens and socks, make the coverlets, quilt the quilts, see that the children's shoes for Sunday were greased with tallow every Saturday night, nurse the sick, give " sheep saffron" for the measles, and do all the cooking. All this too without " protection, tariff, rebate, or combine." About every family had a cow, dog, cat, pig, geese, and chickens. The town gave these domestic animals the right to " life, liberty, and the pursuit of happiness." Of course, under these sanitary conditions, the town was alive with fleas, and every house was full of bedbugs. Bats were numerous, and the "public opinion" then was that the bats brought the bedbugs. This may be given as an illustration of the correctness of public opinion. However, we were contented and happy, and used to sing,—

> "Home, home, sweet, sweet home,
> Be it ever so humble, there's no place like home."

In 1840 there were doubtless many fine horses in Jefferson County yet it seemed to me nearly every horse had stringhalt, ring-bone, spavin, high-step, or poll-evil. Horses with poll-evil were numerous then, but the disease has apparently disappeared. It was an abscess on the horse's head, behind the ears, and was doubtless caused by cruelty to the animal. If a horse did not please his master in his work he would be knocked down with a hand-spike, a rail, or the loaded butt end of a blacksnake whip. Poor food and these blows undoubtedly caused this horrible disease. Sick horses were treated in a barbarous manner, not being allowed to lie down, but were whipped, run, and held upon their feet. I have seen horses held up with handspikes, rails, etc. The usual remedies were bleeding and drenching with filthy compounds. " Bots" was the almost unfailing disease.

The cattle were home stock, big-horned, heavy-bellied, and long-legged. They could jump over almost anything, and could outrun the " devil and his imps." They were poorly fed, received little care, and had little or no stabling. In the spring it was common for cows to be on the " lift." The common trouble with cattle was " hollow horn," " wolf in the tail," and loss of " cud." These were little else than the results of starvation. I have wit-nessed consultations over a sick cow, when one man would declare positively she had hollow horn, and another declare just as positively it was wolf in the tail. After a spirited dispute they would compromise by agreeing to bore her horn and split her tail. If they had called it hollow belly and wolf in the stomach they would have been nearer the truth. A better remedy would have been a bucket of warm slop, a good stable, and plenty of hay. The remedy for " hollow horn" was to bore a gimlet hole in the horn near the head and then saturate a cloth with spirits of turpentine and wrap it around the horn. The cure for wolf in the tail was to split the tail near the end with a knife, and fill the cut with salt and pepper. The cure for " lifts" was to call the neighbors, lift the cow to her feet, and prop her up so she could not lie down again. The cures for loss of " cud" were numerous and filthy. A " sure cure," and common, too, was to roll human excrement in dough and force it down the animal's throat. The same remedy was used for " founder." If the critter recovered, the remedy was the right one; if it died, the reason was the remedy had been used too late. Of course, these conditions were all imaginary. They were only diseases resulting from exposure and want of nourishing food. A wild onion called " ramp," and a shrub called " trip-wood," grew in the woods and were early in their appearance each spring. These, of which the cattle ate freely, were often their only dependence for food. All domestic animals then had to have ear-marks on them, or be branded. Condensed milk was invented in 1849.

The hog of that time was a racer, and could outrun the average horse. His snort when startled was something terrible. He was of the "razor-back" variety, long-bodied, long-legged, and long-snouted. By means of his snout he could plough through everything. Of course he was starved in the winter, like all the other animals, and his condition resulting from his starvation was considered a disease and called "black teeth." The remedy for this disease was to knock out the teeth with a hammer and a spike.

Ignorance was the cause of this cruelty to animals. To the readers of this volume the things mentioned are astonishing. But I have only hinted at the barbarities then inflicted on these domestic animals, which had no rights which man was bound to respect. Not until 1866 was any effort made in this country to protect dumb animals from the cruelty of man. In that year Henry Berg organized the American society in New York, and to-day the movement is felt throughout a great portion of the world. In 1890 there were five hundred and forty-seven societies in existence for the prevention of cruelty to animals, two hundred and twenty-three of them in the United States. "The economic necessity for the existence of societies having for their object the better care and protection of animals becomes manifest when it is considered that our industries, our commerce, and the supply of our necessities and comforts depend upon the animal world. In the United States alone it is estimated that there are 14,000,000 horses, valued at $979,-000,000. There are also 2,330,000 mules, 16,000,000 milk cows, 36,800,000 oxen and other cattle, 44,000,000 sheep, and 50,000,000 swine. The total domestic animals in 1890 were estimated at 165,000,000, valued at over $2,400,000,000." To-day every good citizen gives these humane societies or their agents his support, and almost every one is against the man or men who in any way abuse dumb beasts. It is not a matter of mere sentiment.

Along about 1840 the winters were very severe and long, much more so than now. Regularly every fall, commencing in November,—

"Soft as the eider down,
Light as the spider gown,
Came the beautiful snow, till
Over the meadow lots,
Over our garden plots,
Over the ponds and the lakes,
Lay only beautiful flakes.
Then with this snowing,
Puffing and blowing,
Old Boreas came bellowing by,
Till over the by-ways,
And over the highways,
The snow-drifts were ever so high."

The snow was several feet deep every winter. It came early and remained till late.

I have made frequent reference in these chapters to the old court-house. As I find there is some confusion in regard to its size, and as I find our county history contains this error: " The court-house, a one-story brick building, was finished in ·1832," I deem it of sufficient importance to correct these errors, and to state that the court-house was a two-story building, with a one-story wing on the west extending along Main Street. This wing was divided into two rooms, the first for the prothonotary's office and the other for the commissioners' office. The main building was two-storied, with an attic and belfry. The second story was divided into four good-sized rooms, called jury-rooms. The southwest room was used by the Methodists for a long time for their Thursday evening prayer-meeting. Alexander Fullerton was the janitor. The Union Sunday-school was held here for years also. The northwest room was used as an armory by the Brookville Rifles,—a volunteer company. The other two were used as jury-rooms. I have played in every room of the old building, and know every foot of it. The building cost three thousand dollars. The contractors were John Lucas and Robert P. Barr. It was torn down in 1866 to make room for the present fine structure. Our alley-ball games were all played for years behind the old court-house.

Our first jail was a stone structure, built of common stone, in 1831. It was two stories high, was situated on the northeast corner of the public lot, near Joseph Darr's residence, and fronting on Pickering Street. Daniel Elgin was the contractor. The building was divided into eight rooms, two down-stairs and two up-stairs for the jail proper, and two down-stairs and two up-stairs for the sheriff's residence and office. The sheriff occupied the north part. The early church services in this building were held in the jail part, up-stairs. This old jail has a history, not the most pleasant to contemplate or write about. It was used to imprison run-away slaves, and to lodge them over night, by slave captors. Imprisoning men for no other crime than desiring to enjoy life, liberty, and the pursuit of happiness! There was a branch of the underground railroad for the escape of slaves running through Brookville at that time. As many as twenty-five of those unfortunate creatures have passed through Brookville in one day. Judge Heath, then living in our town,—a great Methodist and an abolitionist,—had to pay a fine of two thousand dollars for aiding two slaves to escape from this old stone jail; a big sum of money to pay for performing a Christian, humane act, was it not? In this stone jail men were imprisoned for debt, and kept in it until the last penny was paid. I have seen some of the best men of that day in our county imprisoned in this old jail for debt or bail money. I have seen Thomas Hall, than whom I knew no better man, no better Christian, an elder in the Presbyterian church, incarcerated in the old stone jail for bail money. He had bailed a relative for the sum of fifty dollars, and his relative let him suffer. Honest, big-hearted, generous, Christian Thomas Hall! Thank God that the day for such inhumanities as those stated above is gone forever. This old jail was rented after the new one was erected, and used as a butcher-shop until it was torn down to make room for the present court-house. The butcher always blew a horn when he had fresh meat to sell.

In these days of fine carriages and Brookville wagons it might be well to describe the wagon of 1840. It was called the Pennsylvania wagon, was wide-tracked, and had wooden axles with iron skeins on the spindles. The tongue was stiff, and reached about three feet ahead of the horses. The horses were hitched to these wagons by iron trace- and long tongue-chains. In rough roads I used to think every time the tongue would strike a horse on the leg it would break it. Old team horses understood this and would spread out to avoid these leg-blows. The wheels were kept in place by means of an iron strap and linch-pin. Every wagon carried its own tar on the coupling-pole under the hind axle. The carriage of that day was called a dearborn wagon. I am unable to describe these, although I used to see them. The making of tar was one of the industries then. It retailed at twenty and twenty-five cents a gallon, and brought from three to four dollars a barrel at Pittsburg. These old wagons would screech fearfully if they were not kept properly lubricated with this tar.

Big political conventions were held in those days, and a great custom was to have a young lady dressed in white to represent each of the different States, and have all these ladies in one wagon, which would be drawn by four or six horses, or sometimes by twenty yoke of oxen.

In the hotels of that day the "bar" was constructed for the safety of the bartender. It was a solid structure with a counter in front, from which a sliding door on iron rods could be shoved up and locked, or shut down and locked; hence the hotel man could "bar" himself in and the drunken men out. This was for safety in dispensing whiskey, and is the origin of the word "bar" in connection with hotels. In 1840 all our hotel bars were so made.

Lumbering in 1840 was one of our principal industries. We had no eastern outlet, and everything had to be rafted to Pittsburg. The saw-mills were nearly all "up and down" mills. The "thunder-gust" mills were those on small streams. All were driven by flutter-wheels and water. It required usually but one man to run one of these mills. He could do all the work and saw from one to two thousand feet of boards in twelve hours. Pine boards sold in the Pittsburg market then at three and four dollars per thousand; clear pine at ten dollars per thousand. Of course, these sales were on credit. The boards were rafted in the creek in "seven-platform" pieces by means of grubs. The oars were hung on what were called thole-pins. The front of each raft had a bumper and splash-board as a protection in going over dams. The creeks then were full of short bends, rocks, and drift. Cables were unknown here, and a halyard made from hickory withes or water-beech was used as a cable to tie up with. "Grousers" were used to assist in tying up. A pilot then received four dollars to the mouth of the creek; forehands, two dollars and expenses. The logging in the woods was all done with oxen. The camp and mill boarding consisted of bread, flitch, beans, potatoes, Orleans molasses, sometimes a little butter, and coffee or tea without cream. Woodsmen were paid sixteen dollars a month and boarded, and generally paid in store-orders or trade.

We usually had three floods on which to run this lumber,—spring, June, and fall. At these times rafts were plenty and people were scarce, and, as time and tide wait for no man, whenever a flood came everybody had to turn out and assist to run the rafts. The boy had to leave his school, the minister his pulpit, the doctor abandon his patients, the lawyer his briefs, the merchant his yard-stick, the farmer his crops or seeding. And there was one great compensation in this,—nearly everybody got to see Pittsburg.

"Running down the creek and gigging back" was the business language of everybody. "How many trips have you made?" etc. It took about twelve hours to run a raft from the neighborhood of Brookville to the mouth, or the Allegheny River, and ordinarily it required hard walking to reach home the next day. Some ambitious, industrious pilots would "run down in the daytime and walk back the same night." James T. Carroll has made four of these trips in succession, Joseph Shobert five, and William Green four or five. Of course, these pilots remained down the last night. This extraordinary labor was accomplished without ever going to bed. Although some may be incredulous, these are facts, as the parties interested are still alive (1895). Pilots sometimes ran all night. Joseph Shobert has started from Brookville at five o'clock P.M. and reached the mouth at five o'clock in the morning. Other pilots have done this also. There were no rubber goods then.

Pine square timber was taken out and marketed in Pittsburg. No other timber was marketable, and then only the best part of the pine could be hewed and rafted. Often but one stick would be used from a tree. In Pittsburg this timber brought from four to eight cents a foot, running measure.

The square timber business was then *the* business. Every lumberman followed it, and every farmer ran one timber raft at least. The "taking out of square timber" had to be done in the fall, before snow came. The trees were felled, "cut in sticks," "scored in," and hewn smooth and square. Each "lumber tract" had its log cabin and barn. The "sticks" were hauled to the creek on a "bob" sled in the snow by oxen or horses, and banked until time to "raft in" and get ready for the "spring flood." It was the timber trade that made the pioneer prosperous and intelligent.

The lumbermen could contract with hewers for the cutting, scoring, and hewing of pine timber, complete, ready to be hauled, for from three-quarters to one and a quarter cents per foot. All timber was generally well faced on one side, and was rafted with lash-poles of iron-wood or white oak, and securely fastened in position by means of white-oak bows and ash pins. Bows and pins were an article of merchandise then. Bows sold at seventy-five cents a hundred, and ash pins brought fifty cents a hundred. Grubs for board rafts sold at two dollars and fifty cents a hundred. Oar stems were then made from small sapling dead pines, shaved down. Pine timber or wild lands could then be bought at from one dollar to two dollars per acre.

Along the lower end of our creeks and on the Allegheny River there lived a class of people who caught and appropriated all the loose logs, shingles,

Rafting on North Fork

boards, and timber they could find floating down the streams. These men were called by the early lumbermen Algerines, or pirates. The name Algerine originated thus: In the war of 1812 " the dey of Algiers took the opportunity of capturing an American vessel and condemning her crew to slavery. Then a squadron of nine vessels commanded by Commodore Decatur, in May, 1815, appeared in the Mediterranean, captured the largest frigate in the Algerine navy, and with other naval successes so terrified the dey that on the 30th of June he made certain pecuniary indemnities, and renounced all future claim to any American tribute or payments, and surrendered all his prisoners."

As there has been considerable agitation over my paragraph on poll-evil in horses, I reprint here a slip that has been sent me:

" ED. SPIRIT,—I am moved by your quotation from Dr. McKnight's article in the *Brookville Democrat* on the old-time nonsense in relation to poll-evil in horses to say that the doctor's explanation of the cause of that severe affliction on the poor brute's head is in part correct; but it was mainly owing to the low door-ways and the low mow-timbers just above the horse's head as he stood in the stall of the old-time log stables. The horse often struck his head on the lintel of the low door-way as he passed in and out; and as he stood in the stall, when roughly treated by his master, in throwing up his head it came in violent contact with the timbers, and continued bruising resulted ultimately in the fearful, painful abscesses referred to. There were those in that day who had reputations for skill in the cure of poll-evil, and their method was this: The afflicted animal must be brought to the doctor before the break of day. An axe was newly ground. The doctor must not speak a word to any person on any subject after the horse was given into his hand until the feat was performed. Before sunrise the doctor took the axe and the horse and proceeded out of sight of any human habitation, going toward the east. When such a spot was reached he turned toward the animal, bent down its head firmly and gently, drew the sharpened blade of the axe first lengthwise, then crosswise of the abscess sufficiently to cause the blood to flow, muttering meanwhile some mystic words; then, just below where the head of the horse was, he stuck the bloody axe in the ground, left it there, turned immediately around, walked rapidly away, leading the animal, and not at all looking back until he had delivered it into the hand of the owner, who was waiting at a distance to receive it, and who took it home at once. The next morning at sunrise the axe was removed, and in due time the cure was effected.

" AN OLD-TIMER.

" SMICKSBURG, PA., September 7, 1894."

The first known person to live within the confines of the present borough was Jim Hunt, an Indian of the Muncy tribe. He was here as early as 1797, and was in banishment for killing a warrior of his own tribe. By an Indian law he was not allowed to live in his tribe until the place of the warrior he had slain was filled by the capture of another male from white people or from other Indians. In 1808 Jim's friends stole a white boy in Westmoreland County, Pennsylvania, and had him accepted into the tribe in place of the warrior Jim had killed. Jim Hunt's residence or cave was near the deep hole, or near the sand spring, on Sandy Lick, and was discovered in 1843 by Mr. Thomas Graham. About 1812 Jim Hunt left and never returned. He was a great bear-hunter, having killed seventy-eight in one winter. He loved " fire-water," and all his earnings went for this beverage; yet he never dared to get so drunk he could not run to his cave when he heard a peculiar Indian whoop on Mill Creek hills. His Indian enemies pursued him, and his Indian friends looked after him and warned him to flee to his hiding-place by a peculiar whoop. Little Snow, a Seneca chief, lived at the sand spring in 1800, and it was then called " Wolf Spring."

The first white person to settle in what is now Brookville was Moses Knapp. He built a log house about 1801 at the mouth of North Fork Creek, on ground now owned by Thomas L. Templeton, near Christ's brewery. The first white child born within the limits of what is now Brookville was Joshua Knapp, on Mr. Templeton's lot, at the mouth of the North Fork, in the month of March, 1810. He is still living (1895) in Pine Creek Township, about two miles from the town. About 1806 or 1807, Knapp built a log grist-mill where the waters of the North Fork then entered the Red Bank. It was a rude mill, and had but one run of *rock*-stones. In 1818 he sold this mill to Thomas Barnett. James Parks, Barnett's brother-in-law, came to run this mill about 1824 (Barnett having died), and lived here until about 1830. Parks came from Westmoreland County, Pennsylvania, and brought with him and held in legal slavery here a negro man named " Sam," who was the *first* colored person to live in what is now called Brookville. He was a large mulatto.

Joseph B. Graham, Esq., of Eldred Township, informs me that he carried a grist on horseback to this mill of one half-bushel of shelled corn for this Sam to grind. Mr. Graham says his father put the corn in one end of the bag and a big stone in the other end to balance the corn. That was the custom, but the 'squire says they did not know any better. Joshua Knapp, Uriah Matson, and John Dixon all took grists of corn and buckwheat to this mill for " Sam," the miller, to grind.

> " Happy the miller who lives by the mill,
> For by the turning of his hand he can do what he will."

But this was not so with " Sam." At his master's nod he could grind his own " peck of meal," for his body, his work, his life, and his will belonged to Parks. Many settlers in early days carried corn to the grist-mill on their own shoulders, or on the neck-yoke of a pair of oxen. I have seen both of these methods used by persons living ten and fifteen miles from a mill.

The census of 1830 gives Jefferson County a population of 2003 whites, 21 free colored persons, and 1 colored slave. This slave was " Sam."

Brookville was laid out as the county seat in 1830, but it was not incorporated as a borough until April 9, 1834. (See pamphlet laws of 1834, page 209.) The first house was erected in August, 1830. The first election held in the new borough for officials was in the spring of 1835. Joseph Sharpe was elected constable. Darius Carrier and Alexander McKnight were elected school directors. The first complete set of borough officers were elected in 1835, and were as follows:

Burgess, Thomas Lucas; Council, John Dougherty, James Corbet, John Pierce, Samuel Craig, Wm. A. Sloan; Constable, John McLaughlin (this man McLaughlin was a great hunter, and could neither read nor write; he moved to Brockwayville, and from there went West); School Directors, Levi G. Clover, Samuel Craig, David Henry, C. A. Alexander, Wm. A. Sloan, James Corbet.

In 1840 the borough officers were:

Burgess, William Jack; Council, Elijah Heath, John Gallagher, Cyrus Butler, Levi G. Clover, John Dougherty, William Rodgers; Constable, John Dougherty.

Of these early fathers the only one now living (1895) is Major William Rodgers. He resides about a mile from town, on the Corsica road.

In 1840 the " itch" was in Brookville, and popular all the year round. As bath-tubs were unknown and family bathing rare, this itch was the seven-year kind. Head-lice among the people and in the schools were also common. Had I been familiar with Burns in my boyhood, many a time, while seeing a louse crawl on and over a boy or girl in our schools, I could have exclaimed,—

> " O, Jenny, dinna toss your head
> An' set your beauties a' abraed;
> Ye little ken what cussed speed
> The beast's a makin'."

The only cure for lice was to " rid" out the hair every few days with a big, coarse comb, crack the nits between the thumb-nails, and then saturate the hair with " red precipity," using a fine-tooth comb. The itch was cured by the use of an ointment made of brimstone and lard. During school-terms many children wore little sacks of powdered brimstone about their necks. This was supposed to be a preventive.

In 1840 the only music-books we had were " The Beauties of Harmony" and " The Missouri Harmony." Each of these contained the old " buck-wheat" notes of me, fa, sol, la. Every one could not afford one of these books. Music-teachers travelled through the county and taught classes. A class was twenty-six scholars, a term thirteen nights, and the tuition-fee fifty cents for each scholar. Teachers used " tuning-forks," and some played a violin in connection with the class-singing. The teacher opened the singing by exhorting the class to " sound your pitches,—sol, fa, la."

In 1840 Billy Boo, an eccentric, intelligent hermit, lived in a hut on the farm in Rose Township now occupied by William Hughey. Although he lived in this hut, he spent most of his wakeful hours in Brookville. He was a man of good habits, and all that he would tell, or any one could learn of him or his nativity, was that he came from England. He was about five feet five or six inches high, heavy set, and stoop-shouldered. He usually dressed in white flannel clothes. Sometimes his clothing, from being darned so much, looked as if it had been quilted. He lived upon the charity of the people and by picking up a few pennies for some light gardening jobs. He died as a charge on Brookville borough in 1863.

Indian relics were found frequently on our hills and in our valleys in 1840. They consisted of stone tomahawks, darts, arrows, and flints.

Prior to and during 1840 a form of legalized slavery was practised in this State and county in regard to minor children. Poor or destitute children were "bound out" or indentured by the poor overseers to masters or mistresses,—boys until they were twenty-one years of age and girls until they were eighteen. Parents exercised this privilege also. All apprentices were then bound to mechanics to learn trades. The period of this indenture was three years. The law was severe on the children, and in favor of the master or mistress. Under these conditions cruelties were practised, and children and apprentices tried to escape them. Of course, there were bad children who ran away from kind masters and mistresses. The master or mistress usually advertised these runaways. I have seen many of these in our papers. I reprint one of these advertisements, taken from the *Gazette and Columbian*, published by J. Croll & Co., at Kittanning, Armstrong County, Pennsylvania, on August 8, 1832:

"$5 REWARD

"Run away from the subscriber, living in the borough of Kittanning, on the 22d inst., an indentured apprentice to the Tailoring business, named Henry P. Huffman, between 18 or 19 years of age, stout made and black hair, had on when he went away a light cotton roundabout, and pantaloons of the same, and a new fur hat. Whoever apprehends the said runaway and delivers him to the subscriber in Kittanning shall receive the above reward.

"JOHN WILLIAMS.

"KITTANNING, July 25, 1832."

In the forties the election for State officers was held on the second Tuesday of October of each year, and in the absence of telegraphs, railroads, etc., it took about four weeks to hear any definite result from an election, and then the result was published with a tail to it,—"Pike, Potter, McKean, and Jefferson to hear from." It is amusing to recall the reason usually given for a defeat at these elections by the unsuccessful party. It was this: "The day was fine and clear, a good day for threshing buckwheat; therefore our voters failed to turn out." The editor of the defeated party always published this poetic stanza for the consolation of his friends:

"Truth crushed to earth will rise again,
    The eternal years of God are hers,
While error, wounded, writhes in pain,
    And dies amidst her worshippers."

In a Presidential contest we never knew the result with any certainty until the 4th of March, or inauguration-day.

In 1840, according to the census, the United States contained a population of 17,062,666 people, of which 2,487,113 were slaves. The employments of the people were thus divided: Agriculture, 3,717,756; commerce, 117,575; manufactures and trades, 791,545; navigating the ocean, 56,025; navigating rivers, canals, etc., 33,067; mining, 15,203; learned professions, 65,236.

The Union then consisted of 26 States, and we had 223 Congressmen. The ratio of population for a Congressman was 70,680. In this computation five slaves would count as three white men, although the slaves were not allowed to vote. Our territories were populated thus: District of Columbia, 43,712; Florida, 54,477; Wisconsin, 30,945; Iowa, 43,112. The chief cities and towns were thus populated:

New York	312,710
Philadelphia	228,691
Baltimore	102,313
New Orleans	102,193
Boston	93,393
Cincinnati	46,338
Brooklyn	35,234
Albany	33,721
Charleston	29,261
Washington	23,364
Providence	23,171
Louisville	21,210
Pittsburg	21,115
Lowell	20,796
Rochester	20,191
Richmond	20,133
Buffalo	18,210
Newark	17,293
St. Louis	16,469
Portland	15,218
Salem	16,083
Brookville	276

Household or family goods were produced in 1840 to the amount of $29,230,380.

Total amount of capital employed in manufactures, $267,726,579.

The whole expenses of the Revolutionary War were estimated, in specie, at $135,193,703.

In 1840 it was the custom for newspapers to publish in one of their issues, after the adjournment of the Legislature, a complete list by title of all the enactments of that session.

In the forties fruit was naturally scarce and inferior in these woods, and, as " boys were boys then," all kinds of means, both fair and foul, were resorted to by the boys to get a fill of apples. Johnny Lucas, Johnny Jones, Yankee Smith, and Mrs. Fuller used to bring apples and peaches into the village and retail them out on the street. I have seen this trick played frequently on these venders by two boys,—viz., a boy would go up to the wagon, holding his cap with both hands, and ask for a sixpence worth of apples or peaches. The vender would then count the apples and drop them into the cap. The boy would then let go of the cap with one hand as if to pay, when boy No. 2 would snatch the cap and apples out of his hand and run for dear life down the street and into the first alley. The owner of the cap, in apparent anger, would immediately take after this thief, forget to pay, and in the alley help eat the apples.

In 1840 " shingle weavers" brought their shingles to Brookville to barter. A shingle weaver was a man who did not steal timber. He only went into the pine-woods and there cut the clearest and best tree he could find, and hauled it home to his shanty in blocks, and there split and shaved the blocks into shingles. He bartered his shingles in this way: he would first have his gallon or two-gallon jug filled with whiskey, then take several pounds of Baltimore plug-tobacco, and then have the balance coming to him apportioned in New Orleans molasses, flitch, and flour. Many a barter of this kind have I billed when acting as clerk.

Timothy Pickering & Co., Leroy & Linklain, Wilhelm Willink, Jeremiah Parker, Holland Land Company, Robert Morris, Robert Gilmore, William Bingham, John Nicholson, Dr. William Cathcart, Dr. James Hutchinson, and a few others owned about all the land in Jefferson County. This goes a great length to disprove the demagogy you hear so much nowadays about the few owning and gobbling up all the land. How many people own a piece of Jefferson County to-day?

In 1840 the only newspaper published in Jefferson County was the *Backwoodsman*, published in Brookville by Thomas Hastings & Son. Captain John Hastings, who is still living in Punxsutawney, was the son. The terms of this paper were one dollar and seventy-five cents in advance, two dollars if paid within the year, and two dollars and fifty cents if not paid within the year. Hastings & Son sold the paper to William Jack. Jack rented the paper to a practical printer by the name of George F. Humes, who continued the publication until after the October election in 1843, when he announced in an editorial that his patrons might go to h—ll and he would go to Texas. Barton T. Hastings and Clark Wilson then bought and assumed control of the paper, and published it until 1846 as the *Brookville Jeffersonian*. Mr. Hastings is still living (1898) in Brookville.

I reprint here a large portion of the proceedings of an old-time celebration of the Fourth of July, in 1843, in Brookville. We copy from the *Backwoodsman*, dated August 1, 1843, then edited by George F. Humes. The editorial article in the *Backwoodsman* is copied entire. The oration of D. S.

Deering, all the regular toasts, and part of the volunteer toasts are omitted because of their length. Editor Humes's article was headed

"FOURTH OF JULY CELEBRATION

"The citizens of Brookville and vicinity celebrated the sixty-seventh anniversary of American independence in a spirited and becoming manner.

"The glorious day was ushered in by the firing of cannon and ringing of bells. At an early hour the 'Independent Greens,' commanded by Captain Hugh Brady, formed into parade order, making a fine appearance, and marched through the principal streets, cheering and enlivening the large body of spectators, whose attention appeared to be solely drawn to their skilful rehearsals of military tactics; and, after spending some time in a course of drilling, joined the large assembly, without distinction of party or feeling, under the organization and direction of John McCrea, Esq., president of the day, and Samuel B. Bishop and Colonel Thomas Wilkins, marshals; when they proceeded to the court-house, where the Declaration of Independence was read in a clear and impressive tone by L. B. Dunham, Esq., after which David S. Deering, Esq., delivered an address very appropriate to the occasion, touching with point and pathos upon the inducements which impelled our fathers to raise the flag of war against the mother-country. The company then formed into line, and proceeded to the hotel of Mr. George McLaughlin, at the head of Main Street, where they sat down to a well-served, delicious, and plentiful repast, the ladies forming a smiling and interesting 'platoon' on one side of the table, which added much to the hilarity of the celebration. After the cloth was removed, and the president and committees had taken their seats, a number of toasts applicable to the times, and as varied in sentiment as the ages of the multitude, were offered and read, accompanied by repeated cheering and a variety of airs from the brass band, thus passing the day in that union and harmony so characteristic of Americans. It was indeed a 'Union celebration.'

"VOLUNTEER TOASTS

"By John McCrea. Our Brookville celebration: a union of parties, a union of feeling, the union established by our Revolutionary fathers of '76. May union continue to mark our course until time shall be no more.

"By W. W. Corbet. Liberty, regulated by law, and law by the virtues of American legislators.

"By William B. Wilkins. Henry Clay: a man of tried principles, of admitted competency, and unsullied integrity, may he be the choice of the people for the next Presidency in 1844.

"By Evans R. Brady. The Democrats of the Erie district: a *form*, *locked up* in the *chase* of disorganization; well *squabbled* at one side by the awkward formation of the district. If not *locked tight* by the *side-sticks* of regular nominations, *well driven* by the *quoins* of unity, and *knocked in* by the *sheep's foot* of pure principles, it will be *battered* by the *points* of whig-gery, bit by the *frisket* of self-interest; and when the *foreman* comes to *lift it* on the second Tuesday of October, will stand a fair chance to be *knocked* into *pi.*

" By Michael Woods. Richard M. Johnston, of Kentucky: a statesman who has been long and thoroughly tried and never found wanting. His nomination for the next Presidency will still the angry waves of political strife, and the great questions which now agitate the nation will be settled upon democratic principles.

" By Hugh Brady. The citizens of Jefferson County: they have learned their political rights by experience; let them practise the lesson with prudence.

" By B. T. Hastings. The Hon. James Buchanan: the Jefferson of Pennsylvania and choice for the Presidency in 1844. His able and manly course in the United States Senate on all intricate and important subjects entitles him to the entire confidence and support of the whole Democracy.

" By Andrew Craig. Henry Clay: a worthy and honest statesman, who has the good of his country at heart, and is well qualified to fill the Presidential chair.

" By A. Hutcheson. American independence: a virtuous old maid, sixty-eight years old to-day. God bless her.

" By David S. Deering. The Declaration of Independence: a rich legacy, bequeathed us by our ancestors. May it be transmitted from one generation to another until time shall be no more.

" By the company. The orator of the day, David S. Deering: may his course through life be as promising as his commencement.

" By D. S. Deering. The mechanics of Brookville: their structures are enduring monuments of skill, industry, and perseverance.

" By George F. Humes. The American Union: a well-adjusted *form of twenty-six pages,* fairly *locked up* in the *chase* of precision by the *quoins* of *good workmen.* May their *proof-sheets* be *well pointed* and their regular *impressions* a perfect *specimen* for the world to look upon.

" By John Hastings. James Buchanan: the able defender of the rights of the people and the *high wages* candidate for the Presidency in 1844. His elevation to that post is now without a doubt."

In 1840 the mails were carried on horseback or in stage-coaches. Communications of news, business, or affection were slow and uncertain. There were no envelopes for letters. Each letter had to be folded so as to leave the outside blank and one side smooth, and the address was written on this smooth side. Letters were sealed with red wafers, and the postage was six and a quarter cents for every hundred miles, or fraction thereof, over which it was carried in the mails. The postage on a letter to Philadelphia was eighteen and three-quarter cents, or three " fippenny bits." You could mail your letter without prepaying the postage (a great advantage to economical people), or you could prepay it at your option. Postage-stamps were unknown. When you paid the postage the postmaster stamped on the letter " Paid." When the postage was to be paid by the person addressed, the postmaster marked on it the amount due, thus: " Due, 6¼ cents."

In 1840 nearly half of our American people could neither read nor write, and less than half of them had the opportunity or inclination to do so. Newspapers were small affairs, and the owners of them were poor and their business unprofitable.

The candles used in our houses were either " dips" or " moulds." The " dips" were made by twisting and doubling a number of cotton wicks upon a round, smooth stick at a distance from each other of about the desired thickness of the candle. Then they were dipped into a kettle of melted tallow, when the ends of the sticks were hung on the backs of chairs to cool. The dipping and cooling process was thus repeated till the " dips" attained the proper thickness. This work was done after the fall butchering. " Moulds" were made in tin or pewter tubes, two, four, six, eight, ten, or twelve in a frame, joined together, the upper part of the frame forming a trough, into which the moulds opened, and from which they received the melted tallow. To make the candles, as many wicks as there were tubes were doubled over a small round stick placed across the top of the frame, and these wicks were passed down through the tubes and fastened at the lower end. Melted tallow was poured into the trough at the top till all the tubes were filled. The moulds were usually allowed to stand over night before the candles were " drawn." The possession of a set of candle-moulds by a family was an evidence of some wealth. These candles were burned in " candlesticks," made of tin, iron, or brass, and each one had a broad, flat base, turned up around the rim to catch the grease. Sometimes, when the candle was exposed to a current of air, it would " gutter" all away. A pair of " snuffers," made of iron or brass, was a necessary article in every house, and had to be used frequently to cut away the charred or burned wick. Candles sold in the stores at twelve to fifteen cents per pound. One candle was the number usually employed to read or write by, and two were generally deemed sufficient to light a store,—one to carry around to do the selling by, and the other to stand on the desk to do the charging by.

Watches were rare, and clocks were not numerous in 1840. The watches I remember seeing in those days were " English levers" and " cylinder escapements," with some old " bull's-eyes." The clocks in use were of the eight-day sort, with works of wood, run by weights instead of springs. Along in the forties clocks with brass works, called the " brass clock," came into use. A large majority of people were without " time-pieces." Evening church services were announced thus: " There will be preaching in this house on —— evening, God willing, and no preventing providence, at early candle-lighting."

In 1840 the judge of our court was Alexander McCalmont, of Franklin,

Venango County. Our associate judges from 1841 to 1843 were James Winslow and James L. Gillis. Our local or home lawyers were Hugh Brady, Cephas J. Dunham, Benjamin Bartholomew, Caleb A. Alexander, L. B. Dunham, Richard Arthurs, Elijah Heath, D. B. Jenks, Thomas Lucas, D. S. Deering, S. B. Bishop, and Jesse G. Clark. Many eminent lawyers from adjoining counties attended our courts regularly at this period. They usually came on horseback, and brought their papers, etc., in large leather saddle-bags. Most of these foreign lawyers were very polite gentlemen, and very particular not to refuse a " drink."

Moses Knapp, Sr., was our pioneer court crier. Elijah Graham was our second court crier, but I think Cyrus Butler served in this capacity in 1840.

In 1840 there was no barber-shop in the town. The tailors then cut hair, etc., for the people as an accommodation. My mother used to send me for that purpose to McCreight's tailor-shop. The first barber to locate in Brookville was a colored man named Nathan Smith. He barbered and ran a confectionery and oyster saloon. He lived here for a number of years, but finally turned preacher and moved away. Some high old times occurred in his back room which I had better not mention here. He operated on the Major Rodgers lot, now the Edelblute property.

Then " Hollow Eve," as it was called, was celebrated regularly on the night of October 31 of every year. The amount of malicious mischief and destruction done on that evening in Brookville, and patiently suffered and overlooked, is really indescribable. The Presidential contest in 1840, between Harrison (Whig) and Van Buren (Democrat) was perhaps the most intense and bitter ever known in this nation.

The first exclusively drug-store in Brookville was opened and managed by D. S. Deering, Esq., in 1848. It was located in a building where McKnight & Brothers' building stands, on the spot where McKnight & Son carry on their drug business. The first exclusively grocery-store in Brookville was opened and owned by W. W. Corbet, and was located in the east room of the American Hotel. The first exclusively hardware-store in the town was opened and owned by John S. King, now deceased. Brookville owes much to the sagacity of Mr. King for our beautiful cemetery.

In the forties the boring of pitch-pine into pump-logs was quite a business in Brookville. One of the first persons to work at this was Charles P. Merriman, who moved here from the East. By the way, Merriman was the greatest snare-drummer I ever heard. He also manufactured and repaired drums while here. He had a drum-beat peculiarly his own, and with it he could drown out a whole band. He introduced his beat by teaching drumming-schools. It is the beat of the Bowdishes, the Bartletts, and the Schnells. It consists of single and double drags. I never heard this beat in the army or in any other locality than here, and only from persons who had directly or indirectly learned it from Merriman. Any old citizen can verify the marvellous and wonderful power and skill of Merriman with a drum. No pupil of his here ever approached him in skill. The nearest to him was the late Captain John Dowling, of the One Hundred and Fifth Regiment, Pennsylvania Volunteers. It was the custom then for the different bands in the surrounding townships to attend the Fourth of July celebrations in Brookville. The Monger band, father and sons, from Warsaw Township, used to come. They had a peculiar open beat that old Mr. Monger called the 1812 beat. The Belleview band came also; it was the Campbell band, father and sons. Andrew C. and James (1895), after going through the war, are still able on our public occasions to enliven us with martial strains. The Lucas band, from Dowlingville, also visited us in the forties. Brookville had a famous fifer in the person of Harvey Clover. He always carried an extra fife in his pocket, because he was apt to burst one. When he "blowed" the fife you would have thought the devil was in it sure.

In 1847 the town had water-works, the enterprise of Judge Jared B. Evans. The spring that furnished the water was what is now known as the American Spring. The conduit-pipes were bored yellow-pine logs, and the plant was quite expensive; but owing to some trouble about the tannery, which stood on the spot where the American barn now stands, the waterplant was destroyed. Judge Evans was a useful citizen. He died some three years ago.

In 1840 the church collection was either taken up in a hat with a handkerchief in it or in a little bag attached to a pole.

H. Clay Campbell, Esq., has kindly furnished me the legal rights of married women in Pennsylvania from 1840 until the present date. The common law was adopted by Pennsylvania, and has governed all rights except those which may have been modified from time to time by statute. Blackstone's Commentaries, Book I., page 442, says, " By marriage, the husband and wife are one person in law; that is, the very being or legal existence of the woman is suspended during the marriage, or at least is incorporated and consolidated into that of her husband, under whose wing, protection, and cover she performs everything."

You see the rights surrendered by a woman marrying under the common law were two: First, the right to make a contract; secondly, the right to property and her own earnings. To compensate for this she acquired *one right*,—the right to be chastised. For as the husband was to answer for her misbehavior, the law thought it reasonable to intrust him with the power of restraining her, by domestic chastisement, with the same moderation that a man is allowed to correct his apprentice or his children.

In 1840 married women had no right to the property bequeathed to them by their parents, unless it was put into the hands of a trustee, and by marriage the husband became the immediate and absolute owner of the personal property of the wife which she had in possession at the time of marriage, and this property could never again revert to the wife or her representatives. She could acquire no personal property by industry during marriage; and if she obtained any by gift or otherwise, it became immediately by and through the law the property of her husband. This condition prevailed until the passage of an act, dated April 11, 1848, which in some slight degree modified this injustice of the common law. By that act it was provided that all property which belonged to her before marriage, as well as all that might accrue to her afterwards, should remain her property. Then came another modification by the act of 1855, which provided, among other things, that "whenever a husband, from drunkenness, profligacy, or other cause, shall neglect or refuse to provide for his wife, she shall have the rights and privileges secured to a *femme-sole* trader under the act of 1718." Modifications have been made from year to year, granting additional privileges to a wife to manage her own property, among which may be noted the act of 1871, enabling her to sell and transfer shares of the stock of a railroad company. By the act of May, 1874, she may draw checks upon a bank. During all these years of enlightenment the master has still held the wife in the toils of bondage, and it was with great grudging that he acknowledged that a married woman had the right to claim anything. The right to the earnings of the wife received its first modification when the act of April, 1872, was passed, which granted to the wife, if she went into court, and the court granted her petition, the right to claim her earnings. But legally the wife remained the most abject of slaves until the passage of the "married woman's personal property act" of 1887, giving and granting to her the right to contract and acquire property; and it was not until 1893 that she was granted the same rights as an unmarried woman, excepting as to her right to convey her real estate, make a mortgage, or become bail.

The higher education of women in the seminary and college is of American origin, and in 1840 there was an occasional young ladies' seminary here and there throughout the country. These isolated institutions were organized and carried on by scattered individuals who had great persistency and courage. Being of American origin its greatest progress has been here, and at present there are more than two hundred institutions for the superior education of women in the United States, and fully one-half of these bear the name of college. The women who graduate to-day from colleges and high-schools outnumber the men, and as a result of this mental discipline and training women are now found throughout the world in every profession, in all trades, and in every vocation.

> "Preferring sense from chin that's bare
> To nonsense 'throned in whiskered hair."

Women are now admitted to the bar in nine different States of the Union, and by an act of Congress she may now practise before the United States Supreme Court.

In 1840 women had but seven vocations for a livelihood,—viz., marriage, housekeeping, teaching, sewing, weaving, type-setting, and bookbinding. Then female suffrage was unknown. To-day (1895) women vote on an equality with men in two States (Colorado and Wyoming), and they can vote in a limited form in twenty other States and Territories.

In 1840 women had no religious rights. She did not dare to speak, teach, or pray in public, and if she desired any knowledge in this direction, she was admonished to ask her husband at home. The only exception I know to this rule was in the Methodist Church, which from its organization has recognized the right of women to teach, speak in class-meetings, and to pray in the public prayer-meeting.

In 1840 women had no industrial rights. I give below a little abstract from the census of 1880, fourteen years ago, which will show what some of our women were working at then and are working at now.

Artists, 2016; authors, 320; assayists, chemists, and architects, 2136; barbers, 2902; dressmakers, 281,928; doctors, 2433; journalists, 238; lawyers, 75; musicians, 13,181; preachers, 165; printers, 3456; tailors, 52,098; teachers, 194,375; nurses, 12,294; stock raisers, 216; farmers, 56,809; in government employ as clerks, 2171; managing commercial and industrial interests, 14,465. And now in 1894 we have 6000 post-mistresses, 10,500 women have secured patents for inventions, and 300,000 women are in gainful occupations. I confess that this statement looks to the intelligent mind as though "the hand that rocks the cradle" will soon not only move but own the world.

The earliest schools established by the settlers of Pennsylvania were the home school, the church school, and the public subscription school, the most simple and primitive in style. The subscription or public school remained in force until the law of 1809 was enacted, which was intended for a State system, and which provided a means of education for the poor, but retained the subscription character of pay for the rich. This 1809 system remained in force until 1834. The method of hiring "masters" for a subscription school was as follows: A meeting was called by public notice in a district. At this gathering the people chose, in their own way, three of their number to act as a school committee. This committee hired the master and exercised a superintendence over the school. The master was paid by the patrons of the school in proportion to the number of days each had sent a child to school. A rate-bill was made out by the master and given to the committee, who collected the tuition-money and paid it to the master. The terms of these schools were irregular, but usually were for three months.

The studies pursued were spelling, reading, writing, and arithmetic. The daily programme was two or four reading lessons, two spelling lessons,—one at noon and one at evening,—the rest of the time being devoted to writing and doing "sums" in arithmetic. It was considered at that time (and even as late as my early schooling) that it was useless and foolish for a girl to learn more at school than to spell, read, and write. Of course there was no uniformity in text-books. The child took to the school whatever book he had, hence there was, and could be, no classification. Blackboards were unknown. When any information was wanted about a "sum," the scholar either called the master or took his book and went to him.

The first school-master in Jefferson County was John Dixon. His first term was for three months, and was in the year 1803 or 1804. The first school-house was built on the Ridgway road, two miles from Brookville, on the farm now owned by D. B. McConnell. I give Professor Blose's description of this school-house:

"The house was built of rough logs, and had neither window-sash nor pane. The light was admitted through chinks in the wall, over which greased paper was pasted. The floor was made with puncheons, and the seats from broad pieces split from logs, with pins in the under side, for legs. Boards laid on pins fastened in the wall furnished the pupils with writing-desks. A log fireplace, the entire length of one end, supplied warmth when the weather was cold."

The era of these log school-houses in Jefferson County is gone,—gone forever. We have now (1895) school property to the value of $269,300. We have 196 modern school-houses, with 262 school-rooms, 295 schools, and the Bible is read in 251 of these. There is no more *master's* call in the school-room, but we have 131 female and 149 male *teachers*,—a total of 280 teachers in the county. The average yearly term is six and a half months. The average salary for male teachers is $39.50, and for female teachers, $33.00. Total wages received by teachers each year, $64,913.20. Number of female scholars, 5839; number of male scholars, 6073. The amount of tax levied for school purposes is $56,688.23. Received by the county from State appropriation, $42,759.72.

The act of 1809 made it the duty of assessors to receive the names of all children between the ages of five and twelve years whose parents were unable to pay for their schooling, and these poor children were to be educated by the county. This law was very unpopular, and the schools did not prosper. The rich were opposed to this law because they paid all the tax-bills, and the poor were opposed to it because it created a "caste" and designated them as paupers. However, it remained in force for about twenty-five years, and during this period the fight over it at elections caused many strifes, feuds, and bloody noses. This was the *first* step taken by the State to evolve our present free-school system. The money to pay for the education of these "pauper" children was drawn from the county in this way: "The assessor of each borough or township returned the names of such indigent children to the county commissioners, and then an order was drawn by the commissioners on the county treasurer for the tuition-money."

One of the most desirable qualifications in the early school-master was courage, and willingness and ability to control and flog boys. Physical force was the governing power, and the master must possess it. Nevertheless, many of the early masters were men of intelligence, refinement, and scholarship. As a rule, the Scotch-Irish master was of this class. Goldsmith describes the old master well:

> " Yet he was kind, or if severe in aught,
> The love he bore to learning was in fault.
> The village all declared how much he knew,
> 'Twas certain he could write and cipher, too.
> In arguing the parson owned his skill,
> For e'en though vanquished he would argue still."

The government of the early masters was of the most rigorous kind. Perfect quiet had to be maintained in the school-room, no buzzing, and the punishment for supposed or real disobedience, inflicted on scholars before, up to, and even in my time, was cruel and brutal. One punishment was to tie scholars up by the thumbs, suspending them in this way over the door. "Spare the rod and spoil the child" was the master's slogan. Whippings were frequent, severe, and sometimes brutal. Thorn, birch, and other rods were kept in large number by the master. Other and milder modes of punishment were in vogue, such as the dunce-block, sitting with the girls, pulling the ears, and using the ferule on the hands and sometimes on the part of the body on which the scholar sat.

> " What is man,
> If his chief good and market for his time
> Be but to sleep and feed? A beast, no more."

In 1840 the country master boarded around with the scholars, and he was always given the best bed in the house, and was usually fed on doughnuts and pumpkin-pie at every meal. He called the school to order by rapping on his desk with his ferule.

During the twenty-five years of the existence of the pauper schools the agitation for a better system was continually kept up by isolated individuals. This was done in various ways,—at elections, in toasts to a " free-school system" at Fourth of July celebrations, and in conventions of directors. The first governor who took a decided stand in favor of the common schools was John A. Schultze. He advocated it in his message in 1828. Governor Wolf, in 1833, found that out of four hundred thousand school children of the legal age, twenty thousand attended school, and that three hundred and eighty thousand were yearly uninstructed. Therefore, in his message to the

Legislature, he strongly recommended the passage of a law to remedy this state of affairs. William Audenreid, a senator from Schuylkill County, introduced a bill during the session of the Legislature of 1833, which became what is known as the school law of 1834,—the establishment of the common-school system. Our second State superintendent of public instruction was appointed under this law. His name was Thomas H. Burrowes. The first State aid for schools in Jefferson County was in 1835. The amount received was one hundred and four dollars and ninety-four cents.

"Barring the master out" of the school-room on Christmas and New Year's was a custom in vogue in 1840. The barring was always done by four or five determined boys. The contest between the master and these scholars was sometimes severe and protracted, the master being determined to get into the school-room and these boys determined to keep him out. The object on the part of the scholars in this barring out was to compel the master to treat the school. If the master obtained possession of the school-room, by force or strategy, he generally gave the boys a sound flogging; but if the boys "held the fort," it resulted in negotiations for peace, and in the master eventually signing an agreement in writing to treat the school to apples, nuts, or candy. It took great nerve on the part of the boys to take this stand against a master. I know this, as I have been active in some of these contests.

In 1840 a woman could teach an A, B, C, or "a-b ab," school in summer; but the man that desired to teach a summer school was a lazy, worthless, good-for-nothing fellow. Cyrus Crouch taught the first term in Brookville under the common-school law of 1834.

In the forties the school-books in use were the New England Primer, Webster's Spelling-Book, Cobb's Spelling-Book, the English Reader, the New England Reader, the Testament and Bible, the Malte Braun Geography, Olney's Geography, Pike's Arithmetic, the Federal Calculator, the Western Calculator, Murray's Grammar, Kirkham's Grammar, and Walker's Dictionary. A scholar who had gone through the single rule of three in the Western Calculator was considered educated. Our present copy-books were unknown. A copy-book was then made of six sheets of foolscap-paper stitched together. The copies were set by the master after school hours, when he also usually made and mended the school-pens for the next day. Our pens were made of goose-quills, and it was the duty of the master to teach each scholar how to make or mend a goose-quill pen. One of the chief delights of a mischievous boy in those days was to keep a master busy mending his pens.

The first school-house in Brookville that I recollect was a little brick building on the alley near the northeast side of the American Hotel lot. Mrs. Pearl Roundy was the first teacher that I went to. She taught in this house. She was much beloved by the whole town. I afterwards went to Hamlin and others in this same house.

When the first appropriation of seventy-five thousand dollars was made by our State for the common schools, a debt of twenty-three million dollars rested on the Commonwealth. A great many good, conservative men opposed this appropriation, and "predicted bankruptcy from this *new* form of extravagance." But the great debt has been all paid, the expenses of the war for the Union have been met, and now (1895) the annual appropriation for our schools has been raised to five and a half million dollars. This amount due the schools for the year ending June 5, 1893, was all paid on November 1, 1893, and our State treasurer had deposits still left, lying idle, in forty-six of our banks, amounting to six and a half million dollars, which should have been appropriated for school purposes and not kept lying idle. This additional appropriation would have greatly relieved the people from oppressive taxation during these hard times.

The act of May 18, 1893, completed the evolution in our school system from the early home, the church, the subscription, the 1809 pauper, the 1834 common, into the now people's or *free* school system.

This free school is our nation's hope. Our great manufacturing interests attract immigrants to our land in large numbers, and to thoroughly educate their children and form in them the true American mind, and to prevent these children from drifting into the criminal classes, will task to the utmost all the energies, privileges, and blessed conditions of our present free schools. In our free schools of Pennsylvania the conditions are now equal. The child of the millionaire, the mechanic, the widow, and the day laborer all stand on the same plane. We have now. for the first time in the history of our State, in addition to the free school-houses, free desks, free fuel, free blackboards, free maps, free teachers, free books, free paper, free pens. free ink, free slates, free pencils, free sponges, and, in short, *free schools.*

In 1840 our houses and hotels were never locked at night. This was from carelessness, or perhaps thought to be unnecessary. But every store window was provided with heavy outside shutters, which were carefully closed, barred, or locked every night in shutting up.

Then every merchant in Brookville was forced, as a matter of protection, to subscribe for and receive a weekly bank-note detector. These periodicals were issued to subscribers for two dollars and fifty cents a year. This journal gave a weekly report of all broken banks, the discount on other State bank-notes, as well as points for the detection of counterfeit notes and coin. The coin department in the journal had wood-cut pictures of all the foreign and native silver and gold coins, and also gave the value of each.

Money was scarce then, and merchants were compelled to sell their goods on credit, and principally for barter. The commodities that were exchanged for in Brookville stores were boards, shingles, square timber, wheat, rye, buckwheat. flaxseed, clover-seed, timothy-seed, wool, rags, beeswax, feathers, hickory-nuts, chestnuts, hides, deer-pelts, elderberries, furs, road orders, school and county orders, eggs, butter, tow cloth, linen cloth, axe-handles, rafting bows and pins, rafting grubs, maple-sugar in the spring, and oats after harvest.

In those days everybody came to court, either on business or to see and be seen. Tuesday was the big day. The people came on horseback or on foot. We had no book-store in town, and a man named Ingram, from Meadville, came regularly every court and opened up his stock in the bar-room of a hotel. An Irishman by the name of Hugh Miller came in the same way, and opened his jewelry and spectacles in the hotel bar-room. This was the time for insurance agents to visit our town. Robert Thorn was the first insurance agent who came here, at least to my knowledge.

In 1840 every store in town kept pure Monongahela whiskey in a bucket, either on or behind the counter, with a tin cup in or over the bucket for customers to drink free of charge, early and often. Every store sold whiskey by the gallon. Our merchants kept chip logwood by the barrel, and kegs of madder, alum, cobalt, copperas, indigo, etc., for women to use in coloring their homespun goods. Butternuts were used by the women to dye brown, peach-leaves or smartweed for yellow, and cobalt for purple. Men's and women's clothing consisted principally of homespun, and homespun underwear. Men and boys wore warmusses, roundabouts, and pants made of flannels, buckskin, Kentucky jean, blue drilling, tow, cloth, linen, satinet, bed-ticking, and corduroy, with coon-skin, seal-skin, and cloth caps, and in summer oat-straw or chip hats. The dress suit was a blue broadcloth swallow-tail coat with brass buttons, and a stove-pipe hat. " Galluses" were made of listing, bed-ticking, or knit of woollen yarn. Women wore barred flannel, linsey-woolsey, tow, and linen dresses. Six or eight yards of " Dolly Var-den" calico made a superb Sunday dress. Calico sold then for fifty cents a yard. Every home had a spinning-wheel, some families had two,—a big one and a little one. Spinning-parties were in vogue, the women taking their wheels to a neighbor's house, remaining for supper, and after supper going home with their wheels on their arms. Wool-carding was then done by hand and at home. Every neighborhood had several weavers, and they wove for customers at so much per yard.

About 1840, Brookville had a hatter,—John Wynkoop. He made what was called wool hats. Those that were high-crowned or stove-pipe were wreath-bound with some kind of fur, perhaps rabbit-fur. These hatters were common in those days. The sign was a stove-pipe hat and a smoothing-iron. A Swiss in 1404 invented the hat. There was a standing contest between the tailors, hatters, and printers in drinking whiskey (doctors barred).

Then, too, coopers were common in every town. These coopers made tubs, buckets, and barrels, all of which were bound with hickory hoops. Our cooper was a Mr. Hewitt. His shop was on the alley, rear of the Commercial Hotel lot. These are now two lost industries.

In 1840 there was but one dental college in the world,—the Baltimore College of Dental Surgery, established in Baltimore, Maryland, in 1839,— the first dental college ever started. Up to and in that day dentistry was not a science, for it was practised as an addenda by the blacksmith, barber, watchmaker, and others. In the practice no anatomical or surgical skill was required. It was something that required muscular strength and manual dexterity in handling the "turnkey." With such a clumsy, rude condition of dentistry, is it any wonder that Tom Moore wrote these lines?—

> "What pity, blooming girl, that lips so ready for a lover,
> Should not beneath their ruby casket cover one tooth of pearl,
> But like a rose beneath a church-yard stone,
> Be doomed to blush o'er many a mouldering bone."

The pioneer native American dentist was John Greenwood.

All the great discoveries and improvements in the science and art of dentistry as it is to-day are American. Dentistry stands as an American institution, not only beautified, but almost perfected upon a firm pedestal, a most noble science; and, through the invention, by Charles W. Peale, of Philadelphia, of porcelain teeth, our molars shall henceforth be as white as milk. If Moore lived to-day, under the condition of American dentistry, he might well exclaim, in the language of Akenside,—

> "What do I kiss? A woman's mouth,
> Sweeter than the spiced winds from the south."

In 1796, when Andrew Barnett trod on the ground where Brookville now stands, slavery existed throughout all Christendom. Millions of men, women, and children were held in the legal condition of horses and cattle. Worse than this, the African slave-trade—a traffic so odious and so loudly reproved and condemned by the laws of religion and of nature—was carried on as a legal right by slave-dealers in and from every Christian nation. The horror with which this statement of facts must strike you only proves that the love of gold and the power of evil in the world is most formidable. The African slave-trade was declared illegal and unlawful by England in 1806–07, by the United States in 1808, by Denmark, Portugal, and Chile in 1811, by Sweden in 1813, by Holland in 1814–15, by France in 1815, and by Spain in 1822.

When Andrew Barnett first trod the ground where Brookville now stands the curse of slavery rested on Pennsylvania, for in that year three thousand seven hundred and thirty-seven human beings were considered "property" within her borders and held as slaves.

"Chains him and tasks him, and exacts his sweat
With stripes, that Mercy with a bleeding heart
Weeps when she sees it inflicted on a beast."

In 1840 slavery still existed in Pennsylvania, the total number being 75, distributed, according to the census of that year, as follows: Adams County, 2; Berks, 2; Cumberland, 25; Lancaster, 2; Philadelphia, 2; York, 1; Greene, 1; Juniata, 1; Luzerne, 1; Mifflin, 31; Union, 3; Washington, 2; Westmoreland, 1; Fayette, 1.

It will be seen that no slave was held or owned in Jefferson County. There is not, to-day, a slave in all Christendom, after a struggle of nearly two thousand years.

"Little by little the world grows strong,
Fighting the battle of Right and Wrong.
Little by little the Wrong gives way;
Little by little the Right has sway;
Little by little the seeds we sow
Into a beautiful yield will grow."

In 1840, according to the census, there were fifty-seven colored people and no slaves in Jefferson County. The most prominent of these colored people who lived in and around Brookville were Charles Southerland, called Black Charley; Charles Anderson, called Yellow Charley; John Sweeney, called Black John; and George Hays, the fiddler. Charles Southerland came to Jefferson County and settled near Brookville in 1812. He came from Virginia, and was said to have held General Washington's horse at the laying of the corner-stone of the national capitol at Washington. He was a very polite man, a hard drinker, reared a family, and died in 1852, at the advanced age of nearly one hundred years.

Charley always wore a stove-pipe hat with a colored, cotton handkerchief in it. He loafed much in Clover's store. The late Daniel Smith was a young man then, and clerked in this store. Mr. Smith in his manhood built the property now owned and occupied by Harry Matson. Charley Southerland, if he were living now, would make a good Congressman, because he was good on appropriations. One day there was no one in the store but Smith and Charley. There was a crock of eggs on the counter. Smith had to go to the cellar and left the store in the charge of Charley. On returning he glanced in the direction of the eggs, and discovered that Charley had pilfered about a dozen of them. Where were they? He surmised they must be in Charley's hat; so stepping in front of Southerland, he brought his right fist heavily down on his hat, with the exclamation, " Why the h—ll don't you wear your hat on your head?" Much to the amusement of Smith and the discomfort of Southerland, the blow broke all the eggs, and the white and yellow contents ran down over Charley's face and clothes, making a striking contrast with his sooty black face.

27   417

The lives of many good men and women have been misunderstood and clouded by the thoughtless, unkind words and deeds of their neighbors. Good men and women have struggled hard and long, only to go down, down, poisoned and persecuted all their days by the venomous and vicious slanders of their neighbors; while, strange to say, men and women who are guilty of all the vices are frequently apologized for, respected, and are great favorites with these same neighbors.

It is unfortunate enough in these days to have been painted black by our Creator, but in 1840 it was a terrible calamity. A negro then had no rights; he was nothing but a " d—d nigger;" anybody and everybody had a right to abuse, beat, stone, and maltreat him. This right, too, was pretty generally exercised. I have seen a white bully deliberately step up in front of a negro, in a public street, and with the exclamation, " Take that, you d—d

Western entrance to Brookville, 1840

nigger!" knock him down, and this, too, without any cause, word, or look from the negro. This was done only to exhibit what the ruffian could do. Had the negro, even after this outrage, said a word in his own defence, the cry would have been raised, " Kill the d—d nigger!" I have seen negro men stoned into Red Bank Creek, for no crime, by a band of young ruffians. I have seen a house in Brookville borough, occupied by negro women and children, stoned until every window was broken and the door mashed in, and all this for no crime save that they were black. It used to make my blood boil, but I was too little to even open my mouth. A sorry civilization, was it not?

The accompanying cut represents Brookville as I first recollect it,— from 1840 to 1843,—a town of shanties, and containing a population of two hundred and forty people. It is made from a pencil sketch drawn on the ground in 1840. It is not perfect, like a photograph would make it now. To understand this view of Main Street, imagine yourself in the middle of the then pike, now street, opposite the Union or McKinley Hotel, and looking eastward. The first thing that strikes your attention is a team of horses hauling a stick of timber over a newly-laid, hewed-log bridge. This bridge was laid over the deep gully that can now be seen in G. B. Carrier's lot. Looking to the left side of the street, the first building, the gable end of which you see, was the Presbyterian church, then outside of the west line of the borough. The next, or little house, was Jimmie Lucas's blacksmith-shop. The large house with the paling fence was the residence and office of John Gallagher, Esq., and is now the Judge Clark property. The next house was east of Barnett Street, and the Peace and Poverty Hotel. East of this hotel you see the residence and tailor-shop of Benjamin McCreight. Then you see a large two-story house, which stood where the Commercial Hotel now stands. This building was erected by John Clements, and was known as the Clements property. Then there was nothing until you see the court-house, with its belfry, standing out, two stories high, bold and alone. East of this and across Pickering Street, where Harry Matson now resides, was a large frame building, occupied by James Craig as a store-room for cabinet-work. Rev. Gara Bishop resided here for a long time. Next to this, where Guyther & Henderson's store now stands, were several brick business buildings belonging to Charles Evans. Next came Major William Rodgers's store, on what is now the Edelblute property. Then came Jesse G. Clark's home; then the Jefferson House (Phil. Allgeier's house), and the present building is the original, but somewhat altered. Then across the alley, where Gregg's barber-shop now is, was the Elkhorn, or Red Lion Hotel, kept by John Smith, who was sheriff of the county in 1840. The next house was on the Mrs. Clements property, and was the home and blacksmith-shop of Isaac Allen. Then came the Matson row, just as it is now down to the Brownlee house, northeast corner of Main and Mill Streets.

Now please come back and look down the right-hand side. The first building, the rear end of which only can be seen behind the tree, was the first foundry built in town. It stood near or on the ground where Fetzer's brick building, the rear end of which, only, can be seen behind the tree, was the first was afterwards the Evans foundry. When built it was outside the borough. The second house, with the gable next the street, was the house of James Corbet, Esq., father of Colonel Corbet, and it stood where the gas-office now is. The next and large building, with the gable-end next the street, was called the James Hall Building, and stood on the ground now occupied by the Bishop Buildings. This building was used for day-school and singing-school purposes. I went to day-school here to Miss Jane Clark then, now Mrs. E. H. Darrah. It was also used by a man named Wynkoop, who made beaver hats. The next building was a house erected by a Mr. Sharpe, and was located on the lot west of where the National Bank of Brookville now stands. The building having the window in the gable-end facing you was the Jack Building, and stood on the ground now occupied by McKnight & Son in their drug business. East of this, on the ground now occupied by R. M. Matson's brick, stood a little frame building, occupied by John Heath, Jr. It cannot be seen. East and across Pickering Street you see the Franklin House and its sign. Here now stands the Central Hotel of S. B. Arthurs. East of the Franklin House, but not distinctly shown on the picture, were the houses of Craig, Waigley, Thomas M. Barr, Levi G. Clover, Mrs. Mary McKnight, Snyder's row, and Billy McCullough's house and shop, situate on the corner of Main and Mill Streets, or where the Baptist church now stands.

The buildings on each side of Pickering Street, east of the court-house, you will see, are not very plain or distinct on the picture.

These recollections were published in 1895.

CHAPTER XXII

"Have we not all one Father? Hath not one God created us?"

IN 1893 the Rev. Robert Audely Brown, D.D., of New Castle, Pennsylvania, in writing of the United Presbyterian Branch of the Presbyterian Church of one hundred years ago, says,—

"We can only imagine the labors of these men as they worked after the ideal of the Scottish pastorate in the new part of the new world. We cannot doubt their fidelity. But no record, printed or written, remains of their visits from house to house and other kindred pastoral labors.

"More durable, however, than marble, is their influence among the living forces of to-day. To estimate their labors better, let us remember the contemporaneous civil and political events that embarrassed their pastorates.

"The Indian wars had called for soldiers from their communities and congregations up till now. It was only this very year that Wayne's victory ended these wars. Sons, brothers, and fathers were many of them in the field. Fort Pitt was the rendezvous and point of departure of troops gathered from the surrounding counties of Western Pennsylvania. As late as 1791 St. Clair's defeat had brought sorrow to many families and terror to homes in prospect of bloody raids and massacres that might follow in Pennsylvania and Virginia.

"More distracting and injurious to religion than Indian wars was the Whiskey Insurrection, which from 1791 until 1794 filled men's minds, and which was crushed only in the latter year. The three Pennsylvania pastors were located in the very centre of the excitement; armed resistance, fire, and bloodshed, signalized ground only a few miles from where we are now met. The member who represented this district in Congress was an elder in the pastoral charge of Matthew Henderson. This was William Findley, of Westmoreland County, grandfather of the late Dr. William Findley, long connected with Westminster College. Standing on the side of justice, law, and order, as our predecessors necessarily did, it cannot be doubted but that they felt the force of adverse currents where in the various communities in which they lived men rose to the point of insurrection against what was conceived to be a hardship and injustice in having that one industry taxed which brought them money, and that from far-off markets east, reached by rugged mountain roads or by long and perilous voyage down the Ohio and Mississippi Rivers to New Orleans.

" But these pastors found a worse enemy still to counteract their work. Worse than Indian wars, worse than the Whiskey Insurrection, was whiskey itself. Whiskey was the chief manufacture of the West and eminently of the two regions which this Presbytery occupied, and certainly this seems a singular fact. Old Monongahela whiskey in Pennsylvania and Old Bourbon whiskey of Kentucky occupied the very centre of these fields which God had allotted the new Presbytery; and as the Prince of Persia withstood the Angel Michael, in Daniel's vision, so this agency of Satan impeded and impaired the sacred work of the laborers for the gospel. Many of the more well-to-do owners of the farms (nearly all were farmers), were the owners also of stills, and for themselves and less prosperous neighbors turned grain into whiskey, in which more portable form their harvests reached a distant market, and so commanded money. There was hard toiling amid the stumps. The belief that whiskey was ' a good creature of God' infested men's minds. So in practice they were true to principle. What was good for others was certainly good also for themselves. They were consumers as well as producers. The farmer and his boys all drank. The store-keeper kept liquor free for his customers, on the counter. The guest in respectable homes was treated to it universally. The pastor was expected to drink it as a pledge of hospitality on entering a dwelling, and again to drink at his departure. If he made twelve visits in a day he had taken twenty-four drinks. It is a wonder that religion survived. Many members of the church were tipplers; some were often (in common phrase) ' the worse for liquor,' and some were confirmed drunkards and died such. How many of the baptized of the church and the unbaptized and those out of the church were lost, who can tell? But the loss was fearful. It included the loss of souls and bodies and standing. It changed the course of lives, it wasted fortunes. It ruined the individual, and doomed his family and friends to be losers by all the interests they had in him. And it inflicted a burden and a blight on the community and the church. These, indeed, grew, but it was not liquor made them grow, but the wonderful wealth of a new and virgin land rewarding the productive industry of a new people, and causing them to grow despite the fearful drain upon their resources. The church has gained even with the curse of the drinking usage its chief enemy. But what it might have achieved but for liquor no man can estimate. Even the ministry, in instances, became victims; more than one wreck caused pain and shame later, and demanded discipline in the form of admonition, warning, suspension, or deposition. But this statement does not apply to the fathers of the Presbytery; and only to a few of those who afterwards became members. It was no wonder some of them were drunkards; it is, on the contrary, a wonder they were not all drunkards. It is a proof of the grace of God and the truth of Christianity that it survived,—an evidence that the church has a living power from God that it grew, though thus weighted down and fettered, until a time came when another principle became ascendant,—namely, that instead of the drinking of an intoxicant being a just use of 'one of God's good creatures,' the making and use of alcoholic poisons as beverages is an essential immorality."

BUTLER COUNTY

PRESBYTERIAN CHURCH

Butler in 1813. Middlesex, in 1802, by Rev. Abraham Boyd. West Minister, in 1835, by Rev. Abraham Boyd. Buffalo, in 1843, by Rev. Abraham Boyd. North Butler, in 1846, by Rev. Coulter. Bear Creek, in 1800, by Rev. William Morehead. Concord, in 1804, by Rev. John McPherrin. Harrisville, in 1807. Martinsburg, in 1822. Muddy Creek, in 1799, by Rev. John McPherrin. Pleasant Valley, in 1844, by Rev. Joseph Moore. New Salem, in 1847. Scrubgrass, in 1802, by Rev. Robert Johnston.

Rev. John McPherrin was the pioneer Presbyterian preacher in Butler County in 1805.

M. E. CHURCH

Butler, in 1825, by Rev. John Chandler. Lancaster, in 1841. Harmony, in 1842. Forward, in 1827. Knox, in 1823. Prospect, in 1844, by Rev. Samuel Crouse. Centreville Borough, in 1831. Harrisville Borough, in 1833. Martinsburg, in 1834, by Rev. Gilmer. Washington, in 1842.

LUTHERAN CHURCH

St. Mark's, in 1827. Grace, in 1843, by Rev. Bassler. Zion, in 1840, by Rev. Schweitzerbarth. St. Paul's, in 1831, by Rev. Schweitzerbarth. Prospect, in 1842, by Rev. Bassler.

ECONOMITE CHURCH

In 1804, by Rev. John Rapp.

UNITED PRESBYTERIAN CHURCH

Evansburg, in 1837, by Rev. Isaiah Niblock. Mt. Pleasant, in 1847, by Rev. Guthrie. Glade Run, in 1817, by Rev. Bruce. Prospect, in 1825, by Rev. Greer. Slippery Rock, in 1807, by Rev. John Anderson. Harmony, in 1800. Venango, in 1800, by Rev. Thomas McClintock. Centreville Borough, in 1848, by Rev. Findley, D.D.

ROMAN CATHOLIC CHURCH

Butler, in 1822, by Rev. Charles Perry. St. Mary's, in 1841. St. Patrick's, Millerstown, in 1801, Father Lanigan.

BAPTIST CHURCH

Zion, in 1841, by Rev. Daniel Daniels.

HISTORY OF NORTHWESTERN PENNSYLVANIA

CRAWFORD COUNTY

PRESBYTERIAN CHURCH

Cochranton, in 1848. Fairfield, in 1810, by Rev. Robert Johnston. Rome Township, in 1815, by Rev. Amos Chase. Evansburg, in 1811, by Rev. Robert Johnston. Spartansburg, in 1844, by Rev. Hampson. Conneautville, in 1835, by Rev. Hassinger. Harmonsburg, in 1829, by Rev. David McKinney. Titusville, in 1815, by Rev. Amos Chase.

The Rev. Elisha McCurdy and Rev. Joseph Stockton were the first ordained ministers who preached within the bounds of what is now Crawford County,—to wit, in 1799.

Rev. Stockton was the first stated preacher in Meadville in the year 1800. The Second Presbyterian Church of Meadville was organized in 1839.

CONGREGATIONAL CHURCH

Centreville, in 1841, by Rev. Lucius Parker, Meadville, in 1825, by Rev. John M. Merrick. Richmond, organized and maintained by John Brown, of Ossawatomie fame.

LUTHERAN CHURCH

The pioneer Lutheran preacher in Crawford County was Rev. S. Muckenhaupt. He preached at Meadville, Conneaut Lake, and Venango from 1803 to 1808.

Saegertown, in 1826. Meadville, in 1815, by Charles W. Colson. Freewill Baptist, Greenwood Township, in 1832, by Rev. George Collins.

EPISCOPAL

Meadville, in 1825, by Rev. J. H. Hopkins.

CUMBERLAND PRESBYTERIAN

Meadville, in 1834.

UNIVERSALIST

Titusville, in 1844.

M. E. CHURCH

Beaver Centre, in 1839. Bloomfield, in 1840. Cambridge Borough, in 1832. Freys, in 1818. Cochranton, in 1839, by Rev. Patterson. Geneva, in 1820. Hayfield, in 1826, by Rev. Tackett. Coons Corner, in 1844. Mead, in 1812, by Rev. J. Graham. Espyville, in 1831. Centre Chapel, in 1825, by Rev. Thomas Carr. Hydetown, in 1847. Guys Mills, in 1822. Richmond, in 1822, by Rev. Hatton. Hartstown, in 1840. Saegertown, in 1839. State Line, in 1819, by Rev. E. Morse. Gravel Run, in 1810, by Rev. Joshua Monroe. Meadville, in 1825, by Rev. Robert C. Hatton. North Richmond, in 1840. Centreville, in 1831. Evansburg, in 1840. North Bank, in 1824, by Rev. Charles Thorn. Spartansburg, in 1827, by Rev. I. H. Tackett.

424

HISTORY OF NORTHWESTERN PENNSYLVANIA

Spring Borough, in 1828, by Rev. Daniel Richie. Steuben, in 1845. Dicksonburg, in 1801, by Rev. James Quinn. Harmonsburg, in 1840. Union, in 1826, by Rev. John Leach. Skelton in 1843, by Rev. Schofield. Venango, in 1842, by Rev. Kellar. Vernon, in 1843.

UNITED PRESBYTERIAN CHURCH

Hartstown, in 1830, by Rev. S. F. Smith. Evansburg, in 1815. Shenango, in 1801, by Rev. Daniel McLain. Cochranton, in 1827, by Rev. Samuel Smith. Fairfield, in 1834, by Rev. Snodgrass. North Shenango, in 1849.

BAPTIST CHURCH

Cambridge Borough, in 1812. Carmel, Cussewago Township, in 1805, by Rev. Thomas G. Jones. Mead, in 1838, by Rev. Enos Stewart. Guys Mills, in 1820. Bloomfield, in 1820, by Rev. James Williams. Spring Township, in 1837, by Elder Keith. Spring Borough, in 1833. Townville, in 1836. Meadville, in 1831, by Rev. Adrian Foote.

ROMAN CATHOLIC CHURCH

Crossingville, in 1833. Frenchtown, in 1837.

CLARION COUNTY

PRESBYTERIAN CHURCH

New Rehoboth, in 1802. Licking, in 1802. Concord, in 1807. Richland, in 1823. Bethesda, May 19, 1836. Callensburg, in 1838. Clarion, May 15, 1841. Greenwood, June 3, 1841. Leatherwood, May 14, 1842. Mill Creek, April 22, 1844.

LUTHERAN CHURCH

The pioneer preacher was a travelling missionary named Rev. Peter Rupert, in the year 1814. The pioneer resident minister was Rev. Henry Koch.

St. John's, about 1811. Mt. Zion, in 1823, by Rev. Gabriel Reichart. St. John's, Fryeburg, in 1825, by Rev. Reichart. Salem, in 1830, by Rev. H. D. Keyl. Emanuel, in 1839, by Rev. George F. Ehrenfield. Mt. Zion, Licking, in 1846, by Rev. Ehrenfield. St. John's, Smithland, in 1846, by Rev. William Uhl.

ROMAN CATHOLIC CHURCH

A mission existed at Fryeburg in 1820. St. Nicholas Church was organized between 1827 and 1833. The log-church was erected in 1833. A congregation was formed in Clarion in 1841.

The pioneer church erected in the county was of logs (Rehoboth) in 1808. The Methodists were in the saddle before 1812, the pioneer preacher being Francis Asbury Montjar.

425

PIONEER UNITED PRESBYTERIAN CHURCHES

In 1802 Rev. John Dickey preached in cabins and barns.

In 1808, a congregation was organized at Rimersburg, calléd Cherry Run, by Rev. John Dickey.

In 1849, the United Presbyterian Presbytery of Clarion was organized by four ministers,—to wit, Rev. John Todd, Rev. John Hindman, Rev. John McAuley, and Rev. John Telford.

ELK COUNTY

METHODIST CHURCH

Ridgway, in 1833, Mission, by Revs. Benjamin F. Sedwick and Abner Jackson.

Pioneer Sunday-school in Ridgway, April 14, 1850, by Rev. R. L. Blackmar.

ROMAN CATHOLIC CHURCH

St. Mary's, in 1842, by Father Alexander, and in 1843 by Father Burgess. St. Boniface (now Kersey), before St. Mary's. Father Smith, first resident priest.

PIONEER PRESBYTERIAN CHURCH

Rev. John Wray was the first Presbyterian minister in 1851 to regularly "cry aloud" to the people of Ridgway, "Repent, for the kingdom of Heaven is at hand. Come buy wine and milk without money and without price." During my two years' stay he preached regularly once in four or six weeks. He may have had a few female members in his church, but to my observation the people generally preferred the "world, the flesh, and the devil," whiskey and New England rum.

In 1855 the pioneer Protestant church building was commenced in Elk County. I was then living in Ridgway and working in the *Advocate* office.

All I know about that is this: One day a large, fine-looking, well-dressed man came into the printing-office and requested Mr. Powell to subscribe something for a church. Mr. Powell was poor, and demurred. The man persisted, but Mr. Powell further objected, whereupon the stranger became indignant, and vehemently declared, "It is a G—d d—n shame there isn't a Protestant church in the county, and I'll be G—d d—d if I stop till there is one!" At the end of this Christian exhortation Mr. Powell subscribed five dollars. The scene was so dramatic and ridiculous that I inquired who the stranger was, and Mr. Powell told me he was Alfred Pearsall, from Jay Township. I understood afterwards Mr. Pearsall succeeded and erected his church, called Mount Zion Methodist Church.

426

PRESBYTERIAN CHURCH

The pioneer Presbyterian minister to preach in what is now Jefferson County, was a Rev. Greer, a friend of Joseph Barnett. He came in 1801, remaining two weeks, and preached several times. He returned to Port Barnett in 1802, and again preached. Joseph Barnett was an ultra Presbyterian. Preaching seems to have been in the settlement in June, 1809. At that time a communion service was held in the house of Peter Jones, on the farm recently occupied by John McCullough, a mile east of Brookville. Robert McGarrah administered the Lord's Supper there. He was then pastor of Licking and New Rehoboth, now in Clarion County. He had come to the Clarion region as a licentiate of the Presbytery of Redstone, in the fall of 1803. Whether he visited Port Barnett settlement at that time cannot now be ascertained. At all events, when he returned from Fayette County with his family, June, 1804, and was ordained pastor of Licking and New Rehoboth churches, November 12, 1807, he seems to have taken the Port Barnett settlement under his care. When he " held the communion," June, 1809, certain persons were received into the church in such a way that he baptized their children. This much is plain from the memory and Bible record of Mrs. Sarah Graham, daughter of Joseph Barnett.

Rev. McGarrah was highly educated, and able in prayer, yet, like Moses, slow of speech, often taking two and three hours to deliver a sermon. He preached without notes, and with great earnestness pleaded with his hearers to forsake their sins and the errors of their way and turn to the Lord. So earnest would he become at times that great tears would roll from his eyes to the floor. It was often said that he preached more eloquently by his tears than by the power of his voice. He lived poor and died poor, and preached in the clothes in which he worked.

How long Robert McGarrah continued to preach in the house of Peter Jones remains uncertain. In 1823 religious services were held in the house of Samuel Jones, west of Brookville, on the farm now owned by W. H. McAninch. The church was fully organized in a school-house, near the present site of the Jefferson United Presbyterian church, on the Andrews farm, now in Clover Township. That seems to have been in 1824. The Allegheny Presbytery reported to the Synod of Pittsburg twenty-three churches in 1823. In 1824 the Presbytery reported twenty-five churches, and among them Bethel and Zelienople, so that the record of the Synod establishes conclusively the fact that in the year 1824 Bethel for the first time was recognized as a separate congregation. The next record is in the minutes of the Allegheny Presbytery, April, 1825. It there appears as vacant, and, shortly afterwards, as connected with Red Bank, both having sixty-eight members.

Bethel church, or Brookville, as organized in the Jefferson school-house, was removed in the fall of 1824, to a farm on the pike from Brookville to Clarion. The farm was east of and adjoining the farm now owned by Peter B. Cowan, in Union Township, and distant from Brookville three miles. There they built a church, and dedicated it " The Bethel" of Jefferson County. The church was built of logs, small and closely notched together. It stood to the right of the road as one goes toward Clarion, near the pike, and on a line between it and the " Old Graveyard." The latter is still in existence, but all traces of the old meeting-house are gone. The floor was genuine mother-earth, and the seats slabs or boards on logs. A board on two posts constituted the pulpit stand, and a seat was made out of a slab or block of wood. The first stated preacher in that log-church was Rev. William Kennedy. His name appears as a stated supply, October 13, 1825; also April, 1827. Bethel was then connected with Red Bank. He ceased to be a member of the Allegheny Presbytery after April, 1827. He was dismised to Salem Presbytery, Indiana Synod. He became a member of Clarion Presbytery January 17, 1843, and died November 2, 1850, aged sixty-seven years and four months. The last year of his life was devoted to the congregations of Mount Tabor and Mill Creek. He lived and died a mile north of Roseville, Jefferson County, Pennsylvania.

Rev. William Kennedy was born July 4, 1783, in Chester County, Pennsylvania, and educated at ——. He was a Latin and Greek scholar. His father was born in Ireland, and his mother, Susan Kennedy, née Doak, was from Scotland. His pioneer ministerial career appears to have been in the Huntingdon Presbytery at Lewistown, Mifflin County, Pennsylvania. He married Mary McClure, who died May 31, 1861.

He was installed and ordained over two churches in 1810,—viz., Lewistown and West Kishacoquillas, in Mifflin County, Pennsylvania. He preached at these two points for twelve years, at a salary of four hundred dollars per year. He was released from the Huntingdon Presbytery in October, 1823, and joined the Presbytery of Erie or Allegheny that same year. Under his ministrations Bethel had eighty-six members. His pioneer elders were Thomas Lucas and James Shields. His church-building was burned down about 1832.

Pisgah, Corsica, in 1833, by John Shoap. Beechwoods, Washington Township, in 1832, by Cyrus Riggs. Perry, Perry Township, in 1836, by John Reed. Mount Tabor, Eldred Township, in 1840, by David Polk.

A regular Presbyterian Church had been formed in Punxsutawney in 1826, and in about 1833 they built a brick church in the Public Square, but the feeble organization was not permanent.

METHODIST CHURCH

Punxsutawney or Clayville, in 1821, by Rev. Elijah Coleman (local). Brookville, in 1829, by Rev. John Johnson. Summerville, in 1830, by Rev.

Jonathan Ayers. Crenshaw, in 1845, by Rev. J. K. Coxson. Mead Chapel, in 1847, by Rev. J. R. Lyon. Hopewell, in 1839, by Rev. R. Peck. Barton, in 1839, by Rev. John Monks. Zion, in 1849, by Rev. Dean C. Wright. Pioneer missionaries in Ringgold, in 1816. Missionary service in Summerville, in 1822. Missionary service at Crenshaw, in 1829, by Rev. Oliver Ega.

The pioneer circuit riders at Punxsutawney were Rev. Ezra Booth and Rev. William Wesley.

In 1822 there were forty-two appointments on this circuit.

The pioneer Methodist church-building in the county was at Punxsutawney, in 1834. A frame building was erected and cost one thousand three hundred and fifty dollars. Methodist services were held in what is now Warsaw Township, in 1842, near the Temple graveyard, by the Rev. John Graham.

The history of Episcopal Methodism in what is now Washington Township is quite obscure. It is known that Rev. Abner Jackson in 1833 preached occasionally in the old log school-house on Waite's farm, but with what success is unknown. Next it is known that Rev. John Graham, the "Boy Preacher," made the old log (Smith) school-house a point in 1843. Graham was then on the Luthersburg charge. Daniel Groves was probably the pioneer resident Episcopal Methodist. He migrated to the settlement in 1841 and connected himself and wife with the Luthersburg church by letters, that being the nearest class and in the Meadville district, Rev. John Bain being the presiding elder. Rev. Elisha Coleman, a county local, ministered in the Smith school-house at intervals. Daniel Groves was the father of Methodism in the township.

LUTHERAN CHURCHES

Zion, in 1836, by Rev. J. G. Young. St. John's, in 1838, by Rev. J. G. Young. Mt. Zion, in 1849, by Rev. John B. Breckenridge.

The pioneer Lutheran services held in the county were by Rev. N. G. Scharetts, in 1826. Missionaries who held services in the county in 1829 were Rev. Henry D. Keyl and Rev. G. Schultze.

ROMAN CATHOLIC CHURCHES

The pioneer Roman Catholic services were by Father John O'Neil, in 1832.

The pioneer priest stationed in Brookville was Father Dean, in 1847.

MERCER COUNTY

PRESBYTERIAN CHURCH

Young Presbyterian ministers as missionaries visited every community in the county before the close of 1800. It is impossible to determine which was the pioneer church. Fairfield was organized September, 1799. Neshannock was organized about 1800, Rev. William Wick, pastor. Hopewell, about the same time by the same pastor. Coolspring was organized in 1800; Rev. Samuel Tait was pastor. Lower Neshannock, now New Castle, was organized in 1803, Rev. Alexander Cook, pastor. Plain Grove was organized in 1800, Rev. William Wood, pastor. Centre was organized in 1801, Rev. William Wood, pastor. First Presbyterian, of Mercer, was organized in 1804, Rev. Samuel Tait, pastor. Rocky Springs was organized in 1801, Rev. Robert Lee, pastor. Amity was organized in 1825. Upper Sandy, now George-town, was organized in 1799. Moorfield was organized in 1802, Rev. James Satterfield, pastor. Sandy Lake was organized in 1835. Greenville was organized in 1825, Rev. James Alexander, pastor. Big Ben was organized in 1825, Rev. James Alexander, pastor. The United Presbyterian Church of Greenville is the old Seceder organization of 1802, Rev. Daniel McLain, pastor. Unity Church of Greenfield was organized in 1832. Orange-ville was organized in 1825. Shenango Township Beulah Church was organized in the fall of 1839.

METHODIST CHURCH

The pioneer preacher in the county was Rev. R. R. Roberts, afterwards Bishop Roberts, in the spring of 1801. At this date the whole region was in the Baltimore Conference. This was the beginning of Methodism in Mercer County. The M. E. Church of Mercer Borough was organized about 1820. Sharon M. E. Church was organized in 1805. Greenville M. E. Church was organized in 1828. Sharpsville M. E. Church was organized in 1836. Sheak-leyville M. E. Church was organized in 1830. Clarksville M. E. Church was organized in 1820. Millbrook M. E. Church was organized in 1816. Henderson M. E. Church was organized in 1833. Salem M. E. Church was organized in 1807. New Vernon was organized in 1840. Springfield Naza-reth Church was organized in 1822.

BAPTIST CHURCH

Sharon was organized in 1802, Rev. David Phillips, pastor. Greenville was organized in 1847, Rev. Jeremiah Hazen, pastor. Georgetown Church was organized in 1807, Thomas G. Jones, pastor. West Salem Baptist Church was organized in 1807, Rev. Thomas Jones, pastor.

UNITED PRESBYTERIAN CHURCH

Mercer was organized in 1801, Rev. Thomas McClintock, pastor. Second United Presbyterian Church, Mercer, was organized about 1805. Greenville was organized about 1802. Sheakleyville United Presbyterian Church was organized in 1818. Middlesex United Presbyterian Church was organized in 1829. Clarksville United Presbyterian Church was organized in 1848.

Mercer, Grace Episcopal, was organized in 1827. Lutheran was organized in 1840. Congregational was organized on March 27, 1847. Sharon, Christian Church was organized on June 28, 1828. Protestant Methodist Church was organized in 1836. Sacred Heart Catholic was organized in 1845. Greenville Congregational Church was organized in 1840. St. Michael's Catholic Church was organized in 1838. Delaware Township, St. John's Lutheran Church was organized in 1837. Methodist Church was organized in 1820. Jackson Township, umberland Presbyterian was organized about 1841. Jefferson Township, All Saints' Catholic Church was organized about 1838. West Salem Township, Good Hope Lutheran Church was organized in 1805.

REVOLUTIONARY PATRIOTS WHO SETTLED IN MERCER COUNTY

Godfrey Carmes, in 1801; Captain James Duncan, William Simonton, David Hayes, Captain Abraham DeForest; Benjamin Kaster, in 1802; Captain William Findley, in 1799; Jacob Junkin, in 1806; Benjamin Stokely, John Carmichael; Peter Wilson, in 1797; William Gill; Daniel Harper, in 1797; William Egdert, in 1800; Joshua Cook, James Young, Mr. Dumars, Christopher Irwin, Samuel Waldron, John Perry, William Dougherty, Captain Cyrus Beckwith, Archibald Titus, Garrett Cronk, William Nickle, Captain John Elliott; Captain Samuel Quinby, in 1808; John Morford, William McCalimans.

POTTER COUNTY

METHODIST CHURCH

Coudersport, in 1823. The first Methodist circuit riders in this county, in 1823, covered the following territory: Coudersport to Canoe Place (now Port Allegheny), eighteen miles; thence ten miles to dividing ridge; thence fourteen miles to Portage; thence down Sinnemahoning twenty-four miles; thence three miles to North Creek; thence two miles to West Creek; thence seven miles to Big Run; thence twenty-three miles to Kersey; thence twelve miles to Brockway's; thence twenty-three miles to Bennett's Branch and Driftwood Branch; thence sixteen miles to the mouth of Sinnemahoning; thence fifteen miles to Youngwoman's Town (North Point); returning *via* Potato Creek and Smethport to Coudersport, a distance of two hundred and forty-nine miles.

These circuit riders always travelled on horseback. The horse was usually " bobbed," and you could see that he had a most excellent skeleton. These itinerants all wore leggings, and carried on the saddle a large pair of saddle-bags, which contained a clean shirt, a Bible, and a hymn-book. The sermon was on a cylinder in the head of the preacher, and was ready to be graphophoned at any point or time.

The Baptist (regular) and the Seventh Day both held services in the county as early as 1833.

Coudersport Catholic Church, in the forties.

Genesee Township Roman Catholic Church in 1844, by Bishop O'Connor, Fathers Smith and Gallagher.

VENANGO COUNTY

PRESBYTERIAN CHURCH

As early as 1801 systematic efforts by the Presbyterian synod of Pennsylvania to send ministers into Venango County had occurred. The records of the Presbytery of Erie, of 1802, speak of supplies preaching at Franklin, Pithole, McGurls, Oil Creek, and Scrubgrass.

Rev. James Satterfield preached in 1801. To hear these ministers people came five, ten, and twenty miles.

Later, churches were erected of rough logs and with no arrangements for fire in the winter.

First Presbyterian Church in the county, now Utica, in 1800, by Rev. William Wylie. Scrubgrass, 1802-03, by Rev. Robert Johnson. Presbyterian, Franklin, in 1801, pioneer sermon. Amity Presbyterian, Irwin Township, in 1800, by Rev. Robert Lee. Concord Presbyterian, Allegheny Township, in 1826, by Rev. Thomas Anderson. Scrubgrass Presbyterian, Scrubgrass Township, in 1800, by Rev. William Moorehead. Academia, Richland Township, in 1823, by Rev. Robert McGarrough. Cherrytree, Cherrytree Township, in 1837, by Rev. G. W. Hampson. Sunville, Plum Township, in 1839, by Rev. Thomas Anderson. Rockland, Rockland Township, in 1822, by Rev. Robert McGarrough. Sugar Creek, Jackson Township, in 1814. Pleasantville, Oil Creek Township, in 1844, by Rev. Hogg.

METHODIST

Peters, Irwin Township, in 1845. Asbury, Allegheny Township, in 1804, by Rev. Andrew Hemphill. Big Bend, Scrubgrass Township, in 1835, by Rev. J. H. Jackson. Nicklin Chapel, French Creek Township, in 1833. Reynolds, French Creek Township, 1840 or 1845. Fairview, Cherrytree Township, in 1836, by Rev. Reuben Peck. Sunville, Plum Township, in 1844, by Rev. John Abbott. Rockland, Rockland Township, in 1830, by Rev. J. C. Ayers. Luther Chapel, Canal Township, in 1830. Sandy Creek, Sandy Creek Township, old church, by Rev. Ira Eddy.

Early Methodist service in Oakland, in 1806, by Rev. Wiley. Methodist Church, Clintonville, in 1828. Methodist services, Pleasantville, in 1804, by Rev. Andrew Hemphill. Centre Methodist Church, Mineral Township, in 1844. Pleasantville Methodist Church, Irwin Township, about 1840. Salem, Cranberry Township, 1845-50, by Rev. Richard Caruthers.

The Methodist circuit rider was an early visitor in Venango County. The pioneer Methodist service in Franklin was in 1804.

In 1804 the Baltimore conference appointed Thornton Fleming presiding elder and Andrew Hemphill preacher of the Monongahela District, which included Mercer, Crawford, Erie, Venango, and Butler Counties. This old circuit, called the Erie, was in existence as late as 1820. It was four hundred miles round and had forty-four apointments to fill every four weeks.

ROMAN CATHOLIC CHURCHES

St. Catharine's, in 1834. St. Patrick's, Franklin, in 1749, by Father Bonecamp.

CUMBERLAND PRESBYTERIAN CHURCH

Scrubgrass, in 1835, by Rev. S. Murphy. Pine Grove, in 1842, by Rev. Hatten. Irwin, in 1843, by Rev. J. Murphy. Church of God, Irwin, in 1839, by Rev. Thomas. Pine Grove, in 1842, by Rev. Werts.

BAPTIST CHURCH

Cherry Tree Baptist, in 1835, by Rev. Samuel Miles. Canal, Freewill Baptist, in 1827, by Rev. J. H. Lamchier.

EPISCOPAL CHURCH

St. John's, Franklin, in 1825, by Rev. Charles Smith.

UNITED PRESBYTERIAN CHURCH

Plumer, in 1828, by Rev. Daniel McLain.

WARREN COUNTY

METHODIST CHURCH

Warren, in 1830, by Rev. James Gilmore. Brokenstraw, in 1809. Pine Grove, in 1830. Deerfield, in 1826. Kinzua, in 1830. Eldred, in 1840. Sugar Grove, in 1840.

BAPTIST CHURCH

Farmington, in 1831. Warren, in 1834.

PRESBYTERIAN CHURCH

Warren, in 1822, by Rev. Amos Chase. Sugar Grove, in 1821, by Rev. Amos Chase. Deerfield, in 1828. Pittsfield, in 1845.

CONGREGATIONAL CHURCH

Sugar Grove, in 1838. Farmington, in 1830.

CHAPTER XXIII

"WHERE ODD FELLOWS CAME FROM

" THE English Odd Fellows date back, so far as recorded, to Loyal Aristarchus Lodge, No. 1, of 1745, at Southwark, a schism, perhaps, from Masonic sources, or possibly in emulation of that craft. At first it was 'pipes and ale' and later the 'friendly society' beneficiary features. Daniel De Foe made reference to its existence and the poet Montgomery wrote an 'Ode to Odd Fellowship.' The society grew under varying 'Odd Fellow' titles until the end of the eighteenth century, when it began to split into numerous Odd Fellow societies, the parent, or Grand United Order, dropping to second place in membership compared with its offspring, the Manchester Unity of 1812, from which the Independent Order here descended.

"THE IMMIGRANT BLACKSMITH

" What George Washington was to the American Republic, Thomas Wildey was to American Odd Fellowship,—a humble English blacksmith, who had emigrated to America, and who, with four comrades at Baltimore, formed the first Odd Fellows' Lodge in the new world which had more than a transitory existence.

" Wildey and John Welch had both been made Odd Fellows in England, and conceived the idea of establishing the Order here. To that end they published a call for such brethren as might see the notice, and John Duncan, John Cheatham, and Menard Rushworth responded on April 13, 1819. They were, most of them, members of the British United Order, by the usages of which any five Odd Fellows could organize and constitute a legal lodge where none existed, and this they did on the 26th of April in that year.

" Lodges of British Odd Fellowship had appeared at Baltimore in 1802, at New York in 1806 and others after the war of 1812, but none of them lived long.

" Washington Lodge, No. 1, that formed by Wildey and his friends, received an English charter from a Lodge of the Independent Order, and in 1821 this was formally confirmed with the additional prerogatives of a Grand Lodge. Thomas Wildey was the first Grand Master, under the British Independent Order, Manchester Unity allegiance, and Subordinate Lodges Washington, No. 1, and Franklin, No. 2, were promptly chartered by him.

" One may imagine the difficulty Wildey and his lieutenants had in keeping alive the fires of enthusiasm over the newly transplanted Odd Fellowship in those early days of difficult intercommunication, and during the period 1826–1835, when the entire East was ablaze with the flames of not only anti-Masonry but antagonism to all secret societies. Yet within five years they formed Grand Lodges in Pennsylvania, New York, and Massachusetts, and in 1825 the first Grand Lodge of Odd Fellows in the United States at a time when the total membership was only five hundred in nine Subordinate Lodges. Wildey, of course, was made Grand Sire of the new Grand Lodge, and in 1826, when he visited England, ' he was joyfully received by Odd Fellows as the founder of the Order in America.'

" HEAVY GROWTH IN MEMBERSHIP

" The jump from five hundred members in 1825 to two hundred thousand in 1861, in which year Wildey died, was a testimonial to not only the character of the founder of the institution, but a tribute as well to the principles inculcated, which, when implanted, steadily grew and spread. But striking as was the gain in membership in those forty-two years, the last forty-four years offer quite as remarkable an exhibit, with an addition, net, of one million to the brotherhood.

" The history of Odd Fellowship is punctuated with more schisms than that of any other secret society in the world, which is saying a good deal.

" The American Order has not failed to keep up with the procession, and has itself constituted a schismatic branch since 1842, at which time it dropped its allegiance to the British Manchester Unity, the latter the largest British Odd Fellows' Society, which branched off from the parent or Grand British Order in 1812.

" The negro Odd Fellows in the United States, strange as it may seem, some one hundred and fifty thousand in number, are a loyal branch of the Grand United (parent) British Order, having been instituted here through the efforts of Peter Ogden, a New York negro of education, a sailor, who had been made an Odd Fellow in Liverpool."—*Albert C. Stevens.*

JEFFERSON COUNTY

The pioneer Lodge of Odd Fellows organized in Jefferson County was Brookville Lodge, No. 217, I. O. O. F. It was chartered December 21, 1846, with the following members,—to wit: Pearl Roundy, David S. Deering, John Hastings, James S. McCullough, and William McCandless. The Lodge was opened and the officers installed by John L. Cuttle, of Clearfield, Pennsylvania, February 8, 1847.

The hall occupied by the Order for that purpose was above what was called " The Philadelphia Cheap Store," or in the second story of the building on East Main Street, now (1902) occupied by Norman D. Matson as a residence.

The pioneer officers thus installed were Pearl Roundy, Noble Grand; David S. Deering, now of Independence, Iowa, Vice-Grand; John Hastings, Secretary; James S. McCullough, Assistant Secretary; and William Mc-Candless, Treasurer. Meetings were held regularly every Saturday night.

The pioneer applications for membership were Uriah Matson, Dr. James Dowling, D. B. Jenks, James C. Matson, Barton T. Hastings, Daniel Smith, W. F. Clark, now (1902) living at Maquoketa, Iowa; and John Reichert; date, February 8, 1847.

Public opinion in Brookville, as well as in the churches, was violently opposed to this organization being created in our midst. It was "a revival of Freemasonry;" it was "immoral," and "in league with the devil." Married women, as a rule, were bitter, and serious trouble arose between some pioneer members and their wives. An order founded on so grand a tripod as Friendship, Love, and Truth could not be destroyed by this "babbling gossip of the air," but rapidly increased in numbers under the light of the knowledge that the United States in this year (1846) had nine hundred and sixty-two Subordinate Lodges and a membership of ninety thousand seven hundred and fifty-three, with a revenue from these Lodges for benevolence to widows, orphans, and afflicted brothers of $708,306.40; and the total amount paid that year for sick brethren, widows, and orphans was $197,317, which proved conclusively that the practical workings of this order were anything but from the devil, and that all the predicted woes and calamities of the enemies of the order were imaginary and but the darkness of ignorance.

Brookville Lodge rented a room in the upper story of the American Hotel, which Judge Heath was then building, and on Wednesday, June 30, 1847, the members of the Lodge, accompanied by the charter members of Mahoning Lodge, No. 250, and a delegation from Clearfield Lodge, No. 198, met in and left the old hall, above Matson's store, at fifteen minutes past one o'clock, preceded by the Clarion brass band, and marched up Main Street to the Presbyterian church. Addresses were delivered there by Rev. John Rugan, a Lutheran minister, and D. B. Jenks, Esq., on the order and its objects, after which the procession reformed and marched to their new hall in the American building, where the dedication ceremonies were performed, when the new hall was thrown open and a reception held for the ladies and the public. The following was the programme:

"ORDER OF EXERCISES, TO BE OBSERVED AT THE PROCESSION AND DEDICATION OF THE I. O. O. F. HALL, AT BROOKVILLE, PENNSYLVANIA, ON THE 30TH OF JUNE, 1847—OFFICERS OF THE DAY

"Grand Master, John L. Cuttle; Master of Ceremonies, David S. Deering; Chief Marshal, John Hastings; Assistant Marshals, Peter Clover, H. B.

Beissel; Chaplain, J. K. Coxson; First Herald, James S. McCullough; Second Herald, Evans R. Brady; Third Herald, Michael Frank; Fourth Herald, A. M. Hills; Outside Guardian, John Reichart; Inside Guardian, Henry Pride.

" The citizens who are desirous of being present will assemble in the Presbyterian church at one o'clock P.M. The members of the Order will leave the old Hall, in procession, under the direction of the Marshals, at fifteen minutes past one o'clock P.M., and proceed to the church. On the arrival of the procession at the church exercises will be conducted as follows,—viz.:

" 1. Prayer. 2. Music. 3. Address by Rev. Mr. Rugan. 4. Music. 5. Prayer. 6. Address by a Brother of the Order. 7. Music. 8. Benediction.

" The procession will then re-form in the same order and march to the New Hall, where the Ceremonies of Dedication will be performed. In consequence of the size of the Hall none will be admitted but members of the Order."

By reason of the burning of the American Hotel, together with the furniture and paraphernalia of Brookville Lodge, except the Charter and Due Book, the Charter was surrendered in 1856. Up to that date one hundred and seventy-four members had been regularly received.

And now (1902) the Odd Fellows have a membership of over one million in the world, and have paid, for sick and funeral benefits and the care of widows and orphans, the magnificent sum of eighty-eight million dollars.

The second organization of Odd Fellows in Jefferson County was Mahoning Lodge, No. 250, I. O. O. F., of Punxsutawney. This Lodge was organized May 31, 1847, and became defunct in 1858. No record can be found, and no information can be obtained about the organization, and but little about the Lodge. Some of the pioneer members were Obed Nordstrum, John B. Wilson, W. E. Bell, P. W. Jenks, Rev. Thomas Wilson, Dr. A. J. Johnson, Major Joseph B. Hucheson, and others.

CRAWFORD COUNTY

The Independent Order of Odd Fellows organized Cupewago Lodge, No. 108, in Meadville, April 21. 1825.

MERCER COUNTY

Mercer Lodge, No. 321, I. O. O. F., was organized July 4, 1832. Alhambra Lodge, No. 293. I. O. O. F., in Greenville Borough, was instituted January 31, 1848. Sharon Lodge, No. 347, I. O. O. F., was instituted on the 19th of February, 1849.

VENANGO COUNTY

The pioneer Odd Fellows' Lodge in Franklin, Venango Lodge, No. 255, I. O. O. F., was instituted October 26, 1847.

CHAPTER XXIV

"Reading maketh a *full* man."

PREVIOUS to 1793 there were no postal or post-office facilities. Letters and papers had to be sent with friends, neighbors, or by special carriers. The first newspaper started in the western part of the State was the *Pittsburg Gazette.* It was published by John Scull, and issued in 1786. It was distributed to patrons by special carriers.

BUTLER COUNTY

The pioneer newspaper in the county was the *Palladium and Republican Star,* published August 17, 1818. John Galbraith, editor and publisher.

Butler Repository, March, 1823. In 1842 it was published by McLaughlin & Zeigler. *Democratic Herald* in 1842–50.

CRAWFORD COUNTY

The pioneer newspaper of Northwestern Pennsylvania was the *Crawford Weekly Messenger,* published and edited by Thomas Atkinson and W. Brendle. The first number was issued January 2, 1805, published every Wednesday morning; terms, two dollars per year. The newspaper was a four paged sheet, four columns to a page, and seventeen by twenty inches in size. Atkinson continued to publish it until 1833. In 1835 it was discontinued.

The *Crawford Democrat and Northwestern Advertiser* was started in 1835 by E. McFarland. In 1831 the *Meadville Courier* was started by W. W. Perkins. Name changed in September, 1837, to *Crawford Democrat and Meadville Courier;* in 1840, to *Crawford Democrat* to 1848. The *Crawford Journal* was started in 1848.

CLARION COUNTY

The pioneer newspaper was the *Republican* printed at Strattonville, April 1, 1839, by James McCracken; moved to Clarion in 1840. The *Republican and Iron County Democrat* was started in 1842, by B. J. Reed and Samuel Duff, merged into the *Clarion Democrat* in 1844, William Alexander, proprietor.

438

HISTORY OF NORTHWESTERN PENNSYLVANIA

ELK COUNTY

The pioneer newspaper in the county was the *St. Mary's Republican*. The first number was issued January 5, 1850, by C. B. Cotton. This paper only lived a short time. *Elk County Advocate*, Ridgway, in 1850.

FOREST COUNTY

Forest Press (pioneer), 1866, Peter O. Conver. *Forest Republican*, 1868, Colonel J. W. H. Reesinger; 1879, J. E. Wenk.

JEFFERSON COUNTY

In the year 1832 John J. Thompson established, in Brookville, Jefferson County, Pennsylvania, and issued the first number of the pioneer paper within

John Jamieson Ypsilanti Thompson

the confines of the county. This paper was printed on coarse paper, thirteen inches wide and twenty inches long. The terms of subscription were the same as printed for the *American*. In politics it was Democratic. In 1833 Thomas Reid purchased a half-interest in the establishment. The paper then

439

was published as a neutral or independent, and still called *Gazette*. Thompson and Reid not agreeing, Reid retired, and Thompson and James P. Blair continued the publication.

In 1833 Thompson disposed of his interest to Dr. R. K. Scott, and the firm became Blair & Scott. Some time after 1833 and before 1835 Thompson added Ypsilanti to his name.

Judge Thompson's grandfather was Robert Thompson. His grandmother was Mary Thompson, *née* Gordon. In what year they came from Ireland (whither they had gone from Scotland), and settled in Franklin County, Pennsylvania, is not known. In the year 1790 they migrated to Indiana County, and settled on a farm near Altman's Run. Robert Thompson died on this farm in 1802, aged seventy years. Mary, his wife, died in 1846, aged ninety-five years. These were Judge Thompson's grandparents.

Robert Thompson and Mary Gordon Thompson had one daughter, named Ruth, who married James Lattimer; they also had four sons, Alexander, Moses, Adam, and William.

William Thompson married Miss Agnes Jamieson, daughter of Rev. John Jamieson, and from this union there were three sons and two daughters,—to wit: Hon. John Jamieson Ypsilanti Thompson, Rev. Robert Thompson, William Gordon Thompson, Agnes Thompson, otherwise called Nancy, and Mary Thompson, otherwise called Polly. William Thompson and wife settled on a farm near Lewisville, Indiana County, Pennsylvania. This farm was deeded by Rev. John Jamieson and Agnes, his wife, to William Thompson and Agnes Jamieson Thompson, his wife, the deed being dated March 26, 1817, and the consideration being twenty dollars. The farm contained two hundred acres, and was afterwards known as the " John Gallagher farm."

On this farm the Hon. J. J. Y. Thompson was born, in 1805. He received his entire education in a little cabin school-house on an adjoining farm owned by Adam Elliott. For seven years he went to Master Adam Elliott, who was the teacher. Master Elliott's school was a subscription one, and was conducted under the law of 1809. He was a great mathematician and a fine penman, and taught young Thompson practical surveying. Of the early boyhood days of the subject of this sketch we have little knowledge, save that he was an acknowledged leader among his schoolmates, beloved by his associates and esteemed by his master. He excelled in civil engineering and surveying, and when such work was to be done was invariably selected as assistant. His father dying in 1817, of smallpox, he was thrown upon his own resources, and at an early age left the home roof and became a clerk in the store of Nathaniel Nesbitt, Blairsville, Pennsylvania. In a short time after this he embarked in business for himself, but his venture not proving successful, he abandoned it, and in 1831 removed to the wilderness of Jefferson County.

July 25, 1833, John J. Y. Thompson was married to Miss Agnes Susan

Kennedy, and commenced married life in Brookville. Miss Agnes Susan Kennedy was a daughter of Rev. William Kennedy and Mary Kennedy, *née* McClure, and was born near Lewistown, in Mifflin County, Pennsylvania, in the year 1813. Her father was the pioneer to locate as a minister in Jefferson County, and was a Presbyterian divine. Mrs. Thompson was a remarkable woman, a model wife and mother, and was beloved by everybody.

In the fall of 1834 Mr. Thompson moved to Dowlingville, Jefferson County, where he remained until the summer of 1837, when he returned to Brookville, and, in the ensuing November, built a saw-mill on Sandy Lick, at the present site of Bell's Mills. Here he remained until the summer of 1840, when he sold his mill to Alpheus Shaw and returned to Brookville. He remained in Brookville three months, and then removed to Heathville, Jefferson County, returning to Brookville in 1841. He then moved to the farm in Union Township now owned by Arthur Morrison, where he lived one year.

In 1843 Mr. Thompson purchased a tract of land from Daniel Stannard, of Indiana, Pennsylvania, known as Warrant No. 681, where he erected a hotel and engaged in the hotel business and in merchandising. He secured a post-office for the place, which he had named Corsica, and was appointed postmaster in 1844. In 1847 Mr. Thompson surveyed and laid out the town of Corsica. He served as justice of the peace, was elected a number of times county surveyor, and was prothonotary, register, etc., from 1845 to 1848. He continued, however, to do business and to reside at Corsica until 1852, when he again removed to Brookville, having purchased the "Arcade" and "American" buildings, at the price of twenty thousand dollars. It was then the largest and finest business block in the place. He occupied the American, and continued in the hotel business until the two buildings, with all their contents, were destroyed by fire, May 24, 1856. This fire left Mr. Thompson without money and financially embarrassed; but nothing daunted, the third day after the fire he and his boys commenced to clear away the débris and began preparation for rebuilding. Owing to his well-known business integrity and great energy, he surmounted every obstacle and completed and occupied what is now known as the American Hotel, owned and managed by Buffington and Brady.

In 1861 Mr. Thompson was elected associate judge. In 1865 he sold the "American" and removed to Portsmouth, Ohio, and was engaged in the lumber business until he was suddenly removed by death, August 19, 1865, in the sixtieth year of his age.

Judge Thompson was a man of fine presence, pleasing address, and popular manners. He was identified with all the early history of Jefferson County, aiding in every public enterprise of his day. For many years he surveyed every purchased piece or parcel of land in the county. His name and face became familiar in every cabin, and the hand of friendship was universally extended to him alike by young and old. Being of a genial and social disposition himself, his presence inspired all with whom he came in contact, and he influenced them in a measure with his own sunny disposition. Indeed, in this wilderness he seemed to be " one of the spirits chosen by heaven to turn the sunny side of things to human eyes." In politics he was a Democrat until 1860, when he became a Republican. He lived and died a United Presbyterian.

Judge Thompson was a man of rare intelligence, charitable, kind, sympathetic, outspoken, benevolent, and bold, with a Scotch temper that would at times break out, when due provocation was given, with " I'll be dod danged to Harry," and " I'll be dod danged to dangnation." But with this explosion over, everything with him was just as tender and serene as if no thunder-clap had jarred the atmosphere.

In June, 1838, Thomas Hastings and son started and published in Brookville a new paper called the *Backwoodsman*. In 1841, Colonel William Jack bought this paper and had it published by George F. Humes. This was not a success, and Humes, in a valedictory to his patrons, told them to go to h—ll and he would go to Texas. In 1843 the paper was owned and published by David Barclay and Barton T. Hastings. In short time Barclay retired and Hastings continued the publication. Those papers were all printed on the old Ramage or Franklin press, and every publisher made his own " roller" out of glue and molasses, in the proportion of a pound of glue to a pint of molasses. In Brookville the " youngest devil" in the office carried to the residence of each subscriber his or her paper. The boy who delivered these papers was called the " carrier." Each New Year's day this carrier would have an address in poetry, written by some local bard, recounting the events of the year just closed. This New Year's address he offered for sale to his patrons.

LAWRENCE COUNTY

The first newspaper in New Castle was founded in 1826 by David Crawford. It lived two years. The *Intelligencer* was issued August 18, 1836. The *Sentinel* was issued in 1837; it was discontinued in 1838. The town had no newspaper from this time until August 14, 1839, when the *Mercer and Beaver Democrat* was issued. The first issue of the *Lawrence Journal* was May 23, 1849. A Democratic paper was published in New Castle on July 13, 1844, by George F. Humes.

M'KEAN COUNTY

The pioneer paper *Forester* was issued in the spring of 1832 by Hiram Paine. The *McKean County Journal* was issued in 1834, by Richard Chadwick; changed to *Beacon and Journal*, 1837. The *Settler and Pennon* was issued in September, 1837, by William S. Oviatt. The *McKean County Yeoman and Elk County Advertiser* was issued December, 1846.

MERCER COUNTY

Western Press, in 1811, by Jacob Herrington. *Express,* in 1848, by J. W. Mason.

POTTER COUNTY

Potter County Journal, in 1848, by William McDougall.

TIOGA COUNTY

The *Tioga Pioneer,* in December, 1825, by Rankin, Lewis & Co. This was the first newspaper in the county, and changed to the *Phœnix,* August, 1827, by Benjamin B. Smith. The *Tioga Phœnix and Potter County Gazette,* in 1838, by Hartman, Howe & Ramsey. *Tioga County Herald,* in December, 1846, by George Hildreth, merged into the *Wellsborough Advertiser* in 1849.

VENANGO COUNTY

The pioneer newspaper in Franklin, Venango County, was the *Herald,* in September, 1820, by John Evans. The *Venango Democrat,* in March, 1824, finally merged into the *Spectator* in June, 1849. The *Democratic Arch,* July 11, 1842. The *Franklin Intelligencer,* in 1834. The *Franklin Gazette,* in 1843. The *Advocate and Journal,* in 1847, was the pioneer temperance paper, by E. S. Durban.

WARREN COUNTY

The pioneer paper was the *Conewango Emigrant,* issued July 24, 1824, suspended in the spring of 1826. *Voice of the People,* in 1829; discontinued in 1835. *Warren Bulletin,* in May, 1836. *Democratic Advocate,* in 1840; in 1847, suspended and bought by S. J. Goodrich; *Warren Standard,* in May, 1847, by S. J. Goodrich; destroyed by fire March, 1849. *Ledger,* in 1849, by S. J. Goodrich. *Allegheny Mail,* in July, 1848, by J. Warren Fletcher.

CHAPTER XXV

BUTLER COUNTY was erected March 12, 1800. It was named for General Richard Butler. It was formed out of Allegheny, and then bounded: "Beginning at the mouth of Buffalo Creek on the Allegheny River; thence by a straight line running due west, until it strikes the line on Beaver County; thence north by the line of said county to the northeast corner of said county; thence by a line north thirty-five degrees east fourteen miles; thence by a line running due east, continuing said course to where a line running due north from the mouth of Buffalo Creek, the place of beginning."

Butler, 1843

Adiel McLure, James Amberson, and Wm. Elliott, were appointed to purchase or receive a grant of land and erect a court-house and prison thereon. The place of the county seat was not to be a greater distance than four miles from the centre of the county. By an act, March 8, 1803, the trustees were directed, "to cause to be surveyed three hundred acres of land, which Robert Graham, John and Samuel Cunningham, had granted to the governor, for the use of the county, on the north side of the Conequenessing,

444

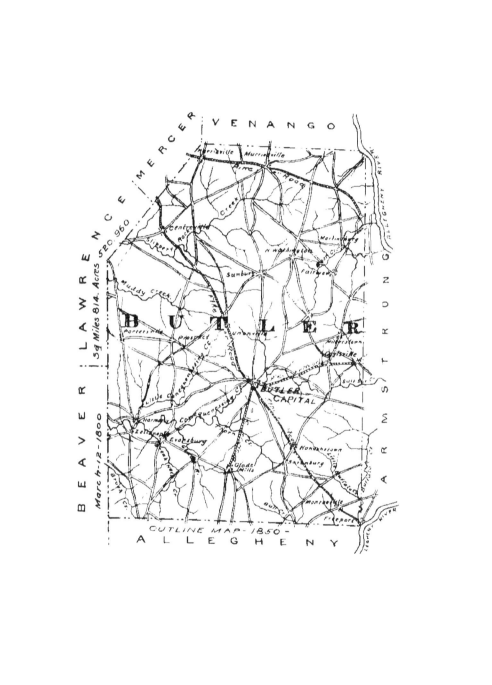

near Cunningham's mill, to lay out a lot, etc., for the public buildings, and the residue in town lots, to be sold by auction."

Butler County is bounded on the north by Venango; on the east by Armstrong; on the south by Allegheny; and on the west by Beaver and Mercer. Length, thirty-three miles; breadth, twenty-three miles; area, seven hundred and eighty-five square miles; and contains five hundred and two thousand four hundred acres of land. Population in 1810, 1346; in 1820, 10,193; in 1830, 14,681; in 1840, 22,378.

Butler Borough is situated on the Conequenessing Creek, in the bend thereof, on an eminence that commands an extensive and picturesque view of the surrounding country, " embracing rolling land, variegated with copse of woodland, country seats, verdant meadows, and the silvery waters of the creek meandering among them."

The town was laid out in lots in 1803, and a public sale held in August of that year. Butler contains the usual county buildings,—a brick court-house, a prison, an academy, and several well-built churches, Presbyterian, Lutheran, Methodist, Episcopal, etc. The borough was incorporated February 26, 1817. Population in 1830, 580; in 1840, 861. On the creek there are several mills, and a salt-works.

Harmony is on the south bank of Conequenessing Creek, fourteen miles southwest of Butler; and Zelienople, on the same creek, is about one mile southwest of Harmony, and was laid out about forty years ago, by Dr. Miller. It contains between forty-five and fifty-five houses, three hundred and twenty-five inhabitants, principally German, and mostly intelligent and enterprising. The soil around the village is fertile. Besides these, there are many other villages,—Centreville, Harrisville, Woodville, Murrinsville, Portersville, Prospect, Evansville, Summersville, North Washington.

No river passes through the county, but the Allegheny River touches the northeast and southwest corners. The county is well watered by a number of creeks, giving an abundance of water-power to grist-mills, saw-mills, oil-mills, woollen-factories, etc. Springs of pure water are abundant.

Several graded roads called turnpikes, though not covered with broken stones, and hence called " clay pikes," cross the county in different directions.

Education receives considerable attention. There is an academy at the seat of justice, established in 1811, and endowed by the Legislature with two thousand dollars and a tract of land. There are twenty school districts in the county, nineteen of which reported that in these were one hundred and fifty-two schools in operation, in which three thousand nine hundred and one males, and two thousand eight hundred and forty-two females were taught five months in the year 1845. A school tax of $5593.86 was assessed, and the State appropriation was $3257.21. The whole cost of instruction was $6484. 55.

The various religious persuasions are Presbyterians, Seceders, German

Reformed, Lutherans, Universalists, Unionists, Covenanters; but the Catholics are the most numerous.

One of Captain Samuel Brady's adventures occurred on the waters of Slippery Rock Creek, probably somewhere in this county:

" The injuries inflicted on the Indians by the troops under General Broadhead quieted the country for some time. He kept spies out, however, for the purpose of watching their motions, and guarding against sudden attacks on the settlements. One of these parties, under the command of Captain Brady, had the French Creek country assigned as their field of duty. The captain had reached the waters of Slippery Rock, a branch of Beaver, without seeing signs of Indians. Here, however, he came on an Indian trail in the evening, which he followed till dark without overtaking the Indians. The next morning he renewed the pursuit, and overtook them while they were engaged at their morning meal. Unfortunately for him, another party of Indians were in his rear. They had fallen upon his trail, and pursued him, doubtless, with as much ardor as his pursuit had been characterized by; and at the moment he fired upon the Indians in his front, he was, in turn, fired upon by those in his rear. He was now between two fires, and vastly outnumbered. Two of his men fell; his tomahawk was shot from his side, and the battle-yell was given by the party in his rear, and loudly returned and repeated by those in his front. There was no time for hesitation; no safety in delay; no chance of successful defence in their present position. The brave captain and his rangers had to flee before their enemies, who pressed on their flying footsteps with no lagging speed. Brady ran toward the creek. He was known by many, if not by all of them; and many and deep were the scores to be settled between him and them. They knew the country well; he did not; and from his running toward the creek they were certain of taking him prisoner. The creek was, for a long distance above and below the point he was approaching, washed in its channel to a great depth. In the certain expectation of catching him there, the private soldiers of his party were disregarded; and throwing down their guns, and drawing their tomahawks, all pressed forward to seize their victim.

" Quick of eye, fearless of heart, and determined never to be a captive to the Indians, Brady comprehended their object and his only chance of escape, the moment he saw the creek; and by one mighty effort of courage and activity, defeated the one and effected the other. He sprang across the abyss of waters, and stood, rifle in hand, on the opposite bank, in safety. As quick as lightning (says my informant) his rifle was primed; for it was his invariable practice in loading to prime first. The next minute the powderhorn was at the gun's muzzle; when, as he was in this act, a large Indian, who had been foremost in pursuit, came to the opposite bank, and with the manliness of a generous foe, who scorns to undervalue the qualities of an enemy, said, in a loud voice, and tolerable English, 'Blady make good jump!' It may, indeed, be doubted whether the compliment was uttered in derision; for the moment he had said so he took to his heels, and, as if fearful of the return it might merit, ran as crooked as a worm-fence—sometimes leaping high, at others suddenly squatting down, he appeared no way certain that Brady would not answer from the lips of his rifle. But the rifle was not yet loaded. The captain was at the place afterwards, and ascertained that his leap was about 23 feet, and that the water was 20 feet deep. Brady's next effort was to gather up his men. They had a place designated at which to meet, in case they should happen to be separated; and thither he went, and found the other three there. They immediately commenced their homeward march, and returned to Pittsburg about half defeated. Three Indians had been seen to fall from the fire they gave them at breakfast."

When Butler County was first organized, Mr. William Ayres was appointed prothonotary, and had for his clerk and law student, Mr. H. M. Breckenridge, since a distinguished Member of Congress from Allegheny County. The following graphic sketch is from his "Recollections of the West":

"On my arrival at Butler there were a few log houses just raised, but not sufficiently completed to be occupied. It was not long before there were two taverns, a store, and a blacksmith's shop; it was then a town. The country around was a perfect wilderness, with the exception of a few scattered settlements. The business of the office requiring but little of my time, and having an unbounded liberty, with a most exquisite relish for its enjoyment, no small portion of it was passed in wild and uncertain rambles through the romantic hills and valleys of Butler. The mornings and evenings were devoted to study, but generally the day was sacred to liberty.

"The first court held in Butler drew the whole population to the town, some on account of business, some to make business, but the greater part from idle curiosity. They were at that time chiefly Irish, who had all the characteristics of the nation. A log cabin just raised and covered, but without window-sash or doors, or daubing, was prepared for the hall of justice. A carpenter's bench, with three chairs upon it, was the judgment-seat. The bar of Pittsburg attended, and the presiding judge, a stiff, formal, and pedantic old bachelor, took his seat, supported by two associate judges, who were common farmers, one of whom was blind of an eye. The hall was barely sufficient to contain the bench, bar, jurors, and constables. But few of the spectators could be accommodated on the lower floor, the only one yet laid; many, therefore, clambered up the walls, and placing their hands and feet in the open interstices between the logs, hung there, suspended like enormous Madagascar bats. Some had taken possession of the joists, and big John McJunkin (who until now had ruled at all public gatherings) had placed a foot on one joist, and a foot on another, directly over the heads of their honors, standing like the Colossus of Rhodes. The judge's sense of propriety was shocked at this exhibition. The sheriff, John McCandless, was called, and ordered to clear the walls and joists. He went to work with his assistants, and soon pulled down by the legs those who were in no very great haste to obey. McJunkin was the last, and began to growl as he prepared to descend. 'What do you say, sir?' said the judge. 'I say, I pay my taxes, and his as good a reete here as iny mon.' 'Sheriff, sheriff,' said the judge, 'bring him before the court.' McJunkin's ire was now up; as he reached the floor, he began to strike his breast, exclaiming, 'My name is John McJunkin, d'ye see—here's the brist that niver flunched, if so be it was in a goode caase. I'll stan iny mon a hitch in Butler County, if so be he'll clear me o' the la'.' 'Bring him before the court,' said the judge. He was accordingly pinioned, and, if not gagged, at least forced to be silent, while his case was under consideration. Some of the lawyers volunteered as *amici curiæ*, some ventured a word of apology for McJunkin. The judge pronounced sentence of imprisonment for two hours in the jail of the county, and ordered the sheriff to take him into custody. The sheriff, with much simplicity, observed, 'May it please the coorte, there is no jail at all at all to put him in.' Here the judge took a learned distinction, upon which he expatiated at some length, for the benefit of the bar. He said there were two kinds of custody: first, safe custody; secondly, close custody. The first is, where the body must be forthcoming to answer a demand, or an accusation, and in this case the body may be delivered for the time being out of the hands of the law, on bail or recognizance; but where the imprisonment forms a part of the satisfaction or punishment, there can be no bail or mainprize. This is the reason of the common law, in relation to escapes under *capias ad satisfaciendum,* and also why a second *ca. sa.* cannot issue after the defendant has been once arrested and then discharged by the plaintiff. In like manner a man cannot be twice imprisoned for the same offence, even if he be released before the expiration of the term of imprisonment. This is clearly a case of close custody—*arcta custodia,* and the prisoner must be confined, body and limb, without bail or mainprize, in some place of close incarceration.' Here he was interrupted by the sheriff, who seemed to have hit upon a lucky thought. 'May it please the coorte, I'm just thinken that may be I can take him till Bowen's pig-pen—the pigs are kilt for the coorte, an it's empty?' 'You have heard the opinion of the court,' said the judge, 'proceed, sir; do your duty.'

"The sheriff accordingly retired with his prisoner, and drew after him three fourths of the spectators and suitors, while the judge, thus relieved, proceeded to organize the court. But this was not the termination of the affair. Peace and order had hardly been restored, when the sheriff came rushing to the house, with a crowd at his heels, crying out, 'Mr. Jidge, Mr. Jidge; may it please the coorte.' 'What is the matter, sheriff?' 'Mr. Jidge,

Mr. Jidge,—John McJunkin's got aff, d'ye mind.' 'What! escaped, sheriff? Summon the posse comitatus!' 'The pusse, the pusse—why now I'll jist tell ye how it happen'd. He was goin' on quee-etly enough, till he got to the hazzle patch, an' all at once he pitched aff intil the bushes, an' I after him, but a lumb of a tree kitched my fut, and I pitched three rad off, but I fell forit, and that's good luck, ye minte.' The judge could not retain his gravity; the bar raised a laugh, and there the matter ended, after which the business proceeded quietly enough."

The pioneer court was held in 1803 by Judge Jesse Moore; Associate Judges, Samuel Findley and John Parker; John McCandless, sheriff. Moore wore knee breeches, powdered wig, etc.

The pioneer school-house was near Whitestown, Nicholas Willison, master. It was a German school. Of course, the school-houses were logs and in every particular were conducted like the pioneer schools in other counties.

Butler academy was built in 1811.

The pioneer doctor was Dr. George Miller, about 1816. Butler County was well represented in the war of 1812. Colonel John Purviance raised a regiment of twelve companies and marched to the front.

Butler City was laid out in 1803, and incorporated as a borough February 26, 1817. General Lafayette passed through the borough on his way from Pittsburg to Erie, June 1, 1825.

Conequenessing Lodge, No. 278, I. O. O. F., was instituted December 11, 1847.

The pioneer grist-mill was a small log one erected in 1805 by Alexander Bryson.

Saxonburg was incorporated August 11, 1846. The pioneer election was held September 5, 1846.

Prospect Borough was laid out in 1825 by Andrew McGowen, and was incorporated as a borough in 1846.

Portersville Borough was laid out in 1828 by Robert Stewart, and in 1845 was incorporated as a borough.

Centreville was laid out by William Hill in 1820, and was incorporated as a borough in 1841.

Harrisville was laid out in 1825, and was incorporated as a borough in 1847.

Thomas Robinson, Esq., of Butler City, kindly loaned me a history of Butler County, from which I have gleaned most of these data.

Although the streams afforded the principal means of communication for the Indians (and for the few whites who ventured into the wilderness in the last century), there were numerous trails crossing the country. The great "Kittanning path," which led westward from Philadelphia to the Indian town of Kittanning on the Allegheny, was continued through what is now Butler County, passed the site of the seat of justice, and thence probably led to Beaver Creek or the Ohio, or merged with other trails which extended to those streams. There is traditionary evidence that an Indian path, well defined when the county was settled, extended from the site of Butler in an almost straight line to Pittsburg. In Buffalo Township a trail has been identified which ran in a north and south direction. It probably extended northward a considerable distance, and again approached the Allegheny River near the northeastern angle of the county, cutting off the big eastern bend of the river.

There were other trails, however, compared with which those we have alluded to were mere by-paths.

The lands which now form the western part of Butler County were traversed by two Indian trails, of which very distinct traces remained when the first settlers came into the county in 1796, and which, indeed, can be identified in some localities at the present day. The more important of these was the trail from the forks of the Ohio (the site of Pittsburg) to Venango, an old Indian town at the mouth of French Creek, on the Allegheny River, where is now the town of Franklin. The old Pittsburg and Franklin road, as originally laid out, closely followed the ancient path of the red men. Entering the present limits of the county on the south line of Cranberry Township, the trail extended almost directly northward.

It can still be detected on the lands of Christian Goehring and Israel Cookson, in Cranberry, and it is probable that, after passing northward into what is now Jackson Township, it bore slightly eastward, following a small run to Breakneck Creek, which it must have crossed very near Evansburg. From this point it extended northward through Forward and Conequenessing, Franklin, Brady, and Slippery Rock, and so onward to Venango. It is highly probable that it crossed the lands upon which the village of Prospect has been built, and it was doubtless at that locality that the trail from Logstown intersected it. This latter trail is supposed to have traversed the sites of Zelienople and Harmony.

Another Indian trail crossed the lands now embraced in Cranberry, from the northwest to the southeast, running in a line approximately parallel to Brush Creek. This connected "the forks," or the site of Pittsburg, with the Indian village of Kosh-kosh-kung. David Garvin, a settler of 1796, is authority for the statement that for many years this ancient pathway could be distinguished upon the farm now owned by J. Dambach.

In the year 1753, more than two score years before there were any white men resident in Butler County, no less a personage than George Washington travelled on foot through the wilderness along the trails between "the forks" and Venango, and between Logstown, on the Ohio, and the site of Prospect.

Robert Morris, the Revolutionary patriot, and Washington's Secretary of the Treasury, became a large owner of Butler County lands, and many of the land-owners of to-day hold title through this celebrated but unfortunate personage.

Morris located three hundred and eleven warrants in that part of Cunningham's district of depreciated lands, lying within Butler County, and was the owner of from seventy to ninety thousand acres of land, including the site of Butler borough.

Litigation concerning title was more common within the limits of this immense purchase than elsewhere in Butler County.

Robert Morris's effects were sold in 1807 at marshal's sale, in Philadelphia, and the warrants for the Butler County lands came into the hands of Stephen Lowrey, of Maryland, and other speculators. Lowrey became the owner of one hundred and seven tracts. Upon many of these tracts, and upon those of other speculators, settlers were located, who had made improvements, but who held no warrants for the lands. Many of them were summarily dispossessed of their squatter homes, and others were compelled to make terms with the speculators for occupancy. As a rule, the land jobbers were sustained by the law. The feeling against them ran very high, and, considering the character of the frontiersmen with whom they had to deal, it is surprising that war did not result from the controversy other than that which was carried on in the courts. As it was, much ill-feeling was engendered, and on one occasion, at least, bloodshed ensued.

In the "new purchase," as the territory in Northwestern Pennsylvania released from Indian claim in 1784 was called, the price set on lands from the 1st of March, 1785, to the 1st of March, 1789, was £30 ($80) per hundred acres; from the 1st of March, 1789, to the 3d of April, 1792, £20 ($53.33⅓).

Lands in the "new purchase" lying north and west of the Ohio and Allegheny Rivers and Conewango Creek, from the 3d of April, 1792, to the 28th of March, 1813, were £7 10s. ($20) per 100 acres. Undrawn donation lands from the 1st of October, 1813, until the 25th of February, 1819, were one dollar and fifty cents per acre, and upon the latter date were reduced to fifty cents per acre.

The first white man who is positively known to have built a habitation within the present limits of Butler County was James Glover.

James Glover was of Holland Dutch descent; was born in Essex County, New Jersey, where he lived until the breaking out of the Revolutionary War. At that time, being of suitable age, and patriotically disposed, he enlisted in the colonial army. He served his first term of duty in the New Jersey Line, and, on its expiration, enlisted in the Pennsylvania Line, the expiration of his former term of service finding him in this State or colony. He served until the close of the war; was at the battle of Princeton, at Germantown, with Washington crossing the Delaware, and was one of the soldiers who passed the memorable and terrible winter at Valley Forge. He was a very skilful blacksmith, and was engaged much of the time as an armorer. His pure patriotism was attested by the fact that he was among those who steadfastly refused to draw pay from the government for services rendered. After the close of the war he went with his wife to Pittsburg, and there followed his trade. His shop was upon Diamond Alley, between Market and Wood Streets. After a few years he purchased a farm on the north side of the Allegheny River, and took up his residence upon it. This farm is now in the heart of Allegheny City, and some of the finest buildings of the busy town stand upon the ground where Glover followed agricultural pursuits. He lived to see the city built up, but realized very little from it pecuniarily. Shortly after the close of the war of 1812 he leased the farm in perpetuity for seventy-five dollars per year, and that amount is now received annually by some of his heirs, one city lot paying the rental. This lease of Glover's, and one or two others, operated to bring about prohibitory legislation in the State of Pennsylvania, so that leasing in perpetuity is now an impossibility. Mr. Glover died on the place where he settled, in Adams Township, in September, 1844, aged ninety-one years. His family consisted of two daughters,—Mary and Nancy. Mary married the Rev. Daniel McLean, for many years a resident of Crawford County, and Nancy married Barnet Gilleland, in 1802, who, with his father, settled in Butler County, in the locality now known as Buhl's Mill, in 1796.

The pioneers of the county were nearly all Irish, Scotch, or Scotch-Irish, and mostly from " beyond the mountains."

The early German pioneers came into the county through the influence of a few individuals. Detmar Basse came from Germany in 1802, settled in Jackson Township, and in 1803 founded Zelienople, which has ever been practically a German village. George Rapp founded Harmony in 1805, bringing into the county a colony of Germans who constituted the Harmonist or Economite Society. When that society removed, in 1815, the community still remained German, Abraham Zeigler, who settled there in 1814 and bought the lands, bringing in a large number of settlers of his nationality from Western Pennsylvania.

The road from Pittsburg to Mercer was laid out as a State road in 1805–06.

The pioneer bridge built in the county was across the Conequenessing, south of Butler, in 1805.

The court-house of 1807 was a small stone building, and stood upon the ground occupied by the present court-house.

In 1803 Butler County was divided into six election districts.

In 1804 the county was made into fourteen townships.

Very primitive methods of marketing necessarily prevailed in pioneer times. Hogs were frequently carried to market on horseback—there was no other way. The legs of two hogs were tied together by a hickory withe and the load balanced thus upon the pack-saddle, a hog on each side of the horse. Ploughs were made after the most ancient pattern, mostly of wood. John Burtner, after his settlement, used to make them for the whole neighborhood. They were very rude affairs, and so light as to require the greatest patience and dexterity from the operator. Thomas Lardin had one of the first metal ploughs. It was called the "patent plough," and when it had been tested and found to work well, other settlers soon purchased ploughs like it. Harrows were made entirely of wood, including the teeth. Horse-collars were made of husks or oatstraw, and sewed together with a tow string. Traces were made of hickory withes.

CHAPTER XXVI

CRAWFORD COUNTY—FORMATION OF COUNTY—LOCATION OF COUNTY SEAT—
TRAILS—ROADS—SETTLERS—LAKES—THE MEADS—TURNPIKE—HOLLAND
COMPANY — CHURCHES — CANALS — BOATING — ANIMALS — OIL —
ELKS — PIGEONS — SALT WELL — WEEKLY MAIL — MURDER — LAWYERS
—VILLAGES—SOLDIERS OF 1812—BOROUGHS—STAGE ROUTE

" CRAWFORD COUNTY was taken from Allegheny County by the act of
March 12, 1800. It received its name in honor of Colonel William Crawford, one of the heroes of the Western frontier, who was burned by the
Indians at Sandusky. Length, forty-one miles; breadth, twenty-four miles;
area, nine hundred and seventy-four square miles. Population in 1800, 2346;
in 1810, 6178; in 1820, 9397; in 1830, 16,030; in 1840, 31,724.

" The land generally is undulating, of good quality; better adapted, however, to the raising of stock than of grain, but there is nevertheless an ample
proportion suitable for the latter. French Creek, formerly known as Venango
River, enters from Erie County, and, meandering centrally through the
county, passes out through a corner of Mercer into Venango County, emptying into the Allegheny River at Franklin. It is a beautiful stream, navigable
for large boats and rafts during high-water, and affords an abundant supply,
at all seasons, for the various mills along its banks. Several other small
streams water the county, as Cussewago, Big and Little Sugar Creeks, Oil
Creek, Woodcock Creek, Muddy Creek, and Conneauttee Creek.

" ' According to the pronunciation of the venerable Cornplanter, the first
of these names should be spelt Kos-se-wau-ga. Tradition states that the
Indians, on coming to the creek for the first time, discovered a large blacksnake, with a white ring round his neck, among the limbs of a tree. The
snake exhibited a wonderful protuberance, as if it had swallowed a rabbit.
They hence called the creek *Kossewauga*, which means *big-belly*.

" ' Conneaut, or Conneot, means something about *snow*, or the *snow
place*. It was noticed that the snow remained some time on the ice of the
lake after it had disappeared in the vicinity. Con-ne-aut-tee is a diminutive,
formed by the American, from the name of the larger lake.'—*Rev. Mr.
Alden.*

" There are three handsome lakes in the county. The Conneaut is a
beautiful sheet of water, about four miles by two, abounding with fine fish.
The other two are of smaller size, but equally picturesque. Agriculture is

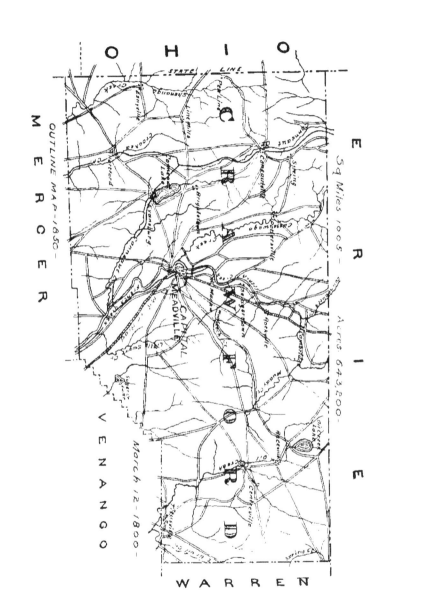

the main object of pursuit. The manufactures of the county are chiefly for the consumption of its own citizens. Iron ore is found in many localities. The French Creek feeder, which supplies the canal from Pittsburg to Erie, and is of the same size, runs from Bemis's dam, three miles above Meadville, down French Creek eleven miles, and then up the valley of Conneaut outlet, to the summit level near that lake. Slackwater navigation also extends down French Creek to the Allegheny."—*Day's Collections.*

Previous to the white man's advent here this wilderness had public highways, but they were for the wild deer and savage Indians. These thoroughfares were called "deer paths" and "Indian trails." These paths were usually well beaten, and crossed each other as civilized roads now do. The first trail discovered and traversed by the white man was the Indian Chinklacamoose path, which extended from what is now Clearfield town to what is now Kittanning. This Indian trail passed through what is now Punxsutawney, and over this path and through this Indian town Allegheny Indians carried their white prisoners from the eastern part of the State to what was then called Kittany, on the Allegheny River. From a most careful and thorough search to ascertain when the first path or trail of the white man was made through this wilderness, I find it to be in the year 1787. In this year of grace two hardy and courageous men, David and John Meade, were living in what is now Sunbury, Pennsylvania, where John was keeping an inn or tavern. These two brothers having read General George Washington's report to Governor Dinwiddie, of Virginia, of the rich lands and valleys that were unoccupied in what is now called Venango and Crawford Counties, Pennsylvania, determined to explore that region for themselves. To reach this uninhabited section they were compelled to open a path from east to west, through what is now Clearfield, Jefferson, Clarion, Venango, and Crawford Counties. From Franklin the trail went up French Creek to where Meadville now is. This path is now called in history Meade's trail. This trail passed through what is now West Reynoldsville, Port Barnett, and Brookville, in Jefferson County. It entered Clarion County where the pike does and crossed the Clarion River at Clugh's Riffle.

These men, with their goods packed on four horses, passed through where Brookville now is in 1788, and settled in and around what is now Meadville, then Allegheny County. Meade's trail commenced at the mouth of Anderson's Creek, near Curwinsville, Clearfield County, Pennsylvania, and over this trail until 1802 all transportation had to be carried into or through this wilderness on pack-saddles by pack-horses. A pack-horse load was from two to three hundred pounds. In 1802–03 the first wagon-road, or the old Milesburg and Waterford State Road, was opened for travel. The Meade settlers in Crawford County in 1788 comprised the pioneer permanent settlement in Northwestern Pennsylvania.

Soon after David Meade and his neighbors reached their new home the great chief of the Six Nations, accompanied by a number of his tribe, made these pioneers a social visit. This chief was Cornplanter, and he was then chief over our Indians who belonged to this confederation. In one of these friendly visits Meade discovered that five white men who had been captured when boys were reared by the Indians and were then living under Cornplanter; that these boys had all attained manhood and three of them had married Indian women. The five white men were Lashley Malone, of Bald Eagle Valley, Pennsylvania; Peter Krause, of Monongahela; Elijah Matthews, of Ohio; Nicholas Rosencrants and Nicholas Tanewood, of Mohawk Valley, New York State.

In 1789 Darius Meade, father of David and John, Robert F. Randolph, and Frederick Baum passed over this "trail" on their way to what is now Meadville. Many of the pioneers who travelled over this trail to the northwest were captured and murdered by the Indians in the raids of 1791–92 and 1793. In 1791 Darius Meade was captured by two Indians while ploughing in a field. His captors were Captain Bull, a Delaware chief, and Conewyando, a Seneca chief. Meade in an effort to escape got possession of Bull's knife and killed Bull with it, and after a fierce struggle with Conewyando was killed, but Conewyando died in a few days from the wounds Meade gave him. Two of our soldiers buried Meade and Bull side by side where they fell.

"Indian trails were 'bee lines' over hill and dale, from point to point. Here and there were open spots on the summits, where runners signalled their coming by fires when on urgent business, and were promptly met at stated places by fresh men."

The ancient Indian path from Fort Venango to Fort Le Bœuf, was on the eastern side of French Creek, not far from the present lower road to Meadville, where it crossed and stretched over the island opposite the town, and continued on the western side a number of miles, and again crossed the creek. Major George Washington followed this path in 1753, on his journey to visit the French commander at Le Bœuf.

After the French had departed, this region remained a cheerless solitude for many years. In 1788 the cheerful sound of the pioneer's axe broke upon the solemn stillness of the forests of Cussewago. David Meade and his brother John, two brothers of the Randolph family, Stophel Seiverling, James Miller, and Cornelius Van Horn came out from Northumberland County, by the way of Bald Eagle and the old Chinklacamoose path to the mouth of French Creek, and thence up the creek until they discovered the beautiful flat where Meadville now stands. Several of these gentlemen had held lands in Wyoming Valley, under the Pennsylvania title, from which they had been driven by Connecticut claimants. Knowing well the quality of land and the value of a good title, they were cautious and judicious in their selections, as the fine estates now in possession of their families will show. Subsequent events, however, threatened to shake the foundation of their titles, and cast them out upon the wilderness for a new selection. The vexed questions, and numerous delays and lawsuits growing out of the land law of 1792, had a dispiriting influence upon the early settlers of Crawford County, until settled by the decision of the great Holland Land Company case, and others of a similar nature. Besides the gentlemen above mentioned, several others came a few years later, among whom were Mr. Heidekoper, Mr. Bennet, Mr. Lord, Mr. Morgan, Mr. Reynolds, on Oil Creek, and others.

The biographies of several of these pioneers have been preserved, and furnish an excellent history of the county. The following is abridged from Rev. Timothy Alden's *Allegheny Magazine*, published at Meadville in 1816:

"The Hon. David Meade, the first settler of the pleasant village which bears his name, was born at Hudson, New York. His father, Darius Meade (also an early settler in this county), when David became of age, removed to the Wyoming country, where they both had purchased lands under the Pennsylvania title. In consequence of the adverse claims, and the superior force of the Connecticut claimants, they were obliged to abandon their lands, and settled near Northumberland. David Meade became a citizen of Sunbury, where he kept an inn for a number of years. After various discouraging struggles with fortune, with the Indians, and the Wyoming boys, Mr. Meade resolved to leave that region, seek a new home, and commence a new career on the lands west of the Allegheny River. In 1788 he visited this section of the country, then a wilderness, in company with his brother John and several others. In 1789 he removed his family. Some time afterwards he obtained a remuneration from the State in lands, for those of which he had been dispossessed at Wyoming.

"After several years of incessant toil and hardship, his prospects began to brighten; but they were soon overcast with a gloomy cloud. Another Indian war menaced the infant settlements of the West. Many fled; those who remained were exposed to constant perils and privations. Mr. Meade, having an important interest here, continued on his plantation, resolved to brave every danger, and bear every privation while the war should exist. The war was at length happily terminated by General Wayne, in 1795. For several months in 1791, when the Indians were daily expected to attempt the extermination of the people on French Creek, Mr. Meade with his family resided at Franklin, that he might have it in his power to repair to the garrison in that place as a last resort. During this period his father was taken, by two Indians, from a field where he was at work, and carried to the vicinity of Conneaut Lake. Some days afterwards he was found, together with one of the Indians, both dead, and bearing such marks of violence as showed they had had a contest; and it was deemed probable that the other Indian had been wounded in the encounter, from the circumstance of his companion having been left unburied.

"Mr. Meade held the office of justice of the peace both at Wyoming and here. In 1800 he became one of the associate judges for Crawford County. He was also a major-general in the militia. He was a man of uncommon bodily strength, standing six feet three, and large in proportion—in deportment sedate and grave, but affable, easy of access, and without ostentation. His vigorous mind was ever actively engaged upon public or private business. His first wife was Agnes Wilson, of Northumberland County; his second, Janet Finney, daughter of Robert Finney, Esq. His mansion was noted for hospitality, and in his later years the morning and evening sacrifice arose from his family altar. He died on the 23d of August, 1816, in the sixty-fifth year of his age."

The following is from the *Crawford Messenger*, of July, 1830: ·

"Died at his farm, near Meadville, on the 16th inst., Robert F. Randolph, in the eighty-ninth year of his age. The deceased was born in Woodbridge Township, Essex County, New Jersey. He married when young, and in 1771 removed to Northampton County, Pennsylvania, where he resided two years; from whence he removed to Northumberland County, then on the frontier of this State, there being hardly a white inhabitant above the spot where Northumberland now stands. There he resided until the year 1776, when hostilities commenced upon the inhabitants of the county, and they were driven from their homes by the savages. He with his family fled to Bucks County, but returned to his residence the same year. He then joined the regiment commanded by Colonel William Cook, and was with it in the memorable battle of Germantown. Shortly after his return from the army, the county of Northumberland, by one desolating sweep, was cut off, and its inhabitants driven out by the cruel and unrelenting hand of the savages. Finding no prospect of peace or safety for his family, he returned to his native State, where they would be at least secure from the terrors of the scalping-knife. He then re-entered the army of the United States, in which capacity he served until the close of the war.

"When peace was restored he returned, in 1783, to Northumberland County, and settled on Shamokin Creek, where he continued to reside until 1789, when he with his family emigrated to this county, at that time one entire wilderness; and on the 6th of July, the same year, arrived on French Creek, near where the village of Meadville now stands, and settled on the farm upon which, till his death, he has ever since resided. When he made his selection and took possession, there were none to dispute his right but the tawny sons of the forest, from whose pitiless hands he had much to fear. But that spirit of enterprise, with an honest view of procuring a permanent home for himself and family, which had induced him to the wilderness and cheered his pathless way into it, continued to support him under every privation, difficulty, and danger incident to the settlement of a new country. His zeal in the cause of freedom was unwavering. Of this fact, the following will serve as an illustration: In one of the alarms occasioned by the approach of the enemy to the town of Erie, during the late war, like the patriarch of old, he mustered a strong band of his own household, consisting of his four sons and two or three grandsons, put himself at their head, and thus armed and equipped marched to meet the expected foe."

Mr. Cornelius Van Horn has been named as one of the early pioneers. He was still (1843) enjoying a quiet old age, on the farm, near Meadville, earned and cleared by the toils and exposures of his youth. The following story of his adventures was derived by the compiler of this work, in conversation with a member of Mr. Van Horn's family:

"Mr. Cornelius Van Horn had been a settler in Wyoming Valley under the Pennsylvania title, and relinquished his possessions there under the compromise, receiving compensation from the State. In 1788 he was persuaded by David Meade (who had also been a Pennamite) to make one of a party of nine to come out and settle in Crawford County. They took the route from Bald Eagle, in Centre County, over the Allegheny Mountains, nearly on the route of the present turnpike, struck the mouth of French Creek, and thence followed it up until they discovered the beautiful flat upon which Meadville is now seated. They here selected their lands, and entered upon their labors. Until 1791 nothing of special importance occurred, except that one day, as he was returning from Pittsburg with pack-horses, he was overtaken by an Indian near a lonely swamp; but he proved to be friendly. His name was McKee; and from this friendly interview and exchange of provisions, courtesies, etc., commenced an acquaintance, which was afterwards probably the means of saving Van Horn's life.

"In the month of May, 1791, Mr. Van Horn, Thomas Ray, and Mr. Gregg were ploughing on the island opposite the town. Gregg and Ray had gone in to fetch the dinner, when Van Horn, who continued ploughing, observed his horses take fright, and turning suddenly he saw a tall Indian about to strike him with his tomahawk, and another just behind. As quick as thought he seized the descending arm, and grappled with the Indian, hugging him after the manner of a bear. While in this close embrace, the other Indian attempted to shoot Van Horn; but the latter, who was no novice in frontier tactics, kept turning round the Indian in his arms so as to present him as a shield against the bullet, and thus gained time enough to parley for his life. No fine-spun diplomacy was practised in this treaty: a few words of broken Indian on one side, and broken English on the other, resulted in a capitulation, by which he was to be taken prisoner, together with his horses. He was pinioned and taken to the top of the hill above the college, where they met the old chief and a fourth Indian. After some parley, the chief mounted one of the horses and the prisoner the other, and pursued their way towards Conneaut Lake; while the three other Indians returned to the island for further adventures. Gregg and Ray had just returned to their work, and were deliberating over the meaning of the tracks in the field, when they

descried the three Indians. Gregg took to his heels, Ray calling to him to
stand his ground like a man; but he was pursued, killed, and scalped. Ray
was taken prisoner.

"The old chief had tied Van Horn by a thong to a tree, in a sitting
posture, with his arms behind him; but the thong working a little loose,
the chief pulled it obliquely up the tree to tighten it, and laid himself down
in the bushes to sleep. Van Horn, by raising himself, loosened the thong
enough to allow him to get a small knife out of his cuff,—he had previously,
to conciliate his good-will and allay suspicion, presented the chief with his
jack-knife, powder flints, tobacco, etc.,—and cut himself loose from the tree,

Pioneer farm

but could not unpinion his arms. He made his way back to the settlement,
where he found an officer from Fort Franklin, who ordered the whole colony
to repair for safety to that place, lest there might be a larger force of Indians
in the vicinity than had yet appeared. Van.Horn pleaded hard for permission
to remain, and learn the fate of Ray and Gregg; and as the officer's horse
had been lost, he was allowed to remain if he could get another to remain
with him. A friendly Indian, by the name of Gilloway, agreed to remain;
and for some other reason it was thought necessary (this was to catch the
horse) that another friendly Indian, McKee, should remain also. They found
the horse, and, taking some bear-skins, furs, etc., in the canoe, embarked for

Franklin. Gilloway, as he was the least of the two, volunteered to ride the horse, while the others went in the canoe; but he rode the horse a little too far, and in the wrong direction, not being heard of again until he was seen at Sandusky. Van Horn afterwards had reason to think that Gilloway had remained behind to murder him, but that his plan had been frustrated by the determination of McKee to stay also; and he then stole the horse.

"Van Horn and McKee determined to return from Franklin; and, by way of getting an early start, to lodge in a deserted cabin, a mile or two this side of Franklin. The commanding officer urged in vain the danger of a surprise and attack from savages. Van Horn and his comrade thought themselves competent to the defence of their position. In the night, however, the officers and soldiers of the garrison determined to make good their surmises, and have a little fun, by raising a whoop, and surrounding the cabin where Van Horn lay. The latter, hearing the noise, was on the alert; and while the soldiers were listening at the door, they heard Van Horn make arrangements with his comrade that he should stand by to haul them into the cabin, while he cut them down at the door with an axe. This was a kind of sport for which the party was not prepared, and they withdrew, laughing at the frustration of their own scheme. Van Horn soon after went to Jersey to attend to his Wyoming business, and then returned. Some few parties of Indians skulked about until after Wayne's treaty, when they all disappeared.

"When the three Indians with Ray had arrived at Conneaut Lake, and waked up the old chief, and found his prisoner gone, they told Ray that it was fortunate for him, as they could have taken only one prisoner away with them. They took him to Sandusky, where he recognized an English trader, who bought him off for a keg of whiskey. He returned by the lake to Olean, and thence down the Allegheny. On passing Franklin he inquired of those on shore for his 'Sally,' and being told she was in Pittsburg, pursued his way down there, where he found her.

"James Dixon, another old settler, better known as Scotch Jemmy, was surprised by a number of Indians in the woods, and shot at several times. He turned his face toward them, levelled his rifle, and dared the rascals to come out of the woods like men, and give him fair play. 'Noo coom on wi' your wee axe,' said Jemmy. With his rifle thus presented, he continued to walk backward until out of reach of their fire; and reached the old block-house, that stood where the blacksmith's shop is, near Bennett's tavern. This occurred about 1793 or 1794."

In a number of the *Messenger*, published in September, 1828, the editor, T. Atkinson, Esq., says,—

"In two months more, *twenty-five* years will have elapsed since we arrived in this village with our printing establishment, being the first, and for several subsequent years, the only one northwest of the Allegheny River. How short the period, yet how fruitful of interesting events! Our village at that time consisted of a few scattered tenements, or what might properly be termed huts. It is now surpassed by few, if any, in Western Pennsylvania for its numerous, commodious, and, in many instances, beautiful dwelling-houses, churches, academy, court-house, with a splendid edifice for a college; all affording pleasing evidence of the enterprise, the taste, and the liberality of its inhabitants. Then we were without roads, nothing but Indian-paths by which to wind our way from one point to another. Now turnpikes and capacious roads converge to it from every quarter. Then the mail passed between Pittsburg and Erie once in two weeks; now eighteen stages arrive and depart weekly. Then we had not unfrequently to pack our paper on horse-back upward of two hundred miles; on one hundred and thirty miles of this distance there were but three or four houses; now, however, thanks to an enterprising citizen of the village, it can be had as conveniently as could be desired. Our country is marching onward."

Meadville, 1843

Meadville was named after General David Meade. Twenty-three years after the organization of Crawford County the county-seat remained a village, but on March 29, 1823, it was incorporated as a borough.

Its growth is as follows: In 1800, one hundred and twenty-five people; in 1810, three hundred people; in 1820, six hundred and sixty-six people; in 1830, eleven hundred and four people; in 1840, thirteen hundred and nineteen people.

The pioneer burgess was Thomas Atkinson, in 1823.

The pioneer post-office was established in 1801, with Frederick Haymaker, postmaster.

The pioneer cemetery was an acre of ground on what is now Park Avenue. It was a Presbyterian graveyard.

Day says, in 1840,—

" The churches are a Presbyterian, Cumberland Presbyterian, Episcopal, Methodist, Baptist, and Unitarian. There is also an academy, several paper-mills, an oil-mill, an edge-tool manufactory, and quite a number of other mills, driven by the ample water-power in the vicinity.

" On the northern border of the town Colonel Magaw, the inventor of straw paper, had formerly a commodious mill for its manufacture. He had previously conducted a rag-paper establishment. On examining some straw which had been placed at the bottom of a barrel of leached ashes, he observed that it looked soft, and thought it might make paper. Perceiving its toughness and adhesive quality, he chewed some of it, rubbed it on a board, and placed it in the sun to dry. He succeeded in making paper on a small scale, obtained a patent-right, and erected his straw paper mill. It is said an edition of the New Testament was printed upon it, costing only five cents per copy."

" A canal-boat was launched at Meadville on the 28th of November, 1828, built of materials that were *growing* on the banks of French Creek the day before! The boat left for Pittsburg on the 30th, having on board twenty passengers, and three hundred reams of paper manufactured from *straw*."—*Crawford Messenger.*

The Rev. Charles William Colson, or Von Colson, who died at Meadville December 20, 1816, was the founder and pastor of the Lutheran Church of Meadville.

In 1790 David Meade completed a log saw-mill, and the first raft of lumber that ever descended French Creek and the Allegheny River to Pittsburg was from this mill, in the spring of 1790. In the fall of 1790 a grist-mill was attached. A distillery was added to the mills in 1805.

The pioneer bank of Crawford County was established in Meadville on October 28, 1814. The bank was located on the east side of Water Street above Walnut. In 1820 it had financial troubles, and in the fall of 1822 closed its doors.

The pioneer Masonic Lodge was instituted September 23, 1817, with the following officers: Robert L. Potter, W. M.; David Logan, S. W.; David Molthrop, J. W.; J. T. Cummings, Treasurer; John D. Morrison, Secretary. This lodge disbanded about 1833. The new Masonic Lodge was instituted in Meadville as Crawford Lodge, No. 284, F. and A. M., organized November 14, 1848.

The pioneer travelling circus was Harrington's, in the fall of 1819. He had a living African lion.

In pioneer days it was not unusual for Crawford County people to go ten, twenty, and more miles to a log grist-mill through the pathless forest, to be benighted and on their road home chased by wolves. A wagon was a wonder in those days, and the man that had one usually did the milling for the whole settlement.

In 1797 three kegs of seneca oil were appraised at fifty cents each.

The wild animals were the same as in the other parts of the Northwest Purchase, as were the birds, snakes, and reptiles.

A French Memoir written in 1714 said buffaloes are found on the south shore of Lake Erie, but not on the north.

The amount paid out for bounty in Crawford County for wolf and fox scalps from 1803 until 1835 was five thousand nine hundred and seventy-six dollars.

In 1806 the premium for full-grown wolf's ears was eight dollars, and three dollars for a puppy. In 1819 the premium was twelve dollars and five dollars, respectively.

Bee-trees were numerous; also wild turkeys and pheasants, and the small streams abounded in trout. The elk was rarely seen west of the Allegheny River.

In 1811 black squirrels were very numerous, but the gray squirrel did not appear until some years after the county began to be settled. In consequence of the devastation of these vermin and the premium offered by the State, regular squirrel-hunts were organized up to as late as 1840. On these days of contest hundreds of squirrels were slain by the contesting parties.

Pigeons clouded the country in the spring and fall. Their roosting-places, however, were the Conneaut and Pymatuning marshes, feeding on the beech-nuts and acorns. Panthers were scarce and not often seen, and seldom heard.

In 1819 the bounty on a panther's scalp was twelve dollars, and five dollars for a cub. The beaver inhabited the Conneaut and Pymatuning marshes.

Horse-flies were so numerous that horses exposed to them would die through pain and loss of blood.

Salt was an early trade, and in 1805 sold at Meadville at eleven dollars per barrel, and at Pittsburg at thirteen dollars per barrel.

In 1815 a salt-well was sunk in Beaver Township by Samuel B. Magaw and William Clark, of Meadville. Salt water was found at a depth of one hundred and eighty-six feet, but little was accomplished.

In the *Messenger* of November 7, 1818, we find the following: " The salt-works of Messrs. Shryock & Co. are now in operation in the west end of this county. The production at present will average about ten bushels per day. The water appearing sufficient, it is intended to increase the number of boilers, when double the quantity can be made. The salt is of excellent quality." The shaft was finally sunk to the depth of three hundred feet, with the hope of tapping a still richer vein, but instead of pure salt water being found, the fluid came forth mixed with petroleum, and therefore became useless for any purpose. An effort was still made to continue the works, but they did not pay and were abandoned in 1821. This undoubtedly was the pioneer oil-well.

" The hauling of the salt over the portage between Erie and Waterford.

and the floating of it down French Creek, gave employment to many citizens of this part of the State. To some farmers the trade was really a Godsend, as their land barely furnished food for their families, and, there being no markets for the little they had to sell, they were obliged by necessity to spend a part of their time at some other employment to raise money for taxes, groceries, and clothing. This was especially the case just before and immediately after the war of 1812–15, when the times were very hard. It is estimated that when the trade was at its best, one hundred teams and as many persons were constantly on the road between Erie and Waterford. The time for making each trip was calculated at two days, and the average load for a four-ox team was fourteen barrels. The price paid at first was from one dollar and fifty cents to three dollars per barrel, which was finally reduced to one dollar, and at the close to fifty cents. Prior to the completion of the Erie and Waterford Turnpike, the road was always bad, and it was not unusual for a wagon-load of freight to get stuck in the mud, and be four days in crossing the portage. On many occasions a part of the burden had to be abandoned on the way, and a second trip made to get it to its destination. A number of warehouses were erected on the bank of Le Bœuf Creek at Waterford for storing the salt until the water was at a suitable stage for floating it down French Creek. The salt was bought at Salina for sixty cents per bushel, and the price at Meadville ranged from five dollars to twelve dollars a barrel. It required from two to three months to convey it from the place of manufacture to Pittsburg. There was a period when salt was one of the circulating mediums in this region of country. Oxen, horses, negro slaves, and land were sold to be paid for in so much salt. As a sample, Hamlin Russell, father of N. W. Russell, of Belle Valley, Erie County, exchanged a yoke of oxen for eight barrels, and Rufus S. Reed purchased of General Kelso a colored boy, who was to be held to service under the State law until he was twenty-eight years old, for one hundred barrels. The price that season was five dollars per barrel, making the value of the slave five hundred dollars. The discovery of salt-wells on the Kiskiminitas and Kanawha, about 1813, cheapened the price of the article at Pittsburg, so that Salina could not compete, and the trade by way of Erie steadily diminished until it ceased altogether in 1819."

Work commenced on the Waterford and Erie Turnpike in 1806, and the road was completed in 1809. This turnpike was a paying property until 1845, when it was abandoned to the township.

The Mercer and Meadville Turnpike Company was incorporated in 1817. In 1821 it was completed and open for travel. This was a through line from Lake Erie to the Ohio River.

In 1810 there were roads to all points south, east, and west. The roads were poor; horseback riding and a foot-back were the usual modes of travelling.

The pioneer bridge over French Creek, in Crawford County, was built about 1810 or 1811.

"In 1801 a weekly mail route was established between Erie and Pittsburg, *via* Waterford, Meadville, and Franklin. By 1803 it had been reduced to once in two weeks, but was soon changed back to the original plan, and in 1806 the route changed to pass through Mercer instead of Franklin. The mode of transportation for some years was on horseback, and it is said that the mail was often so insignificant as to be easily carried in the driver's breeches pockets. During a good part of the time the pouch was carried on the back of a single horse; then the mail increased in size so that two horses were required, one carrying the driver and the other the mail; and later a horse and wagon became necessary. A semi-weekly mail was established through Meadville, from Erie to Pittsburg, Harrisburg, and Philadelphia, in 1818; a tri-weekly in February, 1824; and a daily in 1827.

"The first stage-route was established over the Susquehanna and Waterford, and the Erie and Waterford Turnpikes, from Bellefonte to Erie, by Robert Clark, of Clark's Ferry, in 1820, the first stage-coach arriving at Meadville, on November 7. By 1824 the route was completed through to Philadelphia *via* Harrisburg. In 1821 the route to Pittsburg, by way of Mercer and Butler, was completed. Gibson's Hotel was the stage depot at Meadville. By 1835 a daily line of steamers connected with the stages at Erie, and the fare from Pittsburg to Buffalo was but six dollars."

The pioneer murder in Meadville was the killing of his squaw by a drunken Indian in 1805. Another early murder was the killing of Hugh Fitzpatrick by George Speth Van Holland, on February 7, 1817. He was tried in May, 1817, convicted and sentenced, and executed July 26, 1817. David Lamphier was hanged at Meadville in the fall of 1822 for the murder of a constable by the name of Smith.

The pioneer session of the court in Crawford County, which was in 1800, was held by Associate Judges Meade and Kelso in the upper story of William Dick's residence, corner of Water Street and Cherry Alley. In April, 1801, Alexander Addison, Presiding Judge, William Bell, and Judge Kelso held the regular term of court in that house, as well as all others up until 1804, when the log court-house was erected. The jurisdiction of this court extended then over the counties of Crawford, Erie, Mercer, Venango, and Warren, all of which were organized for judicial purposes under the name of Crawford County.

In 1843 there were several small villages in Crawford County,—to wit, Centreville, Titusville, Cambridge, Rockville, Saegerstown, Evansburg, Hartztown, Adamsville, Espyville, Harmonsburg, and Conniotville.

Lawyers then usually rode the circuit, and when stopping at the taverns, if expected, were fed on chickens, dried apples, maple sugar, corn dodgers, and old whiskey.

HISTORY OF NORTHWESTERN PENNSYLVANIA

In this history I have to contract. It is only intended to be outlined, and many things that I would like to mention I have to entirely abnegate. I can say little of the war of 1812.

" The following is a partial list of army officers of the Northwest who participated in the war, most of whom made Erie their head-quarters: Quartermaster-General, Wilson Smith, 1812–14. Commissary-General, Collendar Irvine. Major-Generals, Sixteenth Division, David Meade, 1812–14; John Philips, 1814; Roger Alden, 1814–15. Brigadier-Generals, First Brigade, Sixteenth Division, John Kelso, 1812–14; Henry Hurst, 1814. Second Brigade, Thomas Graham, 1812. Brigade Inspector, First Brigade, Sixteenth Division, William Clark; Second Brigade, Samuel Powers. Paymaster, John Philips, 1812–13. Colonel David Nelson, Major and Lieutenant-Colonel Dr. John C. Wallace, Majors Ralph Marling, James Herriott, Patrick Farrelly, John Brooks, and William Moore. Commissaries, Rufus S. Reed, Stephen Wolverton. Captains, Isaac Mason, James Cochran, John Collom, Thomas Havlin, and James McKnight.

" Though a treaty of peace between the two nations was signed at Ghent, Belgium, December 24, 1814, the news did not reach the United States in time to prevent the battle of New Orleans, fought January 8, 1815, and which yet shines as one of the most brilliant victories in the history of the nation. Peace was publicly proclaimed February 18, 1815, and on that date the glad tidings reached Crawford County by an express which had left Washington, D. C., the previous Tuesday for Erie, Pennsylvania, passing through Meadville in its route."

TITUSVILLE

The village was planned by Jonathan Titus, although Mr. Titus had settled there in 1796. In lumbering days, 1820, Jonathan Titus's cabin was a regular stopping-place.

Titusville was incorporated by act of Assembly, approved March 6, 1847. The pioneer Burgess was Joseph L. Chase, in 1848.

The pioneer school structure was log, erected in 1817.

The Presbyterian church was erected in 1815, was log, and was used for several years for school purposes.

BOROUGH OF CONNEAUTVILLE

Incorporated by act of Legislature in 1843–44. The pioneer Burgess was John E. Patton. Alexander Power was the founder of the village.

Rockville was incorporated by act of Assembly in 1844, and named Woodcock. Henry Minium laid it out and christened it Rockville in the spring of 1819. He did not live in Rockville until 1824.

BOROUGH OF SAEGERSTOWN

The village was incorporated by act of Assembly in 1838. The pioneer post-office was established in 1833. Daniel Saeger settled here in 1824.

CHAPTER XXVII

"CLARION COUNTY was established by an act passed March 11, 1839, which defines the boundaries as follows: 'That all those parts of Armstrong and Venango Counties, lying and being within the following boundaries,—to wit, beginning at the junction of the Red Bank Creek with the Allegheny River, thence up said creek to the line dividing Toby and Saratoga Townships in Venango County, thence along said line to the corner of Farmington Township, in Venango County, thence a straight line to the mouth of Shull's Run, on the Allegheny River, thence down said river to the place of beginning, be and the same is hereby declared to be erected into a county, henceforth to be called Clarion.'

"By the same act James Thompson, John Gilmore, and Samuel L. Carpenter were appointed commissioners, to fix upon a proper and convenient site for a seat of justice. Mr. Thompson resigned, and by the act of June 25, John P. Davis, of Crawford County, was appointed to supply the vacancy.

"Clarion is bounded on the north by Venango County, on the east by Jefferson, on the south by Armstrong, and by the Allegheny River on the west, separating it from Armstrong, Butler, and Venango. By the return of the census of 1840, its population and general statistics are included in that of Armstrong and Venango Counties. The number of inhabitants within the new county exceed fifteen thousand. Average length, twenty-five miles; breadth, twenty-four miles; area, five hundred and ninety-five square miles.

"Education receives considerable attention. Nearly all the districts had, a few years ago, adopted the general system of common schools. Besides ninety common schools, there is an academy of advanced standing in the county town.

"The prevailing religious denominations are Presbyterians, Baptists, Methodists, Lutherans, and Catholics, all of whom have houses for public worship. The inhabitants are generally characterized for industry, sobriety, and morality. Few idlers are to be found in this county. They are literally '*worked out.*' The people do not *stand* lounging.

"Clarion, the county seat, situated on the east side of the Clarion River,

474

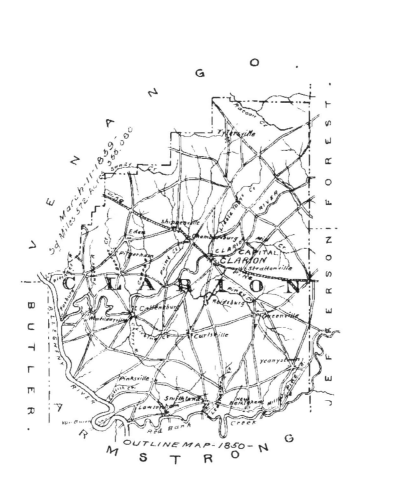

on the Bellefonte and Meadville turnpike road, was laid out by the commissioners in 1840. The land had been owned by General Levi G. Clover, James P. Hoover, Peter Clover, Jr., heirs of Philip Clover, of Strattonville, and the Hon. Christian Myers. ' These persons made a donation of the town site to the county, on condition of receiving half the proceeds from the sales of lots. Space for the county buildings and a public square, were reserved from sale.'

" The public buildings are a neat court-house of brick, surmounted with a cupola, a county prison, built of sandstone, and a spacious academy, built of brick. The borough is well laid out, neatness and much taste are displayed

Clarion, 1843

in both public and private buildings, and a brisk air of enterprise is presented everywhere in this town. There are several churches here.

" Besides the county town, there are several thriving towns and villages in this county. The principal ones are Strattonville, Shippensville, Curlesville, Greenville, Callensburg, Edinburg, Reimersburg, etc.

" Strattonville was laid out by Mr. John Stratton, from New Jersey, in 1830. It is on the turnpike road, about three miles east of the county town. It had seen, until lately, better days. It was the principal place of business for an extensive circle of thrifty and industrious farmers. Business has been principally diverted from this village to Clarion. There are several churches in, and near this village.

" Shippensville, called after its proprietor, the Hon. Judge Shippen, of Meadville, who laid out this town in 1826, is on the turnpike road, seven miles west of Clarion. It is a place of considerable business, and will undoubtedly increase rapidly. A few years ago the Lutherans erected a church in this town.

" Curlesville is a small village on the right bank of Licking Creek, near the township line, between Red Bank and Toby Townships. Greenville is situated near the head of Piney Creek, on the right bank, about one mile northwest of the Olean road. Callensburg is on the right bank of Licking Creek, at its mouth."—*History of Western Pennsylvania.*

The court-house was built by Edward Derby and Levi G. Clover, cost ten thousand six hundred and thirty-six dollars, and was completed in 1842.

Clarion was made a borough April 6, 1841. The pioneer burgess was James Sloan. The pioneer storekeeper was John Potter. The pioneer postmaster was David Wilson, in 1840. In 1841 Clarion contained seven hundred and fourteen people. The Presbyterian church was organized May 15, 1841, in the jail, and the pioneer church-building was completed in 1844.

Clarion County is bounded on the north by Forest County, on the west by Venango County, on the south by Red Bank Creek and the Allegheny River, and on the east by Jefferson County.

It was stipulated in the act of March 11, 1839, that the county organization for judicial purposes should go into effect on September 1, 1840, and the county was attached to the Sixth Judicial District, composed of the counties of Erie, Crawford, and Venango. Hon. Alexander McCalmont, of Franklin, was the pioneer judge: Christian Myers and Charles Evans were the pioneer associate judges. The pioneer court was held the first Monday in November, 1840, in a private house. At this court twenty-three lawyers were present.

John Sloan plotted the town of Clarion in 1839, and but one house then stood on the present site. The pioneer sale of lots was in October, 1839. The court-house and jail were put under contract in the fall of 1839. The court-house was not finished until 1843, and the upper story in the jail was used for court and church purposes until that time. The pioneer election for officers was held October 13, 1840. The following were chosen: James Hasson, for sheriff; James Goe, for prothonotary, etc.; John Reed, for coroner; George L. Benn, Jacob Miller, and Gideon Richardson, for commissioners; John Elliot, Joseph C. King, and George Means, for auditors. Joseph K. Boyd was the first resident lawyer.

The Clarion River divides the county in about the centre.

In 1844 the waters of what is now called the Clarion were as clear as crystal, pure as life, and gurgled into the river from mountain springs. No tannery or other refuse was to be found in it. In 1749 the French named the stream Gall River. It was declared a public highway, as Toby's Creek, by an act of the Legislature, March 21, 1798, up to the second great fork.

In early times this river was known as Stump Creek, and sometimes as Toby's Creek. It was called Toby's Creek as early as 1758. In 1819 we have the first official notice by an act of the Legislature designating the river Clarion.

In an act to authorize the erection of a dam, passed in 1822, this stream is designated as " Toby's Creek, otherwise called Clarion River."

Of the pioneer settlers who came over Mead's trail and settled in what is now Jefferson and Clarion Counties, Judge Peter Clover, of Clarion County, in 1877, wrote as follows:

" As stated in the outset, I will give a brief account of the pioneer settlement of Jefferson County. In 1800, Joseph Barnett and Samuel Scott settled forty miles west of Curwensville, Clearfield County. They were men of great energy and industry, and soon made valuable improvements. They built a saw-mill, which was a great help to the people, providing them with boards, etc. They settled among the Indians of the Seneca tribe, who were, however, civil. Joseph Barnett was a very eccentric, high-minded man, and took a leading part in all the business transactions of the day; a man long to be

Hon. Peter Clover

remembered by those who knew him. Shortly after their mill was made, perhaps as early as 1802, Henry Fir, a German, and a number of other families settled on the west of Mill Creek,—Jacob Mason, L. Long, John Dickson, Freedom Stiles, and a very large negro by the name of Fudge Vancamp, whose wool was as white as the wool of a sheep and whose face was as black as charcoal, and yet he was married to a white woman(?).

" In about 1802 John Scott came to Jefferson County and settled on the farm where Corsica now stands, and about 1805 Peter Jones, John Roll, Sr., the Vastbinder families, and Elijah Graham, and, in 1806, John Matson and some others settled near where Brookville now stands. In the southern part of Jefferson county, near Mahoning, John Bell settled at an early day. He was a man of iron will and great perseverance, afraid of neither man nor beast, and was a mighty hunter. Moses Knapp was also an early settler. ' Port Barnett,' as the settlement of Barnett and Scott was called, was the only stopping-place from Curwensville for all those who came in 1801–02 through or for the wilderness over the ' trail.' We imagine that these buildings would have a very welcome look to those footsore and weary travellers,—an oasis in the desert, as it were.

"In the year 1801, with a courage nothing could daunt, ten men left their old homes and all the comforts of the more thickly settled and older portions of the eastern part of the State for the unsettled wilderness of the more western part, leaving behind them the many associations which render the old home so dear, and going forth, strong in might and firm in the faith of the God of their fathers, to plant homes and erect new altars, around which to rear their young families. Brave hearts beat in the bosoms of those men and women who made so many and great sacrifices in order to develop the resources of a portion of country almost unknown at that time. When we look abroad to-day and see what rapid strides have been made in the march of civilization, we say all honor to our forefathers who did so great a part of the work. It would be difficult for those of the present day to imagine how families could move upon horseback through an almost unbroken wilderness, with no road save an ' Indian trail,' the women and children mounted upon horses, the cooking utensils, farming implements, such as hoes, axes, ploughs, and shovels, together with bedding and provision, placed on what were called pack-saddles, while following upon foot were the men with guns upon their shoulders, ready to take down any small game that might cross their path, which would go toward making up their next meal. After a long and toilsome journey these pioneers halted on their course in what was then called Armstrong County (now Clarion County), and they immediately began the clearing of their lands, which they had purchased from General James Potter, of the far-famed ' Potter Fort,' in Penn's Valley, in Centre County, familiar to every one who has ever read of the terrible depredations committed by the Indians in that part of the country at an early period of its history.

"The names of the men were as follows: William Young, Sr., Philip Clover, Sr., John Love, James Potter, John Roll, Sr., James McFadden, John C. Corbet, Samuel Wilson, Sr., William Smith, and Philip Clover, Jr. Samuel Wilson returned to Centre County to spend the winter, but death removed him. In the following spring of 1802 his widow and her five sons returned,—namely, Robert, John, William, Samuel, and David. Those who did not take their families along in 1801 built their cabins, cleared some land, put in some wheat, raised potatoes and turnips, put them in their cabins and covered them with earth for safe-keeping for the next summer's use, and when they got all their work done, in the fall they returned to their families in Centre and Mifflin Counties. In the spring of 1802 those, with some others, who also came at an early date, James Laughlin and Frederick Miles, built a saw-mill in 1804, at or near the mouth of Pine Creek, and they were the first to run timber to Pittsburg from what is now Clarion County.

" The food and raiment of the first settlers made a near approach to that of John the Baptist in the wilderness. Instead of locusts they had wild turkey, deer, and bear meat, and their raiment consisted of home-spun woollen, linen, or tow cloth, the wool and flax being all prepared for weaving by hand, there being no carding-machines in the county for many years after its first settlement; then women carded by hand. When woollen cloth was wanted for men's wear, the process of fulling was as follows: The required quantity of flannel was laid upon the bare floor, and a quantity of soap and water thrown over it; then a number of men seated upon stools would take hold of a rope tied in a circle and begin to kick the flannel with their bare feet. When it was supposed to be fulled sufficiently, the men were released from their task, which was a tiresome one, yet a mirth provoking one, too, for, if it were possible, one or so must come from his seat, to be landed in the midst of the heap of flannel and soapsuds, much to the merriment of the more fortunate ones. Flax was prepared by drying over a fire, then breaking, scutching, and hackling before being ready to spin. The linen and tow cloth supplied the place of muslin and calico of the present day. That which was for dress goods was made striped, either by color or blue through the white, which was considered a nice summer suit, when made into what was called a short gown and petticoat, which matched very well with the calfskin slippers of that day. The nearest store was at Kittanning, thirty-five miles distant, and calico was fifty cents per yard, and the road but a pathway through the woods.

" In those days men appeared at church in linen shirts with collars four inches wide turned down over the shoulders, linen vest; no coat in summer. Some wore cowhide shoes, others moccasins of buckskin, others again with their feet bare. In winter, men wore deerskin pantaloons and a long loose robe called a hunting-shirt, bound round the body with a leathern girdle, and some a flannel warmus, which was a short kind of a coat, the women wearing flannel almost exclusively in the winter.

" During the first two years after the first settlement the people had to pack their flour upon horseback from Centre, Westmoreland, and Indiana Counties; also their iron and salt, which was at ten dollars per barrel; iron fifteen cents per pound. Coffee and tea were but little used, tea being four dollars per pound, coffee seventy-five cents. Those articles were considered great luxuries, both from the high price at which they came, and the difficulties attending their transportation through the woods, following the Indian trail. As to vegetables and animal food, there was no scarcity, as every one had

31   481

gardens and the forest abounded with wild game, and then there were some expert huntsmen that kept the settlement supplied with meat. Those who were not a sure shot themselves would go and work for the hunter while he would go out and supply his less fortunate neighbor. Many, however, got along badly, some having nothing but potatoes and salt for substantials. I knew one hunter who killed one hundred and fifty deer and twenty bears in the first two years of the settlement, besides any amount of small game. When people began to need barns and larger houses, one would start out and invite the whole country for miles around, often going ten or twelve miles, and then it often took two or three days to raise a log barn, using horses to help to get up the logs."

Judge Peter Clover says,—

"The first white man who settled within the limits of Clarion County was Captain Samuel Brady, who settled on the land upon which East Brady now stands, about the close of the Revolutionary War, and remained long enough to obtain a settlement right.

"Captain Brady was born on the Susquehanna, near Northumberland, and his father and mother were both killed by the Indians. He swore eternal vengeance against the whole savage tribe, and became during the Revolutionary War a noted Indian hunter and scout, and conducted many small expeditions through Western Pennsylvania and Ohio against the Indians for General Broadhead, who was the commander of Fort Pitt. A description of these will not be of interest in this sketch, except what relates to Clarion County.

"The Indians had become very troublesome along the Allegheny River, and had committed many depredations on the lower settlements. General Broadhead started with a considerable force up the river after them. Captain Brady, who was in advance with a small body of scouts, discovered the Indians on the flat where East Brady and Mr. Cunningham's farm now are, and, with the eye of a commander of no small merit, he took in the situation in a moment. He, being familiar with the locality, concluded the Indians would make for the narrow pass where the steep hill puts in between East Brady and Catfish. So, without giving them any notice of his presence, he stationed himself and his men along the rocky cliff. The Indians, as soon as the main army approached, retreated up the river with intent to gain the narrow pass, which a small force could easily defend against a large one. But when they arrived there they found Captain Brady and his men in this impregnable position, who opened fire upon them, and with the main army in their rear escape seemed impossible; and few did escape. Some attempted to cross the river where the water is always dead, and nearly the whole party were killed or taken prisoners.

"Captain Brady had only a cabin on this land, and followed hunting game and Indians after the war closed. He was indicted in Pittsburg for killing an Indian, and gave the Brady's Bend tract of land to Judge Ross, who was an attorney in Pittsburg at that time, for defending him, and who succeeded in having him acquitted. Judge Ross did obtain the title to this land, but the recital in the deeds on record do not show how or from whom he received his title.

" During the war of 1812 Captain Neely raised a company of volunteer minute men for the protection of the harbor of Erie. He was the captain, James Thompson first lieutenant, and Nathaniel Lang second lieutenant. They held themselves in readiness to march at any moment, and were under command of General Meade. In 1814 they were ordered out just in harvest time. In a few hours they were on their march to Lake Erie, leaving the harvest, then just ripe, to the care of the women and children, taking with them their provisions and bedding not furnished by the government, but by themselves. This company was composed of the old settlers I have named, and many others. There were, during that war, many who went with General Robert Orr (then major) in his memorable campaign to Fort Meigs. Among these may be mentioned Colonel John Sloan, the noted Indian fighter. The second settler was Absalom Travis, about 1792.

" The first settlements on Red Bank Creek were made in 1801-2-3-5, by Archibald McKelip, Henry Nulf, Jacob Hetrick, John Shafer, John Mohney, Jacob Miller, the Doverspike family, Moses Kirkpatrick, William Latimer, John Ardery, John Wilkins, John Washy, and Calvin McNutt. Some of the above-named came from Westmoreland County, some from Lehigh County.

" The first child that was born in the county was Mary Guthrie, and the second was Thomas Young.

" The first church that was organized was the Presbyterian. Its first regular pastor was the Rev. Robert McGarrah. When he first began to preach I do not know, but it must have been as early as 1804. He was ordained in the year 1806, at Thomas Brown's, near Reidsburg. The pioneer Presbyterian Churches were Licking and New Rehoboth, both organized in 1802 by Rev. John McPherrin.

" The first store was kept where Rimersburg now stands, by a good old man by the name of James Pinks, in 1812. People from a great distance went there to make their purchases.

" At the breaking out of the war of 1812 there was a draft made in Clarion County, and a number of our neighbors were drafted into the army. It was a sad day for all. I well remember, as a boy, the morning they started. They were all to meet at my father's, and when they were all ready to go they discharged their guns in a tree-top that stood near by, and amid many tears they marched away. The army was gathered along the lakes and at the different forts, this being after Hull's surrender. The names of those that were drafted were Captain John Guthrie, Alexander and Thomas

Guthrie, William Maffett, Robert Allison, John, James, and Joshua Rea, John Wilson, Jacob Fiscus, Hugh Reid, Henry Goheen. James Guthrie went as a substitute for William Maffett and Hugh Reid; Captain Guthrie was discharged at Pittsburg, Captain Wallace taking command. Out of all who went, none were lost; they all returned.

" In 1840 the townships comprising Clarion County, and the population of each, although reported in the census returns of the county to which they had formerly belonged, were as follows:

"Townships from Armstrong County: Clarion, 2239; Madison, 1305; Monroe, 1151; Perry, 1122; Redbank, 3070; Toby, 1829.

"Townships from Venango County: Beaver, 1611; Elk, 585; Farmington, 799; Paint, 491; Richland, 1388.

" Total population, 15,590.

Turning a boat

" In the forties the lumber and boat-building business was very flourishing in this county.

" The iron business was commenced here about 1830. Shippen, Black, Hamilton, Humes, and Judge Myers were the pioneers.

" At one time twenty-seven or twenty-eight furnaces were in full operation, making nearly if not entirely forty thousand tons of iron each year. It was then called the iron county. These furnaces were all run with charcoal, and made a superior quality of metal; but all have ceased operations and many have disappeared, so that no vestige of them remains except large piles of cinders that centuries will hardly obliterate.

" We find traces of the example of the Indian in the first white men. The first settlers above Titusville, on Oil Creek, in 1809, took their bags of grain on their backs, walked to Erie, fifty-three miles, to the mill, and brought home their flour in the same way. The lumbermen at Warren and on the Brokenstraw, as related in the address of Judge Johnson to the old settlers of Warren County, rafted their lumber to New Orleans, and walked home."

The pioneer post-office was in 1818, at the house of James McGonagle, two miles east of Strattonville. This was a horseback route; Josiah Copeley, carrier. The route was from Indiana once a week *via* Greensburg, Freeport, Roseburg, Lawrenceburg (Parker), to Butler; thence back *via* Kittanning to Indiana. There were mail routes through, but no post-office in the county before this one. In 1830 venison hams sold for one and a half cents a pound.

The pioneer grist-mill was built in 1803, on Catfish Run, by Jonathan Mortimer. The pioneer road was the old State Road. (See chapter on that subject, page 181.) It crossed the Clarion in Mill Creek Township. Robert Henry, John Allison, and Thomas Guthrie were the contractors for the Clarion portion of the road.

On February 23, 1829, the pioneer steamboat ascended the Allegheny to the mouth of the Clarion. In 1830, steamers began to make regular trips.

CHAPTER XXVIII

CAMERON COUNTY, named for the Hon. Simon Cameron, was organized by act of Assembly, March 29, 1860, from parts of Clinton, Elk, McKean, and Potter Counties. It contains three hundred and eight-one square miles, two hundred and forty-three thousand eight hundred and forty acres, and is within the purchase of October 23, 1784, known as the New Purchase. Its history is not germane to this book, but I will give some reminiscences of the pioneer settlers, being mostly writings of John Brooks and taken from the county history.

The same Indians were here in great numbers that inhabited the north-west purchase, and countless thousands of rattle- and other snakes. If the man "who eats them alive" had been one of the pioneers, he soon would have weighed four hundred pounds.

The celebrated battle of Peter Groves with the Indians took place at the mouth of a creek called Groves Run, just near the first fork of the Sinnemahoning. It occurred long before the whites were there. John Rohrer was the pioneer surveyor in the county in 1786. Sinnemahoning was surveyed in 1805. The pioneer preaching in the county was by a circuit rider in 1810, at Sinnemahoning.

The pioneer settlement was at second fork, now called Driftwood. In 1804 John Jordan, a mighty hunter, settled there. In 1808, William Nanny settled a short distance up the Bennett's branch. The pioneers jocularly called him "Billy Nanny." Other settlers located in this vicinity. In 1810 John Earl, Sr., was the pioneer to settle on the site of what is now Emporium.

"The immigrants made their entrances by the Indian paths on foot or on horseback, or by canoes or Indian boats propelled against the current by setting poles. These boats or canoes were manned by a bowman and a steersman, who, by placing their poles with steel-pointed sockets upon the bottom of the stream, threw their weight upon the poles thus placed, and by frequent and repeated processes and propulsions (guiding the boat at the same time) often made fifteen to twenty-five miles a day against the current with a cargo of three-quarters to one ton weight in their boats. On some occasions, in case of low water in the streams, the boat's crew would be compelled to remove the gravel and fragments of rock from the line of their course, and wade for miles at a time, carrying and dragging their boats forward by their almost superhuman strength; such frequent exercises developed an unusually vigorous muscle, and it would seem fabulous to relate the extraordinary feats frequently performed by these athletics of pioneer life."

" The early settlers were a hardy, active, energetic, go-a-head class of people, hailing mostly from eastern and middle Pennsylvania, from the State of New Jersey, and from the New England States. As a class they were rude, yet honest in their dealings; though boorish, they were hospitable and generous. The first settlers in America brought with them the traditions of Europe, and the fearful condemnations for witchcraft began at Salem, in 1692. Three children of Rev. Dr. Parris complained of being tortured by witches. The excitement soon spread, and others, both adults and children, complained of being bewitched, and accused those against whom they held some pique. Rev. Cotton Mather, Rev. Mr. Noyes, of Salem, the president of Harvard College, and many others encouraged arrests, as the result of which twenty persons, suspected of witchcraft, were executed in one year, while many others were banished. Some of the pioneers of this county, in order to protect themselves from witchery, would burn hen's feathers, and assafœtida, for incense, and shoot silver slugs at rudely drawn portraits of those who were suspected of witchcraft. A kind of lunacy also prevailed to some extent; potatoes and other vegetables were planted in the moon, or rather when the horns of the moon indicated the proper time. Houses were roofed when the horns of the moon were down, so that the shingles would not cap and draw the nails; fences were laid when the horns of the moon were up, that the rails might not sink into the ground, and the medicinal wants of these primitive people were not administered to in any degree in accordance with the practice of more modern times."

" The early settlers were for a long time compelled to bring all their supplies from Big Island in canoes. Lock Haven did not then exist. Three men named Moran, Hugh Penny, and McKnight kept store at ' Big Island,' who used to furnish the settlers with their supplies and take their timber-rafts as pay. The nearest store in 1820 was six miles above Clearfield town, and kept by John Irvin. Notwithstanding, the store at Big Island, though more remote, was for most purposes most convenient to trade with. Being along the river, it could be reached with the canoes, and besides, for the same reason, it was easier to convey the timber in exchange."

" A considerable amount of whiskey was consumed, and a canoe was not considered properly laden unless at least one barrel of the stimulant was among the stores. The trip up was generally made lively by its cheering influence. The article was then, as now, potent in its influence over the hearts of men. He who had a bottle of whiskey in his hands and a barrel in his canoe possessed the open sesame to every heart and every house. They were also compelled to convey their grain in the same manner down the river to Linden, near Williamsport, to be ground, and then pole it back again to their residences, nearly one hundred miles. Some used hand-mills for their corn, and in time small grist-mills were established at various places in the county. The first grist-mill erected within the limits of the county was located near the mouth of Clear Creek, about 1811. It had no bolt attached to it. The same year Colonel Chadwick built his saw- and grist-mill at the mouth of North Creek. This had a good bolt attached, and is said to have made good flour."

"Early in the 'thirties' William Lewis, of Shippen, tracked a wolf to his rocky den, and then called on Ben. Freeman to assist in the capture. The latter was left at the mouth of the cave to shoot the animal, while Lewis entered to hunt him out. After a long creep through the darkness, Lewis saw the glaring eyes of the animal, but on went the hunter, until the scared wolf jumped past him, only to be shot by Freeman. Lewis, proceeding farther, caught two whelps, and carried them home."

"In 1832, when the salt-works were running on Portage Creek, a strong lumberman named Magee went to the deer lick, a mile from the works, to watch for deer. Looking from his blind in the early evening, he saw two gleaming eyes among the lower branches of a tree not far away. Thinking it was a wild cat, he took a steady aim, fired, and in an instant he saw the body of a huge panther fall to earth. Without halting, he fled to the works. Returning with help next morning, the men found the panther dead, the largest ever known in this section of Pennsylvania. . . . George Parker, who resides three miles above Sizer's Springs, killed three thousand deer, three hundred elks, ten panthers, one hundred and fifty black bears, and other game, with a gun which he purchased in 1839. This was exclusive of his heavy hunting here in earlier years." He is now dead.

John Brooks, speaking of pioneers, says,—

"Occupying, as they did, the remote outskirts of civilization, they were subjected to many privations incident to this rugged section of country. Several of these early immigrants had done efficient service in the Revolutionary War and in the war of 1812. Almost all of the vocations of the industrial classes were represented, and all could aid in the work of extemporizing a cabin for the accommodation of the recent immigrant. Among these early pioneers there were but few who professed Christianity, practically; most of them, however, held some theory of religion, mostly Baptist or Presbyterian in their views. Profanity was the common spice of conversation, and God was, if 'not in all their thoughts,' in all their mouths, and invoked in execrations and imprecations more frequently than by benedictions.

488

The use of whiskey was general; used by clergymen and at funerals, and upon all occasions; some more recent immigrants kept no cow, but always kept whiskey in their houses, alleging that a barrel of whiskey was of more value in a family than a cow."

Some of the descendants of the early settlers yet have a remarkable prescience, and they prognosticate seasons and storms with great assurance. Their prevision enables them to anticipate all the changes of the weather, and they are remarkable for their generosity, essaying upon every opportunity to gratuitously advise all who may hear their converse of the future approaching vicissitudes, and mutations, that so much concern the lunatics. Some consult the milt or spleen of the hog, that organ situate in the left hypochondrium, and which was supposed by the ancients to be the seat of anger and melancholy; and from this organ they augur the severity of the approaching winter. Some would quench their fires to prevent the generation of salamanders. The shrunken sinews in the shoulder of a horse were cured by placing some of the hair in auger-holes, in some peculiar places, at some pecular lunation. Incised wounds also were more readily healed by anointing the instrument that made the wound. Blood was stayed, pain mitigated, and bots in horses cured by pow-wowing or reciting some cabalistic phrase.

J. J. Chadwick, in his sketch of the Methodist Church, states: "About 1806 Joseph Ellicott opened a road from Dunstown, opposite Big Island, on the Susquehanna, to Ellicottville, New York. Along its course, through the valley of the Sinnemahoning, twenty or thirty families settled previous to the general survey of the region, and, as hunting was the general amusement, every adult male had a rifle and every family a supply of hounds."

John Brooks was the pioneer historian in the county. The pioneer school was taught in the summer of 1817 by Miss Eliza Dodge, in a barn at the mouth of North Creek. The pioneer physician to practise within the county was Dr. Kincaid, father of the great Baptist missionary in India, Eugenio Kincaid. An amusing incident occurred in the doctor's practice,— viz.: He was treating a patient at the old Dent place on Bennett's Branch. Leaving his pill-bags near the creek while he went into the house, a cow ate the pill-bags and all their contents, and when the doctor returned for them, the cow was quietly chewing her cud. I suppose the patient recovered. I don't know about the cow.

Some time about 1830 "Buck" Clafflin settled at Sinnemahoning and started a store. It was here that Victoria (Mrs. Woodhull) and Tennie C. Clafflin were born, and ran barefoot until from three to five years old. The Shafer house was erected on the Clafflins' old home.

The pioneer election of county officers was held October 11, 1860. The pioneer sessions of court had to be held in a frame school-house. The Philadelphia Land Company had, however, already become alive to the advantages of the situation, and this corporation donated five thousand dollars toward a court-house, on condition that it should be located on lands owned by them, about a quarter of a mile west of the rising village. The situation suggested was eminently desirable, being a sightly knoll; and, as individual enterprise furnished the remainder of the necessary funds, the pioneer court-house required no levy of taxes. In December, 1860, a newspaper, called *The Citizen*, opened a journalistic career, although there was at the time only twenty-seven buildings and not more than one hundred and ten inhabitants in the village, which was incorporated as a borough in 1864. Previous to incorporation it was known as Shippen, being a part of Shippen Township. But a century previous, a shrewd reasoner, that cities are the result of geographical situation, had cut the name " Emporium" on the bark of a tree when its site was naught but a savage wilderness, and this name was put in the act of incorporation as a borough, with the confident expectation that the conceptive possibility would swiftly crystalize.

In 1900 I. H. Musser wrote the following data of Cameron County:

" FIRST SETTLEMENTS

" Before the advent of the white man the Indians had a town on the Sinnemahoning just east of the First Fork, and in historical times it was called ' The Lodge.' Many relics have been discovered on the site of it. This is probably the only place within the present limits of the county for which there is undisputed evidence of an Indian town.

" The first settlement by a white man was on the site of Driftwood, then called the Second Fork, as the site of the village of Sinnemahoning was called the First Fork. This was in 1804, and the settler was John Jordan, who, with his family of wife and five sons, made the wilderness his home, built his cabin, and began a clearing. But if the country was a wilderness in every sense of our modern acceptation of the term, it was a paradise in one respect, and that was in its home for game. The deer, the elk, the bear, the panther, the wolf, not to speak of smaller game, the delight of the present huntsman, such as pheasants, quails, squirrels, etc., made the mountains and the well-watered bottoms their home and roamed almost unmolested through the dense forests of pine, hemlock, oak, and other woods. The streams were alive with the gamiest of trout, salmon, pike, and the other members of the finny tribe that have always appealed the strongest to the sportsman. And last, but by no means the least dangerous, was the rattlesnake, which even to this day does not hesitate to continue the losing contest for the maintenance of its ancient rights with the aggressive human member of the animal kingdom. Jordan was a hunter, and this perhaps more than anything else influenced him in the selection of his new home. He was at the time about forty years of age, and in the prime of life. He is said to have killed ninety-six elks, besides any amount of other game.

HISTORY OF NORTHWESTERN PENNSYLVANIA

" In 1806 Levi Hicks, Andrew Overturf, and Samuel Smith settled on lands between the First and the Second Forks, Hicks occupying what in recent time is known as the Shaeffer farm. Smith was a single man. The same year was opened the public highway, leading from Dunnstown, nearly opposite the present Lock Haven, up the river to Cook's Run, thence across the mountains to Driftwood, and from thence northward to Ellicottville, New York, where the Holland Land Company had an extensive scope of territory. This company was instrumental in no small degree in having the road laid out. In 1811 the pioneer grist-mill in the county was built at the mouth of Clear Creek. In 1812 Hicks sold out to Jacob Burge, who had come to the vicinity a year or two previous, and moved up the Bennett's Branch. He (Hicks) made the first raft and floated it down the Sinnemahoning, and was thus the pioneer in an occupation that was the chief industry along that stream for many years.

" GAME

" As stated before, game was plenty, and formed a most important article for the table. The woods were full of game of all kinds, and the hunter had every opportunity to indulge in the sport, dangerous though it may have been sometimes.

" DESPERADOES

" It is not to be supposed that a section of country as wild as the West Branch was a hundred years ago would not furnish at least some desperate characters. Of such were Lewis and Connely who for a number of years infested what is now Centre, Clinton, and Cameron Counties. They committed so many deeds of outlawry, and the local officers seemed so far unable to deal with them, that the state offered a reward of six hundred dollars for their apprehension, dead or alive. Having done considerable robbing in the vicinity of what is now Lock Haven, they escaped to the Sinnemahoning country and, continuing their lawlessness, were finally surrounded at a house on Bennett's Branch, where both were wounded, Connely mortally, dying in a short time, and Lewis, being captured and taken to the Bellefonte jail, died soon after.

" The pioneer store was opened in 1829 or 1830, at Sinnemahoning, by Buckman Clafflin. Here Mrs. Victoria Woodhull and Tennessee Clafflin were born.

" The *Cameron Citizen* was the first to enter the journalistic arena in the county. It had been founded at Smethport by F. A. Allen in 1853. Allen sold it to Lucius Rogers in 1858, who moved the plant to Emporium on the formation of the new county, and on December 28, 1860, the first number was issued. William R. Rogers was a member of the firm at Emporium. The next year Lucius Rogers received an appointment to recruit a company for the war, and, leaving for the field, the *Citizen* was discontinued in the latter part of August, 1861.

" The *Cameron County Press* was founded in 1866 through the efforts of a number of Emporium gentlemen who wanted a Republican paper, and who purchased the material of the defunct *Citizen*. They then sent for Mr. C. B. Gould, who at that time was a resident of Binghamton, New York. Mr. Gould came, and after meeting with much discouragement, not the least of which was the condition of the printing material, issued the first number of the *Press*, March 8, 1866, and thus began a career in the county that was distinguished for honor and integrity not less than for success in the editorial field. The paper was a small affair at first, but, with increasing prosperity, it was enlarged until at present it is an eight-page, forty-eight column paper. In 1877 the office was burned with all its contents, and without any insurance, but Mr. Gould began anew, and success again crowned his efforts. On May 25, 1897, Mr. Gould died, and he was succeeded by Mr. H. H. Mullin, his son-in-law, as editor and publisher. Mr. Mullin has been connected with the office for thirty-two years, and prior to Mr. Gould's death had for some years been the *de facto* editor.

" DRAINAGE

" No county in the State has a better drainage system than Cameron. Except the extreme northwest, the entire county is drained by the Sinnemahoning and its tributaries, and this stream flows into the West Branch of the Susquehanna at Keating Station, in Clinton County, not more than seven or eight miles from the Cameron County line. The divide between the Susquehanna and the Allegheny River systems crosses the northwest corner of the county, barely a mile from the boundary, but within that area rises a small stream that mingles its waters with the streams of the Mississippi system. The main stream of the Sinnemahoning rises in Potter County, within perhaps a mile of the Allegheny River, and, flowing almost due south, is joined by the Driftwood Branch at the village of Sinnemahoning, and thence flows southeastward, leaving the county near Grove Station. It receives within the county, after its juncture with the Driftwood, Wyckoff and Upper Jerry Runs.

" AREA

" The area of the county is three hundred and eighty-one miles, or two hundred and forty-three thousand eight hundred and forty acres. It is therefore one of the smaller counties of the State, there being but nine less in size.

" POLITICAL DIVISIONS

" Cameron County contains five townships—Shippen, Portage, Lumber, Gibson, and Grove—and two boroughs,—Emporium and Driftwood. The villages of more or less importance are Sinnemahoning, Sterling Run, Cameron, and Sizerville.

" There is but one recorded conflict that took place on the Sinnemahoning during the period of the Revolutionary War. Farther down the West Branch numerous actions took place that in almost every case could be designated by no other name than massacres, for whether it was the Indian or the white man, each fought only from ambush and tried to exterminate the ambushed party. Perhaps the most important event of the war was what was called ' The Great Runaway.' This was in 1778, immediately after the Wyoming massacre, when, the news reaching the people along the West Branch, they hastened down the river to Fort Augusta, leaving their fields and crops to the savage. A few ventured to return shortly after to gather their crops, and a number were killed by the Indians, among the rest James Brady, whose son Captain Sam Brady amply avenged his death and became the hero of perhaps more exploits than any other border-man of his time.

" In 1780 occurred the affair on the Sinnemahoning. The Indians had made an incursion into Buffalo Valley, Union County, and had committed depredations as far as Penn's Creek, fully twelve miles back from the river. The Groves, noted Indian fighters, lived a few miles east of the present Mifflinburg, where their descendants are still to be found. The elder Grove was killed, but by whom or in what way was not known until a pretended friendly Indian, while drunk, revealed the manner to Peter Grove, a son of the murdered man, by imitating the elder Grove undergoing tortures inflicted by the ' friendly' and his companions. Peter wisely said nothing, nor did he by his countenance reveal any idea of revenge, nor of horror at the recital of the revolting crime, but he immediately after headed a scouting party in pursuit, and at Grove's Run in the present village of Sinnemahoning they attacked the party of twenty-five or thirty Indians while they were asleep and killed a number of them, but as there were only five or six in Grove's party, the Indians rallied and drove them off, without, however, any injury being sustained by Grove and his friends. Five or six Indians were killed in this engagement. On their return the whites waded the creek for a considerable distance to avoid pursuit."

CHAPTER XXIX

THE TOWNSHIP OF RIDGWAY

RIDGWAY TOWNSHIP was originally formed as a part of Jefferson County in 1826, and remained there until 1843, when it was taken from that county, by the following act of Assembly, to create the county of Elk:

" AN ACT ERECTING PARTS OF JEFFERSON, CLEARFIELD, AND M'KEAN COUNTIES
INTO A SEPARATE COUNTY, TO BE CALLED ELK.

" SECTION I. Be it enacted by the Senate and House of Representatives of the Commonwealth of Pennsylvania in General Assembly met, and it is hereby enacted by the authority of the same:

" That all those parts of the counties of Jefferson, Clearfield, and Mc-Kean, lying between the following boundaries,—viz., beginning at the northeast corner of Jefferson County, thence due east about nine miles to the northeast corner of lot number two thousand three hundred and twenty-eight, thence due south to Clearfield County, thence east along said line to the east line of Gibson Township, and thence south so far that a westwardly line to the mouth of Mead's Run shall pass within not less than fifteen miles of the town of Clearfield, and thence westwardly to Little Toby's Creek, along said line to the mouth of Mead's Run, thence in a northwesterly direction to where the west line of Ridgway Township crosses the Clarion River, thence so far in the same direction to a point from whence a due north line will strike the southwest corner of McKean County, thence along said line to the southwest corner of McKean County, and thence east along the south line of McKean County to the place of beginning, be and the same is hereby erected into a separate county to be henceforth called Elk.

" SECTION II. That Timothy Ives, Junior, of Potter County, James W. Guthrie, of Clarion County, and Zachariah H. Eddy, of Warren County, are hereby appointed commissioners, who, or any two of whom, shall ascertain and plainly mark the boundary lines of said county of Elk; and it shall be the duty of the said commissioners to receive proposals, make purchase, or accept donation land in the eligible situations for a seat of justice in the

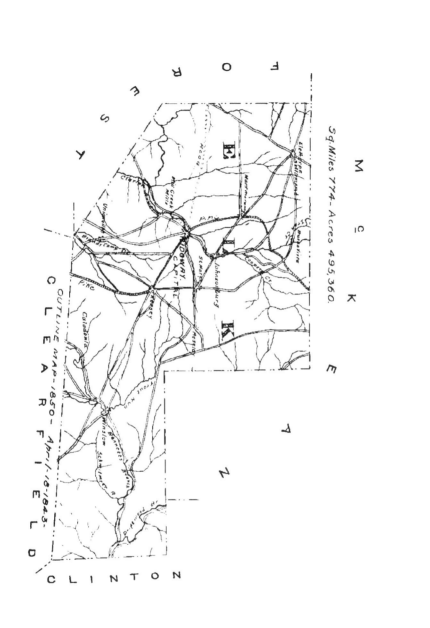

Sq.Miles 774 - Acres 495,360.

OUTLINE MAP - 1850 - April 18 1843.

RIDGWAY CAPITAL

ELK

CLINTON

FOREST

McKEAN

CLEARFIELD

said county of Elk, by grant, bargain, or otherwise, all such assurances for payment of money and grants of land that may be offered to them, or their survivors, in trust for the use and benefit of the said county of Elk; and to lay out, sell, and convey such part thereof, either in town lots or otherwise, as to them, or a majority of them, shall appear advantageous and proper, and to apply the proceeds thereof in aid of the county.

"Provided, that before the commissioners aforesaid shall proceed to perform the duties enjoined on them by this act, they shall take an oath or affirmation before some judge or justice of the peace, well and truly and with fidelity to perform said duties according to the true intent and meaning of this act;

"Provided also, that as soon as the county commissioners are elected and qualified, the duties enjoined on the said commissioners shall cease and determine, and shall be performed by the county commissioners so chosen and elected.

"Section X. That it shall be lawful for the commissioners of the county of Elk, who shall be elected at the annual election in one thousand eight hundred and forty-three, to take assurances to them and their successors in office of such lot or lots, or piece of ground as shall have been approved of by the trustees appointed as aforesaid, or a majority of them, for the purpose of erecting thereon a court-house, jail, and offices for the safe-keeping of the records.

"Section XI. That the judges of the Supreme Court shall have like powers, jurisdictions, and authorities within the said county of Elk, as by law they are vested with, and entitled to have and exercise in other counties of this State; and said county is hereby annexed to the western district of the Supreme Court.

"Section XII. The county of Elk shall be annexed to, and compose part of, the eighteenth judicial district of this Commonwealth; and the courts in the said county of Elk shall be held on the third Monday of February, May, September, and December in each and every year, and continue one week at each term, if necessary.

"Approved the 18th day of April, one thousand eight hundred and forty-three."

The pioneer court held in the county was at Caledonia, twenty miles east of Ridgway, on the Milesburg and Smethport turnpike, in Jay Township. The judges present were: Associates, James L. Gillis and Isaac Horton; Prothonotary, etc., W. J. B. Andrews; Commissioners, Reuben Winslow, Chauncey Brockway, and John Brooks. But little business was transacted. Attorneys present: George R. Barrett, Ben. R. Petriken, and Lewis B. Smith. The first court held in Ridgway was in the school-house, February 19, 1844, Alexander McCalmont, president judge; Isaac Horton, associate judge; and Eusebius Kincaid, sheriff.

The pioneer court crier was Nathaniel Hyatt, from Kersey. Colonel Corbet, who clerked for Gillis in 1845, informs me that the court-house was built in the summer of that year. The contractors were General Levi G. Clover and Edward H. Derby. The supplies for the men were furnished through the store of James L. Gillis. S. M. Burson was the first lawyer to locate in Ridgway. In 1854 the court crier was M. L. Ross. On public occasions he wore a blue broadcloth swallow-tailed coat, with brass buttons in front. "This coat had pocket-holes behind for thirty years or more." The commissioners were E. C. Schultze, C. F. Luce, L. Luther.

The following lawyers, afterwards distinguished, then attended the courts: Brown, Curtis, and Johnson, of Warren; Barrett, Wallace, McCullough, and Larimer, of Clearfield; I. G. Gordon, W. P. Jenks, McCahon, and Lucas, of Jefferson; and Goodrich and Eldred, of McKean.

The pioneer settler was "a pioneer hunter named General Wade and family, with a friend named Slade, who came to the head-waters of the Little Toby in 1798, and settled temporarily. In 1803 the party returned east, but the same year came hither and built a log house at the mouth of the Little Toby on the east bank. In 1806, while Wade and Slade were hunting near what is now Blue Rock, they saw an Indian girl watching them. Approaching her, Wade enticed her to follow him to his home, and there introduced her to Mrs. Wade. In 1809 this Indian girl married Slade, Chief Tamisqua performing the ceremony. Slade removed with his wife to where Portland now is and established a trading house there."

But Amos Davis was the real pioneer settler in 1810.

Of the early settlers, Dr. A. M. Clarke wrote as follows:

"About the time of the 'late war' with England, in 1812, some venturesome men pushed their way up the Susquehanna River and up the Sinnemahoning Creek to the mouth of Trout Run on Bennett's Branch, at which place Leonard Morey located and built a saw-mill. Dwight Caldwell, John Mix, and Eben Stephens came at the same time. These were the first settlers on Bennett's Branch. About the same time a large tract of country, containing some one hundred and forty thousand acres, which had been surveyed on warrants issued in the name of James Wilson, had come into the possession of Fox, Norris & Co., Quakers, of Philadelphia, who sent William Kersey as agent to construct a road into their lands and build a mill. The road started from a point on an old State road leading to Waterford, Pennsylvania, about eight miles west of the Susquehanna River, passed through the woods over Boon's Mountain, crossed Little Toby's Creek, without a bridge, where Hellen Mills now stand, followed up the creek seven miles to the point of Hogback Hill, up which it went, though steep and difficult, continued over the high and undulating grounds to the spot which had been selected for a mill site on a stream which was afterwards called Elk Creek, where the mill was built, about two miles from the present Centreville. Jacob Wilson

Jail

Pioneer court-house, 1845

Recorder's office

was the miller who for many years attended this mill. Often the old man had to go a mile and a half from his own house to the mill to grind a small grist of a bushel, brought on horseback; but his patience was quite equal to the emergency, and he did it without complaining.

"A few settlers came into the county about the time the Kersey Mill was built; of these I may mention Elijah Meredith, James Green, Josiah Taylor, J. R. Hancock, David Reesman, John Kyler, and John Shafer, with their families; these constituted the Kersey settlement."

One of the pioneers of Ridgway Township was James L. Gillis. In June, 1820, he left his home in Ontario County, New York, to look over the land, and in December, 1820, he moved his family into the wilderness. They came in sleds, and it required two days; they had to camp out over night. Gillis was an agent for Ridgway, and was furnished ample means for all expenses. He cleared five hundred acres of land, erected a large frame house, and built a grist-mill and a carding-machine. Reuben A. Aylesworth and Enos Gillis came with his family.

James L. Gillis was a man of State celebrity. He was absent nearly all the time, lobbying at Harrisburg, Pennsylvania, or at Washington.

In 1826 William Morgan, of Batavia, New York, was abducted from his home at night and never heard of afterwards. Morgan had been a Mason, and published the alleged secrets of the Masonic Fraternity. The Masons were charged with abducting and murdering him. Mystery surrounds his disappearance to this day. Intense excitement prevailed all over the nation.

Mr. Gillis was a Mason, and was arrested at Montmorenci and carried to New York State, and there tried for the abduction and murder of Morgan. In the trial he was cleared.

Mr. Gillis was a cavalry soldier in the war of 1812, and took part in several severe engagements. He was taken prisoner by the British and suffered severely. He was a model man physically, and by nature endowed with much intelligence. This, added to his extensive travels and political experience, gave him a prominence in the State and nation that few men possessed. Gillis was the Patriarch in Ridgway Township. He migrated in 1821 to what he named Montmorenci, Pine Creek Township, then in Jefferson County. He brought his children and brother-in-law with him.

For five years he was monarch of all he surveyed; and without any post-office nearer than fifty miles of him. He came to Port Barnett, near Brookville, to vote, was liable to and for militia service, and for all legal business had to go to Indiana, Pennsylvania, a distance of ninety miles.

While at Montmorenci in 1826 Mr. Gillis was instrumental in securing a mail-route from Kittanning to Olean, New York. This gave him mail service once in two weeks. He was a great horseman and a horseback rider.

Gillis was related to Jacob Ridgway, one of the richest men in the State, and he was agent for all his land in Jefferson County. Gillis was slow and methodical in his habits, was fond of games,—viz., chess, backgammon, checkers, and euchre. He carried a snuff-box that held about a pint of the choicest snuff, in which was buried a Tonka bean, that imparted to the snuff a delightful aroma. He walked with a gold-headed cane and in winter he wore a panther-skin overcoat. Physically he was a large man and was social and agreeable. In 1830 he moved to where Ridgway now is. He was elected to several offices, including Congress. He moved to Mount Pleasant, Iowa, where he died in 1881, aged eighty-nine years.*

> " Sleep soldier, though many regret thee,
> Who pass by thy cold bier to-day ;
> Soon, soon shall the kindest forget thee,
> And thy name from the earth pass away.
> The man thou didst love as a brother
> A friend in thy place will have gained,
> And thy dog shall keep watch for another
> And thy steed by a stranger be reined."

Ridgway, the county seat, was laid out in 1833. It was called for Jacob Ridgway.

Jacob Ridgway, who died in 1843, has been regarded as the wealthiest man in Pennsylvania since Stephen Girard. His property is valued at about six million dollars, and is of various kinds; all of which is the result of a long life of untiring industry and perseverance. In early life he was a ship-carpenter. He subsequently was appointed United States Consul at Antwerp, where he resided during a portion of the great war of the European powers, and when the rights of American citizens stood in need of protection from the blind encroachments of angry belligerents. After residing a short time in Paris, he returned to the United States, where he continued engaged in laudable and useful enterprises to the day of his death. His real property is very extensive, lying in various parts of the Union, but principally in Pennsylvania, New Jersey, and Delaware. His heirs are a son and two daughters, Mrs. Dr. Rush and Mrs. Roatch. The latter is a widow. Mr. Ridgway is represented as an amiable, kind-hearted man, kind to his workmen, indulgent to his tenants, and liberal toward his friends and the distressed.

In 1840 the principal part of Elk County was covered with white pine and hemlock. Pine-lands could be bought for from three to five dollars an acre. Hemlock had no value only for farm lands. The bark even was not used for tanning. Pine was about the only timber manufactured.

The streams were alive with pike, sunfish, bass, chubs, magnificent trout, and other fish. Every fall and spring hunters with dogs and fishermen from

---

* A more extended account of James L. Gillis, taken from the Pittsburg *Daily Post* of July 30, 1881, will be found in the Appendix, page 718.

the adjoining counties and from across the line in New York State would flock to these hills, valleys, and streams for recreation or profit. The principal owners of all this wild land lived in Philadelphia,—viz., Ridgway estate, Jones estate, Parker estate, and Fox and Norris estate.

Big trout eat little trout and the eggs or fry of other trout. A trout will not spawn until it is six inches long. Some trout never grow longer than seven inches, maturing and attaining their full size in about eighteen months, while others continue to grow for three years, and will attain from twelve to eighteen inches in length.

One of the pioneer roads was the State road from Kittanning to Olean. There was great excitement and enthusiasm by the land-owners and settlers over this State road. But it all came to naught, for the road has never been used to any extent. It is still known as the Olean road where it is not grown up and abandoned.

The Ceres road was laid out in 1825 and finished in 1828. The Milesburg and Smethport Turnpike Company was incorporated in 1825, and the road was finished about 1830.

Caleb Dill was the "post-boy" in 1828.

The pioneer tannery was started in 1830. Enos Gillis, owner; James Gallagher, tanner.

Dr. A. M. Clarke writes us of his advent in Elk County in 1818:

"When in Russell, St. Lawrence County, New York, I attended a term in the village school, two miles from our home. How much I was benefited by it I know not—I cannot remember that I learned anything. Shortly afterwards my father disposed of his property there, in Russell, New York, and we came to Pennsylvania. The journey was long and tedious, about six weeks. We moved with oxen and wagon; a canvas cover over the wagon gave us shelter from sunshine and storm. I was eleven years old, being the oldest of the children; there were three of us. I had sometimes to drive the team while father supported the wagon to keep us from upsetting. When we got through at last into the wilderness of Pennsylvania our people were much disappointed. In Pennsylvania we came on an old road, the old State Road. The Susquehanna and Waterford turnpike was being built at that time. When we arrived at Neeper's tavern, about four miles east of where Luthersburg now is, we took the Fox, Norris & Co. road over the mountain, which was really a path, and followed our journey over the hills and mountains. Finding we could not get through in a day, we had to stop over night at a place where the road-makers of Fox, Norris & Co. had built a shanty which had been burned, so it was called the 'burnt shanty.' Here our wagon-cover gave us a good shelter, and a good spring of water to drink from was pleasant, indeed. The next day we crossed over Boone's Mountain, came to the crossing of Little Toby near where was built, many years afterwards, the 'Oyster House.' We pursued our journey onward to Kersey settlement.

when my father thought best to examine the land, for which he had exchanged his New York property, before going any further. He was utterly disappointed and disgusted with these lands, so that he made explorations in various directions in search of a mill site, and finally located and erected a round log cabin, with greased paper for windows, where Brockport now is. Here he built, in 1821, a saw-mill, the first ever built on this stream. He put a small grist-mill with bolts into the saw-mill, which mill answered the

Taking out a timber stick

requirements of the neighborhood for a time. He then built a good grist-mill, which did good work for the people until the great flood in 1844 carried it off. My father died in Brockwayville, January, 1852.

"Isaac Horton, since Judge Horton, Hezekiah and Zebulon Warner, and Alanson Viall began improvement on Brandycamp in 1820. Chauncey Brockway, Sr., moved there in 1821. In 1822 Dr. Jonathan Nichols came there to make his home. He was for a long time the only minister who had regular services every Sabbath."

In 1840 labor was cheap. Pine boards of the finest quality sold in Louisville, Kentucky, at seven and nine dollars per thousand. If the operator cleared twenty-five or fifty cents on a thousand feet he was thankful.

All goods and groceries were dear; they had to be hauled from Olean, New York, or Waterson's Ferry on the Allegheny River. Money was scarce, the people social and kind. Whiskey and New England rum was three cents a drink.

Nelson Gardner and Mary, his wife, pioneers of Elk County. Nelson Gardner was
a mighty hunter, and killed the last panther in Elk County

The pioneer and early teamsters from St. Mary's to those points were John Walker, Charles Fisher, and Joseph Wilhelm. The merchandise carried from Pittsburg to this region was by canal to Freeport, by keel-boat and steamboat to Kittanning and Waterson's Ferry. The teamsters loaded their wagons with wheat flour, etc., in barrels bound with hickory hoops, bacon and salt and whiskey in barrels bound with *iron* hoops. But, strange to say, there was always a soft stave in these whiskey-barrels through which a " rye straw" could be made to reach the whiskey for the teamster and his friends while *en route* home.

EARLY HOME OF THE WILD PIGEON

In 1845 Ridgway Township was the nesting and roosting home of the wild pigeon. There was a roost at or near what is now Bootjack, one near Whistletown, and another near Montmorenci. These big roosts were occupied early in April each year. They were usually four to five miles long and from one to two miles wide. Every tree would be occupied, some with fifty nests. The croakings of the pigeons could be heard for miles.

The wild pigeon laid one or two eggs, and both birds did their share of incubating, the female from two P.M. until nine A.M., and the male then to two P.M. These roosts were great feeding-places for animals as well as for man. As late as 1851 the American Express Company carried in one day, over the New York and Erie Railroad, over seven tons of pigeons to the New York markets. A wild pigeon can fly from five hundred to one thousand miles in a day.

Like the buffalo and elk of this region, the wild pigeon has been doomed.

In 1836 J. S. Hyde reached Ridgway clothed in overalls, and with all his possessions tied up in a handkerchief. He entered the store of George Dickinson and wanted to buy an axe on credit; on being refused credit, he told the store-keeper to keep his axe and go to h—ll, that he would see the day when he could buy the whole store. He was ambitious and an untiring worker. Mr. Hyde had great force and a habit of carrying his hands in front of him with the " thumbs up," especially if he was in earnest or excited. Whenever his thumbs were up in the presence of any one, there was sure to be something happen,—an explosion of Christian indignation.

Mrs. Penelope Goddard Clarke planted the first nursery in the county, at what is now Brockport, and supplied the neighbors with fruit-trees.

The most noted hunters of Elk County were George Nolf, Erasmus Morey, Peter Smith, George Smith, Nelson Gardner, and William Eastman.

These men were professionals. Chasing the wild deer was their daily life and delight. They all possessed in a high degree the agile, cat-like step, the keen eye, the cool nerve, and the woodcraft of the " still hunter."

I knew them well, but was not intimate enough to learn the story of their encounters and adventures. The buffaloes that once roamed in great numbers, the beavers that built their dams, and the stately elks that once traversed the forests of Elk are now extinct, and I believe the screaming panther and the prowling wolf can now, too, be so classed.

In 1853 the county paid for panther- and wolf-scalps two hundred and twenty-five dollars and fifty cents.

Ralph Hill settled at Portland Mills about 1832. He came from Massachusetts to the wilds of McKean in 1825. He lived the life of a hermit and hunter. Portland becoming too much in civilization, he moved up Spring Creek, and lived in Forest County, the companion of wild animals, "where his right there was none to dispute." He died at a ripe old age.

The pioneer justice of the peace was Reuben A. Aylesworth, appointed February 18, 1832.

In the year 1833 there were seven families in what is now Ridgway,— viz., Reuben Aylesworth and Caleb Dill west of the river, and Enos Gillis. James W. Gallagher, H. Karns, Thomas Barber, and Joab Dobbins, who was the pioneer shoemaker, on the east side. In 1833 Ralph Hill and a man named Ransom were living in a shanty at Beech Bottom.

In 1839 James Watterson, of Armstrong County, Pennsylvania, settled at the mouth of Spring Creek, and he and Job Paine built a saw-mill.

About 1840 common hands on the river received one dollar per day and board. Pilots, two and three dollars per day and board. The "head" sawyer on the Red Mill received twenty-five dollars per month and board; the assistant, eighteen dollars per month and board; and common hands, fifteen dollars a month and board.

The usual religious exercises on Sunday at the Red Mill, in 1842, were wrestling, fishing, pitching quoits, shooting at mark, running foot-races, and "jumping by the double rule of three."

In the winter of 1832 L. Wilmarth, Arthur Hughes, and George Dickinson erected the red saw-mill. Ridgway was laid out for a town in 1833.

"In 1834 the first bridge was put across the Clarion River. This was a toll-bridge. It was built of twelve by sixteen inch stringers resting on cribbing. Before this time teams forded the river, and in high water boats were used. The country was covered by a thick growth of hemlock-trees. Game, such as elks, deer, bears, panthers, and wild-cats were found in great abundance, fish abounded in the streams," and rattlesnakes and other reptiles were numerous and dangerous.

Up to 1835 Ridgway Township included all that portion of Snyder Township that is now Brockwayville borough, and even west of Sugar Hill, as well as a good portion of what is now Washington Township. Ridgway in 1836 was a small village. At the west end of the town was George Dickinson's boarding-house, then Henry Gross's home, then Dickinson's saw-mill and barn, Caleb Dill's home, justice office, and blacksmith-shop, Stephen Weis's home and John Cobb's house, Hon. James L. Gillis's home and store,

Skidding logs

E. C. HALL, Photo

George Dickinson's home and store, and on the east side of the Clarion was the Exchange Hotel, owned by David Thayer, then Edward Derby's old red house, then the Lone Star Hotel, owned by P. T. Brooks.

When P. T. Brooks, who was quite a wag, very polite and demonstrative, was keeping this hotel in the wilderness, two finely dressed and appearing gentlemen rode up one day in front of and stopped at his hotel for dinner. Of course, this was an opportunity for Mr. Brooks to be demonstrative and polite. After seeing that the horses were properly cared for, Brooks approached the gentlemen in this way: " What kind of meat would you gentlemen prefer for dinner?" " Why, Mr. Landlord, we would prefer venison."

Banking logs

" I am sorry that we are just out of venison." " Oh, well," said the strangers, " a little good beef or mutton will do." " Well, well," replied Mr. Brooks, " I am sorry to say we are just out of beef and mutton." At this the strangers were a little nonplussed, but finally said, " We will be satisfied with fish." " Well, well," replied Mr. Brooks, rubbing his hands, " I am sorry to say that we are just out of fish, but we have some very excellent pickled pork."

Uncle Eben Stevens, an old hunter who came to the Sinnemahoning region about 1812, told me there was an Indian graveyard at the mouth of

Mill Creek, that he used to go up there and hunt with the Indians, and in the spring they would paint their canoes red with that "iron paint" on the Clarion.

And down the Toby Creek—

> "Where the rocks were gray and the shores were steep,
> Where the waters below looked dark and deep,
> Where the shades of the forest were heavy and deep the whole day through,"

Stevens and the Indians in these red canoes would carry their game, skins, and furs to the Pittsburg market.

In 1854 Elk County was one vast wilderness, and was so called on account of the great herds of elks that once roamed through those wilds. There were no elks killed during my residence, but Grandpap Luther told me that in 1852 a drove of twelve or fifteen was found by two hunters near the village of Ridgway, and seven were killed of that drove. Elks are gregarious. Where Portland now is, was a great rendezvous for elks. It was a great wintering place for them. All other wild animals were numerous.

The pioneer effort to erect what is now the county of Elk was on Tuesday, February 28, 1837, when an act to erect the county of Ridgway was reported in the State Senate.

The present town or borough of St. Mary's was established in 1842. Father Alexander had the colony in charge then. Early in the summer of 1842 a number of Germans in the cities of Baltimore and Philadelphia associated themselves in a society to form a German settlement on the community plan, and appointed John Albert, Nicholas Reimel, and Michael Deileth to select the place for settlement. This committee selected Jefferson County, Pennsylvania, and the site where the borough of St. Mary's and the adjoining settlement now is. For this colony they purchased thirty-five thousand acres Father Alexander had the colony in charge then. Early in the summer of settlers—one from Philadelphia and one from Baltimore—reached John Green's, in Kersey. From Kersey these men, in two instalments, opened a path to where St. Mary's now is, and immediately set to work to erect their log cabins on St. Mary's Street. In December, 1842, they moved their families to these cabins, and the county of Elk was organized in 1843.

I copy an editorial from an *Advocate* of June 10, 1854, giving a *résumé* of the stage in operation at that time:

"STAGING—As an evidence of the rapid increase of the business of this county, and of its general prosperity, it is not necessary to refer to every branch of business that is conducted here; but a reference to the single item of staging will make it clear to all that we are a rising nation. Two years ago there was no mode of communication through these interminable forests except that only true republican way, a ' foot-back,' and wading through the mud up to your knees, at least, into the bargain.

"About that time the pioneer stager of the county, Townsend Fall, coroner of Elk County, and landlord in McKean County, commenced running a one-horse mud boat from Bellefonte to Smethport. That was considered a great enterprise, and every body predicted that Fall must get lost in the mud, and his hazardous undertaking would certainly be the ruination of that visionary man. These predictions would probably have all been verified had it not been for the fact that Mr. Fall is one of those live Yankees who is always ready to whittle out a wooden nutmeg while waiting for his horse to gain wind when stuck in the mud.

"He added another branch of trade to his staging which served to make up the losses that caused him, and assisted him in keeping body, soul, horse, and mud boat together. He procured a quantity of steel traps suitable for bears, wolves, and such animals, which he stationed along at intervals, and while waiting for his old horse to browse he could examine them and take care of their contents without losing any time. The furs, skins, and scalps he thus procured soon enabled him to purchase another horse to put by the side of the old veteran that had long served him so faithfully.

"From that day his prosperity and the prosperity of the stage interests of this region has been rapidly onward. He soon was enabled to get a wagon with a top to it; the first trip was a proud day for Elk County. Now Mr. Fall is running a tri-weekly line of splendid four-horse coaches between Smethport and Ridgway, for particulars of which see advertisement in this paper."

"NEW ARRANGEMENT.

"THROUGH AND BACK BY DAYLIGHT!

" HAVING taken the contract for carrying the mail from Bellefonte to Smethport, the subscriber is happy to announce to the travelling public and the world in general, that he is going to ' crack her threw' regularly rain or shine, hot or cold, mud or dust, from this time forth, leaving Smethport every Monday morning, arriving at Ridgway same evening, passing along so as to reach Bellefonte on Wednesday night. On the return trip leaves Bellefonte on Thursday morning, arrives at Ridgway Friday night and Smethport Saturday night.

"☞ Good horses and coaches and *sober* drivers, will always be kept on this route.

"☞ Particular attention will be paid to baggage, which will be carried at my risk where freight is paid. Also, all kinds of errands promptly attended to, along the line. Patronage is respectfully solicited.

" TOWNSEND FALL.

" CENTREVILLE, July 9, 1852.   14-tf"

PIONEER COAL OPERATORS

Dr. C. R. Earley lived at Kersey. The year he came to Elk I do not know. He was energetic, kind, and industrious. He had to keep himself busy, and

33   513

for some time he and Jesse Kyler, rival pioneers, were the baron soft coal kings of the county. Earley's and Kyler's cards, published in the newspapers of that period, are here given:

"IMPORTANT FROM THE MINES

" Having recently commenced operations at the new ' placer' in the ' San Francisco' coal-mine, the subscriber wishes to inform the public that he is prepared to furnish those wishing it an article of coal far superior to any ever before offered in Elk County at his mines in Fox Township. He would also say that he has a lime-kiln in full blast at the mines aforesaid, and will keep constantly on hand a superior article of lime. All of which will be sold on reasonable terms.

" C. R. EARLEY.

" SAN FRANCISCO, Feb. 8, 1851. 48-tf"

" COAL

" The subscriber, thankful for the very liberal patronage he has hitherto and is still receiving, takes this opportunity to inform his friends and the public generally, that he still continues the mining and sale of coal at his old establishment, being the centre of the coal basin, and the identical bed recently opened in another place. He is unwilling to admit inferiority, nor is he bombastic enough to claim superiority, where neither one nor the other can possibly exist. In respect to the quality of coal, it is true, by removing the dirt from the top of the out crop, coal may be got in larger chunks and will seem to burn more free, because the air circulates through it better. But he that buys a bushel of coal by measure, mixed coarse and fine together, gets more for the same money in mining under. However, no section of the country has an advantage over another, and but little can be obtained without. He will therefore furnish coal as usual in quality and price, and abide the judgment of a discerning public.

" JESSE KYLER.

"January 10, 1851. 49-6t."

The pioneer school taught within the present limits of Elk County was at Medix Run, now in Benezette Township, by Master Cephas Morey, in the year 1821. The pioneer master in what is now Fox Township was Dr. William Hoyt, in 1823.

The pioneer school in what is now Horton Township was taught by Miss Olive Brockway, in 1826; salary, one dollar per week.

The pioneer school in what is now Jay Township was taught in 1822 by Captain Potter Goff.

The pioneer school in Jones Township in 1842 was taught by Peter Hardy.

The pioneer school in Millstone Township was started in 1834.

The pioneer school in what is now Spring Creek Township was taught by John Knox.

In the fall of 1846, or in the spring of 1847, the first public school was opened in Benziger Township. Frederick Clarinaar, master.

The pioneer school in the village of Ridgway was held in the year 1826. "There were three families in the settlement at that time, and the fact that they started a school immediately speaks plainly the great value at which they held the culture of their children. The building was partitioned by suspending bedquilts from the ceilings, which partitions certainly had their advantages as well as disadvantages. The memorable teacher who here guided the little flock in wisdom's ways was Miss Hannah Gilbert, a sister of Mrs. Gallagher. It was a subscription school, and the wages were about seventy cents per week. The text-books were very few and often read. The ink was of home manufacture, and the pens were calculated to inspire lofty thoughts, for they were made of the plucked pinions of the birds of flight. The next schools were held also in private dwellings, in what is known as the old red house, for instance, and the teachers were Ann Berry, Betsy Gyant, and others. The first school-house was built in 1834, immediately on the adoption of the common school system, and it was situated on the west side of the Clarion River, near Judge Dickinson's residence. It is said that Miss Betsy Hyatt was about the first teacher who held pedagogic sway therein. The second school building was erected a little prior to 1840, and was located also on the west side of the Clarion, not far from the first one. This was a large building for a graded school."

The pioneer physician was Dr. Rogers, in 1809.

Joseph Smith Hyde was born in the village of Tamworth, Carrol County, New Hampshire, August 30, 1813, and died at Ridgway, Elk County, Pennsylvania, June 30, 1888.

His life presents an illustration of the possibilities of our country. The history of his early struggles, his laborious youth, and final success is pregnant with meaning to all young men. At the age of nineteen he was constrained to quit the parental roof and seek a living for himself. He went to Bangor, Maine, where he secured work on a saw-mill at a salary of thirteen dollars a month. He remained in that vicinity working in mills and in the lumber-woods for a period of nearly five years, during a large portion of which time his wages were remitted to his father. In the fall of 1836 he went to Baltimore, where he remained a year. In 1837 he came for the first time to Elk County. He remained a short time at Caledonia and then drifted to Ridgway, where he worked at digging on an embankment for Enos Gillis. He then secured a contract from Mr. Gillis to run his saw-mill, but this not proving profitable, he moved, in 1840, to St. Croix, Wisconsin, where he remained for about one year. While there he was taken with a severe illness,

515

and, thoroughly disheartened and discouraged, decided to return to Ridgway, where he again went to work in the lumber-woods. His sister Adaline at this time came on from New Hampshire and kept house for him in the " Red House." Mr. Hyde's stories of his poverty at this time, and the makeshifts to which they were at times reduced in order to have both ends meet, were both laughable and pathetic. On the 25th day of July, 1842, he married Jane, daughter of Enos Gillis. They lived at Montmorency about two years and then moved to Sharpsburg, Pennsylvania. He there found some work about the foundries, but not enough to keep him busy, and in 1846 he re-

Joseph Smith Hyde

turned to Elk County, determined to cast his final lot there. He took up his quarters at the Gillis & McKinley mill. The following year he bought the mill and about four hundred acres of land adjoining, on credit. From this date his untiring industry was rewarded, and his indomitable will commanded success. He lived there three years, at the end of which time he was worth three thousand dollars. He then opened a small store. He also bought timber lands as fast as his credit warranted, until he became the leading lumberman of the county. At his death he was undoubtedly the wealthiest man in Elk County. Mr. Hyde was twice married.

Joseph Smith Hyde despised dishonesty and idleness, but loved the honest and faithful, however lowly. He was a man of magnificent physique and fine personal appearance, and up to the time of the illness which caused his death was wonderfully preserved for his years. He was the very type of the courageous, hardworking, tenacious, brainy New Englander, and his career is a monument to tireless industry and clean-handed business integrity. I can say all this from a personal acquaintance. When riding as a pioneer physician over and through Elk County, I met Mr. Hyde every hour of the day and night.

A HUNTER HUNTED

In 1855–56 Ben McClelland, then a young man, was driving team for Sheriff Healey. In the winter he was sent to Warren with two horses and a sled. On his way home he expected to stop over night at Highland. Before Ben reached "Panther Hollow," a few miles north of Townley's, it became quite dark.

At the hollow Ben's horses snorted, frightened, and ran. In the dark Ben quickly recognized the form of a panther after him. The horses had the beaten track, the panther the deep snow alongside and afraid to attack the heels of the horses on account of the sled, the horses crazy and furious.

It was a neck-to-neck race for Highland. The panther never gave up the race until the cleared land was reached. Ben was a hunter, but he was unarmed and almost dead from fright. When Townley's farm was reached the horses were all in a lather of sweat and nearly exhausted. A posse of hunters started in the early morning, and found the big brute near the hollow and killed him.

CHAPTER XXX

FOREST COUNTY (OLD)—FORMATION OF COUNTY—COUNTY SEAT—PIONEERS—
PIONEER ROADS AND PATHS—PIONEER ELECTIONS, MAILS, OFFICERS—
BOAT-BUILDING

FOREST is the only county in the State created by a joint resolution of the Legislature.

" The joint resolution, approved April, 1848, establishing Forest County, detached the territory within the following described boundaries, from Jefferson County: From termination of a straight line running west on the south side of Elk County; thence due west to intersection of north and south line on the west side of Jefferson County; then along Jefferson County line to its termination; thence east along the line of that county to the line of Elk County; along the line of Elk County to the place of beginning. The Commissioners to locate such lines, as well as the county seat, were Joseph Y. James, of Warren County, W. P. Wilcox, of Elk County, and Hiram Payne, of McKean County, who were ordered to report to the Commissioners of Jefferson County, to which Forest was to remain attached for judicial and county purposes until organized, and township elections were to be held without reference to county lines until that period. The act approved April 15, 1851, placed the new county in the eighteenth judicial district, when organized. In April, 1850, an act of the Legislature fixed the southern boundary of Forest County at the north bank of the Clarion River, from a point where the east line of Clarion County crosses that river to the west line of Elk County."

" The undersigned Commissioners to locate the seat of justice for Forest County will meet at Branch's Tavern on Tuesday, the 17th of October, next, and at Cyrus Blood's on the 18th, for the purpose of selecting a proper site, etc.

" WM. P. WILCOX.
HIRAM PAYNE.
J. Y. JAMES.

" September 26, 1848."

Wild land sold in the county then for from fifty cents to two dollars an acre.

Cyrus Blood was the pioneer of Forest County. He brought his family

518

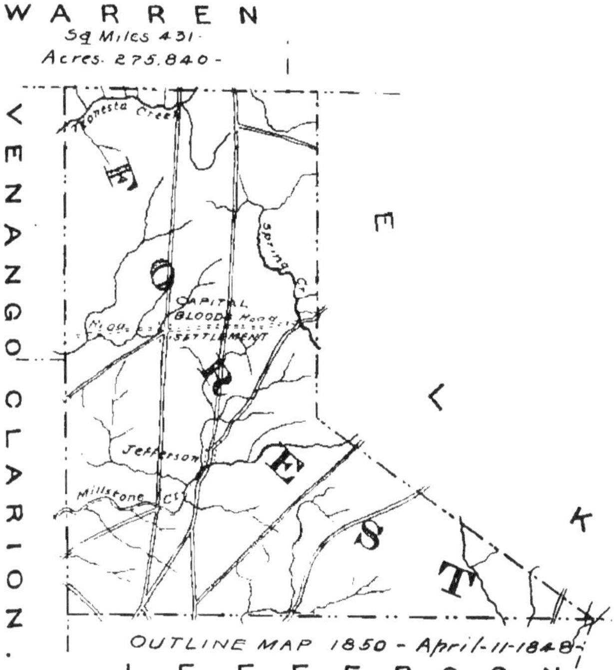

WARREN
Sq Miles 431.
Acres. 275.840 -

V E N A N G O   C L A R I O N .

Tionesta Creek

H)

Spring Cr.

E

CAPITAL
BLOOD Mary's
Niou SETTLEMENT

O E E

Jefferson

L

Millstone Cr.

K

E

S

T

OUTLINE MAP 1850 - April-11-1848.

J E F F E R S O N

into this wilderness in 1833. For years his farm was called the "Blood settlement." When he settled there the region was full of panthers, bears, wolves, wild-cats, and deer. Mr. Blood was a powerful man, of great energy and courage. He was well educated and a surveyor.

Cyrus Blood was born at New Lebanon, New Hampshire, March 3, 1795. He was educated in Boston. When twenty-two he migrated to Chambersburg, Pennsylvania, where he was the principal of the academy. He was afterwards principal of the Hagerstown Academy, Maryland. He accepted and served as a professor in the Dickinson College, at Carlisle, Pennsylvania.

Ambitious to found a county, Cyrus Blood made several visits into this wilderness, and finding that the northern portion of Jefferson County was

Cyrus Blood

then an almost unbroken wilderness, he finally purchased a tract of land on which Marienville is now located, and decided to make his settlement there.

It was understood when Mr. Blood purchased in Jefferson County from the land company that a road would be opened into it for him. In 1833, when Mr. Blood arrived where Corsica now is, on the Olean road, he found, to his annoyance, that no road had been made. Leaving his family behind him, he started from what was then Armstrong's Mill, now Clarington, with an ox team, sled, and men to cut their way step by step through the wilderness twelve miles to his future home. Every night the men camped on and around the ox sled. When the party reached Blood's purchase, a patch of ground was cleared and a log cabin reared. In October, 1833, Mr. Blood and his five children took possession of this forest home. For many years Mr. Blood carried his and the neighbors' mail from Brookville. Panthers were so plenty that they have been seen in the garden by the children, playing like dogs. For years they had to go with their grist to mill to Kittanning, Leatherwood, or Brookville.

The pioneer path or trail was opened by Cyrus Blood from Clarington to Blood's settlement. This was in the year 1833. The pioneer road was this "path" widened and improved by Blood several years later.

The pioneer tavern was the home of Cyrus Blood. Mr. Blood built the pioneer saw-mill in 1834 and the pioneer grist-mill in 1840. These mills were erected by him on Salmon Creek.

The pioneer school-master was John D. Hunt. He taught in the winter of 1833–34 in Mr. Blood's home.

The pioneer preacher was Dr. Otis Smith. The pioneer sermon to white people was preached in Mr. Blood's house.

Brookville was the post-office for this settlement from 1833 to 1843.

The pioneer court-house of Forest County was built in Marienville, of hewed logs, and afterwards weather-boarded and painted white. The work was done by Bennett Dobbs. (See illustration.)

What is now Marienville was called for many years "the Blood settlement."

"AN ACT ORGANIZING FOREST COUNTY FOR JUDICIAL PURPOSES:

"SECTION 1. *Be it enacted, etc.* That the county of Forest, from and after the first day of September, Anno Domini, one thousand eight hundred and fifty-seven, shall be entitled to, and at all times thereafter have all and singular the courts, jurisdictions, officers, rights, and privileges to which other counties of this State are entitled by the constitution and laws of this Commonwealth.

"SECTION 2. That the several courts in and for the said county of Forest shall be opened and held in the town of Marien, at such house therein as may be designated by the commissioners of said county, until a court-house shall be erected in and for said county, as is hereinafter directed, and shall then be held at the said court-house.

"SECTION 3. All suits between Forest County citizens to be transferred to Forest County courts, etc.

"SECTION 4. Relates to the bonds of the public officers.

"SECTION 5. That the sheriff, coroner, and officers of Jefferson County, who have exercised authority over said Forest County, shall continue to do so until similar officers shall be appointed or elected agreeably to law in said county of Forest; and the persons who shall be elected associate judges of

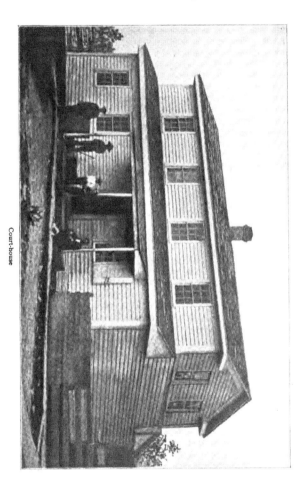

Court-house

the county of Forest shall take and subscribe the requisite oaths and affirmations of office before the prothonotary of Jefferson County, who shall file a
record of the same in the office of the prothonotary of the court of record in
the county of Forest.

"SECTION 6 attached it to the Western District of the Supreme Court.

"SECTION 7. The county shall be annexed to and compose part of the
eighteenth judicial district.

"SECTION 8. Prisoners shall be kept in the Jefferson County jail.

"SECTION 11. Election of county officers, etc.

"Approved May 20. 1857."

John Conrad, Esq., pioneer lawyer

Notification of this act and its purposes was published June 11, 1857,
in the Jefferson County papers for three months, by David C. Gillespie, the
prothonotary of Jefferson County.

The pioneer election authorized by this act was held October 13, 1857,
and the following officials were chosen:

Associate Judges, Cyrus Blood and Milton Gibbs; Prothonotary, G. W.
Rose; Sheriff, John F. Gaul; Coroner, Archibald Black; Commissioner,
Samuel Kincaid; and Auditor, Timothy Caldwell.

525

The pioneer court under this act was held December 21, 1857, in what was then called Marien (now Marienville). President Judge, John S. McCalmont; Associate Judges, Cyrus Blood and Milton Gibbs. W. W. Corbet, as prothonotary of Jefferson County, was present and swore in the Associate Judges.

Thomas B. Mayes was appointed by the court to proclaim the opening. At the suggestion of the judge, W. P. Jenks and L. D. Rogers, of Brookville, were admitted to the "bar" of Forest County. These were the pioneer admissions to the bar of foreign lawyers. It was ordered by the court that Thomas B. Mayes be appointed court crier, and William Walton, of Jenks Township, to act as tipstaff. The rules governing the Jefferson County bar were adopted to govern the Forest County court. On motion of W. P. Jenks, B. F. Lucas, of Brookville, was admitted to the bar. James D. Flick was appointed constable for Barnett Township. Cyrus Blood was appointed county surveyor. Wolves were still killed in this year, 1857, in Forest County.

John Conrad, the local lawyer, was admitted at this term. John Conrad was born in Siebenhausen, Hesse Cassel, Germany, February 18, 1832. His father emigrated to Indiana County, Pennsylvania, in 1833, and settled in Rayne Township, on a farm. John read law with A. W. Taylor, of Indiana, Pennsylvania; was admitted to the bar in Cambria County, Pennsylvania, in 1855; moved to Forest County in the summer of 1857, and was the pioneer lawyer to locate in that county. He was the pioneer district attorney of Forest County from 1858 to 1860; came to Brookville in the spring of 1859, where he lived until he died.

After the adjournment of the court an evening meeting was called of the citizens and visitors. G. W. Rose was chosen president, General Seth Clover and Charles J. Fox were chosen vice-presidents, and W. W. Corbet was chosen secretary. This meeting was addressed by Messrs. Jenks, Rodgers, McCalmont, Clover, Fox, and John Conrad.

The appropriation for schools in 1850 was, Jenks, $10.56; Barnett, $63.96; Tionesta, $4.10. Heath had a population of 187, and Barnett, 479.

About March 8, 1851, the sun was darkened for one week with pigeons. On April 1, 1854, the same conditions existed. '

The pioneer election in Forest County was in October, 1852. The State vote counted with Jefferson.

PIONEER OFFICERS FOR FOREST COUNTY (OLD)

County Commissioners, Cyrus Blood, three years; John Wynkoop, two years; Charles J. Fox, one year; B. Sweet, commissioners' clerk; treasurer, John D. Hunt; auditors, Cyrus W. Hant, William M. Clyde.

The pioneer hunter was John Aylesworth. He came to Barnett Township, Jefferson County, or what in 1838 became Jenks Township, Jefferson County, and is now Jenks Township, Forest County, in 1834. He was a

Connecticut Yankee, but came to this wilderness from Ashtabula, Ohio. He was the most noted and famous hunter in that section of Jefferson County.

Beavers made their homes here in the early thirties, in the great flag swamp or beaver meadows on Salmon Creek. These meadows covered about six hundred acres. Furs were occasionally then brought to Brookville from these meadows by trappers.

The pioneer justice of the peace, John L. Williamson, was elected in 1840.

There appears to have been no election from 1845 to 1849, when a full set of township officers, including the pioneer constable, Thomas Patterson, was elected.

The pioneer coal for Forest County was mined at Balltown.

The best deer-licks in the township were on the Blue Jay.

Rafting timber, Clarion River

Ebenezer Kingsley was the pioneer hunter of Tionesta. He settled in that section in about 1825. Kingsley was a very eccentric man, and a great hunter and trapper. He named nearly all the streams in that section, such as Bear Creek, because he shot a bear there; Jug Handle Creek, because he broke the handle off his jug at its mouth; Salmon Creek, because he shot a salmon at its mouth, etc.

The pioneer saw-mill was built about 1823, by Isaac Ball, Luther Barnes, and William Manross, at the place now called Balltown. The usual food at this mill was said to be one barrel of flour and two barrels of whiskey.

Retailers of foreign merchandise in 1854 were Howe & Co., C. C. Johnson, Shippen & Morrisen, and P. Woodward.

Licensed hotels: Clarington, 1855. Peter G. Reed and Oramel Thing.

Colonel John D. Hunt was appointed postmaster for Marienville, September 25, 1851.

Early mail service March, 1856, from Brookville by Clarington to Marienville (horseback), twenty-six miles and return, once a week.

Dr. D. Bachman located at Clarington May 29, 1857. His stay was short.

The pioneer store was opened at Cooksburg by Hon. Andrew Cook, in 1852.

The pioneer post-office was established in 1871, in Cooksburg, and Andrew Cook was appointed postmaster.

Voters in 1847: Jenks, 10; Barnett, 57; Tionesta, 7.

PIONEER SALE OF LOTS IN MARION (OLD COUNTY SEAT)

" NOTICE.—The public is informed that the sale of lots in Marion, Forest County, has been adjourned on account of the inclement weather, until May or June next, when timely notice will be given.

" CYRUS BLOOD.

" January 16, 1849."

The pioneer school in what is now Forest County was in what is now Tionesta Borough, in 1820. The pioneer school in old Forest County was at Marienville, in 1840. Cyrus Blood, master.

The pioneer missionary to locate and preach in what is now Forest County was the Rev. David Zeisberger, in October, 1767.

PIONEER FLAT-BOATS—PIONEER TIPPLES, ETC.

The pioneer boats in what is now Jefferson County were built at Port Barnett for the transportation of Centre County pig-metal. In 1830 they were built on the North Fork for the same purpose. In after-years, when tipples were used, boats were built and tipples erected at the following points, —viz.: at Findley's, on Sandy Lick, by Nieman and D. S. Chitister; at Brookville, by John Smith; at Troy, by Peter Lobaugh; at Heathville, by A. B. Paine and Arthur O'Donnell; at the mouth of Little Sandy, by William Bennett; at Robinson's Bend, by Hance Robinson. This industry along Red Bank was maintained by the charcoal furnaces of Clarion and Armstrong Counties. The boats were sold at the Olean bridge at Broken Rock, and sold again at Pittsburg for coal-barges. Some of the boats were sold for the transportation of salt to the South from Freeport. The industry on Red Bank ceased in the fifties.

Anthony and Jacob Esbaugh built scaffolds and boats for the dealers on Red Bank. The pioneer boat was sixteen feet wide and forty feet long. These boats were always built from the best lumber that could be made from the choicest timber that grew in our forests. Each gunwale was hewed out

528

of the straightest pine-tree that was to be found,—viz.: twenty-eight inches high at the " rake," fourteen inches at the stern, ten inches thick, and forty feet long, two gunwales to a boat. The ties were hewed six inches thick, with a six-inch face, mortised, dove-tailed, and keyed into the gunwale six feet apart. The six " streamers" for a boat were sawed three by twelve inches, sixteen feet long, and " pinned" to the ties with one pin in the middle of each streamer. These pins were made of white-oak one and a half inches square and ten inches long. The plank for the " bottoms" were first-class white-pine one and a half inches thick, and pinned to the streamers and gun-wales with white-oak pins, calked with flax or tow. All pioneer boats were built on the ground and turned, by about ten men,—and a gallon of whiskey,

Building boat on Clarion River

—over and on a bed made of brush to keep the planks in the bottom from springing. All boats were " sided up" with white-oak studding two and a half by five inches and six feet (high) long. Each studding was mortised into a gunwale two feet apart. Inside the boat a siding eighteen inches high was pinned on. These boats were sold in Pittsburg, to be used as coal-barges for the transportation of coal to the Lower Mississippi. The boats were manned and run by two or three men, the pilot always at the stern. The oar, stem and blade, was made the same as for ordinary rafts. The pioneer boats were tied and landed with halyards made of twisted hickory saplings. The size of these boats in 1843 was eighteen feet wide and eighty feet long,

34

built on tipples similar to the present method. The boats are now made from one hundred and twenty to one hundred and fifty feet long and from twenty to twenty-four feet wide, and from spliced gunwales.

Sixty years ago boats were built on the Big Toby at Maple Creek, Clarington, Millstone, Wynkoop, Spring Creek, Irvine, and Ridgway. The pioneer boat was probably built at Maple Creek by William Reynolds. The pioneer boats were gems of the art as compared with those made to-day. Now the gunwales are spliced up of pieces to make the required length, and the boats are made of hemlock. The industry, however, is carried on more extensively on the Clarion now than ever, and for the same market.

From this time forth, as has been the case for several years of the past, the boat bottom will be of hemlock, patched of many pieces, spiked together instead of built with long oak pins, and they will have to be handled with care to serve their purpose. Of such a kind of boat bottoms there is small danger of scarcity.

CHAPTER XXXI

JEFFERSON COUNTY—FORMATION AND ORGANIZATION—PIONEER SETTLERS—
TREES—JOSEPH BARNETT—INDIAN NAMES OF STREAMS—WAGONS—ROADS
—STORES—MURDERS—COURT-HOUSE AND JAIL—PHYSICIANS—MILITIA—
BRIDGES—ASSESSMENT AND SETTLERS—OLD FOLKS' PICNIC

WHEN William Penn came to what is now the State of Pennsylvania and organized what has become our present Commonwealth, he erected three counties, which were Bucks, Philadelphia, and Chester. Chester County extended over the western portion of the State at that time. In reality, it had jurisdiction over only the inhabitable portion, but its boundary lines extended west of what is now Jefferson County.

On May 10, 1729, Lancaster County was erected from Chester. On January 27, 1750, Cumberland County was erected from Lancaster. On March 9, 1771, Bedford County was erected from Cumberland. March 27, 1772, Northumberland County was erected, and for twenty-four years our wilderness was in this county. On April 13, 1796, Lycoming County was erected from Northumberland, and on March 26, 1804, Jefferson County was erected from Lycoming County. Thus you will see that this wilderness was embraced in six other counties before it was erected into a separate county. The name of the county was given in honor of Thomas Jefferson, who was then President of the United States. The original area of Jefferson County contained twelve hundred and three square miles, but it now has only about 413,-440 acres; highest altitude, from twelve hundred to eighteen hundred and eighty feet above sea-level; length of county, forty-six miles; breadth, twenty-six miles.

" Jefferson County is now in the fourth tier of counties east of the Ohio line, and in the third tier south of the New York line, and is bounded by Forest and Elk on the North, Clearfield on the east, Indiana on the south, and Armstrong and Clarion on the west. Its south line now runs due west twenty-three and one-third miles from the Clearfield-Indiana corner; its west line, thence due north twenty-eight and one-quarter miles to the Clarion River; its north line, first up the Clarion River to Elk County, thence due south one-half mile, thence southeast thirteen and three-quarter miles, to Clearfield County; its east line runs first southwest ten miles, thence due south fifteen and one-third miles, to the starting-place at the Clearfield-Indiana corner.

"The original boundary lines enclosed an area of more than one thousand square miles, embracing much of what is now Forest and Elk, beyond the Clarion River. At what time the present boundaries were erected is not certain; but much shifting took place, especially along the northern border, until comparatively recent years.

"The pioneer people were mainly of Scotch-Irish descent, with a considerable intermixture of the German element, industrious, prudent, and thrifty."

It was first attached to Westmoreland County for judicial purposes, and afterwards to Indiana.

Population in 1810, 161; in 1820, 561; in 1830, 2025; in 1840, 7253.

There are no mountains in the county, but the surface is hilly. The rocks pertain to the series of coal measures lying on the outskirts of the Pittsburg coal basin. Coal is found all through the county.

In 1840 wild lands sold at from one dollar to two dollars per acre. For many years after its establishment the county was but a hunting-ground for whites and Indians.

FOREST-TREES

"The southern portion of Jefferson County was mostly covered with white oak, black oak, rock oak, chestnut, sugar, beech, and hickory.

"The rock areas of northern Jefferson were covered with pine and hemlock, with scarcely a trace of white oak. There is still a considerable quantity of marketable hemlock left.

"White oak, chestnut, sugar, beech, and hickory were the principal kinds of wood on the cleared lands.

"White oak was found mostly on the high uplands.

"W. C. Elliott says of trees, ' There were four kinds of maple, four of ash, five of hickory, eight of oak, three of birch, four of willow, four of poplar, four of pine, and from one to three of each of the other varieties. The following are the names of all of them; some of the trees are not correctly named, but the names given are the only English names by which they go. Their Latin names are all correct and would be given, but would not be understood. Sweet-bay, cucumber, elkwood, long-leaved cucumber, white basswood, toothache-tree, wafer-ash, spindle-tree, Indian-cherry, feted buckeye, sweet buckeye, striped maple, sugar-maple, white maple, red maple, ash-leaved maple, staghorn sumach, dwarf sumach, poison elder, locust, coffee-nut, honey-locust, judas-tree, wild plum, hog-plum, red cherry, black cherry, crab-apple, cockspur, thorn, scarlet haw, blackthorn, Washington thorn, service-tree, witch-hazel, sweet-gum, dogwood, boxwood, sour-gum, sheep-berry, stag-bush, sorrel-tree, spoonwood, rosebay, southern buckthorn, white ash, red ash, green ash, black ash, fringe-tree, catalpa, sassafras, red elm, white elm, rock elm, hackberry, red mulberry, sycamore, butternut, walnut, bitternut, pignut, kingnut, shagbark, white hickory, swamp white

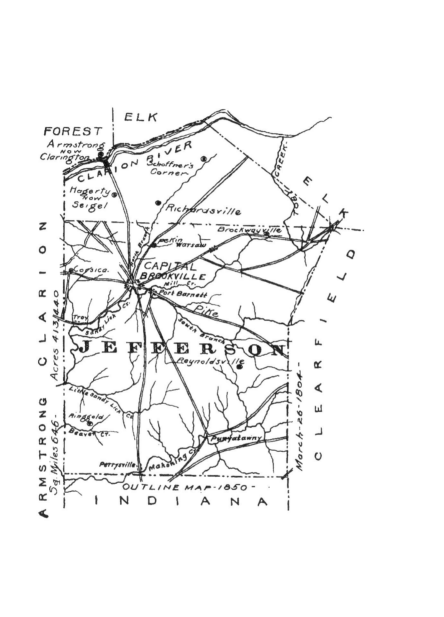

oak, chestnut oak, yellow oak, red oak, shingle oak, chinquapin, chestnut, iron-wood, leverwood, beech, gray birch, red birch, black birch, black alder, speckled alder, black willow, sand-bar willow, almond-willow, glaucous willow, aspen, two varieties of soft poplar, two varieties of cottonwood, two varieties of necklace-poplar, liriodendron (incorrectly called poplar), white cedar, red cedar, white pine, hemlock, balsam, fir, hickory, pine, pitch-pine or yellow pine, red pine, Virginia date, and forest olive. In addition to the above were numerous wild berries, vines, etc.' "

Many of these trees were lofty, magnificent, and valuable, and were not surpassed in any State in the Union. There were over one hundred varieties. The State school-book of 1840 taught that two of our varieties were dis-tinctive and peculiar to Pennsylvania,—viz., the cucumber and umbrella-tree, or elkwood. I will stop to say here, that the woods then were full of sweet singing birds and beautiful flowers; hence some old pioneer called the settle-ment " Paradise."

For the last fifty years a great army of woodmen have been and are yet, to-day, " hacking down these monarchs of the forest," and floating or con-veying them or their product to market. I need not mention our tanneries or saw-mills of to-day. But now

" Look abroad: another race has filled these mountain forests, wide the wood recedes,
And towns shoot up, and fertile lands are tilled by hardy mountaineers."

In regard to the first settlement and early history of the county I have made diligent research, and find, what is not unusual, some conflicting ac-counts and statements. These I have endeavored to compile, arrange, and harmonize to the best of my ability.

From the best information I am enabled to gather and obtain, Andrew Barnett and Samuel Scott were sent in 1795 by Joseph Barnett, who was then living in either Northumberland, Lycoming, or Dauphin County, Penn-sylvania, to explore the famous region then about French Creek, now Craw-ford County, Pennsylvania. But when these two " explorers" reached Mill Creek, now Port Barnett, they were forcibly impressed with the great natural advantages of the place for a saw-mill. They stopped over two or three days to examine the creek. They explored as far down as to where Summer-ville now is, and, after this careful inspection, concluded that this spot, where " the lofty pine leaned gloomily over every hill-side," was just the ideal home for a lumberman.

They went no farther west, but returned east, and informed Joseph Barnett of the " Eureka" they had found. In the spring of 1797, Joseph and Andrew Barnett, Samuel Scott, and Moses Knapp came from their home at the mouth of Pine Creek, then in Lycoming County, to the ideal mill-site of Andrew, and so well pleased were they all that they commenced the erection of the pioneer cabin and mill in the wilderness, in what was then Pine Creek

Township, Lycoming County. The cabin and mill were on the present site of Humphrey's mill and grounds at Port Barnett. The Indians assisted, about nine in number, to raise these buildings, and not a stroke of work would these savages do until they had eaten up all the provisions Mr. Barnett had. This took three days. Then they said, "Me eat, me sleep: now me strong, now me work." In the fall of the same year Joseph Barnett returned to his family, leaving his brother Andrew and Scott to finish some work. In a short time thereafter Andrew Barnett became ill and died, and was buried on the north bank of the creek, at the junction of Sandy Lick and Mill Creek, Scott and two Indians being the only attendants at the funeral. Joseph Barnett was, therefore, soon followed by Scott, who was his brother-in-law, bringing the melancholy tidings of this event, which for a time cast a gloom over the future prospects of these sturdy pioneers.

In 1798, however, Joseph Barnett, Scott, Knapp, and a married man by the name of Joseph Hutchison, came out with them and renewed their work. Hutchison brought his wife, household goods, also two cows and a calf, and commenced housekeeping, and lived here one year before Joseph Barnett brought his family, who were then living in Dauphin County. Hutchison is clearly the pioneer settler in what is now Jefferson County. He was a sawyer. In that year the mill was finished by Knapp and Scott, and in 1799 there was some lumber sawed. In November, 1799, Joseph Barnett brought his wife and family to the home prepared for them in the wilderness. Barnett brought with him two cows and seven horses, five loaded with goods as pack-horses and two as riding or family horses. His route of travel into this wilderness was over Meade's trail.

The first boards were run in 1801 to what is now Pittsburg. About four thousand feet were put in a raft, or what would be a two-platform piece. Moses Knapp was the pioneer pilot.

Joseph Barnett, the patriarch of Jefferson County, was the son of John and Sarah Barnett, and was born in Dauphin County, Pennsylvania, in 1754. His father was born in Ireland, and located in Pennsylvania in the early part of the eighteenth century, and was a farmer up to the time of his death in 1757. His mother died a few years later, and Joseph was "brought up" by his relatives. He was raised on a farm, and was thus peacefully employed when the Revolution commenced. As a son of a patriotic sire he could not resist taking part in the struggle, and so joined the army and served for some years. The exact duration of his service cannot now be ascertained, but this we learn: "he was a brave and efficient soldier, and never faltered in the path of duty." He also served in the State militia in the campaign against the Wyoming boys. After the war he settled in Northumberland County, where he owned a large tract of land, but was dispossessed of it by some informalities of the title. Here he was married to Elizabeth Scott, sister of Samuel Scott and daughter of John Scott, July 3, 1794.

I find Joseph Barnett assessed in Pine Creek Township, Northumberland County, April 28, 1786. I find him, in 1788, assessed in the same township and county with a saw-mill and as a single freeman. This was his saw-mill at the mouth of Pine Creek, and the mill on which he lost his eye. The property is now in Clinton County. After losing his mill and land Barnett returned in the nineties to Dauphin County, Pennsylvania, and engaged in contracting for and building bridges. In 1799 I find him again assessed in Pine Creek Township, then Lycoming County, Pennsylvania, with two hundred and twenty-five acres of land. This was his Port Barnett property, where he migrated to with his family in November, 1799; and here he engaged in the erection of mills and in the lumbering business that eventually made Port Barnett, then in Lycoming County, the centre of business for a large extent of territory. In a short time a tub grist-mill was added to his saw-mill, and, with his " Port Barnett flint-stone binns," he made an eatable, if not a very desirable, quality of flour. The Indians (Cornplanters and Senecas) then in the country were good customers, and what few whites there were for forty miles around would make his cabin a stopping-place for several days at a time. His log cabin became a tavern, the only one in a seventy-five miles' journey, and was frequented by all the early settlers.

" His Indian guests did not eat in the house, but would in winter make a pot of mush over his fire and set it out in the snow to cool; then one fellow would take a dipper and eat his fill of the pudding, sometimes with milk, butter, or molasses; then another would take it and go through the same process until all were satisfied. The dogs would then help themselves from the same pot, and when they put their heads in the pot in the Indian's way he would give them a slap over the head with the dipper."

He kept a store, rafted lumber on Sandy Lick and Red Bank, and at the same time attended to his saw- and grist-mills. I find him assessed in Pine Creek Township in 1800 as a farmer.

" The Senecas of Cornplanter's tribe were friendly and peaceable neighbors, and often extended their excursions into these waters, where they encamped, two or three in a squad, and hunted deers and bears, taking the hams and skins in the spring to Pittsburg. Their rafts were constructed of dry poles, upon which they piled up their meat and skins in the form of a haystack, took them to Pittsburg, and exchanged them for trinkets, blankets, calicoes, weapons, etc. They were friendly, sociable, and rather fond of making money. During the war of 1812 the settlers were apprehensive that an unfortunate turn of the war upon the lakes might bring an irruption of the savages upon the frontier through the Seneca nation.

" Old Captain Hunt, a Muncy Indian, had his camp for some years on Red Bank, near where is now the southwestern corner of Brookville. He got his living by hunting, and enjoyed the results in drinking whiskey, of which he was inordinately fond. One year he killed seventy-eight bears,—

they were plenty then; the skins might be worth about three dollars each,—nearly all of which he expended for his favorite beverage.

"Samuel Scott resided here until 1810, when, having scraped together, by hunting and lumbering, about two thousand dollars, he went down to the Miami River and bought a section of fine land, which made him rich.

"It is related that Joseph Barnett at one time carried sixty pounds of flour on his back from Pittsburg. Their supplies of flour, salt, and other necessaries were frequently brought in canoes from that place. These were purchased with lumber, which he sawed and rafted to that city, and which in those days was sold for twenty-five dollars per thousand. The nearest settlement on Meade's trail eastward of Port Barnett was Paul Clover's, thirty-three miles distant, on the west branch of the Susquehanna, where Curwensville now stands; and westward Fort Venango was forty-five miles distant, which points were the only resting-places for the travellers who ventured through this unbroken wilderness. The Seneca Indians, of Cornplanter's tribe, heretofore mentioned, often extended their hunting excursions to these waters, and encamped to hunt deer and bears and make sugar. They are said to have made sugar by catching the sap in small troughs, and, after collecting in a large trough, hot stones were dipped into it to boil it down."—*Day's Collections.*

About the year 1802 Joseph Barnett consented to act as banker for the Indians around Port Barnett. The Indians were all "bimetallists," and had the "silver craze," for their money was all silver; and bringing their mono-metallism to Mr. Barnett, he received it from them and deposited it in their presence in his private vault,—viz., a small board trunk covered with hog-skin, tanned with the bristles on. On the lid were the letters "J. B.," made with brass tacks. The trunk was now full; the bank was a solid financial institution. In a short time, however, the red men concluded to withdraw their deposits, and they made a "run" in a body on the bank. Barnett handed over the trunk, and each Indian counted out his own pieces, and according to their combined count the bank was insolvent; there was a shortage, a deficiency of one fifty-cent piece. Mr. Barnett induced the Indians to recount their silver, but the fifty-cent piece was still missing. The Indians then declared Mr. Barnett must die; they surrounded the house and ordered him on the porch to be shot. He obeyed orders, but pleaded with them to count their pieces the third time, and if the fifty-cent piece was still missing, then they could shoot him. This the Indians considered fair, and they counted the silver pieces the third time, and one Indian found he had one more piece than his own; he had the missing fifty-cent piece. Then there was joy and rejoicing among the Indians. Banker Barnett was no longer a criminal; he was the hero and friend of the Indians.

The cheapest and most expeditious method of obtaining such supplies as could not be produced on the ground was to go to Pittsburg for them.

Rafts of sawed lumber were run to Pittsburg in the spring of the year. A canoe was taken along, and when the raft was sold most of the avails would be invested in whiskey, pork, sugar, dry goods, etc. These goods were then loaded into the canoe, and the same men that brought the raft through to market would "pole" or "push" the loaded canoe up the river and up the creek to Port Barnett. This was a "voyage" that all men of full strength were very desirous of making, and was the subject of conversation for the remaining part of the year.

These canoes were hewed out of a large pine-tree, large enough to receive a barrel of flour crosswise. A home-made rope of flax was attached to the front end of the canoe to be used in pulling the canoe up and over ripples. The men with these canoes had to camp in the woods wherever night overtook them, and their greatest terror and fear was rattlesnakes, for the creek bottoms were alive with them.

INDIAN NAMES OF STREAMS

Da yon on dah teh go wah (Big Toby, or Alder) gah yon hah da (creek), Big Toby Creek.

Da yon on dah teh we oh (Little Toby, or Alder) gah yon hah da (creek), Little Toby Creek.

Oh non da (Pine) gah yon hah da (creek), Pine Creek.

Oh twenge ah (red) yoh non da (bank), gah yon hah da (creek), Red Bank Creek.

Oh ne sah geh jah geh da geh gah yon hah da, Sandy Lick Creek.

Ga de ja hah da gah nos gah yon hah da, Mahoning Creek.

Oh to weh geh ne gah yon hah da, North Fork Creek.

Oh nah da gon, Among the Pines.

Among the pioneer industries was tar-burning. Kilns were formed and split fagots of pitch-pine knots were arranged in circles and burned. The tar was collected by a ditch and forced into a chute, and from there barrelled. John Matson, Sr., marketed on rafts as high as forty barrels in one season. Freedom Stiles was the king "tar-burner." Pioneer prices at Pittsburg for tar was ten dollars a barrel.

PIONEER WAGONS IN JEFFERSON COUNTY, AND PIONEER DRAYING IN BROOKVILLE

The pioneer wheeled vehicle made in what is now Jefferson County was a wooden ox-cart, constructed by Joseph Barnett in 1801. The wheels were sawed from a large oak log, and a hole was chiselled in the centre for the hickory axle. Walter Templeton, a very ingenious man, and forced to be a "jack-of-all-trades" for the people who lived in what is now Eldred Township, made two wooden wagons in 1829, one for himself and one for his neighbor, Isaac Matson. These wagons were all wood except the iron linch-pin to keep the wheel in place. The wheels were solid, and were sawed from round oak logs. The hind-wheels were sawed from a larger log, and a hole was chiselled in the centre of each for the axle.

Matson hauled, in 1830, the stone spawls for our pioneer jail in his wagon, with two large black oxen, called " Buck" and " Berry." Matson's compensation was one dollar and fifty cents a day and " find" himself.

Draying in those days was usually by two oxen and a cart; but Daniel Elgin bought these black oxen from Matson, and used one of them for some time for a one-ox dray in Brookville.

The pioneer tar to grease these axles was made in this way: Pitch-pine knots were split fine and dropped into an iron kettle; a piece of board was then placed over the mouth of the kettle, and then the kettle was turned upside down over a little bed of earth prepared for it. This bed had a circular drain around it, and this circular drain had a straight one, with a spout at the end. Everything being completed for the burning, the board was taken from under the kettle, and the kettle was then covered with fagots. The wood was fired and the heat from the fire boiled the tar from the split knots and forced it into and through these drains, and from the spout of which it was caught in a wooden trough.

The pioneer road was the Indiana and Port Barnett, for the creation of which the petition of a number of citizens of Jefferson County and parts of Indiana County was presented to the Indiana County Court at the September term, 1808. The points of the road were from Brady's mill, on Little Mahoning Creek, Indiana County, to Sandy Lick Creek, in Jefferson County (Port Barnett), where the State (Milesburg and Waterford) road crosses the same. The Court appointed as viewers Samuel Lucas, John Jones, Moses Knapp, and Samuel Scott, of Jefferson County, and John Park and John Wier, of Indiana County, to view and make a report at the next term. This road was probably built in 1810.

The pioneer justice of the peace was Thomas Lucas, appointed January 16, 1809.

The early settlers to erect cabins on the Indiana road in Pine Creek Township were Joseph Carr in 1817, Manuel Reitz, George Gray, and Samuel McQuiston in 1827, John Matthews in 1830, Elijah Clark in 1833, Andrew Hunter and William Wyley in 1834, and Isaac Swineford in 1835. The pioneer school-house in this settlement was built in 1830; the pioneer graveyard was on the McCann farm in 1830.

" FINES FOR MISDEMEANORS.—In the early days of the county's history the penalties prescribed by the laws of the Commonwealth for any offence against any of the statutes was rigorously enforced, seemingly without regard to the social standing of the offender. Sabbath-breaking, swearing, and intoxication seem to have been the sins most vigorously punished by the arm of the law.

" The earliest recognition of the observance of Sunday as a legal duty is a constitution of Constantine in 321 A.D. enacting that all courts of justice and all workshops were to be at rest on Sunday. Charlemagne, in the West, forbade labor of any kind on Sunday. At first the tendency was to observe the Sabbath (Saturday) rather than Sunday. Later the Sabbath and Sunday came to be observed at the same period, but after the time of Constantine the observation of the Sabbath practically ceased. Sunday observance was directed by injunctions of both Edward VI. and Elizabeth.

" The first election in the county was held at Port Barnett, and up to 1818 it was the only polling and election precinct in and for the county. At the last election (when the township was the whole county), in 1817, Friday, March 14, the names of the contestants for office and the votes were as follows,—viz.: Constable, Elijah M. Graham, 22 votes; John Dixon, 13 votes. Supervisors, Joseph Barnett, 25 votes; Thomas Lucas, 28 votes. Overseer of the Poor, Henry Keys, 9 votes; John Matson, 6 votes. Fence Appraisers, Moses Knapp, 7 votes; William Vastbinder, 7 votes. Town Clerk, Elijah M. Graham, 22 votes.

" Signed and attested by the judges, Walter Templeton and Adam Vastbinder."

The pioneer store was opened by the Barnetts and Samuel Scott, who, in 1826, sold it out to Jared B. Evans, and he, in the fall of 1830, removed it to Jefferson Street, Brookville, Pennsylvania.

The pioneer murder in Jefferson County was committed on May 1, 1844. Daniel Long, one of the mighty hunters of Pine Creek Township, and Samuel Knopsnyder were murdered in Barnett Township, now Heath, near Raught's Mills. There was a dispute between Long and James Green about a piece of land. The land was a vacant strip. James Green and his son Edwin took possession of Long's shanty on this land while Long was absent. On Long's return to the shanty in company with Knopsnyder, Long was shot by young Green as he attempted to enter the shanty, with Long's own gun. Knopsnyder was so terribly cut with an axe in the hands of the Greens that he died in a few days. The Greens, father and son, were arrested, tried, and convicted of murder in the second degree, and each sentenced to four years in the penitentiary.

James Green, the father, served a year and was pardoned. Edwin served his time and returned to Jefferson County a few days only, as he was in terror of the Longs. He therefore returned to Pittsburg, and settled down somewhere and lived and died highly respected.

The second murder was in Washington Township in 1845. It occurred at a frolic at the house of James Ross. A dispute arose between Thomas Brown and James Smith. Brown struck Smith with a hand-spike, which caused his death in twenty-four hours. Too much whiskey was the cause of the dispute and blow. Brown was tried in Brookville, convicted, and sentenced to the penitentiary for six years, but was afterwards pardoned out.

The pioneer graveyard in the county was located on the property now of William C. Evans, deceased, near the junction of the Ridgway road with the pike. I found this graveyard in my boyhood, and thought they were Indian graves. My mother told me its history. The graves are now lost and the grounds desecrated. The second graveyard in the township was laid out in 1842, on Nathaniel Butler's farm, and is still called Butler's graveyard.

BROOKVILLE

This borough, the seat of justice of Jefferson County, commenced its first building in June, 1830. After the lots were sold, it being then in the

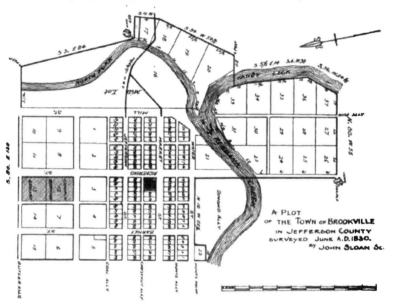

A PLOT
OF THE TOWN OF BROOKVILLE
IN JEFFERSON COUNTY
SURVEYED JUNE A.D.1830.
BY JOHN SLOAN &c.

boundary of Rose Township, its citizens voted with the township till 1848, when it was set apart as a distinct polling-place. It was named after, or on account of, the springs on its hills,—*Brook*, attached with the French *ville* or Latin *villa*, a country seat, in common English a town,—these put together form the name. The taxables in 1849 were 177; in 1856, 273. The population in 1840 by census was 276.

PIONEERS AND PIONEER EVENTS IN BROOKVILLE

"The deeds of our fathers in times that are gone,
Their virtues, their prowess, the toils they endured."

Day says, in 1843, " Brookville is situated on the Waterford and Sus-quehanna Turnpike, forty-four miles east of Franklin, and at the head of Red Bank Creek. The town was laid out by the County Commissioners in 1830; the lots were sold in June of that year at from thirty to three hundred dollars per lot. The town is watered by hydrants, supplied by a copious spring."

A road leads from Brookville to Ridgway, a settlement of New England and New York people, made some years since on the Little Mill Creek branch of the Clarion River, in the northeastern corner of the county. It took its name from Jacob Ridgway, of Philadelphia, who owned large tracts of land in this vicinity.

Punxstawney is a small village with fifteen or twenty dwellings, on a branch of Mahoning Creek, about eighteen miles southeast from Brookville.

Brockway is a small settlement on Little Toby's Creek, at the crossing of the road between Brookville and Ridgway.

Somerville, or Troy, is a small cluster of houses on the right bank of Red Bank, seven miles below Brookville. Not far from this place is a Seceders' church, one of the first built in the county.

BROOKVILLE'S PIONEER SCHOOL

The pioneer school-house in the town was built in the summer of 1832. It was a small, one-story brick building about twenty feet square, and stood where the American House barn now (1905) stands. I remember it well. This house was erected under the provisions of the law of 1809, was paid for by voluntary subscriptions, and was heated by a ten-plate stove that burned wood. My father, Alexander McKnight, taught the first term of school in Brookville in this building, in the winter of 1832-33. I can name but a few of his scholars, —to wit, James Wilson, W. W. Corbet, Rebecca Jane Corbet, mother of Cyrus H. Blood, Esq.; John Heath, Sarah Clements, Daniel Smith, Oliver George, Susan Early, John Hastings, Barton T. Hastings, and John Butler. There was no classification of books and no system in teaching. Each scholar recited from his own book.

School-masters who taught in Brookville subscription schools under the law of 1809: 1832-33, Alexander McKnight, pioneer; 1834, Miss Charlotte Clark, Charles E. Tucker; 1835, John Wilson; 1836, Hannibal Craighead.

Masters who taught under the common school law of 1834: 1837, Cyrus Crouch, had sixty scholars; Rev. Jesse Smith, a Presbyterian minister; 1838, Rev. Dexter Morris, a Baptist preacher; 1839, John Smith, father of Mrs. S. C. Christ; 1840, S. M. Bell, Mrs. M. T. H. Roundy; 1841, D. S. Deering.

543

In this little brick house the Methodists for years held their weekly prayer-meetings. The principal members were Judge Heath, Aarad Marshall, John Dixon, John Heath, David and Cyrus Butler, David Henry and wife, and Mary, Jane and Sarah Gaston.

The first persons to teach in the academy building that succeeded it were, in 1843, R. J. Nicholson, Miss Elizabeth Brady, afterwards Mrs. A. Craig, who died in April, 1905; 1846-50, R. J. Nicholson and Miss Nancy Lucas.

In 1835 Brookville contained about one hundred and thirty-five people. The village had six merchants,—viz., Evans & Clover, William Rodgers, James Corbett, Jared B. Evans, Jack & Wise, and Steadman & Watson. Each storekeeper had a large dry pine block, called " upping block," in front of his store-room, to assist men and women to mount or alight from their horses. The stores were lighted with candles and warmed with wood-fires. Wood-fires in stoves and chimneys were very dangerous, on account of the accumulation of wood-soot in the chimney; for when this soot gathered in quantity it always ignited, burned out, and endangered the shingle roof. Towns and cities then had men and boys called professional " chimney-sweeps." These " sweeps " entered the chimney from the fireplace, climbing up and out at the top by the aid of hooks, announcing their exit in a song and looking as black as an African negro. In 1835 some of the legal privileges of the town were: " That no citizen of the town shall be permitted to keep on Main Street, at one time, more than ten cords of wood, not more than enough brick to build a chimney, or before his door more lumber than will build a spring-house; not more than two wagons and a half-sled; a few barrels of salt, five thousand shingles, or twenty head of horned cattle." Of course, there was no legal restriction as to the number of " chickens in the garden" or geese and hogs on the street. On dark nights the people then carried lanterns made of tin, holes being punched in them, and the light produced by a candle. The lantern had a side door to open, to light, blow out, and replace the candle.

" MAIL ARRIVALS AND DEPARTURES IN 1835

" The Mail arrives from Philadelphia by way of Harrisburg, Lewistown, and Bellefonte every Monday evening, Wednesday evening, and Friday evening in a four Horse Coach.

" From Erie, by way of Meadville, Franklin, &c., every Monday, Wednesday, and Friday evening, and returns the same day, in a four Horse Stage.

" From Washington City, by way of Chambersburgh, Indiana, &c., every Friday and returns same day—carried on a Horse.

" From Pittsburg by way of Kittanning every Friday, and returns on Tuesday—carried on a Horse.

" Arrive at this place every Tuesday, from Smethport, McKean County, by way of Gillis Post-office, and returns on Friday—carried on a Horse."

The pioneer court-house was contracted for in 1830, and finished in 1833. Our first jail was a stone structure, built of common stone, in 1831. It was two stories high, was situated on the northeast corner of the public square lot, near Joseph Darr's residence, and fronting on Pickering Street. Daniel Elgin was the contractor. The building was divided into eight rooms, two down-stairs and two up-stairs for the jail proper, and two down-stairs and two up-stairs for the sheriff's residence and office. The sheriff occupied the north part. It cost eighteen hundred and twenty-four dollars and twenty-three cents.

Previous to and as late as 1850 it was the rule for mill-men, woodsmen, and laboring men generally to stop work every Saturday at noon. The idea was to better prepare for the observance of the Sabbath. As far as my observation reminds me, I can assure you that spiritualizing was practised freely on these Saturday afternoons.

In 1799, when Joseph Barnett settled at the mouth of Mill Creek, there were but two Indian families at that place,—viz., Twenty Canoes and Toma-hawk. The two Hunts were there, but only as individuals, and they were cousins. Jim Hunt was on banishment for killing his cousin. Captain Hunt was an under chief of the Muncey tribe. These Munceys were slaves to our Senecas, and captain was the highest military title known to the Indians. Other Indians came here to hunt every fall, even to my early days. Of two who came about 1800, I might mention John Jamison (Sassy John), who had seven sons, all named John; the other was Crow; he was an Indian in name and in nature. He was feared by both the whites and Indians. He was a Mohawk, and a perfect savage. Caturah and Twenty Canoes stayed here for several years after the Barnetts came. The Hunts were here most of the time until the commencement of the war of 1812. Jim dare not go back to his tribe until the year 1808 or 1809, when his friends stole a white boy in Westmoreland County and had him adopted into the tribe in place of the warrior Jim had slain. . . .

Twenty Canoes and Sassy John were back once to see " Joe Blannett"— they could not pronounce the name of Barnett. The last visit of Caturah was in 1833, he being then over ninety years of age.

The following is from *Hazzard's Register*, 1830:

" Brookville, the spot selected by the commissioners as the seat of justice for Jefferson County, and confirmed by act of Assembly, etc., has lately been laid out in town lots and out lots bearing this name. At the sale, which took place last week, town lots were sold from thirty dollars to three hundred dollars each; the last day's sale averaged above fifty dollars, without in-cluding a mill-seat (Barr's) sold for one thousand dollars. Proceeds of sale will no doubt be sufficient to build a court-house. This may be considered high rate for lots, most of which still remain in a state of nature—but the advantages and prospects of this new county town attract a crowd of strangers. Persons were known to be present from twelve neighboring counties. The location of Brookville is a good one, and it has been judiciously laid out by Mr. Sloan, the artist."

These purchasers stopped with James Parks, near what is now Christ's brewery, and with David Butler, on the east side of the North Fork, at the head of what is now Wayne Cook's dam. A number also stopped with John Eason in his shanty on Main Street. The first sale of produce in what is now Brookville was in June, 1830. Samuel Sloan, of Armstrong County, was then teaming to and from Bellefonte. John Eason had erected a shanty in the woods to board the surveyors of the town plot. He observed, one day, Samuel Sloan on the pike, and Eason bought from his wagon butter, hams, and flour.

The pioneer physician in the county was John Jenks, M.D. In 1818 Dr. John W. Jenks came from Bucks County, Pennsylvania, and settled in

Robert Hamilton, of Perry Township, pioneer, farmer, and financier; born 1813; died 1902

what is now Punxsutawney, where he built a cabin, made improvements, and reared a family. He was quite a prominent man, and filled positions of profit and trust. He was one of the first associate judges, and father of Judge W. P. Jenks, Hon. G. A. Jenks, and Mrs. Judge Gordon.

PIONEER MAJOR SURGICAL OPERATION

Moses Knapp moved to what is now called Baxter in the spring of 1821, and while cutting timber he got a foot and leg crushed so that his limb had to be amputated above the knee. Dr. Stewart, of Indiana, and Dr. William Rankin, of Licking, now Clarion County, performed the amputation in the summer of 1821. Knapp that year was constable, having been elected in the spring election.

PIONEER MILITIA LEGISLATION—AN ACT AUTHORIZING THE FORMATION OF THE MILITIA OF JEFFERSON COUNTY

" A FURTHER SUPPLEMENT TO THE ACT ENTITLED ' AN ACT FOR THE REG-
ULATION OF THE MILITIA OF THIS COMMONWEALTH'

" SECTION I. And be it further enacted by the authority aforesaid, That the part of the ninety-ninth regiment of the fifteenth division of Pennsylvania militia, lying within the county of Jefferson, shall form a separate battalion, and shall be entitled to elect one lieutenant-colonel and one major, and the election of the officers thereof shall be held as soon as convenient, agreeably to the act to which this is a supplement; the field officers of this battalion shall, as soon as practicable, proceed to organize said battalion into companies, so that the number of officers, non-commissioned officers, and privates in the several companies thereof may, if they think it expedient, be reduced to fifty.

" Approved April 10, 1826."

The election under this act was held at Port Barnett, November 6, 1826, when the following officers were elected for the pioneer battalion of Jefferson County:

Lieutenant-colonel, Hance Robinson; major, Andrew Barnett.

There appears to have been no company numbered 1, but the officers elected for company No. 2 were as follows: Captain, Obed Morris; first lieutenant, John Hess; second lieutenant, Benoni Williams. This was a company from and around Punxsutawney.

Of the third company, Samuel Jones was captain; Thomas Robinson, first lieutenant; John Walters, second lieutenant.

Fourth company, Frederick Hetrick, captain; Caleb Howard, first lieutenant; James Crow, second lieutenant.

About 1828 the second election was held for this battalion, when Andrew Barnett was elected lieutenant-colonel, and James Corbet was elected major.

Late in the twenties, or early in the thirties, a volunteer militia company was organized in Punxsutawney, known as the Indiana and Jefferson Greens. I am unable to give precise dates, as these cannot be found on the records at Harrisburg. The pioneer officers were, Samuel Kerr, captain; David McPherson, first lieutenant; Abraham Brewer, second lieutenant. This company had numerous other officers, and had an existence for seven years.

The second volunteer company organized in Punxsutawney, and distinctly belonging to Jefferson County, was the Jefferson Rangers. It was in the third battalion, One Hundred and Forty-fifth Regiment, fifteenth division, and must have been organized in 1839. The pioneer officers were: James H. Bell, captain; William Long, first lieutenant; John Weaver, second lieutenant. In 1842 William Long was captain; James L. Perry, first lieutenant; John Simpson, second lieutenant. About 1846 or 1847 Phineas W. Jenks was captain; Charles B. Hutchinson, first lieutenant; James B. Miller, second lieutenant. This company, under Long, offered its services during the Mexican War, but was not accepted. Long was in office for seven years. It disbanded about 1848.

All marching in the militia was done to the tune of " Yankee Doodle" or the " Girl I left behind me." Marching was in single file. In drill it was "by sections of two, march." Instead of " file right" or " file left," it was " right" or " left wheel." Instead of " front" it was " left face."

The militia of Pennsylvania ceased to muster in 1849, under the provisions of the act of April 17 of that year, entitled "An act to revise the military system and provide for the arming of such only as shall be uniformed."

The pioneer county bridge was petitioned for January 19, 1836; approved by the court, September, 1836. The bridge was let by the commissioners December 15, 1836, to Messrs. Thomas Hall and Richard Arthurs, contractors. The contract called for the completion of the bridge by September, 1837. The accepted contract bid was seven hundred and ninety-five dollars. When finished the bridge was a good solid structure, but was a curious pile of wood and stones.

This pioneer, county, covered bridge was a wooden one, made of pine timber. It was erected across Red Bank Creek in the borough of Brookville, a few feet west of where the present iron structure on Pickering Street now stands. There were no iron nails used in its construction, and only a few *hand-made* iron spikes. The timbers were mortised and tenoned, and put together with wooden pins. This was a single-span bridge of one hundred and twenty feet in length, with no centre pier, and of the burr-truss plan. It had two strings of circle arches, resting on the stone abutments.

Many memories to the old citizen clustered around this bridge, but time has effaced the bridge and will efface the memories. On its planks generations have met, passed, and repassed, and from its stringers fishers dropped many a hook and line. Up to and later than 1843, Brookville had three natatoriums, or swimming-pools,—viz., one at the head of what is now Wayne Cook's dam on the North Fork, one at the " Deep Hole" near the Sand Spring, on the Sandy Lick, and one at or underneath the covered Bridge on Red Bank. In those days, from the time we had May flowers until the chilling blasts of November arrived, one of the principal sports of the men and boys was swimming in these " pools." We boys, in summer months, all day long played on the bosom of these waters or on the border-land. The busy men, the doctor, the statesman, the lawyer, the parson, the merchant, the farmer, the mechanic, and the day laborer, all met here in the summer eve with boisterous shouts of joy and mirth to welcome up the moon. Of course, we had some skilful plungers and swimmers, who were as much at home in these waters as the wild ducks and geese of that day. An artist could swim on his back, on either side, under the water, float on his back, tread or walk in the water, and plunge or dive from almost any height. The beginner or boy. though, always commenced his apprenticeship in this graceful profession by swimming with his breast on a piece of plank, board, or old slab. But alas to the pioneer,—

> " Swimming sports, once deemed attractive,
> Haunts amidst the bloom of laurel flowers,
> Radiant charms that pleased my senses
> In my boyhood's sunny hours,
> Have departed like illusions,
> And will never more be ours."

Alexander McKnight located in Brookville in 1832. He taught the first term of school in the first school building, was the first school director elected for the new borough, held the office of justice of the peace, lieutenant-colonel in the militia, had served a year as private in the regular army of the United States, and was county treasurer when he died, in 1837, aged twenty-seven years.

Samuel Craig located in Brookville in 1832, Hugh Brady, Esq., in 1832, and John Ramsey, the pioneer wagon-maker, in 1834. Hugh Brady and family came from Indiana, Pennsylvania, in a Conestoga wagon drawn by four horses,—the lead horses having bells on. That was the wagon of that period. There was a bridge across the North Fork. They came *via* Port Barnett. John Showalter located here in 1843. He lived. in Snyder's Row, was a gunsmith, and had a confectionery. James R. Fullerton located in Brookville in 1833. The pioneer gunsmith was Isaac Mills. He located where Thomas L. Templeton now resides. The pioneer doctor was Alvah Evans; he came in September, 1831. He was a young, handsome, portly man. He remained four or five months and left. Where he came from or where he went to nobody knows. The second doctor was C. G. M. Prime. He came in the spring of 1832. Dr. Prime amputated the arm of Henry (Hance) Vastbinder. During his residence here he married a Miss Wagley. He was a hard drinker. He left here April 3, 1835, for Mississippi, where he was shot and killed at a card-table. He became a lawyer while here, and delivered political speeches and Fourth of July orations.

The pioneer merchant to sell drugs and medicines in Brookville was Major William Rogers, in 1831. He sold Dover's powder, Hooper's pills, mercurial ointment, wine, brandy, whiskey, quinine, etc.

The pioneer fire-engine was bought June 29, 1839. Cost, two hundred and fifty dollars. It was a hand-engine. This same year it was resolved by the council that "the timber standing or lying on the streets and alleys be sold for the use of said borough." The first volunteer fire company in the United States was at Philadelphia, 1736.

The pioneer saddle and harness manufactory in Brookville was opened by John Brownlee, on May 8, 1834, in the rear of his lot facing Mill Street, and opposite D. E. Breneman's residence.

Pioneer academy

—— McDonald started the pioneer cabinet and furniture factory in 1831-32.

The pioneer foundry was started by a man named Coleman, in 1841. It was located where the Fetzer building now is.

The pioneer grist-mill and saw-mill were both built by Moses Knapp.

The pioneer borough election was in 1835.

The pioneer silversmith and watch- and clock-maker was Andrew Straub, in 1833-34. Watches were then assessed as property.

The pioneer graveyard was on lands now owned by W. C. Evans, on Litch's Hill. The second one is now called the "old graveyard."

The pioneer dentists were Dr. A. M. Hills and T. M. Van Valzah.

These were travelling dentists, and came here periodically. The first dentist to locate was William J. Chandler.

In 1832 Peter Sutton built and kept a tavern on the corner of Taylor Street, across the North Fork, now Litchtown. In 1832 or 1833 there was a frame tavern adjoining the Franklin Tavern. It was kept for a number of years by a man named Craig, Mrs. Wagley, and others.

The pioneer tannery was built in 1831 by David Henry, on the lot now occupied by the United Presbyterian church. As late as 1843 a great gully crossed Main Street, carrying the water from this institution over and through the lot now occupied by that model institution of the town, the National Bank of Brookville.

Miss Julia Clark opened the pioneer millinery and mantua-making business in Brookville. Prices: bonnets, leghorn, $5; silk, $2.50; gimp, $1.50; straw, $1. In her advertisement she says, " She can be seen at her residence, four doors east of E. Heath's store, on Main Street. Persons, so wishing, can be supplied by her with ladies' leghorn hats, flats and crown, from No. 32 to 42; ladies' Tuscan and French gimp; Italian braid hats; Leghorn braid, Tuscan and Italian edge, Misses' gimp hats, Tuscan; French gimp by the piece. She hopes, by giving her undivided attention to the above business, to merit a share of public patronage. Brookville, July 13, 1834."

The pioneer tinner was Samuel Truby. He came from Indiana, Pennsylvania, arriving here on January 1, 1834. The last thirteen miles of the journey was through a dense forest, without house or clearing. They stopped at John Eason's tavern, and as soon as possible he commenced to cut down the trees on and clear his lot, corner of Jefferson and Pickering Streets, preparatory to building a house, a contract for the building of which was taken by the late R. Arthurs, he agreeing to furnish all the material and finish it as specified by April 1 for the sum of forty dollars, which was paid in silver quarters. The house was sixteen feet square and one and a half stories high.

Hon. Thomas Hastings came in May, 1831. " Nearly all of what is now the principal part of the town—Main Street and Jefferson Street—was then a forest. Only three houses had yet been built,—the Red Lion Hotel, where Dr. Gregg's barber-shop now is, the hotel now occupied by P. J. Allgeier."

The pioneer settler to locate where Brookville is was Moses Knapp. The pioneer to locate in the county seat was John Eason, father of Rev. David Eason. He bought the lot on the corner of Main Street and Spring Alley, and erected the pioneer house in the county seat,—viz., in August, 1830, and opened it for a tavern. Mr. Eason died in 1835. In 1831 William Robinson lived in a little log house on the corner of Mill and Water Streets. This log house and log stable had been built by Moses Knapp in 1806. The next person to locate was perhaps Thomas Hall. Benjamin McCreight was an early settler. Mr. McCreight was a tailor and carried on the business. He was an honorable and useful man, and held many responsible positions during his life here. Thomas M. Barr came here in 1830. He was a stone-mason and bricklayer, and assisted to build up the town by taking contracts. The pioneer blacksmith was Jacob Riddleberger, in 1832–33. William Clark, Sr., came to Brookville in 1830, and erected a tavern on the northwest corner of Pickering and Jefferson Streets. In the fall of 1830 Jared B. Evans moved his store from Port Barnett to Brookville, and was appointed the pioneer postmaster for Brookville. Brookville, by post-road, was one hundred and sixty-five miles northwest of Harrisburg, Pennsylvania, and two hundred and thirty-eight miles northwest of Washington, D. C. Mr. Evans's was the pioneer store. The second store was opened three days later by Major William Rodgers. Thomas Hastings located in 1831, and built the Jefferson Tavern. Robert P. Barr came in 1830. He was a useful and public-spirited man. He built the saw-mill and flouring-mill on the North Fork. Joseph Sharpe was the first shoemaker and the first constable. He lived on the lot now occupied by the National Bank of Brookville.

The first assessment for the county was made for the year 1807, and was as follows:

Joseph Barnett, one hundred acres of land, distillery, one horse, and five cows; total valuation, $329.

John Dixon, weaver, one horse and one cow; total valuation, $66.

E. M. Graham (no property assessed).

Joseph Hutchison, one horse, but no valuation.

Peter Jones, blacksmith, one hundred acres of land, one horse and two cows; total valuation, $195.

John Jones, one horse and one cow; total valuation, $61.

Moses Knapp, two horses and one cow; total valuation, $108.

Thomas Lucas, grist- and saw-mill, two horses and two cows; total valuation, $499.

William Lucas, tailor, one cow; total valuation, $19.

Samuel Lucas, three cows; total valuation, $59.

Ludwick Long, distillery, two horses and one cow; total valuation, $185.

Jacob Mason, one cow; valuation, $14.

Alexander McCoy, three cows; total valuation, $54.

John Roll, carpenter, two horses and two cows; total valuation, $132.

Samuel Scott, miller, one hundred acres of land, saw- and grist-mill, four horses and five cows; total valuation, $600.

John Scott, one hundred acres of land, two horses and two cows; total valuation, $222.

Jacob Vastbinder (single man), one hundred acres of land, one horse; total valuation, $247.

William Vastbinder, one hundred acres of land, one horse and three cows; total valuation, $201.

HISTORY OF NORTHWESTERN PENNSYLVANIA

Adam Vastbinder, one hundred acres of land, two horses and two cows; total valuation, $222.

John Vastbinder (single man) ; total valuation, $100.

Taxables, twenty; land taxed, seven hundred acres; grist- and saw-mills, two; horses, twenty-three; cows, thirty-five; aggregate valuation, $3313. Samuel Scott seemed to be the richest man in the county, with a total valuation of $600.

The pioneer settlers in what is now Punxsutawney were Dr. John W. Jenks and Elijah Heath, in the spring of 1818. The pioneer log cabin was erected for and by Dr. John W. Jenks, who was the pioneer physician. He was a graduate of Pennsylvania University in 1816. He kept open house and free entertainment for years. The pioneer minister was the Rev. David Barclay, in 1818 (Presbyterian).

The town was laid out as a white man's town by Rev. Barclay, in 1821, and the plot recorded in Indiana County. The present public square was a gift by him to the people. The Rev. Barclay and Mr. Jenks built a saw-mill on Elk Run, in 1824. The pioneer white male child born in what is now Punxsutawney was Phineas W. Jenks. The pioneer white female child was Cornelia Gaskill. The pioneer cemetery was what is known as the old grave-yard, the land for which was donated by Messrs. Jenks and Barclay. Pioneer interment, Hugh McKee, in 1821.

Other early settlers were Charles C. Gaskill, James E. Cooper, Isaac P. Carmalt, J. B. Henderson, John Hess, William Campbell, Thomas Mc-Kee, John R. Reece, Ephraim Bear, William Davis, George R. Slaysman, John Drum, and James St. Clair.

The pioneer store was opened by Charles R. Barclay, in 1820. The second by Dr. Jenks, in 1830.

Punxsutawney was made a borough February 25, 1850.

The pioneer hotel was opened in a log house by Adam Weaver, in 18—. This tavern stood a little east of where Joseph Shields's drug-store now (1902) stands. Weaver had no license until in the thirties.

The pioneer hotel that was licensed was the Eagle, now known as the City Hotel, kept by Elijah Heath, in 1822, and Elizabeth Winslow and Joseph Long, in 1829. Other early tavern-keepers were James St. Clair, Isaac Keck, William and James Campbell, and John McCoy.

Pioneer lawyer, David Barclay, December, 1849. Pioneer law student, Phineas W. Jenks, in 1852-54.

The pioneer church was built of hewed logs in 1826. It was Presbyterian. The pioneer school-house for that locality was built about 1823.

In 1832 Punxsutawney contained fifteen dwellings, two taverns, one church, one school-house, Barclay & Jenks's store, and one doctor.

The pioneer lodge of Odd Fellows in Punxsutawney was Mahoning Lodge, No. 250, I. O. O. F., and was organized May 31, 1847.

. 553

David B. McConnell, one of the very oldest residents of the Beechwoods settlement now living, was eighty-three years of age September 24, 1904. His parents moved into the Beechwoods in 1832, when he was a boy of eleven years. They came from Centre County, over the Waterford and Susquehanna turnpike, when there was an almost continuous wilderness from Curwensville to Brookville. Only two or three houses occupied the present site of Reynoldsville, and there were only four or five small clearings on the turnpike between Reynoldsville and Brookville.

The picnic in honor of his eighty-third birthday anniversary, Thursday, September 29, 1904, was held in the fine grove on the farm of his son, Ray McConnell, on the Ridgway road, nearly three miles from Brookville. Ray had prepared the grove for the occasion, by erecting a platform, placing seats, putting up nice tables, and providing chairs for the old people to sit on. We have seldom seen such comfortable arrangements.

Had rain not threatened, a big crowd would have been present. As it was, about a hundred and fifty people, a large number of them elderly persons, but still a good many young folks, were in attendance.

A splendid dinner was furnished, nearly all those who came bringing well-filled baskets with them, and everything was enjoyed in common. There was enough and to spare. After dinner a meeting was organized by electing J. G. Allen president, and all the men who were over eighty vice-presidents. Rev. A. E. Bartlett acted as secretary. Short addresses were made by Archie McCullough, of the Beechwoods; Dr. W. J. McKnight, of Brookville; W. A. Andrews, of Pine Creek, and others. Photographer Knapp was present, and took two or three pictures of the company. W. L. McCracken made the following list of persons in attendance who are sixty years old and upward. The list is not complete, as some who were there did not report to him:

NAME	AGE
Mrs. Frank Kelty	61
Mrs. C. H. Shobert	62
Ninian Cooper	79
James McFadden	81
Jerry Oiler	80
James Butler	76
Samuel Butler	72
A. J. Bartlett	73
Jacob Moore	70
Jesse Thompson	85
Dr. W. J. McKnight	69
Archie McCullough	76
Mrs. Archie McCullough	70
Andrew Moore	72
George Cook	87
John Ostrander	83

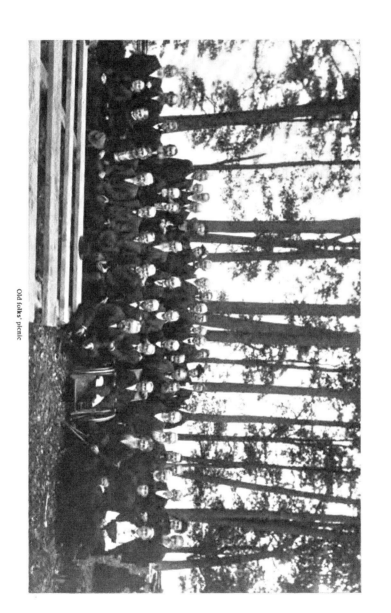

Old folks' picnic

NAME	AGE
Robert Richards	89
David Chitister	71
Mrs. David Chitister	67
David McConnell	83
Ed. Snyder	78
J. P. Lucas	68
E. Perrin	68
Mrs. W. Butler	72
John McMurray	67
Mrs. J. M. Pierce	67
James Harris	72
Perry Butler	66
Joseph Thomas	78
E. Weiser	71
Mrs. J. T. Carroll	68
E. McGarey	66
Nelson O'Connor	71
Wm. Kirkman	63
Robert Matson	85
C. H. Shobert	62
W. A. Andrews	72
Joe Ishman	75
John Clark	80
J. B. Jones	74
Dr. John Thompson	70
Dr. T. C. Lawson	61
John Shick	66
S. R. Milliron	60
James L. Moore	69
W. H. Arthurs	61
J. G. Allen	64
Daniel Burns	63
J. B. Henderson	62
Mrs. Rachel Barber	73
Mrs. W. J. McKnight	68
Mrs. S. Butler	65
C. B. McGiffin	69
T. T. Montgomery	65
R. F. Milliron	62
Mrs. M. L. Hinderliter	60
M. L. Hinderliter	60
D. S. Orr	82
Frank Walters	69
Wm. E. McGarey	63
Mrs. E. Perrin	62
Geo. McClellan	63
Mrs. John McMurray	61

Mr. McConnell was present, in excellent health, and enjoyed the occasion greatly. He was warmly greeted by all in attendance, and every one heartily wished him many more years of pleasant life.

CHAPTER XXXII

LAWRENCE COUNTY was erected out of portions of Beaver and Mercer Counties, by an act of Assembly, approved March 20, 1849, the organization to take place September 1, 1849. William Evans, of Indiana County, William F. Packer, of Lycoming, and William Potter, of Mifflin, were appointed commissioners to run and mark the boundary lines. Mr. Packer did not attend, and his place was supplied by James Potter, of Centre County. Henry Pearson, Esq., of New Castle, was the surveyor who performed the work of running the boundaries. The county is bounded north and south by the counties from which it is taken (Mercer and Beaver), east by Butler, and west by the Ohio line. New Castle was selected as the county seat.

The county was named after Perry's flagship in the battle of Lake Erie, which was named in honor of Captain James Lawrence, U.S.N., whose brilliant naval career was terminated by his obstinate defence of the frigate "Chesapeake" against the British ship "Shannon," in which conflict Lawrence was mortally wounded, and heroically uttered, as they carried him below, the memorable words, "DON'T GIVE UP THE SHIP!"

Like most of the counties west of the Allegheny River and north of the Ohio, it was settled chiefly by the Scotch-Irish, or the descendants of that race, who migrated from the older counties of Western Pennsylvania, the eastern counties, and some directly from Ireland itself. Cumberland, Franklin, Westmoreland, Fayette, and Washington furnished the greater number; but some came from other counties, and a few from the States of Delaware, Maryland, and Virginia. A considerable German element also was early introduced, and constituted a valuable portion of the population, whilst a few of English and Dutch ancestry came from New Jersey.

New Castle is the county seat, and is one of the most flourishing towns west of Pittsburg in the State. It was laid out in 1802, by a Mr. J. C. Stewart, who came to this locality, April, 1798, from the neighborhood of New Castle, in Delaware, and the name was probably given in honor of that old Swedish town.

The population of Lawrence County when organized was 21,079 people, including one hundred and thirty-two colored people. The population of

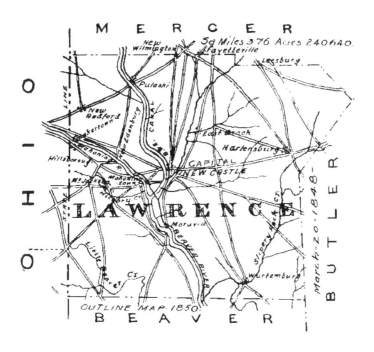

New Castle at that time was 1614, including fifty-one colored people. The pioneer election was held in the fall of 1849. The pioneer court was held in Lawrence County in the First Methodist Episcopal Church, in New Castle, on Monday, January 7, 1850. It was presided over by Hon. John Bredin, assisted by Hon. Jacob Bear.

The attorneys admitted at that term, belonging to Lawrence County, were Jonathan Ayres, L. L. McGuffin, J. K. Boyd, David Craig, Lewis Taylor, W. P. Buchanan, D. B. Kurtz, J. Hoffman, D. C. Cossitt, John M. Crawford, Geo. W. Watson, John N. McGuffin, and James Pollock. Attorneys were also present and admitted to practice from Beaver, Butler, Mercer, and Indiana Counties.

The court-house was not completed ready for occupancy until 1852, the contract for which had been let August, 1850, to Messrs. James M. Craig and William Hamilton for the sum of twelve thousand dollars.

The county at its organization was divided into thirteen townships.

The first white settlers after the Moravians came to Mahoning Township in 1793. When this region was first settled the roads were Indian trails.

The State of Pennsylvania, as early as 1805, appointed viewers to lay out and establish roads, then and now known as State roads. One of the earliest through this section ran from Scrubgrass, in Venango County, by the way of New Castle, to Youngstown, Ohio.

So far as this history will relate, New Castle comprises most of its history.

John Elliott erected the pioneer grist-mill in New Castle, in 1800.

Deer, wolves, bears, panthers, and rattle-snakes existed innumerable in and around New Castle.

The pioneer store was opened by Joseph Townsend, Jr., in a log cabin, in 1800.

The first death in New Castle was in 1802,—a daughter of William McComb.

The pioneer post-office was established in 1812. The pioneer postmaster was Joseph T. Boyd. Before 1812 the mail was obtained at Beaver.

The pioneer fire company was organized on the 29th day of September, 1836.

In 1840 New Castle contained 611 inhabitants. In 1850, the census gave New Castle Borough 1563, fifty-one of whom were colored.

The pioneer telegraph office was opened in the summer of 1849.

In 1806 New Castle contained but twenty houses.

New Castle was made a borough on the 25th day of March, 1825.

In 1813 New Castle had about thirty log buildings, and one hundred and fifty population.

Joseph Thompson started the first tannery in 1805.

Isaac Jones opened a shop for the manufacture of hats in 1805.

The pioneer linseed oil-mill was opened in 1841–42 by the Griswolds.

James D. White completed the Ætna Iron-Works in the fall of 1838.

Joseph S. White started the planing-mill about 1840.

In 1801, in Sandy Lake Township, Joseph Alexander had one mulatto slave man.

In 1810 Arthur Chenowith, of Virginia, came to New Castle, then Mercer, now Lawrence County, Pennsylvania, bringing with him one negro man, a slave,—to wit, " Black Jack."

In 1840 Day says,—.

" New Castle is located at the junction of Shenango and Neshannock Creeks, sixteen miles southwest from Mercer, and twenty-four miles from the confluence of the Beaver and Ohio Rivers. It was laid out about the year 1800; in 1806 it contained about twenty houses. Its population in 1840 was 611. The surrounding country is well adapted for the growth of wheat and wool. Its healthy and picturesque situation has been much admired by visitors.

" The Pennsylvania Canal, which is to connect Lake Erie with the Ohio River, passes through the town, and when completed will open another channel for the rich productions of the neighborhood. Iron ore is found in abundance for fifteen miles around; on the run near the town a furnace is being built, and a rolling-mill and nail factory in town. Bituminous coal, fire-clay, and quartz suitable for making glass exist in abundance in the neighboring hills. The water-power of the Neshannock and Shenango is immense; and, if all brought into use, must create a large manufacturing town. At three different points, powers may be created with a sufficiency of water, and from sixteen to twenty-eight feet fall. The town is passing the second stage in improvement, from frame buildings to brick. There are here Presbyterian, Seceder, and Methodist Churches, and a ' Protestant Methodist' Church is organized."

The Erie Canal was completed from New Castle to Erie in February, 1845.

The court-house was commenced in 1850 and completed in 1852.

The village of Croton was settled by William Crow, from Bucks County, Pennsylvania, about 1846. It now forms a part of the city.

The first regular preacher in charge of the Methodist Episcopal Church in Croton was the Rev. John Graham, the boy preacher.

Wampum Borough was first settled by Robert and John Davidson in March, 1796. Wampum was made a borough February 19, 1876.

Clinton was laid out by James Davidson in 1830.

Newburg was settled about 1798 by Bryce McGeehan.

Ennon Valley (old town) was laid out and lots sold in 1838 by Enoch Marvin.

The use of tokens was discontinued at communion seasons in 1867.

Lawrence County Court-House, 1852

The first settler in what is now the village of Pulaski was Daniel Ault, in 1800.

The village of Princeton was laid out by John Randolph in March, 1841.

The village of Rose Point was settled about 1803 by Mr. Stickle.

Parkstown was settled in the fall of 1800, by a colony from Virginia, consisting of William Park and others.

Fayetteville was laid out into thirty lots, and sold at auction February 8, 1828. William Mays was the first settler.

The oldest church organizations were the Old School Presbyterian and the United Presbyterian, both of which were introduced into the county about 1800.

The pioneer Baptist Church was organized in 1842, and the one in New Castle in 1843. The Catholics held services in what is now Lawrence County in 1831. The first organization in New Castle was about 1850. The Lutherans organized in New Castle in 1848.

The first discovery of coal was made by John Stockman, in Big Beaver Township, in 1810.

The agitation for the creation of Lawrence County began as early as 1820, and was persistently agitated until the spring of 1849, when it was made a success.

The Beaver division of the Pennsylvania Canal was completed to five miles above New Castle in November, 1833, and was open for business. The pioneer boat was the "General Mercer." This was exclusively a passenger boat.

MAIL FACILITIES

In the autumn of 1836 the mail arrangements were as follows:

ARRIVALS

From Beaver—Mondays and Thursdays, at eleven A.M.

From Mercer—Tuesdays and Fridays, at eleven A.M.

From Zelienople—Thursdays at noon.

From Poland, Ohio—Fridays, at ten A.M.

From New Bedford—Fridays, at eleven A.M.

DEPARTURES

For Beaver—Tuesdays and Fridays, at noon.

For Mercer—Mondays and Thursdays, at noon.

For Zelienople—Thursdays, at one P.M.

For Poland—Thursdays, at one P.M.

For New Bedford—Fridays, at one P.M.

JOSEPH T. BOYD, P. M.

In 1841 there were in New Castle one Seceder, one Methodist Episcopal, one Presbyterian, and one Protestant Methodist Church, and three Sabbath-schools.

August 22, 1849, President Zachary Taylor and Governor Johnston, of Pennsylvania, visited the town on their way to Beaver; this incident was the cause of great merry-making.

The pioneer barber was Thomas D. Berry, a colored man.

The pioneer market in New Castle was held in 1846.

The pioneer daguerrean gallery was established in 1847 by Richmond & Pomeroy.

" The first schools of which we have any knowledge were taught in private houses. These will date as early as the year 1800. A school-house was built near Harlansburg, and another in Little Beaver Township, in 1800. These were the first houses built for school purposes. James Boyles was, perhaps, the first teacher in the latter place, and Cornelius Stafford in the former. Stafford is mentioned as an Englishman, who made teaching a business. He taught in different parts of the county. Houses were built and schools taught, in 1802-03, in New Bedford, in Pulaski Township; in North Beaver, near the present location of Westfield Church; also in the northeastern part of the county, Washington and Plain Grove Townships. James Walker was among the first teachers in the vicinity of New Bedford. He taught in a log building erected by the Presbyterian Church, and afterwards in his own house. He is spoken of as a good teacher in the early schools, and continued in the work a number of years. George Monteith was one of the first teachers in the neighborhood of Pulaski, in 1804-05. About this time, houses were built and schools in operation in Perry Township, southeastern part of the county. Some of the early teachers were Samuel Sterritt, John Hines, and, later, Andrew Elliott. Schools were opened in Quakertown, in the western part of the county, in 1806-07; also, in Shenango Township, near Moravia, now Taylor Township; John Gallagher was one of the first teachers. Near the same date, 1806-07, James Leslie taught in North Beaver. Sampson Dilworth and Joshua Hartshorn, in what is now Little Beaver Township. John Byers, near Pulaski. John Gibson taught in Shenango Township, in one of the first school-houses, and was considered a successful teacher. A house was built as early as 1806-07, on the Lindall farm, and William Arnold was the first teacher. The first school-house in the present limits of Washington Township was built in the fall of 1803, on the Jordan farm, west of the present residence of Henry Jordan. Joseph Campbell was the first teacher. There were about twenty-five pupils, many of whom came a distance of several miles to attend school. Another house was built in 1807, and John Mitchell was the first teacher. The first school in Union Township was in 1806, in what is called Parkstown. A man by the name of Shearer was the first teacher. A school-house, southwest of

Princeton, in Slippery Rock Township, was built about 1808; and another on the Young farm, in 1810–11. A man by the name of Lewis was one of the early teachers. In the northern part of the county, the earliest schools were in private dwellings, about 1812–13. In what is now Neshannock Township, Miss Sarah De Wolf was the first teacher, and she appears to have been successful. A school was afterwards opened on the King farm, and James Galbreath taught several years. A house was erected a short distance east of King's Chapel, and Samuel Richards taught in 1823, and for some time after this. Houses were built and schools opened in different parts about this time. In Wilmington, school-houses were built in 1810, or near that time. Some of the early teachers were Master McCready and Hugh Watson.

" Hon. Thomas Pomeroy taught several terms; Dr. Popino also was a teacher for several years.

" Hon. William M. Francis, who was a member of the State Senate, was a member of the school board for over fifteen years, and also examined the teachers of the township during the same length of time. Most of the early teachers were males, and the schools were open for about three months in the winter.

" The schools were supported by subscription, each scholar paid so much per month or quarter. Often pupils had to travel along paths two and three miles to reach the nearest school.

" All the houses were built of logs, and most of them had a large fireplace, in which wood was burned, and this fuel was prepared by the patrons and older pupils. A part or whole log was cut out of the building, and over this opening greased paper was pasted to give light. Houses were floored with puncheons, and seats were made of slabs. These kind of houses were generally in use until the adoption of the present school law, when more and better houses were built. The branches taught in these schools were spelling, reading, writing, and arithmetic. The books used were few, the Bible as a text-book in reading; for advanced classes the spelling-book and arithmetic.

" The authentic history of the early schools of New Castle is very meagre, and can only be learned from the old residents, whose memory of many of the events, so far in the past, must necessarily, in many instances, be very indistinct.

" The earliest schools were supported by subscription, and were taught in private houses. According to the most reliable information, the first school was taught by one Robert Dickey, and was opened about the year 1804. The next teacher was John Dickey, a younger brother of Robert.

" The name of Richard Shearer is mentioned as the third teacher. About the year 1806 the fourth teacher, Joseph Thornton, came here from Chambersburg, Franklin County; his abiding faith in the use of the birch is the principal characteristic remembered by his historian. Next on the roll of early teachers appears the name of Alexander Duncan. After him we find the name of Miss Sarah De Wolf, said to have been the first regular female teacher of a New Castle school.

"Matthew Calvin is enrolled as the next teacher. He appeared upon the scene about 1814, and taught in a house on Beaver Street, nearly opposite the residence of Joseph Justice, Esq.

"The borough of New Castle was incorporated March 25, 1825, and originally embraced all the territory now constituting the first and second wards of the present city, except that portion lying south of County Line Street, in the point between the Neshannock and Shenango Creeks, which was taken into the borough at some subsequent period.

"About this time a frame house, the first building erected exclusively for school purposes, was built upon the lot belonging to the First Presbyterian Church, now the "Old Brewery." Our history informs us, however, that the first house used for school purposes was a log cabin, about eighteen feet square, situated near the spring, at the base of ' Shaw's Hill.' "—*School Report, 1877.*

The first regular doctor who settled in New Castle and in Lawrence County was Dr. John Dickey.

George P. Shaw was the first lawyer in New Castle.

REVOLUTIONARY SOLDIERS

North Beaver Township.—William McCord, James Alsworth, Francis Nesbit, William Carson, John Coleman, Jacob Justice, and Jeremiah Bannon were all out for some length of time during the Revolution, some of them for several years.

Perry Township.—Matthew Murray, Matthew Stewart, John Stewart.

Plain Grove Township.—John Gealey, James Ramsey.

Pulaski Township.—James Stevenson.

Scott Township.—Colonel Bernard Hubley, William Locke.

Shenango Township.—William Tindall.

Washington Township.—Henry Gordon, 1st.

Taylor Township.—John Butcher, Joseph McMurray, " Scotch John Moore," a deserter from the British army.

Neshannock Township.—John Moore, William Richards.

Mahoning Township.— —— Ashton.

New Castle.—Captain Jonathan Smith.

CHAPTER XXXIII

M'KEAN COUNTY—FORMATION OF COUNTY—LOCATION OF COUNTY SEAT—
OFFICERS—ROADS—PIONEER SETTLERS—INDIAN NAMES OF STREAMS—
HUNTERS—SLAVES—HARDSHIPS—LANDS, ETC.

McKEAN COUNTY was separated from Lycoming County by the act of March 26, 1804. It was named in honor of Governor Thomas McKean. Previous to 1814 the county was for a time attached to Centre County, and the records were kept at Bellefonte. In 1814 McKean was attached to Lycoming for judicial and elective purposes. The counties of McKean and Potter were then as formerly united, having one treasurer, one board of commissioners, and one board of auditors. The commissioners held their meetings at the house of Benjamin Bents, on the Allegheny River, and a little east of the county line.

Hon. W. O. Smith says,—

" The Allegheny is a beautiful river, with a volume of water sufficient to carry the commerce of an empire, well confined within its banks and lined on either side with vast stores of mineral wealth, consisting of coal, iron, limestone, fire-clay, glass-sand rock, and building stone. This magnificent stream, three hundred miles in length, with a watershed of nearly twelve thousand square miles, an average width of about twelve hundred feet, and discharging at low stage seventy-five thousand cubic feet of water per minute, courses through a country rich in mineral resources, where the business energies of man have reached their highest development."

McKean County is situated on the northern border of the State, being the third county seat from the west line thereof. It has a length on the State line of nearly forty miles, and a depth of about twenty-five miles, containing about one thousand square miles.

The population of the county in 1810 was 142; in 1820, 728; in 1830, 1439; in 1840, 2975.

CERES ROAD

In 1825 the Ceres road, a State road, afterwards incorrectly called the Serious road, was laid out from Ceres, McKean County, near the New York State line, through Smethport and what is now Reynoldsville, to the town of Indiana, in Indiana County, Pennsylvania. It was completed in 1828.

I now quote from Day's " Historical Collections:"

" The great east and west State road, opened in 1816–18, runs from

Kenjua, on the Allegheny, through the centre of the county to Coudersport and Wellsborough. Another road, opened in 1827–29, runs from Smethport, through Caledonia and Karthauss, to Milesburg, near Bellefonte; another, by way of Coudersport, to Jersey Shore, in Lycoming County.

"The greater part of this county is, and has been for many years, owned in immense tracts by gentlemen residing in the lower part of the State, and by the Holland Land Company. The principal individual owners are Messrs. John Keating & Co., Richards and Jones, and the heirs of William Bingham and Jacob Ridgway, of Philadelphia, James Trimble, Esq., of Harrisburg, and B. B. Cooper, Esq., of New Jersey. These gentlemen have done much by their enterprise and capital toward opening roads and establishing schools in the county. Most of them have agents in the county, from whom their lands may be purchased at from one dollar to three dollars per acre, with a credit of from five to ten years, payable by instalments.

"Smethport, the county seat, a pleasant town, is situated on the left bank of Potato Creek, where the great east and west road crosses, and at the confluence of Marvin Creek. It contains the court-house, substantially built of brick, an academy, a Methodist church, and two Congregational societies who attend service in the public buildings; two printing-offices, seven stores, three taverns, grist-mill, saw-mill, and clothing-mill. The following facts relating to the early settlement of this place, and of others in the county, are derived from a communication in Hazard's *Register* for 1832, by O. J. Hamlin, Esq.

"'Smethport was laid out under the superintendence of John Bell, Thomas Smith, and John C. Brevost, in 1807. The first house was erected by Captain Arnold Hunter, in 1811; another was built in 1812; but both abandoned in 1814. No permanent settlement was commenced until 1822. About this time the first county commissioners were elected, and held their office in a small building erected by Dr. Eastman, at the lower part of the town plot. The first commissioners were Rensselaer Wright and Jonathan Colegrove, for McKean, and John Taggart, for Potter County; Joseph Otto, treasurer. This county was organized for judicial purposes in 1826; and the first county court was held in September of that year. The court-house, a respectable brick building, was erected this year. At this time there were but about half a dozen dwelling-houses. A weekly mail arrives here from the north, the east, the southeast, the south, and west; and a stage commenced running to Coudersport, thence to Jersey Shore, or to Wellsborough. By the Legislature an appropriation of two thousand dollars was made for an academy' at Smethport. Several years ago John Keating, Esq., gave five hundred dollars and one hundred and fifty acres of land adjoining the village, as a donation toward such an institution, and individuals of McKean County have subscribed rising of five hundred dollars for that purpose. These amounts have been vested in productive funds.

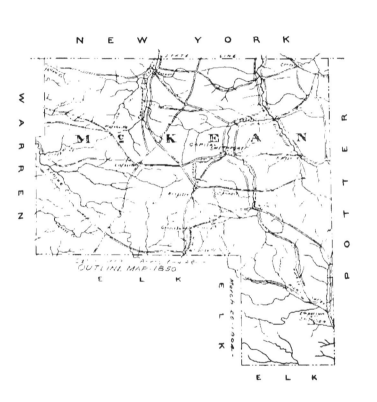

N E W   Y O R K

W A R R E N

M C K E A N

P O T T E R

OUTLINE MAP 1850

E L K

E L K

E L K

" ' Several years previous to 1810 the first settlement commenced in the county began. A Mr. King, an enterprising English gentleman, with several friends of his from England, settled on the Oswaya Creek, in Ceres Township, twenty-five miles from Smethport. There is now a flourishing settlement here, and some of the oldest orchards are in that neighborhood. This neighborhood is usually called King's settlement.

" ' The first settlers of this county suffered great inconveniences; so much greater than those of the present day that there is scarce a comparison. They found here a dense wilderness, without a road, or an inhabitant, save the beasts of the forest, some of which were of a very ferocious character, while others served as a slender support to those who practised hunting. The first settlement of which I have a correct account was made by six families from the State of New York, who came on about the same time, and located on Potato Creek, from three to seven miles north of Smethport, in 1810. They had great difficulty in getting to their new homes, having to bring their families and goods up the stream in canoes. There was no settlement within many miles of them; and they were even obliged for a time to bring their provisions in by canoes or on pack-horses. All kinds of eatables were very dear, even at the nearest settlements. This settlement suffered many privations; but those settlers are now well compensated, for they are the owners of flourishing farms, and are themselves in a prosperous condition. It is usually known by the name of the lower settlement.

" ' Norwich settlement, lying along the Potato Creek, commencing about four miles southeast from Smethport, and extending up that stream, was commenced in 1815, when fourteen families came on, having exchanged their property in Norwich, Chenango County, New York, with Messrs. Cooper, McIlvain & Co., for those lands where they now reside, being then an entire wilderness. Having no roads, they were obliged to ascend the Potato Creek, with much labor and expense, in canoes, with their families and movables. They were under much embarrassment for the first year or two, for want of roads and provisions; and were often obliged to get their provisions, grain, etc., in Jersey Shore, a distance of more than one hundred miles, on pack-horses. Corn was worth, when got here, two dollars per bushel, and salt was sold for fourteen dollars per barrel. This settlement went on vigorously, and in two or three years raised more than sufficient for their own consumption. It is now in a flourishing situation.

" ' A settlement had been commenced at Instanter, four miles west of the Norwich settlement, a short time previous to the latter; and in 1821 or 1822 four hundred acres of land were cleared on one farm, belonging to Jacob Ridgway, Esq., under the superintendence of P. E. Scull, who has always been an active man in furthering the improvement of this county. Judge Bishop, now one of our associate judges, was the first settler at that place. Since those settlements were formed, others have been commenced and carried on in different parts of the county. The townships of Bradford and Corydon have within the last three years been rapidly increasing.

" ' In 1831 the manufacture of salt was commenced by Messrs. Allen Rice & Co., at a salt spring in the southeastern part of Sergeant Township. The operations were found quite favorable, and large boiling works erected. Salt was made of an excellent quality, and the water found to bear a good per cent.'

" Port Allegheny is on the Allegheny River, ten miles east of Smethport, near the confluence of the Portage branch. The Canoe Place is about two miles above. It was here that the early settlers of Warren County came about the year 1795, constructed a canoe, and floated down to the mouth of the Conewango.

" Bradford is a small village recently started in the forks of Tunenguant, on land purchased from the United States Land Company, better known as the Boston Company.

" Ceres, formerly King's settlement, is a smart and flourishing village, inhabited by New York and Yankee lumbermen, on Oswaya Creek, in the northeastern corner of the county. It contains a Methodist church, several stores, mills, etc.

" Teutonia is the name of the new German town, situated on the right bank of Stanton Creek, five miles southwest of Smethport. This town is the property of ' The Society of Industry.' It was started in March, 1843, on the plan and by the enterprise of Mr. Henry Ginal, a German now residing in Philadelphia, and agent of the Society. It contains at present about four hundred and fifty inhabitants. A school-house is built, but no church. Some seventy or eighty log houses have been erected, besides a steam saw-mill, a large tannery, and a store furnished with every article necessary for food and clothing. The Society is in possession of forty thousand acres of land, a considerable part of which is already cleared, and they keep from forty to fifty hands at chopping, all of them members of the Society. Excellent bituminous coal, iron ore, limestone, brick-clay, etc., abound on the lands. The soil is generally of good quality. The Society is founded on the principle of community of property, money and furniture excepted, and is sustained by the co-operation of its members; an equal distribution of the profits being made half-yearly. In its fundamental principles it differs from Fourier's system. The Society has about forty thousand dollars capital; some sixteen thousand dollars of which is invested in land. This stock is divided into six hundred and sixty shares, of which three hundred and sixty are already sold. When the balance is sold the number will be limited, and shareholders will be admitted only by buying out others. The shares are now worth about two hundred dollars; originally they were only worth one hundred dollars, but have risen with the improvements. The land is divided into several districts; in the centre of each there is to be a town, with houses built in

Paul Darling, born in Smethport, November 5, 1823, school-master, financier, philanthropist, now deceased

uniform style, and the stables and barns will be outside of the village. Marriage is not only allowed, but encouraged, and each family resides in its separate house, possessing its own furniture and money. Clothing of a plain and uniform kind, provisions, fuel, etc., are regularly distributed by rations from the society's common stores. An individual becomes a member by purchasing a share of stock, going on the ground, and working with the rest. The society will build him a house if married; or furnish him or her with a lodging if single. Children, when grown up, become members by conforming to the rules of the Society. Married women are not obliged to work for the community, but devote their attention to the care of their own families."

"Near Port Allegheny the earliest settlers were Judge Samuel Stanton, Jonathan Foster, and Dr. Horace Coleman. Judge Stanton and Dr. Coleman were active and public-spirited men, did all in their power to help on the settlement of the country, and were highly esteemed by the then few settlers of the county. Judge Stanton died many years ago while absent at Bellefonte upon some public business. Mr. Foster was accidentally shot by his son. He and his son were out hunting wolves. Each wore a wolf-skin cap, and each was ignorant of the vicinity of the other. It was the custom with wolf-hunters to howl in imitation of the wolf, and thus decoy their prey to within rifle-shot. After being out some time one howled; the other, thinking that he had heard a wolf, answered; both were deceived, and each began cautiously to creep toward his supposed prey. A succession of calls and counter-calls were kept up with sufficient accuracy of imitation to keep both deceived as to the real character of the other. Finally, after much manœuvring on both sides, and conducted after the known habits of the wolf, they approached very near each other, when the quick eye of the younger man caught sight of the wolf-skin cap of the elder as he raised his head to peer over a log, and he instantly fired. What must have been the feelings of that son as he walked triumphantly up to his prey, and found lying before him, not the body of the savage wolf, but that of his dying father! Could life be sufficiently long or busy to eradicate that scene from his memory? Dr. Coleman lived to ripe old age, and died respected by all, and surrounded by a large family, who do ample credit to the efforts of their sire in their behalf." —*Egle's History of Pennsylvania.*

The pioneer court held in McKean County was presided over by Hon. Edward Herrick, on September 25, 1826. The Associates were Joseph Otto and Joel Bishop. The court was held in the court-house, which had been completed. The jail was in process of erection at that time, and was completed soon after. Up to that time the courts of McKean County had been held in Coudersport, Potter County.

The prominent pioneer hunters were Eben Burbanks, Samuel Beckwith, Daniel Corneline, Rufus Cory, Ralph Hill, Nathan White, Henry Willard, Arthur Young, and Stephen Young.

The first coal found in the county was at Instanter, in 1815. Prior to 1840 wild lands were assessed at fifty cents per acre. Asylum Peters was born at what is now the city of Bradford in 1793. He was a negro slave, sold to William Ayres for one hundred dollars, who moved to Potter County in 1808. Peters's father and mother must have been slaves in what is now McKean County.

The pioneer physician was Dr. George Darling at Smethport, in 1827.

The pioneer school was at Instanter, in 1809.

Indian names for streams were, Kinzua, fish; Tunnanguant, bull-frog; Nien-un-dah, potato creek. Marvin Creek took its name from the pioneer who settled on its banks. The second story of the pioneer court-house was used for religious services until after 1830. Up to that date there was not a church structure in the county.

The panther-hunters in 1827 were Joseph Silverkeel, an Indian, Dan. Killbuck, an Indian, Simon Beckwith, William and Dan. Lewis, and Ralph Hill. Panthers were killed years after this, but not so many.

The first mention of petroleum oil in history was by Herodotus, four hundred and forty years before Christ. The Cuba Oil Spring in New York was discovered July 18, 1627. In 1806 Nathaniel Carey established a business on Oil Creek, Venango County. In 1819 John Gibson struck oil on the Conemaugh River near Georgetown, Westmoreland County, at a depth of two hundred and seven feet. He was boring for salt.

The pioneer school in Smethport was in the Eastman building, in 1823–24; Ira H. Curtis, master. The pioneer school in Port Allegheny, under the law of 1834, was taught by Miss Eliza Manning.

CHAPTER XXXIV

MERCER COUNTY is one of the range contiguous to the western boundary of the State. It was taken from Allegheny County by the act of March 12, 1800. Length, thirty-two miles; breadth, twenty-six miles; area, seven hundred and sixty-five square miles. Population in 1800, 3228; in 1810, 8277; in 1820, 11,681; in 1830, 19,729; in 1840, 32,873.

Mercer County was a wilderness until several years after the passage of the celebrated land law of April, 1792, providing for the survey and settlement of all the lands "north and west of the Ohio and Allegheny Rivers and Conewango Creek." Soon after peace was restored to the frontier, in 1795, settlements were made extensively about the southern end of Mercer County, in the forks of Mahoning, Shenango, and Neshannock Creeks.

The adventures of these worthy pioneers were few, and of little general interest. The county was for many years retarded in its growth, and the actual settlers were greatly harassed by the various and conflicting titles to land growing out of the acts of 1785 and 1792.

The pioneer settlers were principally Scotch-Irish, and all Presbyterians.

"The surface of the county is undulating, but little broken, and peculiarly well watered. It is covered with springs and small streams running into the larger creeks. These creeks consist of the Big Shenango on the west, which rises in Crawford County; Neshannock in the centre, with heads all over the northern central portion of the county, and Wolf Creek on the east. These streams all run in a southerly direction, and eventually are swallowed up in the Big Beaver, that empties itself into the Ohio River at Rochester. In addition to these there is the Little Shenango, that runs across a portion of the northern end of the county from east to west, rising six or seven miles east of the central line from south to north, and that empties into the Big Shenango at Greenville; and also Sandy Creek, that takes its rise in Crawford County, and, running diagonally through the northeast quarter, empties itself into the Allegheny River about twelve miles below Franklin. Sandy Lake, a sheet of water about a mile and a half long and half a mile wide, situated near the centre of the northeast quarter of the county, discharges its surplus water into Sandy Creek. The character of its general surface, its bountiful supply of water, and richness of soil was well calculated to make it the foremost agricultural county in this part of the State; nor has it disappointed the anticipations of its early settlers, for it is now not only a fine agricultural, but a heavy and prosperous mining and iron county, notwithstanding that it lost nearly a fourth of its territory in the erection of Lawrence County.

The territory comprising Mercer County was filled with Indians and wild animals before the white man's advent, and for several years after. The Indians were Senecas and popularly called Cornplanters. They lived by hunting and fishing.

There were three large Indian towns, one where Mercer is now, containing seventy lodges; one at the big bend, and the other at Pine Swamp, what is now Jackson Township.

About 1804 a noted hunter, James Jeffers, entered this region. " There are a number of incidents related concerning his hostility to the Indian race, which had been aroused on account of the cruelty with which some of his relatives had been treated by the savages. Whether these are true or not cannot now be determined. They belong, however, to the folk-lore of the county, and as such deserve recital. It is said that on one occasion, while roaming through the forest, he suddenly met two Indians. They instinctively knew him to be a foe, and both at once dodged behind the cover of friendly trees. Jeffers perceived that the contest of one against two would be an unequal one, if carried on squarely, so he resorted to artifice to overcome the odds. Taking off his cap he placed it over the muzzle of his rifle, and exposed it, apparently incautiously, to the view of his antagonists. This had the desired effect. Thinking it was his head which they saw, one of them instantly shot and sent a ball through the empty cap. Jeffers dropped the cap to the ground, giving a death-like groan as he did so. The two Indians at once sprang from cover, and were rushing forward to secure the scalp of their supposed victim, when the latter stepped forth, cocked his rifle and prepared to shoot. He was at first at a loss to know which of the two had the loaded rifle, but perceiving one of them lift his weapon to his shoulder, he surmised that he was the dangerous foe, and accordingly shot him. The remaining savage sprang forward with a huge knife and engaged in a hand to hand conflict, but the superior cunning of the white man caused victory to perch on his side. As the savage was about to make a final thrust, Jeffers deflected the course of the knife, and it sheathed itself in the breast of the Indian himself, instantly killing him."

The wild animals in what is now Mercer County were the usual kind that inhabited this region, and the following story will give you an idea of the snake inhabitants.

About 1800, or 1803, John Johnson lived on a piece of land near the

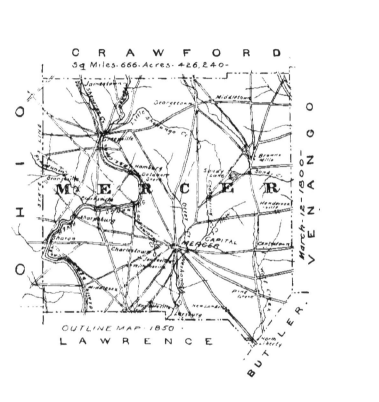

CRAWFORD
Sq. Miles. 666. Acres. 426,240.

OHIO

MERCER

VENANGO
March 12. 1800

OUTLINE MAP. 1850.

LAWRENCE

BUTLER.

Asa Arnold farm. This farm is situated on the west of Yankee Ridge. Johnson's wife went out from her cabin early one morning to get her cows. She had not gone far until she found herself surrounded with rattlesnakes. They were in such numbers that she was compelled to climb a dogwood that stood near by. Her cries for help reached her husband, and he came to her relief. In excitement, he said, " Polly, I can't relieve you myself, there are too many snakes;" and then running to his neighbor, Asa Arnold, he came back with new courage. With hickory poles, these two men cut their way through the snakes until Mrs. Johnson was relieved. Both men sickened in this work and had to rest for a time, and then go at the destruction again. The yellow rattlesnakes were counted and piled, two hundred in number, while there were many black and other snakes left on the ground uncounted. Some of the rattles counted as many as twenty-five. The rattlers of Northwestern Pennsylvania are the banded variety, called timber rattlers.

Mercer, 1843

In the fall of the year 1806 several families came in from Westmoreland, Allegheny, and Washington Counties, and made an opening. The only one remaining over that winter was John Findley, but the others came back in the spring. John Findley's neighbors at that time were John Pugh, James Braden, John Garvin, William Alexander, Mr. Hawthorn, and Mr. McCullough.

" Mercer, the county seat, is situated near the Neshannock Creek, on elevated ground, fifty-seven miles northwest from Pittsburg by the turnpike. It was laid out in 1803 by John Findley, William Mortimore, and William McMillan, trustees, on two hundred acres of land given to the county by John Hoge, of Washington County, who owned large tracts of land in the vicinity. The hill on which it is situated was formerly a dense hazel thicket. The first courts were held in an old log court-house. The court and county officers are now accommodated in elegant public buildings of brick, surrounded by a verdant lawn planted with trees, and enclosed by a neat white fence. In 1807 there were only two or three houses in the place. In 1840 it had a population of seven hundred and eighty-one. The dwellings are neat and substantial, and display a pleasing variety of architectural embellishment. Besides the county buildings, there are in the town an academy, Methodist, Union, Seeder, Old and New School Presbyterian churches, a foundry, and the usual stores and taverns. Daily lines of stages pass through on the Pittsburg and Erie turnpike.

" West Greenville is situated in the northwestern part of the county, on the Shenango River, and is surrounded by large bodies of fine land. The Erie Extension Canal passes through the town, affording every facility to commerce. There are in the immediate vicinity extensive beds of iron ore and mines of very superior coal, which will form an important article of export to the lake. The rapid growth of the town, and the taste and beauty exhibited in its embellishments, indicate the advantages of its location. Seven years since the population was not more than three hundred; it numbered in 1840, six hundred and twenty-six. The Shenango River affords a very ample water-power, which drives several large mills, and is still not all occupied."—*Day's Collections.*

In 1840 there were twelve churches in the county, and special attention was paid to common school education.

The public road from Pittsburg to Erie, through Mercer, Meadville, etc., was authorized and laid out when the territory was under the control of Crawford County.

In 1817 the Mercer and Meadville Turnpike Company was chartered. In 1821 the company opened the line for general traffic. The streams of the county at first had to be forded, but later temporary wooden bridges were erected.

BEAVER AND ERIE CANAL

In 1822-23 the Legislature authorized a survey. In 1824 the United States government did the same. In 1827 the Legislature passed an act for the construction. Ground was broken on the French Creek feeder at Meadville, August 24, 1827, and it was completed to Conneaut Lake in 1834.

In 1843 ninety-seven miles of the main line had been finished, and four million dollars had been expended on the improvement by the State. The work was now turned over without cost to the Erie Canal Company, and was finished by the company December 5, 1844, when the first two boats, the " Queen of the West," a passenger packet, and the " R. S. Reed," loaded with Mercer County coal, passed through to Erie.

William Fruit, of Clarksville, was a pioneer in the coal business, and made this his first shipment of coal to Erie. The canal-boat held twenty-seven tons of coal.

At Erie his new fuel was not in demand. He eventually sold it at two dollars per ton.

Other coal operators were General James Pierce and Rev. George McCleery.

In 1806 a weekly mail was established from Pittsburg to Erie by the way of Mercer,—a horseback route; a semi-weekly in 1818; a tri-weekly in 1824.

In 1821 a stage route was opened, and a daily mail line was authorized in 1827.

Mercer, July 1, 1805, Cunningham S. Semple. Sharon, August 11, 1819, Elias Jones. Greenville, January 9, 1828, Alexander P. Waugh. James-town, April 3, 1833, John Williamson, Jr. Clark, July 14, 1833, John Fruit. New Vernon, July 20, 1837, John M. Montgomery. Perrine, February 16, 1833, William H. Perrine. Salem, March 6, 1832, William Leech. Sandy Lake, January 30, 1833, Thomas J. Brown. North Liberty, January 15, 1840, Robert Shaw. West Middlesex, August 30, 1839, Robert B. Young. Grove City, July 11, 1844, William Fleming. Centretown, January 9, 1840, John Tumelson. Leesburg, December 3, 1836, Arthur Johnston. London, March 16, 1848, David Gilson. New Lebanon, December 17, 1849, James A. Leech.

IRON FURNACES

In 1846 there were ten iron furnaces in Mercer County.

The pioneer agricultural society was in existence as early as January 5, 1828. Joseph Justice was president, Nathaniel McElevey, secretary, and Joseph Emery, treasurer.

The *Mercer Whig* began June 15, 1844, John B. Butler, editor. In 1830 the *West Greenville Gazette* was started by Richard Hill. In 1848 J. W. Mason started the *Weekly Express*. In 1852, the paper was purchased by the Rev. William Orvis, and was published as an antislavery educator. This antislavery paper was in Greenville.

PIONEER DOCTORS

Who the pioneer doctor was in Mercer County is not known. Among the early ones were Dr. Clark, the two Cossitts, Dr. Magoffin, Sr., Dr. Magoffin, Jr., and two Mehards.

The antislavery agitation began in Mercer County about June 15, 1835, by the Rev. Nathaniel West and others.

THE PIONEER JUSTICE

Alexander Dumars was appointed justice of the peace in 1810. Allan Hill prosecuted Joseph Nesbit before Squire Dumars for damages done by Nesbit's cows to Hill's cornfield.

" The parties to the suit appeared. Nesbit claimed that it was Hill's fault; that he would not keep up a fence around his field; that he had himself worked to repair and put up his fence, and had also sent hands for that purpose, but that Hill would do nothing to preserve his own grain. The Squire said, ' If that is the kind of a man Hill is, he ought to be loaded with powder and blown to hell.' The wily Irishman, Nesbitt, immediately said, ' If that is the judgment of your honor, please give us an execution, and let us have it carried out at once.' "

INDUSTRIES

The pioneer industries were saw-mills, grist-mills, and whiskey distilleries, built as early as 1801–02, and flaxseed oil-mills in 1812.

A fulling-mill was erected in 1803 by Benoni Tuttle.

" In 1849 the townships of Mahoning, Neshannock, and Slippery Rock, together with a strip of territory of about half a mile in width taken from the southern sides of the townships of Springfield, Wilmington, and Shenango, were detached from Mercer to contribute to the erection of Lawrence County. In these townships were the villages of Harlansburg, New Wilmington, Pulaski, New Bedford, Hillsville, Edenburg, Eastbrook, and the borough of New Castle, containing altogether quite a third of the population of the county. And thus stand the bounds of Mercer County, with its subdivisions into townships in the one hundred and twelfth year of independence, and the eighty-eighth year of its erection as a separate county by the Legislature of Pennsylvania."

The pioneer fire company of Mercer Borough was organized June 28, 1824.

The pioneer missionary society in Mercer County held its first meeting in Mercer on June 11, 1834, Rev. Samuel Tait, president; Rev. J. L. Dinwiddie, secretary. It was a Presbyterian society.

The first school-house in the borough of Mercer was a one story brick about twenty feet square, heated by a ten-plate stove.

I copy the following from Egle's " History of Pennsylvania:"

" Although declared a county by act of Assembly in 1800, for all practical purposes it constituted a part of Crawford until February, 1804, when the first and second courts were held at the house of Joseph Hunter, situated on Mill Creek, on the mill property near Mercer, now owned by the Hon. William Stewart, in February and May of that year. The commission of Hon. Jesse Moore, as president judge of the circuit composed of the counties of Beaver, Butler, Mercer, Crawford, and Erie, was read; also the commissions of Alexander Brown and Alexander Wright as judges for Mercer County. The various commissions of John Findley (who was the eldest son of the historic William Findley that was so prominent in Congress in the support of Thomas Jefferson) as prothonotary, clerk of the courts, etc., was also read; so also that of William Byers as sheriff, James Braden as coroner, and John W. Hunter as deputy prosecuting attorney. The sheriff and coroner, as well as a board of county commissioners, consisting of Robert Bole, Andrew Denniston, and Thomas Robb, it is presumed were elected in October, 1803.

The attorneys admitted to practice at the first court were John W. Hunter, Joseph Shannon, C. S. Sample, S. B. Foster, A. W. Foster, Ralph Marlin, Edward Work, Patrick Farrelly, William Ayres, Henry Baldwin, and Steel Sample. The two Fosters, Farrelly, Ayres, Baldwin, and Steel Sample, all afterwards turned out to be men of mark and ability.

At the second term of court, held in May, the commission of William Amberson as an additional judge for Mercer County was read. This gave three associate judges. The writer of this, who, as a little boy, occasionally dropped into the court-house, along between 1814 and 1820, was indelibly impressed with the grand dignity of the president judge. He was a heavy, solemn-looking man, retaining the costume of the old-style gentleman,—small clothes, shoe-buckles, knee-buckles, bald head, but hair long behind and done up in a queue, and head and hair and collar of the black coat covered with a white powder sprinkled thereon. He has since seen the Supreme Court of the United States in session. The black gowns of the judges sitting in a row, the low colloquial tone in which causes are argued, and the quietness enforced certainly gave it a very dignified aspect, but still there was lacking the grand old powdered head and queue that gave Judge Moore the advantage in solemn and imposing dignity.

It was with the funds arising from the sale of town lots that the first court-house, standing in the centre of the public square, was built. On the 19th of May, 1807, John Chambers, John Leech, and William McMillan, the then county commissioners, contracted with Joseph Smith and John McCurdy for the building thereof, for the sum of seven thousand one hundred and sixteen dollars. It was a square brick building, two stories high, with wings for the offices. In 1840, there was an addition put to it to get better office accommodations, at a cost of about two thousand dollars. The first court-house and jail, however, was a log structure on the ground now occupied by the First National Bank, the lower story for a jail being built of squared logs let down flat and dove-tailed at the corners, and the court-room above, which was reached by stairs on the outside of the building. Until this construction was ready for prisoners, the county prison was a room in the house of James Braden, which the commissioners rented and fitted up for that purpose.

" The travelled route through northwestern Pennsylvania was that established by the French in 1752,—water communication up the Allegheny River to the mouth of French Creek, then up that stream to Waterford, and from thence by an opened road to Erie. It was this route that was followed by Colonel Washington in 1753, when sent by Governor Dinwiddie, of Virginia, to demand from the French an explanation of their designs in establishing military posts on the waters of the Ohio. This route left Mercer County entirely to the west, and may explain why settlements in Venango, Crawford, and Erie, which it traversed, preceded those formed in Mercer. There were no settlements made in it until after Wayne's victory over the Indians and the peace with them that followed in 1795. After this, in the fall of 1795, the surveyors began their labors, followed closely by the first settlers. Benjamin Stokely now occupies the farm on which his father thus commenced the settlement.

"Among the first settlers along the Shenango were the grandfathers of the present generations of the Quinbys, Budds, Carnes, Beans, McKnights, McGranahans, Campbells, Hoaglands, Mossmans, Leeches, Fells, Hunters, and Christys. In the Neshannock and Mahoning regions, the Byers, Sankeys, Fishers, Watsons, Chenowiths, and Pearsons made their first settlement. In the centre, the Stokelys, Zahnisers, Garvins, Alexanders, Findleys, Junkins, Dennistons, McCulloughs, Pews, Rambos, Coulsons, and Hosacks. In the southeast corner, the Roses, McMillans, Breckenridges, McCoys, and Courtneys. In the Sandy Lake and French Creek region, the Gordons, McCrackens, DeFrances, Carnahans, Browns, Carmichaels, Carrols, Kilgores, Riggs, Condits, and McCloskeys. In the way of startling adventure, these men were not history-makers. Their mission was to open up a wilderness for the use of civilized man, and secure to themselves and posterity comfortable homes. In striving to do this they underwent many privations. It took time to open out fields and get them under cultivation, so that bread could be got without transportation on horseback from Pittsburg or the settlements in Washington County, and before they could provide properly for the keeping of their stock over winter. The first stock was only wintered by the felling of maple- and linwood-trees to enable the cattle to browse on the buds. The forest then afforded them bear meat, venison, and turkey in abundance, but their appetites tired of this as the only food, and "hog and hominy," diversified with mush and milk, was the first change they could hope to make in their diet. Wolves, panthers, and bears were by no means scarce, but as other game was plenty, these animals did not indulge in the more dangerous chase of man. A wolf scalp then brought a premium of eight dollars out of the county treasury, and was a source of profit to quite a number of hunters.

"In the war of 1812 the people of Mercer County were frequently called upon to give their aid in the defence of Erie, where the fleet of Commodore Perry was being built. On these alarms, which were about as frequent as a vessel of the enemy hove in sight in the lake offing, the whole county would be aroused by runners in a day, and in a very few hours most of the able-bodied male population, whether belonging to a volunteer company or the militia, would be on their march to Erie. On one occasion the news came to Mercer on a Sunday while the Rev. S. Tait was preaching in the court-house. The sermon was suspended, the startling news announced from the pulpit, the dismissing benediction given, and immediate preparations for the march commenced. On the next day the military force of the county was well on its way to Erie. At another time the news of a threatened invasion came in the middle of the grain harvest. This made no difference; the response was immediate. It was on this occasion that Mr. John Findley dropped the sickle in his tracks in the wheat-field, hastened to his house, and, seizing his gun, with such provisions as his wife had at hand to put in his haversack, started on his way to the defence of his country. On his return, six weeks afterwards, the sickle was found by him where it had been dropped. It was on one of these occasions that but a single man was left in the county town,—Cunningham Sample, an old lawyer, completely unmanned by age and obesity.

" The history of Mercer County schools is commensurate with the or-ganization of the county in 1800. Although at that time there were no school-houses in the county, the education of the children was not entirely neg-lected. At that time, we find in some localities, schools were organized in families, and teachers secured for seventy-five cents or one dollar per week. Five or six years passed away in this manner, when, in 1805, two school-houses were built in the western part of the county, one in Salem Township, in what is now known as the Fell settlement, another in the present Hickory Township; and in the same or following year, in the southern part of the county, one was built in the Henderson settlement, in the present Worth Township; also one near that time in Pine Township. These were round log cabins. For ceilings, poles were thrown across overhead and brush placed on these poles and covered with earth. Above this was a clapboard roof held down by weight poles. Some of the better class of houses had puncheon floors (the floors in many of the dwelling-houses were constructed in the same way); others had nothing but the green sward, as nature left it. For light, a log was left out of the building, and newspapers greased and pasted in this opening. Seats were rude benches made of split logs, and desks were con-structed by boring into the logs and placing a slit piece of timber on pins driven into these holes. The fireplace, made of stone, mortar, and sticks, in-cluded the entire end of the building. Wood for this huge fireplace was hauled from surrounding forests by neighbors, who would appoint a day, and all turn out with oxen and sleds, and thus the wood was brought to the door, and there cut in suitable lengths by the larger boys in turn. It was also the rule for the larger boys to build the fires in turn, which required very early rising. The distance to the school-house from many of their homes was often five or six miles, and even farther. The time taught was eight hours per day. Boys were seen winding their way at daybreak along the trackless paths, save the track of a wolf, or perchance that of a passing bear.

"In 1800 Mercer County was divided into six townships,—Salem, Pymatuning, Neshannock, Wolf Creek, Cool Spring, and Sandy Creek. Afterwards, twenty-five subdivisions were made, each independent in their local school affairs, containing a number of houses, ranging from three to twenty-three (boroughs excepted), Wolf Creek the least, and Hickory the greatest number.

"Before the 'free school system' the amount of subscription was about fifty cents per month for one scholar. The houses were built in a day. The site agreed upon, the neighbors would assemble on an appointed day, with axes and ox-teams, and erect a rude structure, considered 'good enough to keep school in.'

"No test of scholarship was required, further than an article of agreement for parents to sign was written by the proposed teacher, setting forth his terms, what he proposed teaching, and how far. A teacher who proposed in a winter school to teach as far as the 'double rule of three,' now called compound proportion, was considered quite proficient in mathematics. He who proposed to lead a class through 'tare and tret' (custom-house business) was thought a master mathematician. This article of agreement was all the patrons had by which to judge his ability.

"No black-boards were used; no classes heard, except reading and spelling. Pupils were required to copy all their examples in a blank-book prepared for the purpose, for future reference.

"But little moral suasion was used in the schools. Corporal punishment was almost the sole remedy for all offences. One of the favorite modes was what is termed 'cut jackets.' This was resorted to in case two were to be punished. Each offender selected his rod, and, at a given signal, they began a most furious attack upon each other, and would continue in the most brute-like and wicked manner, until often the blood would trickle down on the floor, and clothes were lacerated by the infuriated contestants, and the boy with the most physical strength and endurance was the envy of the school, a terror to those who had to 'cut jackets,' and the boasted pride of his parents. Another barbarous mode of punishment was sometimes practised, taken, doubtless, from the old Indian mode of massacring the whites. A day was selected to carry the offender, on his back, in a prescribed circle, around the stove, and two or three boys selected to stand in convenient distances of the line, at regular intervals, with rod in hand, whose business it was to strike once at the offender as he was carried past. After he was carried a few times around the circle (according to the nature of the offence) he was considered sufficiently punished, which was often brutally severe. This was termed 'running the gauntlet.'"

The number of schools in the county in 1846 was two hundred and fourteen. Average number of months taught, five months and five days. Number of male teachers, one hundred and seventy. Number of female teachers, one hundred and forty-five. Average salary for males, thirteen dollars. Average salary for females, six dollars and nine cents. The pioneer school-teacher is not positively known. It may have been Thomas Rigdon, in 1800.

The pioneer Masonic Lodge was organized July 4, 1822. The Lodge grew until 1827, and its warrant was vacated February 6, 1837. The Lodge was known as Mercer Lodge, No. 182, A. Y. M.

INCORPORATION OF BOROUGHS

Sharon, October 6, 1841, M. C. Trout, pioneer burgess. Greenville, May 29, 1837. Clarksville, May 5, 1848.

CHAPTER XXXV

POTTER COUNTY was separated from Lycoming, by the act of March 26, 1804. Length, thirty-seven miles; breadth, thirty miles; area, eleven hundred and six square miles. Population in 1810, 29; in 1820, 186; in 1830, 1265; in 1840, 3371.

The county comprises the high, rolling, and table-land, adjacent to the northern boundary of the State, lying on the outskirts of the great bituminous coal formation. Its streams are the sources of the Allegheny, the Genesee, and the west branch of the Susquehanna; and a resident of the county says that all these streams head so near together that a man in three hours may drink from waters that flow into the Gulf of the St. Lawrence, the Gulf of Mexico, and the Chesapeake, respectively. The names of these sources are the Allegheny, the Genesee, the east branch of the Sinnemahoning, Kettle Creek, Pine Creek, and Cowanesque. In the south part of the county bituminous coal is found.

Coudersport, the county seat, was in 1844 a small but thriving town, situated on the right bank of the Allegheny, at the crossing of the great east and west State road. Another road leads to Jersey Shore, on the West Branch. The place contains a stone court-house and jail, an academy, three stores, two taverns, a carding-machine, mills, and dwellings. Stated preaching, by ministers of different denominations, is regularly enjoyed on the Sabbath.

John Keating, Esq., of Philadelphia, who owned immense tracts of wild lands in this region, presented one-half of the town-plot for the use of the county, and five hundred dollars for the academy. He also gave fifty acres of land to each of the first fifty families that settled on his land; and many other benevolent acts of that gentleman are gratefully remembered by the early settlers.

The court-house was finished in September, 1835. Coudersport then contained forty-seven people.

The history of the early pioneers is one of extreme toil and hardship, yet health and competence have been their reward; and where they found naught but a howling wilderness, traversed only by the Indian, the bear, the wolf, the panther, the elk, and the deer, they now see cultivated fields, abounding

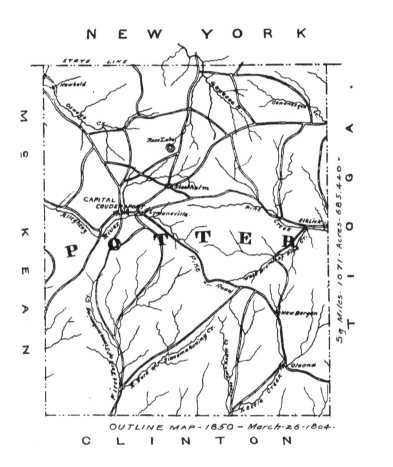

OUTLINE MAP - 1850 - March-26-1804-

with cattle and sheep, and an industrious population, furnished with mills, schools, and manufactories. The following extracts are from the correspondence of respectable citizens of the county. An early settler, Benjamin Birt, Esq., says,—

" In the year 1808 an east and west road was opened through Potter County. Messrs. John Keating & Co., of Philadelphia, owning large tracts of land in the northwest part of the county, agreed with Isaac Lyman, Esq., to undertake the opening of the road. In the fall of 1809 Mr. Lyman came in, with several hands, and erected a rude cabin, into which he moved in March, 1810. He then had but one neighbor in the county, who was four miles distant. I moved in on May 4, 1811, and had to follow the fashion of the country for building and other domestic concerns,—which was rather tough, there being not a bushel of grain or potatoes, nor a pound of meat, except wild, to be had in the county; but there were leeks and nettles in abundance, which, with venison and bear's meat, seasoned with hard work and a keen appetite, made a most delicious dish. The friendly Indians of different tribes frequently visited us on their hunting excursions. Among other vexations were the gnats, a very minute but poisonous insect, that annoyed us far more than mosquitoes, or even than hunger and cold; and in summer we could not work without raising a smoke around us.

" Our roads were so bad that we had to fetch our provisions fifty to seventy miles on pack-horses. In this way we lived until we could raise our own grain and meat. By the time we had grain to grind, Mr. Lyman had built a small grist-mill; but the roads still being bad, and the mill at some distance from me, I fixed an Indian samp-mortar to pound my corn, and afterwards I contrived a small hand-mill, by which I have ground many a bushel,—but it was hard work. When we went out after provisions with a team, we were compelled to camp out in the woods; and, if in the winter, to chop down a maple-tree for our cattle to browse on all night, and on this kind of *long fodder* we had to keep our cattle a good part of the winter.

" When I came here I had a horse that I called ' Main Dependence,' on account of his being a good steady old fellow. He used to carry my whole family on his back whenever we went to a wedding, a raising, a logging-bee, or to visit our neighbors, for several years, until the increasing load comprised myself, my wife, and three children, five in all.

" We had often to pack our provisions eighty miles from Jersey Shore. Sixty miles of the road was without a house; and in the winter, when deep snows came on and caught us on the road without fire, we should have perished if several of us had not been in company to assist each other.

" The want of leather, after our first shoes were worn out, was severely felt. Neither tanner nor shoemaker lived in the county. But ' necessity is the mother of invention.' I made me a trough out of a big pine-tree, into which I put the hides of any cattle that died among us. I used ashes for tanning them, instead of lime, and bear's grease for oil. The thickest served for sole leather, and the thinner ones, dressed with a drawing-knife, for upper leather; and thus I made shoes for myself and neighbors.

"I had fourteen miles to go in winter to mill with an ox-team. The weather was cold and the snow deep; no roads were broken, and no bridges built across the streams. I had to wade the streams, and carry the bags on my back. The ice was frozen to my coat as heavy as a bushel of corn. I worked hard all day and got only seven miles the first night, when I chained my team to a tree, and walked three miles to house myself. At the second night I reached the mill. My courage often failed, and I had almost resolved to return; but when I thought of my children crying for bread, I took new courage."

Mr. John Peat, another old pioneer, in a communication in the *Forester* in 1834, says,—

"It will be twenty-three years the 23d day of May, 1834, since I moved into Potter County. Old Mr. Ayres was in the county at that time, and had been in the county about five years alone. In the fall before I came, three families—Benjamin Birt, Major Lyman, and a Mr. Sherman—moved to the county. The east and west State road was cut out the year before I moved in.

"It was very lonesome for several years. People would move in, stay a short time, and move away again. It has been but a few years since settlers began to stick. I made some little clearing, and planted some garden seeds, etc., the first spring. We brought a small stock of provisions with us. On the 3d day of July I started, with my two yoke of oxen, to go to Jersey Shore, to mill, to procure flour. I crossed Pine Creek eighty times going to, and eighty times coming from mill, was gone eighteen days, broke two axle-trees to my wagon, upset twice, and one wheel came off in crossing the creek.

"Jersey Shore was the nearest place to procure provisions, and the road was dreadful. The few seeds that I was able to plant the first year yielded but little produce. We, however, raised some half-grown potatoes, some turnips, and soft corn, with which we made out to live, without suffering, till the next spring, at planting time, when I planted all the seeds that I had left; and when I finished planting we had nothing to eat but leeks, cow-cabbage, and milk. We lived on leeks and cow-cabbage as long as they kept green —about six weeks. My family consisted of my wife and two children; and I was obliged to work, though faint for want of food.

"The first winter the snow fell very deep. The first winter month it snowed twenty-five days out of thirty; and during the three winter months it snowed seventy days. I sold one yoke of my oxen in the fall, the other yoke I wintered on browse; but in the spring one ox died, and the other I sold to procure food for my family, and was now destitute of a team, and had nothing but my own hands to depend upon to clear my lands and raise provisions. We wore out all our shoes the first year. We had no way to get

more,—no money, nothing to sell, and but little to eat,—and were in dreadful distress for the want of the necessaries of life. I was obliged to work and travel in the woods barefooted. After a while our clothes were worn out. Our family increased, and the children were nearly naked. I had a broken slate that I brought from Jersey Shore. I sold that to Harry Lyman, and bought two fawn-skins, of which my wife made a petticoat for Mary; and Mary wore the petticoat until she outgrew it; then Rhoda took it, till she outgrew it; then Susan had it, till she outgrew it; then it fell to Abigail, and she wore it out."—*Day's Collections.*

I here quote from Hon. M. E. Olmstead's Centennial speech:

" SINNEMAHONING COUNTY ORIGINALLY

" The Legislature whose act created this county assembled at Lancaster, then the seat of government. Propositions to create separate counties out of parts of Lycoming and Huntingdon had been considered, but failed of passage, at two preceding sessions. The matter having been referred to the members from those counties, Mr. Hugh White, of Lycoming, reported on the 13th of January, 1804, bill No. 47, entitled ' An Act to erect parts of Lycoming, Huntingdon, and Somerset Counties into separate county districts.

" It may surprise some of you, as it did me, to learn that the bill as it passed the House did not call this county ' Potter,' but gave it the beautiful Indian name, ' Sinnemahoning.' It created the six counties of Jefferson, McKean, Clearfield, *Sinnemahoning*, Tioga, and Cambria. But in the Senate there was a determination to honor the memory of General James Potter. The attempt was first made by Senator Pearson, from Philadelphia, seconded by Senator McWhortor, from Luzerne, to change the name of McKean to Potter. Had that prevailed our McKean County friends would be living in Potter County to-day, and we should be celebrating the centennial of Sinnemahoning County. But it was defeated by the friends and admirers of the popular governor after whom that county was named. Thereupon Senator Harris, of Centre, seconded by Senator Norton, of Beaver, moved to change Sinnemahoning to Potter. That motion prevailed and the House afterwards concurred in the change.

" A WILDERNESS IN 1804

" Within the limits of what was then declared to be Potter County, the bear, the wolf, the panther, the deer, and the fox walked forth by day and the horn of the hunter was not heard on the hill; the panther's nightly screech fell on no human ear; beautiful, red-speckled, and gamey trout swarmed in every pool, and knew not the cast of the angler; wild-eyed pigeons built their nests in every tree; their countless thousands in morning and evening flight obscured the sun, and the snare of the fowler was set for them not; the otter, the mink, and the musk-rat went forth by day and by night and feared no 'dead fall;' the soil had not known the plough, nor the tree the woodman's axe; here was the forest primeval, unbroken, pathless, magnificent; the smoke from an occasional Indian camp-fire had from time to time curled its way upward through the evergreen branches of the pine and hemlock, but, so far as history records, no white man lived, or ever had lived, within the splendid wilderness which, by the statute of 1804, was set apart and designated as the county of Potter. In the history of the whole Commonwealth there is probably no other instance of the erection of a county in which no human being lived at the time of its erection.

" THE FIRST SETTLER

" Although Coudersport (so-called in honor of Coudere, the French friend of John Keating, who, with other extensive land-owners, contributed lands for public purposes and lands and money for the erection and support of an academy) was decreed by legislative act of 1807 to become the 'seat of justice,' nobody yet lived in it, nor in the county, unless we admit the claim that there settled in 1806, near the mouth of the Oswayo, the Frenchman named Jaundrie, who is said to have built the house, 'clap-boarded with shingles,' from which the place derived and retains the name of 'Shingle House.' The honor of being the first settler is usually accredited to William Ayers, whose settlement in 1808 upon the Keating farm five or six miles east of Coudersport is well established. He brought with him his wife, three children, and a negro boy fifteen years old, named Asylum Peters, whom he purchased from General Brevost at Ceres for one hundred dollars, upon consideration that he give him a fair common education and set him free when of age. This negro, who lived to the age of eighty-seven, and died November 24, 1880, at the house of Walter Edgcomb in Homer Township, was the only slave ever owned in Potter County.

" Major Isaac Lyman, the agent of Keating, came in 1809 and founded Lymansville, where he built the first grist-mill constructed from lumber cut with a whip-saw on the Keating farm.

" Benjamin Burt settled in 1811 where Burtville now stands. In the same year there was a settlement at the mouth of Fishing Creek, and in 1812 Samuel Losey settled on Pine Creek and John Peet near Coudersport. Shortly after that came John Taggart and Daniel Clark. Among the prominent names in the history of the county from that time down until, say, two decades after its complete organization in 1835, I readily recall such as Ives, Sartwell, Nelson, Cartee, Ross, Jones, Freeman, Lewis, Cushing, Raymond, Olmstead, Baker, Kilbourn, Austin, Cole, Stebbins, Reese, Hall, Knox, Mann, Benson, McDougall, Haskell, Butterworth, Armstrong, Colcord, Crosby, French, Stout, Colvin, and many others too numerous to be mentioned here—important guiding characters in the early history of the county.

" The first Potter County exemplification of the fact that all the world is ruled by love occurred in 1810, when Laura Lyman was married to Silas McCarty, of Muncy.

" GRADUAL ORGANIZATION OF THE COUNTY

" By act of 1824 Potter and McKean were partially cut loose from Lycoming and attached to each other; McKean to elect two county commissioners and Potter one, the three to hold their office at the house of Benjamin Burt, in Potter, near the county line. In 1824 Potter was still attached to McKean for certain purposes, and its elections had to be returned to ' Smethport.' But each county had its separate commissioners. Ephraim Fuller, John Lyman, and Leonard Taggart constituted this first board. Finally, in 1833, it was enacted that on and after September 1, 1833, Potter County should cut loose from her neighbors, stand upon her own feet, and walk alone, with the full organization and all the rights, powers, and privileges of a separate and independent county. Within how short a space her greatness has been accomplished is seen when we reflect that there are persons yet living who were in life when the county was erected, and that sixty-nine years only have elapsed since her complete organization.

" The first associate judges were Timothy Ives, Jr., and Seneca Freeman. The first prothonotary, clerk of the court, register of wills, and recorder of deeds was Isaac Strait; the first sheriff, Ansel Purple, and the first coroner, Daniel M. Hunt. The first commissioners under full organization were W. H. Warner, Samuel Cushing, and Elisha Mix, and they awarded the contract for the first court-house to Timothy Ives and Almon Woodcock. The first law judge to hold court in it was Nathaniel B. Eldred, appointed by the governor for the counties of Potter, McKean, Warren, and Jefferson. Prior to that, litigation was a luxury, as Potter County suitors had to go to Williamsport until 1823, and then to ' Smethport.' The judges who have presided here since Eldred have been McCalmont, Williston, White, Williams, and Olmstead."

" There are some things connected with Potter County, closely allied to the lives of our hunter settlers, which, although they might be passed over, are still interesting, and, therefore, as being a portion of the early events, deserve a place here. That the lives of our old settlers had much romance and adventure, mingled with the terrible hardships they underwent, cannot be gainsaid. The untimely meeting of an enraged bear, or a panther, meant at times a life-and-death struggle—a narrow escape at all events.

" The Jamison Fork, a small stream running into the East Fork of the Sinnemahoning, takes its name from a tragical incident which took place at or near its mouth. An Indian, known as James Jamison, while hunting in the East Fork country, was attacked by a panther that sprang upon him from a tree, as local tradition has it. The Indian having but a knife with which to defend himself, the fight was a terrible affair, which had its termination in the killing of both the Indian and the panther. W. W. Thompson, who gave us this item, slew a bear upon the same ground. This is still (1890) a fine hunting territory."

I here quote from Rhoads's " Manuals of Pennsylvania and New Jersey," 1903:

" The following notes by my valued correspondent, Mr. E. O. Austin, of Potter County, Pennsylvania, regarding the habits of the wapiti in that county are of much interest. Under date of March 4, 1901, he writes: ' I settled at my present residence, now in the borough of Austin, in 1856, then a perfect wilderness. When I came into this region, a young man, I could not be surfeited with the stories told by old settlers and hunters as to what they had seen. On the First Fork of the Sinnemahoning near Prouty Run [Potter County] was the " Great Elk Lick" of this region. About 1835 or 1836 the first settlers came into this region. The elks with other wild creatures then reigned here in their glory. Clifford Hoskins, Charles Wykoff, the Jordans, and John Glasspy, with others, were among the prominent men of the time. They were all settled within three or four miles of this lick. They all told me that they would go to the elk-lick to get a deer as often as they wanted one in the summer-time. Here sometimes fifty or more could be seen at a time, with the fawns playing around like young lambs. Cliff. Hoskins said he went there once to get a deer when he saw several elks in the lick and more in the clearing around it. It being the first time he had seen elk there he gazed in wonder, when more came in until forty or fifty had congregated. He watched their grim play for some time and then shot one. The rest started back, then stamped around their fallen comrade gazing in a bewildered way, and stampeded with the noise of thunder when Hoskins approached. Aunt Eleanor Wyckoff lived a mile and a half from Elk Lick. She told me she thought her brother, Mr. Jordan, was telling one of his big yarns when he told her of a similar view of elks, but one day after, when the men found they were around again, she went with her husband to see them. She said, " First some came, then more, until the clearing seemed full of them and the men said there were about fifty there." Regarding the clearing above mentioned—where the elks frequented a big lick they rubbed their horns against the trees, sometimes in play or to rub off the velvet or skin from the new horns. This process soon kills all the trees except some big old ones, so that a clearing of two, three, or four acres is made around the lick. A few thorn trees come up on it which grow so low and stout as to defy them, when it is called a " Thorn Bottom." Elks are gregarious, living in small herds if un- molested, likely in families, but they congregate at the licks in summer in considerable herds.'

" I have no account of their ' yarding' in this county. Their food in summer was nettles, elk or cow-cabbage, elk grass [a wide-bladed bunch-grass common to the woods], and the tender growing twigs of most deciduous trees; and in the winter this elk grass, which keeps green all winter, the edible brake or cow-brake or fern, and browse of deciduous trees, elk wood, bass wood, etc. They migrate in families from section to section of the country, much like deer, but farther away.

"John Glasspy told me of taking a contract to catch elks alive for some fancier. They find and single out their elk, when two men with a small dog, and each a coil of rope and well-filled knapsack of grub, start on the chase, and a long chase it is. But after three or four days the creature halts to see what is following him. They then let loose the little dog. The elk seems to wonder if he has been frightened by that little whiffet. The men have chosen

Edwin Haskell

their time and place not far from some rocky ridge or large rock, accessible to the elk. The dog attacks him with a great noise, and not much else. The beast runs for a rock as the best fort of defence from the attack. While his attention is absorbed by the antics of the little dog, it is easy to put a rope over his horn with a long pole, or by throwing it noosed, and with two ropes on his horns and two strong men, wide apart, to hold him, he soon becomes tired and docile enough to be led out and home. This was not an unfrequent occurrence in those times."

The pioneer term of school in the county was in 1816–17, on Ayers Hill, taught by Master Harley Knickerbocker; the term was three months, and there were but twelve pupils. In 1840 the Coudersport Library Association was organized by a number of women. The pioneer murder in the county was on August 11, 1838. Joshua Jones, of Genessee Township, killed his wife. He was hung May 31, 1839. Pine Creek was declared a highway in 1805; Sinnemahoning, in 1804; Oswayo, in 1807, and the Allegheny, in 1816. About 1816 the pioneer mail route was established from Olean, New York, or what was then Hamilton, New York, to Jersey Shore, Pennsylvania. The pioneer postmaster in the county was Isaac Lyman, and the office was at Lymanville. The service was by horseback. In 1816 the pioneer religious services were held in the county at Lymanville by the Baptists. From February to June 1, 1816. Jacob Van Natter caught seventeen wolves,

Mahlon J. Colcord

besides seven wolf puppies. Up to and long after 1850 Potter County was a veritable menagerie of wild beasts. A large volume could be written about the adventures, perils, and escapes of the pioneer settlers and hunters with wild animals.

The most famous hunters of pioneer times were Jacob Van Natter, Samuel Losey, Nathan Turner, George Taggart, George Ayers, Charles Carlin, Wat. Trowbridge, Cephas Nelson, and Joshua Jackson. Early hunters were John Jordan, Joseph Nelson, and others.

The pioneer newspaper was the *Democratic-Republican*, published at

Coudersport in 1839. Edwin Haskell, a member of the firm of Haskell & Colcord, publishers of the *Potter County Journal*, is one of the early journalists of Northern Pennsylvania. He learned the printer's trade on the *Journal* when it was first published, and has been connected with it much of the time since.

Mahlon J. Colcord is a grandson of John Peet, the fourth settler in Potter County, whose early hardships and indomitable spirit are related in part in this history. The success of the celebration held at Coudersport August 9, 10, 11, and 12, 1904, commemorating the one hundredth anniversary of the erection of Potter County, was largely due to the efforts of Mr.

Head-waters of the Allegheny River

Colcord, who was president of the Centennial Commission, and had general supervision of the work.

"The Allegheny * River rises in Potter County, within a few miles of the head-waters of the Sinnemahoning Creek, and in its course winds through the State of New York about twenty-five miles, and re-enters Pennsylvania, and after meandering through Warren, Venango, Armstrong, and Allegheny Counties, a distance of one hundred and eighty miles, unites with the Monongahela at Pittsburg. ' It is remarkable for the clearness of its waters and the general beauty of the stream, being studded with many islands, and flow-

---

* The Delaware Indians who inhabited this region called this river Alligewisipo; the Iroquois called it Ohio,—that is, *The Beautiful River.—Loskiel.*

ing through a highly picturesque country. During high and middling stages of water, it is navigable for steamboats of light draught as high as Olean Point, in the State of New York. A number of steamboats are now on this river from Pittsburg to Freeport, Kittanning, Franklin, and Warren; and in the summer season, when the river is low, small keel- and flat-boats are employed to do the carrying trade.' The benefit of the trade on this river to our western counties, and indeed to many of the Western States, is incalculable. Out of it has been floated nearly all the pine timber, boards, and shingles that have been used in the valley of the Mississippi, from Pittsburg to New Orleans. Rising of four hundred large arks, or flat-boats, from sixty-five to one hundred and twenty feet long, come down the Allegheny annually, loaded with lumber and produce. These boats are generally sold at Pittsburg to the coal merchants, who reload them with coal for Cincinnati, Louisville, Natchez, and the intermediate ports. The ascending trade of the Allegheny consists chiefly of Pittsburg manufactures, groceries, and foreign and domestic goods for the supply of the upper country; but the descending trade is much greater, embracing a vast amount of all kinds of lumber, logs, and shingles, pot and pearl ashes, whiskey, cheese, cabinet-ware, patent tubs and buckets, hay, oats, potatoes, hoop-poles, bark, etc., a large quantity of salt from the Kiskiminetas, and of pig metal from the great iron establishments in Venango and Armstrong Counties."—*History of Western Pennsylvania in 1846.*

CHAPTER XXXVI

" TIOGA COUNTY was separated from Lycoming by the act of March 25, 1804; in 1806 the seat of justice was established at Wellsborough; in 1808 county commissioners were first elected, and in 1812 the county was fully organized for judicial purposes. Length, thirty-six miles; breadth, thirty-one miles; area, eleven hundred and eight square miles. Population in 1810, 1687; in 1820, 4021; in 1830, 9071; in 1840, 15,498. Area, eleven hundred and twenty-four square miles, and 719,360 acres; mean elevation, 1300; maximum, 2280.

" The county is traversed by the high undulating ridges skirting the northwestern base of the Allegheny Mountains, or rather of Laurel Hill, which sweeps past the southeastern corner of the county. These ridges pertain generally to the hard sandstone strata of formations X. and XII. of our state geologists, and the lower strata of formation XIII., which comprehends the coal measures. The uplands in the vicinity of the larger streams are well covered with white pines of a superior quality; the sugar-maple abounds in many places, and large quantities of sugar are produced from it. The county is well supplied with navigable streams, having the Tioga River, a south branch of the Chemung, on the east, which is navigable for rafts and arks about thirty miles above the New York line; the Cowanesque Creek on the north, navigable about the same distance; and Pine Creek on the west, also navigable; so that no part of the county is distant more than ten miles from descending navigation. A very extensive lumber business has been done on these streams, especially on Pine Creek, whence a vast amount has annually been sent down the Susquehanna. The recent crisis in monetary affairs has tended in some measure to check this trade. Several men from the cities, with more capital than industry, and more enterprise than prudence, had embarked in the business, and driven it beyond its profitable limit.

" Until the year 1796–97 Tioga and the neighboring counties were a howling wilderness, 'entirely cut off from the West Branch settlements by the lofty barrier of the Allegheny Mountains, and trodden only by the beasts of the forest, and the savage on his hostile expedition to the lower settlements. In 1792 a Mr. Williamson, of New York, an agent for Sir William Pulteney, first opened a rough wagon-road through this wilderness, across the mountains from the mouth of Lycoming Creek to the sources of the Tioga, and thence down that river to Painted Post, in New York. This road was made at the expense of Sir William Pulteney for the purpose of render-· ing his lands in the State of New York accessible to German or other emigrants coming up from Philadelphia and Baltimore. Old Mr. Covenhoven (Crownover), of Lycoming County, and Mr. Patterson superintended the workmen on the road, who were principally German redemptioners.* This

John Du Bois, born March 3, 1809, at Owego, Tioga County, New York; died at Du Bois City, Pennsylvania, May 5, 1886

road became a great thoroughfare, and was extensively known as the ' Blockhouse road,' from a log house (called blockhauss by the Germans) erected by Williamson near the mountains for the accommodation of travellers.

"It is still (1843) a tavern stand and the site of a post-office, about twelve miles south of Blossburg. This house was kept in the primitive times by one Anthonyson, a sort of half French and half Dutchman. Anthony, according to his own story, had spent most of his life as a soldier, during

* See chapter on Redemptioners, page 329.

the stormy times of the French Revolution; and he had thereby neither improved his morals nor his fortune. He made no scruple, by way of amusing his guests, of boasting of his bold-faced villany; there was no one of the ten commandments which he had not specifically broken, time and again. With the habits of the old soldier, he had little disposition to get his living by tilling the ground, and found the military code of pillage much more to his taste. He raised no oats, but always charged travellers for the use of his troughs, and for sleeping before his fire. Whiskey was the staple commodity at his house, serving both as meat and drink. Many of the early emigrants to the Genesee country drove their young cattle along. There was a wide track of some fearful tornado, not far from Anthony's house, in which he had contrived to cut an open space, with a narrow passage into it, making a kind of unseen pen. To this spot the cattle of his guests were very apt to stray in the night. In the morning the poor emigrants were hunting, far and near, for their cattle, with Anthony for their guide; but on such occasions he never happened to think of the windfall.

"The unsuspecting guests, after two or three days of fruitless search, would leave, paying roundly for their detention; and instructing the old scoundrel to hunt the cattle, and when found, to write to a certain address, with a promise of reward for his trouble. Anthony never had occasion to write, but it was always remarked that he kept his smoke-house well supplied with what *he* called elk-meat. When or where he caught the elks was never known. Some lone travellers, who stopped at his house, it is strongly suspected, never reached their intended destination.

"After the opening of this road, many of the pioneers from the Wyoming country, and from New England, came into the eastern part of the county, and took up lands under the Connecticut title. For quite a number of years the uncertainty of this title gave rise to much wrangling and litigation. A Mr. Gobin, an assistant surveyor under the Pennsylvania title, was shot in his camp, but not killed. At length the litigation was ended by the compromise at Trenton; the settlers quietly acknowledged the validity of the Pennsylvania title, and compromised their claims with the agents of the land-holders from Philadelphia. A large portion of the lands in the eastern section of the county belongs to the Bingham estate.

"Soon after the cutting of the Block-house road, Mr. John Norris, from Philadelphia, first came, about the beginning of the year 1799, to the south-western part of the county, as an agent for Mr. Benjamin Morris, who owned lands in that region. He was accompanied by his brother-in-law, Mr. Mordecai Jackson, then a young lad. On Mr. Norris's arrival he erected a grist- and saw-mill, on the waters of Little Pine Creek, just within the boundary of Lycoming County. This establishment was generally known as Morris's Mills. The country was then a complete wilderness, and in traversing its wilds these first adventurers endured the many hardships incident to a pioneer's life; such as sleeping on the ground in the open air, often without fire, searching for the blazes on the trees at night, to find the way through the forest, and travelling long journeys for their provisions, to the older settlements, for one or two years after their first arrival. These hardships were doubly severe to young men reared among the comforts and luxuries of Philadelphia. After remaining at Morris's Mills for five or six years, and inducing some half-dozen settlers to immigrate, Mr. Norris removed to the vicinity of the Big Marsh; and subsequently, in 1807, to within a mile of Wellsborough. The mill at that place had been built the year previous (1806), by Samuel W. Fisher, of Philadelphia; and the same year the county seat was fixed at Wellsborough. Among the first settlers at or near Wellsborough, besides Mr. Norris, were Benjamin W. Morris, David Linsey, Alpheus Cheney, and Daniel Kelsey, Esq.

"Wellsborough, the county seat, is located near the centre of the county, three miles from the navigable waters of Pine Creek, on the great State road, passing through the northern range of counties. The north and south road, from the mouth of Lycoming Creek to the one hundred and ninth mile-stone, on the State line, also passes through the place. The village is built upon level ground, on a long and wide street, sheltered on the north and east by high hills. There existed for many years a great strife for the removal of the county seat. The towns on the Tioga and Cowanesque, appearing to be most favored with the increase of population and improvement, contended for the removal; and settlers were consequently diverted from selecting a location at or near Wellsborough. This had a blighting effect upon the place: and in 1831 the village paper describes the place as containing only ' forty or fifty indifferent dwelling-houses, a court-house and jail, of no very reputable appearance,' etc. At length, in 1835, a majority of the citizens of the county authorized the erection of the new stone court-house and county offices, which confirmed to the place its title as the seat of justice.

"Since that time it has greatly improved, and many new frame buildings have been erected, among them an Episcopal and a Methodist church, in a very neat style of architecture. There is also an academy. The private dwellings are built with much taste, and even some of the stores and taverns exhibit the tasteful proportions of Grecian architecture. Pleasant front yards, gardens, and green blinds indicate the origin of the population from New York and New England. The court-house is a fine edifice of white sandstone, surmounted with a cupola. A tri-weekly stage runs to Covington, twelve miles east. Population in 1840, 369. Coal has been discovered about seven miles south of the borough.

"Covington is a large and flourishing village, at the intersection of the great State road with the Tioga River. The railroad of the Tioga Navigation Company also passes through the village. Mr. Washburn, Mr. Elijah Putnam, and Mr. Mallory settled at Covington ' corners' previous to 1806. Mr.

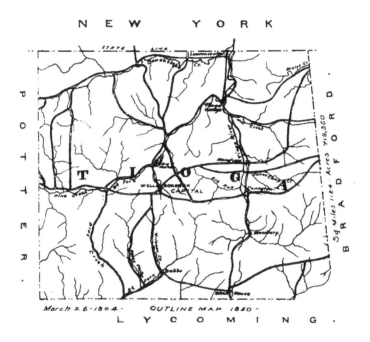

NEW YORK

POTTER.

TIOGA

BRADFORD.

Sq Miles 1124 Acres 719,360

March 26-1804.   OUTLINE MAP 1850-

LYCOMING.

Bloss and Mr. Hovey had settled about the year 1801, two miles below; and Mr. Sacket also lived near the same place. The land titles were for a long time in dispute between the Connecticut and Pennsylvania claimants. When at last they were settled in favor of the Pennsylvanians, or ' Pennamites,' as the ' Connecticut boys' called them, Mr. William Patten came in as their agent and laid out the town, about the year 1822, and started a store and tavern. For some years the place increased very slowly, and was only known as ' The Corners.' In 1831 it assumed the dignity of a borough; soon afterwards the great fever of internal improvement and speculation began to rise, and Covington, being an important point, rose with it.

"Lands both for farming and timber, and town lots, were eagerly taken up, and passed from hand to hand, sometimes doubled and trebled in value at each transfer; coal-mines and iron-mines were opened, and water-powers were sought out and improved; saw-mills, furnaces, houses, stores, and taverns went up as if by magic; bank-notes poured in from New York and Towanda, and everybody was to be getting rich. But at length, in 1841–42, the bubble burst—bank-notes melted in the hand, property became unsalable, and the whole community embarrassed. The fever had subsided, and left in its place a hard-shaking ague.

" The following tragic tale is copied from the newspapers of February, 1842, and will serve to explain much of the embarrassment that has overtaken Covington and the vicinity.

" ' PHILADELPHIA, 17th February, 1842.—This morning, at about six o'clock, Mr. J. G. Boyd, late cashier and agent of the Towanda Bank, killed himself at his residence in Schuylkill Seventh Street, by firing a loaded pistol into his mouth. Previously to his late dismissal as the cashier of the bank, it was ascertained that he had, as the signing officer of the relief issues of that bank, put out some thousands of dollars on his own account. The Penn Township Bank, one of the losers by this fraudulent issue, and by some of his other transactions, had commenced a suit against him, and it was while in the custody of the sheriff, and when he saw that the whole fraud must be exposed, that he committed the melancholy act. About two years since he had married an interesting young lady at Trenton, New Jersey, and was keeping house with her at the time of his suicide in Philadelphia. He had furnished this house splendidly, had settled upon his wife a farm near Germantown, worth about eight thousand dollars, and had made many munificent presents to her relatives. But it appears that all this time he had another wife, a most estimable lady, at Covington, Tioga County, by whom he had several children, and with whom he was living on most affectionate terms whenever his business called him to that vicinity. With his Philadelphia wife he passed as Mr. Henry Seymour, represented himself as a drover having large transactions with the interior counties, and often spoke of his intimate friend, Mr. John G. Boyd. So adroitly was the deception maintained, that neither of these unfortunate ladies ever suspected the least impropriety in his conduct, or alienation of his affections.

" ' Mr. Boyd had come out from the State of New York to Tioga and Bradford Counties some three or four years since. He was a man of about thirty-five years of age, with a gentlemanly, but plain and business-like exterior, exhibiting extraordinary tact and readiness in matters of business, and a good degree of common sense, apparently, in the management of his enterprises. Although comparatively a stranger, yet so plausible was his address that he soon gained the confidence of wealthy men, who intrusted him with means to enter largely into the lumber business, and afterwards into the iron business and coal land speculations in Tioga County. He had several large mills near Covington, a furnace at Blossburg, and was engaged in many of the most prominent schemes for improving these two places. His business led him into intimate connection with the Towanda Bank; and he was successively appointed clerk, agent for the transaction of the bank's business in Philadelphia, and cashier. The latter office, after the credit of the bank began to decline, he was compelled to give up. He still, however, secretly continued his fraudulent issues of Towanda relief notes in Philadelphia, until a short time previous to the tragic close of his career.'

" Covington, however, though shocked and thrown back by this calamity, added to the ordinary embarrassment of the times, still has many advantages for becoming a prosperous town, particularly an extensive farming and lumbering country constantly opening to the west of it, which finds here the most convenient depot for its produce and lumber. Quite a brisk business is still done. No church has yet been erected in the place (1843). The Presbyterians worship in a school-house. The Baptists and Methodists have it in contemplation to erect churches soon. The extensive lumber establishment of Boyd & Clever is about half a mile below the town.

" Blossburg took its name from the aged Mr. Aaron Bloss (now of Covington), who originally settled here and owned the property. Before Mr. Bloss removed here, about the year 1802, one Gaylord, a worthless fellow, had kept a tavern. Mr. Bloss removed from near Covington, and bought him out. The place at that time went by the name of ' Peters's camp.' This Peters was a German, who did the baking in an immense oven for the large company of German redemptioners at work on the Block-House road.* Peters was not remarkable for cleanliness of person; and his comrades, unable any longer to tolerate his filth, caught him and commenced the necessary ablution by pouring sundry buckets of cold water upon his head, stroking and smoothing down his hair in a becoming manner, and were about to complete the process by putting him into the river, when the superintendent of the road interfered.

* See chapter on Redemptioners, page 330.

" Blossburg is situated on the Tioga River, at the head of the railroad connecting the bituminous coal- and iron-mines of Tioga County with the Chemung River and Canal, and promises to become a point of some importance when all the natural resources in its vicinity shall be properly developed.

" The railroad from Blossburg, through Covington, to Corning, in the State of New York, forty miles, was constructed by the Tioga Navigation Company, instead of a canal or slackwater navigation, and was opened for locomotives in July, 1840. This road opens a connection between the coal mines of Blossburg and the Chemung Canal of New York.

" A large iron-furnace stands at the upper end of the village, which had been leased by Mr. Boyd and another person. It was originally wrought with charcoal, but had been altered for coke ; and the workmen were conducting a successful blast with the latter, when Mr. Boyd's catastrophe occurred, and the hearth was allowed ' to chill.' The same blighting *chill* came over many of the enterprises in this region from the same cause. Blossburg has become quite a village since the opening of the mines and the railroad. Like most other coal towns in Pennsylvania, it resembles an army with its tents pitched in different detachments,—here one row of uniformly built houses, and there another. The houses are constructed with good taste, principally of wood. The country around is wild and rugged. The Tioga, here but a narrow stream, flows in a deep and narrow valley, surrounded on both sides by precipitous hills.

" Tioga, or Willardsburg, situated at the confluence of Crooked Creek and the Tioga River, was settled about the year 1800 by Mr. Willard. The opening of the country to a market has given it an impetus, and it has rapidly increased, until it rivals the towns above it on the river. It contains Methodist and Baptist churches.

" Mansfield is on the right bank of the Tioga, at the mouth of Canoe Camp Creek, three miles below Covington. Mainsville is four miles east of Mansfield, on the road to Towanda. Not far from this place, in Union Township, in September, 1835, Major Ezra Long is said to have discovered a considerable quantity of lead ore, the specimens of which were equal to the best lead ores of the West.

" Lawrenceville is a small village just within the State line."

Tioga County has always been celebrated for intelligence and patriotism ; and no wonder ! Forty of its pioneer settlers served in the Revolutionary army, and over forty did service in the War of 1812.

" The first prominent settlers within what is Tioga County—Jesse Losey and his wife—were historic characters. They located in the county in 1786, at least two years earlier than a local historian has credited Samuel Baker and wife with doing so. Losey had been of the Continental army, in which he served throughout the Revolutionary War. He had heard the solid shot, shell, and red-hot ball that rained at Yorktown for more than a week against Cornwallis's fortified lines, and he had listened to the music to which that British general's army marched out, on October 19, 1781, when he surrendered his forces to the Americans.

"In the spring of 1786 Jesse Losey and his wife anchored their birch-bark canoe where Tioga village is now situated and built a cabin on the site of the present Episcopal church in that borough."—*Agitator*.

A settler or two had located at the Block-House as early as 1795. In 1797 Gad Lamb located; Dr. Willard, the pioneer doctor, in 1799. A colony came from Virginia, Delaware, Maryland, and Philadelphia, in 1800, and settled about Wellsboro.

In 1812 the county was organized, and in 1813 the pioneer court was held in the log court-house that was erected in 1812.

The pioneer court was held by John Bannister Gibson, president judge, assisted by associate judges Samuel Wells Morris and Ira Kilburn. The pioneer sheriff was Alpheus Cheney. The present court-house was built in 1835.

Wellsboro was declared the county seat in 1806, and named for Mrs. Mary Wells Morris. It was incorporated as a borough in 1830, with about fifty families or two hundred and fifty people.

Benjamin B. Smith, the editor of the *Phœnix*, who was a member of the council, and had a hand in making the new laws, referred to them in his issue of July 3, 1830, and defended them in these words:

"At last our by-laws are published, and we hope soon to see our streets cleared of sheep, hogs, and cattle, which have hitherto been really a nuisance, especially in the night. Depredations have already been commenced on some of our gardens, and unless cattle are shut up at night we can expect nothing but that our vegetables will, as last year, be entirely destroyed. We borough folks expect now to be quite happy. The squalling of geese at day-light, the bellowing of cattle, the kicking of horses, the audacity of swine, and the 'innomi nutus' odor of sheep, accompanied with their disagreeable bleating, shall entirely cease from annoying us, and we shall go forth at morning and evening, at sunsetting and sunrising, and fear no evil except from dogs, which, by the by, our burgess and council have entirely forgotten —and mad dogs, too, are they not subjects of legislation as well as geese? We expect, however, to have a 'revised code,' and then all things will be perfect." This was the second borough ordinance.

On December 3, 1825, Ellis and Rankin Lewis started the first news-paper in the county, called the *Pioneer*. This was Willardsburg.

In 1802 William H. Wells migrated from Delaware to what is now Wellsboro.

"I know it has always been stated by our learned historians that Wells-boro was named in honor of Mary Hill Wells, the wife of Benjamin Wistar

Morris. It may be so. But at the time Wellsboro was named just a little way out on the old road toward Stony Fork lived William Hill Wells, a man so distinguished in civil life that he had sat in the United States Senate from 1799 to 1804, and resigned his seat in order to move to the ' Beechwoods' of Tioga County, with his negro slaves and other material wealth; a man so distinguished that after his return to Delaware he again represented that State in the United States Senate from 1813 to 1817. Gideon Wells, another brother of Mary Morris, a contractor and builder of the State roads running through this town on the line of Main Street during that formative period, also lived and owned lands in this immediate vicinity. Possibly Wellsboro was named in honor of the Wells family."—*Hon. Charles Tubbs.*

The principal streams are the Pine Creek, declared a public highway by the Legislature, March 16, 1798; the Cowanesque River, Crooked Creek, Lycoming Creek, and the Tioga River. Crooked Creek is the principal tributary of the Tioga River.

Indian trails were numerous, also Indian villages and Indian graveyards. Of the pioneer hunters, Wilson Freeman, in 1808, received sixteen dollars bounty for two panther heads. I might say here that panthers were killed in this wilderness measuring, from tip of nose to end of tail, ten, eleven, and even twelve feet. In May, 1808, Timothy Coats, Isaac Gaylord, and James Whitney received thirty-two dollars for wolf and panther heads. Other hunters who received bounty that year were Aaron Freeman, Nathan Brown, Joshua Reynolds, Timothy Culver, Rufus Adams, and Titus Ives. President Theodore Roosevelt entirely underrates the courage and savagery of the panther of 1800. The panther has intelligence, and he thoroughly understands the improved fire-arms of to-day. Previous to 1784 the Indians carried captives from Pennsylvania over their trails to below Fort Niagara. French explorers, Moravian missionaries, hunters, and scouts passed over these trails previous to 1784.

Eleazer Seelye, whose father was a very early settler, says,—

" My father erected a cabin of bark set against a large pine log, and lived in it for a year and a half. He then built a log house. In this he lived the first winter without a floor, there being no saw-mill nearer than Painted Post. For a grist-mill we used a stump hollowed out by fire for a mortar, and a spring pestle. In this we pounded our samp for bread and pudding timber for two years. After a while several of the settlers clubbed together and purchased a pair of millstones about two feet in diameter, which we turned by hand. At first we could only raise corn. Wheat blasted, rusted, and would not mature. This state of things lasted seven or eight years, when wheat, rye, and oats began to be raised. The family dressed chiefly in deer-skins, and I was ten years old before I had a pair of shoes."

General John Burrows, in a little pamphlet, gives his experience of a trip into Tioga County in 1802. He says,—

" In 1802 I was elected a (Lycoming) county commissioner. About this time I received a letter from Dr. Tate introducing William Hill Wells to me, who had settled in the woods (near) where Wellsboro now stands, the county seat of Tioga.

" Mr. Wells applied to me to furnish him with provisions in his new settlement. He had brought a number of negroes with him from the State of Delaware, where he moved from. I put eighty-eight hundred-weight of pork on two sleds and started to go to him with it. It was fine sledding, but dreadful cold weather. In crossing the Allegheny Mountains the man I had driving one of the teams froze his feet up to his ankles. I was obliged to leave him, and the next morning put the four horses to one sled, and the pork on it, and started for Wells's. I had to cross Pine Creek six times. A man coming into the settlement from that part of the county had frozen to death the day before. I passed him lying in the road.

" The second crossing of the creek was about fifty yards wide; when the foremost horses got to the middle of the creek the ice broke with them; the ice was about mid-side deep; and in their attempting to get on the ice again, drew the other horses and sled into the creek and pulled the roller out of the sled. I got the horses ashore and tied them, and then went back to the sled, and found the water running over the pork. I had to go partly under the water to get an axe that was tied to the sled, to cut a road through the ice to get the sled ashore. Sometimes I was in the water up to my middle, and sometimes I was standing on the ice. The water following the stroke of the axe would fly up, and as soon as it touched me was ice.

" When I got the road cut to the shore I went to the sled, and, getting a log chain, reached under water and hooked it first to one runner and then to the other; then backed the horses in through the road, hitched to the sled, and pulled it out.

" It was now dark. I had six miles to go and four times to cross the creek, without a roller in my sled to guide it. On descending ground it would run out of the road, when I had difficulty to get it in the road again. There was not a dry thread on me, and the outside of my clothes was frozen stiff. It was twelve o'clock (midnight) before I got to the mill, the first house before me; and there was neither hay nor stable when I got there. I thought my poor horses would freeze to death.

" Next morning, as soon as the daylight appeared, I cut a stick and put a roller to my sled—the very wood seemed filled with ice. I started from there at ten o'clock, and had fifteen miles to go to Wells's. The snow was two feet deep and there was scarcely a track in the road. I met Mr. Wells's negro five miles this side of his house, coming to meet me, on horseback, about sunset. He said there was a by-road that was a mile nearer than the one I was on, and he undertook to pilot me, but soon lost the path and we wandered about among the trees till at length my sled pitched into a hole and upset. I then unhooked my horses from the sled and asked the negro if he thought he could pilot me to the house, but he acknowledged himself lost.

"I looked about and took a view of the stars, and started with my four horses, leaving the pork in the wood, and fortunately reached Wells's. When I got there he had neither hay nor stable, or any kind of feed, nor any place to confine my horses, and I had to tie them to the trees. He had a place dug in a log that I could feed two of my horses at a time.

"All the buildings that he had erected were two small cabins, adjoining each other,—one for himself and family, about sixteen feet square, that I could not stand straight in,—built of logs, with bark for an upper floor, and split logs for the lower floor. The negro cabin was a little larger, but built of the same material. I sat by the fire until morning. It took me all that day to get my pork to the house and settle. I started the next morning for home without any feed to give my horses, after they had stood there two nights, and the snow was up to their bellies. I have been particular in detailing the circumstances of this trip, leaving you to judge of the hardships that I had to endure. But it is only a specimen of much of the kind that I have had to encounter through life." This experience was on the State road built in 1799.

The pioneer horse-races occurred in September, 1796, and continued for several weeks. (See Potter County history.)

The pioneer distillery was erected, in 1815, by Joshua Colvin. Rye and corn were used exclusively. The barter was six quarts of whiskey for one bushel of rye or corn.

The pioneer grist-mill was built about 1810 by Thomas and Beecher.

Lumbering boards and timber was carried on at an early date, but without much profit.

Tanneries were erected before 1812. Coal was discovered as early as 1792. To David Clemons is due the credit of being the pioneer operator and shipper of coal in and for the county. This was probably in 1815.

The pioneer meeting of the commissioners was held in Wellsboro, October 20, 1808, in the Friends' log church, the first church edifice in the county.

Wellsboro post-office was opened January 1, 1808, and Samuel Wells Morris was the pioneer postmaster.

"The mail at that time was carried weekly, on horseback, over the State road from Williamsport. A pair of saddle-bags were sufficient to contain all the matter, with room to spare. Newspapers were few in those days, the *Lycoming Gazette* being the only paper printed within a radius of a hundred miles; and as postage was high, few letters were written. No envelopes were in use then; letters were written on foolscap and made as long as possible, covering all the available space, leaving only room enough for the address, when the sheet was folded and sealed with red wax or a wafer. A stamp or signet of some kind was used to press the paper into the wax or wafer, which left an impression and gave the enclosure an official appearance. The amount of postage was written, usually, on the upper right hand corner of the letter, and the price was governed by the distance carried. It was collected at the end of the route from the party to whom it was addressed. The name of the first mail-carrier has not come down to us, but in those days the duty was generally performed by a bright, active, venturesome boy. The route from Williamsport lay through a gloomy wilderness nearly all the way. The log cabins of settlers were few. Panthers and wolves roamed the forest, and their howls frequently caused the mail-boy to spur up his horse and dash swiftly through the gloom.

"One of the early mail-carriers was John Sheffer, Jr., born in Williamsport, February 8, 1803. When thirteen years of age he carried the mail from Williamsport to Painted Post on horseback, a distance of seventy-nine miles, by the way of the State and Williamson roads. The former started at Newberry and passed through Wellsboro. It required nerve in those days to make this journey, and when the youth of the rider is considered, it is still more remarkable.

"It is probable that he either went by this route on going out, or on returning, as he could make a complete circuit by doing so. The Williamson road passed through Block-House, Blossburg, Covington, and Tioga. The first post-office in the county was established at the last-mentioned place January 1, 1805. At Wellsboro he could leave the State road and proceed to Covington by the East and West pike, as it was called, or *vice versa*. It is highly probable therefore, that he made the round trip in this way."

The pioneer tavern-keeper in Wellsboro was X. Miller.

"The old-time tavern was a place of good cheer and social enjoyment. Whiskey in those days cost three cents a drink, or five for a shilling; twelve for twenty-five cents, and a long credit for three cents net, when marked down. The method of charging was a straight mark for a drink, and a tally mark for five, with the creditor's name at the top of a page. This method was adopted as a necessity, as it would sometimes have required two or three clerks to make the charges in the regular way."

The pioneer teachers in the old meeting-house were Lydia Cole, Chauncey Alford, and Benjamin B. Smith. These were subscription schools under the law of 1809. The first public-school building in Wellsboro, was built of logs in 1835. The pioneer church building was erected about 1802.

The Presbyterian church of Wellsboro was organized February 11, 1843. Rev. Thomas Foster was the supply for a year.

The pioneer Methodist church service in Wellsboro was about the year 1802. Rev. Caleb Boyer preached.

Up to 1850 Tioga County had no conviction or execution for murder.

Nearly all the facts as given in this history of Tioga County are taken or quoted from the history of Tioga County in 1897.

CHAPTER XXXVII

" VENANGO * COUNTY was taken from Allegheny and Lycoming by act
of March 12, 1800, and was organized for judicial purposes by act of April
1, 1805. In 1839 its limits were curtailed by the establishment of Clarion
County, the Clarion River having been previously the southeastern boundary.
The county now forms a very irregular figure, with an area of about eight
hundred and fifty square miles. Population in 1800, 1130; in 1810, 3060;
in 1820, 4915; in 1830, 9470; in 1840, 17,900.

" The Allegheny River flows through the centre of the County in a direction so very circuitous that there is not a point of the compass to which it
does not direct its course. The country along its banks is exceedingly wild
and rugged, the river-hills being high and precipitous. The valley is narrow, but bounded alternately on either side by elevated alluvial lands, which
furnish excellent sites for farms. French Creek, which comes in at Franklin,
and Oil Creek a short distance above, are the other two principal streams.
Raccoon, Tionesta, Pit-Hole, Sandy, and Scrubgrass Creeks, are streams of
minor importance. All these streams flow in deeply indented valleys, ren-
dering the general surface quite hilly; and many of the component rocks of
these hills pertaining to the lower conglomerates of the coal formation, make
on the whole a rugged country. Still there are large bodies of what may be
called good farming land. All the hills abound with iron ore of excellent
quality. Bituminous coal is plenty in the southern part of the county, and
some has been found within two or three miles of Franklin. Limestone
abounds in the southwestern end of the county. A great advantage possessed
by this county, is its pure water, which promotes good health. Fine water-
powers exist on all the tributaries of the Allegheny, especially on French
Creek.

---

* Venango River was the name given by the French to French Creek. The word
Venango is a corruption of the Indian word *In-nun-gah*, which had some reference to
a rude and indecent figure carved upon a tree, which the Senecas found here when they
first came to this region.

HISTORY OF NORTHWESTERN PENNSYLVANIA

PIONEER STEAMBOATING ON THE ALLEGHENY RIVER, 1824–62—EXTRACTS TAKEN FROM NEWSPAPER WRITINGS OF WITHIE REYNOLDS, OF KITTANNING, PENNSYLVANIA, THE VETERAN STEAMBOAT AND RAILROAD MAN—HIS SKETCHES WERE PUBLISHED IN 1879

" Now that there are some improvements being made at different points on the Allegheny River, perhaps a few lines from an old timer may be of some interest. From the occasional accounts given of the Allegheny, one would infer that the steamers that formerly plied on the stream were of but little importance as to size, speed, and comfort. True, the boats of early days were of small dimensions, their carrying capacity being about twenty-five tons, and their accommodations for passengers being correspondingly limited, but as time rolled on the demand for larger boats became a necessity.

" PIONEER BOATS

" The first steamboat that ever passed up the Allegheny was named the ' Duncan.' She was very small and a side-wheeler. Her first trip was made to Franklin in 1824 or 1825. Captain James Murphy was her pilot. The Captain is still living (1879) and resides four miles above Freeport.

" The next boat was the ' Allegheny,' a stern-wheeler, and was quite an improvement on the ' Duncan.' Then came the ' Beaver,' ' Pulaski,' and ' Forrest.' Then the ' Allegheny Belle No. 1,' commanded by Captain John Hanna. She was the first boat on the river that had a bell and a whistle, and Captain John took pains to let the people along the banks know it. About this time two boats, one named the ' Clarion' and the other the ' Justice,' were placed in the trade.

" After these came the ' Cornplanter,' Captain T. H. Reynolds; ' Clara Fisher,' Captain E. Gordon; ' Allegheny Belle No. 2,' Captain W. Hanna, and ' Allegheny Belle No. 3,' the machinery of the No. 1 being placed on the latter. These four boats had the river to themselves for quite a time.

" About 1855 the ' Venango' was built by and commanded by Captain Tom H. Reynolds, and the same year the ' Echo' was built by and commanded by Captain E. Gordon. After them, the ' Leclaire No. 1,' ' Leclaire No. 2,' ' Echo No. 2,' ' Allegheny Belle No. 2,' ' Ida Reese,' and ' Urilda;' also the ' Sam Snowden' and ' Allegheny Clipper.' The two latter were on the river about 1850.

" All of these boats had a carrying capacity of from two hundred to two hundred and fifty tons each, full-length cabins, and all the modern improvements (up to that time) in the way of machinery, etc.

" Before the completion of the Allegheny Valley Railroad to Oil City these boats had all the business they could do, the up-trip consisting of boilers and engines for the oil country, returning with all the oil they could carry at two dollars and a half and three dollars per barrel; and to look back it seems

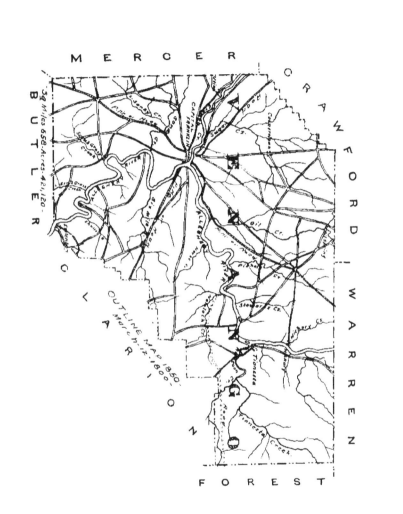

like a miracle that no accident occurred from fire. But to return to the days of the 'Planter,' 'Belle No. 2,' and 'Fisher.' These boats were the fastest that were ever on the Allegheny, and they made racing a business. The 'Planter' and 'Belle No. 2' would always back out from the Allegheny wharf together, 'red hot,' and about the only time you could not see the blaze from the tops of the chimneys would be when they were lowered to pass under the bridges. I have frequently heard Jim Conner, pilot of the 'Planter,' call down to Tom O'Donnell that the 'Belle' was 'coming up on us.' 'All right,' would be the answer, 'I have 160, will soon be 190, and the rest easy, Jim, and say good-by to the "Belle."' Both these boats had four boilers, sixteen-inch cylinders, and six-feet stroke. When the water was too low in the Allegheny the 'Planter' would sometimes go into the Pittsburg and Wheeling trade against the 'Diurnal' and 'Forrest City,' and I have seen her pass these boats while all were under way, so you may judge of her speed.

"There are men still living who remember when all the freight of the upper country was carried on 'dug-outs,' or 'canoes,' that were propelled by sheer muscle from Pittsburg to Warren, and that carried large quantities of freight to the scattered landings, whence they were transported by pack-horses through a comparative wilderness to the interior. Then came the era of keel-boating, and this was followed by the steamboat, an invention of incalculable advantage to the times.

"The *Pittsburg Gazette* of May 28, 1830, gives a long account of the first trip of the 'Allegheny.' She left Pittsburg on her third trip on the 14th of May, 1830, with sixty-four passengers and twenty-five or thirty tons of freight, and arrived at Warren at nine o'clock on the 19th,—three and one-half days running time,—and on the same evening she departed from Warren for Olean. At nine o'clock the next day she arrived opposite the Indian village of Cornplanter. Here a deputation of gentlemen waited on this ancient and well-known Seneca chief, and invited him on board this new and, to him, wonderful visitor, a steamboat. He was in all his native simplicity of dress and manner of living, lying on his couch, made of rough pine boards, and covered with deer-skins and blankets. His habitation, a two-story log house, was in a state of decay, without furniture, except a few benches, and wooden bowls and spoons to eat out of. The venerable chief was a lad in the French war, and fought at Braddock's defeat. He was a smart, active man, seemingly possessed of all his strength of mind and perfect health. He, with his son, Charles, sixty years of age, and his son-in-law, came on board and remained until she passed six miles up, and then returned in their own canoe, after expressing great pleasure. At eleven A.M. on Friday, the 21st of May, the 'Allegheny' landed safely at Olean Point. The boat experienced much trouble and delay in procuring wood, much of which was so green as to prevent, in a great measure, the raising of a proper head of steam.

"*Hazzard's Register* for September, 1830, gives an account of a steamboat celebration at Franklin, in honor of which an elegant banquet was set, and among the honored guests of the occasion is mentioned the name of our venerable townsman, Philip Mechling, Esq. Frederick Crary, father of the late T. G. Crary, of this place, was president of the meeting, at which were assembled some of the most notable men of that day and section. The following is a list of the steamboats that succeeded in the trade:

" ' Forest,' November 5, 1840, to April 9, 1844; ' Pauline,' February 2, 1841, to May 10, 1841; ' Pulaski,' April 20, 1841, to May 4, 1843; ' Allegheny Belle,' April 15, 1843, to December 11, 1850; ' Allegheny Belle No. 3,' March 5, 1851, to May 5, 1858; ' Mary Ann,' November 4, 1846, to December 29, 1848; ' Arrow,' March 20, 1845, to November 30, 1846; ' Arrowline,' October 13, 1847, to May 27, 1848; ' Arena,' October 23, 1847, to December 6, 1849; ' Allegheny Belle No. 2,' March 15, 1850, to June 28, 1858; ' Allegheny Belle No. 4,' March 19, 1859, to April 21, 1861; ' Allegheny Clipper,' November 11, 1848, to August 26, 1850; ' Franklin,' October 28, 1844, to February 16, 1846; ' Fort Pitt,' December 30, 1848, to May 26, 1849; ' Hope No. 2,' April and May, 1848; ' Oneoto,' October 24, 1846, to August 5, 1847; ' Reveille,' April 5, 1850, to June 20, 1850; ' Thomas Scott,' November 15, 1849, to February 24, 1852; ' Star,' November 3, 1850; ' Virginia,' November 29, 1850, to May 10, 1851; ' Wave No. 2,' November 16, 1848, to May 11, 1850; ' Cornplanter,' April 9, 1851, to May 23, 1856; ' Clarion,' August 1, 1851, to March 12, 1853; ' Clara Fisher,' May 8, 1852, to December 7, 1857; ' Echo,' March 22, 1858, to November 15, 1861; ' Justice,' December 1, 1851, to May 25, 1853; ' Thos. P. Ray,' December, 1852; ' J. B. Gordon,' December, 1852; ' Sam Snowden,' March 26, 1853, to December 28, 1853; ' Nebraska,' October 12, 1853, to June 2, 1856; ' Acquilla,' November, 1855; ' Venango,' February 1, 1858, to April 27, 1862; after which, on the completion of the Allegheny Valley Railroad to Kittanning, the steamboat trade began to decline, although some of the finest boats of the trade continued for several years. The ' Echo No. 2,' ' Leclaire No. 1,' ' Petrolia No. 1,' ' Petrolia No. 2,' ' Peerless,' ' Cottage,' ' Urilda,' ' Ida Reese,' and ' Belle' were steamers famous for their speed and accommodation. During the war a number of these last were subsidized by the government for service in the South, and terminated their career in the service as transports.

" During the days of steamboating on the Allegheny it was quite a sight to witness the immense quantities of freight that were piled on the Duquesne wharf in Pittsburg awaiting shipment. The entire wharf from what is now the suspension bridge to the St. Clair Street bridge would be filled with piles of freight, and in the rafting season from five hundred to six hundred passengers left daily on the different boats. They were a rude, jolly, and good-hearted set of men, these woodsmen, who earned good wages on their semi-annual trips, and spent with a reckless liberality and outlay their well-earned money. In those days Jim Lynch's saloon on Irwin Street, in the rear of what is now the Hotel Boyer, was a famous resort for raftsmen, and the quantity of 'old Monongahela' consumed there during the progress of a rise was something fearful to contemplate.

" During these excursions the Pittsburg policemen had their hands full, as these sons of the forest were generally powerful and stalwart men, as capable of executing as they were ready to threaten to whip their ' weight in wild-cats.' After they had indulged in a close and familiar inspection of the ' elephant' they would turn up on the wharf with a twenty-five-cent oil-cloth satchel or carpet-sack filled with peanuts, a bottle of whiskey in each pocket, and a remnant of their wages, happy and contented and ready for another year's hard service. The Cornplanter Indians furnished some of the finest raft pilots on the river. Their intimate and intuitive knowledge of the water in all stages made their skill invaluable to the craft, and the vast amount of money invested in the immense fleets of lumber rendered their service a very important duty. The wild orgies they held during the return trip, generally in good humor, made the passage anything but a desirable one to timid people, and bad as the Indian generally is, he was less harmful than the white savage, though the aboriginal nature would often assert itself in war-whoops and suggestions of the scalp-dance. Among the motley crowd were generally a lot of fiddlers, who carried their instruments with them to while away the hours, and dancing to the sprightly measures of ' Hell on the Wabash' was a favorite pastime.

" The Allegheny River in those early days was the only highway of transportation for the immense lumber product of the pine-forests on the head-waters of the Allegheny, and in the spring and fall such large quantities of it was afloat in the river that the perils of navigation were very great, as they were compelled often to run day and night. It required the greatest skill and accuracy of vision to steer clear of these immense flotillas in the night time that often floated in the dim light without lights sufficient to be discerned at any distance on a cloudy night.

" The prominent landings of the river above Kittanning were Catfish, where all the freight for upper Clarion and Jefferson Counties was delivered. Red Bank was the chief point for Clarion County and Gray's Eddy, and Mahoning for Jefferson County through to Punxsutawney. An immense freight traffic was carried on at these points during the season, and the warehouses of James Watterson, at Red Bank; Gould, at Catfish; Elisha Robinson, at Parker's Landing; Captain Robert Thompson, at Gray's Eddy; and Jere Bonner, at Mahoning, were, during the fall and winter seasons, crowded to their utmost capacity with the immense bulk of freightage necessary to supply the adjacent regions.

" The first oil, of that important traffic that has grown to such gigantic proportions, was transported to Pittsburg by the steamer ' Venango,' from Oil City, in the fall of 1859. There were fifty barrels of the greasy substance that in those days brought large prices for uses that have since been so largely extended. The wildest visionary could scarcely have dreamed anything more fabulous or so unlikely as the history of this great product, that from those incipient beginnings of little note has grown to a business that extends throughout the whole of the civilized world. The romance of Alladin's lamp has been more than realized in the colossal fortunes it has compassed in success and failure and the great benefits its discovery has conferred upon the civilized world. In mention of the speed made by the boats of that day we may note that the ' Cornplanter,' under command of Captain Thos. H. Reynolds, made daily trips from Pittsburg to Catfish Landing, leaving Pittsburg in the evening and reaching her destination at ten

Rafting to Pittsburg on the Allegheny River

o'clock the next day, returning to Pittsburg for her evening trip, a distance of one hundred and fifty miles.

"Among the noted resorts, too, of Pittsburg that were most frequented by rivermen in the good old days, we must not forget to mention Ben Trimble's Varieties, that were carried on with such liberal patronage from the up-river men. This noted resort was in the building adjoining Joseph Horne's famous dry-goods house, and in its days was one of the most entertaining places of amusement in the city. In the rafting season it was crowded with rivermen, who roared themselves hoarse at the broad fun and farce that characterized the extended programme.

"Among the pilots of the past we remember Thos. McLemmon, who still resides in Kittanning (1879), Good Mead, Jim Hulings, Jake Magee, Henry Bolinger, Nelse Bartholomew, Bill Watterson, Robert Conner, John Conner, Bill Conner, Matt Conner, Thos. Murphy, Alf. Russell, John Russell, Wm. Russell, Peter A. Smith, G. A. Renshaw, Dan Jack, Cal Russell, James McCain, Hugh McCain, Geo. London, and many others whose names have escaped our memory.

"The Susquehanna and Waterford Turnpike road passes diagonally through the county, crossing the Allegheny River at Franklin on a splendid new bridge. The French Creek Canal and Slackwater Navigation, a division of the public improvements of the State, opens a communication from Franklin to Meadville, and thence by means of the Beaver and Erie extension (nearly completed in 1843) to Lake Erie. The principal productions of the county for export are lumber and iron. There are several furnaces in operation in a circle of ten or twelve miles around Franklin. This trade for a few years was driven with great activity, so much so as to absorb all the agricultural produce of the region; but for one or two years past it has been depressed in common with other departments of industry.

"There are several natural curiosities in the county, the most remarkable of which is the peculiarly inflammable oil found floating on the surface of Oil Creek. The following interesting extract from one of several historical numbers which appeared in the (Franklin) *Democratic Arch*, in 1842, relates to this subject:

"'The Seneca oil from the oil springs on Oil Creek was used by the Seneca Indians as an unguent, and in their religious worship. It is almost as celebrated as the far-famed naphtha of the Caspian Sea. With it the Senecas mixed their war-paint, which gave them a hideous glistening appearance, and added great permanency to the paint, as it rendered it impervious to water. What a startling spectacle the oil-anointed warrior of the Senecas must have been as he gave forth the fearful war-whoop, or paddled his light canoe along the dark blue waters of the Allegheny and Venango!

"'The other use made of the oil was for religious worship. Here I cannot better describe it than in the imaginative language of the commandant of Fort Duquesne to his Excellency General Montcalm, the unfortunate hero of Quebec. "I would desire," says the commandant, "to assure your Excellency that this is a most delightful land. Some of the most astonishing natural wonders have been discovered by our people. While descending the Allegheny, fifteen leagues below the mouth of the Conewango, and three above Fort Venango, we were invited by the chief of the Senecas to attend a religious ceremony of his tribe. We landed and drew up our canoes on a point where a small stream entered the river. The tribe appeared unusually solemn. We marched up the stream about half a league, where the company, a large band it appeared, had arrived some days before us. Gigantic hills begirt us on every side. The scene was really sublime. The great chief then recited the conquests and heroism of their ancestors. The surface of the stream was covered with a thick scum, which burst into a complete conflagration. The oil had been gathered and lighted with a torch. At the sight of the flames the Indians gave forth a triumphant shout, that made the hills and valley re-echo again!" Here then is revived the ancient fire-worship of the East; there then are the " Children of the Sun."

" A more appropriate region could hardly be selected for the residence of an Indian tribe. The rugged hills, clothed with forests, and abounding with game; the pure sparkling streams flowing among these hills. furnishing both excellent fishing-grounds and the means of communication, bordered here and there with fertile bottom lands, as sites for their villages and cornfields, and overlooked by remarkable headlands and ' high places' for their graves and places of worship; some of these hills containing lead, too, and perhaps other metals greatly prized by them,—these were strong attractions for the red natives of the forest. Accordingly we find in almost every direction traces of a numerous Indian population once inhabiting this region. Remains of villages are found at the mouth of Oil Creek. and about the mouth and along the waters of French Creek.

" About five miles directly south of Franklin, and nine by the river, on the left bank of the Allegheny, is a remarkable rock, known to the present inhabitants as ' the Indian God.' "—*Day's Collections.*

" The next important personages who made their appearance upon these shifting scenes were the sires of those who now occupy the soil. A few, indeed, of the original settlers still remain. The original adventurers, who came in under the act of 1792, were from different sections of the country; some from New England, some from Wyoming Valley, and many from the middle counties of Pennsylvania. They endured the usual hardships of a frontier life until after Wayne's treaty, in 1795, when alarms ceased, population flowed in more rapidly, and they continued to prosper, especially after the litigation that originated under the land law of 1792 had been quieted.

" The following description of Fort Franklin is from a writer in the *Democratic Arch:*

" ' In the spring of 1787 a company of United States troops, under the command of Captain Hart, arrived at this place from Fort Pitt, now Pittsburg. They amounted in number to eighty-seven, including officers. There were, perhaps, a dozen of other persons not immediately connected with the corps, and this constituted the whole force at that time. Immediately on their arrival, they commenced erecting what they called Fort Franklin, and from which the name of our town is derived. In place of locating it at the mouth of French Creek, so as to command that stream, as well as the Allegheny River, they made their location about one hundred and eighty rods above the mouth of the former, and at a point that would not at all command the latter. The road from Fort Pitt to Le Bœuf crossed the creek within a few rods of the fort, and, bad as the reason may appear, it was perhaps the only one that induced the selection. It was a mere path then, but the fording was good, and the ascent of the opposite hill was the most practicable from it. Indeed, the existence of this path, and the erection of the fort near it, induced those who settled here at an early period to make their locations also as near as possible to both these supposed advantages. The road, or path, was the only inland thoroughfare to the place, and on it, in the town, was established the hotel, and near this the merchant erected his stall, and the mechanic his shop. Thus was that town in time built upon its present site, far from where strangers think it ought to have been located.

" ' Fort Franklin was located immediately above and west of the south end of the French Creek bridge, and consequently on the south bank of French Creek. Like old Fort Venango, it is a parallelogram, the out-works including about one hundred feet square. These works consisted of high embankments, outside of which arose tall pine pickets, sixteen feet high. There were four bastions, surmounted by small cannon. Within the area formed by the ditches was the block-house, with a huge stack of chimneys in the centre. In this building were the magazine and munitions. The huts of the soldiers were in the ditch around the blockhouse, and within the pickets. This fort was situated on a bluff bank of the creek, twenty-five or thirty feet high, and nearly perpendicular. To this day is distinctly to be seen a deep ditch running along the top, and near the edge of this bank, some one hundred and twenty feet in length, up the creek. This was intended for a covered way leading from the fort to a small redoubt at the very margin of the creek, which was surmounted by two guns—4-pounders, I think. The garrison had what they called a green-house, or cave, in which they kept vegetables and meat, within a few feet of the excavation now being made at the end of the bridge for the site of a new toll-house. A garrison of near one hundred, including officers and men, was kept at Fort Franklin until 1796, when what is familiarly known as the " Old Garrison," at the mouth of the creek, was erected by the troops at the fort, at a point more convenient for receiving provisions and munitions brought up by boats and canoes from Pittsburg. It was a strong wooden building, a story and a half high, and perhaps thirty by thirty-four feet in length. It was picketed in, but not calculated to be mounted with cannon. Indeed, the necessity for this had ceased, as the treaty of General Wayne with the Indians at Fort Greenville had been made in August, 1795, and was then believed, as it turned out to be, a lasting peace. The troops at this position removed from the fort, which was from that time suffered to dilapidate, and occupied the garrison. This they continued to do until 1803, when they were withdrawn from Franklin altogether. Fort Franklin soon went entirely to ruin. The stone in the chimneys, like those in Fort Venango, were hauled away by the citizens of the place, and used in building foundations and chimneys for private dwellings. The " Old Garrison" was occu-

pied from the organization of the county, in 1805, until 1819 as a common
jail, when the county jail was completed. It remained standing, though in
ruins, until 1824, when the last vestige disappeared. Indeed, I am told that
the very foundation on which it stood has been washed away, and is now part
of the bed of French Creek.'

"Franklin, the county seat, was laid out by the commissioners, General
William Irvine and Andrew Ellicott, under the act of 1795, at the same time
with the Waterford Turnpike, and the towns of Erie and Waterford. It contains the usual county buildings, and Presbyterian, Methodist, and Cumberland Presbyterian churches. It is situated upon a broad plain, a little above
the mouth of French Creek, and is surrounded with scenery highly picturesque.
There are in the vicinity a furnace, a forge, and several mills, and the place
derives considerable trade from several iron works in the surrounding region.
The French Creek division of the Pennsylvania canal terminates here, and
when the Beaver and Erie canal is completed, a communication will be open
from here to the lake. The Allegheny is navigable, in high water, for steamboats to Pittsburg—distance, by water, one hundred and twenty-four miles.
The distance by land is only sixty-eight miles. Two dams on the French
Creek navigation, within a mile of the town, afford an immense water-power;
and there are several other dams farther up the creek. A splendid new
bridge crosses the Allegheny here, and there is also one across French Creek.
Population in 1840, 595. It was made a borough April 14, 1828."—Day's
Collections.

"Among the first settlers at this place were Mr. George Powers and Mr.
William Connolly. Mr. Connolly came from Meadville in 1800. Mr. Powers
came out, in 1787, to assist in erecting the barracks, and subsequently came
in 1793 on his own account, and established a store to trade with the Indians.
Samuel Ray and John Andrews came in 1795. In 1797 there were only three
or four white families in Franklin.

"In the war of 1812 this county was well represented. A call was
issued for all the able-bodied men to go to Erie, to protect the frontier from
an anticipated attack at that point. All who could be spared from their
homes repaired to the scene of expected action. Of the regiment that was
formed from this and some of the neighboring counties, Samuel Dale was
elected lieutenant-colonel. He was a native of Union County, but had resided
in Franklin for many years. About this time the Seneca chief, Cornplanter,
came to see Colonel Dale, to inquire into the cause of the war. When this
was explained to him, he declared his willingness to accompany him with two
hundred warriors. He insisted on the propriety of his going. The corn was
planted, and the young men could go as well as not to assist in the war with
their white neighbors. Colonel Dale could satisfy him only by agreeing to
call upon him should it be actually necessary. During the war Franklin
presented quite a busy aspect. All the military and naval stores were brought

up from Pittsburg in keel-boats, thence up French Creek to Waterford, and thence by teams to Erie. It was a matter of surprise to the British how Perry's fleet was equipped under the circumstances, as they were ignorant of this inland communication with Pittsburg. All these boats were pushed up by hand, with the assistance of the captain, in places where the water was specially rapid.

"From the organization of the county, in 1800, to 1805 it was associated for judicial purposes with the neighboring counties of Warren, Butler, Mercer, Erie, and Crawford, with the seat of justice at Meadville. The first court held was presided over by Judge Alexander Addison. By act of April 1, 1805, Venango was fully organized for judicial purposes, with Franklin as the county seat. The first court was held in a log house on Liberty Street, facing West Park. Jesse Moore was the first judge. He was succeeded by N. B. Eldred, in 1839. The first court-house was erected in 1811. It was of stone, on West Park, and facing what is now Plumer's Block. A second court-house was built of brick in 1848, on South Park, and facing up Liberty Street.

"The old garrison was used as a jail from 1805 to 1819, when a small stone building was erected for the purpose, on the South Park. There was a yard attached to one end of it, surrounded by a stone wall about twelve feet in height, with a well in the inclosure. The cells were lined with oak plank about five inches in thickness.

"Franklin, the county seat, is the oldest town in the county. It was located on lands belonging to the State. On the 24th day of March, 1789, it was resolved by the General Assembly 'that not exceeding three thousand acres be surveyed for the use of the Commonwealth, at the Fort of Venango.' By act of April 18, 1795, commissioners were appointed to survey one thousand acres of the reservation at the mouth of French Creek, and lay off thereon the town of Franklin. The commissioners designated for this purpose were General William Irvine and Andrew Ellicott. Mr. Ellicott had charge of the surveying, and General Irvine of the military escort of fifty men. The name was probably suggested by the name of the fort. The plot selected lies along the south branch of French Creek and the west bank of the Allegheny River. The valley in which it is situated is about two miles in length and about half a mile in breadth, surrounded on every side by bold, precipitous hills, rising to the height of about one hundred feet. The town is beautifully laid out with wide streets, crossing each other at right angles, with the exception of Twelfth Street, where there is an acute angle to accommodate a flexure in the creek.

"The pioneer school-house of Venango County was built of logs and covered with clap-boards, which were held to their places by 'weight-poles.' The heating apparatus consisted of an old-fashioned 'fireplace.' A wide, sloping board, attached to the walls, and a plank or a slab, with peg-legs, and without a back, served respectively for desk and seat. The floor was laid with puncheons.

"For windows, a log on each side of the room was sawed out, and in the winter these openings were covered with greased paper.

"In such a house James Mason taught the first school in Franklin, in 1801–02. The first academy building was erected in 1815 or 1816, and Mr. Kelley taught in it until 1823."

The pioneer academy was erected in Franklin in 1815. The pioneer mail route in the county was in 1802, from Erie to Pittsburg, carried on horseback, and came once every three weeks. The carrier's name was Ash. He carried a tin horn to announce his coming. Mr. Ash carried the mail from Meadville to Franklin, and afterward from Franklin to Warren.

For some time after the pioneer court-house was erected, court was called by a long tin horn purchased at the county's expense. This horn was used by John Morrison, who opened the pioneer court in Mercer, Crawford, and Warren Counties.

The pioneer doctor in Franklin and Venango Counties was T. G. Symonds. Whence he came no one knows.

The pioneer effort to organize an agricultural society was in Franklin in 1838.

The pioneer navigation of the Allegheny by the white man was the expedition of Celoron in 1749. This river has had several names. The Shawnee Indians called it Palawa-Thoriki; the Delawares named it Alligawi Sipu, after a race of Indians which they believed had once dwelt upon the stream. This tribe was called Alleghans by Colden in the London edition of his work, and Lewis Evans, on his map published in 1755, called the river the Alleghan. The Senecas called it Ho-he-u, which name the French adopted, connecting it with the Ohio as the same stream.

The pioneer to make his home in Franklin was George Powers, in 1787. Thomas Skelley McDowell was the first white child born in the town, April 26, 1803.

"The first successful steam navigation of the Allegheny River occurred in 1828, and marks the beginning of a new era in economic development and internal communication in Western Pennsylvania. The following account of the first steamboat appeared in the *Venango Democrat* of March 4, 1828:

"'A STEAMBOAT ON THE ALLEGHENY

"'On Sunday evening, the 24th of February, the citizens of this place were somewhat alarmed by the discharge of a field-piece down the Allegheny River. Another report soon followed; then the cry, "A steamboat!" resounded in all directions, and the citizens, great and small, were seen flocking to the river to welcome her arrival. She proved to be the "William D. Duncan," of one hundred and ten tons, Captain Crooks. She left Pittsburg on Friday at three o'clock P.M., and arrived at Kittanning, a distance of forty-five miles, the same evening; left Kittanning at ten A.M., and arrived at this place on Sunday at five P.M., after stopping at Lawrenceburg (now Parker) and other places. The actual time occupied in running the whole distance, one hundred and forty miles, was twenty-eight hours, averaging five miles an hour. We understand she could have made the trip in much less time, but, it being the first, her engineer was afraid of applying her full power to the current. She had on board several tons of freight, and about one hundred and fifty ladies and gentlemen from Pittsburg, Freeport, Kittanning, and Lawrenceburg came as passengers. On Monday morning a party was got up in town, who took an excursion of eight miles up the river to Oil Creek furnace, for the double purpose of the pleasure of the trip and as a remuneration to the enterprising owners for the visit. She steamed the current at the rate of between five and six miles an hour, and came down in twenty-one minutes. The day was fine, the trip pleasant, all were highly gratified, and the accommodation was excellent. On Tuesday morning she took her departure for Pittsburg, where, we understand, she arrived next morning, without meeting with a single accident to mar the pleasure of their experiment. We learn that two other boats are making preparations for ascending the Allegheny, and that one of them may be expected here on Friday or Saturday next. It is expected they will ascend the river as far as Warren, for which place we understand they have been chartered. This, it is expected, will put an end to the controversy between the citizens of Pittsburg and Wheeling as to which is located at the head of steamboat navigation.'

"The pioneer steamboat built for the river was the 'Allegheny,' in 1830. Her first trip to Franklin was April 16, 1830, and to Warren, April 23, 1830. It went up to Olean, New York, and returned to Pittsburg.

"Stern-wheel steamboats were introduced upon the western waters in 1830. This innovation in nautical construction was the invention of a Mr. Blanchard."

It was not an unusual thing to see a large Olean raft on the river, with a team of horses, a cow, a girl cooking, and the mother spinning flax; these were emigrants going to Ohio or Indiana State. Previous to steamboating, all commerce on the river was carried on by canoes or keel-boats pushed by men. From and after 1828 steamboats carried men and goods up and down the river. The Pennsylvania Canal was finished to Freeport about 1828. Two surveys were made of the river by the United States, with a view to digging a canal along the valley,—viz., one in 1829 and one in 1837.

The pioneer road through Venango County was the Le Bœuf. There is no record, but it was probably opened in 1754.

The Pittsburg, Kittanning and Warren Railroad was chartered April 4, 1837.

The pioneer weekly mail route was opened in 1801 between Pittsburg and

Erie, by way of Butler, Franklin, Meadville, and Waterford. Horseback was the mode of transportation.

The pioneer post-office in the county was in 1801, at Franklin. Alexander McDowell was postmaster.

The pioneer protestant minister to preach in the town was a Presbyterian, in 1801. The services were held in David Irvine's home.

The pioneer Sunday-school in Franklin was founded in 1824 by Rev. Timothy Alden; it was a union school.

The pioneer merchant in Franklin was George Power.

There were Indian paths that led in several directions from Franklin. The old Venango trail led down until it struck the Ohio at Logstown; another led northeast to the lakes.

Ferries were the first means of crossing the streams. French Creek had two ferries.

On one occasion a preacher was crossing the Allegheny Ferry, which was kept by a stout Dutchman who was very just and honest. The preacher thought to let the Dutchman know the nature of his cloth, and inquired, " How much do you charge preachers?" The reply was, " Vell, we do not charge them any more as we do other fellows. We don't take no advantage of de breacher any more as we do of de farmer."

Irwin Township is older than Venango County. The pioneer settlers in Irwin Township were Adam Dinsmore and Henry Crull, in 1796.

The pioneer hotel in Irwin Township was a log house erected about 1800 and kept by Henry Crull.

The pioneer grist-mill in Irwin Township was built in 1805 by John Crain.

" In June, 1817, owing, no doubt, to a scarcity of the necessaries of life, for at this period Irwin Township was but a wilderness, John J. Kilgore with two companions went to Franklin, hired a canoe, and paddled down the river to Pittsburg, where they bought a load of provisions and returned, pushing the canoe up the stream with poles, and making the trip in ten days. During that time they slept but one night under a roof. Game was abundant in those days. In 1819 there was a heavy fall of snow, and it is related by Mr. Kilgore's son that his father, in company with his hired man, killed sixteen deer in one day.

" It is related that a Mormon preacher named Snow came to Irwin Township in 1837, and among his converts were Henry Stevenson and several daughters and a man by the name of David McKee. These two and their families were taken to Salt Lake City by Snow."

Among the early settlers in Venango County were about twenty-five Revolutionary soldiers.

CHAPTER XXXVIII

" WARREN COUNTY was taken from Allegheny and a portion of Lycoming County by the act of March 12, 1800. By the act of 1805 the county was annexed to Venango for judicial purposes. On the 16th of March, 1819, the county was fully organized, and the seat of justice fixed at Warren. Length, thirty-two miles east and west, breadth, twenty-six miles; area, eight hundred and thirty-two square miles. Population in 1800, 230; in 1810, 827; in 1820, 1976; in 1830, 4706; in 1840, 9278. The county was named for General Joseph Warren.

" The Allegheny River runs, with its meanderings, not less than fifty miles within the county, entering at the northeast corner and leaving at the southwest. It consists of extensive sheets of dead water and short ripples, and furnishes power to drive several extensive saw-mills at different points. The Conewango Creek, which enters the county from the State of New York, and meets the Allegheny at Warren, is also a large and navigable stream, and turns many valuable mills. The other principal streams are the Brokenstraw, Little Brokenstraw, Tionesta, Tidioute, Kinjua, Stillwater, Coffee, and Fairbank Creeks, and Jackson's, Alkley's, Valentine's, and Morrison's Runs, etc.,—on all of which the lumbering business is carried on extensively (1843).

" The surface of the county is undulating, and, near the large streams, deeply indented and sometimes rocky. The lands in the townships contiguous to the State line are generally of good quality, and will admit of dense settlements; and the same may be said of those between Brokenstraw and Conewango Creeks, except the river hills. ' The land between the two Brokenstraw Creeks,' says another writer, ' for several miles is stony and broken indeed. A land speculator from " the land of steady habits," once travelling over it, where " stones peep o'er stones, and rocks on rocks arise," remarked, that " it would never be settled till it was *settled* by an *airthquake*." ' Beyond this, near the Crawford County line, is a large body of good land. On all the rivers of the county are broad alluvial margins, producing corn and wheat abundantly when properly cultivated. Previous to the year 1827 that part of the county southeast of the Allegheny River was but little known or explored, and the land abandoned by its owners was principally sold for taxes; but since the titles could be perfected, settlers have moved in, and found the region to be well timbered, supplied with abundant water-power, and containing much good arable land.

"In a letter written by General William Irvine, of the Revolutionary army, to General Washington, after the close of the war, concerning the best means of opening a water communication between Lake Erie and the Ohio, he makes allusion to the traces and traditions then existing of an old road cut by the French over the portage between Chautauqua Lake and Lake Erie, and intimates his belief that it was once or twice used by them and afterwards abandoned for the Presque Isle portage. This must have been between the years 1728 and 1750. Previous to this, and subsequently, this whole region was owned and occupied by the Seneca Indians. In the year 1784 the treaty to which Cornplanter was a party was made at Fort Stanwix, ceding the whole of Northwestern Pennsylvania to the Commonwealth, with the exception of a small individual reserve to Cornplanter. The frontier, however, was not at peace for some years after that, nor, indeed, until Wayne's treaty, in 1795. About the time of Wayne's treaty (and some say even previous to that event, and as early as 1790, but it is not at all probable) several adventurous Irishmen started from Philadelphia, and, passing up the Susquehanna and Sinnemahoning, penetrated the wilderness of McKean County, built canoes, and launched them upon the waters of the Allegheny at Canoe Place, two miles above Port Allegheny. Floating down past Olean to the mouth of Conewango, they left the river, and made the first settlement in Warren County, among the beechwoods of Pine Grove and Sugar Grove Townships. Their names were Robert Miles, John Russel, John Frew, John and Hugh Marsh, and Isaiah Jones. When they arrived upon their lands, their whole stock of ' specie and specie funds' was only three dollars!

"About the year 1795 the venerable James Morrison (who died in 1840, at the age of one hundred and four years) came out, and took up the large island at the mouth of Kinjua Creek. He was also the owner of Morrison's Island, at the mouth of Morrison's Creek, a few miles above Warren. At Irwinville James Harriot built the first mills, about the year 1812 or 1813. Messrs. Faulkner, Wilson, Smith, and Hall were the first settlers near Pine Grove, about the years 1816 to 1820. The McKinney family were also early settlers: John settled on Brokenstraw, and Barney and Michael on the Conewango. Major Robert Andrews, and Messrs. Hicks, Wilson, Youngs, and Kinnear, were also early settlers on Brokenstraw. Most of them were lumbermen. Tomes, an Irishman, and Daniel McQuay, also settled on Brokenstraw.

"'Among the earlier settlers and most enterprising lumbermen of the county was Jacob Hook, better known, perhaps, as "Jake Hook." He emigrated either from Boston or Maine somewhere about the year 1798, bringing

N E W   Y O R K.

OUTLINE MAP-1850 -
V E N A N G O   F O R E S T

March-12-1800

with him, as his stock in trade, a package of the bills of some bank that had failed so recently "down east," that Jake had time to circulate his bills here before the failure became known. This served to start him; and eventually, by dint of sharp bargains and hard work, rolling saw-logs, digging mill-races, and other speculations appurtenant to a lumber country, Jake arrived to the dignity of owning more mills and running more lumber than any other man in the county. In connection with some of his speculations, the charge of perjury had been fastened upon him, and he had made himself extremely obnoxious to many of the citizens. A party attempted to arrest him for trial, and he killed one of them in the affray, was tried for his life, but escaped by an informality in the legal proceedings. The following is from the *New York Censor*, copied into the *Conewango Emigrant* of July 21, 1824: "It was proved on this trial that seven men, headed by one Asa Scott, went to the house of Hook, about four miles above Warren, on the left bank of the Allegheny, between sunset and dark on the 25th of March, for the avowed purpose of taking Hook to Warren that night. They all admitted that they intended to use force is necessary. One said that they meant to take him at all events. These persons were inimical to Hook with one or two exceptions, and had with them one or two loaded rifles. On arriving at Hook's they found his doors fastened. One of the company endeavored to prevail on him to surrender; but he refused, alleging that he feared to trust himself with such men. About nine o'clock Scott and his followers went to the house and demanded admittance; but he persisted in stating that he considered himself in danger, and that he looked upon them as a mob. Scott also stated that, on his demanding admittance, Hook informed him, by a token peculiar to a particular society, that he was in danger, and that he (Scott) assured him that he would be safe. Scott immediately burst open the outer door with considerable violence; and almost at the same instant a gun was fired off within the house, by which one of the assailants (Caleb Wallace) was killed, and another wounded. On the trial, the counsel for the prosecution attempted to show that Scott was a deputy-sheriff, and had a legal warrant for Hook for perjury. The court, however, on examining the deputation under which he pretended to act, decided that it was void, and gave him no authority." Hook was acquitted on that ground. He had always been at sword's points with the Warren people, and this affair had no tendency to heal the breach. He died about 1829 or 1830.

" The settlement of Warren County, more than of any of the neighboring counties, was greatly retarded by the misconstructions and litigation resulting from the land law of 1792, and the peculiar management of the Holland Land Company. This company, under the act of 1792, had taken up the greater portion of the best lands in the county, northwest of the Allegheny and Conewango; and, by way of aiding and encouraging settlers upon their lands, they established a large store at Warren—one of the first buildings erected in the place. Daniel McQuay had charge of it. Pine lumber, however, was the great object of pursuit in this county, and not agriculture, and so long as a lumberman had but the color of a title, he would remain long enough on the land to cut the timber, and then set up a claim to a new tract. Many thus made entries under the act of 1792 upon land claimed by the Holland Land Company, and were in consequence in continual conflict with the company's agents. The latter refused to sell to such persons anything from their store, or in any way to countenance them, without a compromise with the company. During this uncertainty the better class of settlers were deterred from purchasing, and the population in 1810 was only eight hundred and twenty-seven, and in 1820 was less than two thousand. On the southeast of the Allegheny the Lancaster Land Company had taken up a large tract, which had been disposed of by lottery, or in some such other way as to scatter the titles among various unknown and distant owners, who came at length to abandon their lands as of no value, and they were sold for taxes. This part of the county is still comparatively unsettled. By the great speculations of 1828 to 1840, the demand for lumber throughout the great West was increased, the value of pine lands enhanced, and great activity was infused into the lumber business along the Conewango and Allegheny.

"' Warren, the county seat, is situated on a plain of about three hundred acres, on the right bank of the Allegheny, just below the mouth of Conewango Creek. The town is principally built along the river bank, which is about thirty-five feet above the water, and commands a picturesque view above and below. A noble bridge here crosses the Allegheny.

"It is allowed to be one of the most eligible sites on the river. The town was laid out and the lots sold by General William Irvine and Andrew Elliott, commissioners appointed by the State. The borough was incorporated in 1832. Near the centre of the plot is the public square or *diamond*, around which are situated the court-house and public offices, of brick; and the jail, of stone; a bank, of stone,—a solid structure without, but broken within.—and an academy, of brick. The population of the place (seven hundred and thirty-seven in 1840) is not yet commensurate with its original plan, and the consequence is that the public buildings make rather a lonely appearance, separated as they are at some distance from the compact business street along the river. There are three churches,—Presbyterian, Methodist, and German Methodist. There are also Baptist and German Lutheran congregations, who have not yet erected houses of worship. The dwellings and stores are generally of frame, neatly built, and painted white. The place is one hundred and twenty miles from Pittsburg by land, and twenty-two from Jamestown, on the outlet of Chautauqua Lake.

" Warren, in common with the county, was retarded in its improvement by the causes mentioned above, and in 1813 it boasted but five houses. The Holland Land Company at an early day erected their store-house on the river

Old Warren

bank, just above the blacksmith's shop; and Daniel Jackson built another house on the corner. Abraham Tanner, Esq., who is still living, came to Warren from Trumbull County, Ohio, embarked in the lumber business, and pursued it for some years with success. Robert Falconer, Esq., a Scotch gentleman of considerable fortune, came to the place a few years after Mr. Tanner. In 1816 Samuel Dale surveyed the Lancaster lands opposite the town, across the river. The lands on the hills north of the river, and west of the Conewango, and one mile from each, are called the State's lands; they extend from one to two miles in width, nearly through the county, being lands which the Holland Company did not include in their survey.

"The business of Warren varies with the season of the year. In the midst of winter or summer the place is exceedingly dull; but at the breaking up of the ice in the spring, and during the subsequent floods, the town, and the whole country above, on the Conewango and Allegheny, is alive with the bustle of preparation among the lumbermen. Large rafts are continually coming down the Allegheny, and smaller ones down the Conewango, and rounding in at Warren to be coupled into rafts of immense area, sixty or seventy feet wide, and from two hundred and fifty to three hundred feet long, in which shape they pursue their course to Pittsburg and Cincinnati. Large boats, too, or 'broad-horns,' as they are called, from the width of their oars, form part of the fleet.

"These rafts, like immense floating islands, form at once the vehicle and the temporary residence of several families on their way down the river. Old and young, from the gray-haired pioneer of sixty down to the boy of twelve years, are interested in their departure, and compose the crews to navigate them. There is not probably a boy of twelve years old living on any stream in Warren County who has not made his voyage to Cincinnati, perhaps to 'Orleans.'

"It is a cheering sight to see the bright broad raft floating slowly down the picturesque passes of the Allegheny, with its little shanties, and busy population; some lifting the long heavy oars, some cooking at the great fire, some eating their bacon from a broad clean shingle,—superior to French porcelain,—some lounging in the sun, and some practising their coarse wit upon the gazers from the shore, and making the wild hills echo with their shouts. The unsettled habits induced by these semiannual voyages are far from being congenial to the agricultural interests of the county. Among those who have become distinguished in the lumber business is Guy C. Irwin, Esq., who resides on the Conewango, a short distance below Pine Grove. He is a complete Napoleon in the lumber business. His name, person, and character, are known in every large town from Olean to New Orleans. He owns, or has owned, more pine lands and saw-mills, and 'run' more lumber, than any man on the waters of the Allegheny. While the business was driven to its full extent in 1836–38, he frequently sent to market twenty millions of feet of boards in a season. The shore for a mile or two above Pittsburg is frequently lined with his rafts waiting a rise of the waters. Mr. Irvin came out from the West Branch of the Susquehanna about the year 1817, with little other capital than a strong, comprehensive mind, and an untiring spirit of enterprise.

" The failure of the Lumberman's Bank at Warren, three or four years since, was fraught with disaster to the middle and poorer classes of citizens of Warren County. The history of this bank, could its material be gathered at this day, would be an excellent beacon for similar institutions. By means of the great extent of country throughout which the lumber trade was prosecuted, its bills were widely circulated, as well at home as at Pittsburg, Cincinnati, and farther down. The short and prompt loans originally made, became long ones, and eventually permanent; the borrowers were few, and heavy dealers and land speculators; they soon had the bank in their power; the securities assumed the form of pine lands, and unsalable property, the specie was exhausted, the bank failed, with a circulation in the hands of the needy, who sold at a heavy discount to the large borrowers, who thus paid their debts at an easy rate.

" ' In a note, by the editors of the *United States Gazette*, referring to the ancient village of Ephrata, situated in Lancaster County, in this State, the fact is noted that " one of the first printing-presses introduced into the State" was located in that village. As a small item of history connected with our profession we have to add, that the identical press in question became the property of the editor of this paper in the year 1804. He caused the woodwork to be renewed, and removed it to Meadville in the fall of that year. It was the *first* printing-press introduced into this State northwest of the Allegheny River, and from which the *first* sheet issued in this region. All the *continental money* issued by Congress, while in session at Lancaster and York, during the Revolutionary War, was struck upon it. This relic of antiquity is now, we believe, the property of Mr. Purvance, of the neighboring county of Warren, and from which the *Union*, a very respectable sheet, is issued. Long may it continue to administer to the welfare, prosperity, and happiness of the Union.'—*Crawford Messenger, 1830*.

" ' The Hon. Joseph Hackney departed this life at Warren on the 20th of May, 1832, at the age of sixty-nine years.

" ' He was distinguished for stanch integrity, uprightness, and generosity in his intercourse with the world; modest, unobtrusive, amiable, and possessing reliance, for at least the last year of his pilgrimage, on the atonement of the blessed Redeemer.

" ' A development of the murderous outrage upon the happiness of his paternal roof by a savage foe would harrow up the feelings of sensibility. He was a soldier with Colonel Harmar, at the building of Fort Harmar, at the mouth of the Muskingum, in 1785.

" ' In 1789 he went with Major (afterwards General) Doughty, up the Tennessee River, to conciliate the Indians in that region by a distribution of presents from the United States. The party, consisting of fifteen, landed at the encampment of the first Indian village. The tawny natives seemed to manifest great friendship, but the discerning Major Doughty descried something which foreboded treachery. He put his men on their guard, and, having bestowed the presents designed, the Indians all gave them their hands in token of their pretended amicable feelings, but Doughty and his men had scarcely wheeled their boat in order to proceed to another village, when the savages levelled their muskets and killed eleven at the first fire. Mr. Hackney escaped with his life, as did the two officers and one more; but one of his arms was broken by a ball, and hung useless at his side. With the other he managed the boat. The enemy pursued, to the number of sixty, yet by the well-directed fire of the three uninjured warriors, using the loaded guns of their fallen brethren, they killed many of their pursuers, beat off the residue, and defeated them!

" ' Mr. Hackney then repaired to a Spanish fort on the Mississippi, where, with surgical aid and the blessings of Heaven, his limb was fully restored.

" ' He was afterwards with Harmar on his campaign in 1790. During this memorable period, he was sent out under Major Willis and Lieutenant Ebenezer Frothingham, on what may with propriety be called a *forlorn hope*, as one of a battalion intrusted with a duty, in the region of the Sandusky. The Indians killed every member of the battalion except eleven, of which Mr. Hackney was one.

" ' In 1793 he settled in Meadville, diligent in his lawful pursuits, happy in his domestic relations, and beloved by all his acquaintance. He was colonel of the first regiment in Crawford County.

" ' He removed to the banks of the Konnewonggo, in 1817, and gained by his urbanity, hospitality, and correct conduct the esteem of his fellow-citizens, and their suffrages for various offices. He was appointed an associate judge, on the organization of Warren County for judicial purposes, and discharged the duties of the office with dignity, establishing his character as an upright and useful judge till the close of his life.'—*Crawford Messenger.*

" Pine Grove is situated on the right bank of the Conewango, seven miles above Warren, at the head of the rapids. It is compactly built, containing some forty or fifty dwellings, store, taverns, etc. Russel's mills are situated here, on one of the best water-privileges in the county. Three saw-mills and a grist-mill, besides other works, are in operation here, and nearly a mile below is another large saw-mill. Establishments like these, it is said, might be erected on each mile between Pine Grove and Warren.

" Youngsville is situated on both sides of Big Brokenstraw, three miles from its mouth. It contains about twenty dwellings and a Methodist church. Some of the largest and best-cultivated farms in the county surround this

village. Sugar Grove is situated in the township of that name, one and a half
miles south of the New York State line. It contains some twenty or thirty
dwellings, a saw- and grist-mill. It is pleasantly situated, and surrounded
with groves of sugar-maple,—hence the name. Lottsville is in the same township, on the Little Brokenstraw. Fayette is on a branch of the Big Brokenstraw, in Columbus Township. At all these places there are good water-
privileges. At each of these villages there is a post-office, as also at Deerfield,
Kinjua, Spring Valley, and Irvine.

  " A colony of German Protestants have recently purchased (May, 1843)
ten thousand acres of land in Limestone Township, which they are about
settling on the principle of community of property. It is believed, however,
that they intend to retain the common property organization for only five or
ten years, or until the land is fully paid for, when they expect to divide the
shares. A similar colony, of the Catholic denomination, have also purchased a
tract in the eastern part of the county, near the boundary of McKean County.

  " About six miles below Warren, near the mouth of Brokenstraw Creek,
the traveller, who has thus far passed the usual plain log or frame cottages
by the roadside, is struck with the appearance of an elegant mansion of stone,
of a chaste and neat design, standing a little back from the road, with a fine
farm around it. A short distance beyond he sees another, after the same
model, adorning a similar farm; a little farther on, another still, and near it,
by the roadside, the ' Cornplanter Hotel,' built of freestone, in a style and of a
magnitude that would do honor to Chestnut Street, in Philadelphia. Opposite
the hotel is a row of stores, in the same style of architecture; a neat bridge
crosses the creek; on one side are the wild rocky hills, and on the other the
broad alluvial meadows that border the Allegheny. Besides the buildings enu-
merated above, there is a mill and miller's house; two other elegant stone cottages below the creek; and about a mile below, near the Allegheny, is the mansion of the proprietor. This village, intended eventually to become the town of
Cornplanter, was erected and is owned entirely by Dr. William A. Irvine. It
stands on a large tract of fine land inherited from his father, the late Commissary-General Callender Irvine, who was the son of General William Irvine
of the Revolutionary army. The village was built in anticipation of the construction of the Sunbury and Erie Railroad, which was located directly
through it, and was to pass up the Brokenstraw valley. It will be some years
before this road is constructed.

  " On the flats below the village once stood an Indian village, called Buck-
aloon, which was destroyed by a detachment under Colonel Broadhead from
Pittsburg, in 1781. It required a siege of some days to drive out the Indians,
who retreated to the hills in the rear of the village. Several days afterwards
Major Morrison (afterwards a distinguished citizen of Lexington, Kentucky)
returned to reconnoitre, and had stooped to drink at the mouth of the creek,
when a rifle ball from an Indian splashed the water in his face. This fact

was long after confirmed to Dr. Irvine by one of Cornplanter's men. General William Irvine was for several years engaged as commissioner for the State in superintending the surveys of land northwest of the Allegheny, under the land law of 1792; and either he or his son, General Callender Irvine, took up large tracts on Brokenstraw Creek. The latter came to this place in 1795, erected a cabin, and placed in charge of it, by way of perfecting ' an actual settlement,' a faithful old negro slave. A very affectionate intimacy subsisted between General Irvine and Cornplanter, and reciprocal visits were often made by them. One day while General Callender Irvine was staying at the cabin, two Monseys, a small clan of whom lived in the vicinity, came to the cabin for some salt. Salt in those days was as precious as silver, being packed on horses over the mountains. The old negro took out his measure of salt to give them a little, but they wanted the whole, and vowed they would have it by fair means or foul. General Irvine here interfered and drove them off. A few days afterwards one of Cornplanter's men came down to visit and hunt, and spent a fortnight with the general. This was no uncommon occurrence at his hospitable cabin, and he thought nothing of it. Months afterwards Cornplanter told the general that the Monseys had threatened his (the general's) life, and that he had sent the Indian down secretly to watch their movements.

" Kinjua is a small village on the left bank of the Allegheny, at the mouth of Kinjua Creek, and twelve miles above Warren. Five miles above Kinjua, on the right bank of the Allegheny, and four miles below the State line, is the reservation and late residence of Cornplanter, the distinguished Seneca chief. The Allegheny reservation of the Seneca nation is above the State line, extending for thirty miles along the river, and one mile in breadth. The Senecas were by far the most numerous and warlike of the Six Nations. The peculiar organization of that confederacy, and the rank which the Senecas held in it, have been mentioned on page 6 of the Outline History. The history of their wrongs at the hands of land speculators, and of the gradual diminution of their numbers, belongs more properly to the history of New York than to that of Pennsylvania. By various treaties they have been deprived of one piece of their fair domain after another, until they were crowded upon four small reservations, one at Tonawanta, eight or ten miles northwest of Batavia, one three miles east of Buffalo, one at Cattaraugus Creek, twenty-eight miles south of Buffalo, and the fourth on the Allegheny, as mentioned above. At each of these reservations, except the Tonawanta, the American Board have a mission station, with a church and schools. The following is from the *Dayspring* of February, 1842 :

" ' The whole number of schools on all the reservations is twelve, containing two hundred and ten pupils. In addition to these are eight Sabbath-schools, embracing one hundred and fifty-five pupils. To the four churches about fifty members have been added during the year 1842. And there has been a very great advance in the cause of temperance. For three years past there has been great excitement and alienation growing out of their political difficulties. In 1838 a treaty was obtained from them, in which the Senecas sold all their reservations except the last two, and that portion of the Tuscarora which the Tuscaroras held by purchase. By the conditions of this treaty they were to receive one hundred thousand dollars, also one hundred and two thousand dollars for their improvements; and the United States government was to furnish four hundred thousand dollars to remove them west of the Mississippi and support them one year in the West. It has been estimated that the allowance made them for their improvements will not be half adequate to enable them to make as good houses and fields on the new lands to which they go, as they had on those which they leave, and that by this bargain, should it be carried into effect, they would lose more than half their available property, and be for some years to come comparatively poor and destitute. A compromise was effected last spring, by which they sell only a part of Tuscarora and the whole Tonawanda and Buffalo reservations, and receive a proportionable part of the compensation stipulated in the former treaty; but they receive nothing for removal and subsistence. The case at present stands thus. The Indians on the ceded part of the Tuscarora reservation must remove to that part which is not sold. Here they will have land enough for their present wants. The Indians on the Tonawanda and Buffalo reservations must all remove. Cattaraugus and Allegheny remain for the present undisturbed. The Indians from Tonawanda and Buffalo intend, most of them, to settle at Cattaraugus. Some say they will go west of the Mississippi, some to Canada, and a few will probably go to Allegheny. Two years are allowed by the treaty for removing, nearly eighteen months of which still remain. The present number of Indians on these reservations is about three thousand.'—*Day's Collections.*

"The year 1800 was made memorable in the history of Pennsylvania by the erection of several new counties in the northwestern quarter of the State, from territory which had been temporarily attached to organized counties whose seats of justice were hundreds of miles distant. Thus, by an act of the State Legislature passed March 12, of that year, the counties of Beaver, Butler, Mercer, Crawford, Erie, Warren, Venango, and Armstrong were formed from territory previously embraced by Westmoreland, Washington, Allegheny, and Lycoming Counties. Warren was formed from Allegheny and Lycoming Counties, and the clause of the act relating to its boundaries reads as follows:

"'That so much of the counties of Allegheny and Lycoming, as shall be included within the following boundaries,—viz., Beginning at the southeast corner of Crawford County, in the north line of the sixth donation district: thence the course of the said line eastwardly across the Allegheny River, until it shall intersect the line dividing Johnson's and Potter's districts, in the county of Lycoming; thence northerly along the said line to the line of the State of New York; thence westwardly along the line of the said State to the corner of Erie County; thence southerly by the eastern boundaries of the counties of Erie and Crawford, to the place of beginning.'

"The same act further provided that the place for holding courts of justice within the county should be the town of Warren. Also, that the governor be empowered to appoint three commissioners to run, ascertain, and mark the boundary lines of the county; that the commissioners be paid the sum of two dollars per day while so engaged, and that the boundaries described be run 'on or before the 15th day of June next.' William Miles, Thomas Miles, and John Andrews, the latter being then a resident of the county, were appointed, but what their duties were, or what they did, if anything, does not appear.

"It was further provided by this act that the counties of Crawford, Mercer, Venango, Warren, and Erie ('until an enumeration of the taxable inhabitants within the aforesaid counties respectively shall be made, and it shall be otherwise directed by law') should form one county under the name of Crawford County. Meadville thus became the seat of justice for a vast, sparsely settled region, and people of to-day can hardly realize the vicissitudes experienced by the pioneers who, when obliged to visit the county seat to transact legal or other business, or were summoned to attend courts, etc., were compelled, in going and returning, to travel from seventy-five to one hundred and fifty miles through dense forests, and along winding, partly overgrown Indian trails, providing the 'trails' led in the right direction; otherwise the undertaking was still more hazardous.

"Only a few weeks had passed after the passage of the above-mentioned act ere the county of Crawford was duly organized as a separate division of the State, and its first officers installed in office. The first session of court was held in the upper story of William Dick's residence, on the northeast corner of Water Street and Cherry Alley, in Meadville. The record of this session begins as follows: 'At a Court of Common Pleas held and kept at Meadville, for the county of Crawford, the seventh day of July, Anno Domini, One Thousand Eight Hundred, before David Mead and John Kelso, judges, present, and from thence continued by adjournment until the ninth day of the same month inclusive.' Mead and Kelso were only associate judges, and not learned in law. Their attention at this time was chiefly directed to the admission of attorneys, to the erection of townships, the issuing of licenses, and the appointing of certain township officers.

"During the second session of the court of Crawford County, held at the place above described in October, 1800, Hon. Alexander Addison presiding, the first grand jury met. It was during this term, also, that the township of Brokenstraw (the original township of Warren) was erected. The order of court respecting this subdivision reads as follows: 'In pursuance to sundry

651

petitions presented, the court directed the following townships to be laid off. . . . Also all that part of Warren County situate west of River Allegheny and Conewago Creek be erected into a township and the name thereof to be Brokenstraw.' (See Docket No. 1, page 11, Judicial Records of Crawford County.) Judge Addison resided at Pittsburg, and was a gentleman possessed of a fine mind and great attainments, but he was subsequently impeached and removed from office, because of his absolute refusal to allow an associate judge to charge a jury after his own charge had been delivered.

"On the 21st of February, 1801, another act was passed relating to the new county of Warren, by the provisions of which it was denominated the First Election District of Crawford County, and the electors residing therein were directed to hold their general elections at the house of Robert Andrews, who then lived in the Brokenstraw valley, or where Pittsfield now stands.

Pioneer court-house

" This arrangement continued until April 1, 1805, when an act was passed providing for the organization of Venango County from and after September 1 of that year. By the same legislative act Warren County was detached from Crawford and annexed to Venango, for judicial and all other purposes of government; thus becoming part of the Sixth Judicial District, of which the Hon. Jesse Moore was then serving as president judge."

The pioneer court in Warren was held Monday, November 29, 1819, Sheriff Bowman, Prothonotary Alexander McCalmont, and Court Crier Morrison were there from Venango County to help organize the court. The president judge was Jesse Moore, of Meadville, assisted by Associate Judges Hackney and Connelly. The pioneer local lawyer was Abner Hazeltine.

652

"In December, 1806, Daniel Jackson, of the town of Warren, and Giles White, of Brokenstraw Township, were recommended to the governor by the court as suitable persons to keep houses of public entertainment. One year later Salmon Fuller, a millwright, was licensed to keep a public house in Conewango Township. These were the first persons licensed to 'keep tavern' in Warren County of whom we have authentic knowledge.

"In the summer of 1816 Rev. Timothy Alden, before mentioned as the founder of the Allegheny College, set out on a brief missionary tour among the Indians residing on the upper waters of the Allegheny, and spent some days at the village of the venerable chieftain, Cornplanter. Upon his return to Meadville he wrote a letter to the Rev. Joseph McKean, of Harvard University, giving an account of his labors, etc., wherein he says, 'Cornplanter, as soon as apprised of our arrival, came over to see us, and immediately took charge of our horses. Though the chief Sachem of his tribe, and having many around to obey his commands, yet, in the ancient patriarchal style, he chose to serve himself, and actually went into the field, cut the oats, and faithfully fed our beasts from time to time, while we continued in the place, *in ipsa persona propria*. . . .

"'Cornplanter has been the greatest warrior the Senecas have ever had; yet he has always been remarkable for his humane treatment of the women and children of his enemies, who at any time have fallen into his hands. He is a man of strong mind and masterly eloquence. At the treaty of Fort Stanwix he greatly distinguished himself by his talents and address, insomuch that by general suffrage he has ever held the first place of power among the chiefs of his nation.

"'He appears to be about sixty-eight years of age.' (Mr. Alden was mistaken as to Cornplanter's age. He was born about 1732, and in 1816 was eighty-four years old.) 'His countenance is strongly marked with the lines of intelligence and reflection. Contrary to the aboriginal custom, his chin is covered with a beard three or four inches in length, and upon his head are many of the blossoms of age. His house is of princely dimensions compared with the generality of Indian huts, and has a piazza in front. He is the owner of about fifteen hundred acres of excellent land, six hundred of which encircle the ground plot of his little town. From the United States he receives, annually, according to stipulation, two hundred and fifty dollars, besides his proportion of nine thousand dollars equally divided, one-half in goods and one-half in money, among those of every age and condition in the tribe.' "

We again quote from Warren County History of 1887:

"For five years the inhabitants of Warren County had plodded their weary way from their log cabins in the wilderness, over the hills to Meadville, when it was necessary to transact public or legal business, and for fourteen years more had they made toilsome journeys to Franklin, a distance of sixty-five miles from the then hamlet of Warren, when business of the same nature imposed its duties upon them. This condition of affairs at last became too onerous and irksome to be longer borne without an effort being made to effect a change. Hence in the winter of 1818–19 Colonel Joseph Hackney, of the town of Warren, then representing Venango County in the State Legislature, introduced a bill providing for the separate and independent organization of the county of Warren. His efforts were crowned with almost immediate success, and on the 16th day of March, 1819, an act containing the legislation desired was passed.

" This act provided that Warren should be organized as a separate county from and after October 1, 1819, and be attached to the Sixth Judicial District. Also, that the legal electors should choose county officers at an election to be held on the second Tuesday of October of that year, whose duties were to be considered as commenced from the first day of October, 1819. We have no evidence, however, that such an election was held, and from the fact that Lansing Wetmore's commissions as prothonotary, clerk of courts, register and recorder, etc., were signed by the governor, September 25, 1819, it is believed that all the chief officers of the county at the beginning were appointed by the same authority.

" The Hon. Jesse Moore was the first judge in the order of time, from 1819 to 1824. He was a gentleman of the old school, dignified but courteous, learned but not brilliant, characterized by stern integrity and freedom from all prejudice. He was a short, thick-set man, and some still remember his benignant countenance, partially bald head, well-powdered hair, and broad-brimmed, drab-colored hat. He died suddenly, when still in the prime of life and maturity of intellect, honored and lamented by all.

" Henry Shippen succeeded him from 1825 to 1835. His characteristics were common sense and sound judgment. Many here will remember his inflexible honesty, his fidelity to truth, and his contempt for trickery and fraud. A single instance will suffice to illustrate: In 1834 a notorious personage of a neighboring county, by fraud and false interpretation, had procured a judgment note from the venerable old Cornplanter for three thousand dollars, entered judgment, and issued execution on it. Application was made by counsel, in behalf of the old chief, to open the judgment and let him into a defence. As the evidence of the villany was disclosed, the judge became very nervous. Anger flashed from his eye, and before the counsel got through his evidence the judge told him to stop, and, leaning over the bench, in a voice hoarse with indignation, said, ' Mr. Clerk, set aside that writ and strike that judgment from the records of this court !'

" Next came, in 1835, Judge Nathaniel B. Eldred, the accomplished gentleman, brimful of honor, honesty, and sympathy. His quick perception, sound judgment, and stern impartiality guided him to the justice of a case, without the aid of much legal learning, so that his decisions were seldom appealed from and were seldom reversed. With but a year of interruption he remained

N. B. Eldred

L. D. Wetmore

S. P. Johnson

W. D. Brown

Rasselas Brown

Warren pioneer judges

with us until 1843, when he was removed by appointment to the Harrisburg district. His social qualities and public spirit, as well as official conduct, had greatly endeared him to the hearts of the people of this and other counties, who parted with him with much reluctance and regret.

"In 1839, after the death of Judge Shippen, Judge Eldred was appointed his successor in the sixth district, out of which this county had been taken in 1835 to form part of the eighteenth, and without our solicitation or knowledge Alexander McCalmont was appointed to fill his place in the eighteenth district, including Warren County. His administration was so short and unsatisfactory that I will be excused for passing it over in silence. The next year, by legslative act, this county was restored to the sixth district, and thus

Methodist church, 1835

again came under the jurisdiction of Judge Eldred. He was the only judge of the first seven that ever resided in Warren."

The pioneer Methodist minister to visit Warren was Rev. R. R. Roberts, in 1806. The pioneer Presbyterian minister to visit Warren was in 1822. The pioneer school-teacher was in 1804,—a Mistress Cheeks; she had a Dilworth Speller and a copy of the New Testament. The pioneer frame schoolhouse was erected in 1820 on the public grounds. The pioneer jail was made of stone in 1829. The pioneer court-house was of brick, in 1827; all courts held previous to that were convened in a house that stood where the Carver Hotel now stands. A steamboat was built in 1830 to run from Warren to

42   657

HISTORY OF NORTHWESTERN PENNSYLVANIA

Olean; she was called the "Allegheny," and made but one trip. Warren Borough has an existence since April 18, 1795. The town of Warren, as originally laid out, consisted of five hundred and twenty-five lots, each fifty-eight by two hundred and thirty-three feet. An order for the sale of the lots in Warren, Erie, Waterford, and Franklin was issued by Governor Mifflin on the 7th day of May, 1796. All this territory was then Allegheny County. These lots were directed to be sold at Philadelphia, Carlisle, and the borough of Pittsburg. The pioneer permanent building was erected in 1796, and belonged to the Holland Land Company. Warren contained but few white people then, but many Indians. In 1813 the town had but five houses. In 1832 Warren was made a borough, with a population of three hundred and eighty-five. In 1840 it had a population of seven hundred and thirty-seven. The pioneer saw-mill on the upper waters of the Allegheny was erected about 1799. A grist-mill was built at Ceres in 1801. The pioneer raft to float down the Allegheny, from near Warren, was in 1801. In that year there were two saw-mills in the county,—one on the Brokenstraw, and one on Jackson Run. A small raft from each of these mills was run down in 1801.

The pioneer four-horse stage-coach arrived from Dunkirk to Warren May 24, 1826. In 1840 you could go by stage from Buffalo to Pittsburg in less than three days. In 1848, by a line established by Richard T. Orr and others, a traveller could go from Pittsburg, Pennsylvania, to Buffalo, New York, in less than three days. The distance from Pittsburg by way of Erie to Buffalo was two hundred and twenty-four miles.

TAXABLE INHABITANTS IN NORTHWESTERN PENNSYLVANIA

	1835	1842	1849
Butler	4,322	5,535	7,490
Crawford	5,164	7,516	8,130
Clarion	not erected	3,311	5,087
Elk	not erected	....	877
Jefferson	902	1,788	2,622
Lawrence	not erected	....	4,425
McKean	....	1,089	1,213
Mercer	5,196	7,356	6,923
Potter	556	681	1,346
Tioga	2,485	4,091	5,237
Venango	3,014	3,127	4,027
Warren	1,600	3,593	3,149
	23,239	38,087	50,526

CHAPTER XXXIX

ALLEGHENY CITY, IN THE PURCHASE OF 1784

Allegheny City is situated on the right bank of the Allegheny River, near the junction with the Monongahela, opposite Pittsburg, with which it is connected by three bridges. It was incorporated in 1828. This city presents many fine residences, in commanding situations, occupied by many persons doing business in Pittsburg, who are pleased to retire from the bustle, smoke, and coal-dust of the principal city. Its commercial and manufacturing business, properly its own, is considerable.

The pioneer mayor was Robert Simpson Cassatt, father of the president of the Pennsylvania Railroad.

Day, in 1843, says,—

" Passing over to Allegheny City, there may be seen the Western Theological Seminary of the Presbyterian Church, founded by the General Assembly in 1825, and located in Allegheny town in 1827. The edifice was completed in 1831. It stands on a lofty, insulated ridge, about one hundred feet higher than the Allegheny River. It is, indeed, quite a task to ascend this hill of science and religion, but one is amply repaid by the pure air and magnificent prospect. It contains a library of about six thousand volumes, and has connected with it a workshop for manual labor. Rev. Francis Herron, D.D., is president of the board of directors; Rev. David Elliott, Rev. L. W. Green, Rev. Robert Dunlap, professors.

" The Theological Seminary of the Associate Reformed Church, located in Allegheny City, was established in 1826. It is under the charge of Rev. John T. Pressly, D.D., possesses a valuable library, and numbers about thirty students.

" The Allegheny Theological Institute was organized by the general synod of the Reformed Presbyterian Church in 1840; Rev. James R. Wilson, D.D., senior professor; Rev. Thomas Sproull, junior professor. The seminary possesses a valuable library. Measures are in progress to erect a large edifice in Allegheny City.

" The Western Penitentiary is an immense castle, built in the ancient Norman style, situated on the plain behind Seminary Hill, and on the western border of Allegheny City. It was completed in 1827, at a cost of $183,-092, including its equipments. Notwithstanding some glaring defects in

659

its original construction and arrangement, it has now become an efficient institution. It is conducted on the 'Pennsylvania system' of solitary confinement and labor. Weaving, shoe-making, and oakum-picking are the employments of the prisoners. About eight hundred prisoners had been received, in 1842, since the commencement of the institution."

The population in 1830 was 2801; in 1840, 10,089. It has fifty-eight stores, with a capital of eighty-three thousand four hundred dollars; nine lumber-yards, with a capital of fifty thousand dollars; one furnace, and one forge; value of hardware and cutlery manufactured, fifty thousand dollars; three cotton factories, with fourteen thousand two hundred and seventy spindles; two tanneries; one brewery; one rope walk,—total capital in manufactures, $726,640, and several churches.

A PIONEER HISTORY OF DU BOIS CITY

(Written for the *Courier* by the well-known historian, Dr. W. J. McKnight.)

George Shaffer and wife, with their six children, Frederick, Michael, George, Jr., and three daughters, migrated from Dauphin County, Pennsylvania, in 1812 to where Du Bois City now stands. On May 13, 1812, a part of the family arrived and erected a "bark shanty" near where the old Heberling farm and "Inn House" stood, and "beside the spring which bubbles and sparkles to-day as it did then." On the night of the 14th Frederick and Michael Shaffer slept in this shanty, which they erected in what is now the First Ward of the city, the other members of the family stopping with Jacob Ogden, a pioneer who lived at what is now Carlisle Station on the Buffalo, Rochester and Pittsburg Railway, south of Du Bois. The Shaffers cleared two acres of land on the ridge or hill-side in that year. Charles C. Gaskell was agent for the land, and George Shaffer, Jr., afterwards bought the land from him.

In 1815 and for many years after Clearfield was known as " Old Town;" the county was not organized until 1822 and this township was not formed until 1826 and was named after the celebrated Captain Sam Brady, the great Indian fighter. The Shaffer property passed from their hands in 1853 to Jacob Heberling, who sold to his son David, who owned and occupied the land until 1865, when he sold the two hundred and fifty acres of it to John Rumbarger. David Heberling was a prosperous farmer and kept a house of entertainment. John Rumbarger was a jobber for Bell and Rogers, and upon his purchase moved in 1865 into the Heberling house, where he farmed, jobbed and "entertained strangers." His house was always open to Methodist preachers and for the holding of religious service. From a personal knowledge of Rumbarger I can say that he was truly an "honest man." His first attempt to change his general surroundings into a town was in the spring of 1872. P. S. Weber, of Du Bois City, bought the first two lots sold in the coming city; the deeds bear the date of July 10, 1872. The conditions of

Alexander Johnston Cassatt, now President of the Pennsylvania Railroad System, born in Allegheny City, in 1839

that time will be best shown by the following advertisement Rumbarger had inserted in the *Clearfield Journal* and the *Brookville Republican*. Who wrote this advertisement for him I do not know :

"ONE HUNDRED LOTS FOR SALE IN THE TOWN OF RUMBARGER, IN BRADY TOWN-
SHIP, CLEARFIELD COUNTY, PENNSYLVANIA

"The subscriber has laid off one hundred lots, which he offers for sale at reasonable rates to all those who feel disposed to move in that direction. The town is beautifully situated on Sandy Creek within eighty rods of the Allegheny Valley Railroad now under completion. It is also situated on the public road leading from Luthersburg to Brockwayville. In this town liberal inducements are offered to mechanics and enterprising business men, being in a thickly settled farming community. Those in want of lots should buy early, as they are being disposed of very rapidly. He also offers for sale a lot of ten acres adjoining the town with a stream of water running through it, sufficient to run a machine shop, carding-mill, etc., and excellent situation for a tannery. He will sell his Tavern House and about one acre of land in said town, well situated for a hotel, being large and commodious, and having the necessary out-buildings and stabling attached.

"There is a large steam saw-mill and general lumbering establishment now under construction by John Du Bois, adjoining the town, that will give employment to not less than one hundred hands.

"There are several springs of good water in the town, and those wish-ing to sink wells can obtain water in from ten to fifteen feet.

"The town is in a healthy part of the county and easy of access from Luthersburg, Salem, West Liberty, Reynoldsville, Rockdale, and the Beech-woods Settlement.

"Come and see the place before purchasing elsewhere.

"JOHN RUMBARGER, *Proprietor.*

"July 17, 1872, 3 months."—*Brookville Republican.*

In the last of February or the first of March, 1873, Mr. Rumbarger came to my office in Brookville, Pennsylvania, and told me that he thought the time had arrived to more thoroughly advertise his proposed town, "and as you are a good writer I would like you to write one for me." As he and I were close personal friends I wrote the following, which he inserted in the *Brookville Republican:*

"ONE HUNDRED TOWN LOTS FOR SALE IN THE TOWN OF RUMBARGER, CLEAR-
FIELD COUNTY, PENNSYLVANIA

"To those unacquainted with Rumbarger we would say that it is a beautiful site for a town. Not too level or too hilly, but just right for proper drainage, and that it is situated in a healthy locality. The soil is rich and the country is fruitful, located on the banks of the Sandy Lick Creek. A public road from Luthersburg to Brockwayville passes through it.

"The great 'Low Grade,' or Bennett's Branch Extension of the Allegheny Valley Railroad, skirts the entire length of the town, and we have assurances that first class depot buildings will be constructed this summer for the accommodation of the citizens. Further, it is confidently asserted that the Falls Creek Railroad will be commenced, and probably completed this summer. In any event, whenever completed, this road will cross the 'Great Low Grade' at and pass through Rumbarger. This, it will be observed, gives the town the advantage of two great lines of railroad, a northern outlet as well as the main line.

"Rumbarger, being located in a rich mineral country, and surrounded by vast forests of the choicest pine and other timbers, and supplied with such railroad facilities, must of necessity become a great commercial centre and shipping point. The country around it is good for agricultural purposes, much better than is generally found in this western part of the State.

"Among the improvements now under construction are two saw-mills, one of which will be the largest in the State. These mills will contain all the modern improvements, such as lath, sash and door, and planing mills, and other improvements. It is enough to say that these mills are owned and will be conducted by John Du Bois, Esq., of Williamsport, Pennsylvania, who is also erecting about thirty dwelling-houses to accommodate his workmen. Other mills and buildings are now under construction, and from the way lots are selling and present appearances a great many dwellings and business houses will be commenced as soon as the spring will permit.

"The lots we offer are 60 feet front and 180 feet deep. Good water can be had from springs or by digging wells. Favorable time and reasonable terms will be given purchasers of lots. Strangers visiting the town will find good hotel accommodations and persons to show them the town and surroundings.

"The cars will be running as far as Rumbarger on the Bennett's Branch Railroad by July or August next.

I also offer for sale one hundred and fifty acres of land adjoining the town, fifty acres improved and the remainder well covered with pine, hemlock, and oak timber. This land is like all the surrounding lands, valuable for its minerals, containing coal in large quantities, the veins being from seven to ten feet thick.

"For particular information address JOHN RUMBARGER, Jefferson Line, Clearfield County, Pennsylvania.

"March 12, 1873."

After I read to him the above advertisement, he was highly pleased, took out his pocket-book, and proposed to pay for my labor. I said, " Oh, no," and remained firm. He then insisted that I come up, make him a visit, and pick out a lot which he would donate to me. To this generous offer I replied, " My dear friend, what do I want with a town lot up there in the woods?" Mr. Rumbarger lived long enough to walk with me in Du Bois City and ask me this pertinent question: " Doctor, which one of these lots would you have picked for yourself had you made me that visit as I re- quested?"

Du Bois City lies within the 1784 purchase.

Pioneer post-office, Rumbarger, 1874; George L. Glasgow, postmaster. Post-office name changed to Du Bois in 1876. Pioneer merchants in the town, J. B. Ellis, Thomas Montgomery, C. D. Evans & Bro., in 1873. Pioneer doctor, W. J. Smathers, 1873. Pioneer hotel-keeper, William Corley, 1874. The town was incorporated as a borough and named Du Bois, after the post-office, at January Court, 1881. Lewis A. Brady was elected first burgess.

Beaver City, in Beaver County, also lies within the 1784 purchase. Of this city, Day, in his " Collections of 1843," says,—

" BEAVER

" The place known by this name to travellers and others at Pittsburg, whence so many little steamers are seen plying for this destination, is not,

Beaver in 1843

properly, one town, but a little cluster of towns—a sort of United States in miniature, situated around the mouth of Beaver River, and for four or five miles up that stream. And it is a singular fact, that to a traveller passing on the Ohio scarcely any village at all can be descried at the place, although there is here a population of some six thousand.

" Beaver borough, the seat of justice, is a quiet, orderly, old-fashioned county town, with its respectable society and the usual number of stores and taverns. It is built principally upon a long street running parallel with the Ohio River, upon an elevated plateau, some forty rods back from the river. A dangerous gravel shoal, formed by the confluence of the Beaver with the Ohio, lies directly abreast of the town, which accounts for the fact of there being no business street along the river. The court-house, jail, and three churches, all substantial buildings, stand around an open square, through which runs the main street. Population in 1840, 551. The borough was incorporated March 29, 1802.

" The annexed view [page 665] shows the court-house, jail, etc., on the left, and the churches on the right, with the main street beyond.

" ' By the act of 28th September, 1791, the governor of the State was instructed to cause to be surveyed two hundred acres of land in town lots, near the mouth of Beaver Creek, "on or near the ground where the old French town stood," and also one thousand acres adjoining, on the upper side thereof, as nearly square as might be, in out-lots, not less than five, nor more than ten acres each. By the same act, five hundred acres, near the town, were granted for an academy. Daniel Leet surveyed the town plot. The probable motive at that day for locating the county seat at a distance from the great manufacturing advantages at the Falls, was the existence of the well-known shoal just below the mouth of Beaver, a difficult and dangerous passage to the keel-boats and other craft in use at that day. By the location here, the town was accessible alike to the lower and upper trade, and the obstructions themselves would probably throw considerable business into the place. The idea of erecting Lowells and Rochesters had not as yet entered the heads of speculators in land. Samuel Johnston first settled at Beaver in 1796. He kept an inn on the bank of the river, near Fort McIntosh. Some traces of the old fort are still to be seen near his house. Jonathan Porter, Abraham Laycock, David Townsend, Joseph Hemphill, John Lawrence, Mr. Small, Mr. Alison, were also early and prominent settlers. Judge Laycock filled many important offices in the county and State, and held a seat in the Senate of the United States. On the present site of New Brighton, there existed an ancient "blockhouse," at which Sergeant-Major Toomey commanded when Mr. Alison first came here, on a visit, in 1793. General Wayne was encamped at Legionville, on the river, below Economy. The only road in those days was " Broadhead's," which led across the country from where Phillipsburg now is.' "

CITY OF TOWANDA, IN 1784 PURCHASE

" Towanda, the county seat of Bradford County, is situated near the centre of the county, on the right bank of the Susquehanna. A part of the village is on the river bank, and a part on several successive benches gently rising from the river, and presenting a most enchanting prospect. The dwellings are built with taste, generally of wood, painted white, imparting a remarkably bright and cheerful appearance to the town as one approaches it from the Wysox valley, just opposite. Besides the usual county buildings, the town contains Presbyterian, Methodist, and Episcopal churches, an academy, and a bank, very extensively known. A noble bridge crosses the river at the town. Just below the bridge is the dam and lock of the North Branch Canal, which here crosses the river by a pool, thus forming a convenient basin opposite the town. Part of the dam was swept away in the flood of 1841 or 1842. In former times the people of Towanda numbered fresh shad among their luxuries, but the construction of the dams in the river has excluded them entirely. Population, 912.

"Towanda was first laid out in 1812, by Mr. William Means, who re-

Southeast view of Towanda in 1843, from the hill near the Wysox road. In the foreground is the bed of the North Branch Canal, laid bare (in 1841) by the destruction of the dam below. Over the centre of the bridge is the Presbyterian Church; on the hill is the Academy, and on the right the Methodist and the Episcopal churches

sided here at that time. The act organizing the county directed the courts to be held at his house until public buildings were erected. Old Mr. Fauks, a German, and his son-in-law, Mr. Bowman, lived then on the point below Towanda. Mr. Fauks had settled there before, or during the Revolution, having been attached to the British side in that contest. The village for several years was called Meansville, and so marked upon the maps. Other names were also occasionally *tried on*, but did not fit well enough to wear long. The *Bradford Gazette* of March 4, 1815, says, 'The name of this village having become the source of considerable animosity, the editor (Burr Ridgway), willing to accommodate all, announces a new name,—*Williamston;* may it give satisfaction and become permanent.' But subsequently, in that same year, the *Gazette* appears dated Towanda; and in 1822, again the *Bradford Settler* was dated at Meansville. Towanda was incorporated as a borough in 1828, and its name was thus permanently fixed. The location of the canal, the discovery of coal-beds in the vicinity, and the establishment of a most accommodating bank gave a great impetus to the growth of the place between the years 1836 and 1840; but the subsequent disastrous failure of the bank, in the spring of 1842, following, as it did, the already severe commercial distress, and the suspension of the public works, spread a gloom over its prospects. The natural advantages of the place, however, are too great to be annulled by any temporary cause, and Towanda must soon shake off the load, and eventually become a place of considerable business. Besides the great valley of the Susquehanna, three smaller valleys, rich in the products of agriculture, centre here, and must pour their trade into the stores of Towanda."—*Day's Collections, 1843.*

APPENDIX

In the spring of 1864 we had thirty thousand human, living skeletons in rebel prisons. The war had been carried on for three years. The following great and sanguinary battles had been fought,—viz.: Bull Run, Seven Pines, Fort Donelson, Fort Pillow, Shiloh, Seven Days' battle in Virginia, second battle of Bull Run, Antietam, Fredericksburg, Stone River, Chancellorsville, Gettysburg, Chickamauga, Cold Harbor, Spottsylvania, and the Wilderness. These battles, or most of them, had been the bloodiest that modern history had recorded. In our sorrow and despair, the most bitter antagonisms existed at home between the war and anti-war people. A new President was to be elected that year, and in order to save the country and to punish rebellion, nearly all patriots—this included war Democrats—believed that the re-election of Lincoln was absolutely necessary. Actuated by these impulses, Judge Joseph Henderson, of Brookville, was chosen our Congressional delegate to the national convention, which was to meet on the 7th of June, 1864, in Baltimore, Maryland. Judge Henderson, Major Andrews, and myself were warm friends. The judge was a great friend of Lincoln and Johnson. On the 5th of June I accompanied the judge to Baltimore. Our State delegation consisted of fifty-two men,—forty-eight district delegates and four at large,—viz., Simon Cameron, W. W. Ketcham, Morrow B. Lowry, and A. K. McClure. Simon Cameron was made chairman of the delegation. The following States were represented in that body: Maine, Vermont, New Hampshire, Massachusetts, Rhode Island, Connecticut, New York, New Jersey, Pennsylvania, Delaware, Maryland, Louisiana, Arkansas, Tennessee, Ohio, Indiana, Illinois, Michigan, Wisconsin, Iowa, Minnesota, California, Oregon, West Virginia, Kansas, Nebraska, Colorado, Nevada, and Missouri. There was a dispute as to the right of Tennessee to representation, but the convention voted them in. In this the judge voted aye, and on the first ballot Lincoln received every vote except Missouri, which cast a solid vote for General Grant. For Vice-President, Andrew Johnson, of Tennessee, was nominated on first ballot over Hamlin, of Maine, Dickinson, of New York, and Rosseau, of Kentucky. It was thought by the convention expedient to strengthen the ticket by nominating a man for this office who was

669

known to be a war Democrat and from the South, and as this was a convention of freemen, wise leaders, and not of bosses, the people and wisdom ruled.

From Baltimore I went to Washington on business to see Stanton. I found him haughty and austere. I therefore sought and received an audience at the White House. I had heard Lincoln denounced verbally and in the newspapers as "Lincoln, the gorilla," "Lincoln, the ape," "Lincoln, the baboon," etc., and, true enough, I found him to be a very homely man, tall, gaunt, and long-limbed, but courteous, sympathetic, and easily approached. My business with him was this: In 1863 a boy fourteen years two months and fifteen days old, from Jefferson County, whose father had been killed in battle, was recruited and sold for bounty into the Fourteenth United States Regulars at Pittsburg, Pennsylvania. After a few months' service, this boy, tired of military life, was told by his soldier companions that he could not be held in the service, and, instead of demanding his discharge in a proper way, unceremoniously left and deserted, for which he was afterwards arrested, court-martialled, and sentenced to be shot. As early as April 28, and after that, legal efforts were put forth, and military influence used by myself and others to save this boy, but without avail.

"ADJUTANT-GENERAL'S OFFICE,
"WASHINGTON, D. C., April 28, 1864.

" SIR,—I have the honor to acknowledge the receipt of your communication of the 9th ultimo, requesting the discharge of —— —— from the military service of the United States, of the Fourteenth United States Infantry, on the ground of minority, and to inform you in reply that he is now under arrest for trial by court-martial for desertion, and no action can be taken for his discharge, or that will prevent his punishment if found guilty.

"I am, sir, very respectfully,
"Your obedient servant,
"THOMAS M. VINCENT,
"*Assistant Adjutant-General.*

"W. J. McKNIGHT, Brookville, Pa."

My business was to save the boy's life, and while everything else had been done by legal talent and military influence, I went to Lincoln with a sad heart. He was at that time perhaps the busiest man in the world. He listened patiently to my story, and then said, "Is all this true, Dr. McKnight, that you have told me? Will no one here listen to you?" I replied, "Yes, Mr. President, it is all true." He arose, reached for his hat, and remarked to me, "I'll be a friend to that fatherless boy." He put his arm in mine and took me to Stanton's office, and, after a few minutes' talk with the Secretary, he turned to me and said, "You can go home, doctor, and if that boy has not been shot, you can rest assured he will be discharged." In due time, after my return home, I received by mail the following:

> "ADJUTANT-GENERAL'S OFFICE,
> "WASHINGTON, D. C., July 13, 1864.
>
> "SIR,—I have the honor to inform you that, by direction of the President, —— ——, *alias* John Scott, Fourteenth United States Infantry, was discharged the military service of the United States, by special orders No. 204, Par. 25, current series, from this office.
>
> "I am, sir, very respectfully,
> "Your obedient servant,
> "SAMUEL BRECK,
> "*Assistant Adjutant-General.*

"MR. W. J. McKNIGHT, Brookville, Pa."

Washington at this time was the greatest panorama of war in modern times. It took me days to secure an audience with Mr. Lincoln. I was then, and am yet, perhaps too ultra and bitter a Republican, but after this humane act of President Lincoln I was as bitter a partisan as ever, and, in addition to that, a personal admirer of Lincoln from the crown of my head to the end of my toes.

The call for our county convention that year was issued July 13, 1864, as follows,—viz.:

> "DELEGATE ELECTION
>
> "The Republicans of Jefferson County will meet in their respective townships and boroughs on Tuesday, the 2d of August, between the hours of two and six o'clock P.M., to elect two delegates of each township and borough, to meet at the court-house in the borough of Brookville, on Friday, the 5th day of August, at one o'clock, to nominate candidates to be supported for the different county offices.
>
> "M. M. MEREDITH,
> "*Chairman County Committee.*"

The county then had twenty-three townships and four boroughs, giving us fifty-four delegates. The date fixed for the primaries was on the day set by the law of the State, passed in the spring of that year, for the special election for three amendments to our Constitution, one of which was to permit the soldiers in the field to vote. The date fixed for this call was a shrewd policy, as it materially assisted in bringing out a full Republican primary, and was a great aid in carrying that "soldier vote" issue in the county, which we did, as the full return gave fourteen hundred and ninety-seven for this amendment and twelve hundred and twenty against it, a majority of two hundred and seventy-seven. This issue was bitterly fought. After the national convention I had been appointed a member of the Union State Central

Committee by Simon Cameron, who was then chairman of that committee, and this soldier campaign in the county was conducted by Captain Meredith. The county convention was held on August 5, as called, and the following ticket selected: For District Attorney, A. C. White; County Commissioners, I. C. Jordan, Eli B. Irvin; Auditor, Joseph P. North; Trustees of Academy, P. H. Shannon, M. M. Meredith, Calvin Rodgers.

G. W. Andrews was made county chairman. Our Representative district was Clarion and Jefferson, and on September 9, at Corsica, Hunter Orr, of Clarion County, was declared the nominee for the Legislature. On September 15 G. W. Schofield was declared in Ridgway our nominee for Congress. Dr. A. M. Clarke and S. W. Temple were our conferees there. This completed our ticket. There were no State officers to be elected. Nothing but district and county tickets in that October election. I do not recollect who was the Democratic chairman, but it is immaterial, for ex-Senator K. L. Blood dominated and controlled the Democratic party in this county then, and a bold, wiry, vigorous antagonist he was. Our Democratic Dutch friends used to make this reply: " I do not know how I votes. I votes for der Kennedy Blute anyhows." School-house meetings were held in all the townships. Local speakers were scarce. Most of them were in the army, and this labor then principally devolved upon Andrews and myself. Dr. Heichhold was furloughed about October 20 to help us. In our meetings we all abused Blood, and he in return abused us. Major Andrews was a great worker, and usually took a number of papers and documents to read from. What little I said was off-hand. The major would always say in his speeches that " the common people of the Democrats were honest, but the leaders of that party were rascals, traitors, and rebels." He was a Maine Yankee. We elected him to the State Constitutional Convention in 1872, and after his service there he removed to Denver, where he lived and died.

For the August and October elections we had no funds except our own, and we were all poor alike. Our newspaper editor was John Scott, Esq. He was poor, too; paper was high and hard to get, and, as a consequence of this, our organ, the *Republican*, was only published occasionally, and often only half-sheets: hence our meetings had to be advertised verbally and by written and printed posters. I had one horse. I traded some books for a second-hand buggy, and bought another horse that I would now be ashamed to own, and in this buggy and behind this team the major and I drove the circuit in October and November, stopping for dinner and over night, Methodist preacher fashion, with the brethren. It was a rainy fall, and all through October and November there was mud,—mud rich and deep, mud here and there, mud on the hill and everywhere, mud on the ground and in the air, and to those who travelled politically it was a mud-splashing as well as a mud-slinging campaign. We had a mass-meeting on October 8 in Brookville, and on that day we had a strong address published, reviewing the issues to the people, signed by I. G. Gordon, Philip Taylor, T. K. Litch, A. S. Rhines, R. G. Wright, and J. P. Wann. The speakers for the mass-meeting were Chairman Andrews, Colonel Childs, of Philadelphia, Congressman Myers, and A. L. Gordon. J. W. Pope, the great campaign singer, from Philadelphia, by his patriotic songs, impelled us all to greater earnestness. In the October struggle we lost our county and Representative ticket, but Schofield was re-elected to Congress. A Congressman then never thought of having one or two bosses in a county to dispense post-offices. The Democrats carried the State on the home vote; but, with the aid of the soldiers, we carried the State by a small majority. The anti-war Democrats greatly rejoiced at their victory on the home vote, and they confidently expected, as McClellan was a Pennsylvanian, that State pride would carry him through in November. The two elections were about one month apart. The soldier vote was denounced as the " bayonet vote" and " bayonet rule." Simon Cameron, our State chairman, was greatly disappointed at the loss of our State on the " home vote." After the October election Cameron sent me a draft for two hundred dollars in " rag-money," which I expended as judiciously as I knew how. We gained in the county sixty votes for the November election. I am sorry that I cannot give the manner of expenditure of this money. My accounts were all audited and the settlement-paper left with G. W. Andrews. McClellan had been the idol of the army and the people, and although he and Pendleton were nominated at Chicago on August 31, 1864, on a peace platform that the war had been a failure and a call to suspend hostilities, there never was a day that McClellan would not have been overwhelmingly elected in 1864, until in September, when Sherman captured Atlanta and Sheridan went whirling through the valley of Virginia. Everybody, Lincoln and all, knew this. These two victories gave the Union people great heart for hard work. After these victories, Fremont and Cochrane, who had been nominated at Cleveland, Ohio, on May 31, 1864, for President and Vice-President by radicals of the Republican party, withdrew, and both supported Lincoln. Our army before Richmond was idle, and, to effectually stop the " bayonet rule" charge, Meade furloughed five thousand soldiers for two weeks. Sheridan did the same, making ten thousand in all, and they went home and voted. This gave us the State on the home vote by about five thousand, and with the " bayonet vote" by about twenty thousand. In this election our county went as follows:

	Lincoln.	McClellan.
Home vote	1614	1756
Army vote	207	111
Total vote	1821	1867

In the November election our county went Democratic; but we Republicans had a grand jubilee after the returns came in from the nation, as McClellan only carried three States,—viz., Kentucky, Delaware, and New Jersey.

Brevity requires many things that I would delight to say about Lincoln and this campaign to be omitted. Republican success gave assurance to the world that "the war for the Union would still be prosecuted," and it was, and Pennsylvania performed her duty, both politically and on the battle-fields. Pennsylvania gave to the national government during the war three hundred and eighty-seven thousand two hundred and eighty-four soldiers, including emergency men. Three times during the war Pennsylvania was invaded, and it remained for the Rebellion to receive its Waterloo at Gettysburg and from a Pennsylvania commander.

In conclusion, it was the soldiers' bayonets and the "bayonet voters" of "Lincoln's hirelings" that crushed the rebellion and saved the Union.

THE TEACHERS' INSTITUTE

(Extract from the Proceedings held in Brookville, Pennsylvania, November 23, 1896.)

The Jefferson County Teachers' Institute met in the court-house, Brookville, on Monday, at two P.M. After the enrolment of teachers, and the selection of T. T. Millen as secretary, the following address of welcome to the teachers was delivered by Dr. W. J. McKnight, of Brookville:

"MR. CHAIRMAN AND TEACHERS,—This is an assemblage of teachers, called an 'institute'—the institute of Jefferson County. What is its history? Let us lift the veil from the past and ascertain. The Rev. John C. Wagaman, of Punxsutawney, was our first county superintendent, elected in 1854, and paid a salary of three hundred dollars a year. He resigned in 1856, and Samuel McElhose, of Brookville, succeeded him by appointment. Our first county institute was held by McElhose in the old Academy building, in Brookville, in October of 1856, continuing two weeks. The published call for it reads as follows:

" ' TO TEACHERS

" ' Believing that much good can be done to the cause of common school education, by means of a county institute for the benefit of teachers, I hereby issue this call to teachers and those who wish to teach, requesting and urging each one of them to meet in Brookville, on Monday, the 20th day of October, at which time will commence, in the Academy, the first session of the Jefferson County Teachers' Institute. It will last two weeks.

" ' Professor S. W. Smith will be present during the session. He is a graduate of the best of the New England schools, and has the advantage of several years practice as a teacher. The course of instruction will extend to a general review of the branches required to be taught in our common schools. It will be one leading object to treat at large on the subjects of school government, classification of scholars, and the improved methods of teaching.

" ' Persons who attend the institute will be at no expense except for their own boarding. Several gentlemen have tendered their services and will deliver lectures on topics connected with education at the proper times in the session. We again solicit the attendance of those who desire to teach in this county, and also extend a cordial invitation to the friends of education in this and other counties to be present.

" ' S. McELHOSE,
" ' *County Superintendent.*

" ' BROOKVILLE, December 22, 1856.'

" This institute was opened with prayer by Professor Smith. The work consisted largely of daily class drills, conducted by Professor Smith and Superintendent McElhose. Professor Smith was an educated gentleman, and died in Brookville a few years ago, after serving two terms as county superintendent most acceptably.

" The evening lectures before this first institute were free, delivered in the Presbyterian church, by local talent. They were by Rev. Thomas Graham on ' The Duties of Teacher,' A. L. Gordon, Esq., on ' Self-Knowledge,' and I. G. Gordon, Esq., on ' Discipline.' All these evening entertainments were announced to be held at ' candle lighting.' Day lectures were given before the institute by Superintendent McElhose, Professor Smith, on ' Astronomy,' and Dr. Cummins, on ' Physiology.' Numerous essays were read by the teachers present, on the beauties of nature, on education, on teaching, etc. Of the forty-two teachers who attended, I can recall but these: A. H. Brown, A. L. Gordon, J. C. Wilson, William Monks, T. Evans, John H. McKee, A. J. Monks, R. A. Travis, J. Kelso, Misses Maggie Polk, Jennie Craig, M. Kinnear, Abbie McCurdy, Martha Dennison, Emma Bishop, Mary McCormick, H. Thomas, Martha McCreight, and Messrs. C. M. Matson, David Dickey, and S. A. McAllister. The last three named are present with us to-day.

" Extended discussion was had, and resolutions were passed in regard to the construction of school-houses, and concerning school furniture and school-books. The county then had one hundred and five school-houses, and sixty-eight male and fifty female teachers.

" Samuel McElhose served as superintendent a part of a term by appointment and two full terms by election, at a yearly salary of five hundred dollars. He was an educated and popular gentleman, a great worker, and the first in the county to agitate institutes. He held many of these, sometimes three or four in a year, some lasting three or four weeks. He was a good citizen, and a patriot, and died a private soldier in the army in 1863.

" Ninety-two years ago, in the winter of 1804, John Dixon, father of the venerable John Dixon of Polk Township, taught the first school in this county. It was a subscription school, and the term was three months. The ' school-house' was two miles east of Brookville, on what is now the McConnell farm. It was twelve feet wide and sixteen feet long, was built of rough logs, and had no window-sash or glass. The light was admitted to the school-room through chinks in the walls, over which greased paper was plastered. The floor was of 'puncheons,' and the seats of broad pieces split from logs, with pins underneath for legs. The roof was covered with 'clapboards' held down by poles. Boards laid on pins driven into auger-holes in the walls furnished writing desks. A log fireplace, occupying an entire end of the room, supplied warmth when the weather was cold.

"The second school was taught by John Johnson, in 1806, on the old 'State Road,' near the present residence of William C. Evans, between Port Barnett and Brookville. The house was similar to the first one named, with the exception of a single window of six lights of 8 x 10 glass. This school cabin was heated by a ten-plate wood-stove, the invention of Franklin in 1800, and called by the people 'The Little Devil.' This was a subscription school also, and was known in those days as a 'neighborhood,' to distinguish it from the 'family' school. The building was erected by those interested. The tools used in constructing it were a pole-axe and an auger. The Master was hired by a committee of three, elected by the people at their own time and in their own way. This committee supervised the school. Children had to travel three or four miles in some cases, over trails and paths, where the Indian lurked and the wild beast prowled.

"Although Penn had declared, in founding his colony, that 'wisdom and virtue must be carefully propagated by a virtuous education of the youth,' and although the constitution of 1790 declared in favor of the establishment of schools throughout the State that the poor might be taught gratis, yet it was not until 1809 that the Legislature attempted to obey this mandate. Colleges and academies were, it is true, sparsely inaugurated, but they were not for the poor. Education was carried on by voluntary effort. The law of 1809 simply provided that it should be the duty of the county commissioners and assessors of the townships to ascertain from the parents the names of all the children between the ages of five and twelve years who reside in each township, and whose parents were unable to pay for their schooling. These children then had the privilege of attending the nearest subscription school, under the restrictions of the committee, and the county had to pay for each pauper scholar by the month the same as the subscribers paid. This law was in existence for twenty-five years. It was despised by the poor and hated by the rich. The poor would not accept it because it declared them paupers. Its existence, however, kept up an agitation for a better system, which culminated in 1834–36, in what is known as the common school law.

"In 1833 Governor Wolf ascertained, by careful inquiry, that under this law of 1809, out of four hundred thousand children in the State between the ages of five and twelve years, only twenty thousand attended any school whatever.

"The pioneer school-house in the southern part of the county was built of logs, in the fall of 1820, near John Bell's, a little more than a mile northeast of Perrysville. It was built after the fashion of the first school-house in the county, lighted, warmed, and furnished in the same manner. John B. Henderson taught the first school in this pioneer house in the winter of 1820.

"Our oldest schoolmaster in the county is Joseph Magiffin—hale and hearty at the age of ninety. He taught near Dowlingville, in 1827. The books used in the pioneer schools were generally the Bible, Columbian Reader, Murray's Grammar, Pike's Arithmetic, Catechism, United States Speller, and New England Primer. As a matter of care and economy, these books were covered by the mothers with paper or cloth, generally calico or bed ticking. The pioneer school-masters were nearly all Irishmen, and, as a rule, well educated. In the winter they usually wore a red flannel warmus, and sometimes white flannel pants. They taught their scholars from the proverbs of the poets, from the maxims of the surrounding forests, and from the tenets of the blessed Bible, whose apocalypse is love. Is it any wonder then that the log cabin and log school-house proved to be the birthplace and nursery of mental giants, of men who have blessed our country as rulers, statesmen, soldiers, scholars, orators, and patriots? What nation, old or new, has produced the equal of our Washington? What nation has equalled our Jefferson, with his Declaration ' that all men are created free and equal'? What nation has equalled our Lincoln, born and reared in a cabin, one of the people and for the people? With a heart alive to pity like an angel of mercy, he was ever at home in his office of President to the most humble citizen. This I know by personal experience. What nation has produced the superior of Chief Justice Marshall? What orators have been more eloquent than Clay or Webster? What nation has produced a greater than our military chieftain, Grant? who commanded larger armies, fought more battles, and won more victories than any other general history records. Napoleon's career is pigmy-like when compared to Grant's successes. What nation has equalled our inventors? Fulton, born in Pennsylvania's woods, who harnessed steam to water craft; Whitney, who invented the cotton-gin; Morse, who sought out the telegraph; McCormick, who made the reaper; Howe, who made the sewing-machine, and Edison, the intellectual wonder and marvel of the world—born in Ohio and reared in the woods of Michigan? Such a mental genius as he is could only be the son of an American ' school-marm.'

"I have not time to recapitulate the history of our country and its achievements. I can only say that what we are to-day we owe to the log cabin, the log school-house, and the pioneer school-master.

"We live in the age of steam and railroads, telegraphs, telephones, and of a free school system. 'We live in an age on ages telling; to be living is sublime.' Yet you are pioneers, pioneers of a new era, an era of moral courage, of the fatherhood of God and the brotherhood of man; an era of honesty, of temperance, of plenty, of virtue, of wisdom, and of peace. And you, teachers, are the leaders in this grand new era. As such we welcome you to Brook-

ville. We welcome you most heartily as friends and neighbors. We welcome
you as citizens of our county, whose hills and valleys are sacred to us. We
welcome you as the children of noble, courageous, patient, toiling pioneer
heroes and heroines, who subdued the savage and the wild beasts of the forests,
and reclaimed these lands. We welcome you as teachers under the free school
system of the great State of Pennsylvania—made great by her forests, her
fertile valleys, her mountains of coal, rivers of oil, and the enterprise of her
sons and daughters, and whose free school system is the continued assurance
of American liberty. We welcome you as teachers in an empire whose State
insignia proclaims to the world Virtue, Liberty, and Independence. We
welcome each one of you to Brookville for your individual worth, and we
welcome you as an aggregation of intelligent force assembled in our midst for
the public good. Finally, we welcome you as teachers convened to learn more
thoroughly how to impart intelligence, teach virtue, wisdom, and patriotism
under our flag, the emblem of all that is dear to man and woman in and
for the best government on the face of the earth."

EARLY POSTAL ROUTES AND RIDES

" More than sixty-seven years ago the first Tuesday of April, 1830, a
bright, beautiful morning, I started forth from my log cabin home with a
United States mail-bag, on my black pacing horse Billy, with Bob Thompson,
then about my own age (twelve years), on his dwarf mule Bully, to penetrate
the wilderness through a low grade of the Allegheny Mountains, between the
Allegheny River at Kittanning and the west branch of the Susquehanna River
at Curwensville, sixty-five miles and return each week, Robert going along
to show me the way.

" I have climbed the Rockies with a burro since that period in search of
gold and silver, but I have never met either so primitive a people or a rougher
route of sixty-five miles than that wilderness route. The post-offices were
Glade Run, Smicksburg, Ewing's Mill, Punxsutawney, and Curwensville.
The first of these was eighteen miles from Kittanning, near where is now the
little town of Dayton.

" In about three months the route was changed up the Cowanshannock,
and the Rural Valley post-office established about two miles above Patterson's
mill. The changed route intersected the old one at Glade Run post-office.
The next place east of Glade Run was the residence of George McComb,
where I rested for dinner and fed my horse. A stretch of over two miles
brought me to Smicksburg, as now spelled, but the original founder spelled
his name Schmick. Mr. Carr, the blacksmith, was postmaster. For more than
four miles there was not a single house on the road, though a cabin was to be
seen in the distance, until I reached Ewing's Mill, another post-office. My
place of lodging for the first night was with James McComb, four miles from
Punxsutawney, and never did a boy find a more pleasant home.

"The second day I rode ten miles for breakfast, passing Punxsutawney, where Dr. Jenks was postmaster. The town was a mere hamlet, principally a lumbering camp, surrounded with the finest of white pine, which was rafted in hewed logs down Mahoning Creek to the Allegheny River, and thence to Pittsburg. It is a rapid, rocky, crooked stream, and the logs were hewed square to make their transit over safe, both by reducing their size and securing a smooth, even surface. Six miles farther on was a farm, a few acres, the home of Andrew Bowers, where I ate breakfast, then entered a wilderness of sixteen miles. Those sixteen miles of wilderness were then a most dismal district of country, heavily timbered with pine, spruce, hemlock, and chestnut, with much undergrowth of laurel. In this dreary waste I saw every animal native to the clime, except the panther, of which more hereafter.

"After emerging from this wilderness, in which the sun was never visible, there was a settlement of Quakers, known as the Grampian Hills, near the centre of which was a fine farm, the home of a colored man, Samuel Cochran, where I took dinner, and then passed on to Curwensville, the end of my route. I returned to Cochran's for the second night's rest. The object of this return was to be ready to enter the wilderness and give good time to get through it before the shades of evening had fallen. Once I realized the wisdom of this plan when high water delayed me, so that I was compelled to stop at Bowers's place for the night and ride through the wilderness twice in a day, entering at the dawn of morning and reaching the place of departure amid darkness.

"Was I lonely? If the shriek of the panther, the growl of the bear, the howling of the wolf, the hooting of the owl is society, I was far from lonely. When I realized my situation I drove the spurs into my horse and rushed him with all his speed. My heart-beats seemed to drown the racket of his hoofs upon the stony road. The return was but a repetition of the outgoing journey. I never made such a trip again.

"My predecessor was John Gillespie, of whose history since I know nothing, but there was a story that in his ambition to create a favorable impression of the importance of his charge he frequently horrified a good Presbyterian preacher, who was the Glade Run postmaster, by stuffing the mail-bag with crab-apples, and made indignant the good Mrs. McComb, where he had lodged the night previously, by laying the mischief to the McComb children. A plethoric mail-bag always opened the eyes of the rural postmaster, and it was fun to John to witness the indignation of the good Mr. Jenks and hear the screaming of laughter of the villagers, just arrived to get the latest news, when a peck of crab-apples, but no letter, rolled out on the floor at Punxsutawney.

"Those were the days of William T. Barry as postmaster-general. I used to collect government's moiety in each of the little post-offices in driblets of five to ten dollars, with the plain signature of 'Wm. T. Barry, P. M. G.,' attached to the orders, and looked at the great man's name with admiration, until I really think I could distinguish his handwriting now.

"On more than two-thirds of the little farms no wagon-tracks were to be seen, all the work being done with sleds. Nevertheless, there were occasional freighters through the wilderness, generally loaded with salt. The only stores in that sixty miles were one at Glade Run and one at Punxsutawney. The people made all their own clothes. Nearly every family that had a daughter as old as fourteen years had a weaver. The blooming miss who learned that art was an artist indeed. It was a treat for the boys who had no sister weaver to carry the yarn to the neighbor girl and help her adjust the web for the work. Their clothes were made from the backs of the sheep and the flax in the field. The girls wore linsey-woolsey and the boys linen and tow shirts, and indeed full suits of the same for common work. The fine clothes for the girls were barred flannel of their own spinning, and the boys satinet,—then generally called cassinet,—flax, and wool. The preachers and the teachers were reverenced and respected, but woe unto them if they even seemed to put on airs on account of their ' store clothes.'

"Many were the expedients for social gatherings; but to these brave, industrious pioneers it was essential to unite business with pleasure, and I rarely heard of a party which was not utilized for the advancement of improvements on the farm. The singing-school was the only exception. In the log-rolling, the wood-chopping, the flax-scutching, the sheep-shearing, all the neighbors would go the rounds helping each other, in the spirit of the song,—

> " ' Let the wide world wag as it will,
> We'll be gay and happy still.'

" ' Scutching' was the term used for the primitive mode of separating the woody part of the flax from the fibre used in weaving cloth, and a scutching was a jolly party, in which the boys took the heavier part, and passed the ' hank' to the girls for the lighter, more delicate work of polishing.

"Thus the logs were rolled in the clearings, the flax and wool prepared for the loom, and the firewood made ready for the winter. But the most primitive, most amusing, and the merriest gathering of all was the kicking frolic.

"It is doubtful whether any of the readers of this book have ever seen a kicking frolic. Let me try to describe it. As I have said, the people made all their own clothes in those days. After the web was woven, the next process was fulling, whereby the cloth was properly shrunken for use. Generally it was taken to fulling-mills, but in some parts they were so far away and so expensive that the wits of the pioneers were compelled to invent a substitute. One night, at my journey's end for the day, near Punxsutawney, I was invited to go with the McComb boys to Henderson's kicking. The girls of the whole neighborhood had spent the afternoon at quilting, for the quilting was an accompaniment of nearly all the other frolics, and at dark the boys assembled for the kicking. The good old Mrs. Henderson had prepared a boiler full of soapsuds. The web of cloth was placed on the kitchen floor,—a floor generally made from puncheons,—that is, logs split and smoothed with the axe and adze. Around the web was placed a circle of chairs, with a plough-line or a clothes-line circling the chairs, to hold the circle together for work. Thus equipped the boys took off shoes and stockings, rolled up their pants to their knees, placed themselves on the chairs in the circle, and then the kicking began. The old lady poured on the soapsuds as hot as the boys' feet could stand, and they sent the web whirling and the suds splashing to the ceiling of the kitchen, and thus the web was fulled to the proper thickness and dimensions. Despite the good Mrs. Henderson's protestations that ' the hard work would kill the boys,' I stripped and went in, and never did a boy so sweat in his life. The work was done. The barred flannel was ready for the girls' dresses, the blankets for the beds, and the satinet for the boys' clothes. A merrier time boys and girls never enjoyed, nor did a party ever have a better supper than Mrs. Henderson prepared. There was no dance, but the kissing plays of the time lent zest to the occasions, and

" ' In the wee sma' hours ayont the twal'

all returned to happy homes.

" The threshing machinery was unknown to the farmers anywhere, and the flail did the work of threshing. Even the fanning-mill was uncommon, as I remember of but three on all that route. There was a mode of winnowing grain by three men, one shaking the wheat in the chaff through a ridder or sieve, and two waving a tightly drawn sheet, producing wind to separate the chaff from the grain.

" In places I have seen hand-mills for grinding corn and wheat. They had an upper and nether millstone, the upper stone being turned by a ' handle' standing nearly perpendicularly above the centre of the stone.

" In the wilderness was every animal native to the clime,—the deer, the wild turkey, the fox, the raccoon, the wolf, the porcupine, the bear, and the panther. There I have seen scores of such animals. Frequently I have met bears in pairs, but I never saw a panther, though I frequently heard their familiar screams. It was a shy animal, but considered the most dangerous of all wild animals. On one occasion, when near the middle of that wilderness of sixteen miles, I was startled by the fearful screams of a panther, which, from the sound, seemed fast approaching me. Hurriedly breaking a limb from a spruce tree, I lashed my horse into all his speed; still the screams became more distinct and frightful. I had perhaps run my horse a quarter of a mile, when a bear rushed through the thick underbrush across the road.

not more than two rods ahead of me, the screaming of the panther sounding as if he was not a rod behind in the brush. The bear never stopped to look at me, and I plied my stick to the horse's back, shoulder, and flank with all my power, running him until the sounds gradually died away, and the exhausted horse gave out and I was compelled to slacken my speed. My first stopping-place was at the house of Mr. Andrew Bowers, at the edge of the wilderness. I told him my story, and he replied, ' John, that was a " painter," and that " painter" was after that bear, and if he had come up to that bear when you were near it, he would have jumped onto you quicker than the bear. Now, John,' he continued, ' don't run, nor don't advance on it. If you do either, the " painter" will attack you. But just stop and look the " painter" in the eye, and by and by he will quietly walk off.'

" I have twice seen in the wilderness that rarest of animals, the black fox, whose fur rivals the seal and the sable in ladies' apparel.

" Did I ever see ghosts? Of course I did. What could a poor post-boy know of cause and effect in the wilderness which has since developed some of the most wonderful gas-wells of the age? In that wild country the ignis fatuus was frequently seen. Once I saw a floating light in the darkness, and in my fright was trotting my horse at his best speed, when he stumbled on a rock, throwing me clear over his head, the mail-bag following. I grabbed the bags and was on my horse's back before he could get off his knees. The 'ghost' in the mean time had vanished. At another time, when about half-way between Smicksburg and Punxsutawney, a light as brilliant, it seemed to me, as Paul saw on his way to Damascus, shot up under my horse. I grabbed my hat, as my hair seemed to stand on end. I was so alarmed that I told my story to the postmaster at Ewing's Mill, and he relieved my mind greatly by explaining the phenomenon. He said, ' Was there snow on the ground?' ' Yes.' And then he went on to relieve my fears in the most kindly way, telling me that all the stories about ghosts, spooks, and hobgoblins could be explained on natural principles. He said that at times natural gas exuded from between the rocks, and that the snow confined it, and that my horse's shoe had struck fire from the flinty rock, and the gas exploded. I believed him, and my ghost story was exploded, too, but I would have killed a horse before I would have ventured over that spot in night-time again.

" The boys of that period had as much fun in their composition as those of the present age. One Hallowe'en we sauntered ' on fun intent' near where Dayton now stands. We lodged a yearling calf in a hay-mow, changed the hind wheels of the only two wagons in the neighborhood to the forward axles, and vice versa, robbed a loom and strung the maiden's web from tree to tree across the road, and changed the natural order of things generally. I remember especially that in our mischief we accidentally broke a window in the house of a good old couple. We repaid damages by a boy slipping up and depositing fifty cents on the sill of the broken window. The old people were so universally esteemed that malicious mischief would have been investigated; but whether the motive for recompense was remorse for a bad act or esteem for their two beautiful daughters with raven locks and black eyes, this boy will only confess for himself. The McComb boys reported that one of the girls called on the way to the store the next day for glass and expressed the gratitude of the family for the kind consideration of the boys in making restitution.

" I distinctly remember how we all put in our utmost strength to place a log endwise against the door of Dr. Sims's house, so as to press it inward with such force that an urgent call before morning compelled the doctor to crawl out of the window."—*Punxsutawney News.*

In the fall of 1852 I made my pioneer trip as a mail-boy on the " Star route" from Brookville to Ridgway, Pennsylvania. In 1852 this was still a horseback service of once a week and was to be performed as follows:

Leave Brookville Tuesday at five o'clock A.M. and arrive at Ridgway same day at seven o'clock P.M. Leave Ridgway Wednesday at five o'clock A.M. and arrive same day at Brookville at seven o'clock P.M.

The proprietor of the route was John G. Wilson, then keeping the American Hotel in Brookville. To start the service on schedule time was easy enough, but to reach the destined point in the schedule time was almost impossible. The mail was usually from one to three hours late. Indeed, it could not be otherwise, for the route was through a wilderness, over horrid roads, and about seven miles longer than the direct road between the points.

It was too much work in too short a time for one horse to carry a heavy mail-bag and a boy. On my first trip I left Brookville at five A.M., James Corbet, the postmaster, placing the bag on the horse for me. I rode direct to Richardsville, where William R. Richards, the pioneer of that section, was postmaster. From Richardsville I went to Warsaw, where Moses B. St. John was postmaster. He lived on the Keys farm near the Warsaw grave-yard. From St. John's I rode by way of what is now John Fox's to the Beechwoods, McConnell farm, or Alvin post-office, Alex. McConnell, post-master. From Alvin I went direct to what is now Brockwayville for dinner. Dr. A. M. Clarke was postmaster, and it was at his house I ate, to my disgust, salt rising bread.

The doctor and his father lived in a large frame house near where the old grist-mill now stands. The old up and down saw-mill across the creek was then in operation. C. K. Huhn I think lived near it. The old frame school-house stood on a prominence near the junction of the Brookville and Beechwoods roads. Henry Dull, one of the pioneer stage-drivers in Jefferson County, lived in an old frame building near where D. D. Groves now resides, and John McLaughlin lived in an old log house down by the Rochester depot.

With these exceptions, all west of the creek in what is now Brockwayville was a wilderness. East of the creek the bottom land was cleared and along

683

the road on each side was a log fence. W. D. Murray and the Ingalls family lived near the Pennsylvania depot.

There was no other family or store or industry to my recollection in what is now the beautiful town of Brockwayville.

About five miles up the Little Toby, and in Elk County, Mrs. Sarah Oyster kept a licensed hotel, and the only licensed tavern in that year outside of or between Brookville and Ridgway. Near this hotel Stephen Oyster lived, and had erected a grist-mill and saw-mill. Oyster was postmaster, and the office was named Hellen Mills.

Stephen Oyster's house and mills were alongside or on the pioneer road into this region. The road was surveyed and opened about 1812, and over it the pioneers came to Brandy Camp, Kersey, and Little Toby. Fox, Norris & Co. owned about one hundred and forty thousand acres of land in this vicinity, and desiring to open these lands for settlement, employed William Kersey, a surveyor, to survey, open a road, and build a mill on their lands.

Kersey and his men started his road on the Susquehanna River near Luthersburg, on the old State Road, crossed over Boone's mountain, reached Little Toby at what is now Hellen, went up the creek seven miles, over what is called " Hog Back Hill" to a point on Elk Creek near where Centreville now is, and then located and built " Kersey Mill."

Kersey had an outfit and a number of men, and erected shanties wherever necessary while at his work. One of these he built on Brandy Camp. Among other necessaries, Kersey had some choice brandy with him. The men longed for some of this brandy, but Kersey kept it for himself. One day in the absence of Kersey the cabin burned down.

On Kersey's return he was chagrined, but the men told him that the Indians in the neighborhood had drunk his brandy and burned the shanty. This story had to be accepted, and hence the stream has ever since been called Brandy Camp. " The Travellers' Home Hotel" was on this stream. It was famous for dancing parties, blackberry pies, and sweet cake, but was closed this year and occupied as a private residence by a man named Brown.

Night came upon me at the farm of Joel Taylor, and through nine miles of wilderness and darkness I rode at a walk. There was a shanty at Bootjack occupied by a man named McQuone. From Taylor's to Ridgway was a long ride to me. It was a wearisome time.

I reached Ridgway, a small village then, about nine o'clock P.M. John Cobb was postmaster, and the office was in his store, near where Powell's store is now. My horse knew the route perfectly, and I left all details to her.

Two hotels existed in the village, the Exchange, kept by David Thayer, near the river, and the Cobb House, kept by P. T. Brooks, on the ground where Messenger's drug-store now is. My horse stopped at the Cobb. For some reason the house was unusually full that night, and after supper I expressed to the landlord a doubt about a bed.

Mr. Brooks patted me on the back and said, " Never mind, my son, I'll take care of you, I'll take care of you." Bless his big heart, he did. Boy-like, my eyes and ears were open. I took in the town before leaving it. The only pavement was in front of the Gillis house. I knew of the Judge's reputation as a Morgan killer, and I wanted to see where and how he lived. I had seen him in Brookville many a time before that.

There was a board fence around the public square. Charles Mead was sheriff, and lived in the jail. The village had a doctor, one Chambers. The school-teacher was W. C. Niver, afterwards Dr. Niver, of Brockwayville, Pennsylvania.

Of the village inhabitants then, I can recall these: Judge Gillis, E. C. Derby, M. L. Ross, Henry Souther, Caleb Dill, James Love, J. C. Chapin, Lebbeus Luther, a hunter and great marksman; Lafe Brigham, 'Squire Parsons, E. E. Crandal, Charles McVean, Judge Dickinson, J. S. Hyde, and Jerome Powell, editor of the *Advocate*.

In January, 1855, I carried the mail one trip on horseback to Warren from Ridgway. A man by the name of Lewis was the proprietor, and he boarded at Luther's. I performed this service free, as I was anxious to see Warren.

I had to start from Ridgway on Friday night at nine P.M., ride to Mont-morenci, and stop all night. A family by the name of Burrows lived there. I stopped on Saturday in Highland for dinner at Townley's. There was living in that township then Wells, Ellithorpe, Campbell, and Townley. I arrived in Warren Saturday after dark, and stayed over night at the Carver house. I returned on Sunday from Warren to Ridgway, and the weather being intensely cold, " I paid too dear for my whistle."

PENNSYLVANIA SYSTEM OF RAILROADS—PENNSYLVANIA RAILROAD—INCEPTION, CONCEPTION, AND COMPLETION—HORSE-CAR—ENGINE—PIONEER PRESIDENT—PIONEER RESTAURANT—PURCHASE FROM STATE—RAILROAD AGITATION AND EXPERIMENT—LOCOMOTIVE—FUEL—COACHES—SLEEPERS—UNIFORMS—FREIGHTAGE—ORIGIN OF THE PASS SYSTEM—DISCRIMINATION—WHEN THE PIONEER TRAIN RAN INTO PITTSBURG FROM PHILADELPHIA

I am indebted to Sipes's as well as Wilson's histories of the Pennsylvania Road for some data and facts.

What is now the Pennsylvania system has evoluted from agitation and experience. John Stephens, of New Jersey, advocated, in 1812, the use of steam in land-carriages. When he was seventy-four years old the Legislature of Pennsylvania, at his earnest appeal, passed an act, on March 31, 1823, to " incorporate a company to erect a railroad from Philadelphia to Lancaster." Nine wealthy and influential men were made incorporators. John Connelly, of Philadelphia, was named as president of the company. So little confidence was had in the scheme that five thousand dollars could not be raised from any source to start the enterprise, hence the Legislature, in 1826, repealed the charter. Several charters were granted after this, but they all perished from indifference or opposition. In 1827 the State, through the canal commissioners, ordered a series of surveys to be made, and a report made in 1827 by Major John Wilson, one of the surveyors, induced the Legislature to pass the act of March 24, 1828, authorizing the construction of a railroad by the State, from Philadelphia through Lancaster to Columbia. In April, 1829, forty miles of track were laid, twenty at each terminal. In April, 1834, the single track clear through was opened and connected with the Pennsylvania Canal, and on April 16 the first train of cars with an engine started over the line. To provide against accident, a horse-car followed this train with horse relays. Horse relays were twelve miles apart.

By the first of October, 1834, the last spike was driven in the double track. The act of April 13, 1846, authorized the Pennsylvania Railroad to construct a road from Harrisburg to Pittsburg. This road was chartered February 25, 1847. The company was organized on March 31, 1847, with Samuel Vaughn Merrick, president, and eleven directors.

On April 9, 1847, John Edgar Thompson was chosen chief, and W. B. Foster, Jr., and Edward Miller, associate engineers. Grading commenced at Harrisburg July 7, 1847. This was the beginning of the Pennsylvania Road. In about two years trains were running to Lewistown. In 1850 the road was completed to the Allegheny Portage Railroad. On the 10th of December, 1852, cars were running from Philadelphia, over the Columbia Road, the Portage Road, and the Pennsylvania Road, into Pittsburg. The Portage Road was one of the wonders of America. Passenger changes were at Harrisburg and Dillersburg. Each passenger-car carried an eight-foot plank on which the passengers walked the plank to make these changes.

The pioneer restaurant in 1856 was the "pie-and-cake" stand on the railroad platform. From this was sold pies, "mint stick candy," sour balls, ju-ju-be paste, licorice balls, Baltimore plug, ginger bread, mead, root beer, and half-Spanish cigars.

On June 25, 1847, John Edgar Thompson, for seven and a half million dollars, bought the public works of Pennsylvania, and on August 1, 1857, the Pennsylvania took possession of the main line of public works of Pennsylvania, which embraced the Columbia Railroad to Philadelphia, and on July 18, 1858, the Pennsylvania Railroad ran the first passenger wide car train into Pittsburg from Philadelphia without a change of cars. To this train was attached a Woodruff sleeper and a smoking-car, the first smoker ever used. Up to 1843 the cost of the public works to the State was $14,361,320.25. Horses were used more or less on the Portage Road up to 1850. In 1857 this road was abandoned.

Railroad agitation and experimentation date back to 1773. Oliver Evans then declared he could build and run a carriage with steam. In 1805 he did.

HISTORY OF NORTHWESTERN PENNSYLVANIA

In 1809 Thomas Leiper constructed a tram-road in Delaware County, Pennsylvania, a mile long. It was all wood, and a single horse drew the car. The second railway in Pennsylvania was built in 1827,—a horse-road nine miles long. The first locomotive was used in 1829. The pioneer railroad in Pennsylvania for passengers and freight was the Germantown Road, and the pioneer passenger train left Philadelphia June 6, 1832, drawn by horses. These horse-cars on the level ran about eight miles an hour, and had relays like the stages. The pioneer road into the interior of the State was the Columbia and Philadelphia. The State owned the road-bed, and any or everybody could use it by paying two cents a mile for each passenger he carried and four dollars and ninety-two cents for each coach sent over it, but the coaches were mostly owned and generally managed by old stage men. It was not until 1836 that locomotives were generally used on railroads. The fuel was coke and wood, twenty bushels of coke to one cord and a half of wood.

The first tunnel built in the United States was at Staple Bend, four miles east of Johnstown. It was built by the State.

William B. Sipes says,—

" The Columbia Railroad, being one of the first built in the United States, contained most of the defects of our primitive roads. It was very crooked,— some of the curves being of but six hundred and thirty-one feet radius. Its gradients, owing to the comparatively level country over which it was built and the care of the engineers who located it, were not heavy, in no place exceeding forty-five feet per mile, and that for a very short distance, while the uniform grade was kept at thirty feet. An inclined plane was at each terminus,—that at Philadelphia being two thousand eight hundred and five feet in length, and one hundred and eighty-seven feet rise, while that at Columbia was eighteen hundred feet in length and ninety feet rise. These were at a subsequent period avoided without materially increasing the average gradient of the road. The track was of varied construction, consisting in part of granite or wooden sills, on which were secured flat rails; of edge rails on stone blocks and stone sills, and of edge rails on stone blocks and locust sills. These gradually gave place to modern improvements, and many of the sharper curves were straightened.

" The road having been constructed to be operated by horse-power, the track and turn-outs were adapted for that purpose. For several years these horse-cars were regularly run between Columbia and Philadelphia. They were built something like the old stage-coach, but larger, the entrance door being at the side, and the driver occupying an elevated seat in front. The time of these cars over the road—a distance of eighty-two miles—was about nine hours, the horses being changed every twelve miles.

" The first locomotive put on the road was built in England and named the ' Black Hawk,' after the celebrated Indian chief. As the eastern end of the road was not then completed, this engine was hauled over the turnpike to

Lancaster, where her trips were to commence, and she was to be used between that city and Columbia. The day for her trial trip was a beautiful one, and thousands of people had gathered from the surrounding country to witness the novel performance. Governor Wolf and the State officials were all in Lancaster to participate, and the excitement ran high. Men were stationed along the track to keep the too venturesome boys out of danger, and among these guardians was an Irishman, who made himself particularly officious. Armed with a club, he paraded along the road, shouting to the eager urchins, ' Get out of the track! When she starts she'll go like a bird, and ye'll all be kilt.' The important moment came,—the engineer pulled the lever, but the locomotive would not go. At length, by pushing, the train was got under way; but the wonderful machine did not 'go like a bird.' She proved a failure, in fact, and her history is lost in oblivion.

" Soon after, three smaller engines were imported and put on the road. These did better than their predecessor, and about 1836 locomotives were regularly put to work, to the exclusion of horse-power. From this time on the State furnished the motive power, while all cars used for the transportation of passengers and freight were the property of individuals. A regular rate of toll was charged for the use of the road and for motive power."

Rebates, discrimination, and the pass system originated with the State management in 1834, continued during the public ownership of the works for twenty-one years. So frightful were these abuses under the State management that the State became bankrupt. Now, under private or corporate use the management is healthy and profitable.

The chair-car was introduced on night lines in 1847. The pioneer sleeping-car (Woodruff's) was used in 1837-38; the Pullman sleeper in 1871.

Uniforms were introduced in the Harrisburg division about 1856. The uniform was a blue coat with brass buttons, buff vest, and black trousers. This uniform was so unpopular with the employees and the people that they were abandoned, but the Civil War popularized the uniforms, and the present uniform was adopted in 1876. Up to that period the word " conductor" was worn on the left lapel of the coat. It is now on the cap.

On July 6, 1837, two coal-burning locomotives were tried, but they proved useless.

Travel from Philadelphia to Pittsburg, in 1834, was as follows: Over the Columbia Railroad, eighty-two miles; canal from Columbia to Holidaysburg, one hundred and seventy-two miles; Portage Railroad from Holidaysburg to Johnstown, thirty-six miles; and on canal from Johnstown to Pittsburg, one hundred and four miles; total, three hundred and ninety-four miles. The frequent transfers made the journey long and tedious and the cost of freightage high. Summit tunnel was used January 21, 1854, but was not completed until February 17, 1855. December 10, 1852, an all-rail line was opened from Harrisburg to Pittsburg.

HISTORY OF NORTHWESTERN PENNSYLVANIA

A writer, in 1903, has the following to say of the Pennsylvania system:

" For fifty years the Pennsylvania has been the foremost railroad of the United States. Its operating system and equipment have become the standards toward which practical railroad men strive from year to year. From the beginning a genius in management has built up and strengthened its position, not only deriving from the public unnumbered privileges, which have made expansion and improvement possible, but gaining and holding public endorsement and admiration. To-day it is the undisputed leader among railroads, its far-flung lines drawing power and wealth from the whole eastern half of the continent. Westward to the Mississippi, northward to the lakes, eastward to the seaboard, southward to the Gulf, the Pennsylvania and its systems have an unshaken grip upon the illimitable enterprise of transportation.

" The richest territory between the oceans yields its tribute. The road drives straight through the great manufacturing districts. Its main line and branches reach the coal-mines, the oil regions, the natural gas-fields, and through its connections it extends to the granaries of the West and the steel-mines of the North. More than this, the company is absolute master of the bituminous mining interests, gets a generous share of the anthracite business, and virtually owns two of the largest independent steel plants in the country.

" In transportation the Pennsylvania has a monopoly in effect, if not in fact. By purchase or agreement it controls the Baltimore and Ohio, the Philadelphia and Reading, the Norfolk and Western, the Chesapeake and Ohio, the , Western New York and Pennsylvania, the Hocking Valley, and a score of less important lines. It is the master railroad.

" Translate these generalities to cold figures, and the magnitude of the corporation becomes more striking. The Pennsylvania operates directly three thousand seven hundred and six miles of track, and, by control or affiliation, a total of ten thousand seven hundred and eighty-four miles. Its capital stock is more than two hundred and four million dollars, and the authorized issue is four hundred million dollars. When it is understood that every dollar represents, or will represent, cash investment, the swollen bulk of the Steel Trust shrinks in comparison, and the Pennsylvania Railroad stands forth as the greatest industrial institution in the country.

· " Its growth has been enormous. Forty years ago, with a mileage of eight hundred and fifty-six miles, its gross earnings were $19,500,000; in 1902 its gross earnings were $112,663,000. Including affiliated lines, this corporation earned during that year a little less than $220,000,000. The combined system carried nearly two hundred and seventy million tons of freight, and nearly one hundred and sixteen million passengers. The company owns in stocks and bonds of various roads $318,000,000. During the next two or three years it purposes to spend $67,000,000 in improvement east of Pittsburg. aside from the gigantic operation of tunnelling under the North River to reach the heart of New York city."

William Augustus Patton, now (1905) first assistant to President Cassatt, entered the service of the General Superintendent's office when a boy of sixteen, January 1, 1865, and was promoted to chief clerk of Alexander Johnston Cassatt on August 1, 1872, when Mr. Cassatt was general manager of the road. On October 1, 1882, Mr. Patton was transferred to the president's department, and on April 1, 1884, was appointed general assistant in that department. On May 4, 1884, he was elected vice-president of the New York, Philadelphia and Norfolk Railroad, and on June 14, 1899, he was elected president of that company, and is still serving in that capacity. Mr. Patton is a veteran in the service of the road, having been connected with it continuously for more than forty years. His service has been long, faithful, intelligent, wise, and efficient. He has been a success in every department he has served. He is a natural-born gentleman. His warm heart and genial deportment have made the road a host of friends.

Alexander Johnston Cassatt was elected president of the Pennsylvania system June 9, 1899. He is a Northwestern Pennsylvania product. He was born in Allegheny City, Pennsylvania, in 1839. This city lies within the purchase of 1784. In 1861 Cassatt was appointed rodman on the Philadelphia division. In two years from that date he was made an assistant engineer. In 1864 he was assistant engineer, at Renovo, of the middle division of the Philadelphia and Erie Road. In 1867 he was transferred to Altoona. On April 1, 1870, he was made general superintendent of the Pennsylvania Road. In 1871 he was manager of all lines east of Pittsburg and Erie. On July 1, 1874, he was chosen third vice-president; on June 1, 1880, he was promoted to first vice-president. I am proud of him as a Western Pennsylvanian. I am proud of his courage, skill, enterprise, and prudence. I am proud of the Pennsylvania Road, and under Cassatt and staff's management it is to-day, as a success, a marvel and wonder of the world. (See page 661.)

PIONEER RAILROADS IN NORTHWESTERN PENNSYLVANIA—ACT TO INCORPORATE SUNBURY AND ERIE—CONSTRUCTION COMMENCED—LENGTH OF ROAD— OPENING OF ROAD—WHEN COMPLETED—PIONEER INCORPORATORS—PRESIDENT, ENGINEER, MEETINGS, ETC.

In 1835 the pioneer locomotive railroad cars were running in Pennsylvania. These were three in number, and in this year the public began the agitation of a railroad from Philadelphia to Erie. In 1834 this project was completed from Philadelphia to Harrisburg. In 1837 forty locomotives were in use.

An act to incorporate the Sunbury and Erie, and Pittsburg and Susquehanna Railroad Companies was passed April 3, 1837, and approved by Governor Joseph Ritner. This formed the last link. Under the act commissioners were appointed from different counties of the State to open books and receive

William Augustus Patton

subscriptions to the stock of the company. Those from Northwestern Pennsylvania were as follows:

Erie County, R. S. Reed, P. S. V. Hamot, John A. Tracy, Daniel Dobbins, Josiah Kellogg, Edwin J. Kelso, William Fleming, Isaac G. Williams, John H. Walker, Joseph S. Colt, Thomas H. Sill, Gillis Sanford, William Kelly.

Lycoming County, Joseph B. Anthony, William F. Parker, Dr. W. R. Power, Henry Hughes, Dr. Arthur Davidson, John H. Cowden, William Wilson, Tunison Coryell, Nicholas Funston, William A. Petrikin, Joshua Bowman, Peter Shoemaker, Isaac Bruner, James Wilson, James Gamble, Alexander Hamilton, William Johnson, Jr., Robert Carson, Benjamin Hays.

Warren County, Robert Falconer, Josiah Hall, Stephen Littlefield, Obed Edson, Thomas Struthers, Archibald Tanner. N. B. Eldred, G. C. Irwin, G. A. Irvine, F. W. Brigham.

Pioneer railroad train in the United States

McKean County, Solomon Sartwell, H. Payne, John King, Jonathan Colegrove, Asa Sartwell, Orlo J. Hamlin.

Crawford County, Henry Shippen, David Dick, Stephen Barlow, Andrew Smith, Joseph Douglass, J. Stewart Riddle, David McFaddin.

Venango County, Rowletten Power, Alexander McCalmont, James Kinnear, John Evans, James Thompson, Joseph M. Fox, Christian Myers, David Phipp, Myran Parks, William Raymond, Arnold Plumer, Andrew Bowman, John W. Howe.

Tioga County, Benjamin B. Smith, Robert G. White, Joseph W. Guernsey, Josiah Emery, Samuel Dickinson, Samuel W. Morris.

Potter County, Timothy Ives, John H. Rose, Charles Leyman.

Mercer County, John Findley, Benjamin Stokely, Bevan Pearson, John Hoge, William Maxwell, Samuel Thompson, William F. Clark, James Bredin. Joseph Smith, David T. Porter, Robert Stewart, Abraham Pell, Samuel Holstein, John Ferker, James McKean, Joseph T. Boyd, John Fisher, Robert W. Stuart, Ezekiel Sankey, Thomas Wilson, and Daniel Means.

In this act it is said, " or any three of them, be, and they are hereby appointed commissioners to do and perform the several things hereinafter mentioned, that is to say, they shall, on or before the first day of November next, procure books, one of which shall be opened at Northumberland, Sunbury, Milton, Williamsport, Warren, Wellsborough, Clearfield, Meadville, Erie, Franklin, Harrisburg, Bellefonte, in the city of Philadelphia."

Shares of stock to be one hundred dollars each.

The stock necessary to secure the charter was taken by the United States Bank. Nicholas Biddle, of Philadelphia, was the pioneer president, from 1837 to 1840; Daniel L. Miller, 1851-52. In 1856 Samuel V. Merrick was elected. During the years 1838 and 1839 Edward Miller, the pioneer chief engineer, made exploratory surveys of the different routes suggested, and on March 1, 1840, made a full report to the board of directors, recommending a route two hundred and eighty-six and one-half miles long. In 1838 the time was extended by the Legislature to 1840 for commencement of work. It might be well to state here that the road originally, in 1835, was designed to pass by way of West Branch, Clarion River, and Franklin, in Venango County. The pioneer cars for the Western division were built in Erie.

The only town of importance between the two charter points was Williamsport. Clinton, Cameron, and Elk Counties had not been created. Warren was a small village sustained by lumber-mills and camps, but Erie had great business prominence at that time on account of her canals and prospective extensions. As a city she had an international fame. It was on her lake that Commodore Perry, in 1813, wiped a whole English fleet from the waters of the earth,—the first time such a thing had been done. We whipped England on the ocean in 1776 and in 1812, and now she has for fifty years been trying, annually, to outsail us for a silver cup, and cannot win. The United States has never been defeated on land or sea. American manhood triumphs on land and waters. "Don't give up the ship!" was the cry. And the same American manhood was behind this railroad in the northwest, for thirty years, with the cry, "Don't give up the road!" and it won, as we Americans always have won, in war as well as in industrial and commercial enterprise.

In the speculative times of 1836 non-residents of this wilderness bought largely of the wild lands along the route, which, of course, when railroad and other bubbles burst, was left on their hands. This land had been advertised to contain valuable iron ore and bituminous coal, and much of it could have been bought as late as 1851 at fifty cents an acre.

To build a railroad through a dense wilderness of worthless hemlock, ferocious beasts, gnats, and wintergreen berries, required a large purse and great courage. Of course, there was no subject talked about in the cabin homes of that locality so dear to the hearts of the pioneers as this railroad. Living, as they were, in the backwoods, they were perfectly excusable when the subject of railroads was broached, even if they did cut all kinds of fantastic tricks at celebrations and meetings.

The first railroad meeting held in Ridgway, Elk County, was in the fall of 1845. Gentlemen were present from Erie, Warren, McKean, Centre, Philadelphia, and other counties. The deliberations were held in the old school-house, and there the road was constructed in words, as it was all through the seasons for years afterward.

In any event, I suppose those railroad barons enjoyed themselves in Ridgway, and were fed on elk-steak for breakfast, blackberry-pie for dinner, speckled trout and bear meat for supper, with nothing stronger to *drink than sassafras tea*. This generous diet, in sleep at least, would build railroads.

In 1837 there was not a cabin on the line of this proposed road from Shippen (Emporium) to Ridgway, and but one at Johnsonburg from Ridg-way to Tionesta Creek.

The company commenced grading the railroad from Erie to Warren in 1852, and the pioneer regular passenger-train ran from Erie to Warren December 21, 1859. A great celebration took place in Warren in honor of this event. The pioneer superintendent of the Western division at this time was S. A. Black, whose office was at Erie. The pioneer through regular train from the East was October 4, 1864.

I do not know that it is material to give the trials, failures, and hardships in raising money for the work. They were overcome, and that is sufficient. On March 7, 1861, the name was changed, by an act of Legislature, to the Philadelphia and Erie.

On April 23, 1861, an act was approved by the governor authorizing rail-road companies to lease and operate other roads; and under this law the Phila-delphia and Erie leased to the Pennsylvania for a term of nine hundred and ninety-nine years from January, 1862, the Pennsylvania to pay a rental of thirty per cent. on all gross earnings. At the close of 1859 one hundred and fifty-eight miles had been completed; and on the balance of the line, one hundred and forty miles, the grading and bridging were well along to completion. February 1, 1862, the Pennsylvania assumed control, and the management applied the same business habits, probity, and skill to the road that these officials have always exhibited. Joseph D. Potts was appointed general manager, and under his *régime,* on January 1, 1864, one hundred and sixty-four miles of track, from Sunbury to St. Marys, was laid, as also from Erie to Wilcox. The road was opened for business successively at the following points,—viz., May 2, 1864, Emporium to St. Marys; May 23, Sheffield to Kane; July 6, Kane to Wilcox; October 17, Wilcox to St. Marys; and clear through, October 19, 1864.

For some of these dates I am indebted to local histories. I lived in Ridg-way a number of years while this road was in agitation and construction. My medical practice extended all over the county from March, 1859, to the summer of 1863. I might say here that the original route was from Driftwood to where Du Bois now is, from there through Brockwayville to the Clarion River, and up Spring Creek to Warren; but Philadelphia land-owners in Elk County forced the road from its natural channel.

An Act for the incorporation of the " Pittsburg, Kittanning, and Warren Railroad Company" was passed April 4, 1837, and approved by Governor Joseph Ritner, which reads, in part, as follows:

" SECTION 1. Be it enacted by the Senate and House of Representatives of the Commonwealth of Pennsylvania, in General Assembly met, and it is hereby enacted by the authority of the same, That Benjamin Darlington, Samuel Baird, Isaac Harris, John P. Bakewell, James Ross, Harmar Denny, Francis Kearns, William Robinson, Jr., Robert H. Douthell, George Ogden, George R. White, James Gray, Fourth Street; John Morrison, Samuel B. McKinzey, and John Shoenberger, of the County of Allegheny; Jacob Weaver, James Bole, Robert Lowry, William Coyle, James Green, Samuel Cooper, George Rip, John Michling, Robert Spars, Joseph Buffington, Alexander Colwell, Philip Michling, John Gilpin, David Reynolds, Robert Orr, Samuel Hutchison, Chambers Orr, James Waterson (Terry), William Templeton, David Lawson, and Richard Reynolds, of the County of Armstrong; James Kinnear, George R. Espy, James R. Snowden, Alexander McCalmont, Arnold Plumer, John Evans, Andrew Beaument, Edward Pierce, and R. Power, of the County of Venango; Thomas Struthers, Josiah Hall, Robert Faulkner, Archibald Sanner, Nathaniel B. Eldred, Guy C. Irvine, Galbraith A. Irvine, Thomas Martin, William A. Irvine, Lansing Wetmore, S. J. Johnson, Abraham Hazelton, Henry Sargent, John King, Walter W. Hoges, and F. W. Brigham, of the county of Warren, are hereby appointed commissioners, and they, or any ten of them, are authorized to open books, at such times and places, and upon such notice as they may deem expedient, for the purpose of receiving subscriptions to the capital stock of the company hereinafter directed to be incorporated, and if any of said commissioners shall resign, neglect to act, be absent, or become legally incapacitated to act, during the continuance of the duties devolved upon them by this act, others may be appointed in their stead, by a majority of the persons named in this act."

Capital stock to be two million dollars, in shares of fifty dollars each.

Several routes were surveyed,—one through Brookville, up the North Fork to the Clarion River, and one up the Mahoning to Punxsutawney, through Reynoldsville, Warren, and Olean. These routes were found to be expensive on account of the tunnels, and were abandoned, and the route along the Allegheny River chosen. I here quote Wilson's History:

" In 1847 the time for beginning construction was extended to 1852, and in 1851 again extended to 1855. On the 12th of February, 1852, the company was organized. On April 14, 1852, the name was changed to the Allegheny Valley Railroad Company. Ground was formally broken March 18, 1853, at Pittsburg, and on May 1 the contractors began work, persevering in the face of many obstacles until January 30, 1856, when Kittanning was reached and the road opened for operation. Further progress was suspended for some time on account of financial stringency, but the road was operated between Pittsburg and Kittanning with more or less success. In July, 1860, the road's schedule showed an express train leaving Kittanning at 5.30 A.M., and arriving at Pittsburg, a distance of forty-five miles, at 8.30 A.M. Also a mail-train leaving at 3.30 P.M., making its run to Pittsburg in two hours and forty minutes. An express train left Pittsburg at four P.M. and arrived at Kittanning at 6.50 P.M., and a mail-train at seven A.M. from Pittsburg, arriving at Kittanning at 9.50 A.M."

FIRST OFFICIAL SCHEDULE FOR BUSINESS

ALLEGHENY VALLEY RAILROAD.

THE ALLEGHENY VALLEY RAIL ROAD is now open and in operation between

Pittsburg and Crooked Creek, within four miles of Kittanning.

NOTICE.

ON and after Tuesday, December 11th, Trains for Passengers and Freight will leave Lawrenceville Station (upper wall of Arsenal,)

Regularly every Evening at 3 o'clock,

(*Sundays Excepted.*)

and stop at the following Stations, viz: Sharpsburg, Leland's, Sandy Creek, Verner, Hulton, Logan's Eddy, Logan's Ferry, Parnassus, Arnold, Tarentum, Chartier's, M'Cain's, Freeport, Kiskiminetas, White Rock Eddy, Kelly's, T. Logan's and Crooked Creek.

RETURNING, will leave Crooked Creek at 8 o'clock. A. M., and stop at all the above intermediate Stations.

The Company is prepared to receive and deliver freight for any of the above stations, at their freight depot, corner of Penn and Wayne streets, Pittsburg.

TICKETS can be had at the Company's Office, corner of Penn and Wayne streets, or from the Conductor.

THE EXCELSIOR OMNIBUS LINE

Will leave the corner of Market and Fifth Sts., in connection with the Cars, at 2 o'clock P. M.

NEW CONNECTIONS. — Stages will leave Crooked Creek, on the arrival of the trains, for Kittanning, Catfish, Curlsville, Middlesex, Red Bank, Clarion, Brady's Bend, Reimersburg, Brookville, Smicksburg and Punxsutawney. Fare to Kittanning, $1.25.

A. H. HOPPER,

Dec. 22, 1855.—tf.   *Superintendent.*

"The road was opened and operated to Kittanning January 30, 1856; to Mahoning in 1866; to Brady's Bend, June 27, 1867; and to Oil City, February 2, 1870. Parlor cars used June 15, 1879.

" The *Oil City Derrick,* in its issue of February 12, 1896, in a sketch of the road, said,—

" ' While it serves a large number of manufacturers, carrying to and from them a great variety of products, the road transports also a very heavy tonnage of minerals, mainly coal, of which it moves about two million tons per annum. This tonnage goes mainly to Pittsburg, Buffalo, and points in New York State and Canada. The favorable grades that characterize both of its divisions enable the road to move freight at a minimum cost. Between Pittsburg and Oil City the grade is practically that of the river bed itself, which rises at the rate of about two feet per mile. The Low Grade division, although it crosses the main ridge of the Alleghenies, has a remarkably gentle descent. The average rise per mile from Red Bank to the summit of the mountains, going eastward, is only sixteen feet, while coming westward the average rise per mile from Driftwood to the summit is about the same. The connections of the Allegheny Valley Railway are as follows:

" ' At Pittsburg, in the Union Station, it comes in close touch with the vast Pennsylvania system east and west of that city. It has also at Eleventh Street a connection with the Pennsylvania lines west of Pittsburg, enabling it to exchange freight with these lines without using the tracks at the Union Station. At West Penn Junction, twenty-eight miles north of Pittsburg, it connects with the West Penn division of the Pennsylvania Railroad; at Foxburg with the Pittsburg and Western Railway, and at Oil City with the New York, Pennsylvania and Ohio Railroad, Lake Shore and Michigan Southern Railway, and the Western New York and Pennsylvania Railway, which latter line forms its through route to Buffalo. At Falls Creek, on the Low Grade division, it connects with the Buffalo, Rochester and Pittsburg and Ridgway and Clearfield Railways, and at Driftwood it joins the Philadelphia and Erie Division of the Pennsylvania Railroad.'

" The Presidents of the road have been Governor William F. Johnston, in 1859; F. R. Bruno, 1860; R. F. Morley, 1861; T. J. Brereton, 1862; F. R. Bruno, 1863–64; who was succeeded by Colonel William Phillips, who was in turn succeeded in 1874 by John Scott, who continued in the presidency until his death, March 23, 1889. Mr. Henry D. Welsh succeeded him as president, and served until the reorganization of the company in 1892."

LOW GRADE—CHARTER—EXTENT OF ROAD—GRADIENTS—GRADING COMMENCED — LINE OPENED — PIONEER WRECK — SURGICAL OPERATION — GENERAL OFFICES

This road was constructed under the charter granted to the Pittsburg, Kittanning, and Warren Railroad Company, which was subsequently changed to the Allegheny Valley Railroad Company, and the supplemental acts which became a part of the charter of the last-named company.

This division extends from Red Bank to Driftwood, a distance of one hundred and ten miles, crosses the main ridge of the Allegheny Mountains at a point just east of the Sabula Station, the Summit tunnel being nineteen hundred and twenty-six feet in length, and the height above the sea fourteen hundred and sixty-six feet. This tunnel is one hundred and thirty-four miles from Pittsburg, and thirty-nine miles west from Driftwood. Spencer Mead superintended the tunnel work.

The project lay dormant from 1837 till in the sixties, when J. Edgar Thompson commenced the agitation and brought about the construction of the road. He was then president of the Pennsylvania Railroad Company.

This road extends from the Allegheny River, through the counties of Clarion, Jefferson, Clearfield, and Elk, to the Pittsburg and Erie at Driftwood. It is familiarly called the Low Grade Road, as it is the natural route for a road from the Atlantic coast to the Mississippi Valley. It has a maximum grade of only forty-eight feet to the mile, and that for a very short distance, while every other road between the east and the west has gradients approximately one hundred feet to the mile. It was encouraged, aided, and guaranteed by the Pennsylvania Railroad Company for the purpose of facilitating freight traffic between the east and west. The report of that company for 1869 says,—

" This line is designed chiefly for the transportation of freight at a slow speed, with a view to cheapen its cost so as to compete with the water lines leading to New York. The intention is to extend this line to the Mississippi River, across the tablelands of Ohio, Indiana, and Illinois, and thus afford a medium of transportation at all seasons of the year as cheap and more expeditious than *via* the Lakes and Erie Canal."

Grading began on the Low Grade in 1872. The road was opened for passenger service to New Bethlehem, a distance of twenty-one miles, May 6, 1873; from New Bethlehem to Brookville, June 23, 1873, twenty-one miles; from Brookville to Reynoldsville, fifteen miles, on November 5, 1873. On the eastern end a section from Driftwood to Barrs, nineteen miles, was opened on August 4, 1873. And on May 4, 1874, the entire line was open from Driftwood to Red Bank.

The pioneer wreck on the Low Grade road occurred near Iowa Mills on November 16, 1873. While going around a curve at high speed the engine struck a stone, causing the whole gravel train to jump the track. John McHugh, the brakeman, was thrown in the air, and when the other employees found him he was lying under the wreck, his left arm terribly mangled, a deep cut in his head, severing an artery, and an ugly gash on the back of his head. McHugh was taken to Reynoldsville, where Dr. W. J. McKnight, in the brick tavern, assisted by Dr. B. Sweeney, amputated the arm and dressed his wounds. This was the pioneer major surgical operation on the Low Grade division and in what is now Reynoldsville.

The general offices were moved from Brookville to Reynoldsville in 1885.

HISTORY OF NORTHWESTERN PENNSYLVANIA

On August 1, 1900, the Pennsylvania Railroad Company leased the entire Allegheny Valley Railway for twenty years. Charles Corbet, Esq., of Brookville, Pennsylvania, has been attorney for this road for the past thirty-one years, and is now the legal representative of the Pennsylvania system in its thirty-fifth district.

MILEAGE OF ROADS OWNED AND OPERATED BY THE PENNSYLVANIA SYSTEM IN
NORTHWESTERN PENNSYLVANIA

DIVISION.	BRANCH AND R. R. CO.	COUNTIES.	MILES.
West Penn	Butler Branch, P. R. R.	Butler	18.4
West Penn	Winfield Branch, P. R. R.	Butler	2.0
Buffalo	Main Line, W. N. Y. and P. Ry	Cameron, Potter, McKean	41.3
Buffalo	McKean and Buffalo R. R.	McKean	22.3
Chautauqua	Main Line, W. N. Y. and P. Ry	Venango, Crawford	37.5
Chautauqua	Lakeville Branch, W. N. Y. and P. Ry	Crawford	8.5
Chautauqua	Pioneer Branch, W. N. Y. and P. Ry	Crawford, Venango	8.9
Chautauqua	Oil City to Irvineton, W. N. Y. and P. Ry	Venango, Forrest, Warren	50.2
Chautauqua	Warren to State Line, W. N. Y. and P. Ry	Warren	21.7
Chautauqua	Kinzua Ry.	Warren, McKean	14.0
Chautauqua	Bradford Ry	McKean	2.5
Chautauqua	Kinzua Valley R. R.	McKean	10.0
Chautauqua	Olean, Bradford and Warren Ry	McKean	2.3
River	Allegheny Valley Ry	Clarion, Venango	69.0
Low Grade	Allegheny Valley Ry	Cameron, Elk, Jefferson, Clarion	89.4
Low Grade	Sligo Branch, A. V. Ry	Clarion	10.2
Low Grade	Brookville Branch, A. V. Ry	Jefferson	1.4
Middle, P. and E.	Phila. and Erie R. R.	Cameron, Elk, McKean	79.8
Middle, P. and E.	Johnsonburg R. R.	Elk, McKean	10.7
Middle, P. and E.	Ridgway and Clearfield Ry	Elk, Jefferson	27.1
Western, P. and E.	Phila. and Erie R. R.	Warren, McKean	56.8
		Total	593.0
Western	P. and E. R. R.	Erie	36.6
Chautauqua	W. N. Y. and P. Ry. Main Line	Erie	12.9

Total (including Erie County) 642.5

THE PITTSBURG, SUMMERVILLE AND CLARION RAILROAD COMPANY—CHARTER MEMBERS AND ORGANIZERS—LENGTH OF LINE—CHARLES F. HEIDRICK, ORGANIZER, BUILDER, AND PRESIDENT OF THE ROAD—INDUSTRIES, ETC.

For twenty years or more a railroad from Summerville, Jefferson County, Pennsylvania, to Clarion, Clarion County, Pennsylvania, has been agitated and contemplated. A survey with this in view was made about 1895, and a few years later the Allegheny Valley Railway made an examination along the route with the view of building a road. In 1900 Pittsburg, Beaver Falls, and Clarion gentlemen secured a charter and organized under the name of the Clarion, Summerville, and Pittsburg Railroad Company. This company made a permanent survey, adopted a route, secured considerable right of way, graded a little on the line, when the president of the company died. Internal dissensions followed the death of the president, which resulted in the abandonment of the project. In the fall of 1902 Charles F. Heidrick, a young business man of Brookville, Pennsylvania, conceived the idea of pushing this abandoned project to completion. In September, 1903, he purchased from the Clarion, Summerville and Pittsburg Railroad Company their survey, rights of way, and other assets, and in October, 1903, he let the contract for the construction of the road from Summerville to Clarion to Colonel James A. Bennett, of Greensburg, Pennsylvania, and Daniel Nolan, of Reynoldsville, Pennsylvania. The road was completed and opened for traffic August 27, 1904.

The charter members and organizers of the present Pittsburg, Summerville and Clarion Railroad are, to wit, Charles F. Heidrick, John Q. Heidrick, Emmett R. Heidrick, M. I. McCreight, C. H. Cole, A. L. Cole, Theo. L. Wilson, Charles Corbet, R. M. Matson, and Alfred Truman. The officers of the company are as follows: Charles F. Heidrick, president; A. L. Cole, secretary; John Q. Heidrick, treasurer; the board of directors consists of Charles F. Heidrick, John Q. Heidrick, M. I. McCreight, A. L. Cole, Theo. L. Wilson, R. M. Matson, and J. A. Haven.

The main line of the road is about sixteen miles long; one mile south of Corsica, and two and one-half miles north of Greenville to Strattonville, and thence to Clarion Borough. A branch from the main line extends from Strattonville up along the Clarion River to the mouth of Mill Creek, where a large lumber plant is operated. The road along its entire line taps a large field of undeveloped coal. This coal is now being gradually opened up. The road was a paying proposition from the start.

THE BUFFALO, ROCHESTER AND PITTSBURG RAILWAY COMPANY—WHEN IN-
CEPTED—OFFICERS—CHARTERED ROUTES—PROPOSALS FOR WORK—TRIALS—
EXTENSIONS—CAR SERVICE—PULLMAN CARS—COMPLETED TO PUNXSU-
TAWNEY—THE FIRST THROUGH TRAIN—TRANSPORTATION OF COAL—PRES-
ENT OFFICERS

To my personal knowledge, agitation by the people and the newspapers for this railway commenced as early as 1854. But the first official organization of anything approaching the present road I find in a Rochester newspaper of June 12, 1869, speaking of the directors of the contemplated Rochester and State Line Railroad Company holding a meeting in that city,—viz., president of the road, Isaac Butts, Rochester, New York; vice-president, Oliver Allen, Wheatland, New York; secretary and treasurer, G. E. Mumford, Rochester, New York; executive committee, G. J. Whitney, Rochester, New York; M. C. Reynolds, Rochester, New York; James Wycoff, Perry, New York; directors, Isaac Butts, Rochester, New York; G. J. Whitney, Rochester, New York; Patrick Barry, Rochester, New York; S. M. Spencer, Rochester, New York; M. F. Reynolds, Rochester, New York; Geo. E. Mumford, Rochester, New York; Oliver Allen, Wheatland, New York; James Wycoff, Perry, New York; John A. Thompson, Castile, New York; Miles Dodge, Wiscoy; Luke R. Hutchcock, Canedea; John S. Lee, Wellsville.

The contemplated line was from Rochester to Perry or to Salamanca, but on December 7 of that year the board of directors decided on a western route running through LeRoy, Bliss, Machias, and Salamanca. The line, originally, was to run through Salamanca, Carrollton, LaFayette, McKean County, Ridgway, Brookville, Red Bank, and Kittanning to Pittsburg. This route was very likely located in the sixties.

Through the courtesy of George E. Merchant, late superintendent of the road, I have been shown an extended "map and profile of railroads proposed and under contract connecting Pittsburg, Pennsylvania, and Rochester, New York, (of) February 4, 1854, by McRee Swift, chief engineer, and E. Everett, principal assistant engineer, R. and P. R. R."

The proposed route for the road by this map in the State of Pennsylvania passed through Smethport, Bishop's Summit, Johnsonburg, Richardsville, Brookville, down the Red Bank, through Kittanning, and into Pittsburg.

A change of route was made, however, by Walston H. Brown, in 1882, from the mouth of the Little Toby up the stream to Du Bois, Punxsutawney, and down the Mahoning to Allegheny, Pennsylvania. This change was brought about by the occupancy of the route from Little Toby to Brookville by a survey and right of way obtained by the Clarion and Mahoning road, which, to say the least, was simply a bubble and an obstruction.

The pioneer notice published for work by the directors was as follows:

" Proposals for the work of grading and masonry required in the construction of the Rochester and State Line Railway, between the city of Rochester and the village of Salamanca, Cataraugus County, about one hundred miles, will be received at the office of the company in the city of Rochester, until and including the 25th day of July, 1872. Profile, specifications, and estimated quantities of work to be done will be ready for inspection on and after the 18th day of July, 1872.

(Signed)   " D. McNAUGHTON,
Secretary.

C. S. MASTEN,
" ROCHESTER, NEW YORK, July 9, 1872."   *Chief Engineer.*

Tuesday, October 7, 1873, track-laying was commenced, the pioneer rail being laid at Rochester on that day.

The pioneer schedule issued by the railroad was as follows:

" ROCHESTER AND STATE LINE RAILROAD.

" On and after September 15, 1874, and until further notice, trains on this road will run as follows:

" Leave LeRoy 8.40 A.M.; arrive Rochester 10.10 A.M.; leave Rochester 6.10 P.M.; arrive LeRoy 7.40 P.M.

(Signed)   " M. F. REYNOLDS,
President.

C. S. MASTEN,
Chief Engineer."

August 6, 1877, the line was completed to Warsaw, forty-four miles, and on September 18 of the same year, to Gainsville, fifty-four miles from Rochester.

The road was finished to Salamanca and opened for regular and through freight and passenger business on May 16, 1878.

In July, 1879, the majority of the stock was owned by William H. Vanderbilt, and the road was practically controlled by him until that year. At that time suits were brought against the railroad company by the city of Rochester to recover six hundred thousand dollars which had been contributed toward the construction of the road. The suits were decided against the city and in favor of the company. Mr. Vanderbilt then dropped out of the management, and the road was unable to pay the interest on the first mortgage, which fell due on January 1, 1880, when the road was sold and a receiver appointed June 7, 1880. It was sold under foreclosure January 8, 1881. Mr. Walston H. Brown, of New York city, purchased control and reorganized it under the name of " Rochester and Pittsburg Railroad." Mr. Brown associated with himself an active, able and efficient manager,—to wit, George E. Merchant. Mr. Merchant has been identified with the road ever since that time, and was the general superintendent, managing its great interests with rare tact and skill.

The pioneer officers of this reorganization were as follows,—viz., president, Walston H. Brown, of New York; treasurer, F. A. Brown, of New York; secretary, Thos. F. Wentworth, of New York; general manager, George E. Merchant, Rochester, New York; chief engineer, William E. Hoyt; counsel, C. H. McCauley, Ridgway, Pennsylvania.

" In 1881 three companies were organized in New York in the interest of the Rochester and Pittsburg,—namely, the Rochester and Charlotte, to build from Rochester to Charlotte on Lake Ontario; the Buffalo, Rochester and Pittsburg, to build from Buffalo to Ashford, on the main line; and the Great Valley and Bradford, to build from Great Valley to the Pennsylvania line. At the same time the Bradford and State Line and the Pittsburg and New York were organized in Pennsylvania to extend the road from State Line to Brookville, Pennsylvania. These several companies were consolidated into the Rochester and Pittsburg in 1882. In 1882 the road was completed from Bradford Junction, 1.33 miles north of Salamanca, New York, south to Howard Junction, Pennsylvania, 21.09 miles; from Clarion Junction to Ridgway, Pennsylvania, 9.08 miles; from Du Bois to Falls Creek, Pennsylvania, 2.09 miles; a total of 32.26 miles of the Great Valley-Pittsburg line in that year. On the Buffalo Division track was laid from Buffalo Creek to Hamburg, 7.93 miles, and from Ashford to West Valley, 6.34 miles. In the following year, 1883, the road was completed by laying from Hamburg to West Valley, New York, 30.9 miles; from Ridgway to Falls Creek, Pennsylvania, thirty miles; and from Du Bois to Walston Junction, Pennsylvania, 22.91

miles.   The Beech Tree and Walston Mines branches were also built in 1883.

"An issue of ten million dollars stock, doubling the capital of the company, was made in 1883, the new stock being used in cancelling an intended issue of three million two hundred thousand dollars income bonds of the Buffalo division and in purchasing the capital stocks of the Rochester and Pittsburg Coal and Iron Company and the Brockwayville and Punxsutawney Railroad Company, under the charter of which latter the road from Young Township to Punxsutawney, Pennsylvania, was built and opened September 30, 1883.   In the same year the company purchased the franchises and capital stock of the East Terminal Railroad Company of Buffalo, having the right to build from Howard Street in East Buffalo into the heart of the city.

"In November, 1883, the directors authorized an issue of four million dollars second mortgage consolidated bonds, secured on the entire property of the company, the proceeds to be used in providing seven hundred thousand dollars worth of new equipment, in retiring six hundred thousand dollars second mortgage terminal bonds issued earlier in the same year, and in liquidating the floating debt.   Of these, two million eight hundred thousand dollars were issued February 1, 1884, but one million one hundred and thirty-two thousand five hundred dollars only were taken, so that to meet pressing demands the company was forced to hypothecate the remainder, which was subsequently sold to cancel loans.   Default was made in payment of the first coupon, due August, 1884, on these bonds, and the road was sold under foreclosure on October 17, 1885; it was bid in for one million one hundred thousand dollars by Adrian Iselin, representing the second mortgage bondholders.

"A plan of reorganization was agreed upon by Mr. Iselin and others, which called for the formation of two new companies, one to acquire the part of the road lying within the State of New York and the other the Pennsylvania portion, the two to be ultimately consolidated under the title of Buffalo, Rochester and Pittsburg Railway Company, with a capital of six million dollars preferred and six million dollars common stock, the latter issue, including one million two hundred thousand dollars, representing the Pennsylvania section.   The common stock was issued at the rate of one share for four in exchange for the stock of the company.   The preferred was subscribed for at par and the proceeds used to pay off the second mortgage bonds and floating debt.

"Under the terms of this plan the Buffalo, Rochester and Pittsburg Railway Company was organized in the State of New York, on October 24, 1885, and acquired the property in that State.   The Pittsburg and State Line Railroad Company was organized and acquired the property in Pennsylvania. In consequence of litigation attending the transfer of the property in Pennsylvania, under which the portion of the road in that State was placed in the hands of a receiver on March 23, 1886, the final consolidation of the two corporations was not effected until March 11, 1887, when the receivership was dissolved."—*Poor's Manual.*

The extension of the line from Ashford to Buffalo was completed for freight about June 1, 1883, but regular passenger and mail trains were not run into Buffalo until June 15, 1883. Freight trains carrying coal, with a caboose attached for passengers, were run from Du Bois north about May 1, 1883. Regular passenger and mail trains north from Du Bois were not run until June 16, 1883. The road was completed to Punxsutawney and through passenger trains were running, one to Buffalo and one from Buffalo to that point, September 1, 1883.

About July 25, 1883, there were two passenger trains running on the Beechtree branch, one to and one from Beechtree. Coal was shipped from Beechtree July 1, 1883.

An agreement was entered into on June 6, 1883, by George E. Merchant, of Rochester, and David McCargo, of Pittsburg, superintendents of their respective roads, that a night express should be added by a joint service of the two lines,—to wit, one from Rochester to Pittsburg, and *vice versa,* one from Pittsburg to Rochester, this service to contain a Pullman and day car on each line; each road to exchange their sleepers at Falls Creek. The schedule for this service went into effect on the evening of December 23, 1883, and on that evening the pioneer car of this service was so run. The conductor and engineer of the Valley train was M. J. McEnteer and James Montgomery. The conductor and engineer on the Rochester I know not. The time-table for this joint service was as follows,—to wit, the north-bound train for Rochester, with sleeper, left Pittsburg at 8.20 P.M., passed through Brookville, a flag-station, at 1 A.M., arrived at Falls Creek at 2 A.M., where the north-bound cars were shifted to the Rochester road, and this train arrived at Rochester 7.30 A.M. The south-bound train from Rochester left Rochester about 8.20 P.M., and shifted their Pullman and day coach at Falls Creek to the Allegheny Valley road, which, returning, passed through Brookville, a flag-station, at 3.30 A.M., and arrived at Pittsburg at 7.50 A.M.

"About four years ago the Buffalo, Rochester and Pittsburg entered into a traffic arrangement with the Pittsburg and Western for running trains into Pittsburg from Butler over the Pittsburg and Western tracks. This arrangement, of course, was continued when the Baltimore and Ohio secured the Pittsburg and Western. That agreement was made for twenty years, consequently it has still sixteen years to run."

Surveys for the extension of the road from Punxsutawney to Allegheny City were made in the fall of 1894. The actual construction of the railroad did not begin until March, 1898. The track from Punxsutawney to the Allegheny River Bridge was finished in June, 1889. Track-laying commenced at Butler in January, 1899, and was extended eastward to Mosgrove.

The track was joined at Mosgrove Station in August, 1899, when the last spike, a silver one, was driven by Arthur G. Yates, president of the road.

The first regular train through to Allegheny City was run September 4, 1899, and regular through passenger service from Buffalo and Rochester to Allegheny began October 9, 1899.

That the Buffalo, Rochester and Pittsburg is a good paying proposition needs no exploitation. Their coal territory and its productiveness in both coal and coke is shown in the average daily handling of one thousand cars of coal and two hundred cars of coke. The value is also shown in the numerous spurs that have been built into rich coal regions. The largest of these spurs is the twenty-eight mile extension to Ernest. From Ernest through Indiana County two lines are constructed, with a combined mileage of forty-two miles, one running to Slate Lick and the other to Elder's Ridge. The Slate Lick branch is operated from Indiana. Just outside of Ernest on the new line a tunnel is constructed. The tunnel and new branches are now completed.

At Ernest a fine steel coal tipple has been built by the Rochester and Pittsburg Coal and Iron Company, which is the controlled subsidiary company. The structural steel for the tipple alone cost fifty-five thousand dollars. The main locomotive works, at Du Bois, Pennsylvania, were opened November 4, 1901. They have facilities for making heavy repairs on twenty locomotives per month.

The traffic having reached the limit of economical operation on a single track, the construction of a second track was authorized. During the fall of 1903 the middle division of the main line from Du Bois to East Salamanca, a distance of one hundred and twenty-eight miles, or over one-third of the total mileage, was double tracked. The Pittsburg division is laid on one-hundred-pound steel rails.

The present officers of the Buffalo, Rochester and Pittsburg Railway Company are as follows:

Arthur G. Yates, president, Rochester, New York; Adrian Iselin, Jr., vice-president, 36 Wall Street, New York; John F. Dinkey, auditor and treasurer, Rochester, New York; John H. Hocart, secretary and assistant treasurer, 36 Wall Street, New York; W. T. Noonan, general superintendent, Rochester, New York; J. M. Floesch, chief engineer, Rochester, New York; Robert W. Davis, general freight agent, Rochester, New York; Edward C. Lapey, general passenger agent, Rochester, New York; E. E. Davis, superintendent of motive power, Du Bois City, Pennsylvania; Perkins & Havens, counsel, Rochester, New York; C. H. McCauley, counsel, Ridgway, Pennsylvania. George E. Merchant, ex-superintendent, has been twenty-five years in the service of the road, and is now not in active duty.

Under this efficient board the management of the road has been prudent, bold, aggressive, potential, and successful, and has now a mileage of 557.69 miles.

Paralleling the Buffalo, Rochester and Pittsburg Railway through Brock-wayville is the Ridgway and Clearfield road. It is part of the Pennsylvania system and was completed about October, 1884.

The New York, Lake Erie and Western (branch) was extended into Jefferson County, *via* Crenshaw, about 1882. The coal freightage is and has been large over this road.

The Reynoldsville and Falls Creek road, seven miles long, was finished by Bell, Lewis & Yates, in September, 1885.

The pioneer steam railway in the world was opened in England in September, 1825, and was called the Stockdale and Darlington Road. It was thirty-eight miles long. It is claimed that the Baltimore and Ohio is the pioneer steam railroad in the United States. It was built in 1830. In any event, seventy years later, our railroads are the wonder of the world.

In 1830 the railway mileage in the United States did not exceed sixty; to-day we have 182,746 miles, and the gross earnings of our railroads combined is over three million dollars per day. In 1830 we travelled at high speed, as railroad passengers, at six and ten miles per hour, but now we glide along at the rate of forty or sixty miles an hour as smoothly as our fathers did with their skates on ice or sleds on snow. To-day we telegraph around the world in nine minutes. What next?

In 1850 we had only seven thousand three hundred miles of railway owned and operated by one hundred and fifty-one companies, and with a few exceptions each road was less than one hundred miles in length. The New York and Erie was the only " Trunk Line," with a mileage of three hundred and one miles.

The amount of money now invested (1905) in railway property is about twelve thousand million dollars, and the number of employees are about twelve hundred thousand.

The first stone coal discovered in America was by Father Henepin in what is now Illinois, on the Illinois River, in 1679. In 1684 William Penn granted the privilege to mine the coal at Pittsburg, Pennsylvania. In 1728 coal was discovered in Virginia.

Anthracite coal is bituminous coal coked and condensed by nature.

The first record of bituminous coal-mining is at New Castle, England. This coal was on the market in 1281. Stone coal was first mined and used in Western Pennsylvania near where Pittsburg now is, by Colonel James Burd, in 1759. It was dug from the hills of the Monongahela. In 1807 stone coal was mined in central Pennsylvania and sold as a fertilizer. I quote the following notice from the *Bedford Gazette* of June, 1807,—viz.:

HISTORY OF NORTHWESTERN PENNSYLVANIA

HISTORY OF NORTHWESTERN PENNSYLVANIA

"Huntington, June 4.

"Stone Coal.—Such of the farmers as wish to make experiment with stone coal as a substitute for plaster, in manuring their Indian corn, may be supplied with coal gratis upon application to Peter Hughes, at Mr. Riddle's mines, on the Raystown Branch. The proprietor of the mines offers not only to refund the carriage, but to pay the expenses of applying the coal, if upon a fair experiment it is found to be inferior to plaster, which now sells at two dollars per bushel."

The pioneers to dig coal in Northwestern Pennsylvania were mostly blacksmiths. Previous to the discovery of coal in this wilderness, the blacksmiths burned their own charcoal, and used it for fuel; but it appears they early searched the runs with bags for coal, and picked up loose pieces, and occasionally stripped the earth and dug bags full of what they called "stone coal." They burned this in their fires, either alone or with charcoal.

"In 1784, the year in which Pittsburg was surveyed into building lots, the privilege of mining coal in the 'great seam' opposite that town was sold by the Penns at the rate of thirty pounds for each mining lot, extending back to the centre of the hill. This event may be regarded as forming the beginning of the coal trade of Pittsburg. The supply of the towns and cities on the Ohio and Mississippi Rivers with Pittsburg coal became an established business at an early day in the present century or in 1800. Pittsburg coal was known long before the town became noted as an iron centre.

"Down to 1845 all the coal shipped westward from Pittsburg was floated down the Ohio in flat-bottomed boats in the spring and fall freshets, each boat holding about fifteen thousand bushels of coal. The boats were usually lashed in pairs, and were sold and broken up when their destination was reached. In 1845 steam tow-boats were introduced, which took coal-barges down the river and brought them back empty."

The first carload of bituminous coal hauled east of the Alleghenies came from the Westmoreland Company's "Shade Grove" mine, or what was later called the northside colliery in Irwin. The mine was opened in 1852 by Coleman, Hillman & Co.

The coal was taken out of the mine and hauled to the platform of the freight station and loaded into an eighteen-thousand-pound box car, the standard of those days. It was sent forward as one of about twelve cars of like capacity, hauled by a wood-burning locomotive at about six miles an hour, with Philadelphia as its destination.

The first person to mine coal in Jefferson County for manufacturing purposes was John Fuller.

He was the first person to mine coal in what is now Winslow Township, or, probably, in Jefferson County. He mined for his own use a few bagfuls occasionally from the bed of the creek near to and above the bridge on

708

the pike, in what is now Reynoldsville. He hauled his first coal in a pung to his shop with an ox and a cow.

In what year Mr. Fuller first picked from the bed of the creek his little load of what was then and in my boyhood days called stone coal is not precisely known, but of course it was shortly after his settlement, probably in 1825.

The first person to mine coal in the county for general use was a colored man named Charles Anderson. He lived in Brookville, and was called " Yellow Charley." He was the first to operate, lease, mine, transport, and sell coal. He opened his pioneer mine about 1832, on the Joseph Clement's farm, north of and close to Brookville. The vein he exposed was about two feet thick. He stripped the earth from the top of the vein, dug the coal fine and transported it to Brookville in a little rickety one-horse wagon, retailing the stone coal at family doors in quantities of a peck, half-bushel, and bushel. The price per bushel was twelve and one-half cents, or " eleven-penny-bit," and a " fippenny-bit" for half a bushel, and three cents a peck. It was burned in grates. I had a free pass on this coal line, and rode on it a great deal. To me it was a line of " speed, safety, and comfort." Anderson was a " Soft Coal King," a baron, a robber, a close corporationist, a capitalist, and a monopolist. He managed his works generally so as to avoid strikes, etc. Yet he had to assume the rôle of a Pinkerton or a coal policeman at one time, for there was some litigation over the ownership of this coal-bank, and Charley took his old flint-lock musket one day and swore he would just as soon die in the coal-bank as any other place. He held the fort, too.

Charley was a greatly abused man. Every theft and nearly all outlawry was blamed on him. Public sentiment and public clamor was against him. He tried at times to be good, attend church, etc., but it availed him nothing, for he would be so coldly received as to force him into his former condition. As the town grew, and other parties became engaged in mining coal, Charley changed his business to that of water-carrier, and hauled in his one-horse wagon washing and cooking water in barrels for the women of the town. He continued in this business until his death, which occurred in 1874. · In early days he lived on the lot now owned by Dr. T. C. Lawson. He died in his own home near the new cemetery.

John Dixon who is now (1903) living in Polk Township at the advanced age of ninety-five years, was one of the pioneer miners, and was born in the county. He mined on the present Rose Township poor farm from 1840 to 1847. The pioneers to open and operate banks in Young Township, were Obed Morris and John Hutchison. Their first operations were about 1834 or 1835. The sales were light, the coal being principally used for black-smithing purposes and for a few families who had grates. Coal was sold at the bank for ten cents a bushel, and every bushel was measured in a " bushel box." The mining was done by the families. The census of 1840 reports but two points in the county as mining and using coal,—viz., Brookville and Rose Township. The amount used in Rose Township a year was five hundred bushels, in Brookville, two thousand bushels. Jefferson County coal is now shipped to and used from Arctic ice to tropic sun.

Woodward Reynolds commenced to mine coal for his own general use in the fall of 1838, and for about ten years he, John Fuller, and their neighbors, would mine what they wanted for their own use, paying no royalty for the coal whatever. A coal-miner then received ninety cents for a twelve-hour day.

In the year 1849, about the time Woodward and Thomas Reynolds commenced to mine coal in what is now Winslow Township, the whole output of bituminous coal in that year in the United States was only four million tons. In 1870 it was 36,806,560 tons; in 1880 it was 71,481,569 tons; in 1890 it was 157,770,963 tons.

About the latter part of the year 1863, or the beginning of 1864, Hon. Joseph Henderson, Dr. W. J. McKnight, G. W. Andrews, Esq., I. C. Fuller. P. W. Jenks, and James A. Cathers, and possibly one or two others, organized themselves into a company for the purpose of taking some measure toward bringing the coal lands and other resources of the county to the notice of capitalists who were seeking investments for their money. During the year 1864 geological surveys of the Brockwayville, Reynoldsville, and Punxsutawney regions were made by J. P. Leslie, who has since made the geological survey of the State, and the chemical analysis of the minerals were made by Dr. Guenth, the famous chemist of Philadelphia, after which an exhaustive report was submitted setting forth the advantages of the district. The expenses of this work, amounting to over three thousand dollars, were paid by the above-named gentlemen, who never realized anything from it. They, however, purchased some land during their transactions, and this was afterward disposed of at a profit, lessening their net outlay of money.

In 1865 a number of English capitalists visited this country, and the above-mentioned report was laid before them through the officers of the Catawissa Railroad Company, as will be noticed in the following letter, and it had its influence in securing the building of a railroad through this section. The road spoken of in this letter was never built, but the Pennsylvania Railroad Company, in order to head it off, was compelled to force the building of the Low Grade division of the Allegheny Valley road. The movement of the above gentlemen was, we believe, the first organized effort to bring this county into prominent notice as one of the richest parts of the State in mineral and lumber, and resulted in bringing about the development of the resources of the county which have followed. We therefore record this as a matter of history, to be handed down to future generations:

HISTORY OF NORTHWESTERN PENNSYLVANIA

"OFFICE CATAWISSA RAILROAD COMPANY,
424 WALNUT STREET, PHILADELPHIA, December 16, 1865.
" MESSRS. W. J. MCKNIGHT, JOSEPH HENDERSON, G. W. ANDREWS, I. C. FULLER:

" GENTS,—I return you herewith the copy of Leslie's geological report, kindly loaned me for presentation before the English capitalists on their visit to this country. I feel that it had its influence among other things in deciding the question of building the new route through the counties lying between Milton and Franklin.

" Several corps of engineers are already making surveys to ascertain the most practical route, and it will be pushed forward with energy and despatch, the capital necessary for the same having all been promised. This measure, of course, meets with the utmost hostility from the Pennsylvania Railroad, as it is opposed to monopoly, and it is to be worked upon the principle that railroads are built for the accommodation of the community—trade and travel to be allowed to go and come as the parties may wish. We feel that this portion of the State will not allow their interests to be crushed out by it.

" P. M. HUTCHINSON,
"Vice-President, Secretary, and Treasurer."
—*Brookville Jeffersonian.*

It was not until April, 1874, that coal-mining for a foreign market began in Jefferson County. In that year the Diamond Mine was opened just north of Reynoldsville. The pioneer to ship coal by rail from that mine was H. S. Belnap. He hauled his coal in wagons to the Reynoldsville depot and there from a platform shovelled the coal into the cars, and it was shipped to Buffalo, New York. John Coax, Jr., Thomas Jenkins, and others were his team drivers. The second drift opened in Winslow Township was the Pancoast. The third was the Washington Mine, located near Pancoast flag-station. The fourth was the Hamilton Mine, and the fifth the Soldier Run Mine. Following these, the Sprague Mine was opened at Rathmel, and the Pleasant Valley Mine was opened east of Reynoldsville. The Hamilton and Pleasant Valley Mines were owned by the Hamilton Coal Company, and the Soldier Run and Sprague Mines were owned by Powers, Brown & Co.

On June 25, 1890, Alfred Bell, George H. Lewis, and Arthur G. Yates, known as the firm of Bell, Lewis & Yates, bought out the interest of all these companies with considerable adjoining territory. Of this firm only Arthur G. Yates is now (1903) living, and he is president of the great coal road of this region,—to wit, the Buffalo, Rochester and Pittsburg Railway Company. Mr. Yates is an active, progressive man. His was the pioneer railroad to enter Jefferson County for the transportation of coal. Before the advent in 1883 of Bell, Lewis & Yates, the shipment of coal from this county only amounted to a few thousand tons a year, but by September 1, 1883, the

711

Hamilton Mine employed one hundred and twenty-four men; the Sprague Mine, eighty-five men; Powers, Brown & Co., one hundred and thirty men; Pancoast Mine, thirty-six men; Rochester Mines, four hundred and fifty men; Falls Creek Mine, seventy men; Hildrup, eighty-two; Beechtree, one hundred and eighty-five; and Walston, fifty-five men.

I copy here from the *Pittsburg Times* of May 24, 1890, and as I was well acquainted with the Bells and these events, I have taken the liberty to correct what I quote.

"Alfred Bell came to Jefferson County about 1856 from Nunda, New York. He was a dignified and stately man, precise in his methods, careful in his operations, and with Calvin Rogers he operated a large tract of timber land which they had bought east of Brookville. The Bell holdings extended for miles from Bell's mills, up and around what is now Falls Creek and Du Bois.

"Frederick Bell came to Jefferson County about 1866, with his father, and the young man had his head-quarters in Brookville. A great deal of his leisure was spent in McKnight & Bro.'s drug-store. As the lumber business developed, he perceived the possibilities in the coal that underlay their vast acreage of land. When, in 1873, the Allegheny Valley Railroad pushed up the Red Bank valley, Frederick A. Bell interested with him two congenial spirits, and not long after the firm of Bell, Lewis & Yates was formed, and it speedily became the foremost power in soft coal circles in the Buffalo and Rochester country. Lewis was a Canadian who married Bell's sister, while Yates was a practical coal merchant of Rochester. The firm commenced to mine and ship the splendid soft coal of Clearfield County in March, 1877, making its opening on the Young tract of seven hundred and forty acres, or what is called the Rochester Mine at Du Bois, for which they paid a royalty of ten cents per ton. The firm marketed its coal at that date by the Allegheny Valley and the Buffalo, New York and Pennsylvania roads.

"Putting good coal in the market gave Bell, Lewis & Yates the easy control, and presently the firm had the largest docks on the lakes, and had created an export trade in soft coal, sending fully a third of its product to the international bridge at Black Rock for the Canadian trade.

"Mr. Yates sold the coal, and put the New York Central, the Grand Trunk, and other important concerns on his list, and came home from his selling trip sometimes with single contracts for half a million tons. The firm grew and prospered and opened new mines and bought mines opened by others. But it was hampered by the lack of facilities for getting coal to market. By May, 1883, when the Rochester and Pittsburg road reached Du Bois, the company was ready to and did give it business, and later on when the Pennsylvania road, Ridgway and Clearfield, reached Falls Creek, Bell, Lewis & Yates afforded the roads an enormous traffic. New works were established, additional territory was secured, and one day Bell, Lewis & Yates commenced a tunnel and shaft at Sykesville, seven miles from Du Bois.

Arthur G. Yates, born at Waverly, Tioga County, New York, December 18, 1843

" The firm had extended its operations to Reynoldsville, and the Sykes-ville tunnel was dug miles under ground that the Reynoldsville works could be connected with a proposed new opening, but above all else to afford drain-age to the system, for the coal dips toward Sykes. It was one of the most stupendous engineering feats in this region or in the coal world. The firm was now carrying coal in its own cars, and paying freight on a basis of wheel tollage with the roads. Meanwhile, the Rochester and Pittsburg Coal and Iron Company had been creating extensive mines, and developing great blocks of coal territory in Jefferson County, and in this corporation Bell, Lewis and Yates found a rival that was no mean competitor. In 1890 Bell, Lewis & Yates bought the Buffalo, Rochester and Pittsburg Railway Company, as well as the Coal and Iron Company.

" In 1886 Clearfield and Jefferson Counties did not produce together five million tons of coal, but six years later they totalled more than ten million tons, and the bulk of the increase was that of the Bell, Lewis & Yates interests. Not only that, but a large proportion of the original product of 1886 was from its mines or those that finally came into its hands. In 1898 the product of the two counties climbed to almost twelve million, and the coke ovens of the affiliated interests made Jefferson the third coke-producing county in the State.

" Later, in 1896, Bell, Lewis & Yates sold their coal properties and their railroad—to wit, the Reynoldsville and Falls Creek roads, the Buffalo, Rochester and Pittsburg Railway Company, and the Rochester and Pittsburg Coal and Iron Company—to Adrian Iselin, and this vast property is now in the hands of these corporations.

" The superintendents of the Rochester and Pittsburg Coal and Iron Company have been Franklin Platt, James McLeavey, J. A. Haskell, and, since 1890, L. W. Robinson. The present officers are, president and general manager, Lucius W. Robinson; secretary, George L. Eaton; treasurer, George H. Cune.

" This Coal and Iron Company is now developing Indiana and Armstrong Counties with just the same energy that it developed Clearfield and Jefferson.

" Frederick A. Bell was one of the three men who brought the great enterprises into life, but Arthur G. Yates practically made them what they are. He took interest in Du Bois when the town was a struggling lumber and mining town, and probably has had as much, if not more, to do with its perpetuity and importance than John Du Bois, whose name it bears, for Du Bois is more of a coal and railroad town than it is a lumber town. The pros-perity of Reynoldsville, Brockwayville, Punxsutawney, Big Run, Falls Creek, and the vast region that embraces a population of one hundred thousand in its sixty miles of coal lands, is a monument to the perception and business tact of Arthur G. Yates, who knew what the coal-deposits of Clearfield and Jeffer-son Counties would mean if they were opened for the markets.

" Bell, Lewis & Yates owned the first of the gigantic concerns operating in this vicinity for soft coal. And in these days of great things, the Buffalo, Rochester and Pittsburg interests are still among the great institutions. Bell, Lewis & Yates were pioneers in the field, and they were highly successful.

" Arthur G. Yates, now president of the Buffalo, Rochester and Pittsburg Railway, was and is a wonderfully successful man, and he created a market for coal in northern New York such as never had been dreamed of. Really the firm commenced business at a time most opportune, for when its coal started for market the product of the McKean and Tioga fields was not of the best, while the excellent coal of Jefferson County has never been outclassed.

" The Rochester and Pittsburg Coal and Iron Company operates mines that give employment to ten thousand operatives. New towns and villages have been built, and more in course of construction.

" The first operations of the company were begun in Jefferson County about 1882 immediately after organization, the initial steps being the opening of the mines at Beechtree, Walston, and Adrian, followed by those at Eleanora, Helvetia, Elk Run Shaft, and Florence. In 1896 it absorbed by purchase the extensive interests of the Bell, Lewis & Yates Company, at that time the largest operators in what are known as the Reynoldsville and Du Bois districts. The operations of the mines in these districts were subsequently transferred to a corporation, organized in 1896, known as the Jefferson and Clearfield Coal and Iron Company, for which the Rochester and Pittsburg Coal and Iron Company became selling agents. The mines owned and operated by the Jefferson and Clearfield Coal and Iron Company are by name as follows: Soldier Run Mine, said to have the largest producing capacity of any single mine in this country, if not in the world, situated near Reynoldsville; the Maplewood, Sherwood, Virginia, Rochester, London, and Sandy Lick Mines, all situated near Reynoldsville, Du Bois, and Punxsutawney. The average daily output is twenty-five thousand tons, requiring a large number of trains and crews moving night and day to handle the product.

" The production of coke by the Rochester and Pittsburg Coal and Iron Company is an important auxiliary to the mining industry. This is carried on extensively at Walston, Adrian, Eleanora, Reynoldsville, and Helvetia. The ovens are of the pattern known as beehive, of large capacity and modern construction. At Walston is said to be the longest continuous string of coke ovens in the world, its length being one and one-fourth miles, and containing in all four hundred and twenty-five ovens; there is also a shorter bank of two hundred and seventy-five ovens, a total of seven hundred ovens. At Adrian there are four hundred and seventy-six ovens, at Eleanora two hundred and one, at Helvetia forty, and at Reynoldsville two hundred and sixty-one in operation and one hundred and fifty in course of construction. The daily output of coke is about two hundred cars.

HISTORY OF NORTHWESTERN PENNSYLVANIA

" The output of the mines and the coke ovens finds a ready market in practically all parts of the world. Situated as they are on the line of the Buffalo, Rochester and Pittsburg Railway Company, excellent shipping facilities are enjoyed. At Buffalo and Charlotte there are extensive docking facilities for the enormous lake tonnage while the rail shipment to the North, Northwest, and New England points, *via* the valuable connections of the Buffalo, Rochester and Pittsburg, are very heavy. A large percentage of the tonnage of these mines is also moved East *via* Clearfield and over the New York Central Railroad (formerly the Beech Creek), and the Philadelphia and Reading Railway to the docks at Philadelphia and New York, from which shipments are made by water both north and south. ' The recent extension of the Buffalo, Rochester and Pittsburg to Butler and New Castle gives a valuable Western outlet for the product.

" The main offices of the Rochester and Pittsburg Coal and Iron Company and the Jefferson and Clearfield Coal and Iron Company are at Rochester, while branch offices are maintained in charge of the sales agents of the former company at New York, Philadelphia, Buffalo, and all the larger cities."·

The first instance of the use of wooden rails and a car for the removal of coal from a mine was at New Castle upon Tyne, England, in 1675. The first introduction of that method of removal of coal in Jefferson County was by Jacob Meinweiser, on the Haugh farm, Union Township, in 1852. All miners previous to that date in this county used wheelbarrows.

With some pride I state that the first trip across the ocean in six days and fifteen hours was made by steam from Beechtree coal, and that as a nation we have millions of square miles covered with forest trees and empires underlaid with coal.

Coke was first used in Pennsylvania in 1835 in Huntingdon County; it was then used in a furnace. The first coke-works of any importance in the State were erected in 1860.

The pioneer coal strike in Jefferson County was on September 1, 1883. The men were out about six weeks. To maintain order forty or fifty Pinkerton men were imported and kept on the ground.·

The bituminous coal output of the country has quadrupled since 1885, and it will only require a few years more until the demand in the United States will be a million tons for each day of the year. One-half of the nation's output is now used up by the railroads and steamships. The annual output of the Rochester and Pittsburg Coal and Iron Company and their associate companies is now six million tons a year, and it is safe to say this output will be doubled within a very short time.

Coal is found in twenty-seven of our States and Territories. The bituminous coal-field in Pennsylvania has an area of fifteen thousand square miles. The first shipment of coal from Pittsburg was made in 1803. The first shipment from Clearfield was in 1804, in barges to Columbia, Pennsylvania.

HISTORY OF NORTHWESTERN PENNSYLVANIA

The earliest authentic mention of coal in history is by Theophrastus, about two thousand two hundred years ago. An estimate was made in 1897, by eminent men, of the world's coal-producing territory, the sum total of which was found to be 563,150,000 square miles, distributed as follows,—to wit, United States east of the Rocky Mountains, 192,000; Canada, 65,000; India, 35,000; New South Wales, 24,000; Russia, 20,000; United Kingdom, 11,500; Spain, 5500; Japan, 5000; France, 2080; Austria Hungary, 1790; Germany, 1770; Belgium, 510; China, 200,000.

With our history of only one hundred and twenty-seven years, as a government, the United States leads the world in wealth, mining, and transportation.

(From the Pittsburg *Daily Post*, Saturday, July 30, 1881.)

" THE LATE JAMES L. GILLIS, THE PATRIARCH OF ELK COUNTY—A MOST RE-
MARKABLE CAREER—SOLDIER, STATESMAN, JUDGE, AND LEADING CITIZEN
—HIS ARREST AND TRIAL FOR THE MURDER OF MORGAN—HIS STATEMENT
ABOUT MORGAN—HIS BLAMELESS LIFE

" The death of Judge Gillis, at Mount Pleasant, Iowa, a few weeks ago, calls to mind the man, who he was, and the part he filled in his eventful life, most of which was spent in Pennsylvania. He was born in Washington County, New York, October 7, 1792, and was one of a large number of sons, all sturdy and hardy men. His father lived to a ripe old age and visited his sons, James and Enos, late in life, when they resided at Ridgway, Pennsylvania. A few years prior to the war of 1812 the family moved to Ontario County in the State of New York. There, in 1812, James enlisted in a company of New York volunteers, and was immediately commissioned a lieutenant of cavalry and assigned to a regiment commanded by one Colonel Harris, regular dragoons. He was in the battles of Fort George, Chippewa, and Lundy's Lane. Shortly after the latter battle he was taken prisoner by the British and confined at various places in Canada, and in 1814, while under parole, he was arrested and put on board a transport about to sail for England. Gillis and several others were successful in making their escape by capturing a boat belonging to the transport and gaining the bank of the St. Lawrence River opposite Quebec, at which place the vessel was lying. All were finally retaken. They wandered about for several days, wishing to reach the United States frontier, and made but little headway in that direction. Finally they made terms with a Canadian Frenchman, who promised to guide them toward the boundary, but betrayed them; the red-coats got them, returned them to confinement, and Lieutenant Gillis was not again permitted to escape. He remained in confinement till the close of the war, when he was exchanged at Salem, Mass. When Congress, about 1853, passed a law giving a bounty of one hundred and sixty acres of land to the soldiers

718

of 1812, Judge Gillis had no trouble in proving his title to one. He considered the certificate too sacred to part with, and for years kept it hanging in his house in a gilt frame, which was a luxury in the way of fine art that his neighbors generally could not indulge in.

"IN THE WILDS OF PENNSYLVANIA

"In 1822 he moved to Pennsylvania and located in what was then Jefferson (now Elk) County. His nearest neighbor was sixteen miles distant and nearest post-office about seventy miles. The approach to his location was from Olean Point, on the Allegheny River, and supplies were brought from that place over a rough wagon-road, about thirty miles of which he got over as best he could. He came there as the agent of Jacob Ridgway, of Philadelphia, who owned a large tract of land in Jefferson County, expecting that the country would soon settle up. He built a grist-mill, upon a small scale, to supply his wants in that direction and those of the future settlers, but it was some years before it was used by any one except himself. In 1816, he married a Miss Mary Ridgway, of Philadelphia, a niece of his future employer. By that marriage he had three children,—Ridgway B., Charles B., and Caroline, now the widow of Judge Houk, late of Ridgway. In that wild country he reared these three children. His wife died in 1826, and in 1829 he married a Miss Celia A. Berry, who died in 1855, leaving seven children. In 1830 he moved from his farm, which he cleared six miles from the town of Ridgway to that place, naming the place Ridgway, where he and his family resided for a long time. In that country, where the benefits of education were very limited, he brought up his ten children, giving them such education as the country afforded, and all of them have acquitted themselves very creditably in life. One of his sons, Captain James H. Gillis, U.S.N., did gallant service in the late Rebellion. He was in command of a war-vessel throughout the war, and at the bombardment of Mobile his vessel came in contact with a torpedo, was sunk to her gun-deck, but he fought her as long as there was enough of her above water to stand upon. While he was a midshipman, and the vessel to which he was attached was in a South American port, he called for volunteers from his crew, took one of the ship's boats, and saved the crew of a Chilian vessel which was going to pieces in a fierce storm two miles from the shore. He took the crew from the rigging and brought them safely to land. The act was recognized by the Chilian government in a fitting manner. Another son, B. W. Gillis, has made considerable reputation as a journalist in Virginia. Another son, C. V. Gillis, lives in this State.

"JUDGE AND CONGRESSMAN

"Judge Gillis was first appointed associate judge of Jefferson County by Governor Porter. When Elk County was organized he was appointed one of the associate judges of that county and served one term. In 1840 he was elected to the Legislature of Pennsylvania. He served in all three years in the House and one term in the Senate. He was elected to Congress in 1856, but he wrecked his future political advancement by voting for the Kansas-Nebraska bill. After his Congressional term closed he was appointed agent for the Pawnee tribe of Indians, and he located them upon their reservation, built buildings for them, among others a grist-mill, and was their faithful friend and protector while he remained with them. No act of peculation or crookedness was ever laid to his charge, either there or in any other public office which he held. As an evidence of his kindness and goodness of heart he adopted from the tribe a little Pawnee girl, aged five or six years, under the following circumstances: Both parents of the child were dead; she had no relatives who, under the laws of the tribe, were bound to care for her or support her, and was, therefore, cast off by every one. The story goes that Judge Gillis found her picking the pieces of fat off the entrails of a decayed buffalo. He immediately took her to his own quarters, had her washed, clothed, and cared for as if she were the most precious child in the world. He brought her to Ridgway with him when he returned. She lived in his family while he stayed there, went with him when he moved to Iowa, and died there.

"His Congressional course was but one term; he knew his defeat for the second term would be sure if he favored or voted for the bill having for its end the repeal of the Missouri Compromise. His attachment to President Buchanan led him to vote for it against his better judgment. The President made it a party measure, and when he interviewed Judge Gillis the judge said to him, 'It is defeat for me in either event. If I do not vote for it the politicians will beat me; if I do the people will.' He knew the sentiments of his district. He was renominated by the Democratic Convention in 1858 in his district, but was defeated at the polls by Chapin Hall, of Warren, now deceased. In Congress and in the Legislature of the State he was faithful always to the local interest of his constituents. It was through his efforts at Harrisburg more than that of any other man that the counties of Elk and Forest were organized, and in the contest for the location of the county seat of Elk County he favored, of course, the location at Ridgway, and used his future efforts to keep it there. When in the Senate he passed a resolution which created the county of Forest. It also passed the House of Representatives and is the only instance in the history of the State where a new county has been created by a joint resolution. It was approved by the governor, of course, and thereby became a law. It was near the close of the session, and the joint rules would not allow of its passage in any other form. He did this to oblige a fellow-pioneer in the wilds of the new county, Cyrus Blood. Subsequently, Forest County was enlarged; its primitive limits were quite circumscribed.

" THE ABDUCTION OF WILLIAM MORGAN

" The connection of Judge Gillis with the abduction of William Morgan, of Batavia, New York, the exposer of the secrets of Masonry, rendered him notorious through life. He was tried at Canandaigua, New York, in connection with the affair and charged with being one of the abductors of Morgan. He was accused of being one of the party who helped to convey him from Batavia to Fort Niagara, whither he was taken, no doubt, in a closed carriage, and relays of horses were furnished by the brethren along the route, thus insuring rapid and secret transit. At the trial he was defended by John C. Spencer, a lawyer then of great reputation, of Canandaigua, afterward Secretary of War and of the Treasury, who subsequently became noted in the politics and affairs of the country. The trial resulted in the acquittal of Mr. Gillis, and the affair led to the formation of the party known in politics as the Anti-Masonic party, which held an important part in politics from 1827 to 1832. It held such power in Pennsylvania that in 1834 Joseph Ritner was elected governor by it. The removal of the deposits from the United States Bank developed a new issue, and Morgan and his platform dropped out of politics. At the time Mr. Gillis was arrested he was residing upon a farm, which he was clearing up, in what was then Jefferson County, Pennsylvania, and which is upon the old road known as the Milesburg and Smethport turnpike, six miles northeast from Ridgway. At the time of his arrest he was busily at work clearing the farm, which was known then, and is now, as the Montmorenci farm.

" A deputy sheriff from Ontario County, New York, came there for him. He was a man whom Gillis hated most intensely, but he kept him over night, as the nearest neighbor was sixteen miles distant. The sheriff had come there from the town of Indiana, the seat of justice then, accompanied by a deputy-sheriff of that county. The requisition of the governor of the State had been duly recognized by Judge Young, who was then holding court at Indiana, and the proper warrant had been issued for the arrest. The party started on horseback the next morning for Indiana, a distance of about one hundred miles through the woods. The most part of the way was only a blazed line and a bridle-path for their route. A heavy rain had caused the Clarion, the Red Bank, and other streams to rise very high, and the party was delayed three days over the proper time making the trip. Great anxiety was felt at Indiana, caused by the delay, and the opinion was freely expressed that Gillis had made way with both officers. Late one afternoon, however, the community were relieved by the arrival of the overdue party. Gillis was handed over to the sheriff of the county, who was a Mason, and spent a pleasant night in the town with his brother Masons. The next morning he procured a writ of habeas corpus to be issued by Judge Young. Indiana was the seat of justice then for Jefferson County. Upon the hearing a discharge was refused. He was conveyed to Canandaigua by way of Franklin

46   721

and Erie, Pennsylvania, and Buffalo, New York. Upon the route he lacked neither food, drink, nor lodging. During the whole trip he refused to associate or have anything to do with the deputy-sheriff who nominally had him in custody—would not let him ride inside the stage with him. Gillis pledged his word to the sheriff before leaving Indiana, through a third party, that he would accompany the deputy to Canandaigua peaceably and quietly, but if any harsh means were used he would not be responsible for the consequences, and ironed he would not be. A rescue could have been invited at any point almost along the road. The sheriff knew this well; he also knew that his prisoner was a gentleman who would keep his word, and he relied upon it. When they arrived at Canandaigua he was released immediately upon bail, and he returned to Pennsylvania. At the proper time he went to Canandaigua, stood his trial, and was acquitted. He had the full report of the trial printed in a Masonic paper or magazine, called the *Craftsman*, published at the time, which he kept carefully through life. His special friends had access to it. The writer of this at one time requested Judge Gillis to write up the history and his knowledge of the Morgan affair and leave it sealed, and it should be kept sacred in the hands of the writer till after the death of the former, when it should be published, and thus throw some light upon the mystery. His reply was, 'I don't know, I never did know, what became of Morgan. You know from what you have read and from what I have told you what I was accused of. I have no knowledge as to what became of him. No information was ever imparted to me. He was evidently taken to Niagara Falls and passed into Canada from one set of men to another. At that time most every British man-of-war had a regular Masonic Lodge, acting under a charter from the Grand Lodge of Great Britain. Some of these were stationed at Montreal, Quebec, and Halifax. He could have been easily taken, or passed, from one to another, as being a man who had divulged the secrets of Masonry, till he reached one which was about sailing to a foreign shore, and carried there, kept in such position that he could communicate with no one, and ended his life in a natural way. I never believed that he was murdered, either by drowning, or otherwise, as alleged. At any rate, I can leave nothing behind me which will throw any light on the subject, and would not if I could. There are many persons living now, descendants of those who were implicated in the matter, and respect for them, if nothing more, is sufficient for me not to aid in stirring the subject, now almost forgotten.' He was a truthful, honorable man. What he told me I have no doubt was true.

" HIS SON'S ASSASSINATION

" In 1862 he left Elk County and went to reside with his son Charles at Mount Pleasant, Iowa, the one who was shot dead in his own door last fall by some unknown and undiscovered assassin. The son was a good man, beloved by every one, honest, faithful, true, and what the motive was which impelled any one to assassinate him is unexplained and a mystery. His father was the first one at his side after he fell, and there is no doubt but the shock experienced then very much shortened the father's days. Judge Gillis, after he moved to Iowa, made annual visits to Elk County, and took great comfort and delight in visiting his relatives and early friends. Every house was open to receive him, and he was beloved and welcomed by all. Throughout life he was a Democrat. The 7th day of October last, his eighty-eighth birthday, he was at Ridgway, and at a Democratic meeting he made a speech for Hancock and English and the whole ticket, the last and only one made during the campaign. Those who heard him say that it had the old style ring to it. Judge Gillis's early education was very limited. He was reared in the country, and at a time when school-houses were scarce and an education hard to obtain. He was a great reader. Engaged in a book, past midnight would often, and very often, find him absorbed in it, and if approaching the end of an interesting one the time of day or night was nothing to him till it was concluded. His library contained many of the standard works. Shakespeare, Scott's novels, and poems he was extravagantly fond of. The writings of the politicians and statesmen of this country he took great delight and interest in, and upon the political topics of the day he was always one of the best posted men. As an evidence of his reading power and ability it is a fact that he read through entire that set of public literature published by the Legislature of this State a few years ago, known as the 'Colonial Records and Pennsylvania Archives,' some twenty-five or thirty volumes—probably the only person who ever did it. Much, very much, of interest might be added to this, which would be of interest to the readers of the *Post*, about this man. His life and the part he took in the settlement of that part of Pennsylvania where he lived would make a very readable and valuable book. Probably it will not be written. He was a man of sterling and inflexible integrity, a kind, affectionate, companionable husband, friend, and parent. His conversational powers, fund of information, and anecdote were comprehensive and great; every one loved his companionship and society, and last and best of all he died in the faith of a Christian, a firm believer in God the Father Almighty, and in His Son, and in the resurrection of the dead and life in the world to come.

"HENRY SOUTHER.

"ERIE, PENNSYLVANIA, July 26, 1881."

INDEX

INDEX

INDEX

C

Cabin, pioneer, how built, 254
Call for troops in 1814, 243
Calling wolves, trick of, 158
Cameron County, area of, 486, 492
  desperadoes in, 491
  drainage of, 492
  early settlers in, 487
  first grist-mill in, 488
    newspaper in, 491
  formation of, 486
  game in, 491
  home of the Clafflin sisters, 489
  Indian depredations in, 493
  location of county seat, 490
  pioneer election of officers of, 489
    historian of, 489
    physician of, 489
    sessions of court, 489
    settlement in, 486
    store in, 491
  political divisions of, 492
  Press founded, 492
  salt-works in, 488
  " the great runaway," 493
  transportation in, 486
  whiskey a staple commodity, 487
Campaign of 1864, 669
Campbell, Archie, and Jimmie Kyle, 370
  and the apple-butter, 370
Camp-meeting, description of exercises at, 282
  Dutch, 283
  hymn, 283
  meetings, pioneer, 281
Candles used in 1840, 406
  method of making, 406
" Canoe Place," 55
Canoes, how made, 34
Cassatt, Alexander Johnston, 690
Catamount, or bey lynx, 119, 130
Census of free and slave States in 1840, 329
  of United States in 1840, 402
  returns of negro slavery, 364
Ceres Road, 569
Chair-car introduced on railroads, 688
Children, home training of, 389
Chimney-sweeps, 544
Circuit riders, outfit of, 431

Circus, pioneer travelling, 467
Civil War, Pennsylvania soldiers in, 674
Clarion Baptist Association, organization of, 277
  churches represented in, 277
  constitution for, adopted, 277
  ordained ministers of, 277
Clarion county, boat building in, 484
  boundaries of, 474
  draft in, for war of 1812, 483
  first child born in, 483
    church organized in, 483
    white settler in, 482
  food and raiment of first settlers, 481
  formation of, 474
  iron furnaces in, 484
  location of county seat, 474
  Lutheran church, 425
  pioneer grist-mill, 485
    newspaper in, 438
    post-office in, 485
    settlers in, 479, 480
  population statistics of, 484
  Presbyterian church, 425
  religious denominations in, 474
  Roman Catholic church, 425
  thriving towns in, 477
  United Presbyterian church, 426
pioneer court held in, 478
  judges in, 478
  officers of, 478
  public buildings in borough of, 477
  River a public highway, 478
    boat-building on, 529
    bridge over, 212
    first bridge across, 508
    pioneer steamboat on, 485
  town of, plotted by John Sloan, 478
Clans, Iroquois system of, 23
Clearing land, mode of, 217
Clothing worn in 1840, 415
Clover Harvey, famous fifer, 408
Coal, earliest mention of, in history, 718
  mining for foreign market, 711
Coinage, first, in United States, 342
  metal purchased for, 342
Coke first used in Pennsylvania, 717
Columbia Railroad, 687
    construction of track, 687
    first locomotive on, 687

INDEX

INDEX

INDEX

INDEX

Home-made candles, 406
  occupations of women in 1840, 391
  sweet home, in 1840, 392
  training of children in 1840, 389
Hominy-mills, 35
Honey, basswood, 153
  bee, 151
    wild, bait used in "lining," 154
    wild, "lining," 153
    wild, mode of hunting, 152
Hook, Jacob, arrested for perjury, 641
  mobbed, 641
Horse-car follows train, 686
  cars between Columbia and Philadel-
    delphia, 687
  racing in pioneer days, 373
Hospitality, pioneer, 223
Hotels of 1840, 395
  bar of, described, 395
"How fair is the rose," 387
Hudson Bay or red squirrel, 135
Humming-birds, 150
Hunt, Jim, bear-hunter, 398
Hutchinson, Joseph, pioneer settler in
  Jefferson County, 536
Hyde, Joseph Smith, anecdote of, 507
    sketch of, 515-517
Hymn-books, pioneer, 248

I

Ignorance in 1840, 406
Immigrant blacksmith, the, 434
Implements of stone and copper, 35
  description of manufactured, 35
Importation of passengers, act regulating,
  334
Imprisonment for debt, 333, 394
  act abolishing, 333
Incident on the pike, 168
Indentured apprentices, 330, 401
Indian amusements, 29
  bow, how made, 33
  canoes, 34
  doctors, 30
  express, so-called, 37
  festivals, 45
  names of, 45
  heraldry, 45
  huts, description of, 26
    how built, 25

Indian love-making, 46
  marriage ceremonies attending, 28
  moccasins, 45
  names of streams, 539, 578
  "nunnery," 266
  remedies, 31
  reservations, schools and churches on,
    649
  runners, 34
  stratagem in war, 33
  superstitions, 28
  terms of peace, 33
  the, as a ball-player, 45
    as a runner, 45
  tobacco-pipes, 34
  trails, 38
  treaties at Forts Stanwix and
    McIntosh, 75
  villages, how built, 42
  wampum, 41
  war-dance, description of, 29
  wars, how carried on, 31
    how declared, 32
    preparations for, 32
Indians, how they travelled, 29
  introduction of rum among, 39
  weapons employed by, 33
Industrial rights of women in 1840, 410
Introductory, 17
Iroquois, or Six Nations, 22
  early marriage of, 28
  names of families of, 22
  system of clans, 23
  treachery of, 24
  polygamy among, 24
Irwin, Guy C., Napoleon in lumber business, 645

J

Jamieson, Rev. John, attainments of, 275
  children of, 271, 272
  comes to America, 271
  death of, 275
  deposed from synod, 274
  descendant of noble family, 271
  devotion to duty, 274
  early and adult life of, 271
  erects first county jail, 275
  found guilty of libel, 274
  made moderator, 273
  marriage of, 271

INDEX

736

INDEX

47
737

INDEX

INDEX

INDEX

INDEX

INDEX

Weasel, changes of coat of, with seasons, 134
   homes of the, 134
   physiognomy of, 133
   poultry yard frequently visited by, 134
Weather prognosticators, 489
Weddings in 1780, 19
Wellsborough, county seat of Tioga County, 610
   early settlers near, 610
   first church building erected in, 620
   first public school building in, 620
   incorporated, 616
   origin of name of, 616
   pioneer Methodist church services in, 620
      tavern-keeper in, 620
   post-office opened in, 619
   Presbyterian church of, organized, 620
Wesley, Rev. John, 278
      preaches pioneer Methodist sermon in America, 279
Western Penitentiary, 659
   Pennsylvania, early settlers in, 199
      explored by Christopher Gist, 199
      pioneer settlement of, 199
   Theological Seminary, 659
Westminster confession and catechism adopted, 276
Where Odd Fellows came from, 434
Whigs in Brookville in 1840, 388
Whiskey drinking, evil effects of, 422
   free in 1840, 415
   insurrection, 1791-1794, 421
White slavery, 330
      nature of, in Rome, Greece, and Europe, 310
      origin of, 310
Who skinned the nigger, 290
Wild animals, natural life of, 136
   cat, 130
      habitat of, 130
      nest of, 131
      young of, 131
   pigeon, early home of, 507
   turkey, the, 136, 139, 227
Wildey, Thomas, founder of American Odd Fellowship, 434

Winter amusements in 1840, 389
Winters in 1840, severity of, 393
Wolf, bounty on head of, 119
   endurance in a race, 132
   gray or timber, 118
   habits of the, 177
   in the tail, treatment of, 392
   pen, description of, 122
   persistence in hunting, 132
   pup, raising, 120
   trap, 123
Wolverines, 123
Wolves, act for killing of, 172
   calling, trick of, 158
   how deer are hunted by, 177
Women admitted to the bar, 409
   apparel of, in 1840, 391
   higher education of, 409
   in 1840, home occupations of, 391
   industrial rights of women in 1840, 410
   married, legal rights of, 408
   religious rights of, in 1840, 410
   vocations of, in 1840, 410
Wooden clocks made, 367
Woodpecker, the, 144
   courtship of, 144
   feeding young, 144
   friend of the orchard, 144
   red-headed, 144
   yellow-breasted, 145
World's coal-producing territory, 718

Y

Yates, Arthur G., 711
Year without a summer, 1816, 366
Young deserter sentenced to be shot, 670
   life saved by W. J. McKnight, 670

Z

Zeisberger, Rev. David, 46, 258
      establishes mission of Friedenschnetten, 260
      pioneer missionary in Forest County, 528
      preaches to the Indians, 259